Professional Advancements and Management Trends in the IT Sector

Ricardo Colomo-Palacios
Universidad Carlos III de Madrid, Spain

Information Science
REFERENCE

Managing Director:	Lindsay Johnston
Senior Editorial Director:	Heather Probst
Book Production Manager:	Sean Woznicki
Development Manager:	Joel Gamon
Development Editor:	Development Editor
Acquisitions Editor:	Erika Gallagher
Typesetter:	Jennifer Romanchak
Cover Design:	Nick Newcomer, Lisandro Gonzalez

Published in the United States of America by
Information Science Reference (an imprint of IGI Global)
701 E. Chocolate Avenue
Hershey PA 17033
Tel: 717-533-8845
Fax: 717-533-8661
E-mail: cust@igi-global.com
Web site: http://www.igi-global.com

Library of Congress Cataloging-in-Publication Data

Professional advancements and management trends in the IT sector / Ricardo Colomo-Palacios, editor.
       p. cm.
  Includes bibliographical references and index.
  Summary: "This book offers the latest managerial trends within the field of information technology management, offering a broad variety of case studies, best practices, methodologies, and research within the field of information technology management"--Provided by publisher.
   ISBN 978-1-4666-0924-2 (hbk.) -- ISBN 978-1-4666-0925-9 (ebook) -- ISBN 978-1-4666-0926-6 (print & perpetual access) 1. Information technology--Vocational guidance. 2. Information technology--Management. I. Colomo-Palacios, Ricardo, 1973-
  T58.5.P77 2012
  004.068--dc23
                                  2011045600

British Cataloguing in Publication Data
A Cataloguing in Publication record for this book is available from the British Library.

Table of Contents

Section 1
IT Professionals Human Resource Management

Ricardo Colomo-Palacios, Universidad Carlos III de Madrid, Spain
Edmundo Tovar-Caro, Universidad Politécnica de Madrid, Spain
Ángel García-Crespo, Universidad Carlos III de Madrid, Spain
Juan Miguel Gómez-Berbís, Universidad Carlos III de Madrid, Spain

Darko Galinec, Ministry of Defense, Croatia

António Trigo, Escola Superior de Tecnologia e Gestão de Oliveira do Hospital, Portugal
João Varajão, Universidade de Trás-os-Montes e Alto Douro, Portugal
Pedro Soto-Acosta, University of Murcia, Spain
João Barroso, Grupo de Investigação em Engenharia do Conhecimento e Apoio à Decisão, Portugal
Francisco J. Molina-Castillo, University of Murcia, Spain
Nicolas Gonzalvez-Gallego, University of Murcia, Spain

Raquel Mendes, Instituto Politécnico do Cávado e do Ave, Portugal

Section 2
IT Professionals Education

Section 3
IT Professionals in IT Projects

Detailed Table of Contents

Section 1
IT Professionals Human Resource Management

Chapter 1

Ricardo Colomo-Palacios, Universidad Carlos III de Madrid, Spain
Edmundo Tovar-Caro, Universidad Politécnica de Madrid, Spain
Ángel García-Crespo, Universidad Carlos III de Madrid, Spain
Juan Miguel Gómez-Berbís, Universidad Carlos III de Madrid, Spain

This paper aims to identify technical competency levels relevant to Software Engineering in a spectrum of professional profiles which are found in Spain's main Software Development companies. The research work presents a combination of three initiatives. The first step constitutes a review of the literature related to the characterization of the labor force in the Software Engineering domain. The subsequent step consists of a qualitative study of the practices of a set of organizations, and lastly, this was followed by a quantitative analysis based on investigative surveys administered to a number of representative professionals. The professional career is established from seven consecutive profiles. The pyramidal model for professional careers, identifying one single professional track going from Junior Programmer to IT Director, is still present in the organisations subject to this study. Technical excellence is reached in a determined professional profile, in this case "D". From this point onwards, other competencies which are not uniquely characteristic of Software Engineering gain importance, and stimulate professional development towards higher levels.

Chapter 2

Darko Galinec, Ministry of Defense, Croatia

Human capital management (HCM) inside large systems is very complex and demanding, to achieve successful accomplishment high quality information support is necessary. There are many cases where human capital management process is not conducted in a satisfactory way. Key decisions usually come late, very often because of impossibility to consider a problem in its entirety. The cause of it usually lies in weakness and understatement of the human capital management itself and in this connection data management is not given adequate consideration. Data originating from inside and outside sources within information system (IS) are not integrated in a way which will provide an optimal use. In this connection, this paper examines possibilities to innovate the entire human capital management process through the integration of respective data. Data warehousing (DW) possibilities and position within the integral business intelligence (BI) concept are noted as a first step towards its realization. In this paper the necessity to innovate and promote permanently the quality of human capital management process is considered; the main features of the process are given as well. Business process innovation (BPI) as a systematic approach with a view to achieve significant business process change is presented; its connection with data aspect of IS is given too. According to the research of this paper, HCM BPI is achieved by the data integration within existing IS. DW model intended for HCM has been elaborated as a solution which will innovate the process itself. The position and the role of DW within entire BI organization concept have been established as well. Finally, the benefits achieved by the research are explained.

Chapter 3

António Trigo, Escola Superior de Tecnologia e Gestão de Oliveira do Hospital, Portugal
João Varajão, Universidade de Trás-os-Montes e Alto Douro, Portugal
Pedro Soto-Acosta, University of Murcia, Spain
João Barroso, Grupo de Investigação em Engenharia do Conhecimento e Apoio à Decisão, Portugal
Francisco J. Molina-Castillo, University of Murcia, Spain
Nicolas Gonzalvez-Gallego, University of Murcia, Spain

Nowadays, Universities and other Training Institutions need to clearly identify the Information Technology (IT) skills that companies demand from IT practitioners. This is essential not only for offering appropriate and reliable university degrees, but also to help future IT professionals on where to focus in order to achieve better job positions. In an attempt to address this issue, this study rely on 102 Chief Information Officers, from Iberian large companies, to characterize current IT professionals and what is expected from future hirings. Results revealed that IT Technicians and Senior Analysts are the predominant positions and also that future hiring will request candidates with at least two to five years of work experience. The two most important skills found were core functions at the IT department: business knowledge and user support. In contrast, traditional competences such as web development and management of emerging technologies were less demanded.

Chapter 4

Raquel Mendes, Instituto Politécnico do Cávado e do Ave, Portugal

Despite the evidence of female progress with regard to women's role in the labor market, gender inequality remains. Women are still less likely to be employed than men, occupational gender segregation continues, and females continue to earn less than males. The gender wage gap remains wide in several occupational sectors, among which is the information technology (IT) sector. This paper focuses the determinants of gender wage inequality. More precisely, it investigates for statistical evidence of a glass ceiling effect on women's wages. Based on the quantile regression framework, the empirical analysis extends the decomposition of the average gender wage gap to other parts of the earnings distribution. The main objective is to empirically test whether gender-based wage discrimination is greater among high paid employees, in line with glass ceiling hypothesis. Larger unexplained gaps at the top of the wage distribution indicate the existence of a glass ceiling effect in Portugal.

Chapter 5

Konstantinos C. Zapounidis, Aristotle University of Thessaloniki, Greece
Glykeria Kalfakakou, Aristotle University of Thessaloniki, Greece

This paper's aim is to analyse practices adapted by different enterprises regarding personnel motivation and human resources approaches to increase their productivity and profitability while examining the methodology of human resources recruitment and selection used by different kinds of enterprises, which cannot exist without human manpower. The objective of this paper is to analyse methods and tools used by several enterprises in motivation and in human resources recruitment and selection. Regarding motivation, the basic aim of the process adapted was to define whether each enterprise was closer to the participating or to directive management model. Especially in the recruiting and selecting process IT could add important value since adapted IT processes could lead to quicker and more successful transparent results. IT professionals could organise these processes for every enterprise in order to become standard, formulated, and even more accredited procedures which would lead to successful recruiting and selecting results.

Chapter 6

Macarena López-Fernández, University of Cádiz, Spain
Fernando Martín-Alcázar, University of Cádiz, Spain
Pedro Miguel Romero-Fernández, University of Cádiz, Spain

Over the past years, several researchers have analysed the relational dynamics that takes place inside and between organizations (concept, mediating and moderating variables, effects, etc.) considering it as a resource capable of contributing to the orientation and the strategic positioning of the organizations, and, as a last resort, to the support of the competitive advantages. Nevertheless, there are very few studies that include evidence about how the effective management of certain characteristics and properties of the network, such as the work dynamics developed or the interaction in the group may be useful for the operation of the work group itself in firms that develope its activity in high-tech sectors. Thus, the objectives of this paper is to develop a conceptual framework for studying the relationship between Human Resource Activities and Social Capital while underlining the importance that human resource policies play in the management of this variable in a IT environment.

Section 2
IT Professionals Education

Chapter 7

Tokuro Matsuo, Yamagata University, Japan
Takayuki Fujimoto, Toyo University, Japan

In designing a new teaching system, a challenging issue is how the system intelligently supports learners. This paper describes a methodology and a system design on the intelligent instruction support for software engineering education. For information science courses at a university, software engineering subjects are usually compulsory and students study dominant conceptions of implementation like software architecture, and the methodology of software design in software engineering lectures. To enhance learners' understanding, the authors design a novel instructional model based on the analogical thinking theory. The analogical thinking-based instruction consists of concrete teaching methods like analogy dropping method, self role-play method, and the anthropomorphic thinking method. Questionnaires for learners after the instructions give results of effective education in an actual trial. The contribution of this paper is to provide a new instruction theory, the way of educational practice method, and implementation of the system.

Information technology professionals comprise an important segment of adult learners seeking a four-year undergraduate degree, and it is important to provide programs that address not only the conceptual and theoretical, but also adult learning needs in terms of career orientation and practicality together with providing real-life applications relevant to the needs of the IT job marketplace. The techniques of employing distance learning, providing modular and practical learning segments, emphasizing adult-oriented learning preferences, engaging users toward learning, and providing appropriate course schedules and sequencing are discussed in the context of an actual adult learner program. This program integrates job and career-oriented needs with that of a well-rounded business education. Examples and illustrations are provided to illustrate how an adult-oriented program was customized to provide needs important to adult learners and IT professionals, with the objective of producing superior and useful learning results.

Chapter 9

Specifications such as RSS feeds are opening a new channel of communication for Internet-based learning, which gives a decentralized view of web resources while maintaining the privacy of teachers and students who are consulting the information. This philosophy can be used to create personalized learning tools in which users can take control of resources they want to have access to. In this regard, RSS is XML-based, which makes it easy to complement visual access with audio interfaces, adapting the feeds to different educational contexts and learning styles. This paper discusses the use of feed syndication to create personalized feed readers accessible in visual and voice formats.

Section 3
IT Professionals in IT Projects

This study aims to explore the critical driving and resisting forces that promote or inhibit the implementation and use of project management (PM) software in Qatari Government Organizations in an attempt to determine whether software-based PM methodologies are being effectively implemented in the public sector organizations or not. Research hypotheses were evaluated using ANOVA and Mann- Whitney test. Findings indicated that forces that promote or inhibit software based PM implementation are significantly affected by the managerial interest and nature of existing (traditional or contemporary) PM practices. More importantly our findings identified some driving forces that promote the implementation of software-based PM methodology (SPMM) in Qatari government organizations and also identified some roadblocks that prohibit such implementations. Finally managerial implications for the successful implementation of SPMM are provided and avenues for further research are suggested.

Chapter 11

Adrián Hernández-López, Universidad Carlos III de Madrid, Spain
Ricardo Colomo-Palacios, Universidad Carlos III de Madrid, Spain
Ángel García-Crespo, Universidad Carlos III de Madrid, Spain
Pedro Soto-Acosta, University of Murcia, Spain

Distributed software development is becoming the norm for the software industry today as an organizational response to globalization and outsourcing tendencies. In this new environment, centralized models for software development team building models have to be reanalyzed. Team Software Process (TSP) guides engineering teams in developing software-intensive products and is intended to improve the levels of quality and productivity of a team's software development project. In this paper, the authors assess the difficulty of using TSP in distributed software development environments. The objective of this assessment is twofold; firstly, know the general difficulty for using TSP in these environments, and secondly, know the caveats to be addressed in future software development team building models designed specifically for distributed environments.

Chapter 12

Margarita André Ampuero, Instituto Superior Politécnico José Antonio Echeverría, Cuba
María G. Baldoquín de la Peña, Instituto Superior Politécnico José Antonio Echeverría, Cuba
Silvia T. Acuña Castillo, Universidad Autónoma de Madrid, Spain

The formation of software development project teams is carried out, conventionally, in an empiric manner; however, in this process, multiple factors should be considered. In literature, the works where this process is modeled are scarce, and most do not consider aspects linked to the formation of the team as a whole. In this paper, a group of patterns that contribute to the formation of software development projects teams are identified through the use of the Delphi method, psychological tests, and data mining tools. The paper identifies patterns that are validated experimentally, while psychological characteristics in the process of software team formations are exemplified.

Chapter 13

Alexander Baumeister, Saarland University, Germany
Markus Ilg, Vorarlberg University of Applied Sciences, Austria

There are numerous forecast models of software development costs, however, various problems become apparent in context to practical application. Standardized methods, such as COCOMO II have to be calibrated at an individual operational level on the basis of the underlying database. This paper presents a new activity based approach that is based on business specific cost data that can be easily integrated into existing management accounting systems. This approach can be applied to software development projects based on the unified process in which activity driven budgeting promises several advantages compared to common tools in use. It supports enterprise specific cost forecasting and control and can be easily linked with risk analysis. In addition to the presentation of a conceptual design model, the authors present a framework for activity driven budgeting and cost management of software development projects combined with concrete implementation examples.

Section 4
IT Professionals in Organizations

Chapter 14

David O'Sullivan, National University of Ireland, Ireland
Lawrence Dooley, University College Cork, Ireland

All organisations are now facing one of the largest upheavals in business practice since the 'great depression'. Information technology organisations, who frequently lead the development of change based around ICT, are being asked to develop new products and services that add significant value for customers and to radically change their internal processes so that they are more cost effective. Innovation is process of creating positive change to any organisation and that adds value to customers – internal and external. Innovation is now widely accepted at the only sustainable engine of renewed growth for organisations. Organisations that do not embrace innovation and learn to apply its principles will simply stagnate or be obliterated by competition. ICT organisations that can learn to apply innovation effectively will become key strategic assets in driving costs down and also in adding new dimensions to product and service development. This paper presents an approach to applying innovation in any ICT based organisation, be it a service department within a larger organisation or a commercial business that generates ICT solutions for clients. The process of innovation in ICT based organisations is similar to innovation in any organisation and requires an in-depth understanding and practice of developing innovation goals, the management of innovative actions or projects, the empowerment of human capital or teams and the continuous monitoring of innovation performance. This paper presents a methodology for applying innovation and a case study of how innovation related knowledge can be managed in any ICT organisation.

Chapter 15

Zamira Acosta, La Laguna University, Spain
Jaime Febles, La Laguna University, Spain

Changes in economic activity on a global scale affect organizations due to modifications on their decision criteria, but also for the permanent character of the change. This situation implies an increase of the competition and also the appearance of new markets and opportunities. On the other hand the innovation not only offers major possibilities to guarantee the organization's survival but also it allows to increase their competitive capacity; even turning into a generating element of the change and vice versa. But it will be the organization that inserts appropriately the above mentioned innovation, or that uses it better, the one that will be more competitive. The management of the organizational change, in this sense, turns into an influential factor in the creation of future and in the promotion of the available possibilities. This paper analyzes organizational management more adapted to the innovative processes of the Canary companies, as well as the underlying differences in the types of compared enterprises.

Chapter 16

Helena Campos, Universidade do Minho, Portugal
Luís Amaral, Universidade do Minho, Portugal

Information Systems Technology (IST) has an increasingly central role in today's globalised information society. In this regard, it is imperative to recognise the impossibility of a technological life without ethics. As typical components for an ethics program, the authors use Codes of Ethics/Conduct/Practices (CE/CC/CP) as some professions (physicians, lawyers, etc.) have adopted them. The codes are instrumental in developing sound relations with various stakeholders to reduce the number of legal proceedings and contingencies, negotiate conflicts of interest, and ensure the fulfillment of the law. In view of this, the codes should be dynamic and not static documents, used for the advancement in easy reading, understanding, and structure. This will be instrumental for their followers to more easily consult and understand them, and find guidelines for their key ethical problems and concerns. This paper proposes the voluntary GOTOPS code of the techno ethics governance, that is, ethical problems raised by IST.

Chapter 17

Leisa J. Armstrong, Edith Cowan University, Australia
Dean A. Diepeveen, Department of Agriculture and Food Western Australia, Australia
Khumphicha Tantisantisom, Edith Cowan University, Australia

The ability of farmers to acquire knowledge to make decisions is limited by the information quality and applicability. Inconsistencies in information delivery and standards for the integration of information also limit decision making processes. This research uses a similar approach to the Knowledge Discovery in Databases (KDD) methodology to develop an ICT based framework which can be used to facilitate the acquisition of knowledge for farmers' decision making processes. This is one of the leading areas of research and development for information technology in an agricultural industry, which is yet to utilize such technologies fully. The Farmer Knowledge and Decision Support Framework (FKDSF) takes information provided to farmers and utilizes processes that deliver this critical information for knowledge acquisition. The framework comprises data capture, analysis, and data processing, which precede the delivery of the integrated information for the farmer. With information collected, captured, and validated from disparate sources, according to defined sets of rules, data mining tools are then used to process and integrate the data into a format that contributes to the knowledge base used by the farmer and the agricultural industry.

Chapter 18

Neuza Ferreira, International Association for Scientific Knowledge (IASK), Portugal

This paper aims at stating the main advantages and implications of Web 2.0 by analysing popular social networks in Portugal and addressing some examples of their utility. The authors present results of an empirical study applied to young people, aged between 12 and 20 years old, in a specific Portuguese region. In the first part of the study, main characteristics and differences between Web 1.0 and Web 2.0 are presented. In addition, results of empirical research and concluding remarks are presented and discussed. Achieved results seem to be particularly relevant for academics and industry professionals who might be interested in the application of new technologies for communication and socialization purposes.

Chapter 19

Sara Pinto, Polytechnic Institute of Santarém, Portugal

*Fernando Ferreira, Polytechnic Institute of Santarém and CASEE - University of Algarve Portugal,
& University of Memphis, USA*

Nowadays, few would contest that the contribution of ICT – Information and Communication Technologies – for the progress of the payments system in Portugal has been significant. The continuous irruption of new payment forms, as well as the emergence of more attractive and profitable offers, triggers countless changes. In fact, there has been an organizational restructuring of the banks, aiming at achieving higher efficiency levels, resulting from the use of ICT. In broad terms, the payments system in Portugal has been revealing high levels of modernity. However, is that adhesion to ICT similar in all the regions that are part of the Portuguese territory? The main goal of this study focuses on an empirical analysis which allows to investigate the degree of convergence, regarding the technological dissemination for banking purposes, between the region of Santarém and the national trends.

Preface

Information technology (IT) has been fundamental for improving productivity as well as for the development of knowledge-intensive products and services (Soto-Acosta, Martinez-Conesa & Colomo-Palacios, 2010). Organizations currently use multiple IT/IS solutions to support their activities at all management levels (Trigo, Varajao, & Barroso, 2009). Today, the successful exploitation of IT within the business is dependent upon the availability of IT professionals to design and integrate IT infrastructure and applications (Agarwal & Ferratt, 2002). In this scenario, IT human capital represents a strategic resource for firms, which has the ability to bestow competitive advantages (Bharadwaj, 2000; Wade & Hulland, 2004).Given that a company's human resources can be a source of competitive advantage that is difficult for competitors to imitate (Kuean, Kaur& Wong, 2010), IT professionals are in the eye of the hurricane of firms assets. Following this trend, Josefek and Kauffman (2003) suggest that the possession of IT human capital distinguishes IT professionals from other professionals. Finally, Beard, Schwieger and Surendran (2010) indicated that the skills and knowledge of IT professionals should prove invaluable in seeking and implementing innovations.

However, this importance reveals a serious threat: the shortage of IT professionals all over the world, which has been pointed out by many works and reports (e.g. Acharya & Mahanty, 2008; Agarwal & Ferratt, 2002; Mithas & Krishnan, 2008). The problem presents two different sources. On the one hand, IT is suffering from the erosion of its student base (Hirschheim & Newman, 2010) because of the low attractiveness of the profession in terms of image (García-Crespo et al., 2008) and status (Day, 2007). According to the analysis by Gartner, many people see computer science profession as an unattractive career option: it is both hard work and "uncool." (Morello, Kyte, & Gomolsky, 2007).Moreover, IT stereotypes are widely adopted by a large part of society and have been reported in several studies. For example, stereotypes include nerdy/geeky (Gurer & Camp, 2002; Rashid, 2008; Beaubouef & McDowell, 2008; Fisher & Margolis, 2002), anti-social (Martin, 1998), solitary (Craig, Paradis, & Turner, 2002; Rashid, 2008; Beaubouef & McDowell, 2008), unethical (Martin, 1998), snack food and "pizza and coke" eaters (Rashid, 2008; Timms et al., 2008), poorly dressed (Jemielniak, 2007) and men-only (Lavy, 2008; Anderson et al., 2008; Rashid, 2008; Fisher & Margolis, 2002; Durndell & Thomson, 1997) to name but a few.

This bad image of IT professionals can create also potentially serious problems for IT professionals and their employers since IT human resource practices are based on managers' views (Enns, Ferratt, & Prasad, 2006). In any case, enrollments in computer science university degrees have dropped significantly (Lee & Lee, 2006), causing a severe shortage of new graduates (Allen et al., 2008). According to Pollacia and Lomerson (2006) the decline in the enrollment has declined sixty five percent. On the other hand, lack of career commitment and high turnover rates are threatening IT professional workforce. As a result of this, the supply of human capital possessing the knowledge and skills needed to exploit IT is falling short and all kinds of organizations around the world struggle to maximize the return from their IT investments (Agarwal & Ferratt, 2001). Moreover, the war for talent (Michaels, Handfield-Jones & Axelrod, 2001) in the IT sector has its battlefield outside and inside the company and the internal recruitment of professionals must be done basing selection requirements in competence evidences. Ang and Slaughter(2004) indicated that recruiting and retaining qualified IT workforce continues to be an important endeavor for many organizations. In fact, a recent survey shows that the second highest priority for organizations and IT managers behind IT-business alignment is how to attract, retain and grow IT personnel (Luftman & Kempaiah, 2007). To conclude, the mismatch of supply and demand is a source of concern for business executives and academics alike (Luftman, 2005).

This situation presents another player: Offshoring outsourcing. Offshoring outsourcing is the practice of distributing work, particularly in the area of information technology services and development to workers outside the national borders of the host country (Niederman, Kundu& Salas, 2006). Not in vain, the Information and Communication Technology (ICT) industry is becoming more global regarding ownership and market scope (Aramo-Immonen, Jaakkola & Keto, 2011). Research indicates that offshoring can create wealth for both the countries and companies involved (Farrell & Agrawal, 2003) but in the other hand, the debate about the possible impact of offshoring services on developed country growth rates, wages, and industrial structure is open (Dossani & Kenney, 2007).Few trends in management in recent years have attracted so much interest as outsourcing and today outsourcing is an indispensable tool in the management of information systems (Leeney et al., 2011). Information systems (IS) outsourcing can be defined as the significant contribution made by external providers of physical and/or human resources, associated either with all components or with IT infrastructure specific components in the user's organization (Loh & Venkatraman, 1992). The literature situates the beginning of outsourcing in 1991, subsequent to the success achieved by Eastman Kodak with the outsourcing of its IS (Applegate & Montealegre, 1991), followed by other cases such as Continental Bank (Huber, 1993), and BP (Cross, 1995).The focus of IT outsourcing has been changing, since its creation in the 1960s (Loh & Venkataraman, 1995), from a focus on hardware, to software on the 1970s, to hardware and software standardization on the 1980s, and to total solution on the 1990s (Lee, Huynh, Kwok & Pi, 2003).

In the early 1990s, offshoring of software work to development centers in low wage countries pertained to large Western companies such as IBM and SAP who systematically attempted to take a hold of wage differences and resources of a global market (Winkler, Dibbern & Heinzl, 2008). Now, many Fortune 500 companies produce their business information systems in developing countries (such as China and India) to take advantage of their relatively low-cost labor (Sakthivel, 2007) and large telecommunications and software companies have numerous software development groups around the world (Edwards & Sridhar, 2005). However, one of the implications of this situation is the fear of jobs loosing in western countries (e.g. Casey & Richardson, 2008; Casey & Richardson, 2009; García-Crespo et al., 2010). On the other hand, outsourcing and offshoring is here to stay, and IT professionals in developed countries need to adapt to the new world. Not in vain, cultural diversity is influencing software development and its outcomes (Casado-Lumbreras et al., 2011) in both directions.

According to Mithas and Lucas (2010), among high-skill workers, IT professionals who create the IT infrastructure to support critical business processes of □rms are particularly susceptible to the forces of globalization. IT related jobs also involve high information intensity and often few requirements for physical presence, these jobs are amenable to global disaggregation and can be performed remotely or offshore (Apte & Mason 1995). While, reasons like the difficulties involved in transferring tacit knowledge of customers and developers across geographic locations make it necessary to deploy some IT resources onsite (e.g. Espinosa, Delone & Lee, 2006; Ramasubbu et al., 2008).

The result of all these pressures is that IT personnel are experimenting increasing job demands and constraints (e.g. Riolli & Savicki, 2003, Sethi, Barrier & King, 1999; Thong & Yap, 2002). The IT work has been labeled as "stressfull" (Engler, 1998), although this stress is not equally distributed among junior and senior practitioners (Bradley, 2007). The most significant stressors, according to Love et al. (2007), are: work overload, role ambiguity and conflict, career progression, diverse personalities, changing technology, redundancy, limited resources, financial pressures, budget constraints, and so on. Therefore, one of the ongoing concerns among the IT industries is to mitigate the effects of changes in work environment on job satisfaction, work performance, reliability, health and comfort (Rethinam & Ismail, 2008).

In this highly complex scenario, efforts like the International Journal of Human Capital and Information Technology Professionals (IJHCITP) make sense. The objective of this journal is to offer an outlook on the state of the IT profession from the perspective of human capital. IJHCITP includes the different disciplines within the IT field (Software Engineering, Information Systems, Computer Science, Computer Engineering…), focusing on them from the outlook of professionalism and covering the themes applying a multidisciplinary perspective, which includes visions from fields such as human resource management, sociology, psychology and management.

This book is concerned with opportunities and threats for IT Professional working in the 21st century. All these visions are reflected on the first volume of IJHCITP. This manuscript, as a result of a year of works published in IJHCITP, presents four different sections and nineteen chapters.

SECTION 1

Section 1, *IT Professionals Human Resource Management*, includes six chapters. Given that human resource management policies and practices on firm performance is an important topic (Huselid, 1995), a section devoted to these practices is timely and relevant. Boxall, Purcell, and Wright (2007) distinguish among three major subfields of human resource management: micro HRM (including recruitment, selection, induction, training and development, performance management, remuneration and union-management relations), strategic HRM (which, according to Lengnick-Hall et al. (2009), covers the overall HR strategies adopted by business units and companies and tries to measure their impacts on performance), and international HRM (that is related to practices operating across national boundaries). In the case of the book, the first two subfields are covered in the book.

First, Chapter 1 aims to identify technical competency levels relevant to Software Engineering in a spectrum of professional profiles which are found in Spain's main Software Development companies. Based on a qualitative study of the practices of a set of organizations, and on quantitative analysis based on a survey, Ricardo Colomo-Palacios, Edmundo Tovar-Caro, Ángel García-Crespo and Juan Miguel Gómez-Berbís identify seven consecutive profiles going from Junior Programmer to IT Director.

Chapter 2 is entitled "Human Capital Management Process Based on Information Technology Models and Governance". In this article, O'Sullivan and Dooley present an approach to applying innovation in any IT based organisation, be it a service department within a larger organisation or a commercial business that generates IT solutions for clients.

Chapter 3, "IT Professionals: An Iberian Snapshot" study empirically investigates which skills are most important for current and future IT personnel based on the perceptions of Iberian (Portuguese and Spanish) CIOs. This paper is authored by António Trigo (ESTGOH - Escola Superior de Tecnologia e Gestão de Oliveira do Hospital, Portugal), João Varajão (Centro Algoritmi and UTAD - Universidade de Trás-os-Montes e Alto Douro, Portugal), Pedro Soto-Acosta (University of Murcia, Spain), João Barroso (GECAD - Grupo de Investigação em Engenharia do Conhecimento e Apoio à Decisão, Portugal), Francisco J. Molina-Castillo (University of Murcia, Spain) and Nicolas Gonzalvez-Gallego (University of Murcia, Spain).

Chapter 4, "Glass Ceilings in Portugal? An Analysis of the Gender Wage Gap using a Quantile Regression Approach" focuses the determinants of gender wage inequality looking for statistical evidence of a glass ceiling effect on women's wages.

Chapter 5 is entitled "Recruiting, Selecting and Motivating Human Resources: Methodological Analysis and Case Studies Applications" and is authored by Zapounidis and Kalfakakou. The chapter analyses methods and tools used by several enterprises in motivation and in human resources recruitment and selection.

Chapter 6 is the final chapter in Section 1. It is entitled "Human Resource Management on Social Capital". The objective of the chapter is to develop a conceptual framework for studying the relationship between Human Resource Activities and Social Capital while underlining the importance that human resource policies play in the management of this variable in an IT environment.

SECTION 2

Section 2 is devoted to IT Professionals Education and includes a set of three chapters ranging from seven to nine. The education of IT professionals is facing several challenges in the 21st century: gender misbalance (e.g. Kvasny, Trauth & Morgan, 2009; Rosembloom et al., 2008), race asymmetry (e.g. Goode, 2007; Jackson et al., 2008) or erosion of the student base (Hirschheim & Newman, 2010; Rashid, 2008) to cite just a set of the most important and reported ones. This book tackles some of them in three different chapters.

Chapter 7 by Tokuro Matsuo and Takayuki Fujimotois entitled "Analogical Thinking Based Instruction Method in IT Professional Education". This chapter describes a methodology and a system design on the intelligent instruction support for software engineering education.

Chapter 8 by Jeffrey Hsu, Karin Hamilton and John Wang presents an approach to bridge the gap between industry and education institutions. The aim is to provide ideas and examples of focused methods and techniques that support the educational outcomes needed by adult students, with a particular focus on IT professionals, relating to new or advanced career placement and the acquisition of useful, practical knowledge.

Chapter 9 closes Section 2. "RSS-Based Learning Using Audio" analyses the use of Really Simple Syndication (RSS)in an educational context and finds that this technology enables new ways of communication to be established between students and teachers while, at the same time, allowing information to be personalised by the users themselves, selecting which educational material they wish to consult.

SECTION 3

Section 3 contains four chapters under the *IT Professionals in IT Projects* research field. The management of IT projects is a challenging task with many projects failing to achieve their intended objectives (Standing et al., 2006); not in vain, according to Chen, Zhang & Lai (2009) an information technology project is an inherently uncertain investment. In this unstable environment, IT professionals are expected to perform their jobs with a sufficient level of competence but also experiencing rising levels of work-related stress (Love & Irani, 2007). IT projects are the working environment of most of the IT professionals and this section aims to shed some light into this complex setup.

In Chapter 10, Salaheldin Ismail Salaheldin, Khurram Sharif and Maysarah Al Alami present a study on the critical driving and resisting forces that promote or inhibit the implementation and use of project management (PM) software in Qatari Government Organizations.

Chapter 11, "Team Software Process in GSD Teams: A Study of New Work Practices and Models" deals with Global Software Development and its implications for Team Software Process (TSP), one of the leading team-oriented product and process quality initiatives. The aim of the chapter is to assess the difficulty of using TSP in distributed software development environments by evaluating the difficulties for each activity and goal of each role defined in TSP, in order to know the tune that each role needs for global environments.

In Chapter 12, Margarita André Ampuero, María G. Baldoquín de la Peña and Silvia T. Acuña Castillo present a work in which Identification of patterns for the formation of software development projects teams are presented and validated. In their work, a group of patterns that contribute to the formation of software development projects teams are identified through the use of the Delphi method, and of the application of psychological tests and data mining tools. Identified patterns were validated experimentally. This work seems to be the perfect match between psychology and technology, software engineering and management.

The final chapter in Section 2, "Activity Driven Budgeting of Software Projects", by Baumeister and Ilg, investigates a new activity approach that is based on business specific cost data, which can be easily integrated into existing management accounting systems and applied for software development projects. Besides the presentation of a conceptual design model, this contribution presents a framework for activity driven budgeting and cost management of software development projects.

SECTION 4

Section 4 includes a set of six chapters devoted to shed some light into the work of IT Professionals in Organizations. Since the value of the IT workforce to help organizations survive and excel calls for thoughtful planning and investment (Zwieg et al., 2006), this section will be helpful for both professionals and managers to groom and retain the best IT human capital.

Chapter 14 by David O'Sullivan and Lawrence Dooley is entitled "Collaborative Innovation for the Management of Information Technology Resources". Being innovation one of the leading challenges in all industries this chapter is important, interesting, and timely. The chapter, after a complete overview of the leading processes of innovation, presents a methodology for applying innovation and a case study of how innovation related knowledge can be managed in any IT organization.

Chapter 15 is entitled "The Organizational Management as Instrument to Overcome the Resistance to the Innovative Process: An Application in the Canary Company" and is authored by Zamira Acosta and Jaime Febles from La Laguna University, Spain. This chapter discusses the management of organizational change as an influential factor in the creation of firm innovation through the implantation of innovative processes. Using a sample of 401 firms from the Canary Islands (Spain), the authors analyze the organizational aspects that could influence the resistance to innovative change and the predisposition to innovation thru the importance that companies grant to environmental variables.

Helena Campos and LuísAmaral (Universidade do Minho, Portugal) present Chapter 16 entitled "GOTOPS: Code of Technoethics Governance". This chapter focuses on the GOTOPS code of the technoethics (ethical problems raised by IT) governance. Given the importance of ethics in IT field, authors developed a voluntary code of Technoethical Governance for Sustainable Portuguese Organizations (GOTOPS).This code was created to include ethical problems raised by development and utilization of the IT. This code includes Codes of Ethics/Conduct/Practices fully and includes ethical problems raised by development and utilization of the IT.

The work "An eAgriculture-Based Decision Support Framework for Information Dissemination" is presented in Chapter 17. In this work, Armstrong, Diepeveen and Tantisantisom propose an approach to facilitate the acquisition of knowledge for farmer's decision making processes. The framework comprises data capture, analysis and data processing which precede the delivery of the integrated information for the farmer.

Chapter 18 is "Social Networks and Young People: A Case Study". In this work, Ferreira analyses some of the most popular social networks. The main characteristics and differences between the "Web 1.0" and "Web 2.0" are explained and, then, the results of the empirical research are presented and discussed. The findings presented in the chapter are particularly relevant for academics and industry professionals who might be interested in the application of new technologies for communication and socialization purposes.

Chapter 19, "Technological Dissemination in the Portuguese Payments System: An Empirical Analysis to the Region of Santarém" is the last chapter of the book. This work, by Sara Pinto and Fernando Ferreira, integrates to what extent payment systems are extended in the Santarém Region, Portugal.

CONCLUSION

The objective of this book has been to draw together on one place a year of articles published in IJHCITP. The four sections of this book delve into some of the most prevalent and pervasive concerns that Information Technology professionals are facing. The book includes chapters from around the world. Each contribution provides an interesting and deep study of one of the main issues on the IT professionals' practices and scenarios. Enjoy the reading and raise awareness of the skills and circumstances that make IT professionals successful and competitive.

Ricardo Colomo-Palacios
Universidad Carlos III de Madrid, Spain

REFERENCES

Acharya, P., & Mahanty, B. (2008). Manpower shortage crisis in Indian information technology industry. *International Journal of Technology Management, 38*(3), 235–247. doi:10.1504/IJTM.2007.012712

Agarwal, R., & Ferratt, T. W. (2002). Enduring practices for managing IT professionals. *Communications of the ACM, 45*(9), 73–79. doi:10.1145/567498.567502

Agarwal, R., & Ferratt, T. W. (2001). Crafting an HR strategy to meet the need for IT workers. *Communications of the ACM, 44*(7). doi:10.1145/379300.379314

Allen, M. W., Armstrong, D. J., Reid, M. F., & Riemenschneider, C. K. (2008). Factors impacting the perceived organizational support of IT employees. *Information & Management, 45*(8), 556–563. doi:10.1016/j.im.2008.09.003

Anderson, N., Lankshear, C., Timms, C., & Courtneya, L. (2008). 'Because it's boring, irrelevant and I don't like computers': Why high school girls avoid professionally-oriented ICT subjects. *Computers & Education, 50*(4), 1304–1318. doi:10.1016/j.compedu.2006.12.003

Ang, S., & Slaughter, S. (2004). Turnover of information technology professionals: The effect of internal labor market strategies. *The Data Base for Advances in Information Systems, 35*(3), 11–27.

Applegate, L., & Montealegre, R. (1991). Eastman Kodak organization: Managing Information Systems through strategic alliances. Harvard Business School Case 9-192-030. Boston: Harvard Business School.

Apte, U. M., & Mason, R. O. (1995). Global disaggregation of information-intensive services. *Management Science, 41*(7), 1250–1262. doi:10.1287/mnsc.41.7.1250

Aramo-Immonen, H., Jaakkola, H., & Keto, H. (2011). Multicultural Software Development: The Productivity Perspective. *International Journal of Information Technology Project Management, 2*(1), 19–36. doi:10.4018/jitpm.2011010102

Beard, D., Schwieger, D., & Surendran, K. (2010). A Value Chain Approach for Attracting, Educating, and Transitioning Students to the IT Profession. *Information Systems Education Journal, 8*(7), 1–12.

Beaubouef, T. (2003). Why Computer Science Students Need Language. *ACM SIGCSE Bulletin, 35*(4), 51–54. doi:10.1145/960492.960525

Bharadwaj, A. S. (2000). A Resource-Based Perspective on Information Technology Capability and Firm Performance: An Empirical Investigation. *Management Information Systems Quarterly, 24*(1), 169–196. doi:10.2307/3250983

Boxall, P., Purcell, J., & Wright, P. M. (2007). Human resource management: Scope, analysis and significance, P. Boxall, J. Purcell, P.M. Wright, Editors, The handbook of human resource management, Oxford University Press, Oxford, pp. 1–16.

Bradley, G. (2007). Job tenure as a moderator of stressor-strain relations: A comparison of experienced and new-start teachers. *Work and Stress, 21*(1), 48–64. doi:10.1080/02678370701264685

Casado-Lumbreras, C., Colomo-Palacios, R., Soto-Acosta, P., & Misra, S. (2011). Culture dimensions in software development industry: The effects of mentoring. *Scientific Research and Essays, 6*(11), 2403–2412.

Casey, V., & Richardson, I. (2008). Virtual Teams: Understanding the Impact of Fear. *Software Process Improvement and Practice, 13*(6), 511–526. doi:10.1002/spip.404

Casey, V., & Richardson, I. (2009). Implementation of Global Software Development: A Structured Approach. *Software Process Improvement and Practice, 14*(5), 247–262. doi:10.1002/spip.422

Chen, T., Zhang, J., & Lai, K. K. (2009). An integrated real options evaluating model for information technology projects under multiple risks. *International Journal of Project Management, 27*(8), 776–786. doi:10.1016/j.ijproman.2009.01.001

Craig, A., Paradis, R., & Turner, E. (2002). A gendered view of computer professionals: Preliminary results of a survey. *ACM SIGCSE Bulletin, 34*(2), 101–104. doi:10.1145/543812.543840

Cross, J. (1995). IT outsourcing: British petroleum. *Harvard Business Review, 73*(3), 94–102.

Day, J. (2007). Strangers on the train The relationship of the IT department with the rest of the business. *Information Technology & People, 20*(1), 6–31. doi:10.1108/09593840710730536

Dossani, R., & Kenney, M. (2007). The Next Wave of Globalization: Relocating Service Provision to India. *World Development, 35*(5), 772–791. doi:10.1016/j.worlddev.2006.09.014

Durndell, A., & Thomson, K. (1997). Gender and computing: a decade of change? *Computers & Education, 28*(1), 1–9. doi:10.1016/S0360-1315(96)00034-6

Edwards, H. K., & Sridhar, V. (2005). Analysis of Software Requirements Engineering Exercises in a Global Virtual Team Setup. *Journal of Global Information Management, 13*(2), 21–41. doi:10.4018/jgim.2005040102

Engler, N. (1998). IS managers under stress. *Computing, 12*, 44–48.

Enns, H. G., Ferratt, T. W., & Prasad, J. (2006). Beyond stereotypes of IT professionals: implications for IT HR practices. *Communications of the ACM, 49*(4).

Espinosa, J. A., DeLone, W., & Lee, G. (2006). Global boundaries, task processes and IS project success: A □eld study. *Information Technology & People, 19*(4), 345–370. doi:10.1108/09593840610718036

Farrell, D., & Agrawal, V. (2003). Offshoring and beyond. *The McKinsey Quarterly, 4*, 24–35.

Fisher, A., & Margolis, J. (2002). Unlocking the clubhouse: the Carnegie Mellon experience. *ACM SIGCSE Bulletin, 34*(2), 79–83. doi:10.1145/543812.543836

García Crespo, A., Colomo Palacios, R., Gómez Berbís, J. M., & Tovar Caro, E. (2008). The IT Crowd: Are We Stereotypes? *IEEE IT Professional, 10*(6), 24–28. doi:10.1109/MITP.2008.134

García-Crespo, Á., Colomo-Palacios, R., Soto-Acosta, P., & Ruano-Mayoral, M. (2010). A Qualitative Study of Hard Decision Making in Managing Global Software Development Teams. *Information Systems Management, 27*(3), 247–252. doi:10.1080/10580530.2010.493839

Goode, J. (2007). If You Build Teachers, Will Students Come? The Role of Teachers in Broadening Computer Science Learning for Urban Youth. *Journal of Educational Computing Research, 36*(1), 65–88. doi:10.2190/2102-5G77-QL77-5506

Gurer, D., & Camp, T. (2002). An ACM-W literature review on women in computing. *ACM SIGCSE Bulletin, 34*(2), 121–127. doi:10.1145/543812.543844

Hirschheim, R., & Newman, M. (2010). Houston, we've had a problem…… offshoring, IS employment and the IS discipline: perception is not reality. *Journal of Information Technology, 25*(4), 358–372. doi:10.1057/jit.2010.23

Huber, R. (1993). How continental bank outsourced its 'Crown Jewels'. *Harvard Business Review, 71*(1), 121–129.

Huselid, M. A. (1995). The impact of human resource management practices on turnover, productivity, and corporate financial performance. *Academy of Management Journal, 38*(3), 635–672. doi:10.2307/256741

Jackson, L. A., Zhao, Y., Kolenic, A. III, Fitzgerald, H. E., Harold, R., & Von Eye, A. (2008)… *Cyberpsychology & Behavior, 11*(4), 437–442. doi:10.1089/cpb.2007.0157

Jemielniak, D. (2007). Managers as lazy, stupid careerists? Contestation and stereotypes among software engineers. *Journal of Organizational Change Management, 20*(4), 491–508. doi:10.1108/09534810710760045

Josefek, R. A., Jr., & Kauffman, R. J. (2003). IT human capital and the information systems professional's decision to leave the company. Working paper, MIS Research Center, University of Minnesota, Minneapolis.

Kuean, W. L., Kaur, S., & Wong, E. S. K. (2010). The relationship between organizational commitment and intention to quit: the Malaysian companies perspective. *Journal of Applied Sciences, 10*(19), 2251–2260. doi:10.3923/jas.2010.2251.2260

Kvasny, L., Trauth, E. M., & Morgan, A. J. (2009). Power relations in IT education and work: the intersectionality of gender, race, and class. Journal of Information . *Communication and Ethics in Society, 7*(2/3), 96–118. doi:10.1108/14779960910955828

Lavy, V. (2008). Do gender stereotypes reduce girls' or boys' human capital outcomes? Evidence from a natural experiment. *Journal of Public Economics, 92*(10-11), 2083–2105. doi:10.1016/j.jpubeco.2008.02.009

Lee, J. N., Huynh, M. Q., Kwok, R. C. W., & Pi, S. M. (2003). IT outsourcing evolution: past, present and future. *Communications of the ACM, 46*(5), 84–89. doi:10.1145/769800.769807

Lee, Y., & Lee, S. J. (2006). The competitiveness of the information systems major: an analytic hierarchy process . *Journal of Information Systems Education, 17*(2), 211–222.

Leeney, M., Varajao, J., Trigo-Ribeiro, J., & Colomo-Palacios, R. (2011). Information systems outsourcing in large companies: evidences from 20 Ireland companies. *International Journal of Information Technology Project Management, 2*(4), 44–58. doi:10.4018/jitpm.2011100104

Lengnick-Hall, M. L., Lengnick-Hall, C. A., Andrade, L. S., & Drake, B. (2009). Strategic human resource management: The evolution of the field. *Human Resource Management Review, 19*(2), 64–85. doi:10.1016/j.hrmr.2009.01.002

Loh, L., & Venkataraman, N. (1995). Diffusion of information technology outsourcing: influence sources of Kodak effect . In Khosrowpour, M. (Ed.), *Managing Information Technology Investments with Outsourcing* (pp. 334–358). Hershey, PA: IGI Global. doi:10.1287/isre.3.4.334

Loh, L., & Venkatraman, N. (1992). Determinants of information technology outsourcing: a cross-sectional analysis. *Journal of Management Information Systems, 19*(1), 7–28.

Love, P. E. D., & Irani, Z. (2007). Coping and psychological adjustment among information technology personnel. *Industrial Management & Data Systems, 107*(6), 824–844. doi:10.1108/02635570710758743

Love, P. E. D., Irani, Z., Standing, C., & Themistocleous, M. (2007). Influence of job demands, job control and social support on information systems professionals' psychological well-being. *International Journal of Manpower, 28*(6), 513–528. doi:10.1108/01437720710820026

Luftman, J. (2004). Key Issues for IT Executives 2004. *MIS Quarterly Executive, 4*(2), 269–285.

Luftman, J., & Kempaiah, R. M. (2007). The IS Organization of the Future: The IT Talent Challenge. *Information Systems Management, 24*(2), 129–138. doi:10.1080/10580530701221023

Martin, C. D. (1998). Is Computer Science a Profession? *ACM SIGCSE Bulletin, 30*(2), 7–8. doi:10.1145/292422.296068

Michaels, E., Handfield-Jones, H., & Axelrod, B. (2001). *The War for Talent*. Boston: Harvard Business Press.

Mithas, S. & Krishnan, M.S. (2008). Human Capital and Institutional Effects in the Compensation of Information Technology Professionals in the United States. Management Science, 54(3) 2008, 415-428.

Mithas, S., & Lucas, H. C. (2010). Are Foreign IT Workers Cheaper? U.S. Visa Policies and Compensation of Information Technology Professionals. *Management Science, 56*(5), 745–765. doi:10.1287/mnsc.1100.1149

Morello, D., Kyte, A., & Gomolski, B. (2007). The quest for talent: You ain't seen nothing yet. Gartner Inc. Retrieved November 11, 2011 from http://www.gartner.com/DisplayDocument?ref=g_search&id =569115&subref=advsearch

Niederman, F., Kundu, S., & Salas, S. (2006). IT Software Development Offshoring: A Multi-Level Theoretical Framework and Research Agenda. *Journal of Global Information Management, 14*(2), 52–74. doi:10.4018/jgim.2006040103

Pollacia, L., & Lomerson, W. (2006). Analysis of factors affecting declining CIS enrollment. *Issues in Information Systems, 7*(1), 220–225.

Ramasubbu, N., Mithas, S., Krishnan, M. S., & Kemerer, C. F. (2008). Work dispersion, process-based learning and offshore software development performance. *Management Information Systems Quarterly, 32*(2), 437–458.

Rashid, R. (2008). Image Crisis: Inspiring a new generation of computer scientists. *Communications of the ACM, 51*(7), 33–34. doi:10.1145/1364782.1364793

Rethinam, G. S., & Ismail, M. (2008). Constructs of Quality of Work Life: A Perspective of Information and Technology Professionals. *European Journal of Soil Science, 7*(1), 58–70.

Riolli, L., & Savicki, V. (2003). Information system organizational resilience. Omega . *The International Journal of Management Science, 31*(3), 227–233.

Rosenbloom, J. L., Ash, R. A., Dupont, B., & Coder, L. A. (2008). Why are there so few women in information technology? Assessing the role of personality in career choices. { . *Journal of Economic Psychology, 29*(4), 543–554. doi:10.1016/j.joep.2007.09.005

Sakthivel, S. (2007). Managing risks in offshore systems development. *Communications of the ACM, 50*(4), 69–75. doi:10.1145/1232743.1232750

Sethi, V., Barrier, T., & King, R.C. (1999). Examination of the correlates of burnout in information systems professionals. Information Resources Management Journal, 12(3), .5-13.

Soto-Acosta, P., Martínez-Conesa, I., & Colomo-Palacios, R. (2010). An empirical analysis of the relationship between IT training sources and IT value. *Information Systems Management, 27*(3), 274–283. doi:10.1080/10580530.2010.493847

Standing, C., Standing, A., Lin, C., & Love, P. E. D. (2006). The attribution of success and failure in IT projects. *Industrial Management & Data Systems, 106*(8), 1148–1165. doi:10.1108/02635570610710809

Thong, J. Y. L., & Yap, C.-S. (2000). Information systems and occupational stress: a theoretical framework. Omega . *The International Journal of Management Science, 28*(6), 681–692.

Timms, C., Lankshear, C., Anderson, N., & Courtney, L. (2008). Riding a hydra. Women ICT professionals' perceptions of working in the Australian ICT industry. *Information Technology & People, 21*(2), 155–177. doi:10.1108/09593840810881060

Trigo, A., Varajao, J., & Barroso, J. (2009). A practitioner's roadmap to learning the available tools for Information System Function management. *International Journal of Teaching and Case Studies, 2*(1), 29–40. doi:10.1504/IJTCS.2009.026297

Wade, M., & Hulland, J. (2004). The Resource based View and Information Systems Research: Review, Extension, and Suggestions for Future Research. *Management Information Systems Quarterly, 28*(1), 107–142.

Winkler, J. K., Dibbern, J., & Heinzl, A. (2008). The impact of cultural differences in offshore outsourcing—Case study results from German–Indian application development projects. *Information Systems Frontiers, 10*(2), 243–258. doi:10.1007/s10796-008-9068-5

Zwieg, P., Kaiser, K., Beath, C., Bullen, C., Gallagher, K.P., Goles, T., Howland, J., Simon, J.C., Abbott, P., Abraham, T., Carmel, E., Evaristo, R., Hawk, S., LAcity, M., Gallivan, M., Kelly, S., Mooney, J., Ranganathan, C., Rottman, J., Ryan, T., & Wion, R. (2006). The information technology workforce: Trends and implications 2005-2008. MIS Quarterly Executive, 5("), 101-108.

ADDITIONAL READING

De Marco, T., & Lister, T. (1987). *Peopleware: Productive Projects and Teams* (2nd ed.). Dorset House Publishing Company.

Igbaria, M., & Shayo, C. (2003). *Strategies for Managing IS/IT Personnel*. Hershey, PA: IGI Global. doi:10.4018/978-1-59140-128-5

Jemielniak, D., & Kociatkiewicz, J. (2008). *Management Practices in High-Tech Environments*. Hershey, PA: IGI Global. doi:10.4018/978-1-59904-564-1

Luftman, J. (2004). *Assessing Business-IT Alignment Maturity*. Hershey, PA: IGI Global.

Luftman, J. (2011). *Managing IT Human Resources: Considerations for Organizations and Personnel*. Hershey, PA: IGI Global. doi:10.4018/978-1-60960-535-3

Pankl, E., Theiss-White, D., & Bushing, M. C. (2010). *Recruitment, Development, and Retention of Information Professionals: Trends in Human Resources and Knowledge Management*. Hershey, PA: IGI Global. doi:10.4018/978-1-61520-601-8

Shi, N. S., & Silvius, G. (2010). *Enterprise IT Governance, Business Value and Performance Measurement*. Hershey, PA: IGI Global. doi:10.4018/978-1-60566-346-3

Yoong, P., & Huff, S. (2007). *Managing IT Professionals in the Internet Age*. Hershey, PA: IGI Global.

Acknowledgment

Firstly, editor would like to thank each one of the authors for their contributions. Our sincere gratitude goes to the chapter's authors who contributed their time and expertise to this book.

A special thanks also go to the publishing team at IGI Global for their help and support throughout the process.

Dr. Colomo-Palacios would like to thank his (beautiful) wife Cristina, a constant source of inspiration, encouragement and endless love. And, finally, Rodrigo, every father's dream.

Ricardo Colomo-Palacios
Universidad Carlos III de Madrid, Spain

Section 1
IT Professionals Human Resource Management

Chapter 1
Identifying Technical Competences of IT Professionals:
The Case of Software Engineers

Ricardo Colomo-Palacios
Universidad Carlos III de Madrid, Spain

Edmundo Tovar-Caro
Universidad Politécnica de Madrid, Spain

Ángel García-Crespo
Universidad Carlos III de Madrid, Spain

Juan Miguel Gómez-Berbís
Universidad Carlos III de Madrid, Spain

ABSTRACT

This paper aims to identify technical competency levels relevant to Software Engineering in a spectrum of professional profiles which are found in Spain's main Software Development companies. The research work presents a combination of three initiatives. The first step constitutes a review of the literature related to the characterization of the labor force in the Software Engineering domain. The subsequent step consists of a qualitative study of the practices of a set of organizations, and lastly, this was followed by a quantitative analysis based on investigative surveys administered to a number of representative professionals. The professional career is established from seven consecutive profiles. The pyramidal model for professional careers, identifying one single professional track going from Junior Programmer to IT Director, is still present in the organisations subject to this study. Technical excellence is reached in a determined professional profile, in this case "D". From this point onwards, other competencies which are not uniquely characteristic of Software Engineering gain importance, and stimulate professional development towards higher levels.

DOI: 10.4018/978-1-4666-0924-2.ch001

1. INTRODUCTION

Human Factors represent one of the most important areas of improvement in Software Engineering (SE). Failure rates in software projects are high, and qualified software engineers pertaining to software development teams are key factors in the software development process and their shortcomings and caveats (Pressman, 2005). More precisely, Boehm points out that "After product size, people factors have the strongest influence in determining the amount of effort required to develop a software product " (Boehm, 1981), and "Personnel attributes and Human Resource activities provide by far the largest source of opportunity for improving software development productivity" (Boehm, Horowitz, Madachy, Reifer, Clark, Steece, Brown, Chulani, & Abts, 2000). Competence at the individual level is required for the creation of core competence, crucial for todays organizations at the organizational level. (Bassellier, Reich & Benbasat, 2001).Individual differences have been identified as one of the paradigms for the research of human factors in software development (Curtis, 2002). Research in this area goes back to the 1960s (Sackman, Erikson & Grant, 1968) and continued actively in the 1980s (De Marco & Lister, 1985). Since the 1990s, productive research investigating the role of human factors in software engineering has emerged (Sommerville & Rodden, 1995), (Turley & Bieman, 1995), (Humphrey, 1998), (De Marco & Lister, 1999), which has continued progressively since the beginning of the 21st century (van Solingen, Berghout, Kusters & Trienekens, 2000), (Constantine, 2001), (Tomayko & Hazzan, 2004).

In order to improve the capability of the workforce, several initiatives, such as SEI's People-CMM (Curtis, Hefley & Miller, 2001), describe an evolutionary improvement path which starts from ad hoc, inconsistently performed workforce practices, and progresses to a mature infrastructure of practices for continuously elevating workforce capability. Level 3,"Defined" of the proposed

People-CMM refers to a processing area called "Career Development", which implements the professional career to ensure that individuals are provided opportunities to develop workforce competencies that enable them to achieve career objectives. In order to reach level 3, organisations should determine which different professional careers their employees can undertake, specifying in an explicit way the professional profiles and their corresponding competency levels.

Moreover, competency levels for professional profiles represent one of the fundamental aspects of a professions' maturity level, namely "Professional Development" (Ford & Gibbs, 1996). SWEBOK (Abran, Bourque, Dupuis, Moore & Tripp, 2004), the Software Engineering Body of Knowledge, establishes cognitive levels for each of the components of the 10 knowledge areas. These levels are determined based on levels of apprenticeship described by Bloom's taxonomy (Bloom, 1956). The typology is made for one single profile, being a Software Engineer with four years of experience. In order to complement the capacity levels introduced by SWEBOK, Bourque, Buglione, Abran, & April (2004) have realised an additional competency description of skill levels which three different profiles of Software Engineers should correspond to at different stages of their professional career: at graduation, after four years of professional experience (already included in SWEBOK), and as an experienced Software Engineer. Nevertheless, the study is not complete, as it has been limited to four areas of knowledge: Maintenance, Management, Processing and Quality. Additionally some other efforts had developed recommendations of knowledge and skills required by software engineering professionals in software industry (Eg. Lethbridge, 2000; Turley & Bieman, 1995), the software engineering curricula (Kitchenham, Budgen, Brereton & Woodall, 2005) an the continuous education of IT professionals (Callahan & Perdigo, 2002). Other studies can be found about the competencies necessary for software project managers (Sukhoo et al., 2005), analysts (Misic & Graf, 2004), chief information officers (Bassellier, Reich, & Benbasat, 2001), entry-level IT professionals (McMurtrey, Downey, Zeltmann, & Friedman, 2008) information systems professionals (E.g. Lee, Trauth, & Farwell, 1995; Wu, Chen & Chan, 2007) and IT professionals in general (Kovacs, Caputo, Turchek, & Davis, 2006), to cite some of the most significant examples.

Initiatives such as the one mentioned above are difficult to be implemented directly by HR Departments, as they are either limited – they do not cover all of the sector's professional profiles – or too generic, or exclusively specific to other areas of Human Resource Management (Acuña & Juristo, 2004), referring uniquely to a spectrum of knowledge typically associated with a SE stereotype profile. Identifying competences and skills for IT personnel is not a new research area.

This article will identify a professional career for Software Engineers, described by means of the required competency levels for each of the SE jobs for a specific type of company of significant importance in the software business, as well as a particular geographic area. Specifically, the study has been based on the job profiles identified in actual companies in Spain: large consultancies and software development organisations. In order to define the professional career models as completely as possible, some possibilities were omitted from the research, such as specialisation and dual career paths (technical and managerial).

In order to accurately define the professional careers, Section 2 firstly establishes a professional career and its professional profiles, and analyses appropriate career paths for the companies. Secondly, competency scales of the identified profiles are defined, based on the areas of knowledge established in SWEBOK (Abran, et al, 2004). Section 3 defines the competencies associated with the profiles based on an empirical study.

2. A PROFESSIONAL CAREER PROPOSAL FOR SOFTWARE ENGINEERS

The lack of definitions for professional careers in the field of Information Technology has been highlighted (Lee, 2001). Several studies show the recommendability of making the professional responsible for the planning of his own professional career (Chesebrough & Davis, 1983). However, significant initiatives such as People-CMM (Curtis, Hefley & Miller, 2001) point out the importance of establishing a professional structure with careers which are defined, documented and driven by the organisation.

In this section, a professional career will be defined which can be applied to those Software Engineers who develop their careers in large development and consulting companies in Spain. In order to do so, an analysis will be carried out starting from three different dimensions. Each dimension contributes to the definition of SE professional profiles within the working field of this paper, with additional reference to geographic area and type of company. From the definitions which result, a professional career will be proposed in Section 2.4, based on the following research sources:

- International and local recommendations of professional profiles for Software Engineers (Section 2.1).
- Studies on SE job offers in all types of companies, but restricted to the geographic area covered in this paper (Section 2.2).
- Professional careers present in a sample of companies corresponding to the profile within the domain of this paper (Section 2.3).

2.1. Technical Literature

There are three principal initiatives within the relevant SE literature: METRICA 3 (MAP, 2001), sponsored by the Spanish government, secondly, suggestions proposed by People-CMM (Curtis, Hefley & Miller, 2001), and thirdly, experiences gained by Construx Software (McConnell, 2003).

The methodology used by METRICA 3 (MAP, 2001) defines profiles of participants in software development projects, and describes a total of 5 different professional profiles: Programmer, Analyst, Consultant, Project Manager and Director.

Secondly, one of the objectives of People-CMM's processing area "Development of Professional Careers" (Curtis, Hefley & Miller, 2001) is to define professional profiles, their competencies and requirements for professional career regularisation. The publication offers an example of gradual professional opportunities, including both technical and managerial competency growth within SE. The description of the professional career is shown in Figure 1:

The proposal establishes a dual professional career, starting with mainly technical jobs, branching into Software Team Leader and Project Manager, which later on evolve in parallel within the company, depending to the improvement of either technical or managerial competencies.

Finally, the proposal for professional development made by Construx Software (McConnell, 2003) is based on SWEBOK's (Abran et al 2004) ten knowledge areas. Construx attributes to each of those areas four applicable abilities: Introductory, Competence, Leadership and Mastery. In order to provide its personnel with mechanisms for professional career development, the company establishes a scale with seven professional levels, starting with level 9 and ending with level 15. Figure 2 shows the required competencies for each level, according to the knowledge area.

2.2. Employment Reports in Spain

Spanish employment reports offer a broad range of detailed information on company practices concerning professional careers. The first report which was consulted for the research is issued by the Association of Electronic, IT and Telecommunication Companies. The report is called "Study on Salaries and Labour Policies within the IT Profession" (AETIC, 2004) and has been carried out on a sample of 32.346 employees in the IT field. Out of a total of 22 profiles which have been identified for the technical department, 8 can be applied to Software Engineers: Programmer in training, Junior Programmer, Senior Programmer, Programmer Analyst, Junior Analyst, Senior Analyst, Project Manager and Director.

Another relevant report for analysis is entitled "Infoempleo 2005" (Círculo de Progreso, 2005). The report carries out a review of the Spanish labour market based on 175.362 job offers. The jobs within the IT area which correspond to those performed by Software Engineers are, in order of their position in the hierarchy: Programmer, Programmer Analyst, Functional Analyst, Project Manager, IT Manager or Development Manager and Director.

The last report to be taken into account for definition of the professional career is called

Figure 1. People CMM graduated career opportunities

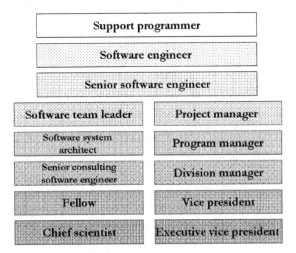

Figure 2. Construx Ladder level requirements via knowledge areas

Level 9	Not applicable			
Level 10	Introductory All K.A.	Competence 3 K.A.	Leadership -	Mastery -
Level 11	Introductory All K.A.	Competence 6 K.A.	Leadership 1 K.A.	Mastery -
Level 12	Introductory All K.A.	Compentence 8 K.A.	Leadership 3 K.A.	Mastery -.
Level 13	Introductory All K.A.	Competence 8 K.A.	Leadership 5 K.A.	Mastery 1 K.A.
Level 14	Intentionally not defined			
Level 15	Intentionally not defined			

"Requirements for Employment within the area of New Information Technologies"(Sedisi, 2004). This report shows the result of analyses made of job offers published in newspapers with national coverage, focussed on offers towards technical specialists. The following profiles are considered for the current work: Low-level Developers, Medium-level Developers, High-level Developers, Project Managers and Directors.

2.3. Industry Practices in Spain

Industry practices will be analysed based on the professional career exams used by three established companies in Spain, which will be called I, II and III for current research purposes.

Company I is a Spanish IT multinational with over 6.000 employees. Due to its size it has different professional careers, however, only those applicable to Software Engineers will be considered here. This company has the following functions in hierarchical order: Technician IV, Technician III, Technician II, Technician I, Mastery, Expert and Director.

Company II is a division of a US-based multinational, specialised in software development. The pyramidal structure of its professional profiles has seven functions, in the following hierarchy:

IT Encoder, Application Programmer, Application Analyst, Systems Analyst, Project Manager, General Manager and Partner.

Finally, Company III is a conglomerate of different European companies which have been merged and acquired. It is currently the most important company in Spain within the business and has a headcount of over 45.000 people worldwide. It has six defined profiles for professional careers related to software, which are in hierarchical order: Programmer, Organic Analyst, Functional Analyst, Project Manager, Business Manager and Director.

2.4. Proposal for Professional Career

The analysis of all the professional profiles identified the previously mentioned sources results in the definition of a professional career that is relevant for the type of development and consulting companies described earlier. The proposal for this professional career is the result of a study of similarity between all of the references consulted. An analysis has been carried out to extract similarities between definitions for each professional profile in all of the research sources. The result of this analysis and the correspondence between profiles is shown in Table 1.

3. COMPETENCY LEVELS FOR THE ESTABLISHED PROFILES

The second step in this study is to define the degree of technical competency with regard to SE, required for each of the professional profiles.

The definition of competency levels within this study, from a professional perspective was considered a very significant factor. Competency studies for Software Engineers (Turley & Bieman, 1995) do not show competency levels, and focus only on the possession of competencies evident in professionals which are relevant for successful job fulfilment. However, during the definition of such competency profiles, distinct professional profiles were not considered, accompanied by the fact that these studies were not performed recently. Therefore, advancement of the profession or shifts in requirements due to the emergence of new paradigms and new technologies have not been considered. Given this current status, it was regarded fundamental to perform a study which analyses the opinions of professionals active in the IT field today. This paper represents an empirical study made in order to support the proposal for competency levels in the previously defined professional profiles. The objective is to establish the professionals' perspective on technical competency levels for each of the professional roles identified. The complete set of competencies corresponds to the ten knowledge areas identified by SWEBOK (Abran et al, 2004).

The quantitative study consists of the application of a questionnaire in order to define competencies for the SE professional profiles defined earlier. A Likert (1932) scale with an even number of values was used, ranging from 1 to 4 points. The description of the scale will be generic for all competencies, showing the following order of values and descriptions:

1= Low Level
2= Medium Level
3= High Level
4= Very High Level

3.1. Sample Description

The sample consists of 50 professionals working in software development jobs within large enterprises (over 500 employees) during a period of at least five years. Alongside the assumption that the professionals held the relevant industry experience, they were interviewed *a priori* with the objective of verifying their knowledge of the discipline, as well as determining whether their knowledge was sufficiently adequate for the aims of the study. As a consequence of this process, three subjects were eliminated from the sample. The distribution of the subjects within the categories identified previously was subsequently established, based on the interviews: 21 "D" (42%), 20 "C" (40%), 5 "D" (10%) y 4 "A" (8%).

The distribution of experimental subjects shows that it was comprised of 6 women (12%) and 44 men (88%). The average age was 35.4, with an average experience in the business of 10.32 years.

3.2. Results

Table 2 shows medium scores (m), standard deviations (sd) and modes (mo) of SE technical competencies for the different profiles identified.

The descriptive analysis of competencies does not clarify sufficiently the objectives of the study. Therefore, additional analyses were required, in order to appropriately address the following research questions: (1) Is there variability between the answers? (2) Which is the most important technical competency? (3) What is the professional profile regarded to require most technical competencies? (4) What is the Evolution of Competencies among profiles?

Table 1 Proposal for professional profiles for software engineers

Proposal	TECHNICAL LITERATURE			COMPANIES			LABOUR MARKETS		
	Métrica 3	People CMM	Construx	I	II	III	RENTIC	Infoempleo	S.E.D.I.S.I.
G			Level 9	IT Technician I	IT Encoder				Programmer in training
									Junior Programmer traditional environments
									Junior Internet Programmer
F	Programmer	Support Programmer	Level 10	IT Technician II	Application Programmer	Programmer	Low level Developer	Programmer	Senior Programmer traditional environments
									Senior Internet Programmer
E		SW Engineer	Level 11	IT Technician III	Application Analyst	Organic Analyst	Medium level Developer	Programmer Analyst	Programmer Analyst
									Junior Analyst
D	Analyst	Senior SW Engineer	Level 12	IT Technician IV	System Analyst	Functional Analyst	High level Developer	Functional Analyst	Senior Analyst
C	Project Manager	Project Manager	Level 13	IT Expert	Project Manager	Project Manager	Project Manager	IT Project Manager	Project Manager
B		Program Manager	Level 14	IT Mastery	General Manager	General Manager		IT Manager	
A	Director	Division Manager	Level 15	Director	Partner		Executive	Director	Director of the technical / development department
		Vice-President							

Table 2. Medium scores, standard deviations and modes for technical competencies of professional profiles

COMPETENCIES	A m	A sd	A mo.	B m	B sd	B mo.	C m	C sd	C mo.	D m	D sd	D mo.	E m	E sd	E mo.	F m	F sd	F mo.	G m	G sd	G mo.
Software Requirements	1,84	,912	1	2,34	,982	2	3,32	,844	4	3,74	,487	4	2,96	,605	3	1,98	,820	2	1,32	,587	1
Software Design	1,4	,535	1	1,76	,797	1	2,82	,941	3	3,78	,507	4	3,5	,580	4	2,46	,813	2	1,56	,733	1
Software Construction	1,22	,465	1	1,42	,642	1	2,22	,79	2	3,04	,781	3	3,58	,538	4	3,44	,733	4	2,58	,971	2
Software Testing	1,24	,431	1	1,72	,784	1	2,8	,948	3	3,5	,735	4	3,56	,611	4	3,1	,839	4	2,32	,999	2
Software Maintenance	1,3	,505	1	1,58	,758	1	2,56	,907	2	3,32	,768	4	3,36	,749	4	3	,969	4	2,12	,961	2
Software Configuration Management	1,54	,762	1	2,04	1,16	1	3,16	,955	4	3,52	,58	4	3,06	,682	3	2,16	,71	2	1,54	,676	1
Software Quality	1,8	,857	1	2,52	1,01	3	3,4	,782	4	3,58	,673	4	3,16	,71	3	2,38	,855	2	1,64	,693	1
Software Engineering Management	2,84	1,08	4	3,42	,835	4	3,66	,593	4	2,86	,969	3	2,26	,944	3	1,62	,667	1	1,12	,328	1
Software Engineering Tools and Methods	1,68	,741	1	2,26	,876	2	3,62	,667	4	3,72	,454	4	3,14	,729	3	2,3	,886	2	1,58	,731	1
Software Engineering Process	2,36	1,08	2	2,88	,961	2	3,76	,476	4	3,4	,67	4	2,58	,785	3	1,68	,653	2	1,16	,37	1

Table 3. Competency level per profile

Competency	G	F	E	D	C	B	A
Software Requirements	1	2	3	4	3	2	1
Software Design	2	3	4	4	3	2	1
Software Construction	3	4	4	3	2	1	1
Software Testing	2	3	4	4	3	2	1
Software Maintenance	2	3	4	4	3	2	1
Software Configuration Management	2	2	3	4	3	2	1
Software Quality	2	2	3	4	4	3	1
Software Engineering Management	1	2	3	3	4	4	3
Software Engineering Tools and Methods	2	2	3	4	4	2	1
Software Engineering Process	1	2	3	4	4	3	2

Variability of Answers

Reviewing standard deviations between scores, which are in general lower than 1 (standard deviations greater than 1 have been highlighted in Table 2), it can be seen that variability in the sample's answers is low. All 4 cases of significant variability occur in the professional roles "A" and "B", equally distributed and for *Software Configuration Management* and *Software Quality* in case of "B" and for *SE Process* and *SE Management* in case of "A".

Most Important Technical Competency

In order to determine the most important technical competency for all professional profiles, Table 3 shows a comparison of totals on averages and modes for each technical competency. According to its total average, *Software Quality* is the most important competency, followed by *SE Tools and Methods* and *Software Testing*. The competency to be considered of least importance is *Software Configuration Management*, followed by *Software Maintenance*. However, it is important to point out that values among competencies are very similar, and there is no significant difference among technical competencies. (See Figure 3)

Professional Role which Requires the Most Technical Competency

In order to determine the relative importance of SE technical competencies, averages and modes (Figure 4) of technical competencies for each professional profile were summed. "D" shows the highest technical competence, followed by "C" and "E". Visualisation of the figure suggests a pyramidal approach of competencies. Technical skills increase to a maximum level, in correspondence with profile "D", from where technical tasks are exchanged for management tasks, often concurring with the professionals' obsolescence.

Figure 3. Average and mode sums of different technical competencies

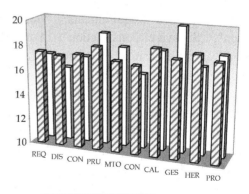

☑ Average Sum ☐ Mode Sum

Evolution of Competencies among Profiles

The establishment of an organisation's competency levels is considered by People-CMM as part of a personal development plan. People-CMM specifically mentions the requirement for a professional to know which competencies he will need for future levels in his career. For this purpose, competency levels - understood as significant differences between scores of technical competencies in related profiles - have been calculated comparing averages by means of Student's T-test for related samples. Comparisons have been made 2 by 2 for each technical competency value, in order to find significant differences which would justify the possible increase, by means of negative T's, or decrease of competencies between related profiles. The results display that significant increases in all of the technical competencies are evident between categories G and F, a similar pattern being visible in the transition between F and E. In the difference between E and D, significant increases in all of the competencies were produced, except with regard to the competency "Software Construction", which held the values t(49)=4,846, p<.05. Examining C, significant increases in "Software Engineering Management" t(49)=- 5,715, p<.05, and "Software Engineering Process" t(49)=-3,527, p<.05 were evident, while a significant decrease could be witnessed in the competencies considered more associated with Software Development, and less to Management, that is,, "Software Requirements", "Software Design", "Software Construction", "Software Testing" and "Software Maintenance". A and B, reflecting a similar pattern to the previous one, display significant differences between all of the competencies, except "Software Engineering Management" and "Software Engineering Process".

Table 3 shows the competency level required for each knowledge area and SE professional profile within the type of companies analysed.

Figure 4. Average and mode sums for professional profiles

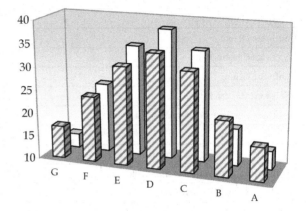

Competency values have been attributed according to the scores given by the experimental subjects, reflecting competency requirements for different professional profiles. Scores, expressed in a Likert scale ranging from 1 - 4, have initially been assigned by rounding the average scores for different professional profiles. Subsequently, they have been refined according to the competency scales which had been defined previously, in order to finally establish the evolution of competencies of employees in the business environment defined.

Thus, the previous description of professional profiles can be completed by adding the associated competency levels outlined and described below:

G: Additionally to the previous aspects, this category requires a high competency level with regard to software construction, with notions of design, quality, testing and configuration management.

F: In addition to what was previously mentioned, employees in this category are highly skilled in software construction, which constitutes a major part of their labour efforts. They possess advanced knowledge of design and testing. Employees should have a medium level in other technical competencies.

E: Workers to be found in this category hold a profound knowledge of design, construction, testing and software maintenance, in addition to a high level of knowledge of other SE technical competencies.

D: Employees in category D are top level in technical competencies. They are highly skilled in Requirements, design, testing, maintenance, configuration management, quality, Tools and process. They also hold a high level of knowledge of management and software construction.

C: From this profile onwards, technical competency is less important, except for issues characteristic of management. Nevertheless, employees still show very high competency levels on Quality, Tools and Process, apart from the already mentioned Management skills, and have high skill level on requirements, Testing and Configuration Management features. On Construction, they have a medium level.

B: Additionally to what was mentioned earlier, this profile shows very high Management skills, and competencies with regard to Process and Quality. Such employees hold medium levels of other competencies, except for Construction, which are of low level.

A: Employees in this category do not focus on technical competencies related to SE, except for managerial aspects, due to commitments to Management and the Software Process.

The most important evidence, shown in Figure 2, is the pyramidal structure of SE professional careers in the targeted companies. The top of the pyramid is represented by profile "D", showing the highest level of technical competency. This characteristic confirms the professional's perception of lesser importance of technical competency in profiles higher up in the hierarchy compared to intermediate profiles, contradictory to the integration and continued competency improvement proposed by Construx (McConnell, 2003) but in the same career path showed by Lannes (2001) in a typical engineering career path.

4. CONCLUSION AND FUTURE WORK

In this paper, a professional career and the competency levels related to the professional profiles identified for the organisations subject to this study is proposed, based on the viewpoint of professionals. The professional career is established starting from seven consecutive profiles, giving concrete form to different levels of technical competency. The global importance *of Software Quality* and knowledge of *Tools and Methods* and *Testing* is reflected in the higher levels of competency required for the different professional profiles. On the other hand, *Software Configuration Management* and *Maintenance* are less valued by professionals. The central professional profile, "D", represents higher competency levels in all technical competencies, except for Management.

The pyramidal model for professional careers, identifying one single professional track going from Junior Programmer to IT Director, is still present in the organisations subject to this study. Technical excellence is reached in a determined professional profile, in this case "D". From this point onwards, other competencies which are not typical of Software Engineering gain importance and stimulate professional development towards higher levels. Controversial aspects of these type of professional structures, on one hand, the technical obsolescence in levels higher up in the hierarchy, and on the other hand, the lack of correspondence between improvement of technical competencies and professional progress, are still valid, despite new initiatives which try to define a correspondence between professional development and progress in the career. This can be explained by the company cultures and behavioural inertia of the individuals, heirs of years of tradition of pyramidal professional models.

As future research, we propose definition of competency levels for non-technical competencies, called general competencies, which are common to all professions. This will provide a frame in which the selected companies can establish competency characteristics for the profiles. On this basis, they can create an evaluation model allowing the identification of strengths and weaknesses of the competencies of their employees, referring to the established standards.

REFERENCES

Abran, A., Bourque, P., Dupuis, R., & Moore, J. W. (2004). *SWEBOK. Guide to the Software Engineering Body of Knowledge*. Los Alamitos, CA: IEEE Computer Society.

Acuña, S. T., & Juristo, N. (2004). Assigning people to roles in software projects. *Software, Practice & Experience, 34*(7), 675–696. doi:10.1002/spe.586

Bassellier, G., Reich, B. H., & Benbasat, I. (2001). IT Competence of Business Managers: A Definition and Research Model. *Journal of Management Information Systems, 17*(4), 159–182.

Bloom, B. S. (1956). *Taxonomy of Educational Objectives: The Classification of Educational Goals*. Chicago, IL: Susan Fauer Company.

Boehm, B. (1981). *Software Engineering Economics*. Englewood Cliffs: Prentice-Hall.

Boehm, B., Horowitz, E., Madachy, R., Reifer, D., Clark, B. K., Steece, B., et al. (2000). *Software Cost Estimation with COCOMO II*. Upper Saddle River: Prentice Hall.

Bourque, P., Buglione, L., Abran, A., & April, A. (2004). Bloom's Taxonomy Levels for Three Software Engineer Profiles. In *Proceedings of the Eleventh Annual International Workshop on Software Technology and Engineering Practice (STEP'04)*.

Callahan, D., & Pedigo, B. (2002). Educating Experienced IT Professionals by Addressing Industry's Needs. *IEEE Software, 19*(5), 57–62. doi:10.1109/MS.2002.1032855

Chesebrough, P. H., & Davis, G. B. (1983). Planning a career path in information systems. *Journal of Systems Management, 34*(1), 6–13.

Círculo de progreso (2005). *Informe Infoempleo 2005: Oferta y Demanda del empleo cualificado en España*. Madrid, Spain: Círculo de Progreso.

Constantine, L. (2001). *Peopleware Papers: The Notes on the Human Side of Software*. Englewood Cliffs, NJ: Prentice-Hall.

Curtis, B. (2002), Human Factors in Software Development. In J.J. Marciniak (Ed.), *Encyclopedia of Software Engineering* (pp. 598-610). Willey & Sons.

Curtis, B., Hefley, W.E., & Miller, S.A. (2001). *People Capability Maturity Model (P-CMM®) Version 2.0*. CMU/SEI-2001-MM-01.

De Marco, T., & Lister, T. (1985). Programmer Performance and the effects of the workplace. In *Proceedings of the 8th International Conference on Software Engineering* (pp. 268-272).

De Marco, T., & Lister, T. (1999). *Peopleware: Productive Projects and Teams* (2nd ed.). New York: Dorset House.

Ford, G., & Gibbs, N. E. (1996). *A Mature Profession of Software Engineering*. Technical CMU/SEI-96-TR-004, Pittsburgh, PA: Software Engineering Institute, Carnegie Mellon University.

Humphrey, W. S. (1998). *Managing Technical People: Innovation, Teamwork and the Software Process*. Reading, MA: Addison-Wesley.

Kitchenham, B., Budgen, D., Brereton, P., & Woodall, P. (2005). An investigation of software engineering curricula. *Journal of Systems and Software, 74*(3), 325–335. doi:10.1016/j.jss.2004.03.016

Kovacs, P. J., Caputo, D., Turchek, J., & Davis, G. A. (2006). A survey to define the skill sets of selected information technology professionals. *Issues in Information Systems Journal, 7*(1), 242–246.

Lanes, W. J. (2001). What is Engineering Management? *IEEE Transactions on Engineering Management, 48*(1), 107–110. doi:10.1109/17.913170

Lee, D., Trauth, E., & Farwell, D. (1995). Critical Skills and Knowledge Requirements of IT Professionals: A Joint Academic/Industry Investigation. *MIS Quarterly, 19*(3), 313–340. doi:10.2307/249598

Lee, P. (2001). Technopreneurial Inclinations and Career Management Strategy among Information Technology Professionals. In *Proceedings of the 34th Hawaii International Conference on System Sciences.*

Lethbridge, T. C. (2000). What Knowledge Is Important to a Software Professional? *Computer, 33*(5), 44–50. doi:10.1109/2.841783

Likert, R. (1932). A Technique for the Measurement of Attitudes. *Archives de Psychologie, 22*(140), 1–55.

McConnell, S. (2003). *Professional Software Development.* Boston, MA: Addison-Wesley.

McMurtrey, M. E., Downey, J. P., Zeltmann, S. M., & Friedman, W. H. (2008). Critical skill sets of entry-level IT professionals: An empirical examination of perceptions from field personnel. *Journal of Information Technology Education, 7*, 101–120.

Ministerio de Administraciones Públicas, M. A. P. Secretaría de Estado para la Administración Pública. Consejo Superior de Informática (2001). MÉTRICA: versión 3 Madrid, Spain: Ministerio de Administraciones Públicas.

Misic, M. M., & Graf, D. K. (2004). Systems analyst activities and skills in the new millennium. *Journal of Systems and Software, 71*(1-2), 31–36. doi:10.1016/S0164-1212(02)00124-3

Pressman, R. (2005). *Software Engineering: A Practitioner's Approach.* New York: McGraw Hill.

Sackman, H., Erikson, W. J., & Grant, E. E. (1968). Exploratory Studies comparing online and offline programming performance. *Communications of the ACM, 11*(1), 3–11. doi:10.1145/362851.362858

SEDISI. (2004). *Estudio sobre Salarios y Política Laboral en el Sector Informático.* Madrid, Spain: SEDISI.

Sommerville, I., & Rodden, T. (1995). Human, *social and organizational influences on the software process.* Technical Report CSEG/2/1995, Cooperative Systems Engineering Group, Computing Department, Lancaster University (pp. 1–21).

Sukhoo, A., Barnard, A., Eloff, M. M., Van der Poll, J. A., & Motah, M. (2005). Accommodating soft skills in software project management. *Issues in Informing Science and Information Technology, 2*, 691–704.

Tomayko, J., & Hazzan, O. (2004). *Human aspects of Software Engineerng.* Hingham, MA: Charles River Media.

Turley, R. T., & Bieman, J. M. (1995). Competencies of Exceptional an Non-Exceptional Software Engineers. *Journal of Systems and Software, 28*(1), 19–38. doi:10.1016/0164-1212(94)00078-2 van Solingen, R., Berghout, E., Kusters, R., & Trienekens, J. (2000). From process improvement to people improvement: enabling learning in software development. *Information and Software Technology, 42*(14), 965–971. doi:10.1016/S0950-5849(00)00148-8

Wu, J. H., Chen, Y. C., & Chang, C. (2007). Critical IS professional activities and skills/knowledge: A perspective of IS managers. *Computers in Human Behavior, 23*(6), 2945–2965. doi:10.1016/j.chb.2006.08.008

Chapter 2
Human Capital Management Process Based on Information Technology Models and Governance

Darko Galinec
Ministry of Defense, Croatia

ABSTRACT

Human capital management (HCM) inside large systems is very complex and demanding, to achieve successful accomplishment high quality information support is necessary. There are many cases where human capital management process is not conducted in a satisfactory way. Key decisions usually come late, very often because of impossibility to consider a problem in its entirety. The cause of it usually lies in weakness and understatement of the human capital management itself and in this connection data management is not given adequate consideration. Data originating from inside and outside sources within information system (IS) are not integrated in a way which will provide an optimal use. In this connection, this paper examines possibilities to innovate the entire human capital management process through the integration of respective data. Data warehousing (DW) possibilities and position within the integral business intelligence (BI) concept are noted as a first step towards its realization. In this paper the necessity to innovate and promote permanently the quality of human capital management process is considered; the main features of the process are given as well. Business process innovation (BPI) as a systematic approach with a view to achieve significant business process change is presented; its connection with data aspect of IS is given too. According to the research of this paper, HCM BPI is achieved by the data integration within existing IS. DW model intended for HCM has been elaborated as a solution which will innovate the process itself. The position and the role of DW within entire BI organization concept have been established as well. Finally, the benefits achieved by the research are explained.

DOI: 10.4018/978-1-4666-0924-2.ch002

INTRODUCTION

Human capital management is the basis to obtain comparative advantages and integral efficiency since human potentials are the most important resources nowadays. Successful functioning and realization of aims defined in the chosen strategy, within functionally oriented and hierarchically structured organizational system it is necessary to upgrade human capital management processes. This can be obtained by innovation of the already existing and development of new processes and procedures which will result in the integration of the information system's data. Improving business processes is the top business priority for CIOs in 2009, while improving enterprise workforce effectiveness is at the 3rd place of business expectations for IT focus on improving current operations and performance (McDonald & Begin & Fortino, 2009). In the organizational context, innovation may be linked to performance and growth through improvements in efficiency, productivity, quality, competitive positioning, market share, etc. All organizations can innovate, including for example hospitals, universities, and local governments. While innovation typically adds value, innovation may also have a negative or destructive effect as new developments clear away or change old organizational forms and practices. Organizations that do not innovate effectively may be destroyed by those that do. Hence innovation typically involves risk. A key challenge in innovation is maintaining a balance between process and product innovations where process innovations tend to involve a business model which may develop shareholder satisfaction through improved efficiencies while product innovations develop customer support however at the risk of costly research and development that can erode shareholder return.

Innovation, like many business functions, is a management process that requires specific tools, rules, and discipline (Davila & Epstein & Shelton, 2006). Information system which usually supports human capital management is not completely satisfying, since the data within it are not integrated on the data model level and because of inherited modularity they are disunited. The aforesaid disunity is manifested through inadequate (insufficient) connection between information subsystems within HCM IS. Possibility to make complex and user defined data analyses on the basis of time dimension which is indispensable in the decision making process are insufficient too. Obtained desired improved process should render possible the integration with other functional areas and processes within an organization. They can also be improved through other different approaches (neither necessarily through data integration, nor by elimination of it). Integration within organization system will be conducted on the basis of chosen and accepted strategy, in conformity with defined priorities, disposed human potentials, organizational procedures and chosen technology. Functional logics should be defined in order to satisfy conceptual unity of the improved process which is the first element of the IS unity. Improved process must be open and connecting point must be provided for. Aforementioned processes should lead to enterprise information integration (EII), as concept of data abstraction in addressing the data access challenges associated with data heterogeneity and data contextualization.

The unanticipated changes in the IT infrastructure forced IT personnel to set new priorities that caused delays in other aspects of their work. There are several problems that information technology (IT) directors must monitor carefully when their organizations introduce complex IT-based projects that have strategic implications. Six major tactics that an organization may employ in order to ensure continuity and flexibility in its IT functions are: retaining by continuous training, evaluation by objectives, reward for smooth operations, reducing stress and burnout by encouraging creative ideas, job rotation, and finally involving IT personnel in the hiring process of new employees (Watad & DiSanzo, 1998).

Stress and burnout are major problems and the IT director must make the work environment more enjoyable. There is a tendency to reward IT personnel who can resolve crises instead of rewarding managers who keep their operations running smoothly (Sturm, 1996). In general, reliability and continuity are more important than crisis handling. Therefore the reward system should be designed to reflect these values. Organizations cannot afford to lose IT personnel during an IT-enabled major organizational change. Retaining IT staff with older skills as the needs of the company change is a challenge. The cost of replacing IT professionals is much higher than retraining them (Champy, 1997). Most IT organizations have someone who is in charge of recruiting but no one is directly responsible for retention (Champy, 1997). IT managers must view successive waves of IT - ranging from mainframe to intranets - as evolutionary rather revolutionary (Babcock, 1996). Therefore, IT managers must institute continuous training programs.

The organization believes that it is the employee's responsibility to develop and maintain the skill sets required to continue to be a contributing member. To that end, the organization will pay and provide all the means necessary for job related training and education where needed. The employee's ability to achieve his or her objectives on time is to be measured by his or her ability to meet project plan objectives on time and is used as a leading indicator of performance. IT employees must be rewarded on the basis of providing a smooth operating environment and meeting their agreed-upon deadlines. Employees may receive additional monetary compensation, recognition or time off for successfully handling crises that are not of their own making. For example, if a hardware failure resulted in a catastrophic loss of data, the employee that worked all weekend to solve the problem would receive some type of reward for actions above and beyond the call of duty.

In an attempt to relieve some of the stress associated with IT, humor is encouraged and an informal atmosphere is maintained in the department. Unit managers and team leaders are encouraged to spend more time with their staff and to take more of a personal interest in their work and lives outside the office. Since much of the work is based on specific deliverables, more leeway is given as to when and how work is performed (in office, over lunch, at home). This management by objective approach allows the IT staff to be flexible in structuring their work. Regular department events are scheduled to increase morale. Picnics, bowling, dinners and holiday parties are all scheduled to help department personnel relieve stress and get to know each other informally. "Crazy Days" are held to aid in the development of new ideas. Crazy Days are quarterly events where the department gathers for lunch and brainstorms on how processes can be improved. The basic idea behind these events is that no idea is too crazy. Crazy Day ideas that generate process improvements are rewarded with a bonus payout that is commensurate with process improvement on a percentage basis.

Job rotation is practiced throughout the IT department. The department is divided into teams that specialize in maintaining and creating select types of applications (office automation, optical scanning, etc.). Employees are cross-trained within each of these teams so that they can perform all of the functions the team may be called on to complete. The team leader has supervisory responsibility for team members. The leader analyzes user requests and assigns tasks with a definite eye toward load balancing and cross training requirements. The team leader is evaluated on his or her ability to achieve successful cross training of team members. Job rotation often results in slower job turn around when a new member who is unfamiliar with the team's applications is added. Nonetheless, the long-term benefits of job rotation outweigh its short-term negative aspects.

An important factor in ensuring effective functioning of the IT department is involving the current employee in the hiring process of prospective employees. Potential new employees have to pass two technical hurdles in order to gain employment. The first step centers on taking a technical test that has been designed to simulate IT issues that occur routinely on the job. The second step is the technical review. The potential employee's peers hold this review. The organization has found that peers are most interested in having any potential fellow employee know as much as or more than they do. This is based on the belief that underachievers will have to be carried and coddled during team projects until they come up to speed or are terminated due to poor performance (Watad & DiSanzo, 1998).

HUMAN CAPITAL MANAGEMENT

People, human capital, human capital management are the key words which are dominant preoccupation of modern managers and organizations. Human capital management is oriented towards successful fulfillment of the organization goals and objectives. Modern business requires process centric approach, i.e. end-to-end (E2E) management and control of business system (Galinec & Vidović, 2007).

HCM Goals

HCM specific goals must be compatible with business goals and objectives. Therefore associated goals can be divided into three basic groups: business and economic, social, goals of flexibility and permanent change as well. Immediate business goal is to ensure: appropriate number of employees with adequate qualification in good time and place. Their potentials achieve organization goals and to increase organization competitiveness and success must be turned to the best account. HCM social goals are identified through fulfillment of needs, expectations and interests of the employees, improvement of their socioeconomic status, use and

development of individual possibilities, insuring permanent full employment and the improvement of working life quality. Key assumptions needed for development and existence of the organizations refer to continuous and prompt adjustments to the outside changes. People are the resource of flexibility and adaptability. In this connection, HCM goals and objectives involve the creation and maintenance of flexible and adaptable potential of all employees, resistance to changes should be reduced. Changes should be viewed as a way of life and complete human potential should be sensitive to quantitative, qualitative and structural changes.

HCM Process

Human potentials include knowledge, skills, abilities, creative possibilities, motivation and loyalty at disposal to an organization. That is intellectual and mental energy which an organization can engage to achieve goals and business development. HCM include a lot of interconnected processes, activities, and tasks by means of which adequate number and structure of employees, their knowledge, skills, interests, motivation necessary to realize actual, developmental and strategic goals will be insured. HCM include the following basic processes:

- Strategic HCM
- Necessary number and structure of employees
- Analyses and shaping of jobs and posts
- Recruitment, installation and disposition of personnel
- Tracking and assessment of efficiency
- Motivation and awarding
- Education and development of employees
- Creation of adequate organization climate and culture
- Social and health protection
- Employment
- Different services to employees

Each of the above mentioned processes includes various and specific activities, professional tasks and duties. As for management and organization managers, these processes and duties correspond to the key questions connected to the business and development problems, as follows:

- Vision of future business and staff planned to be engaged in business development
- Work and business demands at present and in future
- Staff needed for present and future business needs
- HCM strategy which will result in such personnel
- Recruitment of best experts and talents
- Keeping those who are the best and the most qualified, sacking those who are not competent
- Further development of employees' potentials
- Differentiation and awarding of the best employees
- Provide for necessary knowledge and skills of all employees
- Provide for permanent development of employees' proficiency and potentials

For all above mentioned processes, activities and accomplishments, it will be necessary to provide information system support with numerous entities and connections so that big quantities of differently organized data can be stored and processed. Since the data are originating from different resources they should be integrated-consistence in content, titles and formats should be ensured. Data must contain the time dimension as well, during the process data should be snapshot during regular periods of time.

HCM Tools State of the Art

"Human capital management applications are part of the administrative backbone of all organizations" (Otter & Holincheck, 2009, p. 1). Business applications are used to automate administrative and strategic human resources (HR) processes. Although personnel, benefits and payroll administration often are viewed as "commodity" processes, the effective deployment of systems and governance models to support these functions can result in significant operating efficiencies that improve bottom-line performance. These applications also are part of a broader enterprise resource planning (ERP) strategy. These process areas and applications also can become an important foundation for achieving strategic goals - for example, an organization that plans significant global expansion will struggle to accomplish this goal without robust performance and incentive systems that align employee actions and behaviours with these objectives. Similarly, organizations find it difficult to attract, recruit and retain skilled employees without effective HCM systems and strategies.

HCM Technology

HCM applications are fundamental to an organization's business application strategy. Regardless of the industry, these applications form part of the backbone of an organization's business application portfolio. Consequently, the evaluation, selection and implementation of the applications will have a major impact on the overall business application strategy. Most organizations deploy significant systems to improve HCM administrative processes. A combination of system consolidation, process standardization, shared services and self-service has driven considerable cost reductions and quality gains in administrative processes. Organizations will continue to automate and reduce HR administrative overhead. Even after major administrative process transformation, continuous improvements are possible. Business process outsourcing (BPO) is significant component of HR service deliveries. The current economic climate means a stronger focus on cost savings. A renewed interest in employee services, time management and contingent workforce management is seen.

However, relentless administrative process optimization is not enough. Organizations must do more by focusing on strategic processes, including talent management, and by building a more rigorous approach to HCM analytics. Self-service is moving beyond the transactional into the analytical. As organizations grapple with the recession, workforce planning becomes more critical than before. HCM technology provides a way to automate administrative processes, support required compliance activities and leverage talent in the organization. There are three broad categories of HCM technology - core HR management system (HRMS), talent management and workforce management. Core HRMS supports the automation of administrative HR processes, including personnel, payroll and benefits administration. In addition, core HRMS includes employee and manager self-service. It is the employee system of record. Talent management applications focus on attracting, developing and retaining talent. The applications include workforce planning, talent acquisition (e-recruitment and contingent workforce management), employee performance management, career development, succession management, e-learning and compensation management. Workforce management enables companies to optimally deploy talent. Workforce management solutions include workforce planning, task/activity management, labour scheduling, and time and attendance. Historically, most HR systems have focused on a "pull" basis, with HR departments requesting or demanding information from employees and management. Facebook and similar applications have begun to affect HCM more significantly than most other business areas, especially in recruitment, and many vendors are rushing to include social software features into their solutions, and integrate them with mainstream networks. Whether these additions become widely adopted remains to be seen. HCM software as a service (SaaS) continues to grow at two to three times the pace of on-premises. Through 2010 three major trends will continue: the maturing of shared-

service and BPO delivery models and offerings; continued, although markedly slower, growth in talent management solutions and analytics; and social software solutions. These will begin to have a significant impact on HR processes such as recruitment and alumni management. HR master data integration into the broader applications environment will continue to grow in importance and complexity, due partly to compliance and identity management demands. Leading organizations will begin to address the thorny challenge of integrating SaaS and on-premises applications into a consistent HCM process model. Most organizations have a core HRMS. These organizations are looking to leverage talent management, workforce management solutions and analytics to improve their HCM. Leading organizations are beginning to explore social software tools and Web 2.0 in an HR context. We expect an accelerated deployment of consumer tools into HR processes. (Otter & Holincheck, 2009).

Service Oriented Architecture (SOA) and HCM

SOA can be used to address some of the key challenges of HCM applications, such as changing the applications as business needs change, extending the applications to meet business needs and addressing the difficulty in upgrading applications. Initial solutions being delivered to the market will meet some of these challenges, but they need to evolve to deliver all that's promised.

- Well-designed SOA-based solutions should make it easier to change applications as business needs change, as well as improve integration and extensibility. However, it is not the only way to achieve similar goals. Service-enabling application programming interfaces (APIs) can help improve integration, and integrated process modeling can help achieve some of the same objectives.

- Properly designed HCM service-oriented business applications (SOBAs) should reduce implementation and upgrade costs. However, the offerings are still maturing, and the customer experience is too limited to prove this value proposition.
- For evolutionary business changes, a well-designed SOA-based HCM solution should improve flexibility and increase agility by enabling customers to change models and associated configurations without the same level of table maintenance as the traditional approach. However, making business change happen requires more than having the right technology. The right people and skills, as well as processes, are imperative.

Most customers have struggled with the flexibility and agility of the current generation of HCM solutions. During the implementation process, customers have all the options available on how to configure these applications to meet the defined business requirements. However, once implemented, it is often difficult for customers to change the configuration if the business needs change, and it is especially difficult to accommodate transformational change in the business. For example, in a corporate restructuring, it is easy to move entities on an organization chart, but many related configurations may have to be updated.

SOA does not solve flexibility/agility challenges completely. For a transformational business change, nearly all services may be replaced and functionality added, requiring organizations to spend significant time and effort to redesign business processes, model services, architect and configure applications, and help people through the change journey. For more-evolutionary business changes, the self-contained nature of services can make application changes easier and more frequent, thus increasing business agility.

Composite applications represent an opportunity for companies to leverage services for more agility. A composite application can be used to define a new process by leveraging other services. For example, for an employee directory application, a company might combine a service called View Organization Chart with other internal services (such as Launch an Instant Message Session), as well as with external services (such as View Address on Google Maps or Call Out Using Skype) to create a new application (or extend the organization chart application). This is a simplistic example, but more-complex composite applications are possible. The flexibility and agility promised by SOA can be achieved only if the proper governance processes are in place. Selecting the "right" services to leverage - packaged in an application, available over the Internet and custom-built - as well as determining the right level of granularity and ensuring proper reuse are among the issues that SOA governance processes address. HCM customers should consider these applications only if the functionality meets their needs today or if the 12-month road map will fill gaps for culturally aggressive. In addition, customers should expect some growing pains as the offerings mature. Culturally moderate and culturally conservative organizations should monitor the experience of the early adopters (whether they are seeing the benefits) and consider these solutions in a longer-term planning horizon - two to three years (Holincheck, 2008).

BUSINESS PROCESS INNOVATION/IMPROVEMENT

More than ever, business process improvement/reengineering (BPI/BPR) is gaining recognition as a critical success factor in sustaining the growth and profitability of businesses (Wood, 2008). BPI is a systematic approach to help any organization make significant changes in the way it does business. It's about the redesign of business processes and the associated systems and organizational structures to achieve an improvement in business performance. (Rummler & Brache, 1990) defined comprehensive approach to organizing companies around processes, managing and measuring processes and redefining processes. The organization may be a for-profit business, a non-profit organization, a government agency, or any other ongoing concern. BPI works by:

- Defining what the organization's strategic goals and purposes are
- Determining what the organization's customers (or stakeholders) are
- Aligning the business processes to meet the customer's requirements.

The goal of BPI is a radical change in the performance of an organization, rather than a series of incremental changes. This radical model was popularized by Michael Hammer and James Champy, when they stated that the process was not meant to impose trivial changes, (e.g. 10 or 20 percent improvements or cost reductions), but was meant to be revolutionary. Reengineering has earned bad reputation due to the fact that such projects have often resulted in massive layoffs. In spite of the hype surrounding its introduction, reengineering has not lived up to its expectations (Hammer & Champy, 2003). The main reasons seem to be that:

- Reengineering assumes that the factor that limits organization's performance is the in-effectiveness of its processes (which may or may not be true) and offers no means of validating that assumption
- Reengineering assumes the need to start the process of performance improvement with a "clean slate", i.e. totally disregard the status quo
- Reengineering does not provide an effective way to focus improvement efforts on the organization's constraint.

Other organizations did not make radical changes in their business processes, did not make significant gains, and wrote the process off as a failure. Yet others have found that BPI is a valuable tool in a process of gradual change to a business. An organization could be viewed as a network of people sharing information through cross-functional processes to achieve predictable and desirable results (profits and growth). The goal is to use this fundamental notion to design and build systems that would leverage the organization's ability to manage information more effectively and efficiency. There's a big opportunity and impact this knowledge has when applied to the organization as a whole within a Business Process Improvement Methodology (Wood, 2008).

Systematic Approach and Human Capital Strategic Analysis

The Business Process Improvement world is abundant with tools, techniques and methods these days. Yet little can be found on exactly how to do projects in a prescriptive manner (Wood, 2008). The keys to successfully addressing human capital management issues are linking human capital to the mission and strategic direction of the organization and being able to conduct business-driven requirements analysis (LMI Government Consulting, 2008). Building on these keys, strategic analysis practice uses a fully integrated analytical approach to address the many influences on human capital management planning. It begins by creating a business profile of an organization, as a basis for further work, such as human capital planning, change and risk management planning, workforce management analysis, business process innovation evaluations, and the development of unique human capital management systems. The profile also enables to ensure that all proposed workforce and process changes have a business basis and that they link back to the strategic direction and organizational needs of the organization. Fully integrated analytical approach to human capital management planning include the following (LMI Government Consulting, 2008):

- Strategic directions defined in business terms
- Mission interconnected with outcomes, such as products and services
- Business trends and customer requirements integrated into strategic directions, which drive workforce and service delivery requirements
- Initiatives linked to business objectives or needs
- Business-driven workforce plans incorporated into organizational strategies
- Human capital requirements linked to budgets, business needs, and organizational requirements.

The link between organizational stakeholders, business strategies, measurable objectives, cross functional operations and leveraging information technologies is given by following (Wood, 2008):

- Business strategies and objectives only have context to how they deliver value to stakeholders.
- To be effective, these strategies and objectives must be stated in terms that measure the gap between the value delivered today and the value that needs to be delivered to sustain growth and profitability.
- To be deployable, strategies and objectives must be quantified in a way that is readily understandable by those performing the work that achieves them (operations).
- Operations must be viewed cross-functionally in terms of how information is shared and transformed by the actions that are taken in order to achieve desired outcomes.
- The workforce must be systematically and pragmatically engaged and facilitate the discovery of ways to improve the way work is thought about and conducted.
- Information technologies must be tailored to mirror the nature of the information and the form it takes as it passes through the organization.

- This information must be structured to mirror the business model of the organization in a way that is malleable and resilient.
- Processes must be then reengineered to achieve the strategies and objectives of the organization while providing the proper mechanisms to ensure that the data being shared is properly managed and maintained.

To achieve the above requires a systematic and aligned approach. It requires a set of tools and models that integrate together seamlessly so that they flow from strategy through operations to supporting information technologies. These tools must be prescriptive in nature so that no matter who is using them, the results are the same. Thus, variation of the process innovation process is virtually eliminated.

Principles of Business Process Improvement

Most BPI methods and techniques grew out of the Total Quality Management School of thinking (Wood, 2008). This is evidenced by the tools and techniques these methodologies utilize. Many have their roots in organizational behavior and focus more on the "Touchy Feely" and "Political Correctness" aspects of change than on the fundamental need of the organization to adopt pragmatic and systematic methods for improving and sustaining itself. Eight principles of Business Process Improvement are given:

- **Base activities around outcomes, not routines:** BPI is organized around outcomes, not the specific tasks required to reach the outcome. Organizations using BPI seek to eliminate the emphasis on routine that may not work well in an ever-changing political, business or legal climate.
- **Focus on the customer:** Many organizations fail to do this. Routine sets in. Resources within the organization start to

be allocated based on political needs rather than business or policy needs. Meanwhile, customer needs may have changed to the point that the organization may no longer effectively serve the customer and faces economic pressure or political pressure.

- **Process first, not automation first:** Although BPI may use automated planning tools such as enterprise resource planning, automation or information processing is not meant to be a substitute for BPI. An automated but inefficient system does not adequately meet customer requirements.
- **Benchmark regularly:** An organization using BPI must continually and frequently determine if the costs of performing a business process outweigh the benefits. Therefore this organization must establish benchmarks, or a set of standards, against which the process must be measured. The benchmarks themselves must be quantifiable, attainable, and realistic.
- **Establish who owns a business process:** Specific people, the *process owners*, must be placed in charge of a business process, be responsible for the performance and changes in the process, and be responsible for the success or failure of a process. Without personal responsibility, the process may fail.
- **Build control points into a process:** There should be frequent points where the process owners and customers/stakeholders decide if the process is meeting current benchmarks and what they should do with the process. This may include halting the process if it fails to meet realistic benchmarks.
- **Standardize similar processes:** Many organizations rely on an ad hoc approach to business processes. They make them up as they go along and change them without deliberate planning. A standardized system

of preparing processes saves time, effort, staff hours, and money.

- **Make changes now:** The change process should be done repeatedly, not merely once. Waiting for a perfect solution would mean no solution.

Data and Information Processing in Implementation of Business Process Innovation

The scope of Data Governance includes (Bilodeau & Singh, 2007):

- Enterprise-wide data naming convention and standards
- Data planning
- Data quality: availability, timeliness/latency definition
- Data attribute/metric management
- Data delivery vehicle/performance management
- Data user/access management
- Data storage
- Data standards, ownership and compliance.

Effective BPI relies on working in partnership with the people who own and use the process. This approach is adopted because it is the owners and users of the process who have detailed knowledge about the process – how it works and how it can be innovated and, consequently, improved. Carrying out BPI is a project, so all principles of project management and control apply. The first step in BPI is to define the organization's mission, existing structure and processes (*AS-IS*). Then the BPI process owners should determine what outcomes would add value to the organization's mission and objectives (*TO-BE*). Once the outcomes are determined, the organization's work force needs to be reshaped to meet the new missions and objectives, and a series of benchmarks, including cost metrics, should be put into place. It is during these latter steps that much of the resistance to BPI becomes apparent. Although information processing is not meant to be the whole of BPI, it is a significant part of BPI. Successful BPI programs follow guidelines similar to these:

- Do not think of existing procedures when designing new processes
- Put information processing power into the real work that produces the information rather than peripheral processes
- Move towards organization-wide data definitions
- Capture information once, at the source, without duplicating data.

Most resistance to BPI comes from within an organization. Managers do not wish to change existing structures; they reached their positions within the current system. The labor force may resist BPI because of fears of layoffs; however, an organization using BPI on a regular basis, argue many proponents, will already have the proper work force to meet existing business challenges.

HUMAN CAPITAL INFORMATION MANAGEMENT PROCESS

Strategy should enable the company realize broader enterprise goals, one of which is to improve process automation by converting some manual processes to automated processes (Herschel, 2004).

An analysis of the Hackett Group (Kempf & Soejarto, 2003) data shows that three strategies are used to deliver information technology (IT) solutions. Technology-only solutions are easier to implement but fail to consider all the effects technology has on the business process. Strategies include the following:

- **A point solution approach:** Technology is deployed to solve a portion of a business process issue. Variables related to human factors (internal and external human and technological interactions), the impact of the point solution on the entire business process, and how the enterprise measures the process improvements and accesses key data to facilitate decision making are not considered.
- **A multipoint or process solutions deployment:** Technology is used to address the key areas of processes, people and business process information (measuring process improvement and gaining access to data). Each of these interactions is addressed independently. Interaction among the variables is not considered.
- **A multi-variant approach:** Solutions delivery simultaneously addresses four key areas: technology, processes, people and business process information. It addresses each area independently and also addresses how each area affects others.

The business process platform is a model to describe how new software technology can be used to support a business. The value of BPP is to provide, first, business value and, second, IT productivity. Business systems need BPP strategy to coordinate IT resources across business intelligence, business applications and business process management. BPP includes an integrated set of technologies, a business service repository and the process component content that enables the creation and orchestration of business processes. BPP represents the approach that the IT department and business process owners should follow to manage better and reduce the costs of an ever-increasingly complex IT stack. Using a BPP model will help business system consider the process environment as a whole and apply the right sourcing model for IT-enabled processes. Integrated composition environments, BPM and business service repositories are emerging to assist users with managing their BPPs (Genovese & Hayward, 2008).

Place and Role of Data Warehousing for Business Process Improvement through Integration of Information Systems

The rub in selecting the best tools and techniques for BPI approach is in the lack of the proper evaluation and selection criteria upon which to base decisions needed. Knowledge workers (the people who actually perform operational-level work) hold the key to discovering ways to improve cross-functional business processes. However, first they must be briefed on the value gaps that management needs to close. It is only in this context that process mapping has any value in BPI initiatives. BPI methods must provide comprehensive techniques for facilitating knowledge workers in context to the value gaps defined in order to identify and define the innovation opportunities. Furthermore, the techniques used should be facilitator independent as to form and outcomes achieved (Wood, 2008). Among other things DW is needed because of insufficient data connection of transaction system information subsystems. This is manifested in the existence of a number of independently developed and nonintegrated application systems with data bases in different parts of an organization. Such nonintegrated systems are the result of uncontrolled decentralization and redundancy. Even if there is an integrated transaction information system, its data model doesn't satisfy newly risen analytic needs, especially when the quantity of data is extremely big. Improvement of existing transaction system by eliminating weaknesses of data model and application system usually provokes notable costs. It includes big organizational effort and intervention into program code; exchange of the existing procedures and the execution of the new ones, additional burden for the system users because of system testing and development etc.

Even when all necessary upgrades have been successfully performed, such information system supports only processes on operational level; it remains inadaptable for management and decision making support. In the aforesaid case, where data and, consequently, information subsystems processes are not integrated, DW can assume an integration role, since DW makes a new model of higher level. In this way the existing data of transaction system will be cleansed and used in a new way, with a new quality. They will be described in detail and enriched with content from outside data bases with a view to analysis and decision making HCM processes. Data modeled in a new way are integrated, so they become a lever which will advance complex HCM processes; in focus are people, care about their professional development, and their use within organization.

Requirements of Data Warehousing and its Logical Model

Requirements of Data Warehouse (DW), as given in (Kimball, 2002), are:

- To make an organization 's information easily accessible
- To present the organization's information consistently
- To be adaptive and resilient to change
- To be secure bastion that protects our information assets
- To serve as the foundation for improved decision making
- The Business Community must accept the Data Warehouse if it is to be deemed successful.

To accelerate decision making process on the basis of existing transaction systems, logic DW model will be created. DW creation within this work is viewed as a way to achieve HCM BPI by information system data integration, within functionally oriented hierarchic system. HCM processes are supported by star-like data structure-fact tables with associated dimensions on the logic model level. Survey by which an employee is tracked in a specific period of time explains the role/position for which the employee is being prepared within department/section/ division, and/or project, the name of institution and type of training he attended, knowledge level he obtained, costs originating from the training, employee's commitments towards organization etc. Big systems HCM process must be permanently served with data concerning mentioned and similar events within organization to avoid that an employee in whom notable sum of money has been invested is not disposed in the optimal way. Business phenomenon described by all dimensions i.e. model parameters total costs per employee is calculated for a specific period of time. Combined with parameter Performance, ratio between work contribution and respective costs will be defined as well. Tracking of such and similar phenomena and successful management have far reaching consequences for the success of an organization. It is directly connected with future investments into employees' training, better efficiency, satisfaction and motivation of employees and their wish to stay in the system. Depending on the number of phenomena which should be tracked, integrated DW model can contain more star-like structures; see Figure 1 for previously described structure.

Business Intelligence Initiatives for Further BPI through Development of Information System

Data integration technologies come in a variety of forms. Each has different characteristics, uses and design patterns that it commonly supports. Sorting through the available options is not a simplistic task because there is overlap in functionality. Vendor marketing and buyer misconceptions may add further confusion, often leading organizations to select inappropriate tools and limiting the success in their deployment. Data integration technologies commonly found in large enterprises include among others, the following (Friedman, 2005):

- **Extraction, transformation and loading (ETL) tools:** Support the acquisition and integration of data from multiple source databases, and the ability to change the syntax and semantics of that data, and then deliver it to one or more target databases. ETL tools typically support the movement of data for batch-oriented data integration processes, often in the context of building an integrated data structure such as a data warehouse or data marts.

- **Integration brokers:** Commonly applied to problems of near-real-time application-level integration, integration brokers are increasingly considered for solving data integration problems as well. These technologies typically incorporate adapter technology to connect to a variety of application and database types, and the ability to conditionally route transactions according to business rules and transport transactions from source to target with low latency. Integration brokers often form the core of an enterprise's application integration architecture.

DW creation makes a part of infrastructure needed for development of the integral Business Intelligence (BI) concept of HCM process. Further improvement of HCM process, by development of support information system, increases gradually the importance and the force of information system for HCM processes in everyday business. That is a complex procedure which ultimately results in the creation of new HCM sub-processes and produced data will be used for further increase of business effectiveness and efficiency. Further investment into knowledge, employees and equip-

Figure 1. Data warehouse logical model creation in HCM process innovation

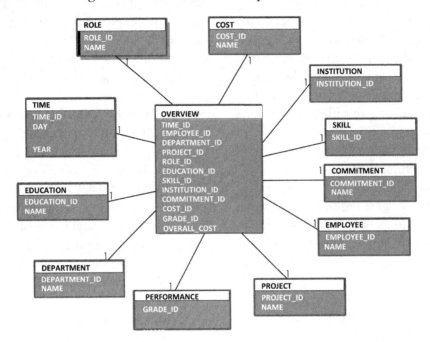

ment will lead to the creation of integral DW on the basis of overall transaction information systems. In this way integral DW will become a part of the basis for the development of functional, organizational and business levels of BI systems. A BI framework enables enterprises to align their various BI initiatives and helps them to determine the right ROI, as presented in Figure 2 (Dresner & Linden & Buytendijk & Friedman & Strange & Knox & Camm, 2002). Enterprises need a BI framework to align their BI initiatives to achieve an optimal result.

The framework suggests that enterprises align their BI initiatives on four levels (Dresner & Linden & Buytendijk & Friedman & Strange & Knox & Camm, 2002). Each of the layers affects the others, and maximum benefit is only achieved if enterprises understand how the layers work together. Just to be complete, the framework also addresses a transactional layer; however, as this is not part of BI, it will not be discussed in detail. Layers have a meaningful return only if viewed in combination with the other layers. It is of little use to have an infrastructure if there is no BI functionality that uses it. And it is of no use to apply BI in a way that doesn't fit the organizational culture. It is crucial for BI to have an infrastructure layer in which the data is collected, integrated and generically made accessible (Dresner & Linden & Buytendijk & Friedman & Strange & Knox & Camm, 2002). Optimally, this is done by a data warehouse fed by an extraction, transformation and loading (ETL) tool, but ETL tools are still only used in a minority of cases.

A data warehouse is not the only possible component of the infrastructure layer. To enable a more real-time approach to corporate performance - a process called "business activity monitoring" (BAM) - enterprise applications integration processes become involved, on top of transactional systems. To deploy BAM, there may be a need for an operational data store (ODS), possibly linked to the enterprise's workflow structures. These structures become increasingly connected.

Figure 2. The BI framework

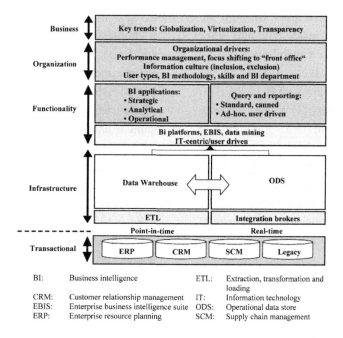

In many cases, the ODS can function as a source for the data warehouse, so it is not necessary to go back to the source systems. In its turn, the data warehouse provides relatively stable analytic context to real-time indicators in BAM, providing a frame of reference. The ROI of the infrastructure is in efficiency and flexibility. The infrastructure generically enables other applications, provides economies of scale for support costs and systems management, and ensures better-quality operations. Aiming at a tangible business result - currently a popular approach - usually leads to creating sets of data marts, not a generic infrastructure.

CONCLUSION

The relation between data and process begins at the point of entry - at the lowest level of details within a process or during the execution of specific tasks or steps. Data can be coming from or be used by more than one process. They can also be stored in one or multiple systems. A lack of

understanding of these relationships often leads to poor business intelligence and communication barriers that ultimately may result in bad business decisions. One of the root causes of this problem is that each process uses the same point of data, but may be carrying a different context for the capture and analysis of this specific point of data. In this scenario, the more data reuse without proper governance, the greater the chance of misinterpretation. Without a clear understanding of the context in which data are captured, and their meaning, a multitude of data quality problems can be encountered. Examples of issue possibilities include poor accuracy, completeness, accessibility, availability, timeliness, volatility, complexity, redundancy, integrity, consistency, cohesiveness, precision, breadth, depth, certification, privacy, etc. (Bilodeau & Singh, 2007).

Thanks to the presented HCM BPI solution model, which includes development and implementation of data integration process through DW creation, initial HCM process is improved. On the other hand, presented solution model render possible development of the integral DW concept on the organizational system level, through the integration of outside and inside data and other important processes. Such a warehouse can be implemented into integral BI concept and further developed. With such an approach to HCM BPI, through creation and usage of DW, intermediary connection between information subsystems of the integral IS HCM is obtained: 1. Connection through data-formerly unconnected data are aggregated and enriched by new dimensions and attributes. 2. Connection through management-the users, on the basis of their position within organization and newly obtained qualitative data level within DW, are given new roles and new authorizations for data handling and data management.

By means of the aforesaid connections, processes leading to an important process data integration (such as HCM) improve it at the same time. Advantages obtained through this research are reflected through the following facts: (a) in complex organizations, functionally oriented and hierarchically structured, improvement of all processes can be hardly achieved by data integration of all business functions, (b) on the other hand, integral HCM process, because of its importance and complexity, should be improved in the acceptable period of time (delay in decision making should be reduced as much as possible) and this can be achieved through the DW creation as a part of BI infrastructure, (c) thus improved HCM process, by means of data model, remains open for further integration with other processes and organization systems, in conformity with defined strategy.

Such approach results in human capital management which is improved through its information system data integration by DW creation for the integral HCM support. Proposed business driven and data structured solution model for business process innovation can be used and applied in other functional areas and processes, with necessary modifications depending on the particular case. Finally, such approach leads to enterprise information integration (EII) as desired

and continuous process within the complex business system.

People who combine business skills and IT experience to establish effective links between separate operations within organizations are keys for successful implementation of IT-enabled process transformations. Because such a program has technical and business implications and integrates technology into the business process, reliable IT infrastructure is extremely important for the program to work. Business managers' cooperation in adjusting policies and procedures is very important so as not to burden IT personnel with impossible tasks such as forcing the technology to solve every business problem. Both sides must cooperate to launch the program successfully. The IT director is the bridge between business managers and IT. Directing organizational change is a key factor in aligning the IT architecture to continuously support changing organizational business strategies: managing IT personnel because they are the key resource that determines the IT flexibility level. They must be retrainable and be willing to update their skills. Furthermore, organizations must use a combination of several reward strategies to ensure effective and flexible IT personnel. The main features of the process transformation are: the deployment of new technologies, automation of the procedures, and acquiring new skills.

Linking IT improvements with the mission and the survival of the organization is a key factor that mobilizes IT personnel to deliver quick and successful implementation. IT management must be responsive and address technical and personnel issues immediately. Executive management must give full support for the program and provided cover for the IT team as it becomes necessary to shelve internal applications. Careful planning continues to be a very important factor for the successful redeployment of reliable information technology architecture. Flexibility of the IT personnel and their ability to respond to problems and to ensure continuity as the improvements are implemented makes the transformation successful (Watad & DiSanzo, 1998).

REFERENCES

Babcock, C. (1996). Taking the long view on IS expertise. *Computerworld, 30*(51).

Bilodeau, N., & Singh, L. (2007). The *marriage of process and data governance: key to BPM and SOA initiatives' success*. BPMInstitute.org.

Champy, J. (1997). It's not who you hire, it's who you keep. *Computerworld, 31*(39).

Davila, T., Epstein, M. J., & Shelton, R. (2006). *Making Innovation Work: How to Manage It, Measure It, and Profit from It "*. Wharton School Publishing.

Dresner, H., Linden, A., Buytendijk, F., Friedman, T., Strange, K., Knox, M., & Camm, M. (2002). *The business intelligence competency center: an essential business strategy*. Gartner, Inc.

Friedman, T. (2005). *Data integration forms the technology foundation of EIM*. Gartner, Inc.

Galinec, D., & Vidović, S. (2007). Methodology framework for process integration and service management. [Faculty of Organization and Informatics Varaždin - University of Zagreb.]. *Journal of Information and Organizational Sciences, 31*(1), 37–49.

Genovese, Y., & Hayward, S. (2008). *What Does It Mean to Implement a BPP?* Gartner, Inc.

Hammer, M., & Champy, J. (2003). *Reengineering the Corporation: A Manifesto for Business Revolution*. Collins Business Essentials.

Herschel, G. (2004). *AGF gains visibility through customer segmentation*. Gartner, Inc.

Holincheck, J. (2008). *The Impact of SOA on HCM Applications*. Gartner, Inc.

Kempf, T., & Soejarto, A. (2003). *Answerthink delivers metric-based process improvements*. Gartner, Inc.

Kimball, R. (2002). *The data warehouse toolkit: the complete guide to dimensional modeling*. Wiley.

LMI Government Consulting. (2009). *Organizations and human capital*. Retrieved January 10th, 2009 from http://www.lmi.org/organizations/ organizations.aspx. LMI Headquarters, McLean.

McDonald, M., Begin, J., & Fortino, S. (2009). *Meeting the Challenge: The 2009 CIO agenda*. Gartner Executive Programs, Gartner, Inc.

Otter, T., & Holincheck, J. (2009). Key Issues in Human Capital Management Software, Gartner, Inc.

Rummler, G., & Brache, A. (1990). *Improving Performance: How to Manage the White Space on the Organization Chart*. Jossey Bass Business and Management Series.

Sturm, R. (1996). When quality of service, not crisis management, is the real standard. *Communications Week, 625*.

Watad, M. M., & DiSanzo, F. J. (1998). Transforming IT/IS infrastructure and IS personnel issues. [MCB UP Ltd.]. *Business Process Management Journal, 4*(4), 322–332. doi:10.1108/14637159810238228

Wood, R. M. (2003). *Uncovering BPI*. Retrieved February 15th, 2009 from http://www.gantthead. com/article.cfm?ID=184452. Gantthead.

This work was previously published in International Journal of Human Capital and Information Technology Professionals, Volume 1, Issue 1, edited by Ricardo Colomo-Palacios, pp. 44-60, copyright 2010 by IGI Publishing (an imprint of IGI Global).

Chapter 3
IT Professionals:
An Iberian Snapshot

António Trigo
*Escola Superior de Tecnologia e Gestão de
Oliveira do Hospital, Portugal*

João Barroso
*Grupo de Investigação em Engenharia do
Conhecimento e Apoio à Decisão, Portugal*

João Varajão
*Universidade de Trás-os-Montes
e Alto Douro, Portugal*

Francisco J. Molina-Castillo
*University of Murcia,
Spain*

Pedro Soto-Acosta
*University of Murcia,
Spain*

Nicolas Gonzalvez-Gallego
*University of Murcia,
Spain*

ABSTRACT

Nowadays, Universities and other Training Institutions need to clearly identify the Information Technology (IT) skills that companies demand from IT practitioners. This is essential not only for offering appropriate and reliable university degrees, but also to help future IT professionals on where to focus in order to achieve better job positions. In an attempt to address this issue, this study rely on 102 Chief Information Officers, from Iberian large companies, to characterize current IT professionals and what is expected from future hirings. Results revealed that IT Technicians and Senior Analysts are the predominant positions and also that future hiring will request candidates with at least two to five years of work experience. The two most important skills found were core functions at the IT department: business knowledge and user support. In contrast, traditional competences such as web development and management of emerging technologies were less demanded.

INTRODUCTION

Information Technology (IT) professionals, such as programmers, analysts, database administrators, network specialists, etc., constitute a critical group of knowledge workers in modern organizations (McMurtrey, Downey, Zeltmann, & Friedman, 2008) which is expected to grow in the near future. According to the "Tomorrow's Jobs" section of the 2008-2009 Occupational Outlook Handbook, two IT related professions, namely "network systems and data communications analysts" and "computer

DOI: 10.4018/978-1-4666-0924-2.ch003

software engineers", occupy the first and fourth places respectively in the list of the top twelve jobs projected to grow faster between 2006 and 2016 (U.S. Department of Labor, 2009).

IT professionals need to possess various skills to perform adequately in their job. They need to have technical skills to work with computers, business skills to apply their technical knowledge to solve business problems, as well as managerial skills and soft skills to be able to work effectively with computer users. IT professionals, therefore, need to be trained in different skills as employers are keen to recruit employees who possess technical as well as non-technical skills (Lee, 2006).

As technology advances and the business environment continues to evolve, organizations and training institutions face a key challenge: to identify critical skill sets for current and future IT practitioners. In an attempt to address this issue, this study surveyed 102 Chief Information Officers (CIOs), from Portuguese and Spanish large companies, to characterize present and future IT professionals. In this sense, this study empirically investigates which skills are most important for current and future IT personnel based on the perceptions of Iberian CIOs. The results offer a comprehensive and updated set of IT professionals skills that will be useful to both public and private organizations, Universities and Technical Institutes, as well as to IT professionals.

To analyze the essential skills for current and future IT professionals, the organizations selected for the study are large companies. This particular audience was preferred because large organizations are generally leaders in technology use and application (Li, McLeod, & Rogers, 2001; Liu & Arnett, 2000; McLeod, 1995) and need to have a well-structured IT department to manage the overall information system architecture.

Considering the above-mentioned points, the key research questions that motivate our work are:

- What characteristics have actual IT professionals employed in large companies?

- What are the most important skills of actual IT professionals employed in large companies?
- What skills will be important for future IT personnel?

The paper is structured as follows: The next section presents the literature review; Following that, the methodology used for sample selection and data collection is discussed; Then, data analysis and results are examined; Finally, the paper ends with limitations and conclusions.

LITERATURE REVIEW AND CURRRENT STATUS

In an IT department of a company we can find various types of professionals. Among others, we have, developers with different levels of experience (junior and senior), analysts (junior and senior), computer technicians and trainees.

The large amount of studies that since the 1980s have been conducted regarding IT workforce issues and IT professionals, confirm the relevance of these topics (Goles, Hawk, & Kaiser, 2008). Among these topics, the characterization of IT skill requirements for professionals is recognized as one of the main areas of research (Ang & Slaughter, 2000).

Prior research in this area has resulted in two broad categories of skills, technical and non-technical (Goles, Hawk, & Kaiser, 2008). Technical skills basically consist of those skills specific to the IT field, including but not limited to knowledge and competencies associated with hardware, systems and application software, and telecommunications (Cash, Yoong, & Huff, 2004). Non-technical skills generally include: business skills, such as knowledge of the organization's structure, strategy, processes and culture and the ability to understand the business environment; management skills as planning, leading, organizing and controlling; and soft skills, which refer to the cluster of personality traits and attitudes that drives one's behavior (Amanda Roan, 2007), such as the ability to communicate or the ability to work in teams (Cash, et al., 2004; Litecky, Arnett, & Prabhakar, 2004).

With regard to previous studies comparing the importance of technical and non-technical skills, results are diverse. Although the general perception is that IT professionals need to put more emphasis on non-technical skills, some studies (Lee, 2006) based on the analysis of job advertisements in the United States, Canada and Hong Kong reveal that technical skills have become increasingly important, in contrast to business skills for system analysts and programmers.

Within the context of IT skill requirements, one issue that Universities, Training Institutions and prospective IT professionals are investigating is related to the skills employers value the most. To shed light on this issue, a set of IT skills (see Table 1) is proposed after a review of recent studies (CIOMAG, 2006, 2007; Lee, 2006; McMurtrey, et al., 2008).

METHODOLOGY

This study is base on a survey that was conducted to investigate several aspects of the Information Technology / Information Systems (IT/IS) situation in large Portuguese and Spanish companies. Specifically for this study, the survey aimed to determine what kind of IT skills are more important for current and future IT personnel. The decision-maker targeted by the survey was normally the person responsible for IT within the company, typically the Chief Information Officer (CIO) or the IT manager. The target population consisted of the 1000 largest companies by gross revenue in Portugal and Spain.

Table 1. List of selected skills

Skill
Project management (PM)
Application development (AD)
Help desk/User support (HD)
Database management (DM)
Network management (NM)
Servers management (SRVM)
Security management (SECM)
Web site and web services development (WS)
Emerging technologies (EM)
Business knowledge (BK)

Questionnaire

A structured questionnaire consisting of open and close-ended questions was developed from previous studies (CIOMAG, 2006, 2007; Varajão, Trigo, Figueiredo, & Barroso, 2007). The questionnaire was divided into several sections, each one with well defined objectives. The formulation and criteria for answering the questionnaire is defined in the Appendix A.

The proposed questionnaire was pre-tested with a small sample of CIOs and used in a previous survey (Varajão, et al., 2007) to validate its content and readability and to improve some aspects of the questions. The necessary changes were made to the final questionnaire, which was edited in an online survey tool. A briefing letter was subsequently sent to the CIOs regarding the scope and goals of the study, including a link to an Internet home page, which allowed the completion of the questionnaire online. In the first and second rounds the letter was sent by email and, in the third round, by post.

Data Collection

The survey was mailed to a sample group of 500 companies in Portugal and a sample of 500 companies in Spain both from the above mentioned target population in each country during February to October 2008. In order to obtain a representative sample, a casual sample method was used, the stratified sample method, opting for a random sample of 50% of the companies in each group of 100 companies, selected according to their position in the INE list of the 1000 largest national companies in Portugal (INE, 2007) and the SABI database list of the 1000 largest firms in Spain.

In the first and second rounds, the number of undelivered and returned questionnaires (by email) was 111 from Portuguese firms and 94 from Spanish companies, quite a significant number perhaps due to the email policies of the companies. In the third round, the invitation letter was sent by post and then the number of undelivered and returned questionnaires was 44 and 23 for Portuguese and Spanish firms, respectively. 102 valid responses were obtained (59 responses from Portuguese companies and 43 from Spanish firms), yielding a final response rate of around 10%.

This response rate did not come as a surprise as it is comparable with the response rates of others studies conducted in the last few years (Enns, Huff, & Golden, 2001; Li, et al., 2001; Lin & Pervan, 2003; Liu & Arnett, 2000; Sohal & Ng, 1998). This may be due to the fact that some subjects are unwilling to respond to unsolicited surveys (Li, et al., 2001), or simply had insufficient time (Lin & Pervan, 2003) and many more companies set a policy of rejecting survey questionnaires (Li, et al., 2001; Lin & Pervan, 2003).

Tables 2 and 3 show the demographics and characteristics of the respondents. The companies of the responding CIOs represent a broad range of companies in terms of their characteristics, which indicates that the results can be used to explain the Portuguese IT/IS adoption in large companies. It is important to note that, although it is true that large organizations generally provide leadership in using information technology, differences do exist between small and large businesses (Liu & Arnett, 2000). Therefore, careful use of the

results should be made, especially regarding their applicability to small businesses.

According to descriptive analysis presented in Table 2, the majority of the sample presented a high number of employees among firms and annual sales between 50 and 250 million euros. Therefore, these firms can be considered as large companies. In addition, approximately 65% of the surveyed companies demonstrate an international presence in more than one country. This figure also proved that selected firms are big enough as the international presence in more than one country requires additional investments that traditionally can only be afford by big companies.

The majority of CIOs that answer the survey were male (90.2%) with a Bachelor's degree (60.8%), in their forties. They have an average tenure within their organization of 10 years and an average tenure in their current position of 8 years.

DATA ANALYSIS AND RESULTS

In order to answer to the above research questions, a questionnaire was developed which asked companies to indicate what type of IT professional they have in their IT department and which IT professionals skills they considered most important for their performance today, as well as the desired skills (and therefore more valued) of the new professionals to hire.

Figure 1, shows the types of IT professionals currently present in large Iberian companies. As expected, most of the companies (more than 80%) possess informatics technicians inside the company. This is not surprising since we have in this group, professionals of several technical areas (e.g. database, network management, etc.) that are usually quite versatile in terms of skills and responsibilities. It is important to notice the significant difference between the number of companies that possess system analysts from those companies that possess software programmers internally. This may due to the growing trend in

Table 2. Demographic characteristics of respondent' companies

Characteristics	Number	%
Total number of employees		
<00	17	16.7
201-500	29	28.4
501-2000	33	32.3
>2000	23	21.6
Total	102	100
Annual sales (million Euros)		
Lss than 10	2	2
10 to below 50	16	15.7
50 to below 250	49	48
Greater than 250	28	27.5
No answer	7	6.8
Total	102	100
International presence (number of countries)		
0	33	32.3
1	13	12.7
2	6	5.9
3-4	7	6.9
5-20	19	18.7
>20	18	17.6
No answer	6	5.9
Total	102	100

the adoption of outsourcing by organizations in the last two decades (Calabrese & Erbetta, 2005; Varajao, Trigo, Figueiredo, Barroso, & Bulas-Cruz, 2009). At the top of most frequently outsourced services, we found recurrently the development of applications and maintenance of applications (CIOMAG, 2006, 2007; Varajão, et al., 2008). However, companies often prefer to outsource services of an operational nature rather than services that are more strategic and essential for the core business. This is a plausible justification for the fact that less than 50% of Iberian large companies possess senior programmers internally and, on the other hand, more than 60% of companies

holding senior analysts. About 30% of companies hire trainees, as this is an important way not only to acquire new elements to the team, but also an opportunity to incorporate new knowledge and create a new dynamic internally. Note also that the companies have identified more than 30% of "other professionals", which include, for example, project managers and help desk / user support staff.

In Figure 2 it is represented the differences between Portuguese and Spanish companies. Note that in all cases, we have more Spanish companies possessing internally IT professionals than Portuguese firms. This is an interesting results and may be due to the fact that larger Spanish companies are bigger than Portuguese companies having therefore larger structures than larger Portuguese companies or maybe due to Portuguese firms have a sourcing structure that recurs more to outsourcing than Spanish companies. In particular, the biggest differences can be found for the Senior programmers, Junior analysts and Senior analysts.

One of the important elements to better understand IT professionals is the set of skills needed for the proper performance of theirs activities. In this study, CIOs were asked to indicate the importance of the skills of professionals in the IT departments, using a Likert scale ranging from 1 to 5, where 1 indicates that the skill is without importance and 5 very important.

In Table 4 and Figure 3 is possible to see the ranking of skills by their raw mean sorted from most important to least important.

Topping the list are two skills closely related to the business: business knowledge and help desk / user support. Clearly the most valued skills relate to understanding the organization and its needs in terms of IT/IS support. In the second group of skills we found a set of skills related to the management of several services such as server management, security management and network management. In line with the type of professionals in internal departments, application development and web site development and web ser-

Table 3. Demographic characteristics of respondents' CIOs

Characteristics	Number	%
Gender		
Male	92	90.2
Female	10	9.8
Total	102	100
Age		
Less than 30	5	4.9
31 to 35	15	14.7
36 to 40	21	20.6
41 to 45	22	21.6
More than 45	39	38.2
Total	102	100
Highest degree earned		
High school	9	8.8
Bachelor's	62	60.8
Post-Graduation	12	11.8
MBA	7	6.9
Master's	8	7.8
PhD	1	1
Other	3	2.9
Total	102	100

vices appear at the bottom of the list. Once again we cannot fail to mention the influence that outsourcing has on the structuring of departments and therefore the set of skills teams need to keep internally.

In Table 5 and Figure 4 are presented the main differences between Spanish and Portuguese IT skills. The results presented, show that in almost all the current skills of IT professionals there is a great alignment between Spanish and Portuguese companies, with even similar results in certain categories. Exceptions to this alignment can be found on the skills of application development and the ability to monitor emerging technologies. In the latter case the difference is quite striking, valuing much more this skill Portuguese companies than their Spanish counterparts.

In order to understand companies' needs of IT professionals, it is also important to understand the skills desired in the new professional to hire. Therefore, using a Likert scale ranging from 1 to 5, where 1 indicates that a skill is without importance and 5 that it is very important, participants in the study were asked to indicate the importance of the skills of IT professionals to hire. Table 6 and Figure 5 show the ranking of skills desired by their raw mean sorted from most important to least important.

Table 4. Iberian IT professionals' most important skills today ranked by their raw mean

Rank	Skill	Mean
1	Business knowledge (BK)	4.25
2	Help desk/User support (HD)	4.23
3	Servers management (SRVM)	4.18
4	Security management (SECM)	4.10
5	Network management (NM)	4.04
6	Project management (PM)	3.93
7	Database management (DM)	3.84
8	Emerging Technologies (ET)	3.58
9	Application development (AP)	3.42
10	Web site and web services development (WS)	2.75

Figure 1. Iberian IT professionals present in companies

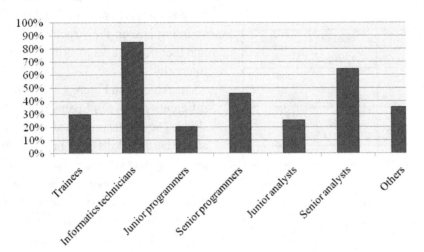

With regard to the desired skills, we find at the top of the list the capacity to monitor emerging technologies, followed by security management, help desk/user support, network management and project management. This is justified by the need to strengthen existing skills, as well as the need to gather new skills internally.

In Figure 6 and Table 7 are represented the desired IT skills in both Spanish and Portuguese companies. In general, similar to what was identified regarding the current set of skills, desired skills there is also a great proximity between the reality of Spanish companies and Portuguese companies. Almost all the Spanish companies report a greater need, excluding cases of web services and web site development and ability to monitor emerging technologies.

Figure 2. Iberian IT professionals present in Portuguese and Spanish companies

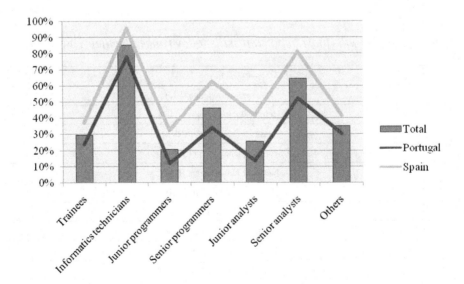

Figure 3. Iberian IT professionals' today most important skills

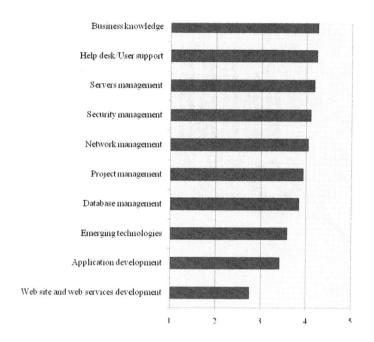

It is important to note that regarding desired skills there is less concordance between companies than in the case of existing skills, which is reflected in the standard deviation of responses as can be seen in Table 7.

Regarding the level of experience that companies requires from new hired professionals, Figure 7, shows that there is a clear preference for professionals with less than five years of experience, reaching 90% the number of companies that refer it. This clearly indicates a favorable Iberian market for professionals and new graduates with few years of professional experience (just giving, theoretically, lower costs for organizations).

Table 5. IT professionals today's competences means comparison between Portugal and Spain

	Origin	PM	AD	HD	DM	NM	SRVM	SECM	WS	ET	BK
Portugal	Mean	3.93	3.20	4.27	3.85	4.08	4.19	4.15	2.75	4.08	4.29
	N	59	59	59	59	59	59	59	59	59	59
	Std. Deviation	1.081	1.323	1.014	1.127	1.134	1.090	1.047	1.294	1.055	.929
Spain	Mean	3.93	3.72	4.16	3.84	3.98	4.16	4.02	2.74	2.88	4.19
	N	43	43	43	43	43	43	43	43	43	43
	Std. Deviation	1.163	1.278	1.153	1.153	1.144	1.067	1.123	1.449	1.159	.932
Total	Mean	3.93	3.42	4.23	3.84	4.04	4.18	4.10	2.75	3.58	4.25
	N	102	102	102	102	102	102	102	102	102	102
	Std. Deviation	1.110	1.323	1.071	1.132	1.134	1.075	1.076	1.355	1.246	.927

Figure 4. Portuguese and Spanish IT professionals' today skills

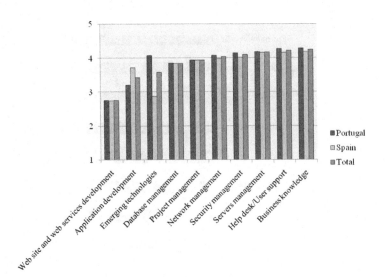

These results may also demonstrate that these low experienced professionals can also be trained easily than more experienced professionals that show lower preferences for new technologies.

LIMITATIONS

The primary limitation of this research, as other studies that use a similar research sample (Li, et al., 2001; Lin & Pervan, 2003; Liu & Arnett, 2000), is that the results cannot be generalized to all business. It is true that large organizations generally provide leadership in using information technology, but differences do exist between small and large business (Liu & Arnett, 2000). Therefore, careful use of the results should be made, especially as to their applicability to small businesses.

CONCLUSION

Hiring properly trained individuals allows organizations to spend less time preparing new staff, and accordingly this allows incorporating them more efficiently into the workplace. For colleges, Universities, and Technical Institutions, understanding the required skill sets is critical for curriculum maintenance and development.

Our study reveals that IT Technicians and Senior Analysts are the predominant positions and that future hiring will request at least from two to five years of work experience.

The two most important IT professionals skills mentioned were: business knowledge; and user support, core functions at the IT department, which underlines the importance of including disciplines from the management field in the IS curriculum. In contrast, traditional competences such as web development and management of emerging technologies were less demanded, which reflects the importance of the outsourcing phenomenon regarding IT services, and can also reveal the need for this kind of IT professionals skills by software and IT service providers companies.

This study provides a snapshot of current Iberian IT professionals, including the set skills most valued by employees, that can be included in today's IS curriculum to help ensure that IT professionals are adequately prepared and trained with skills that will serve them well in their careers.

Table 6. Iberian IT professionals' most desired skills from new employees

Rank	Skill	Mean
1	Emerging technologies	3.82
2	Security management	3.79
3	Help desk/User support	3.71
4	Project management	3.67
5	Network management	3.64
6	Servers management	3.6
7	Business knowledge	3.6
8	Database management	3.52
9	Application development	3.34
10	Web site and web services development	3.11

Since this only a snapshot of today's situation future research and monitoring of skills is required in order to keep up in an ever-changing IT world.

The results obtained in this study can be very valuable from an academic and managerial point of view. The figures and tables commented in this study is an attempt to demonstrate the main differences that arise between Spanish and Portuguese companies in terms of IT professional and desired IT professional skills in both countries. There are some important conclusions that can be found from this analysis.

Note that this study reflects the range of skills that are relevant to big Iberian companies. Skills may have a different relevance in companies in the area of IT service providers, deserving also these companies be target in similar studies in the future studies.

Figure 5. Iberian IT professionals' desired skills

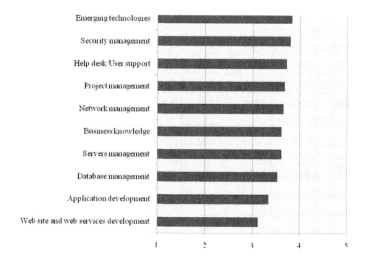

Figure 6. Portuguese and Spanish IT professionals' desired skills

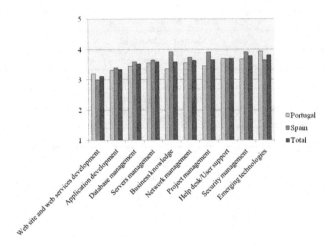

Figure 7. Preferred level of experience from new employees (IT professionals)

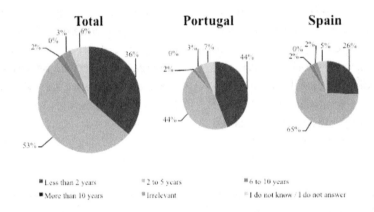

Table 7. IT professionals desired competences mean comparison between Portugal and Spain

Origin		PM	AD	HD	DM	NM	SRVM	SECM	WS	ET	BK
Spain	Mean	3.93	3.40	3.70	3.60	3.74	3.65	3.93	3.00	3.65	3.93
	N	43	43	43	43	43	43	43	43	43	43
	Std. Deviation	1.242	1.383	1.406	1.294	1.329	1.395	1.183	1.574	1.213	1.223
Portugal	Mean	3.47	3.31	3.71	3.46	3.56	3.56	3.69	3.19	3.95	3.36
	N	59	59	59	59	59	59	59	59	59	59
	Std. Deviation	1.344	1.368	1.439	1.394	1.442	1.430	1.441	1.479	1.181	1.297
Total	Mean	3.67	3.34	3.71	3.52	3.64	3.60	3.79	3.11	3.82	3.60
	N	102	102	102	102	102	102	102	102	102	102
	Std. Deviation	1.315	1.368	1.418	1.348	1.392	1.409	1.337	1.515	1.197	1.292

REFERENCES

Amanda Roan, G. W. (2007). Women, information technology and 'waves of optimism': Australian evidence on 'mixed-skill' jobs. *New Technology, Work and Employment, 22*(1), 21–33. doi:10.1111/j.1468-005X.2007.00181.x

Ang, S., & Slaughter, S. (2000). The missing context of information technology personnel: a review and future directions for research. In R. Zmud (Ed.), *Framing the domains of IT management: Projecting the future through the past* (pp. 305-327). Cincinnati, Ohio: Pinnaflex Education Resources.

Calabrese, G., & Erbetta, F. (2005). Outsourcing and firm performance: evidence from Italian automotive suppliers. *International Journal of Automotive Technology and Management, 5*(4), 461–479. doi:10.1504/IJATM.2005.008585

Cash, E., Yoong, P., & Huff, S. (2004). The impact of E-commerce on the role of IS professionals. *The Data Base for Advances in Information Systems, 3*(3), 50–63.

CIOMAG. (2006). The STATE of the CIO '06. *CIO Magazine*.

CIOMAG. (2007). The STATE of the CIO '07. *CIO Magazine*.

Enns, H. G., Huff, S. L., & Golden, B. R. (2001). How CIOs obtain peer commitment to strategic IS proposals: barriers and facilitators. *The Journal of Strategic Information Systems, 10*(1), 3–14. doi:10.1016/S0963-8687(01)00041-5

Goles, T., Hawk, S., & Kaiser, K. M. (2008). Information technology workforce skills: The software and IT services provider perspective. *Information Systems Frontiers, 10*, 179–194. doi:10.1007/s10796-008-9072-9

INE. (2007). *Lista das 1000 maiores empresas portuguesas. Ficheiro de Unidades Estatísticas - FUE - Base Belém*: Instituto Nacional de Estatística.

Lee, P. C. B. (2006). Information Technology Professionals' Skill Requirements in Hong Kong. *Contemporary Management Research, 2*(2), 141–152.

Li, E. Y., McLeod, R., & Rogers, J. C. (2001). Marketing information systems in Fortune 500 companies: a longitudinal analysis of 1980, 1990, and 2000. *Information & Management, 38*(5), 307–322. doi:10.1016/S0378-7206(00)00073-2

Lin, C., & Pervan, G. (2003). The practice of IS/IT benefits management in large Australian organizations. *Information & Management, 41*(1), 13–24. doi:10.1016/S0378-7206(03)00002-8

Litecky, C. R., Arnett, K. P., & Prabhakar, B. (2004). The paradox of soft skills versus technical skills in IS hiring. *Journal of Computer Information Systems, 45*(1), 69–76.

Liu, C., & Arnett, K. P. (2000). Exploring the factors associated with Web site success in the context of electronic commerce. *Information & Management, 38*(1). doi:10.1016/S0378-7206(00)00049-5

McLeod, R. (1995). Systems theory and information resources management: Integrating key concepts. *Information Resources Management Journal, 18*(2), 5–14.

McMurtrey, M. E., Downey, J. P., Zeltmann, S. M., & Friedman, W. H. (2008). Critical Skill Sets of Entry-Level IT Professionals: An Empirical Examination of Perceptions from Field Personnel. *Journal of Information Technology Education, 7*, 101–120.

Sohal, A. S., & Ng, L. (1998). The role and impact of information technology in Australian business. *Journal of Information Technology*, *13*(3), 201–217. doi:10.1080/026839698344846

U.S. Department of Labor. (2009). Occupational Outlook Handbook, 2008-09 Edition Retrieved April 12, 2009, from http://www.bls.gov/oco/oco2003.htm

Varajão, J., Ferreira, N., Fraga, M. d. G., & Amaral, L. (2008, Dezembro de 2008). Outsourcing de Sistemas de Informação nas empresas nacionais. *Revista CXO*.

Varajão, J., Trigo, A., Figueiredo, N., & Barroso, J. (2007, Maio). 2007). TI nas empresas nacionais. *Revista CXO*, *2*, 19–23.

Varajao, J., Trigo, A., Figueiredo, N., Barroso, J., & Bulas-Cruz, J. (2009). Information systems services outsourcing reality in large Portuguese organisations. *Int. J. Bus. Inf. Syst.*, *4*(1), 125–142. doi:10.1504/IJBIS.2009.021606

This work was previously published in International Journal of Human Capital and Information Technology Professionals, Volume 1, Issue 1, edited by Ricardo Colomo-Palacios, pp. 61-75, copyright 2010 by IGI Publishing (an imprint of IGI Global).

APPENDIX

a. How many professionals of the following types does the IT/IS department possess internally?
__ Trainees
__ Informatics technicians
__ Junior programmers
__ Senior programmers
__ Junior analysts
__ Senior analysts
__ Others _____

b. What are the most important skills of your internal IT/IS team (where 1 is without importance and 5 the very important)?
1 2 3 4 5
Project management ○ ○ ○ ○ ○
Application development ○ ○ ○ ○ ○
Help desk/User support ○ ○ ○ ○ ○
Database management ○ ○ ○ ○ ○
Network management ○ ○ ○ ○ ○
Servers management ○ ○ ○ ○ ○
Security management ○ ○ ○ ○ ○
Web site and web services development ○ ○ ○ ○ ○
Emerging technologies ○ ○ ○ ○ ○
Business knowledge ○ ○ ○ ○ ○

c. What are the skills you will need from new employees (where 1 is without importance and 5 the very important)?
1 2 3 4 5
Project management ○ ○ ○ ○ ○
Application development ○ ○ ○ ○ ○
Help desk/User support ○ ○ ○ ○ ○
Database management ○ ○ ○ ○ ○
Network management ○ ○ ○ ○ ○
Servers management ○ ○ ○ ○ ○
Security management ○ ○ ○ ○ ○
Web site and web services development ○ ○ ○ ○ ○
Emerging technologies ○ ○ ○ ○ ○
Business knowledge ○ ○ ○ ○ ○

d. What level of experience do you require of new employees?
   ○ Without experience
   ○ Less than 2 years
   ○ 2 to 5 years
   ○ 6 to 10 years
   ○ More than 10 years

Chapter 4

Glass Ceilings in Portugal?
An Analysis of the Gender Wage Gap Using a Quantile Regression Approach

Raquel Mendes
Instituto Politécnico do Cávado e do Ave, Portugal

ABSTRACT

Despite the evidence of female progress with regard to women's role in the labor market, gender inequality remains. Women are still less likely to be employed than men, occupational gender segregation continues, and females continue to earn less than males. The gender wage gap remains wide in several occupational sectors, among which is the information technology (IT) sector. This paper focuses the determinants of gender wage inequality. More precisely, it investigates for statistical evidence of a glass ceiling effect on women's wages. Based on the quantile regression framework, the empirical analysis extends the decomposition of the average gender wage gap to other parts of the earnings distribution. The main objective is to empirically test whether gender-based wage discrimination is greater among high paid employees, in line with glass ceiling hypothesis. Larger unexplained gaps at the top of the wage distribution indicate the existence of a glass ceiling effect in Portugal.

INTRODUCTION

Gender equality has been a constant concern of national and supranational governments since the latter half of the twentieth century. Viewed as an essential right of all working citizens and an elementary condition for economic, social, and cultural progress, public authorities and academia alike have kept this subject under close scrutiny, making it a point to gather and monitor data on the differences between men and women in all aspects of societal life. This field of study has become a fertile ground for research given the profound effects gender equality, or lack of,

DOI: 10.4018/978-1-4666-0924-2.ch004

may have on economic growth, employment, and social cohesion.

The achievement of gender equality has become a central topic on the policy agenda of the European Union. Implemented in the late 1990s, the European Employment Strategy (EES) brought about a renewed interest in the equality between men and women in the European Union. Two particular aspects of the equality agenda are employment and wages. In the year 2000, the Lisbon Strategy defined increased female participation in the labor force, reduction of unequal access to job opportunities, and equal pay as the top priorities to be achieved in Europe by 2010. More recently, the European Commission defined the strategy of equal economic independence as one of the six priority areas of intervention for the period 2006-2010.

As the year 2010 is approaching, statistics show that the overall employment gender gap in the European Union has been decreasing, as more women have improved their academic and professional qualifications and have actively pursued working careers. General economic conditions and various measures promoting female employment, such as policies fostering better childcare facilities and more flexible working time arrangements, have contributed to women's progress. Also as a result of the gender equality movement, statistics reveal that wage differentials between men and women have decreased in many member states.

Gender equality has also been on the political agenda of Portuguese governments over the past thirty years, and it is regarded as a fundamental element of the development of society and the improvement of the quality of democracy. The country's Constitution of 1976 promoted gender equality as one of its fundamental principles, ensuring women's full legal equality. From the late 1970s onwards, national legal commissions have been set up to promote equal employment opportunities, and national legislation has been passed in order to foster gender equality.

These factors have contributed to the improvement of the position of women in the Portuguese society. Female labor market participation in Portugal ranks among the highest within the European Union. Additionally, statistics reveal an upward trend in women's qualifications as a result of greater levels of tertiary education and a larger portion of women occupying jobs that require higher skills.

Despite the evidence of female progress with regard to their role in the labor market, gender inequality remains. Women have not yet attained full social and economic equality, and their productivity potential is not used at its best. Although women represent an important economic resource for the improvement of society, their role continues underdeveloped. Women are still less likely to be employed than men, and occupational gender segregation continues, with women underrepresented in positions that require higher qualifications and overrepresented in jobs that are traditionally labeled as female jobs. Furthermore, women continue to earn less than their male counterparts. Statistics show that economies across the European Union are still characterized by important wage disparities between men and women. The gender wage gap remains wide with regard to several occupational sectors, among which is the information technology (IT) sector.[1] Male professionals in this sector continue to receive higher salaries, bonuses and raises than their female colleagues. In most developed European countries, women in scientific and technological professions receive substantially lower pay than men.

Why do women earn lower wages than men? There are several empirical studies that investigate the size and components of the average wage gap in Portugal (e.g., Kiker & Santos, 1991; Vieira et al., 2005; Vieira & Pereira, 1993). A key issue in these studies is whether or not the observed wage differentials result from wage discrimination against female employees. In general, the studies conclude that gender-based wage discrimination is important in explaining the observed average gap. Although the studies based on average gaps provide interesting insights on gender wage differentials, they cannot address the question of whether or not a glass ceiling exists. The investigation of the glass ceiling hypothesis implies the analysis of the wage gap across the entire distribution of earnings.

The glass ceiling metaphor is used by the economics literature to describe a specific type of gender inequality in the labor market. A glass ceiling represents a situation whereby the pay disadvantages that women face with regard to men increase systematically as they advance to the higher levels of the pay hierarchy. The existence of a glass ceiling implies that wage discrimination against females is greater at the upper levels of the wage distribution. It implies that female wages fall behind male wages more at the top of the wage scale, impeding qualified women from obtaining the earnings of their highest paid male colleagues.

This paper investigates for statistical evidence of a glass effect on women's wages in the Portuguese labor market. The empirical analysis extends the decomposition of the average wage gap to other parts of the earnings distribution. The main objective is to ascertain how the gender wage gap and its components evolve throughout the entire distribution of wages. Does gender-based wage discrimination explain wage disparities at various parts of the earnings distribution? If so, is it greater at the upper end of the wage scale than it is at the lower end, preventing women from attaining the earnings of their highest paid male colleagues? Is there a glass ceiling effect in the Portuguese labor market?

For empirical purposes, an adaptation of the decomposition methodology derived in Machado and Mata (2000) is applied to the micro data from the *Quadros de Pessoal* (Personnel Records). The adaptation of this quantile regression (QR) decomposition methodology to the gender wage gap analysis extends the widely used approach

derived in Oaxaca (1973) by implementing decompositions at different points of the wage distribution, instead of exclusively at the distribution's mean. Knowing where in the earnings distribution unexplained gender wage gaps lie, and how the magnitude of these gaps evolves throughout the distribution, allows to test whether or not gender-based wage discrimination is greater among high paid employees than it is among low paid employees, in line with glass ceiling hypothesis.

Various empirical studies base the investigation of the glass ceiling phenomenon on the application of the Machado and Mata (2000) decomposition methodology (e.g., Albrecht et al., 2003; Arulampalam et al., 2006; De la Rica et al., 2005; Kee, 2006). For Portugal, there is no known study that relies on this methodology to decompose gender wage disparities at different points of the distribution of earnings in order to test for the glass ceiling effect.

This paper proceeds in the following manner. In the next two sections, respectively, the theoretical explanations for gender wage differentials are briefly reviewed, and the glass ceiling concept is outlined. Next, the methodological framework used in the empirical analysis is described, followed by the report and discussion of the estimated results. Finally, the main conclusions are presented in the last section.

SOURCES OF THE GENDER WAGE GAP

The traditional approach in analyzing the determinants of the wage gap is to consider both the role of gender differences in human capital endowments and labor market discrimination.[2] The human capital theory (Mincer & Polachek, 1974) posits that the earnings of individual workers are a function of their past investment in human capital. The theory suggests that the gap can be explained by the fact that, when compared to men, women have fewer qualifications, such as formal education, labor market experience, and on-the-job training. The results of these differences in human capital are lower levels of productivity for women and, therefore, lower female wages. This theory's explanation for gender differences in acquisitions of human capital is based upon the traditional role of women within the family. Because they tend to have shorter and more interrupted working lives than their male counterparts, women invest less in labor market qualifications (Blau & Kahn, 1999).

In addition to differences in human capital endowments, labor market discrimination is often pointed out as a main source of gender wage differentials. Blau and Ferber (1986, p. 229) consider that labor market discrimination exists when "two equally qualified individuals are treated differently solely on the basis of their sex". Thus, in accordance with the labor market discrimination theory, gender disparities in earnings arise from the unequal treatment of equally productive males and females.[3] The two main theories of labor market discrimination are those referred to as theories of taste discrimination and theories of statistical discrimination (Stenzel, 2001). In Becker's (1957) model of taste discrimination, the unequal treatment of two groups arises from discriminatory tastes or personal prejudices against members of one of the groups. In models of statistical discrimination (e.g., Aigner & Cain, 1977), employers discriminate based on the average differences between two groups in the expected value of productivity or in the reliability with which this value can be predicted (Blau & Kahn, 1999).

More recently, scholars focus on the role of occupational gender segregation in explaining the gap. This type of segregation exists when men and women are employed in different types of occupations (Preston, 1999). The segregation theory suggests that gender differences in pay stem from the fact that female-dominated occupations are generally paid more poorly than those dominated by males (Boraas & Rodgers, 2003). To explain occupational segregation, Ter-

rell (1992) distinguishes between labor supply and demand factors. On the labor supply side, the human capital approach views occupational distribution as a function of occupational choice. The basic idea is that, given their traditional role within the family, women tend to invest less in human capital than men and select occupations on the basis of this role and these investments. On the labor demand side, occupational segregation is explained by employers' discrimination of women in their hiring practices in certain occupations (employment discrimination).

It is important to note that most economists do not necessarily consider mutually exclusive sources of the gender wage gap. Many authors refer to the possibility of more than one factor contributing to the determination of the gap. In her analysis of Portuguese female labor force participation, Cardoso (1996) concludes that gender wage differentials do not result exclusively from lower levels of female human capital and from the concentration of female employment in less regarded occupations or economic sectors. This author considers that disparities between male and female wages are also due to the fact that, at each human capital level and in each occupation or economic sector, women with equal characteristics as that of men are paid less.

GLASS CEILING METAPHOR

The economics literature uses the glass ceiling metaphor to describe a specific type of gender inequality in the labor market. Taken literally, a glass ceiling represents a transparent but real barrier that prevents female employees from advancing as far up an outcome[4] hierarchy as their male counterparts. Qualified women can see further advancement levels beyond the glass ceiling but cannot reach them due to the invisible barrier that blocks any additional upward movement. Below the barrier, female employees advance to higher outcome levels; above it, they do not.

Baxter and Wright (2000) present a looser definition of the term, whereby the glass ceiling metaphor is used to describe a situation in which the disadvantages that female employees face relative to men increase systematically as they move up the outcome hierarchy. Women find themselves at greater relative disadvantages at the upper levels of the outcome hierarchy than at the lower levels. When restricted to its literal meaning, a glass ceiling implies an absolute barrier for the vertical advancement of female employees; when considered more loosely, the metaphor implies intensifying relative disadvantages for female employees as they ascend to the higher rungs of the outcome hierarchy. With regard to the current study, the glass ceiling metaphor is used from here on out in the looser definition of the term.[5]

Based on glass ceiling literature, Cotter et al. (2001) define four specific criteria they consider must be met for a glass ceiling to exist. First, a glass ceiling inequality represents a gender difference that cannot be explained by other labor market characteristics of the employees, such as education and experience. Glass ceilings are measured as residual gender differences after controlling for characteristics. Thus, the first glass ceiling criterion implies labor market discrimination against female employees. Second, a glass ceiling inequality represents a gender difference that is greater at the higher levels of an outcome than at the lower levels. Glass ceilings imply increasing levels of labor market discrimination as one moves up the outcome hierarchy. Third, a glass ceiling inequality represents a gender difference in the chances of advancing into the upper levels of an outcome hierarchy, not merely the proportions of each gender that are currently at those levels. Finally, a glass ceiling inequality represents a gender difference that grows over the course of a career. Glass ceilings imply that gender disadvantages increase as the employee's career progresses.

The current study bases the glass ceiling concept on the criteria outlined in Cotter et al. (2001).

More specifically, the concept is based on the first two criteria, whereby glass ceilings imply increasing levels of labor market discrimination against female employees as they advance to the higher rungs of the outcome hierarchy. On the other hand, although there are different types of work-related outcomes that may reflect the existence of glass ceilings, the concept applied in the current study is based on the earnings outcome. Hence, for the purpose of the empirical analysis conducted in this chapter, the glass ceiling concept is used to describe a situation in which gender-based wage discrimination is greater at the higher levels of earnings than at the lower levels. Glass ceilings imply that female wages fall behind male wages more at the top of the wage distribution than at the bottom, impeding qualified women from obtaining the earnings of the highest paid men. The glass ceiling concept used in the current study is similar to the concept applied in various empirical studies that investigate the glass ceiling hypothesis (e.g., Albrecht et al., 2003; Arulampalam et al., 2006; De la Rica et al., 2005; Kee, 2006).

METHODOLOGICAL FRAMEWORK

The empirical study conducted in this paper is based on an adaptation of the decomposition methodology derived in Machado and Mata (2000). These authors derive a decomposition methodology to study the changes in the Portuguese wage distribution over the period 1986-1995. Specifically, the methodology decomposes the changes in the wage distribution into changes in the employees' characteristics and changes in the returns to those characteristics.

The decomposition procedure is based on the quantile regression (QR) framework. This framework, introduced by Koenker and Bassett (1978), aims at complementing the classical linear regression analysis. In OLS estimation, the main objective is to determine the conditional mean of the dependent variable. The QR approach goes beyond this and enables the full characterization of the conditional distribution of the dependent variable. This is of particular interest in the analysis of gender wage gaps given that "gender-earnings differentials entail much more than the fact that men, on average, earn more than women" (Sakellariou, 2004, p. 460).

The QR model, expressed in a wage equation setting, can be defined as follows:

$$\ln w_i = x_i{}^2{}_\theta + \mu_{\theta i},$$
$$\text{Quant}_.(\ln w_i | x_i) = x_i{}^2{}_\theta \tag{1}$$

where subscript i indicates the ith employee, subscript xi denotes the θth quantile, $\ln w_i$ is the natural logarithm of hourly wage, β_θ is the vector of the coefficients to be estimated, x_i is the vector of covariates that represents individual characteristics, and $\mu_{\theta i}$ represents the error term. The θth ($0 < \theta < 1$) conditional quantile of $\ln w_i$ given x_i is denoted by $\text{Quant}_\theta(\ln w_i | x_i)$. In the classical linear regression model, the normal distribution of the unknown error term μ is specified. In this case, however, the distribution of the error term for the θth quantile is left unspecified, just assuming that $\mu_{\theta i}$ satisfies $\text{Quant}_\theta(\mu_{\theta i} | x_i) = 0$.[6]

The estimation procedure in the QR model minimizes the sum of absolute residuals. In other words, the θth quantile regression estimator of β_θ is obtained by solving the following minimization problem:

$$\min_{\beta_\theta} \left\{ \sum_{i:1 n w_i \geq x_i \beta_\theta} \theta \, | 1 n w_i - x_i \beta_\theta | + \sum_{i:1 n w_i < x_i \beta_\theta} (1 - \theta) \, | 1 n w_i - x_i \beta_\theta | \right\} \tag{2}$$

The solution at different quantiles is obtained by the asymmetrical weighting of absolute residuals. For a positive residual, the weight is θ; for a negative residual, the weight is $(1 - \theta)$.

By using the QR technique, it is possible to estimate the effect of the covariates at various quantiles of the conditional distribution of the dependent variable, rather than just the effect of the covariates upon the conditional mean of the dependent variable. Thus, in a wage equation setting, the estimated QR coefficients are interpreted as the returns to the individual characteristics at the θth quantile of the wage distribution.

Adjusted for the gender wage gap analysis, the decomposition equation derived in Machado and Mata (2000) may be expressed as:

$$(\ln w_\theta^m - \ln w_\theta^f) = \hat{\beta}_\theta^m (\S^m - \S^f) + \S^f (\hat{\beta}_\theta^m - \hat{\beta}_\theta^f) + \text{residual} \tag{3}$$

where superscripts m and f indicate, respectively, male and female gender, subscript θ denotes the θth quantile, $\ln w_\theta^m$ and n $\ln w_\theta^f$ are the natural logarithms of hourly wages, and $\hat{\beta}_\theta^m$ and $\hat{\beta}_\theta^f$ are vectors of the estimated QR coefficients. The terms X^m and X^f represent the matrices of labor market characteristics. Machado and Mata (2000) propose a bootstrap technique whereby the values of the two groups' characteristics are derived at the various quantiles of the wage distribution.[7] This technique is described in the next section.

In decomposition Equation (3), the wage gap measured at the θth quantile is expressed as the sum of three components. The first two components represent the explained and unexplained components, respectively. The interpretation of these components is analogous to the interpretation given to the components of the Oaxaca (1973) decomposition equation. Hence, the explained component captures the portion of the wage gap that is due to differences in the levels of male and female labor market characteristics, whereas the unexplained component represents the portion of the gap that cannot be accounted for on the basis of those differences. The unexplained component stems from differences in the rates of return to the two groups' characteristics and is interpreted as wage discrimination.

The third component, which is not present in the Oaxaca (1973) equation, is residual and represents the portion of the gap that is unaccounted for by the estimation method used to evaluate differentials across wage distributions. Hence, the residual component corresponds to the part of the gap that is left unassigned to either the explained or unexplained components.[8]

The wage decomposition specified in Equation (3) is based on the male wage structure, assuming that in the absence of wage discrimination female employees will have the same rates of return to characteristics as their male colleagues. However, if it is assumed that the female wage structure prevails in the absence of discrimination, then the decomposition equation may be expressed as:

$$(\ln w_\theta^m - \ln w_\theta^f) = \hat{\beta}_\theta^f(\hat{s}^m - \hat{s}^f) + \hat{s}^m(\hat{\beta}_\theta^m - \hat{\beta}_\theta^f) + \text{residual}.$$
(4)

Various empirical studies apply this adapted version of the Machado and Mata (2000) decomposition methodology to investigate the glass ceiling phenomenon. Albrecht et al. (2003), relying on Swedish micro data, find evidence of a strong glass ceiling effect for female employees. Arulampalam et al. (2006) use data from eleven European countries[9] and report evidence of glass ceilings in most countries. De la Rica et al. (2005) stratify their sample of employees by education groups and conclude that glass ceilings exist in Spain for the highly educated. Based on an analysis of the private and public sectors of the Australian labor market, Kee (2006) finds that a glass ceiling effect prevails in the private sector. For the Portuguese labor market, there is no known study that employs the methodology described above to decompose gender wage disparities at different points of the wage distribution in order to test whether or not a glass ceiling exists.

EMPIRICAL EVIDENCE ON PORTUGUESE GLASS CEILINGS

Data

The empirical study is first performed for the year 2004, relying on micro data from the *Quadros de Pessoal* (Personnel Records). The *Quadros de Pessoal* is an extensive data set provided by the Portuguese Ministry of Labor and Social Solidarity. The data set is based on an annual employment survey that each firm in the Portuguese economy with paid personnel is legally obliged to fill in. Excluded from the legal obligation of answering the annual survey are both public administration and employers of domestic related services. For the remaining cases, firms are legally required to answer the employment survey in November of every year, based on information regarding the reference month of October.

The micro data gathered in the *Quadros de Pessoal* cover information at three different levels: the firm level, the establishment level, and the worker level. At the firm level, there is information on each firm's location, legal setting, capital stock, establishments, employment, economic activity, year of constitution, and sales volume. At the establishment level, the data cover information on the location, employment, and economic activity of each one of the firm's establishments. Reported data at the worker level include information on each worker's gender, nationality, occupation, professional situation, qualifications, schooling, age, monthly wages (divided into several components), hours worked, and employment duration regime.

Several constraints were imposed on the total number of observations of the original data set. In relation to the worker's professional status, only wage earners were included in the analysis. Firm owners, unpaid family members, and active members of cooperatives were, therefore, dropped. Employers engaged in the firm's activities and members of cooperatives were not considered since the distinction between wages and profits may not be sufficiently clear and non-subjective. Given that wage inequality is the main theme of this thesis, unpaid family members were also dropped from the original data set. Furthermore, only full-time wage earners, aged 16 to 64, were retained for the analysis undertaken.

Due to their low representation in the data set *Quadros de Pessoal*, observations related to the economic sectors of agriculture, forestry, fishery, mining, public administration, domestic service, and extra-territorial organizations were not included in the analysis. These economic sectors are not adequately covered by the annual survey since either they correspond to economic sectors explicitly excluded from the legal obligation to answer the annual survey, or they correspond to economic sectors that have a very low share of workers in total employment. From a geographical point of view, the empirical study is focused on the Portuguese mainland, therefore excluding observations regarding the autonomous regions of Azores and Madeira. Finally, and given the problems that the existence of missing values in the data set can bring to the computations to be performed, observations with missing data were also dropped from the original data set.

The observations included in the analysis correspond to 1,886,943 employees, the majority of which correspond to males. For the year in analysis, women represent approximately 42% of the employed labor force. Table 1 presents the average descriptive statistics for male and female employees for the year 2004.

The comparison of male and female average hourly wages reveals that women earn on average about 78% of men. Differences in the educational attainments for male and female employees are small: the average number of years of schooling is 8 for men and 9 for women. On average, male employees are older than females and have more work experience prior to their current job. Job tenure is also slightly greater for men than for women.

Although both groups of employees are similarly characterized in relation to the firm's size and location, they are distributed differently across occupations. While a substantial portion of male workers (58%) are employed as production workers, machine operators, assembly workers, middle managers, and technicians, half of the female group is concentrated in administrative, service, and sales occupations. The two groups are also distributed differently across economic sectors. The three leading sectors are "trade", "construction", and "financial intermediation, real estate, renting, and business" for male employees and "trade", "social and personal services", and "financial intermediation, real estate, renting, and business" for female employees.

Gender Wage Gap by Quantile

Figure 1 displays the unconditional gender wage gap at each percentile of the wage distribution. For comparison, the estimated mean wage gap is also displayed. The gender wage gap is measured as the difference between the male and female natural logarithm of hourly wages.

As can be seen from the results presented in the figure, the magnitude of the average gender wage gap remains constant at 0.204 across the entire wage scale. An exclusive focus on the mean of the wage gap may therefore lead to the conclusion that the size of the gender wage gap (and its possible causes) is constant across the entire distribution of wages. Given that the main objective of the current analysis is to test for statistical evidence of a glass ceiling effect, the focus is the magnitude of the gender wage gap measured at different quantiles of the wage distribution, rather than the magnitude of the gap estimated at the distribution's mean.

The results displayed in Figure 1 reveal that male wages are greater than female wages at every percentile of the wage distribution (the exceptions are at the first and second percentiles in which the wages of the two groups are equal). Additionally, the QR estimates reveal that the unconditional

Table 1. Average descriptive statistics by gender, 2004

Characteristics (N=1,886,943)	Mean	
	Males	Females
Share of employees by gender	57.91	42.09
Ln hourly wage	1.54	1.34
Education (years) %:	8.02	8.76
≤ 4	27.91	23.19
6	22.90	20.30
9	21.79	20.32
12	17.94	23.06
≥15	9.46	13.13
Age (years)	37.87	36.39
Previous experience (years)	16.33	14.77
Tenure (years)	7.52	6.88
Ln firm size	3.83	3.74
Region %:		
North Coast	28.79	29.24
Center Coast	15.01	14.65
Lisbon and Tagus Valley	44.28	43.71
Inland	8.44	8.33
Algarve	3.48	4.07
Occupation %:		
Executive civil servants, industrial directors, and executives	5.19	2.72
Professionals and scientists	4.81	5.67
Middle management and technicians	12.73	9.66
Administrative and related workers	11.47	23.81
Service and sales workers	9.47	26.03
Skilled workers, craftsmen, and similar	29.44	14.19
Machine operators and assembly workers	16.23	5.33
Unskilled workers	10.66	12.59
Economic activity %:		
Food, beverages, and tobacco	3.41	3.72
Textiles, clothing, and footwear	4.61	13.42
Wood and cork	1.86	0.87
Paper, printing, and publishing	2.05	1.44
Chemical	2.31	1.52
Non-metal mineral products	2.70	1.45
Metal	4.33	1.21
Machinery and equipment	5.47	3.24

continued in following column

Table 1. Continued

Other manufacturing industries	2.15	1.34
Electricity, gas, and water supply	0.79	0.22
Construction	18.26	2.37
Trade	20.84	21.72
Hotels and restaurants	4.69	9.95
Transport, storage, and communication	8.96	3.52
Financial intermediation, real estate, renting, and business	13.25	13.99
Social and personal services	4.32	20.02

Source: Computations based on Ministério do Trabalho e da Solidariedade Social (2006).

wage gap exhibits an upward tendency as it moves towards the higher quantiles of the earnings distribution. Hence, the results indicate that the Portuguese gender wage gap is larger at the top of the wage distribution than it is at the bottom. Female wages fall behind male wages more at the top than at the bottom of the wage scale. A larger gender wage gap at the higher levels of the earnings distribution may be interpreted as an indicator of the glass ceiling phenomenon.

However, it is important to note that these results are based on the unconditional gender wage gap. They do not, therefore, provide sufficient evidence to conclude whether or not a glass ceiling exists. In order to test for the glass ceiling hypothesis, it is necessary to measure how much of the wage gap estimated at different quantiles of the wage distribution is unexplained by gender differences in the levels of endowments and is due to wage discrimination against female employees. The existence of a glass ceiling implies that gender-based wage discrimination is greater at the upper levels of the wage distribution than at the lower levels. The estimated results of the wage gap decomposition performed at various parts of the wage distribution and based on the adapted version of methodology derived in Machado and Mata (2000) are presented and discussed in the next sub-section.

Figure 1. Gender wage gap (ln) by quantile, 2004 (Source: Computations based on Ministério do Trabalho e da Solidariedade Social (2006))

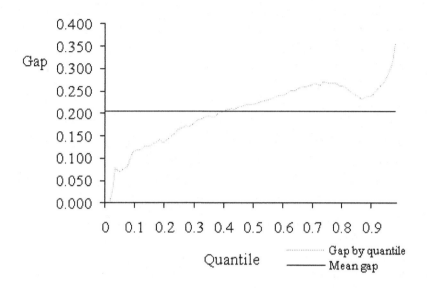

Decomposition Results

As explained in the previous section, Machado and Mata (2000) propose a methodology that implements wage decompositions across the entire distribution of earnings. This methodology combines both QR and bootstrap techniques. The empirical analysis conducted in this chapter employs an adapted version of this methodology to investigate whether or not a glass ceiling exists in the Portuguese economy.

The first step followed is the estimation of separate QR wage equations at different quantiles of the wage distribution based on the male and female data sets, respectively.[10] The dependent variable corresponds to the natural logarithm of hourly wages, and the independent variables are years of previous work experience (and its square), years of job tenure (and its square), the natural logarithm of firm size, and a sequence of dummy variables that represent years of educational attainment, firm location, occupation, and economic activity.[11] According to the results, most of the

estimated regression coefficients are statistically significant at the 0.01 level.

The estimated results reveal that higher educational levels raise earnings and that the returns to each level of education increase with the quantiles of the wage distribution. The results also reveal the extent to which returns to education differ between male and female employees at the different points of the wage distribution. According to the estimated results, male employees receive greater payoffs to education than their female colleagues, particularly at higher quantiles and educational levels.

The wage regression results show that previous experience and tenure have diminishing marginal effects on hourly wages and that the returns to these variables are larger at higher quantiles when compared to lower quantiles. The results also show that the male returns are larger than the corresponding returns for female employees at all parts of the wage distribution. Additionally, the results indicate that the firm's size has a positive effect on hourly wages and that this effect is larger for males than for females throughout the distribution of wages.

The results reveal that the firm's location in the Lisbon and Algarve regions leads to greater payoffs when compared to location in other regions and that these payoffs tend to increase with the quantiles of the wage distribution. Furthermore, the results reveal that the payoffs to these variable dummies are always greater for males than for females. In relation to the occupation dummies, the results show that the returns to top management positions are higher than the returns to other occupations (the exceptions are at the 10th and 25th percentiles in which both groups of employees receive higher premiums as "professionals and scientists") and that these disparities are larger at the top parts of the wage scale. The results also show that males have larger wage penalties than females at all quantiles for the occupations "administrative and related workers" and "unskilled workers". The opposite applies to the occupations "skilled workers, craftsmen, and similar" and "machine operators and assembly workers".

As for the dummy variables for economic activity, the results indicate that "chemical", "electricity, gas, and water supply", and "financial intermediation, real estate, renting, and business" are among the most highly remunerated sectors (the exceptions are at the 10th and 90th percentiles for "financial intermediation, real estate, renting, and business" and "electricity, gas, and water supply", respectively). The progression of the returns along the wage distribution differs by sector and by gender. The results further indicate that the returns to the sector "chemical" are always greater for male employees, whereas the sectors "electricity, gas, and water supply" and "financial intermediation, real estate, renting, and business" have larger effects for females at all quantiles of the wage distribution.

The second step followed is the estimation of the values of both groups' characteristics at each percentile based on bootstrap draws. For each of the male and female data sets, samples of 100 observations are randomly drawn with replacement. Each observation is then sorted by wage, comprising a percentile point of the wage distribution. This process is repeated 100 times in order to obtain 100 observations at each quantile. The average characteristics of the observations of both groups' of employees at each quantile are estimated for the purpose of the decomposition analysis.

The components of the wage decomposition expressed as in (3) and performed at the selected quantiles are presented in Table 2. The results reveal that the unexplained component of the wage gap represents more than 70% of the observed gap at all quantiles.[12] It is shown that even after gender differences in labor market characteristics are considered, substantial portions of the wage gap remain unaccounted for. Hence, the estimated results indicate that for the year in analysis a significant portion of the gender wage gap across the wage distribution is unexplained by differences in male and female endowments and is due to gender-based wage discrimination. The residual component, that is, the portion of the gap that is unaccounted for by the estimation method used, accounts for a relatively small portion of the total gap at all quantiles. If this portion were assigned to either the explained or unexplained components, the qualitative information provided in this study would remain unchanged.

The results provided in Table 2 further reveal that the unexplained component is larger at the top of the wage distribution than it is at the bottom. These findings indicate that gender-based wage discrimination is greater among high paid employees, impeding qualified women from obtaining the earnings of their highest paid male colleagues. Thus, the estimated results indicate the existence of a glass ceiling effect for the year 2004.[13]

Given the restrictive nature of investigating the glass ceiling hypothesis based on only one cross-section of the data set, this study extends the empirical analysis to other years (1986, 1992,

Table 2. Decomposition results, 2004

Quantile	Total wage gap	Explained component	Unexplained component	Residual component
0.10	0.115	0.026	0.090	−0.001
0.25	0.165	0.035	0.134	−0.004
0.50	0.220	0.018	0.216	−0.014
0.75	0.270	−0.008	0.240	0.038
0.90	0.239	−0.043	0.250	0.032

Source: Computations based on Ministério do Trabalho e da Solidariedade Social (2006).

and 1998) of the period 1986-2004. The fact that these four years span over two decades in sub-periods of equal length allows for the detection and explanation of wage inequality patterns.

Figures 2, 3, and 4 plot the unconditional gender wage gap at each percentile of the wage distribution for the years 1986, 1992, and 1998, respectively. According to these results, female employees are at a pay disadvantage across all quantiles of the wage distribution (the exception is at the second percentile for the year 1998 in which the unconditional wage gap is equal to zero). Furthermore, the results reveal that the female pay disadvantage does not occur uniformly across the earnings distribution; it is greater at the top part of the distribution than at the bottom. These empirical findings may be interpreted as preliminary evidence of the glass ceiling effect.

As explained earlier on, in order to test for the glass ceiling effect, it is necessary to measure how much of the wage gap estimated at the different quantiles is unexplained by gender differences in labor market characteristics and is due to gender-based wage discrimination. The decomposition results for all four years are summarized in Table 3.[14]

The estimated results reveal the relative importance of the unexplained component in accounting for gender differentials across the distribution of wages. In all of the years, and for all of the selected quantiles, the results indicate that the majority of the wage gap is unexplained by gender differences in labor market characteristics and is due to wage discrimination against female employees. Overall, the residual component accounts for a relatively small portion of the total

Figure 2. Gender wage gap (ln) by quantile, 1986 (Source: Computations based on Ministério do Trabalho e da Solidariedade Social (2006))

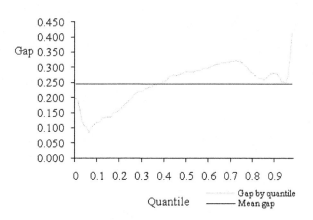

Table 3. Decomposition Results, 1986-2004

	Quantile				
	0.10	**0.25**	**0.50**	**0.75**	**0.90**
1986					
Total wage gap	0.115	0.191	0.284	0.320	0.280
Explained	0.016	0.047	0.067	0.106	0.022
Unexplained	0.088	0.130	0.162	0.165	0.198
Residual	0.011	0.014	0.055	0.049	0.060
1992					
Total wage gap	0.122	0.231	0.336	0.361	0.313
Explained	0.008	0.064	0.088	0.092	0.045
Unexplained	0.065	0.154	0.190	0.200	0.210
Residual	0.049	0.013	0.058	0.069	0.058
1998					
Total wage gap	0.150	0.203	0.270	0.350	0.278
Explained	0.017	0.052	0.041	0.096	0.103
Unexplained	0.085	0.147	0.193	0.201	0.202
Residual	0.048	0.004	0.036	0.053	−0.027
2004					
Total wage gap	0.115	0.165	0.220	0.270	0.239
Explained	0.026	0.035	0.018	−0.008	−0.043
Unexplained	0.090	0.134	0.216	0.240	0.250
Residual	−0.001	−0.004	−0.014	0.038	0.032

Source: Computations based on Ministério do Trabalho e da Solidariedade Social (2006).

gap. If this unassigned portion were incorporated in either the explained or unexplained components, the qualitative information provided by the analysis would remain unchanged.

The results also show that the unexplained wage gap widens as higher quantiles of the wage distribution are considered. Thus, the results indicate that wage discrimination against female employees is greater at the top part of the distribution. As women advance to the higher rungs of the earnings hierarchy, they become more relatively disadvantaged with regard to pay, evidence that is very much in line with the glass hypothesis. In sum, the results of the empirical analysis indicate that a glass ceiling exists and is persistent in the Portuguese labor market.

CONCLUSION

Over the last decades, women in most developed countries have made profound progress with regard to their role in the labor market. In Portugal, this progress is reflected in both quantitative and qualitative changes that have taken place over time. Among these changes are sharp increases in female activity and employment rates, higher levels of female qualifications, and shifts in both employment status and activity patterns of employment. However, and despite these signs of progress, gender inequality remains. Female employment continues lower than male employment, and the labor market continues to be characterized by occupational gender segregation and gender wage

Figure 3. Gender wage gap (ln) by quantile, 1992 (Source: Computations based on Ministério do Trabalho e da Solidariedade Social (2006))

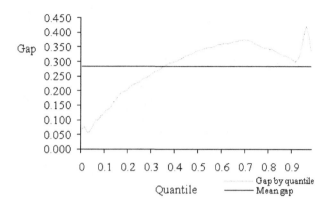

inequality. The wage gap remains high with regard to several occupational sectors, among which is the information technology (IT) sector. Female employees in technological professions continue to receive lower pay than their male counterparts.

This paper focuses on the determinants of gender wage disparities. It investigates how the Portuguese gender wage gap and its components evolve throughout the entire distribution of wages. The main objective was to test for the existence of a glass ceiling, defined as a situation whereby wage discrimination against female employees is greater at the top part of the wage distribution than at the bottom part, preventing qualified women

from earning the highest pay levels of their male counterparts.

For empirical purposes, and relying on the micro data from the *Quadros de Pessoal*, decompositions of wage differentials were performed at various parts of the wage distribution based on an adaptation of the methodology derived in Machado and Mata (2000). The estimated results of these wage decompositions show that the portion of the gap that is unexplained by gender differences in labor market endowments and that is due to wage discrimination accounts for a substantial part of the total gap at all quantiles of the earnings distribution.

Figure 4. Gender wage gap (ln) by quantile, 1998 (Source: Computations based on Ministério do Trabalho e da Solidariedade Social (2006))

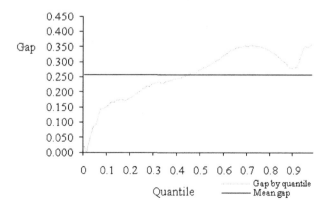

The estimates further reveal that the unexplained component widens as higher quantiles of the wage distribution are considered. The results indicate therefore that gender-based wage discrimination is greater among high paid employees than it is among low paid employees; that women become more relatively disadvantaged with regard to pay as they advance to the upper levels of the wage hierarchy. Hence, the estimated results suggest the existence of a glass ceiling effect on women's wages.

From a policy point of view, and although the debate on the gender wage gap needs to focus on all parts of the wage distribution, the results suggest that particular attention should be given to gender wage disparities among high wage earners given that the disparities among this group of employees is relatively larger and, therefore, motive for greater political concern.

REFERENCES

Ahuja, M. K. (2002). Women in the information technology profession: A literature review, synthesis and research agenda. *European Journal of Information Systems, 11*(1), 20–34. doi:10.1057/palgrave/ejis/3000417

Aigner, D. J., & Cain, G. G. (1977). Statistical theories of discrimination in labor markets. *Industrial & Labor Relations Review, 30*(2), 175–187. doi:10.2307/2522871

Albrecht, J., Björklund, A., & Vroman, S. (2003). Is there a glass ceiling in Sweden? *Journal of Labor Economics, 21*(1), 145–177. doi:10.1086/344126

Arulampalam, W., Booth, A. L., & Bryan, M. L. (2006). Is there a glass ceiling over Europe? Exploring the gender pay gap across the wages distribution. *Industrial & Labor Relations Review, 60*(2), 163–186.

Baxter, J., & Wright, E. O. (2000). The glass ceiling hypothesis: A comparative study of the United States, Sweden, and Australia. *Gender &. Society, 14*(2), 275–294.

Becker, G. S. (1957). *The Economics of Discrimination*. Chicago: University of Chicago Press.

Blau, F. D., & Ferber, M. (1986). *The Economics of Women, Men, and Work*. New Jersey: Prentice-Hall.

Blau, F. D., & Kahn, L. M. (1996). Wage structure and gender earnings differentials: An international comparison. *Economica, 63*(250), 29–62. doi:10.2307/2554808

Blau, F. D., & Kahn, L. M. (1999). Analyzing the gender pay gap. *The Quarterly Review of Economics and Finance, 39*(5), 625–646. doi:10.1016/S1062-9769(99)00021-6

Boraas, S., & Rodgers, W. M. (2003). How does gender play a role in the earnings gap? *Monthly Labor Review, 126*(3), 9–15.

Buchinsky, M. (1994). Changes in the U.S. wage structure 1963-1987: Application of quantile regression. *Econometrica: Journal of the Econometric Society, 62*(2), 405–458. doi:10.2307/2951618

Buchinsky, M. (1998). The dynamics of changes in the female wage distribution in the USA: A quantile regression approach. *Journal of Applied Econometrics, 13*(1), 1–30. doi:10.1002/(SICI)1099-1255(199801/02)13:1<1::AID-JAE474>3.0.CO;2-A

Cardoso, A. R. (1996). Women at work and economic development: Who's pushing what? *The Review of Radical Political Economics, 28*(3), 1–34. doi:10.1177/048661349602800301

Colwill, J., & Townsend, J. (1999). Women, leadership and information technology: The impact of women leaders in organizations and their role in integrating information technology with corporate strategy. *Journal of Management Development, 18*(3), 207–216. doi:10.1108/02621719910261049

Cotter, D. A., Hermsen, J. M., Ovadia, S., & Vanneman, R. (2001). The glass ceiling effect. *Social Forces, 80*(2), 655–682. doi:10.1353/sof.2001.0091

Cukier, W., Shortt, D., & Devine, I. (2002). Gender and information technology: Implications of definitions. *SIGCSE Bulletin, 34*(4), 142–148. doi:10.1145/820127.820188

De la Rica, S., Dolado, J. J., & Llorens, V. (2005). *Ceilings and floors: Gender wage gaps by education in Spain* (Discussion Paper No. 1483). Bonn, Germany: Institute for the Study of Labor.

Dex, S., & Sloane, P. J. (1988). Detecting and removing discrimination under equal opportunities policies. *Journal of Economic Surveys, 2*(1), 1–27. doi:10.1111/j.1467-6419.1988.tb00034.x

García, J., Hernández, P. J., & López-Nicolás, A. (2001). How wide is the gap? An investigation of gender wage differences using quantile regression. *Empirical Economics, 26*(1), 149–167. doi:10.1007/s001810000050

Gardeazabal, J., & Ugidos, A. (2005). Gender wage discrimination at quantiles. *Journal of Population Economics, 18*(1), 165–179. doi:10.1007/s00148-003-0172-z

Hartog, J., Pereira, P. T., & Vieira, J. A. C. (2001). Changing returns to education in Portugal during the 1980s and early 1990s: OLS and quantile regression estimators. *Applied Economics, 33*(8), 1021–1037.

Kee, H. J. (2006). Glass ceiling or sticky floor? Exploring the Australian gender pay gap. *The Economic Record, 82*(259), 408–427. doi:10.1111/j.1475-4932.2006.00356.x

Kiker, B. F., & Santos, M. C. (1991). Human capital and earnings in Portugal. *Economics of Education Review, 10*(3), 187–203. doi:10.1016/0272-7757(91)90043-O

Koenker, R., & Bassett, G. (1978). Regression quantiles. *Econometrica: Journal of the Econometric Society, 46*(1), 33–50. doi:10.2307/1913643

Machado, J. A. F., & Mata, J. (2000). *Counterfactual decomposition of changes in wage distributions using quantile regression.* Paper presented at the Econometric World Society Conference, Seattle.

Machado, J. A. F., & Mata, J. (2001). Earning functions in Portugal 1982-1994: Evidence from quantile regressions. *Empirical Economics, 26*(1), 115–134. doi:10.1007/s001810000049

Martins, P. S., & Pereira, P. T. (2004). Does education reduce wage inequality? Quantile regression evidence from 16 countries. *Labour Economics, 11*(3), 355–371. doi:10.1016/j.labeco.2003.05.003

Mincer, J., & Polachek, S. (1974). Family investments in human capital: Earnings of women. *The Journal of Political Economy, 82*(2), 76–108. doi:10.1086/260293

Mueller, R. E. (1998). Public-private sector wage differentials in Canada: Evidence from quantile regressions. *Economics Letters, 60*(2), 229–235. doi:10.1016/S0165-1765(98)00110-4

Oaxaca, R. (1973). Male-female wage differentials in urban labor markets. *International Economic Review, 14*(3), 693–709. doi:10.2307/2525981

Portugal, Ministério do Trabalho e da Solidariedade Social (2006). *Quadros de Pessoal.* In magnetic media.

Preston, J. A. (1999). Occupational gender segregation: Trends and explanations. *The Quarterly Review of Economics and Finance, 39*(5), 611–624. doi:10.1016/S1062-9769(99)00029-0

Sakellariou, C. (2004). Gender-earnings differentials using quantile regressions. *Journal of Labor Research, 25*(3), 457–468. doi:10.1007/s12122-004-1024-7

Stenzel, T. F. (2001). Why is there a gender wage gap and how can we fix it? *Employee Rights Quarterly, 2*(2), 1–7.

Terrell, K. (1992). Female-male earnings differentials and occupational structure. *International Labour Review, 131*(4), 387–404.

Trauth, E. M. (2002). Odd girl out: An individual differences perspective on women in the IT profession. *Information Technology & People, 15*(2), 98–118. doi:10.1108/09593840210430552

Venkatesh, V., & Morris, M. G. (2000). Why don't men ever stop to ask for directions? Gender, social influence, and their role in technology acceptance and usage behavior. *Management Information Systems Quarterly, 24*(1), 115–139. doi:10.2307/3250981

Vieira, J. A. C., Cardoso, A. C., & Portela, M. (2005). Gender segregation and the wage gap in Portugal: An analysis at the establishment level. *The Journal of Economic Inequality, 3*(2), 145–168. doi:10.1007/s10888-005-4495-8

Vieira, J. A. C., & Pereira, P. T. (1993). Wage differential and allocation: An application to the Azores islands. *Economia, 17*(2), 127–159.

Wardle, C., & Burton, L. (2002). Programmatic efforts encouraging women to enter the information technology workforce. *SIGCSE Bulletin, 34*(2), 27–31. doi:10.1145/543812.543824

ENDNOTES

[1] The role of gender in the information technology (IT) sector is addressed in several studies (e.g., Ahuja, 2002; Colwill & Townsend, 1999; Cukier et al., 2002; Trauth, 2002; Venkatesh & Morris, 2000; Wardle & Burton, 2002).

[2] Blau and Kahn (1996) additionally consider the role of wage structure in determining the magnitude of the gender wage gap. Defined as "the array of prices set for various labour market skills (measured and unmeasured) and rents received for employment in particular sectors of the economy" (Blau & Kahn, 1996, p. 29), wage structure determines the wage penalty or reward related to an individual's position in the wage distribution. For example, if female employees have less formal education than their male colleagues, the greater the return to formal education (regardless of gender), the larger the size of the wage gap. As another example, if males and females are distributed differently across occupations, the higher the premium received by workers employed in male-dominated occupations (regardless of gender), the larger the wage gap.

[3] Dex and Sloane (1988) distinguish two forms of labor market discrimination: wage discrimination and employment discrimination. Wage discrimination occurs when individuals with the same levels of productivity are paid different amounts, whereas employment discrimination occurs when individuals with the same levels of productivity are employed differently across occupations. These authors note that employment discrimination may or may not accompany wage discrimination.

[4] There are different work-related outcomes that may reflect a glass ceiling. For instance, earnings and authority are two outcomes that can be used to demonstrate the glass ceiling effect.

[5] The sticky floor metaphor is also used by the labor economics literature to describe a specific type of gender inequality. Contrary to glass ceilings, sticky floors imply situations in which the relative disadvantages faced by women are greater at the lower

[6] levels of an outcome hierarchy than at the higher levels (Arulampalam et al., 2006).

Although the linear conditional (QR) model is first introduced in Koenker and Bassett (1978), Buchinsky (1994, 1998) further advances the application of QR in the context of wage estimation, analyzing changes in the U.S. wage structure at different points of the earnings distribution. For Portugal, Hartog et al. (2001) and Martins and Pereira (2004) use the QR estimates of returns to education to address the relation between schooling and wage inequality. Machado and Mata (2001) also rely on the QR framework to characterize the evolution of the wage distribution in Portugal over the 1980s and early 1990s.

[7] García et al. (2001), Gardeazabal and Ugidos (2005), and Mueller (1998) also decompose differentials across wage distributions based on the QR framework. However, these authors apply alternative approaches for deriving the two groups' labor market characteristics. García et al. (2001) and Mueller (1998) evaluate gaps by combining the estimated QR coefficients with the means of the covariates distributions. Gardeazabal and Ugidos (2005) obtain empirical realizations for male and female characteristics relying on an auxiliary regression based framework.

[8] The proprieties of OLS estimators ensure that the predicted wage gap evaluated at the vector of mean characteristics is exactly equal to the average wage gap. By using OLS estimation, an exact decomposition of the average gap between males and females is obtained. However, this property is lost in the context of the QR framework.

[9] Austria, Belgium, Britain, Denmark, Finland, France, Germany, Ireland, Italy, Netherlands, and Spain.

[10] In order to test if pooled estimation is appropriate, tests for the equality of regression coefficients across gender groups are performed. The hypothesis of equal coefficients for both groups of employees is rejected. This finding justifies QR estimation stratified by gender. Tests are also carried out to examine the equality of the coefficients across quantiles. The equality hypothesis is rejected in all cases.

[11] In order to save space, QR estimates for male and female employees for the year 2004 are not reported. The results are available upon request.

[12] The residual component, that is, the portion of the gap that is unaccounted for by the estimation method used, accounts for a relatively small portion of the total gap at all quantiles. If this portion were assigned to either the explained or unexplained components, the qualitative information provided in this study would remain unchanged.

[13] Arulampalam et al. (2006) specify a precise criterion for the existence of a glass ceiling. According to this criterion, a glass ceiling occurs when the unexplained gap at the 90th percentile exceeds the unexplained gaps in other parts of the wage distribution by at least two percentage points. The current study uses the term glass ceiling in a looser sense, whereby a glass ceiling occurs when the unexplained gap is greater at the top half of the wage distribution than it is at the bottom half.

[14] In order to save space, the average descriptive statistics and the QR estimates for male and female employees for the years 1986, 1992, and 1998 are not reported. The results are available upon request.

This work was previously published in International Journal of Human Capital and Information Technology Professionals, Volume 1, Issue 2, edited by Ricardo Colomo-Palacios, pp. 1-18, copyright 2010 by IGI Publishing (an imprint of IGI Global).

Chapter 5

Recruiting, Selecting and Motivating Human Resources:
Methodological Analysis and Case Studies Applications

Konstantinos C. Zapounidis
Aristotle University of Thessaloniki, Greece

Glykeria Kalfakakou
Aristotle University of Thessaloniki, Greece

ABSTRACT

This paper's aim is to analyse practices adapted by different enterprises regarding personnel motivation and human resources approaches to increase their productivity and profitability while examining the methodology of human resources recruitment and selection used by different kinds of enterprises, which cannot exist without human manpower. The objective of this paper is to analyse methods and tools used by several enterprises in motivation and in human resources recruitment and selection. Regarding motivation, the basic aim of the process adapted was to define whether each enterprise was closer to the participating or to directive management model. Especially in the recruiting and selecting process IT could add important value since adapted IT processes could lead to quicker and more successful transparent results. IT professionals could organise these processes for every enterprise in order to become standard, formulated, and even more accredited procedures which would lead to successful recruiting and selecting results.

INTRODUCTION

The environment in which enterprises are operating is extremely competitive and in order to survive, they have to react to the new circumstances, including globalisation, new technologies, innovation and collapse of economic barriers. Moreover, low productivity is a common problem faced by an increasing number of organisations world-wide. When in an enterprise the productivity is not managing to keep up pace with the increasing work cost, then effectiveness, but also the existence of the enterprise, is under important threat.

DOI: 10.4018/978-1-4666-0924-2.ch005

Requirement for each enterprise is competitiveness, productivity, quality and finally efficiency. The objective of this paper is to analyse methods and tools used by several enterprises in human resources recruitment and selection, taking into consideration the aforementioned requirements (Vaxevanidou, 2008; Chitiris, 2001) and, moreover, to examine motivation methods used by them.

For this scope important is the role that the human resources recruited provides. The human resources, in the field of organisations and enterprises or the human capital, in the field of society in general, are considered as basic pivot of development and whilst up to now they were defined inductively, a tense is presented to be assessed in knowledge (new and dissemination of existing) and skills (education and training).

Human resources are the only factor that could activate and develop all the production elements, in order an enterprise to operate and successfully accomplish all its objectives. Great and successful enterprises are formed by human capital, whilst enterprises fail or are low efficient, as employers could not or are not willing to participate in the objectives' accomplishment.

Machinery, computers, installations and the rest factors of production, do not think, learn, try and of course do not set objectives in order to decide what and how to perform. Furthermore they are not motivated, they do not act collectively and they do not have expectations and needs to de fulfilled. All these characterise the human nature and action (Chitiris, 2001).

The quality of Human Resources is characterized, without any doubt, first priority for a "competitive economy" and for balanced social development. This recognition is depicted in operational level, through the quest and adaptation of methods used for investment's value assessment and for education and training of production mechanisms.

Regarding motivation, the question that derives is what the reasons of low productivity are. A number of executives are pointing as reason for low productivity the decrease of personal motives and the minimisation of "will to work". Moreover, the decline of devotion to the organisation in correlation with weakening of their commitment to the ethical laws for work is another important factor. The aforementioned explanation has been challenged repetitively by experts on human resources management, based on an important number of results. According to these results, it is proved that, as a rule, an individual human being "wants" to work, "wants" to be productive and to contribute to the organisation's development. Supporters of the so called "motivation school" support that if the productivity of employees is inadequate, management has not succeeded to apply in a right way the conclusions of the modern science related to work environment attitudes. Rivals as the aforementioned lead to the conclusion that it is difficult to define what the "real" answer for low productivity is. To succeed a common accepted answer, a number of parameters should be taken into account as the possibility that motivation experts and academics could be wrong and the option that individuals are not willing to work or are obliged to work and for this reason do not perform in an efficient way.

It is easily perceptible how important Human Resources Management is when it is applied in the right way, in order an enterprise to acquire, preserve and develop capable employers, who will execute their role efficiently and successfully. Indicatively actions that Human Resources Management includes are (Chitiris,2001):

- Planning of Human Resources
- Job analysis
- Recruitment and selection of capable human resources
- Education and Training
- Employers' efficiency evaluation
- Employers; wages
- Employers' protection
- Negotiation of working relations

The aforementioned actions are interrelated and inter-depending in such a degree that the successful or not execution of one influences the rest. It is obvious that the on time and rational planning of human resources influences the efficiency of actions of recruitment, selection and education, whilst the inefficiency of the system influences human resources planning.

In order to highlight the interrelation of human resources actions, it is deliberate to consider them as subsystems of the human resources management system. Each transformation of one of the aforementioned sub-systems (or of their elements) influences the operation and efficiency of the whole system. Human Resources Management, considered as an open system, accepts inputs (human resources) and is being influenced by factors and limitations of the external business environment. Adapting the appropriate processes seeks the accomplishment of specific outputs-objectives, as the qualitative and quantitative performance of the employers, the positive working conditions, high motivation level (Werther, 1996).

As it can be conclude, Human Resources Management is a tough project, multi-sectoral, requiring knowledge and art by all involved individuals (Human Resources Managers or not) (Chitiris, 2001).

Basic factors for the successful and effective function of an enterprise or organisation constitute the recruitment and the selection of ideal executives and workers for any level of hierarchy. The basic aim therefore is that all stages can be comprehensible for an objective and effective selection of the particular candidate for the particular vacancy should be accomplished.

It is vital, that the qualifications and the experience which an enterprise requires to be precisely determined, before the enterprise commences to search for the suitable candidate for the job vacancy. This can be achieved with the meticulous job-description and the thorough definition of the candidate specification (Chitiris, 2001; Hindle, 2001). The job-description is useful as a map and

as a compass on the direction that each employee is obliged to have for the implementation of the work. It describes in every detail all the content and the breadth of work that it should be executed by the holder of the position (Vaxevanidou, 2008). The candidate specification, or personnel specification, as it is frequently called summary of the knowledge, skills and personal characteristics required of the job to carry out the job to an acceptable standard of performance (Cole, 1999).

The next step is the attraction/seeking of human manpower, as it is called the process of inviting of suitable individuals with regard to their knowledge, experience and skills, so that they can correspond to the job required (Leigh, 2001). There are two basic methods of seeking ideal candidates for covering the vacancies: 1) the Internal Attracting/Seeking with the exploitation and upgrade of the existing personnel, and 2) the External Attracting/Seeking via the external environment of the company. Both sources of attracting/Seeking have advantages and disadvantages; thus their combination helps the enterprises to remain competitive in a rapidly altered environment.

The observation of an electronic database with the characteristics of the employees, the notification of the vacancy via the company's table of statements or the company's publications, the internal system of promotion, the workers' references and finally the recruitment of former workers of former candidates constitute the internal seeking process. The external sources of attracting are various and differ in terms of cost and effectiveness. The most usual are the following: the contact with the Offices of Interconnection of the Universities and Polytechnic Colleges of the country, the contact with technical and professional faculties of specialisation, the communication with the Organisms of Employment of Workforce and the local unemployment agencies, the interaction with the private agencies, the collaboration with companies of benefit of services and selection of executives, the communication with relevant enterprises of the branch that proceed in redundancies, the transcription of executives from corresponding competitive enterprises of the branch (Vaxevanidou, 2008; Chitiris, 2001; Hindle, 2001).

Then the process of the selection follows. According to the requirements of each vacancy, a practical combination of examining methods – steps is used, so that all essential information for each candidate arises. In each one of those steps it is possible that the candidate could be rejected; the analytic description of these steps is: First of all, the person in charge (interviewer) examines the CVs and the applications of employment (accompanying letters) that the candidates have sent and divides them into three groups as follows: very suitable - must be interviewed, quite suitable - call for interview if insufficient numbers in previous category, or send holding letter, not suitable - send polite refusal letter, thanking them for their interest in applying (Cole, 1999). If there are numbers of very suitable candidates, then it may be necessary to have one "first" interview of short duration, aiming at the reduction of the suitable candidates who will pass from the "main" selection interview in an acceptable number (Chitiris, 2001).

The next step is the second phase of the selection process, the interview, which is the most common technique used for selection purposes. It is very important to be properly prepared before an interview. It enables the interviewer to feel confident in himself about his key role in the process, and enables him to exploit to the full the information provided by the candidate. It also helps to minimise embarrassment caused by constant interruptions, inadequate accommodation and other practical difficulties.

Questioning plays a vital role in a selection interview, as it is the primary means; which information is obtained from the candidate at the time. Questions have been categorised in a number of different ways, however it is enough to distinguish between closed questions, which require a specific answer or a Yes/No response and open questions that require a person to reflect on, or elaborate

upon, a particular point in his own way. Open questions invariably begin with what? How? Or why? It is usual to ask closed questions to check information which the candidate has already partly supplied on his application form, and to re-direct the interview if the candidate is talking too much and/ or getting off the point. Open questions tend to be employed once the interview has got under way, with the object of getting the candidate to demonstrate his knowledge and skills to the interviewer (Cole, 1999). Open questions are probably more useful in the interview, since they allow the interviewer to observe the communication dexterities of the candidate (Hindle, 2001).

There are three conduct methods of an interview: one-to-one basis, a two-to-one situation and the panel interviews. By the panel interviews it is ensured the fairness of the proceedings, since more interviewers evaluate the candidates and finally agree for the suitability of the candidate. From researches it has been found that it is required relatively few time in order the interviewers to reach a consensus over the suitable candidates. What is critical for the effectiveness of the interview of this type it is the good collaboration and the co-ordination of the examiners. There are several disadvantages, however - the candidate will find it difficult to feel at ease in such a formal atmosphere; the individual; panel members may be more concerned about being cued for their questions than being concerned to listen to what the candidate is saying (Cole, 1999; Roth, 1992).

There are three basic types of an interview; the standardised where concrete rules for all candidates without exception are applied, the structured where predetermined structure is followed but not necessarily common for all candidates, and the "free" interview, with the form of a free flowed dialogue between the interviewer and the candidate.

Besides the interview, the candidate can simultaneously pass from various tests, according to the nature and the requirements of the vacancy. The basic function of the tests is the measurement of the dexterity and the behaviour of the candidate in different cases and under special conditions (Vaxevanidou, 2008).The tests can be divided in a lot of ways; however, the most acceptable way of classification is in two big categories; the attainment tests and the personality tests. With the attainments tests can be measured the possibly highest performance of the candidate, while with the personality tests can be examined the main characteristics of his personality.

The assessment centres is an alternative way of selection in which the candidates for high graded vacancies are subjected to an amount of questions and exercises. The processes, which are applied, are about the evaluation of the candidates' skills with regard to important sectors of professional activity. It is found from researches that the assessment centres, as a selection method, give reliable and valid results. The disadvantage of this method is its high cost and that it time consuming process.

It is vital, after every interview, concerning the suitable evaluated candidates, that a confirmation of the information they give in their CV or during the interview be done, on terms of their signed authorisation.

As far as the selection decision is concerned, there are two methods; the subjective, which is based on the personal evaluation and the objective, which is based on the results of a statistical analysis (Chitiris, 2001).

Furthermore, it is vital for particular jobs that medical examinations are done by the new employee, either because there is a relevant relation to the implementation of his work, or in order to exclude the possibility of transmission of dangerous illnesses in the working place. In any case, the physical health of the candidate should be controlled after offering the job.

The recruitment under trial gives the opportunity to the company to examine the new employee in practice, to find his skills and to be sure that he possesses the ability to perform the job required. This method is applied for a period of time (one or two years) mainly by the most banks and the biggest organisations.

Finally, the employee's integration is the last and most important step, that the companies usually neglect, since it is between the end of the selection process and the beginning that that the employee undertake his new role (Leigh, 2001). The new-employees' integration in the company constitutes one of the main functions of the Personnel Management, since it has an essential role, not only for the employees' performance, but also for their long stay in the company.

Managing a company or an enterprise and achieving its targets requires the cooperation of human resources. The administrative actions are characterized by the efforts to motivate work force and to equate company's objectives with workers' objectives. The presence of a worker in a company's project does not contribute towards the promotion of company's objectives. The contribution could be either positive or negative, depending on the similarity of objectives.

Every project team member is considered to be basically a passive element that could be motivated, could produce, but could not undertake initiatives. Thus the activation of the work force in order to produce is the baseline of every managerial effort. Two are considered to be the basic issues that preoccupy the administrative hierarchy of a company:

1. The finding of the level that employees could support efficiency or could increase efficiency in correlation with overall objectives accomplishment.
2. What are the motives related to the efficiency of the employees, in which level these are related to work productivity and in what degree a motivation system could be adapted, in order to support the effective motivation of human resources towards a predetermined direction.

METHOD

Participants

The scope of the approach adapted was not to compare organizations of similar characteristics but organizations of different fields that could be activated in the same industry (especially in the construction industry). The reason of such a selection was the fact that the type of the offered services affects in an important degree the recruitment and selection process and, moreover, the motivation policy and the level of employees' participation.

Two groups of organisations under investigation were created; one in order to examine recruitment and selection and one in order to examine motivation.

Selecting the organisations that formed the sample for distributing the questionnaires was based on the aim to cover the following 4 axes:

1.   Local Characteristics
2.   Construction industry.
3.   Private and public sector.
4.   Word wide range local enterprises.

The sample of Human Resources' Selection and Recruitment Sample was consisted of the following enterprises:

*   A Societe Anonyme of the public sector, with 278 employers. The Human Resources Manager and responsible of administrative matters answered the questionnaire, whilst more details of the organisation are not publicised due to their request.
*   An important technical construction company, activated and constructing important projects all over Greece and abroad, either by itself or conglomerating with other companies of the sector. It has 100 employers, whilst this number could be increased depending in the number of the undertaken

projects. More details of the organisation are not publicised due to their request.

*   The third company was a local development agency. Its activities are prescribed by the wider European philosophy, for more essential decentralisation, with active contribution in the planning and management of the development resources, through the coordination of all local institutional authorities. The detection, research, promotion, support and realization of integrated proposals for the growth is achieved through the productive exploitation of national and European financial support and development programs. It has 32 employers, depending in the number of projects undertaken.
*   A medium-sized company of the sugar products' sector. 50% of its production is sold in Greece whilst the rest 50% abroad. It has 40 employers. More details of the organisation are not publicised due to their request.
*   A local branch of a private bank (established in 1982). It has 10 employers and the answers were given by the 2nd manager.

The sample of Human Resources' Motivation Sample was consisted of the following enterprises:

*   A technical company constructing private projects (Organisation No.1). The company is activated mainly in the sector of building constructions, covering issuing building permits and constructing private owned buildings (either as constructors-design and build or as developers-design, build and sell). The company employs ten individuals and is operating for more than twenty years. The selection of this company was based on the fact that it reflects the typical example of a small company with two owners (engineers with horizontal re-

lationship). The company is considered as medium sized, at local level.

- An important technical company of general construction operations (Organisation No. 2), employing more than forty individuals. The company is producing private and public works nationally. Moreover, they own concrete production premises, for internal and external, to the company, projects.
- A factory (Organisation No. 3) producing ready to use concrete (last of the construction industry sector). The company employs ten individuals and is operating for more than twenty years.
- A participative company which produces, standardises and trades local agricultural products word widely (Organisation No. 4). It constitutes a pilot pioneering company at national level, exporting products in important markets, as the European Union and Russia. The company employs forty to fifty individuals, depending on the production level.
- As typical sample of the private sector, the local branch of an important Greek bank (Organisation No. 5) was selected, having fifteen employees.
- The local branch of a public sector organisation (Organisation No. 6). For this specific organisation, it must be noted, that the director responsible of answering the questionnaire could not answer all questions, as some of them could not be applied in the public sector. These questions were answered by a private sector expert, of the same profession discipline as the responder.

MATERIALS AND PROCEDURE

Regarding recruitment and selection three types of questionnaires were produced (closed type graded, closed type of two alternatives, open type). The questionnaires were produced for the scope of this paper and were used for first time within this paper's framework.

Regarding motivation, the questionnaire was based on the research work of Dr. E.S. Stanton (1982), Professor of Management in the Business Administration School of St. John University-New York. The initial thirty questions were adapted at local level and the questionnaire was enriched with fourteen more questions. Each question-proposal is graded from one to four depending on its subject. The possible answers to these questions were: totally agree, generally agree, generally disagree and totally disagree. In the end the grades are added, leading to a possible range of total grade between 44 and 176. The answers were weighed in the way that the lowest total grade results to adaptation of directive management model whilst the highest grade results to adaptation of participating management model, by the organisations under examination. All enterprises under examination were based in the same local environment (Pieria, Greece) and a predefined questionnaire of closed type was addressed to them.

Procedure

The completion was consisted of the following steps:

1. Questionnaire composition
2. Distribution of the questionnaires to the executives responsible for human resources management and employment relations.
3. Provision of time in order the questionnaires to be studied and analysed.
4. Predefined on-site meetings and interviews for possible specifications.
5. Questionnaires collection.

RESULTS

Human Resources' Selection and Recruitment Analysis

Graded closed-type questionnaire offered four different possible scaled answers: Always-Often-Sometimes-Never. Regarding the 25 questions of the graded closed-type questionnaire, these were divided in 4 categories: firstly the questions which displayed "absolute identification" of answers; all companies answered "Always" or "Never", secondly the questions which displayed "identification" where the companies answered "Always-Often" or "Sometimes-Never", thirdly the questions which displayed "big dispersion"; in this category the answers "Always" and "Never" occurred simultaneously (possibly the intermediary answers occurring as well) and finally the questions that displayed "small dispersion" with the answers "Often" - "Sometimes" - "Always" or "Often" - "Sometimes"- "Never". Grouping as aforementioned, led to the following results: 12% of the answers displayed "absolute identification" and "identification", while 32% of the answers displayed "big dispersion". The highest percentage of the answers showed "small dispersion", which is 44%.

As far as the closed-type Questionnaire of two alternative choices is concerned, the 12 questions were grouped in 2 categories: in the questions with two alternatives choices as an answer and in the questions with the additional choice "Combination" of the above mentioned answers, as some of the under investigation companies couldn't give as an answer one of the two alternatives excluding the other.

The questions of the opened type questionnaire couldn't be possible to be grouped in any way; thus its answer are analysed further below.

Closed-Type Graded Questionnaire

The answers provided by the under investigation companies/organisations in the closed-type graded questionnaire are presented according to the grouping aforementioned; identification and dispersion of answers.

Absolute identification was pointed in the fact that for each enterprise the general direction is always responsible for the selection process; whilst interviews are always take place within the enterprises premises.

Identification was presented in the fact that the recruitment of formerly rejected candidates is sometimes necessary because of the specialised type of the services (local development agency and public sector company).

Regarding big dispersion, in three companies, the responsibility for the selection process is not taken by the Department of Human Resources Management. This was expected for the two of them (industry of food, local development agency), since they do not have such a Department. The Hu-

Figure 1. Graded questionnaire - Grouping of answers based on identification-dispersion factor

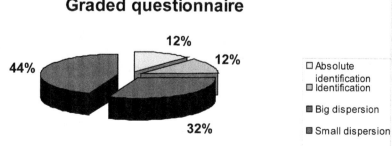

Figure 2. Two alternatives questionnaire – Grouping of answers based on combination or selection one of the answers

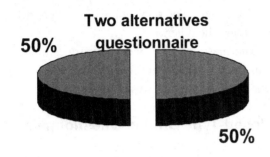

☐ Questions with Combination

☐ Questions answering one of alternatives

man Resources Management Department always decides for the selection only in the Public sector company, where the decision of the selection belongs equally to this department; perhaps because of the enormous size of the human resources that recruits. Relatively to the available database, a high dissemination between the answers is observed. As it is also observed, the companies with limited workforce do not hold a database with the characteristics of its each employee or they occasionally hold; while the companies with considerate workforce do that, always or often. An exception of the sample constitutes the local development agency, which despite the limited number of its personnel, always holds a database, because of the specialised type of services and the limited offer of work at local level.

Regarding small dispersion, the internal recruitment of human manpower is being preferred by the companies that allocate a high number of human resources, compared to the external recruitment (technical company and public sector company). When the personnel is vast, there is the possibility of allocating different responsibilities to people of different sectors, according to the requirements of each position and the experience that they acquired during their professional back-

ground in the company. This is a little more difficult to be achieved by a small sized company, which prefers the exterior attraction of human manpower. Nevertheless, most of the companies often give the possibility of recruitment to candidates from other country - members of the European Union. The reason is the international dimension of the used methodology and the use of the English language that is required for the management of many projects, as well as the use of standardised personnel. Only two companies exclude that possibility (bank and the food industry). For the most companies, former employees of a company are never being recruited again. The companies which are excluded have a lot of contract based projects (local development agency, technical company), so it is very likely that a former employee with experience on that specific field will be recruited. In the rest of the companies the employment is depended, which means that the employee resigns either with his will, or is being fired because his employer is not satisfied with his performance.

General identification can easily be observed in the answers of the local development agency, the Public sector company and the technical company. It can be ascertained that the common characteristic, which the three companies have, is the formality that distinguishes them with regard to practically but at the same time very important subjects of the selection process. It is also remarkable the recruitment of former employees by these companies; a reasonable explanation for that constitutes the specialised work in these companies that requires specific qualifications. Finally, an obvious identification in the negative answers of the food industry company and the bank is equally observed because of the standardised work that is considered at the recruitment of personnel.

Closed-Type Questionnaire of Two Alternative Choices

The conclusion that anyone can easily reach is that most questions - proposals that required the addition of the answer "Combination" concerned the qualifications that the ideal candidate should possess in order to be recruited by the company; such qualifications are for example the experience, the specialisation, the quantitative and qualitative characteristics, the technical and communication skills. Furthermore, the question concerning the preference of men or women for the recruitment constituted an issue of major interest.

The questions that were answered with the two alternative choices concerned the highest percentage the elements of the selection - interview, as for example the type of the questions, the method of the interview and the tests.

The conclusions about the answers that were given in all questions - proposals are presented in groups.

With regard to the qualifications that the ideal candidate should have, the overwhelming majority (60%) of the companies (technical company, food industry company and bank) considered that the time experience at work is more important than the specialization. The 20% (public sector company) considered that the specialisation is more important; while also at the same percentage (local development agency) didn't trace any difference in the degree of the importance between the two qualifications and both of them are being required.

The technical dexterities outweigh the communicational skills, according to 40% (Public sector company and technical company), while just the 20% (bank) answered the opposite. It is also remarkable that the 40% of the companies (the local development agency and the food industry company) answered that both dexterities are equally important; that shows that the candidate is examined on terms of technical and communication skills.

The companies with low manpower are these companies which considered equally important both dexterities. They included the communicational skills, perhaps because in a small working environment proper working relationships and friendly atmosphere enhances performance. On the contrary, in the big enterprises is given priority in the technical dexterities, as usually impersonal relations prevail between the workers.

Particular interest presents the fact that mostly (60%) (technical company, food industry company and bank), the candidates who are overqualified are rejected because of their high economic requirements they will probable demand. The public sector company recruits them only, as the more qualifications do not play any particular role in the salaries of the public sector. Even if it influences the salary, the state budget has the possibility of

Figure 3. Important qualifications

Which of the following qualifications is more important?

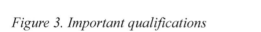

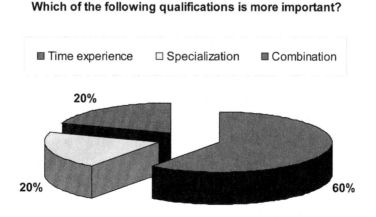

Figure 4. Important dexterities

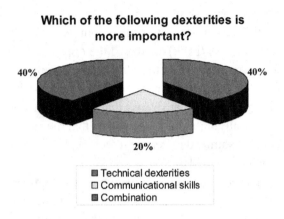

covering the difference. Whether overqualified candidates will be recruited by the local development agency, depends on each project case and on their specialized services.

Particular interest presents also the fact that, the majority of the companies (60%) (public sector company, technical company and local development agency) does not present any certain preference regarding the recruitment of men or women, while 40% (food industry company and bank) prefer men. As it appears, in the companies with high manpower and the necessary academic background a certain preference does not exist. This shows that the women have been henceforth equally accepted with the men in the professional sector. A reasonable explanation for the preference of men over women by the industry of food is perhaps the limited presence of women in that field.

In what concerns the subjects of the selection interview process the following factors should be taken into consideration: The companies use mostly (60%) (technical company, local development agency and food industry company) the method of the "free" interview, while a lower percentage (40%) (public sector company and bank) use the standardised interview. The public sector functions are, in general, more standardised than the private sector. That is also observed in the bank because of its obligatory organisational

structure. All companies prefer to conduct "open" typed questions. All companies also consider the personality tests more important than the learning aptitude tests. On the contrary 80% of companies consider the attainment tests more important than the personality tests. An obvious exception constitutes the bank, as it gives priority to the communicational skills contrary to the technical dexterities.

There is an absolute identification in all answers between the technical company and the food industry company, apart from the question that concerns the preference of men or women at work. In what concerns the interview part absolute identification is traced in the answers among the above mentioned companies and the local development agency. It is remarkable that the public sector company shows an absolute identification with the bank on the interview grounds, whereas an exception is the preference of the attainment tests instead of the personality tests, while in what concerns other issues there is total incoherence. Finally, there is a relative harmony at the answers of the public sector company and the answers of the local development agency.

Open-Type Questionnaire

Although the open-type questionnaire is not susceptible to standardised answers, the following

Figure 5. Overqualified candidates

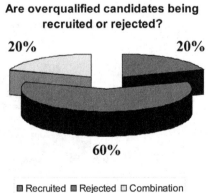

conclusions have been reached after the relative analysis.

As for the question whether the companies have a Department of Human Resources Management, the answers are mainly positive. Only two of our sample (local development agency and food industry company) do not have such a Department and do not also consider its existence important. These companies have a common characteristic which is the small size of their personnel (30-40 individuals); this number is not sufficient to justify the operation of such department. An exception constitutes the bank, which despite the few individuals of its personnel (10 individuals) does have a Department of Human Resources Management, because of its obligatory organisational structure and its total size of the personnel at national level.

The individuals who carry out the interview are mostly two or three. There is always a representative of the Human Resources, if there is such a Department or from the administration of the company (the Director or a C.E.O.), if there is not. There are also one or two executives from the corresponding sector. In the case of the technical company the interview is conducted by the Director of the corresponding department.

Initially most companies always or sometimes recruit the candidate for a trial period of 4 to 12 months. Only the local development agency does not follow this method of recruitment, because the contracts of the company have concrete time duration and keep pace with the programmatic periods which are financed by the European funds.

The examiners are mainly influenced by the combination of the curriculum vitae and the impression that they acquire about the candidate's personality during the interview.

The candidate's body language during the interview has a major impact on all companies provided that the candidate corresponds in the requirements of the position. Characteristically, public sector company supports that the body language may reveal more than the interview itself.

Finally, the candidate is submitted in attainment tests only in two companies (the public sector company and the local development agency), when it is required by the work-position; because the public sector is more standardised, the submission of candidates in tests is expectable. Likewise tests are expected in the local development agency, where specified knowledge is demanded due to the specialized type of the services which offers.

It is therefore concluded that there is an agreement in the majority of the answers that the companies provide. General identification is found in the following companies: food industry company and the bank, the public sector company and the bank. Considerable disagreement is observed in the following companies: the local development agency and the technical company, the public sector company and the technical company.

HUMAN RESOURCES' MOTIVATION ANALYSIS

All organization under examination have gathered total grade above 110 (average grade: $(44+176)/2$), characterizing their management style closer to the participating model.

Despite the differences of each organization under examination, mainly due to the fact that they have different size, they are activated in different industries (construction, agriculture, finance) or in different sectors of the same industry, the grade range was rather narrow, $122-112=10$, leading to $10/176=5,68\%$ of total range.

In the organizations of the construction industry (No.1, No.2 and No.3) there is an important spread, mainly based in the different size but also in the different sector of action (private construction, public construction, concrete production). In this way, organization No. 1 is defined as the most participating, as personal relations are important between the owners but also within the hierarchy. Moreover, the organization size is not so enormous, especially in comparison with organization No.2.

Rather higher than expected proved to be the participation level in the local branches of the private bank (organization No.5) and of the public sector organization (organization No.6). The reasons could be the increased level of familiarity due to local based environment and the obvious tense for participation and collaboration. The higher grade was the one of organization No.4, which was an expected result, since this organization operates based on quality management systems (for management and production) as HACCP and ISO 9001.

Another interesting point that resulted from the analysis is the percentage of coincidence in the answers of all organizations, examining the percentage of coincidence and dispersion in their answers. This analysis was based on the grouping of the answers in four different categories: those that presented total coincidence (either totally agree or disagree), those that presented important coincidence (agree either totally or generally and disagree either totally or generally), those that presented high dispersion and those that presented important dispersion (one of the answers were different than the others).

Six of the forty four questions presented total coincidence of answers, leading to a percentage of 13.64%. The proposals with coincidence are those stating that: the income is determining independently of the age and family status, the employee who works hard should be rewarded accordingly and in time, when tasks are appointed full details should be described, employees should be asked regarding their tasks and plans, not only financial factors affect the employees.

Although the range of total grades is limited to 5.68% (Figure 6), the total and important coincidence is not proved to be so high (13.64+25.00=38.64%). Generally, high dispersion (36.36%) exists, nevertheless all organization were laying in the side of participating model. It is proved thus, that no "rule" exists to characterize

Figure 6. Total grade of each organization

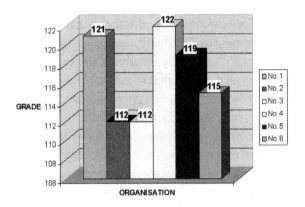

a participating organization, due to the existing disperse of opinions.

Regarding the type of organizations, important results emerged. Local characteristics outweighed the possible barriers of participation in the national public and private bodies (organizations No.5 and No.6). Multi-sector action (even in the same industry) leads to more directive management of human resources (organization No 2). Organizations with typical production process (organization No.3) present limited participating style due to the standardized production process. The requirement for ideas and proposals (organization No.1) leads to higher participation level.

Figure 7. Coincidence-dispersion of answers

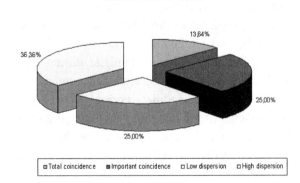

Finally, all responders were rather cautious, whilst public sector responder required full discretion.

All responders agreed that they do not recognize threat as a motivation method, which is rather satisfactory. The sector of Human Resources Management including motivation is not incorporated in the wider management framework of the organizations, which could be expected for local based organizations. Human Resources Management is implemented (in the level that it is possible) by directors-founders-owners and not by experts of the discipline.

DISCUSSION

The general conclusion drawn for human resources' selection and recruitment is that the companies that follow a similar, if not a common process of personnel recruitment are the following: the public sector company and the local development agency, the public sector company and the bank, the food industry company and the bank.

Regarding the recruitment and selection process, the highest percentage of the enterprises applies the following: Firstly, a form of description is drawn up. The internal attraction of the human manpower is preferred especially by those companies who detain a database with the characteristics of the candidates. In general the personal contact does not influence the companies about the selection – decision. Furthermore candidates who were rejected or released in the past are not being recruited. The percentage of the recruitment of women is the same as men. Remarkable is that candidates from other country - members of the European Union are also being attracted. The newspapers are being used more as a source of attracting, whereas under no circumstances the radio is used. With regard to the qualifications that influence the selection - decision, the experience in the subject of the position is more important than the specialisation. The possession of a postgraduate title constitutes an extra qualification and

not a condition for the recruitment. The technical dexterities are also very important, without undermining the importance of the communication skills. Overqualified candidates mostly are not being recruited because of their high economic expectations. The interview is carried out mainly by a committee (a representative of the Human Resources Department and two from the responsible department of the position) in the working place. The method of the free interview with open typed questions is used. The personality tests and the attainments tests are being considered as the most important, although these are not being applied in most companies. Furthermore the initial recruitment is under trial for a period of time. Finally the Management of the Company rather than the Human Resources Department holds total responsibility for the final decision.

IT processes could support several of the aforementioned steps of a selection and recruiting procedure. IT professionals could support these steps by providing tools and methodologies that could add value to the processes but also increase the transparency factor, along with the procedure speed and, overall, lead to successful selection of the more suitable candidate for each working position.

Outcome of the analysis regarding motivation processes was that although organizations motivate their employees, mainly by prompting them to participate in different levels of decision making, and are positioned closer to the participating management model, their approach was rather un-organised and based mainly on interpersonal relations. Generally, it is proved that organizations although positioned closer to the participating management model, they have important opportunities for adapting and developing motivation models and organising leadership tactics. These tactics could be supported by IT professionals that could introduce the required IT tools for successful results in leadership and motivation.

REFERENCES

Berger, F., & Ghei, A. (1995). Employment tests: A facet of hospitality hiring. *Comell hotel and restaurant administration quarterly, 36*(6).

Blake, R. R., & Mouton, J. S. (1982). *Productivity: the human side*. New York: Amacom.

Bolton, R., & Bolton, D. G. (1984). *Social Style/Management Style*. New York: A.M.A.

Borman, W. C., & Hallman, G. L. (1991). Observation Accuracy for assessors of work sample performance. *The Journal of Applied Psychology, 76*(4).

Burke, R. (1999). *Project Management: Planning & Control Techniques*. New York: John Wiley and Sons Ltd.

Chitiris, L. (2001). *Human Resources Management*. Athens, Greece: Publications Interbooks.

Cole, G. A. (1999). *Management theory and practice* (5th ed.). Edinburgh, UK: Letts.

Dimou, N. (2003). *Personnel Management* (2nd ed.). Athens, Greece: Ellin.

Dvorak, D. E. (1988). *References, resumes and other lies*. Industry Week.

Fletcher, C. (1992). Ethics and the job interview. *Personnel management.*

Fyock, C. D. (1991). *Expanding the talent search: 19 ways to recruit top talent*. H.R Magazine.

Hindle, T. (2001). *How to recruit and select*. Athens, Greece: Ellinika Grammata.

Hough, L. M. (1990). Criterion - related validities of personality constructs and the effect of response distortion on those validities. *The Journal of Applied Psychology, 74.*

Iacocca, L., & Novak, W. (1984). *Iacocca: An Autobiography*. New York: Bantam.

Kantas, A. (1995). *Organisational and industrial psychology*. Athens, Greece: Greek Letters.

Leigh, A. (2001). *20 ways to manage better*. London: Chartered Institute of Personnel and Development.

Likert, R. (1961). New patterns of Management. *Industrial & Labor Relations Review, 17*(2), 336–338.

Likert, R. (1967). *The Human Organisation*. New York: McGraw-Hill.

Mathis, R. L., & Jackson, J. H. (1994). *Human resource management*. St. Paul, MN: West Publishing.

Maylor, H. (2003). *Project Management* (3rd ed.). London: Pearson Education Limited.

McDaniel, M. A. (1989). Biographical constructs for predicting employee suitability. *The Journal of Applied Psychology, 74*(6). doi:10.1037/0021-9010.74.6.964

Munchns, G. (1992). *Check references for safer selection*. H.R. Magazine.

Polyzos, S. (2004). *Management and Planning of Projects*. Athens, Greece: Kritiki.

Robertson, I., et al. (1990). The validity of situational interviews for administrative jobs. *Journal of organizational psychology, 11.*

Roth, P. L., & Camprion, J. E. (1992). An analysis of the predictive power of the panel interview and pre-employment tests. *Journal of Occupational and Organizational Psychology, 65.*

Seitanidis, P. (1987). *Personnel Evaluation* (2nd ed.). Athens, Greece: Galaios.

Sherman, A., Bohlander, G., & Snell, S. (1998). *Managing human resources*. Cincinnati, OH: South-Western College.

Stanton, E. S. (1982). *Reality-Centered People Management Key to Improved Productivity*. New York: Amacom.

Storr, A. (2006). *Fraud*. Philadelphia: Naxos/Audiofy.

Tadman, M. (1989). The past predicts the future. *Security management, 33*(7).

Vaxevanidoy, M., & Reklitis, P. (2008). *Human Resources Management Theory and Act*. Athens, Greece: Propobos.

Werther, W. B. Davis, Jr., & Davis, K. (1996). *Human resources and personnel management* (5th ed.). New York: McGraw-Hill.

Zapounidis, K., Kalfakakou, G., & Athanasiou, V. (2008). Theories and Models of Motivation and Leadership, Case Study Application. In *Proceedings of the PM-04 - 4th SCPM & 1st IPMA/MedNet Conference on Project Management Advances, Training & Certification in the Mediterranean.*

Zevgraridis, S. (1985). *Organisation and Management*. Thessaloniki, Greece: Kiriakidis Bros.

Chapter 6
Human Resource Management on Social Capital

Macarena López-Fernández
University of Cádiz, Spain

Fernando Martín-Alcázar
University of Cádiz, Spain

Pedro Miguel Romero-Fernández
University of Cádiz, Spain

ABSTRACT

Over the past years, several researchers have analysed the relational dynamics that takes place inside and between organizations (concept, mediating and moderating variables, effects, etc.) considering it as a resource capable of contributing to the orientation and the strategic positioning of the organizations, and, as a last resort, to the support of the competitive advantages. Nevertheless, there are very few studies that include evidence about how the effective management of certain characteristics and properties of the network, such as the work dynamics developed or the interaction in the group may be useful for the operation of the work group itself in firms that develope its activity in high-tech sectors. Thus, the objectives of this paper is to develop a conceptual framework for studying the relationship between Human Resource Activities and Social Capital while underlining the importance that human resource policies play in the management of this variable in a IT environment.

INTRODUCTION

During the recent decades, the increasing relevance of intangible assets, where the organizational knowledge and background become the leading resources (Drucker, 1992), reveals that human resources are gaining importance in an environment more and more competitive and changeable as high-tech sector.

Human capital, understood as the set of capabilities, skills and knowledge, bears a huge influence on firms' results (Barney, 1991; Snell et al., 1999; Youndt & Snell, 2004). People are considered as a major strategic factor for the organizations (Becker & Gerhart, 1996).

However, the social changes resulting for some time now in an increasing heterogeneity in the labour markets -groups of diverse people as for

DOI: 10.4018/978-1-4666-0924-2.ch006

their age, gender, training level or experience- (Van der Vegt & Janssen, 2003), require us to adopt a different view. It seems that the availability of varied, qualified and trained human resources is not enough anymore (Snell, 1999). Their dissimilar contributions, skills, perspectives and ideas, displaying influence both on workgroups operation and on the organizational performance, must be incorporated. From this point of view, organizations are required to appreciate not only the strategic importance of their human capital, but also the need of integrating and managing the heterogeneous profile of their employees as a source of competitive advantage, which shall allow them to stand against their competitors (Burt, 1992). The organizational success depends now on the network of social interactions where the employees share, combine and transfer knowledge thanks to certain attributes such as trust, identity, sense of belonging and civic awareness (Bontis & Choo, 2001). All in all, social capital is identified as an essential complement of human capital (Coleman, 1988; Burt, 1992). The network of social relationships among employees or organizations, based on trust and cooperation, facilitates communication, interaction and a continuous exchange of information and knowledge, which provides the organization with the opportunity to improve its performance and to obtain sustainable advantage over their competitors.

Therefore, as well as the Theory on human capital, the contributions of the social capital approach are also remarkable (Nahapiet & Ghoshal, 1998; Leana & Van Buren, 1999), since they consider the possibility that the relational ties may be combined with other perspectives in order to analyze the strategic management of human resources. The theories converging through the development of this branch of knowledge offer partial contributions, so that sometimes they may be complementary. Several relevant approaches agree to highlight that an exclusive cumulative human capital policy may not be effective, at least on the long term (Snell, 1999). Certainly,

human capital, understood as the set of skills, knowledge and background is a feature exclusively developed among people (Boxall, 1998; Wright & Snell, 1998). However, we must remark that knowledge and skills achieved from training and professional experience are built and transferred through social relationships *social capital*, particularly through conversation and dialogue (Lesser & Cothrel, 2001).

Considering these ideas, this study approaches the aim of explaining the means available for the organizations in order to manage this wave of communication. In other words, we will analyze the influence displayed by the management of human resources on social capital, by identifying those practices used by the organizations to efficiently manage workgroups operation. With this aim, we will start by reviewing literature on social capital. Particularly, we will analyze the importance gained by social capital as a strategic resource generator of competitive advantage, as well as the main factors affecting the said interpersonal relationships, which often become a "double-edged weapon": source of competitive advantage, but also of conflicts if it is not properly managed. Considering these arguments, we will complete the model by introducing the management of human resources. We will specifically try to explain the way how the policies and human resources practices may manage the social relationships developed among the members of a certain network, reducing the potential interpersonal troubles and increasing the benefits.

SOCIAL CAPITAL

Lately, social capital construct has aroused the interest of experts on various subject matters as a research line. It is generally believed that benefits may be extracted from the relationships established in the networks of the social structures that a certain person belongs to (e.g., Reagans & Zuckerman, 2001; Schmid, 2003). Given that, according to the

Theory of Resources and Capacities, social capital is a strategic resource, which meets the required features to develop a strategy unattainable for competitors (Bourdieu, 1986; Coleman, 1988; Lin, 2001). Considering the Theory of networks, social capital is the mean or link where several resources are connected: information, opportunities, projects, etc. (Bourdieu, 1986; Coleman, 1988; Burt, 1992; Putnam, 1995, Nahapiet &Ghoshal, 1998; Lin, 2001). In this sense, if the actors of a network perceive that the achievements of other members ease the attainment of theirs, in order words, if they appreciate the collectivist culture leading to a better trust, coordination, communication and cooperation among the employees and try to minimize the importance of social stereotypes, then it is possible to access to resources and gain advantages that would be unachievable individually (Cohen & Prusak, 2001; Adler & Kwon, 2002). Added value benefits may be obtained by sharing skills, knowledge and experiences (human capital) among the employees (Davies & Kanaki, 2006). Consequently, social activities are crucial in our current economy, since they allow the possibility of creating and sharing the necessary knowledge to generate sustainable competitive advantage.

Nevertheless, by reviewing literature we conclude that the opportunities for the actors and organizations taking part in the network to access to these benefits is not always the same, but it is variable according to the place, time and context where said relationships are established (Wasserman & Galaskiewicz, 1984). Thus, trying to provide an in-depth explanation of the social relationships which may, to a certain extent, permit the access to assets and opportunities, it is worth mentioning Walker et al. (1997) or Seibert et al. (2001), who concluded that the possibility of opting to these specific resources depends, to a great extent, on the level of the network settings.

There is an agreement somehow among researches that *demographical and psychosocial differences* existing in workgroups bear an influence on interpersonal relationships developed within the network (Chatman & Flynn, 2001). Particularly, the varied researches dealing with this phenomenon prove that the relationships among diverse people may be eventually positive or negative. Sometimes they lead to a better decision making process (Ancona & Caldwell, 1992), an increase on the innovation capacities (Knight et al., 1999), and even to create a great variety of perspectives (Wiersema & Bird, 1993). However, sometimes they just produce the opposite effect, triggering confrontations of points if view and interpersonal conflicts (Jehn, 1997). In this respect, it is necessary to adopt a series of policies aimed at replacing value judgments based on stereotypes by a more accurate mutual knowledge, avoiding the generation of superficial opinions leading to relational conflicts (Lau & Murnighan, 1998).

On the other hand, as Harrison et al. (1998) or Richard and Shelor (2000) pointed, the intensity of the interactions among the members of a group □*network density or cohesion*□ bears also a relevant influence on social capital. In general terms, the approach which states that the more united a workgroup is, the higher its performance will be, is generally supported (Coleman, 1988; Walker et al., 1997). Following Coleman (1988), the closed relationships based on mutual interdependence and interconnectivity encourage communication and trust among the members of a network. This leads to the discussion and confrontation of multiple perspectives, resulting in a higher willingness towards the collective action and, in short, in a reduced interpersonal conflict (Walker et al., 1997; Lankau & Scandura, 2002). Nonetheless, despite there are several studies that, on the contrary, defend the benefits of an "open", non-united and heterogeneous structure (Granovetter, 1985; Burt, 1992) we must highlight that this idea has less and less followers. Authors like Reagans and Zuckerman (2001) states that the structural gaps are not so positive locally, since they hamper mutual coordination and bear a decisive influence in the group disintegration and confrontation. Therefore, we may state that organizations are required to identify the closeness among the actors of a network as a variable allowing the access to the network resources.

Likewise, authors such as Fairhurst and Snavely (1983) suggest that *constant interaction* among the workgroup members is required in order to keep the team properly united. If the actors of a network keep a continuous relationship, the prospect of exchanging objective information increases. That shall produce well founded opinions about the rest of the team and will make more likely to create common work patterns resulting in enhanced interpersonal relationships and, ultimately, in the neutralization of conflicts (Harrison et al., 1998; Lau & Murnigham, 1998). In this sense, it is necessary to develop policies where a continuous involvement and participation of the group members is conceived as another indispensable requirement to achieve the potential benefits of social capital.

Along with these features which determine an appropriate network structure, researchers have proved that, for people who are motivated to work together and share common objectives, it comes to be essential that social relationships are characterized by *trust, cooperation and solidarity* (Fukuyama, 1995; Humphrey & Schmitz, 1998). It has been more and more clearly evidenced that these variables bear a positive influence on the affective dynamics, since they avoid segregation, to a large extent, and maximize the frequency and intensity of communication among individuals, developing group cultures, which make team work easier, neutralize confrontation and, therefore, improve the group performance (Fukuyama, 1995; Putnam, 1995; Nahapiet & Ghoshal, 1998; Adler & Kwon, 2002).

Considering these perspectives, it is particularly interesting to analyze how the effective management of certain network characteristics and properties, such as the work dynamics developed or the group interaction, may be useful for the workgroup operation and, ultimately, for the organizational performance. Thus, this study

approaches the goal of explaining the resources available for the organizations in order to manage this communication flow. A proper staff management is considered as a valid answer to contextual transformations (Hunt, 1984). With this purpose, we moved to review literature on human resources management with a view to modify those orientations that may result in a better exploitation of the benefits of social capital.

HUMAN RESOURCES AND SOCIAL CAPITAL MANAGEMENT

Social changes undergone recently in labour markets demand new requirements for the organizations as for the management of factors related to people. As we have previously remarked, since a long time ago, there is an increased interest concerning the subject of the social factor among researchers (Nahapiet & Ghoshal, 1998; Tsai & Ghoshal, 1998; Leana & Van Buren, 1999; Snell, 1999; Lin, 2001; Adler & Kwon, 2002; Youndt & Snell, 2004), who try to find out from several theoretical approaches, such as the Theory of Resources and Capacities (Bourdieu, 1986; Coleman, 1988; Lin, 2001) or the Theory of Networks (Bourdieu, 1986; Coleman, 1988; Burt, 1992; Putnam, 1995; Nahapiet & Ghoshal, 1998; Lin, 2001), the best way to contribute to the generation of business advantage. That is why a different approach or sensibility is required as regards social relationships occurring among people. Managers are required to identify the importance of this variable, to adopt a different point of view (Wright & McMahan, 1992), and to consider not only the human factor as an essential resource for the organization, but also to take into account the need of managing the informal communication system, considering that it may boost the attainment of the organizational goals (Gruenfeld et al., 2000; Mohrman et al., 2003). Therefore, if companies intend to take part in this new world market, they must be flexible and adaptable, due to the lack of simple and stable industrial environments nowadays, and their human resources departments have to define practice patterns and staff policies so that the company may develop and make the most of the strategic potential resulting from social capital. In outline, the development of the group dynamics will depend, to a large extent, on the capacity of firms to manage this new business framework.

Considering that human resources management may play a very relevant role in order to value the social relationships created within or between organizations, we will emphasize the analysis of the policies that need to be implemented and developed by human resources managers in order to take advantage of the social capital resources.

Based on the assumption of the Universalist perspective, we cannot state that certain policies are always preferred, regardless of the organization peculiarities (Delery & Doty, 1996; Brewster, 1999). Nevertheless, it may be observed that multiple aspects concerning the commitment and cooperation among the employees, the elaboration and deployment of strategies and instruments of open communication, or the creation of mechanisms designed to warranty equal opportunities in the selection process, remuneration, etc., can contribute to reinforce the social relationships among the members of a network (Youndt & Snell, 2004). In this respect, we should identify certain human resource practices leading the organization to effectively manage workgroups operation.

First of all, clear evidences have been offered about the possible usefulness of developing a set of policies aimed at assuring the employees' awareness. As we previously mentioned, empirical literature supports that the demographic composition of the social context where personal relationships are performed has a significant influence on certain factors such as the increase of social stereotypes, commitment or relational conflict (Tsui et al., 1992; Wiersema & Bird, 1993; Riordan & Shore, 1997). Blau (1964) states that said negative influence of heterogeneity upon integration and, especially, upon the social ties is

due to the tendency of individuals to get mixed with other actors whose attributes, interests and skills similar are their own (Messick & Mackie, 1989). This natural arrangement results in the fragmentation of the workgroup in subgroups, who avoid the conctact with other demographically different groups (Ibarra & Andrews, 1993; Haslam et al., 1995). Consequently, it is essential to display a set of policies, efforts and practices aimed at raising the group members' awareness about the importance of team work and about the opportunities resulting from the differences between them. With this purpose, human resources management departments must reconsider the traditional recruitment and hiring means, like some other policies, such as the creation of posts and the performance assessment. Specifically, literature advices organizations to promote *staff recruitment and selection policies* highlighting the mutual goals through more informal techniques (active educational methods like group dynamics, case studies, role play, etc.), by reducing the specification level required and encouraging team work. Inappropriate affection procedures can result in ineffective, demotivated and even problematic employees, and this, consequently, disturbs work climate (McDaniel et al., 1994). Likewise, it is also necessary to develop *performance assessment policies*, based on team criteria, rather than on individual criteria (Wiersema & Bird, 1993), as well as *designing tasks* leading to more interesting, less specialized working routines, promoting team work and increasing employees' motivation. This way, it will be more likely to develop collectivist group cultures (Chatman & Flynn, 2001) so that the employees may further identify themselves with the whole group, rather than with some specific social categories (Gaertner et al., 1990).

The frequency of the interactions between the members of a network -communication policies- (Fairhurst & Snavely, 1983) is also a basic aspect to be taken into account by any human resources management department aiming at obtaining benefits from social capital. Dealing with the importance gained by heterogeneity nowadays, Amason and Sapienza (1997) identified a deep correlation existing between this variable and the frequency of the interactions among the team members. Generally, most of the bibliography referred suggests that the demographical composition of a given network negatively affects the capacity of its members in order to communicate in an effective way, since they are not so willing to interact with those whom they perceive as different (Riordan & Shore, 1997). The lack of contact is a considerable loss for the group operation, since, as we already mentioned, it is necessary to keep a frequent relationship in order to exchange information, get access to resources and make decisions (Zenger & Lawrence, 1989; Ancona & Caldwell, 1992). A group without communication and unwilling to get related is not a group anymore; it simply becomes a set of individuals who share the same work space (Keller, 2001).

In this sense, it is also necessary to emphasize the need that human resources management introduces open communication processes and promotes the creation of shared languages and means because, without them, it would be virtually impossible that frequent contact between the individuals produced the desired positive effect expected (Coleman, 1988; Burt, 1992; Lankau & Scandura, 2002). The constant interaction can lead people to well founded opinions as for the rest of the individuals, since it increases the level of objective information available, weakens the subgroup limits and make more likely to create common work patterns (Lazerson, 1995; Lin, 2001). Thus, other best practices have been defined as well, like *staff socialization* and *training*. It is essential that all the employees feel integrated in the organization, convinced that they can express themselves and that their ideas will be heard and appreciated (Granovetter, 1985), and also that all of them know how to interpret properly the information transferred by colleagues with different communication patterns, since the lack of understanding causes one of the most important

potential problems in the interaction process (Nahapiet & Ghoshal, 1998; Adler & Kwon, 2002).

On the other hand, in order to obtain benefits from the relationships established within the social structure networks, their members are required to satisfy some flairs and behaviours, such as trust, identity, sense of belonging and coexistence (Bontis & Choo, 2001), indispensable in order to interact in the social system (Nahapiet & Ghoshal, 1998) - development policies-. Following authors like Fukuyama (1995), Putnam (1995), Leana and Van Buren (1999), Cohen and Prusak (2001), Lin (2001), or Adler and Kwon (2002), successful networks are those including a climate of trust and honest communication, where mistakes are considered as a part of the learning process, and open discussions help the employees to find out the causes of the problems without blaming anyone. For the development of these behaviours, human resources management is essential, since, by means of organizing *training* programmes it is possible to raise the employees' consciousness about the influence of these variables on affective dynamics, and this will avoid segregation, to a large extent, and maximize the frequency and intensity of the communication among the employees, resulting in an easier team work (Wiersema & Bird, 1993; Smith et al., 1994). Also, the improvement of *carriers' development* programmes may be another valid method in order to promote collectivist culture and the employees' involvement (Richard & Johnson, 2001). Moreover, literature on human resources management assumes that the *performance assessment* practices play an important role too as a motivation method subject to estimulate and keep certain behaviours of the employees. Thus, by emphasizing group incentives, the organization will be able to strengthen the creation of a collectivist culture leading to a higher performance (Gaertner et al., 1990; Chatman et al., 1998).

Those policies designed to warranty equal opportunities and treatment -equal opportunities policies-. Recently, among this kind of policies, literature has particularly highlighted the need to integrate best practices aimed at pursuing Equal Opportunities (EO) in the organization, based mainly on the exploitation of human diversity benefits, especially those derived from gender diversity (Jacobson, 1999). Practices are required to acknowledge that employees are not all the same, and precisely these differences among them contribute to gain a set of benefits and improvements regarding productivity (Kandola & Fullerton, 1994; Ledwith & Colgan, 1996). Therefore, various researches in this regard emphasize the need of integrating objective measures as for staff *recruitment and selection*, by using more unbiased, clear, fair and transparent methods (Robertson & Makin, 1986). It also necessary to introduce *Development procedures* granting equal opportunities for all the employees, increasing fulfillment at work, commitment and interest on the tasks and, ultimately, performance. And finally, it is important to adapt *wage policies* assuring the application of the equality principle, resulting in the improvement of the group affective environment (Barber y Daly, 1996) and in the limitation of relational conflicts (Freedman, 1978). These changes will decrease the differences existing among the varied human resources policies used by organizations, so that business managers put the value of every people according to their merits and their possibility to contribute to the firm, regardless of their origin and/or personal characteristics (Eagly & Steffan, 1984; Falkenberg, 1990).

Many labour environments support the idea that cooperation increases efficiency -cooperation policies- (Jones et al., 2000). Two people who work together by mutual agreement are considered more efficient than working separately. However, has we have remarked, the evidence that the heterogeneity in multiple attributes affects groups dynamics also reflects in this variable. Despite a lot of authors concluded that diverse teams develop more supportive behaviours, there are many more researchers who state the opposite: that in hetero-geneous groups, cooperation behaviours are less frequent because the personal and psychosocial differences generate an individualistic, rather than cooperative, distribution of the tasks (Chatman & Flynn, 2001). Nevertheless, literature remarks the importance of promoting interdependent relationships between the members of a workgroup where open support, effective communication, team spirit, coordination and cooperation are a reality (Saavedra et al., 1993). In this sense, a proper human resources management is indispensable so that individuals can identify the team as whole in order to make the most of their social relationships, rather than intensifying trouble among them. For the purposes of a better cooperation process, human resources management must encourage interdependence and emphasize mutual goals as a vehicle in order to generate trust among the employees and reduce the importance of stereotypes. It is necessary to develop policies leading to a greater contact among the employees so that they can really assess the need of working together, removing excessively individualistic behaviours by the group members (Nahapiet & Ghoshal, 1998; Cohen & Prusak, 2001). In short, the team has to operate actually as a social system and its members must play a leading role in the definition of the goals, the discussion of rules and the elaboration of labour processes.

As a result, staff management practices are considered as tools available for the organization in order to determine the social capital level among its employees. Nevertheless, we must highlight that the definition of this set of best practices is far apart from being systematic. The different researches referred offer very disjointed evidences about the coexistence of the multiple policies, by focusing just on some specific aspects of human resources management. However, we should consider if a better efficiency is obtained by analyzing these works together, since the four approaches offer four different solutions for a single research topic.

Bearing in mind the relationships described above, we can conclude the following set of hypotheses (figure 1):

Hypothesis 1: The development of certain Human Resources policies benefits organizational social capital. Particularly:

Hypothesis 1.1: Organizations that raise their employees' awareness about the importance of diversity and the damages caused by stereotypes have workgroups with high levels of social capital.

Hypothesis 1.2: Organizations establishing open processes of communication have workgroups with high levels of social capital.

Hypothesis 1.3: Organizations developing behaviours and approaches among their employees through training, assessment and promotion policies have workgroups with high levels of social capital.

Hypothesis 1.4: Organizations securing equal opportunities and treatments for their employees have workgroups with high levels of social capital.

Hypothesis 1.5: Organizations encouraging cooperation and interdependence among their employees have workgroups with high levels of social capital.

METHODOLOGY

In order to test the set of relationships identified, this paper approaches a quantitative analysis. Particularly, once we have fulfilled the global consistency of the scales, we will move to search for conclusions about the relationships given among the varied sets of (dependent and e independent) variables, by means of a regression analysis that will allow us to know if it is possible to reduce our prediction mistakes on the criterion variable defining the model —social capital—, starting from the independent variables (human resources policies).

Figure 1. Effects of human resource policies on social capital

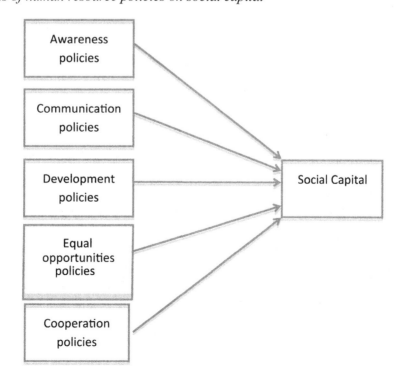

Regarding the measurements, it is worth remarking that we have used instruments available from literature for all the variables, previously tested in other researches. Specifically, in order to measure social capital and communication policies, development, equality and cooperation, we used the items proposed by Youndt & Snell (2004), measured by using a Lickert scale from one (absolutely disagree) to seven (absolutely agree). However, for the variable related to the awareness policy, we have considered, in the same scale, the contribution introduced by Cornelius (2002), based on four items dealing with employees' differences, importance of stereotypes, diversity competences and conflict handling.

As we have previously mentioned, it order to make the proposed model operative, a quantitative analysis will be practiced. Particularly, the most common analysis among researchers and also the most widespread in empirical studies, is a set of linear regressions, as we start from the premise that this multivariant tool will permit us to make clear the relationship existing among the variables in the model, to extract as much information as possible from the available data and to reach a more comprehensive understanding of reality.

CONCLUSION

As it may be observed, this is an in progress work, since the proposed hypotheses have not been tested yet. This study deals with aspects concerning the influence bore by human resources on the level of social capital in the organization. Thus, the relationship existing between both variables is reviewed with the aim of proving how human resources policies encouraging the employees' awareness, communication, and development of behaviours in pursuit of collectivity and equality get higher benefits from the relationships established among the members of a given network.

Despite for a time now researchers have been making us aware of the need to take into consider-

ation the management of the social relationships established between the members of a certain network, in the practice there are few models including this variable. Indeed, we could state that both study fields have been analysed separately so far. Thus, when dealing with human resources literature we may find varied explanations of this conception, its evolution, policies, approaches, etc. These works match up in the remarked strategic importance granted to human capital and its management. Similarly, as regards social capital, most part of the researching efforts deployed have focused on the definition of the concept itself, the specification of its components, its effects and also, but not limited to it, the designation of who benefits from the development of social capital, etc. In this sense, a wide discussion has been open regarding a whole range of aspects of social capital, from the theoretical foundations in different disciplines of social science fields, to more practical issues related with its assessment and measurement. However, few evidences have been offered about the way how this construct may be managed by the organization, and literature advice is a high priority, since both social capitals inherent and external to the organization suppose a different basis for the formulation and implementation of human resources practices, policies and strategies. Considering all the previous points, the next step would be to acknowledge the important role that social relationships management may play on performance and group processes. In this respect, literature on social capital should be integrated on some human resources management models approached. For this reason, we are convinced that this work line can contribute not only to literature on social capital, but also to human resources management. And, we consider that this work in high tech sectors could be interesting. The Human capital is a critical variable for competitiveness in high-tech sectors. It is required of personnel with a high degree of knowledge, abilities, and experiences. However, its interchange for the generation of new ideas is crucial. In this sense, the share capital acquires a great importance and, the management of the same through policies and practices of human resource also.

Social capital, defined as a series of social relationships generated among a group of people, must be properly managed and human resources practices may mean a potential, important contribution. Therefore, we assume that this model can explain the relevance of a suitable management of human resources policies on social capital, even though we are not in position to present empirical results yet. Analysing the consequences that human resources management may bear on social capital may allow us to identify those orientations which are useful for the organization in order to extract the potential benefits from social relationships given between the members of a certain network.

Nonetheless, despite it approaches a very particular analysis, the model, just they we have explained it above, presents certain limitations. For the purpose of building this model, we have incorporated a basic Universalist statement, widely discussed in other literature areas. Since, as Delery and Doty (1996) pointed, only causal, simple explanations have been offered, obviating some essential aspects for the analysis on human resources management. Nevertheless, in order to analyse how is social capital created and administered, the Universalist perspective presents some evident limitations, since a single practice cannot determine the increase or creation of a variable. On the contrary, the varied practices are closely related one another, and all of them interact with a view to reach a shared goal. Besides, we must not get around that there are some incidental factors which ultimately determine the way how the organization operates. In this sense, the practices used for the management of social capital should be designed, for instance, according to other variables influencing this causal relationship (Jackson

& Álvarez, 1992). Contingency variables deal with the influence borne by environmental and organizational elements, as well as by the human resources strategy implemented by the company. On the other hand, there are also contextual factors to be considered, since the inner (work climate, size, organizational structure and individual interests of the people involved, etc.) and external environments (legal, political and institutional framework; social and economic conditions; cultural differences, etc.) have a direct impact on human resources operation.

In this respect, it is worth considering as a future line of research the idea of building an explanatory model on human resources management including all items required for social capital management, approached from the point of view of the integration of the Universalist, contingent, configurational and contextual contributions. According to Brewster (1999), every approach emphasizes one of the basic dimensions of human resources management. Hence, it is necessary to approach the design of an alternative, joint description which tackles the subject matter from all its possible dimensions.

Due to these limitations, we come to the conclusion that in order to make an in-depth internal analysis on human resources management, it would be interesting to study all the practices as a whole, rather than separately, so that they reveal the different approaches used by the organization to face the challenges of social capital.

ACKNOWLEDGMENT

The authors are alphabetically ordered. This study has benefited from financing from the Research Project ECO2008-05171 of the Spanish Ministry of Science and the Research Group SEJ-449 of the Andalusian Government.

REFERENCES

Adler, P. S., & Kwon, S. W. (2002). Social capital: Prospects for a new concept. *Academy of Management Review, 27*(1), 17–40. doi:10.2307/4134367

Amason, A. C., & Sapienza, H. (1997). The effects of top management team size and interaction norms on cognitive and affective conflict. *Journal of Management, 23*(4), 495–507. doi:10.1016/S0149-2063(97)90045-3

Ancona, D. G., & Caldwell, D. F. (1992). Demography and design: Predictors of new product team performance. *Organization Science, 3*(3), 321–341. doi:10.1287/orsc.3.3.321

Barber, A. E., & Daly, C. L. (1996). Compensation and Diversity: New Pay for a New Workforce? In Kossek, E. E., & Lobel, S. A. (Eds.), *Managing Diversity: Human Resource Strategies for Transforming the Workplace*. Cambridge, UK: Blackwell.

Barney, J. B. (1991). Firm resources and sustained competitive advantage. *Journal of Management, 17*, 99–120. doi:10.1177/014920639101700108

Becker, B. E., & Gerhart, B. (1996). The impact of human resource management on organizational performance: Progress and prospects. *Academy of Management Journal, 39*(4), 779–801. doi:10.2307/256712

Blau, P. M. (1964). *Exchange and power in social life*. New York: John Wiley.

Bontis, N., & Choo, C. W. (2001). *Strategic management of intellectual capital and organizational knowledge*. New York: Oxford University Press.

Bourdieu, P. (1986). The forms of capital . In Richardson, J. G. (Ed.), *Handbook of Theory and Research in Sociology of Education* (pp. 241–258). New York: Greenwook.

Boxall, P. (1998). Achieving competitive advantage through human resource strategy: towards a theory of industry dynamics. *Human Resource Management Review, 8*(3), 265–288. doi:10.1016/S1053-4822(98)90005-5

Brewster, C. (1999). Strategic Human Resource Management: the value of different paradigms. *Management International Review, 39*(3), 45–64.

Burt, R. S. (1992). The social structure of competition. In Nohria & Eccles (Eds.), *Networks and organizations structure, form, and action* (pp. 57-82). Boston, MA: Harvard Business School Press.

Chatman, J. A., & Flynn, F. J. (2001). The influence of demographic heterogeneity on the emergence and consequences of cooperative norms in work teams. *Academy of Management Journal, 44*(5), 956–974. doi:10.2307/3069440

Cohen, D., & Prusak, L. (2001). How to invest in social capital. *Harvard Business Review, 79*(5), 86–93.

Coleman, J. S. (1988). Social capital in the creation of human capital. *American Journal of Sociology, 94*, 95–120. doi:10.1086/228943

Davies, M. F., & Kanaki, E. (2006). Interpersonal characteristics associated with different team roles in work groups. *Journal of Managerial Psychology, 21*(7), 638–650. doi:10.1108/02683940610690187

Delery, J. E., & Doty, D. H. (1996). Modes of theorizing in Strategic Human Resource Management: Test of Universalistic, Contingency, and Configurational performance predictions. *Academy of Management Journal, 39*(4), 802–835. doi:10.2307/256713

Drucker, P. F. (1992). The new society of organizations. *Harvard Business Review, 70*(5), 95–104.

Eagly, A. H., & Steffan, V. J. (1984). Gender Stereotypes Stem from the Distribution of Women and men into Social Roles. *Journal of Personality and Social Psychology, 46*, 735–754. doi:10.1037/0022-3514.46.4.735

Fairhurst, G. T., & Snavely, B. K. (1983). Majority and token minority group relationships: Power acquisition and communication. *Academy of Management Review, 8*(2), 292–300. doi:10.2307/257757

Falkenberg, L. (1990). Improving the Accuracy of Stereotypes within the Workplace. *Journal of Management, 16*(1), 107–118. doi:10.1177/014920639001600108

Fukuyama, F. (1995). *Trust: The social virtues and the creation of prosperity*. New York: The Free press.

Gaertner, S. L., Mann, J. A., Dovidio, J. F., Murrell, A. J., & Pomare, M. (1990). How does cooperation reduce intergroup bias? *Journal of Personality and Social Psychology, 59*(4), 692–704. doi:10.1037/0022-3514.59.4.692

Granovetter, M. S. (1985). Economic action and social structure: the problem of embeddedness. *American Journal of Sociology, 91*(3), 481–510. doi:10.1086/228311

Gruenfeld, D. H., Matorana, P. V., & Fan, E. T. (2000). What do groups learn from their worldiest members? Direct and indirect influence in dynamic teams. *Organizational Behavior and Human Decision Processes, 82*, 45–59. doi:10.1006/obhd.2000.2886

Harrison, D. A., Price, K. H., & Bell, M. P. (1998). Beyond relational demography: Time and the effects of surface and deep-level diversity on work group cohesion. *Academy of Management Journal, 41*(1), 96–107. doi:10.2307/256901

Humphrey, J., & Schmitz, H. (1998). Trust and inter-firm relations in developing and transition economies. *The Journal of Development Studies, 34*(4), S32–S61. doi:10.1080/00220389808422528

Hunt, J. W. (1984). The shifting focus of the personnel function. *Personnel Management, 16*(2), 14–18.

Ibarra, H., & Andrews, S. B. (1993). Power, social influence and sensemaking: Effects of network centrality and proximity on employee perceptions. *Administrative Science Quarterly, 38*(2), 277–303. doi:10.2307/2393414

Jackson, S. E., & Álvarez, E. B. (1992). Working through diversity as a strategic imperative . In Jackson, S. E. (Ed.), *Diversity in the workplace: Human resource initiatives* (pp. 13–29). New York: Guilford Press.

Jacobson, B. (1999). Diversity management process of transformational change. In *Proceedings of the Total E-Quality Management Conference*, Nuremberg, Germany.

Jehn, K. A. (1997). A qualitative analysis of conflict type and dimensions in organizational groups. *Administrative Science Quarterly, 42*(3), 234–257. doi:10.2307/2393737

Jones, D., Pringle, J., & Shepherd, D. (2000). Managing diversity´ meets Aotearoa/New Zealand. *Personnel Review, 29*(3), 364–380. doi:10.1108/00483480010324715

Kandola, R., & Fullerton, J. (1994). Diversity: More than just an empty slogan. *Personnel Management, 26*(4), 46.

Keller, R. T. (2001). Cross-functional project groups in research and new product development: Diversity, communications, job stress, and outcomes. *Academy of Management Journal, 44*(3), 547–555. doi:10.2307/3069369

Knight, D., Pearce, C. L., Smith, K. G., Olian, J. D., Sims, H. P., Smith, K. A., & Floods, P. (1999). Top management team diversity, group process and strategic consensus. *Strategic Management Journal, 20*(5), 445–465. doi:10.1002/(SICI)1097-0266(199905)20:5<445::AID-SMJ27>3.0.CO;2-V

Lankau, M. J., & Scandura, T. A. (2002). An investigation of personal learning in mentoring relationships: content, antecedents, and consequences. *Academy of Management Journal, 45*(4), 779–790. doi:10.2307/3069311

Lau, D. C., & Murnighan, J. K. (1998). Demographic diversity and faultlines: The compositional dynamics of organizational groups. *Academy of Management Review, 23*(2), 325–340. doi:10.2307/259377

Lazerson, M. (1995). A new phoenix: Modern putting-out in the modern knitwear industry. *Administrative Science Quarterly, 40*(1), 34–59. doi:10.2307/2393699

Leana, C. R., & Van Buren, H. J. III. (1999). Organizational Social Capital and Employment Practices. *Academy of Management Review, 24*(3), 538–555. doi:10.2307/259141

Ledwith, S., & Colgan, F. (1996). *Women in organizations. Challenging gender politics. Management, work and organizations.* New York: Macmillan Business.

Lesser, E., & Cothrel, J. (2001, spring/summer). Fast friends: Virtuality and social capital. *Knowledge Directions,* 66-79.

Lin, N. (2001). *Social capital: A theory of social structure and action.* New York: Cambridge University Press.

McDaniel, M. A., Whetzel, D. L., Schmidt, F. L., & Maurer, S. D. (1994). The validity of employment interviews: A comprehensive review and meta-analysis. *The Journal of Applied Psychology, 79*(4), 599–616. doi:10.1037/0021-9010.79.4.599

Messick, D. M., & Mackie, D. M. (1989). Intergroup relations. *Annual Review of Psychology, 40,* 45–81. doi:10.1146/annurev.ps.40.020189.000401

Mohrman, S. A., Finegold, D., & Mohrman, A. M. (2003). An empirical model of the organization knowledge system in new product development firms. *Journal of Engineering and Technology Management, 20*(1-2), 7–38. doi:10.1016/S0923-4748(03)00003-1

Nahapiet, J., & Ghoshal, S. (1998). Social Capital, Intellectual capital, and the organizational advantage. *Academy of Management Review, 23*(2), 242–266. doi:10.2307/259373

Putnam, R. D. (1995). Bowling slone: America's declining social capital. *Journal of Democracy, 6*(1), 65–78. doi:10.1353/jod.1995.0002

Reagans, R., & Zuckerman, E. (2001). Networks, diversity, and productivity: the social capital of corporate R&D teams. *Organization Science, 12*(4), 502–517. doi:10.1287/orsc.12.4.502.10637

Richard, O. C., & Johnson, N. B. (2001). Understanding the Impact of Human Resource Diversity Practices on Firm Performance. *Journal of Managerial Issues, 2,* 177–195.

Richard, O. C., & Shelor, R. M. (2002). Linking top management team age heterogeneity to firm performance: juxtaposing two midrange theories. *International Journal of Human Resource Management, 13*(6), 958–974. doi:10.1080/09585190210134309

Riordan, C. M., & Shore, L. M. (1997). Demographic diversity and employee attitudes: An empirical examination of relational demography within work units. *The Journal of Applied Psychology, 82*(3), 342–358. doi:10.1037/0021-9010.82.3.342

Robertson, I., & Makin, P. (1986). Management and selection. A survey and critique. *Journal of Occupational Psychology, 59*(1), 45–58.

Saavedra, R. P., Earley, C. P., Dyne, L. V., & Lee, C. (1993). Complex interdependence in task-performing groups. *The Journal of Applied Psychology, 78*(1), 61–72. doi:10.1037/0021-9010.78.1.61

Schmid, A. A. (2003). Discussion: Social capital as an important level in economic development policy and private strategy. *American Journal of Agricultural Economics*, *85*(3), 716–719. doi:10.1111/1467-8276.00473

Seibert, S. E., Kraimer, M. L., & Liden, R. C. (2001). A social capital theory of career success. *Academy of Management Review*, *44*(2), 219–237. doi:10.2307/3069452

Smith, K. G., Smith, K. A., Olian, J. D., Sims, H. P., & Scully, J. A. (1994). Top management team demography and process: The role of social integration and communication. *Administrative Science Quarterly*, *39*(3), 412–438. doi:10.2307/2393297

Snell, S. A. (1999). Social capital and strategic HRM: It's who you know. *HR. Human Resource Planning*, *22*(1), 62–65.

Snell, S. A., Lepak, D. P., & Youndt, M. A. (1999). Managing the architecture of intellectual capital: Implication for strategic human resources management. *Research in Personnel and Human Resources Management*, *4*, 175–193.

Tsui, A. S., Egan, T., & O'Reilly, C. A. III. (1992). Being different: Relational demography and organizational attachment. *Administrative Science Quarterly*, *37*(4), 549–579. doi:10.2307/2393472

Van der Vegt, G., & Janssen, O. (2003). Joint impact of interdependency and group diversity on innovation. *Journal of Management*, *29*(5), 729–751. doi:10.1016/S0149-2063_03_00033-3

Walker, G., Kogut, B., & Shan, W. (1997). Social capital, structural holes and the formation of an industry network. *Organization Science*, *8*(2), 109–125. doi:10.1287/orsc.8.2.109

Wasserman, S., & Galaskiewicz, J. (1984). Some generalizations of p1: External constraints, interactions, and non-binary relations. *Social Networks*, *6*, 177–192. doi:10.1016/0378-8733(84)90016-9

Wiersema, M. F., & Bird, A. (1993). Organizational demography in Japanese firms: Group heterogeneity, individual dissimilarity, and top management team turnover. *Academy of Management Journal*, *36*(5), 996–1025. doi:10.2307/256643

Wright, P. M., & McMahan, G. C. (1992). Theoretical perspectives for strategic human resource management. *Journal of Management*, *18*(2), 295–320. doi:10.1177/014920639201800205

Wright, P. M., & Snell, S. A. (1998). Toward a Unifying Framework for Exploring Fit and Flexibility in Strategic Human Resource Management. *Academy of Management Review*, *23*(4), 756–772. doi:10.2307/259061

Youndt, M., & Snell, S. A. (2004). Human resource configuration, intellectual capital and organizational performance. *Journal of Managerial Issues*, *16*(3), 337–360.

Zenger, T. R., & Lawrence, B. S. (1989). Organizational demography: The differential effect of age and tenure distribution on technical communication. *Academy of Management Journal*, *32*(2), 353–376. doi:10.2307/256366

This work was previously published in International Journal of Human Capital and Information Technology Professionals, Volume 1, Issue 2, edited by Ricardo Colomo-Palacios, pp. 36-48, copyright 2010 by IGI Publishing (an imprint of IGI Global).

Section 2
IT Professionals Education

Chapter 7
Analogical Thinking Based Instruction Method in IT Professional Education

Tokuro Matsuo
Yamagata University, Japan

Takayuki Fujimoto
Toyo University, Japan

ABSTRACT

In designing a new teaching system, a challenging issue is how the system intelligently supports learners. This paper describes a methodology and a system design on the intelligent instruction support for software engineering education. For information science courses at a university, software engineering subjects are usually compulsory and students study dominant conceptions of implementation like software architecture, and the methodology of software design in software engineering lectures. To enhance learners' understanding, the authors design a novel instructional model based on the analogical thinking theory. The analogical thinking-based instruction consists of concrete teaching methods like analogy dropping method, self role-play method, and the anthropomorphic thinking method. Questionnaires for learners after the instructions give results of effective education in an actual trial. The contribution of this paper is to provide a new instruction theory, the way of educational practice method, and implementation of the system.

INTRODUCTION

As one field of engineer education, software engineering instruction method is proposed by many literatures (e.g., Casado-Lumbreras et al., 2009; Chao et al., 1992; Colomo Palacios et al., 2010; Dewayne et al., 2000; Saiedian et al., 2002; Shaw, 2002). When it is designed as an intelligent instruc-

tion system, system designers consider how the system supports users by taking students' activities and the cognitive analyses into consideration (e.g., Baker, 2007; Garcia-Crespo et al., 2008a; Martin, 1998; Miyake & Masukawa, 2000). In this paper, we discuss the support process and learning process to help learners understand and grasp software engineering issues. Such processes can

DOI: 10.4018/978-1-4666-0924-2.ch007

be implemented into the education support system and intelligent instruction agent in the system.

Nowadays, Universities and other Training Institutions need to clearly identify the Information Technology skills that companies demand from practitioners, including software engineers (Trigo et al., 2010). Universities and educational institutes provide lectures and exercises of software engineering for students who want to take them. In the lecture and exercises, the learning issues include software design, lifecycle models and its history, UML, and so on (e.g., Garcia-Crespo et al., 2008b; Garcia-Crespo et al., 2009b). Learning issues also include the aspect of business model and usability. Students can appropriately understand them by imagining, since many students learn such theories for the first time when they attend university lectures. In many engineering education, students can sometimes visually understand through experiments and exercises (e.g., Behling et al., 1996; Colomo-Palacios et al., 2008; Garcia-Crespo et al., 2009a). However, it is difficult for many students to grasp and design software, since software is not visual. Although the programming exercises in the lectures help learners implement the applications, such applications are quite small and do not have any requirement of industry.

Many students have not studied software engineering when they were a junior high school and high school students. Software engineering has little relationship with the learning subjects in secondary schools. If students have studied subjects such as mathematics, the students would not have many problems with lectures such as information mathematics. On the other hand, there are few students who have learnt about planning and designing software and applications in during secondary school. Law schools and business schools in universities often provide discussion-based lectures since many students are unfamiliar with such learning fields before their entrance into the university. Similarly, software engineering education should also be done based on a method in which students can learn easily.

In this paper, we propose a new software engineering education methodology based on analogical thinking to develop and implement as intelligent tutoring system. Concretely, the analogical thinking-based teaching method consists of the instruction method based on analogical dropping, the instruction method based on self role-play, and the instruction method based on anthropomorphic thinking. We also, in this paper, provide an evaluation of our proposed instruction methodology with data from our experiments. Our research contributes to providing a new instruction theory for software engineering, the way of educational practice based on the new instruction method, and implementation of the tutoring system.

When people understand a certain issue, they sometimes learn it through experience, pre-knowledge, and other stimulus in the environment and course curricula. To develop an instruction system that has such learning process, this paper discusses the methodology of intelligent instruction based on formalization of analogical thinking-based learning model. In our learning model, users' knowledge is enhanced by their pre-knowledge, developmental theme, developmental stage theory. Each issue is mapped as a computer system and device through integration and reuse with each other. The contribution of this paper is to develop new instruction model for e-learning, analyze the learning process, map system's behavior from human growth, and give their perspectives.

The rest of the paper is organized as follows. Section 2 outlines of motivations for this study and investigations in universities. In Section 3, we propose a novel software engineering instruction theory based on analogical thinking. In Section 4, we show the effectiveness of our method by using in actual lectures. After that, in Section 5, we present an example of instruction system that utilizes analogical thinking. Finally in Section 6, we provide some final remarks.

PRELIMINARY DISCUSSION

Lecture and Exercise in Software Engineering Education

In computer science and informatics course at many universities, software engineering education is provided in the form of lectures and exercises (Garcia-Crespo et al., 2009b). There are many types of educational methodology for software engineering, however most of them are provided as just lectures without active practices. In many software engineering lectures, their methodologies are not referred and considered and they mainly depend on just teachers' intentions and ability.

As the actual case example, there are not many universities that provide both "Software engineering lecture" and "Software engineering exercise". Some universities provides the software engineering lecture only includes the network programming exercise, the way of using the UNIX, programming by C language. The reason why some universities cannot provide essential software engineering education is often due to financial constraints. In many universities, there are limitations to employing lecturer, the number of classroom, facilities and so on.

To solve the above problem, we propose distributing an intelligent software engineering education system. In this paper, we propose a new education methodology to implement such a system. The system should be designed so that students can learn and grasp effectively based on cognitive viewpoints and their analyses. As shown in the two sections above, many students are unfamiliar with software engineering theories since they only learn it for the first time in a university lecture. Thus, it is desirable that the instruction method is based on integrated lectures and exercises. Furthermore, we design the instruction method based on concrete thinking and understandable activity. Our proposed method can be applied in other areas and courses where need not prepare the special equipments to enhance an effectiveness of education.

Related Work

Regarding related work in thinking methodology and education, there are some literatures in computer science and educational science. Carbonell et al. (1983) proposed a problem solving method using analogical process. The analogy is produced using a solution included in a problem solved by a computer. The relationship of the analogy is directly connected to it. Thus, the computer guesses a solution for new questions. However, in our paper, we propose a problem solving method using heterogeneous types of experiences.

Nickerson et al. (1985) discussed a thinking method called critical thinking with cognitive analysis. In learning process, the paper shows five approaches for thinking such as comparing and classifying, heuristics, formal thinking, instruction in language and symbol manipulation, and thinking about thinking. This research shows a problem solving method without learners' experiences. On the other hand, our paper shows a concrete problem solving methodology by using students' pre-knowledge and experiences.

Matsuura (2007) proposed a software engineering education method through its actual development. The education activity is based on practical software development experiments and is carried out by students groups. However, in this research, students have already grasped basic software engineering method. On the other hand, the instruction model in our paper focuses on software engineering novices.

Preliminary Investigation

We investigated to university students to grasp the students' conditions of background and preliminary knowledge before the software engineering education. The number of examinees is 87 and all students are third year undergraduate students. Our questionnaires include the advance knowledge and background information, their experiments of operating computers, and so on.

In our investigation, many students have heard of the word "software" before they entered university, however, they have less knowledge of software design and large-scale software system even though they are third grade students. Students also stated the reason why they selected the computer science and informatics course when they entered the university. Ninety percent of them were interested in information science and technology before their entrance to the university. On the other hand, most of them answered that they gradually became interested in software after they entered university. About twenty percent of them did not know the fact of that software is implemented by the programming language during their time as high school students.

Based on the basic questionnaires above, we investigated what the students know about software engineering. The investigation includes mainly software design, manufacturing process, and several other fields. The examinees are the same people as the above students. All of them have obtained the credits for more than 20 subjects related to information science and computer science. They have also received the credits for some programming exercises and basic information science subjects.

The first question is about designing software. Most students cannot imagine the development method for software and has never experienced of implementation based on analyses and design. Even though they have taken lectures related to software engineering such as programming exercises, the theories are different to that of software engineering. Thus, it is difficult for the students to enhance their understanding by using the concepts of learning contents, in which students have already learned.

The second question is about the essence of software engineering. For this question, about eighty percent of students answered that they had never known about the lifecycle model of a software product. About fifty percent answered that they had known about UML and forty percent had known some UML diagram since the UML is being focused on today. The result of the answer shows that students do not have a good chance to use lifecycle model and UML even programming exercise in the university curriculum, since such exercise never handles the implementation like large-scale software. Namely, even though students have just digressionary information engineering skills, they cannot grasp the bigger picture of software manufacturing. It is important for software engineers to be able to plan the manufacturing process as well as the implementation process.

Considering the above condition, students understand the learning contents through the semi-exercise in the lecture. Thus, we propose an instruction system including both integrated lecture and exercise. We propose analogical thinking-based teaching method in the software engineering education support system. By using our proposed method, student's knowledge grows and improves from ambiguous level to clarified level.

Model

Our proposed instruction/learning method is employed in self-education method such as e-learning in addition to actual teaching in universities. Students can learn and understand the subjects effectively by using our method as the learning system. Our system prepares appropriate instruction methods according tot the software engineering education theme. For example, when students learn about life-cycle models for large-scale software, our system gives a lecture and provides an environment where students can rationalize based on analogical dropping. When the students learn about UML diagram, our system provides an environment where students can think based on anthropomorphic thinking. Each instruction method is appropriately employed with each learning subject.

SOFTWARE ENGINEERING INSTRUCTION THEORY

Characterizing Doctrine of Engineering Education

According to the Nicolei Hartmann who was a German philosopher, education is defined as "Erziehung durch den objektiven Geist, zu objektiven Geist" (Hartmann, 1933). Namely, education to an objective ethos is performed successfully with cultural transmission. The objective ethos means all sorts of knowledge, experience, morals, arts, and others. On the other hand, as a civilization rapidly develops, modern engineering education is standing by the Pragmatism, which is the typical philosophy in United States. John Dewey who was a Pragmatism Philosopher, stated that education is acquiring good knowledge and knowledge is obtained through experience (Dewey, 1916). He emphasized that a person's behavior is former than knowledge and thinking is result of the behavior. He also emphasized that knowledge is merely an instrument to think and consider for our behavior. Pragmatism takes things in the opposite way compared to German Idealism. Thus, the Pragmatic process should be inductive and tangible. Engineering education has a greater affinity for Pragmatism than German Idealism. In this paper, its standpoint is projected to the instruction space in engineering education. We also design an instruction theory to transmit special knowledge in software engineering.

New Instruction Theory based on Analogical Thinking

When students learn and acquire something new, sensuous image and example help learners grasp. In the literature (Fujimoto, 2005), imagination is a chain of images. Thus, it is desirable to use the students' preliminary knowledge and experience, when teaching a new learning issue for the first time. In this paper, we show a novel instruction method which is used in engineering education systems. The method includes (1) Analogy dropping method, (2) Self role-play method, and (3) Anthropomorphic thinking method.

Instruction Method Based on Analogical Projection

When a person understands a new learning issue, he/she sometimes understands by relating it to their preliminary knowledge. Dropped a hint as it, we design an instruction method based on analogy dropping. As the existing method, an analogical learning is proposed. By using analogical learning, students understand a new learning issue using their direct preliminary knowledge. On the other hand, our method does not use directly related knowledge. Figure 1 shows the difference between analogical learning and our proposed analogical dropping instruction method. For example, when A' is the price theory, A might be microeconomics. "A" is related with A' directly. On the other hand, in our method, X has no relationship with economics.

The instruction method based on analogical dropping makes clear students' image of learning issues and its problem. In the method, students imagine the indirect analogy against the learning issues and grasp them. A certain behavior such as trips can map and project to the understandable behavior such as planning of requirement analyses. However, when students cannot imagine the behavior as analogy, the image which should be understood by students does not become clear. Figure 2 shows a concept map about the instruction method of analogical dropping. In the education method based on analogical dropping, the knowledge and experiences in which students have are employed. For this method to succeed, the system prepares appropriate students' knowledge and experiences with their development stage based on reversed analogical thinking.

Figure 1. The Relationships between original and analogical knowledge

$$A \rightarrow A'$$
$$(\text{Direct preliminary knowledge} \rightarrow \text{learning issues})$$
$$X \rightarrow A'$$
$$(\text{Heterogeneous experience} \rightarrow \text{learning issues})$$

Instruction Method Based on Self Role-Play

Role-play is sometimes used in psychology education. In role-playing, a player performs a certain character to know his/her problem and characteristics. For example, a few students imagine a situation such as a trade between a buyer and a seller in a shop. Each student performs each character of the situation. The students actually perform the purchasing and selling of an item like a shop manager. Doing such ad-lib play, they can feel the buyer's and seller's behaviors and their patterns. They may also be able to learn the decision making process in the shop. Figure 3 shows the concept of our proposed self role-play method compared with traditional role-play method. In a traditional role-playing method, an independent study cannot be done since each character is performed by different performers. On the other hand, in our proposed self role-play method, one leaner performs all the characters. The student imagines the behavior of each character by himself/herself to understand the situation and solve the special problems.

Instruction Method Based on Anthropomorphic Thinking

Anthropomorphication/personalification can be explained as a certain thing that is thought as people. To apply personalification, we develop a new instruction method based on anthropomorphic thinking. Students can consider and understand some sorts of system design and diagram in UML.

UML is an important concept for designing software based on multiple diagrams. In the anthropomorphic thinking-based method, learners can assume an entity such as a software module as a person. For example, when there is an instrument such as a vending machine, learners consider that the vending machine consists of multiple persons.

Relationships between Learning Issues and Instruction Method

In three instruction methods above, the relationships between learning themes and instruction method are shown in Table 1.

Each relationship is considered as follows. First, instruction method based on analogical dropping is employed when students have some knowledge and ambiguous knowledge of the learning issue. Actually, when the lifecycle model in software manufacturing is being taught, travel planning and cooking process are used as an analogy. This instruction method has high scalability. "Reverse analogical thinking by the system" and "Analogical thinking by learner" is defined as meta-conception.

Secondly, the instruction method based on self role-play is employed in a situation where there are more than two modules communicating and cooperating with each other. Each module performs a specific task while communicating with other modules in the software. Specifically, this method is employed to make students become aware that there are many cooperative objects in the software. For example, a general end-user sometimes proposes his/her requirements without

Figure 2. Concept map about the instruction method of analogical dropping

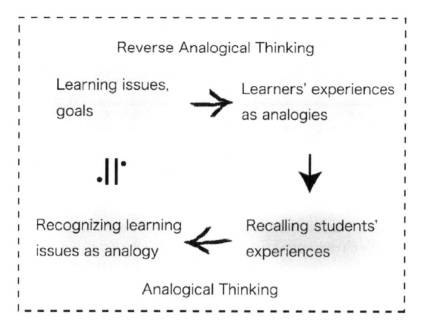

constraints and restriction in implementation, when a systems manager hears them from the end-user. In such situation, learners consider both the implementer and the customer and imagine their discussion, ordering, and negotiation. As the result, learners can understand both customer's selfish and requirement and possibility of implementation.

Third, the instruction method based on anthropomorphic thinking is employed where students act like the system. Thus, the learner can know and grasp the tasks in which the system can do. When there are multiple modules in the system, students can consider that the module need communicate with other module and cooperate with each other. The idea of this instruction model is mapped from the vender machine, which is worked like many shop staffs, such as a checker, stockman, and salesperson.

Figure 3. Concept of role-play and self role-play

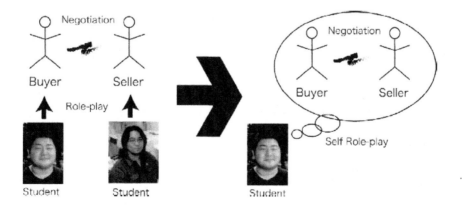

Table 1. Composition of instruction method based on analogical thinking

Our proposed Education Method	Segmented Instruction Method of Analogical Thinking-based Education Method	Role for Instructor and Tutoring System	Features in Learning
Instruction Method based on Analogical Thinking	Analogical Dropping	Preparing appropriate students' preliminary knowledge by reverse analogical thinking	Analogical thinking of learning issues based on their experiences
	Self Role-play	Explanation of characteristics of players	Grasp of situation where there are staffs more than two
	Anthropomorphic Thinking	Preparing tasks that can be done both manually and automatically	Understanding tasks considering that compares the modules to people

Thus, the above three instruction methods can be appropriately applied with each learning issue. Table 2 shows the relationships between the details of learning issues and instruction method based on analogical thinking.

DISCUSSION

Preliminary Evaluation

In this subsection, we show the actual use the above three instruction methods in the lecture to evaluate effectiveness of our proposed teaching methods. We show some of actual trials and the result of evaluation by using questionnaires. The number of students is 84 and all students are third grade of undergraduate in the university.

Instruction using Analogical Dropping

Regarding the instruction method based on analogical dropping, we conducted an actual lecture using the method. The lecture theme was set by Lifecycle model. Lifecycle model is the task flow model that is shown by abstraction of task level in software development. In the lifecycle model, system developers consider and discuss the appropriate protocol of tasks and the order of tasks from requirement analyses to running

and maintenance. Regarding these the iterative steps of phases, it is famous about waterfall, spiral model, prototype model, and so on. In the lecture, we gave the analogical dropping-based instruction methods in learning waterfall model and spiral model. To enhance this learning issue, we use the travel planning as analogy for the lifecycle model since most of students have ever made a plan of their travels. When students have not experienced a travel planning, the cooking process may be available. Each step in waterfall model is mapped to each task of cooking shown in Table 3. We allow sufficient time for students to consider the travel planning. As the result of questionnaires of this instruction, 80 students answered that their knowledge enhanced by using our proposed instruction/leaning method shown in Table 4.

Instruction using Self Role-Play

In the instruction method based on self role-play, we conducted an actual lecture using the method. The lecture theme was set by Requirement Analyses. We set up the problem as that software is ordered by a customer. The ordered software is designed and implemented by a software development company and subcontractors. In current learning of require analyses, it is difficult for students to understand it through reading textbook and simple lecture since most of students have

Table 2. An example of relationships between learning issues and instruction methods

Instruction method	Learning Issues
Analogical dropping method	Lifecycle Model Flowchart Activity Diagram in UML Management and Run etc.
Self role-play method	Estimating costs Require analyses Making Specification etc.
Anthropomorphic thinking method	Sequence Diagram in UML Collaboration Diagram in UML etc.

Table 3. Mapping from waterfall to cooking

Waterfall Model	Cooking Process
Require Analyses	Asking to family what they want to eat.
Design and Architecture	Considering how to cook.
Implementation	Cooking
Testing and evaluation	Running taste tests
Run and maintenance	Eating and seasoning by table salt.

Table 4. Results of investigation of analogical think

Question: How do you think of your grasp using the analogical thinking ?	Number of students.
I think that it is easy for me to understand without examples.	4
I hope that more appropriate example with the special terms of software engineering.	18
As the lecture, I think that it is easy to understand by using experiences and example.	62
No response	1

never experienced in this situation. In the leaning of requirement analyses by using our method, students consider the role of buyers (customer) and sellers (software developer) and do self role-play about the transactions. In this situation, buyers are sometimes naive users and novice. They also sometimes give free expression and say whatever their feels as requirements and requests. In such case, students have a good opportunity to consider how the software developers think and do. In this learning process, 16 students answered that they enhanced their understanding of importance of requirement analyses and business aspects of software engineering shown in the Table 5. Other 62 students answered that they could understand the importance of requirement analyses. For the 62 students, we analyzed their answers and became clear that they did not have good knowledge of characteristics of buyers and sellers. To solve the problem, in our education system, it is desirable to include the actual condition of customers and software developers.

Instruction using Anthropomorphic Thinking

In the instruction method based on anthropomorphic thinking, we conducted an actual lecture using the method. The lecture theme was set by UML. UML is the unified modeling language based on multiple diagrams shown the relationships and flows of tasks and data. In UML, it is difficult for students to understand each diagram and its meaning in short time since there are many types of diagram with their roles in system design phase. Particularly, it is difficult for students who have never studied about concept of object-orientation. In the actual lecture of UML, we used our method to teach sequence diagram and collaboration diagram. In the sequence diagram, information system and software consist of multiple objects and each object performs each tasks. For students, the object-orientation is unknown knowledge as their preliminary background. Our anthropomorphic thinking-based instruction method compares objects to human beings. Namely, students consider the modules and objects to persons. Such modules cooperate with each other and they communicate to perform successfully tasks.

Table 5. Results of investigation of self role-playing

Question: How do you think of your grasp using self role-play?	Number of students.
I think that it is easy for me to understand without examples.	7
I think that the business tasks should be shown before the lecture.	62
As the lecture, it is easy to understand by using examples of software company.	16

Concretely, students considered a vender machines. The machine is basically implemented instead of a shop staff. Namely, we can consider how the shop staffs work.

The process of this thinking method is shown in Figure 4. First, students consider that the system can compare to a certain person. Considering this phase, students consider a person who works in the actual world as similar with the system. For example, an auto telling machine is compared to a bank teller, e-learning support system is compared to a teacher, and so on. Second, they consider whether the system can be separated from some parts of modules/objects or not. Tasks done by such people are separated with multiple roles. For example, vender machine's task is mainly divided three parts, checker, stockman, and salesperson. Third, students consider how these people can perform the tasks about selling items. In actual lecture, many students answered that these people should communicate with each other for this case. This means the message passing and serving among objects.

In this instruction method, 60 students answered that they enhanced their grasps about the sequence and collaboration diagram shown in the Table 6.

Result of Investigation after the Lecture

It is an investigation result concerning the person's of attending a lecture understanding when didactics like is used ahead as follows. Tables 4 to 6 show the result of our survey about our proposed educational methods. Those who attended a lecture about 90 percent answered that analogized idea had helped understanding. There were of those of about 70 percent who attended a lecture by the idea that it was able to understand that it first understood the standpoint and the business of the software development company for the self role-playing, and did the self role-playing afterwards. It was answered that understanding had promoted it by having thought that the student of about 75% was oneself information system for a pseudo-human idea at the end.

Follow-Up Investigation

Evaluation in education is difficult to scale in a reproducible fashion since students are relative. To ensure our instruction method, we conducted follow-up investigation. We had questionnaires from each student seven month later after they got the credit of the lecture. Particularly, we asked

Figure 4. Process of anthropomorphic thinking

Figure 4. Process of anthropomorphic thinking

	Checker	⇐	Thinking his/her role
Task →	Stockman	⇐	Thinking his/her role
	Salesperson	⇐	Thinking his/her role

Table 6. Results of investigation of anthropomorphic thinking

Question: Q: Did you enough understand by imagining the ATM machine ?	Number of students.
Yes	60
No	19
Other opinions	5
No response	1

about lifecycle model and sequence diagram in UML. As the result of investigation, students could answer most completely of waterfall model and spiral mode. Regarding the sequence diagram, all students can answer perfectly. Thus, our instruction method has a certain effectiveness of education.

INSTRUCTION SYSTEM

In our system, the importance for learning is the thinking process rather than the learning issues.

Students can generally understand viewing the textbook when they recall a simple learning item. On the other hand, in software development, it is important for students to understand what the learning items mean and what they relate with. Even though students learn the lifecycle model and several learning issues seeing the words in the textbook, most of them fail to enhance their grasp of the learning issues. When the students learn just the system and programming, they drop off existence of actual users and their requirements. Grounds of this system are to eradicate learning issues for students and to train grasping the external situation. Thus, our system provides the way of thinking as well as the direct knowledge of software engineering.

Figure 5 shows an example of interface of the intelligent instruction system. This figure also shows the users' thinking based on analogical dropping with the example of travel planning. Students recognize that this problem is similar with their experiences. After students' viewing and answering questions, the system gives an

Figure 5. Intelligent instruction system 1

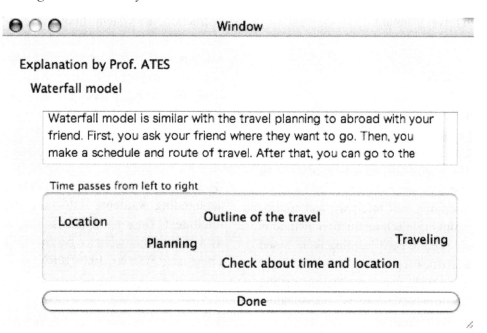

Figure 6. Intelligent instruction system 2

essential question about learning issues. Figure 6 shows the comparison between analogical issues and learning issues. In this display, students can clearly understand that the lifecycle model is quite similar with travel planning.

CONCLUSION

In this paper, we propose a new instruction method based on analogical thinking to develop an intelligent tutoring system in software engineering education. The analogical thinking-based teaching method includes the instruction method based on analogical dropping, self role-play, and anthropomorphic thinking. Each instruction method is appropriately used in each learning issue based on its characteristics of problem. Our preliminary experiments and evaluation shows that our method is effectiveness to enhance learners' understanding and grasp the learning issues.

Our future work includes developing a collaborative tutoring system used by multiple users and makes sure its effectiveness through actual use. When users learn based on discussion-based instruction, the system should have some useful functions that is designed based on psychological analysis. And also, it includes developing extension of the instruction theory and to look-over the application to other special area.

REFERENCES

Baker, S. J. D. R. (2007). Modeling and Understanding Students' Off-Task Behavior in Intelligent Tutoring Systems. *Proceedings of ACM SIGCHI conference on Human Factors in Computing Systems*, 1059-1068.

Behling, R., Behling, C., & Sousa, K. (1996). Software Re-engineering: Concepts and Methodology. *Industrial Management & Data Systems, 96*(6), 3–10. doi:10.1108/02635579610126836

Carbonell, J. G., Larkin, J. H., & Reif, F. (1983). *Towards a General Scientific Reasoning Engine* (Tech. Rep. pp. 445-457). Computer Science Department.

Casado-Lumbreras, C., Colomo-Palacios, R., Gomez-Berbis, M. J., & Garcia-Crespo, A. (2009). Mentoring Programmes: A Study of the Spanish Software Industry. *International Journal of Learning and Intellectual Capital, 6*(3), 293–302. doi:10.1504/IJLIC.2009.025046

Chao, G. T., Walz, P. M., & Gardner, P. D. (1992). Formal and Informal Mentorships: A Comparison on Mentoring Functions and Contrast with Non-mentored Counterparts. *Personnel Psychology, 45*, 619–636.

Colomo-Palacios, R., Gomez-Berbis, M. J., Garcia-Crespo, A., & Puebla-Sánchez, I. (2008). Social Global Repository: Using Semantics and Social Web in Software Projects. *International Journal of Knowledge and Learning, 4*(5), 452–464. doi:10.1504/IJKL.2008.022063

Colomo-Palacios, R., Tovar-Caro, E., Garcia-Crespo, A., & Gomez-Berbis, M. J. (2010). Identifying Technical Competences of IT Professionals. The Case of Software Engineers. *International Journal of Human Capital and Information Technology Professionals, 1*(1), 31–43.

Dewayne, E. P., Adam, A. P., & Lawrence, A. V. (2000). Empirical Studies of Software Engineering. In *Proceedings of International Conference on Software Engineering* (pp. 345-355).

Dewey, J. (1916). *Democracy and Education*. New York: The Macmillan.

Fujimoto, T. (2005). *Imagination of Information Design*. Tokyo, Japan: Pleiades Publisher.

Garcia-Crespo, A., Colomo-Palacios, R., Gomez-Berbis, M. J., & Mencke, M. (2009a). BMR: Benchmarking Metrics Recommender for Personnel issues in Software Development Projects. *International Journal of Computational Intelligence Systems, 2*(3), 257–267. doi:10.2991/ijcis.2009.2.3.7

Garcia-Crespo, A., Colomo-Palacios, R., Gomez-Berbis, M. J., & Paniagua-Martin, F. (2008b). A Case of System Dynamics Education in Software Engineering Courses. *IEEE Multidisciplinary Engineering Education Magazine, 3*(2), 52–59.

Garcia-Crespo, A., Colomo-Palacios, R., Gomez-Berbis, M. J., & Tovar-Caro, E. (2008a). The IT Crowd: Are We Stereotypes? *IT Professional, 10*(6), 46–49. doi:10.1109/MITP.2008.134

Garcia-Crespo, A., Colomo-Palacios, R., Gomez-Berbis, M. J., & Tovar-Caro, E. (2009b). IT Professionals' Competences: High School Students' Views. *Journal of Information Technology Education, 8*, 45–57.

Hartmann, N. (1933). *Das Problem des geistigen Seins: Untersuchgn zur Grundlegung d. Geschichtsphilosophie u. d. Geisteswissenschaften*. Berlin: de Gruyter.

Martin, C. D. (1998). Is computer science a profession? *ACM SIGCSE Bulletin, 30*(2), 7–8. doi:10.1145/292422.296068

Matsuura, S. (2007). Software Engineering Education Based on Practical Software Development Experiments. *Transactions of Information Processing Society of Japan, 48*(8), 2578–259.

Miyake, N., & Masukawa, H. (2000). Relation-making to sensemaking: Supporting college students' constructive understanding with an enriched collaborative note-sharing system. *Fourth international conference of the learning sciences*, 41-47.

Nickerson, R. S., Perkins, D. N., & Smith, E. E. (1985). *The Teaching of Thinking*. Hillsdale, NJ: Lawrence Erlbaum.

Saiedian, H., Bagert, D., & Mead, R. N. (2002). Software Engineering Programs: Dispelling the Myths and Misconceptions. *IEEE Software, 19*(5), 35–41. doi:10.1109/MS.2002.1032852

Shaw, M. (2002). Software Engineering Education: A Roadmap. In *Proceedings of International Conference on Software Engineering* (pp. 371-380).

Trigo, A., Varajão, J., Soto-Acosta, P., Barroso, J., Molina-Castillo, F. J., & Gonzalvez-Gallego, N. (2010). IT Professionals: An Iberian Snapshot. *International Journal of Human Capital and Information Technology Professionals, 1*(1), 61–75.

Chapter 8
Educating IT Professionals Using Effective Online, Pedagogical, and Scheduling Techniques

Jeffrey Hsu
Fairleigh Dickinson University, USA

Karin Hamilton
Fairleigh Dickinson University, USA

John Wang
Montclair State University, USA

ABSTRACT

Information technology professionals comprise an important segment of adult learners seeking a four-year undergraduate degree, and it is important to provide programs that address not only the conceptual and theoretical, but also adult learning needs in terms of career orientation and practicality together with providing real-life applications relevant to the needs of the IT job marketplace. The techniques of employing distance learning, providing modular and practical learning segments, emphasizing adult-oriented learning preferences, engaging users toward learning, and providing appropriate course schedules and sequencing are discussed in the context of an actual adult learner program. This program integrates job and career-oriented needs with that of a well-rounded business education. Examples and illustrations are provided to illustrate how an adult-oriented program was customized to provide needs important to adult learners and IT professionals, with the objective of producing superior and useful learning results.

INTRODUCTION

An evolution in the roles and responsibilities of today's Information Technology (IT) professionals is occurring as employers increasingly view IT as a vehicle to help create a competitive edge in the markets they serve. Companies are looking to their IT professionals to support the development and implementation of strategic initiatives in areas including, but not limited to productivity improvements, streamlining supply chains, aligning and integrating information to create knowledge systems and securing proprietary and increasingly integrated systems (Applegate, Austin, & Soule, 2009; Porter & Millar, 1985). Innovations in computing hardware, software, and networks

DOI: 10.4018/978-1-4666-0924-2.ch008

will further impact the types of expertise needed by companies as new technologies are brought into the market (Koong, Liu, & Liu, 2008). For example, job opportunities for professionals in technical support, network systems and database development as a percentage of total IT employment are growing, with positions in programming slightly decreasing (Information Technology Association of America, 2004).

Technically-skilled individuals, who possess practical skills and are familiar with the intricacies of hardware and software systems, are still highly valued by today's employers. In fact, one critical area of study concerns what kinds of skills are desired and sought after, but are less frequently found among IT professionals, sometimes referred to as the IS/IT skills gap (Kim, Hsu, & Stern, 2006). However, formal education and training are increasingly being viewed by employers as equally important. "Across all NWCET job categories, hiring managers see the combination of previous experience in a related field (46 percent) and a four-year college degree in a related field (41 percent) as the most important preparation for job obtainment" (Information Technology Association of America, 2004). Therefore, knowing which skills are crucial for IT professionals is a critical issue in research literature (Colomo et al., 2010; Trigo et al., 2010), whether coming from formal education or from previous technical training or work experience.

The likely rationale underlying this thinking is that many technically-savvy individuals without a four-year degree are more likely to be self-taught, or have obtained technical job skills through training and/or certification programs, or from on the job experience. As a result, there is likelihood that they typically would lack the overall background and theoretical knowledge base to approach business-oriented and more managerial tasks both holistically and from viewpoint of end users and the organization as a whole. The knowledge gained in a degree program can thereby help to elevate the perspective and critical thinking skills

of technically-skilled individuals beyond solving narrowly defined problems, towards developing the ability to manage more long-term, integrated, and sustainable problems and solutions.

In fact, the need for a formal baccalaureate four-year education in the 21st century goes beyond that of tech-savvy individuals and IT professionals, to encompass a much broader set of students. Beyond traditional secondary and "vocational" schools" the demographics of today's undergraduate population now extend to include older adult students; homemakers returning to the workplace; previously retired persons who desire a second career; and those who desire a career change or have been moved toward change to meet the demand for updated skills in the workplace (National Center for Educational Statistics, 2002).

Most undergraduate university programs are designed to meet the learning preferences and scheduling needs of young, "traditional" high school graduate age students pursuing degrees in preparation for a future career. Adult students, however, pursue degrees for different reasons than their counterparts.

Consequently, educational programs, as well as the tools, curricula, and services designed to address educational needs, should similarly evolve to be appropriate and useful to the new populations they intend to serve. Beyond learning specific skills to complete a job, educational knowledge should be delivered so as to enable adult students to master the problem-solving and critical-thinking skills required of workers in the global economy. This is especially important for IT professionals, who, given the rate of change and the complexities of computing technologies, may focus more on technical skills development, rather than broader goals and abilities required for supervisory or managerial tasks (Information Technology Association of America, 2004).

A study of the means by which university programs can be made more suitable for adults in these areas is the objective of this paper. The intent is to provide ideas and examples of focused methods and techniques that support the educational outcomes needed by adult students, with a particular focus on IT professionals, relating to new or advanced career placement and the acquisition of useful, practical knowledge.

WHO ARE ADULT LEARNERS AND WHY ARE THEY IMPORTANT?

Adult students are increasingly becoming an important market force. According to the NCES, almost half of undergraduate students can be classified under the categories of "non-traditional" or "adult learners" (National Center for Education Statistics, 2002). It is conceivable that very soon the majority of undergraduate students could fall into this category (Horn, 1996). Some of the core characteristics of non-traditional students are that they delayed enrollment (did not enter college after high school; or started and did not finish), are likely to attend school part time, have full-time jobs and careers, and are likely to be married with dependents (National Center for Education Statistics, 2002).

In contrast to traditional students who enroll as the next logical step after high school, 73% of adult non-traditional students attend college for the purposes of career advancement, to improve their knowledge in a subject area, and/or to complete a degree to add to their credentials (U.S. Department of Education, 2002). These aspects help to classify adult learners as a specialized population, together with their educational need for more career and technically oriented content, and their goals of career enhancement and mastering practical (and accompanying conceptual/theoretical) skills.

Adult (or adult learner) students are generally older, and may exhibit less-developed or alternate approaches to learning because of their incomplete educational histories. At the same time, many possess a great deal of professional experience and knowledge, and could benefit from a firmer grounding in a variety of theoretical knowledge

areas and their application to complex real-life challenges found in the workplace. This is especially applicable to IT professionals returning to the classroom who may have been initially hired during the growth of the dot.com era, when practical experience and personal skill in IT were preferred by employers, and who now find themselves in a new job market in which hiring managers favor candidates having a four-year degree in a related field combined with experience (Information Technology Association of America, 2004).

Adult students generally bring to the classroom strong intentions to obtain both short- and long-term value from a learning experience. Many have highly focused career-oriented goals, which make their desire to pursue an education practical and job-based, rather than just the next step in the "schooling" process. If effectively taught, adults can become highly engaged and involved in the learning process, and will seek to master a subject because they understand the benefits provided by enhanced knowledge and its relationship to career performance and advancement. For example, adults tend to ask more questions, demand more class discussion, and seek connections between concepts introduced and practical applications from work. In terms of IT professionals, for example, rather than focusing mainly of technological aspects, adult students can bring experiences from their workplaces, and also share various issues, concerns, and challenges which come about when trying the meet the varying demands of end users, management, and customers.

ADULT LEARNERS AND IT CAREER PROSPECTS

Adults seeking to earn a four-year degree recognize that education is not only desirable, but necessary in today's highly competitive and changing IT global job market. In fact, many future jobs will require higher-level cognitive skills that only a portion of current workers possess (U. S. Bureau of Labor Statistics, 1999). Yet, many programs serving adult learners are conducted by corporate sponsors, rather than by government or educational institutions. In fact, only a portion of existing adult programs are run by traditional colleges and universities, although their number has been increasing. All things considered, there is a shortage of learning opportunities that provide adults with both higher order educational knowledge and advanced analytical and problem-solving skills, which are especially desired by IT employers. Many of these skills are essential for those IT professionals who want to advance in their careers, such as moving from a more technical or staff position, to one with more supervisory or managerial authority.

It is a reality that some, if not many, adult learners may have experienced difficulty in their previous educational work which could impact their new attempts at completing their educations (Knowles, 1984; National Center for Research in Vocational Education, 1987). Yet, adult learners generally exhibit many positive characteristics, including; self-directedness, a desire to immediately apply learned material, a strong practical emphasis, ability to gain experiences related to new learning, and determination to effectively use available time. Ability to think at higher, more critical levels is a strength frequently observed in adult learners. Perry (1970) examined the stages from which students develop critical thinking skills, and Espana (2004) found that adults tend to possess higher levels of thinking; emphasizing contextual relativism (finding supporting information to confirm validity), and the dialectic (handling a problem from different perspectives). This is in contrast to lower levels of thinking including dualism (choosing between right/wrong answers), and multiplicity (considering multiple answers), and more closely associated with traditional undergraduate students. Consequently, adults often expect their instructors to take on

the role of facilitator rather than a lecturer who only imparts concepts and facts (Espana, 2004).

Because the current workplace provides experiences and demands which ultimately shape behavior, the expectations of working adult students can significantly differ from younger, traditional students. These expectations can be related to classroom and course activities, exercises, and tools which employ distance learning and use of technology to supplement the classroom process (Knowles, Holton, & Swanson, 1998; Brookfield, 1991). Workplace behaviors that can translate into classroom preferences include active learning; group-oriented collaboration; solving complex, real-world problems having work-related applications; enhancing decision making; applying experience; and emphasizing practice. Andragogy, the principles and concepts behind teaching adults (Knowles, 1984), provides insight to the unique learning needs of adults. Contrasted to pedagogy, which is defined as the "art and science of teaching children," andragogy emphasizes the need for practicality and application to career-oriented learning. Active learning and self-direction are also critical aspects in that adults need to understand clearly the purpose and rationale of learning something, tend to take much greater personal responsibility, express enthusiasm and eagerness to learn, and are life-centered rather than task-centered (Knowles, 1980; Frey & Alman, 2003).

An important application of Knowles's theory is that feedback, flexibility, and control are most appreciated. This includes not only receiving timely evaluations and being able to understand the value in, and level of what is learned, but also flexible schedules and formats. The fact that learning is intertwined with work and family responsibilities needs to be recognized (Knowles, 1977).

Other related theories which provide insight into adult learners include social context of learning, perspective transformation, critical reflection and transformative learning. The social context of learning theory (Wenger, 1998) emphasizes the fact that many activities can be structured to constitute a "community of practice" involving various individuals in the shared task of learning. Communities of practice can provide academic and social support; as well as address other adult learner needs previously identified (Phelps, 2002)

Perspective transformation (Mezirow, 1990), focuses on viewpoint changes in the learner which can occur through the process of critical reflection and thought. An example of this might a student's initially resistant and negative attitude toward computers which, after further use and discovery, could lead to new appreciation of its utility. Closely related is the concept of critical reflection, in that deliberation can help to bring about new perspectives in the learner (Mezirow, 1997; Frey & Alman, 2003; Cercone, 2008). Transformative learning theory describes the growth that can occur when a student armed with new perspectives approaches a task or skill with greater understanding and insight (Mezirow, 1997; Mezirow, 1990).

Taken from these perspectives, critical reflection, and transformative learning, can play an important role in the education and career development of IT professionals. The ability to better understand the role of information technology throughout an organization, appreciate the difficulties that non-technical colleagues face, and gain insight into the importance of "soft" skills can all have a positive impact on the development of professions in this field (Noll & Wilkins, 2002).

In summary, motivation and interest of adult learners can be improved by providing self-directed, active and flexible course assignments that are more relevant to work and life responsibilities. Rather than merely accumulating new information, adult students thrive when learning provides opportunities to broaden their perspectives, apply and practice new knowledge, tap into collective wisdom, and improve critical thinking skills.

ADULT LEARNER CLASS ENVIRONMENTS

In traditional classes, most students are young and lack context, which requires the instructor to serve as an authority figure. Students are lectured to and then expected to memorize facts for objective tests with the support of textbooks and other printed materials. There is frequently an emphasis on the one "right" answer, with a de-emphasis on discussion.

Transformation from a traditional classroom environment to one which better suited to adult learners, including those in the IT field, should include facilitation and support for more engaged students who participate, offer arguments, debate, and work in groups to solve problems for which there may be multiple solutions, and produce results which may be a beyond the knowledge and expertise of any single individual in the group. Group work would be typical, and a level of engagement and interest associated with higher levels of critical thinking can be developed. Project ideas could be initiated by students, or at least selected from several choices, rather than solely developed by the instructor. Student performance assessment would remain a primary responsibility of the instructor; however, assessments from other students or team members can also be utilized (Hamilton, 2002).

For the instructor, the experience of teaching adult learners can be both interesting and challenging. Some specific pedagogical techniques which can be employed include replacing lecture with student-instructor and student-student dialog, using structured multiple-part assignments, replacing case studies with real-life, "present time" assignments, and emphasizing application over memorization. Using project-based assignments rather than objective tests has been found to be more attuned to adult student learning goals (Hamilton, 2002).

DISTANCE LEARNING AND ADULT LEARNER IT PROFESSIONALS

Distance learning (also online and e-learning) can be defined as students using computing and communications technologies, interactivity, and also asynchronous communications to allow them to learn remotely, without the need for face to face class sessions (Beck et al., 2004; Wahlstrom, Williams, & Shea, 2003) .

Online learning can play a significant role in adult-based programs for IT professionals. Adult learners would likely find online learning highly appealing since they are accustomed to using technology through their jobs, and therefore should adapt well to online coursework. Concurrently, their drive to successfully complete their degrees would facilitate the proper and focused use of online tools, which often require initiative and self-directed concentration. Because DL enables anytime-anywhere communications, it is also conducive to the needs of adult learner students who work in the IT industry.

Several fundamental differences exist between traditional classroom learning formats and Internet-based asynchronous learning. Lectures, discussions, and in-class exercises form the basic elements of traditional classroom learning, and in general, delivery of content is through face-to-face communication. This directly contrasts to online asynchronous learning, where the Internet and online portals are used, and the instructor and students are not necessarily interacting in the same place and time. Instead, they can log in when needed to enter or retrieve information, respond to other posts, and otherwise participate in the course. The fact that some or all of the classroom activities can continue beyond physical face-to-face meetings throughout the week is considered a positive by students who must balance work, school, and family responsibilities. Chaffee (1998) suggested that adult students tend to expect flexibility, convenience, and ease of access, and have no qualms about seeking out these in educational programs. Greater interest and desire for online interaction is related both to the greater work hours and a student's distance from campus (Perez Cerijo, 2006).

Distance learning can be implemented in a number of ways. Some courses can be run completely online, with no face to face sessions. The instructor develops the course content, manages the interaction, and runs the class using e-mail, message boards, and real-time online sessions. This option is best for students who are geographically dispersed, and either have difficulty or no desire to attend on-campus sessions.

Hybrid distance learning provides an alternative that combines face-to-face instruction with interaction outside of class through the Internet and can be implemented in a variety of formats. One could deliver introductory class sessions in a traditional face to face format, followed by online interaction. As an option, both modes could alternate throughout the course. In essence, it allows for the "best of both worlds" where there is classroom interaction and also the ability to continue the discussions and studies outside of the classroom.

Hybrid distance learning is likely to be suitable for IT professionals, as they are familiar with or have previously used these kinds of technologies. This approach also supports the development of "soft skills" which have been found in previous research to be important to career success, yet in many IT professionals tend to be weak or non-existent (Noll & Wilkins, 2002).

A course management system (CMS) such as WebCT or Blackboard is frequently used to support the online portion, since both offer workspaces from which instructors and students can run activities and present information online. Specific tools used may include e-mail, synchronous chat, threaded discussions, message boards, and also online lectures, tutorials, and quizzes (Martyn & Bash, 2002). Online applications can also include m-learning (mobile learning), which supports learning using mobile handheld devices, and the use of learning management systems (LMS) (Seng & Lin, 2004).

Techniques which address the applicability of distance learning for adult learners include self-direction, authentic activities, collaboration; and effectively using discussion boards to provide opportunities for critical reflection.

Given their time constraints and also because most of their time is spent off campus, adult learners need to be self-directed, which is described as being "active participants in their own learning process" (Zimmerman, 2001). Students must take initiative in formulating their own learning goals, selecting materials for learning, and developing strategies for solving a problem (Knowles, 1975).

Effective self-directed online course activities require the instructor to guide and coach students through the learning and also provide meaningful examples for the concepts presented (Young, 2006). While there may be a preference expressed by adult students studying online to work independently, feedback is also critical to the learning process (Knowles, 1980).

Because adult learners seek an education that blends concepts, theory, and application, Reeves, Herrington, and Oliver (2002) argue for the development of authentic classroom activities, which tend to move away from teacher-centered "instructivist" approaches toward those which emphasize "constructivist" learning.

Instructivist, or the more traditional, behaviorist approach is geared towards specific performance often evaluated using objective testing formats. Learning happens when skills are taught and presented in a logical structure or method. As such, instructional activities are designed with the purpose of providing a means for practice, and in such a manner that repeated practice will result mastering a skill.

The constructivist approach is more in line with authentic activities, or those which are complex, constructive, and collaborative; and used to solve more real-life, application-oriented, and "authen-

tic" problems. Of particular relevance to this is the contribution of collaboration through groups, where several minds work together to solve a problem rather than emphasizing individual learning (Reeves, Herrington, & Oliver, 2002; Phelps, 2002). The development of group work and collaborative skills fall into the category of critical "soft" skills which are desired by employers in the IT field (Noll & Wilkins, 2002).

Authentic learning activities provide real-world relevance, opportunities to tackle ill-defined and complex tasks, the ability to de-compose a large problem into smaller steps, and to expand the various resources used in problem-solving. These are what IT professionals need to help them move away from a technical, narrow, single-solution mindset to a more holistic perspective. In addition, these tasks would provide them with greater insight into the problem and challenges that end users and customers face, which in the long run would help them to do their jobs better (Reeves, Herrington, & Oliver, 2002).

Often, more authentic tasks are difficult to represent online. It is easy, for example, to put text up on a screen, but far more challenging to create multimedia presentations which explain complex tasks (Powers, 2005). One means of supporting the learning of a new concept is to offer worked-out examples and demonstrations which can help a student to better understand the specific steps in that kind of problem-solving. This can provide a helpful supplement to improve student confidence and independence in problem-solving (Powers, 2005).

Online portals and related technologies can provide support for several design requirements of authentic learning activities, by providing a diverse range of multimedia tools (documents, graphics, video, links, etc.) and the facility to group students together in collaborative activity using e-mail, discussion boards, real-time chat, or workspaces where documents and other deliverables can be shared. Use of hyperlinks and other non-linear navigation allows students to follow a thought or idea more effectively than the linear approach inherent in most printed and traditional resources. Ability to publish information using weblogs or to have a group collaboratively edit and update information using wikis would be helpful. These tools could help to promote more critical reflection and thought, and also to perhaps bring in the thoughts, idea, and critiques by external experts as well as the instructor.

Another important aspect of authentic activities is collaborative learning, which is defined as "working in a group of two or more to achieve a common goal, while respecting each individual's contribution to the whole (McInerney & Robert, 2004). Higher levels of achievement, connections, and positive psychological factors arise from the collaborative approach, rather than from a competitive or individual approach (Johnson, Johnson, & Smith, 1991; Smith, 1995). Higher order thinking, socialization, and the ability to engage in critical thinking can be realized (Jegede, 2002; Schultz, 2003). Reduced anxiety, increased levels of student feedback, and greater levels of reflection are also cited as benefits.

Effective group online collaboration typically includes individual accountability, whereby each member feels responsible and contributes to the team's output. There should also be a sense of camaraderie within the group; the ability to come to a consensus without diminishing the contributions of anyone; clear instructions about a project or assignment from the instructor; and a proactive team leader who can manage the group and produce positive results and outcomes. Negative factors include the predominance of technical problems and difficulties in communicating through writing, which is the primary format for most online communications (McInerney & Robert, 2004).

IT professionals would likely bring to online collaboration a slightly different skill set; that is, strength in working through technical problems, but a potential gap in written and group communication aspects. Discussion forums generally provide a useful platform for threaded discussions on topics that can be introduced and where dialog is conducted in an organized manner. Through discourse and ultimately learning among participants, discussion forums can help build learning communities (Garrison, 1993). Dialog has been found to be an effective learning tool from the perspective of andragogy (Knowles, 1990), critical evaluation of ideas, and the creation of new ideas (Bloom, 1956). Discussion forums can also facilitate learning new ideas by relating concepts to previous knowledge (Anderson & Garrison, 1995). Many aspects of what makes face-to-face discussions effective can also be found in online discussions (Hiltz, 1990). The social aspect of collaboration and discussion also brings about results in learning which are claimed to be superior to those trying to learn a topic alone (Vygotsky, 1978). Since adults bring a wealth of personal experience to a course, it can be suggested that discussions among adult students is especially useful in sharing knowledge and allowing all participants to learn (Kramlinger & Huberty, 1990).

An inherent problem experienced in discussion forums is the lack of visual clues which are easily noted in face-to-face meetings. In addition, students who are timid, lack interest or knowledge on the subject, or have difficulty in expressing themselves clearly in writing may not participate actively in discussions (Nonnecke & Preece, 2001). Allowing for anonymous participation and assigning credit or grades for participation has been found to improve participation rates.

In summary, the use of distance learning and associated technologies and application seem particularly suitable for adult learner IT professionals, since one of the factors which can often hinder or slow progress in using distance learning is the lack of familiarity with (or resistance to) the technologies used to support class and academic work. The busy schedules and demands placed on IT professionals also make their ability to attend numerous classes on campus challenging. Distance learning can provide an ideal solution, especially if used in a hybrid modality, since it would provide an extension of the learning process outside the classroom and also provide opportunities for soft skill development.

INTENSIVE COURSE SCHEDULING

The length of time needed to obtain a degree for adult IT students who take courses part-time only may be twice as long, or even longer. This can be due to class scheduling constraints, lack of availability of certain courses in certain semesters, and also conflicts between taking courses which are offered only during certain terms and in certain time slots.

The extended time needed to complete a program is perceived negatively by adult learners, and could potentially decrease persistence, resulting in the potential loss of a student to the educational institution.

One possible solution is the use of class formats which are accelerated and intensive, and result in equivalent course instruction time (contact hours), with shorter calendar terms. Course terms can be shortened from 5 to 10 weeks by expanding individual class sessions from 3 to 8 hours. Benefits from this approach include longer sessions that would allow a greater depth of learning, interaction, and critical thinking; as well as faster completion of the course.

Because intensive schedules tend to be associated with evening and weekend programs, they have been the target of resistance from some faculty who perceive them as a vehicle for sacrificing academic standards in the interest of student desires, preferences and convenience (Daniel, 2000; Scott & Conrad, 1991; Scott, 1996; Scott, 1995; Scott, 1994). However, research conducted on the results from full-term versus intensive formats suggests that this not necessarily true. Serdyukov et al. (2003) found that compressed formats, even with courses spanning as little as one month, produced learning outcomes comparable, or even superior to, full semester courses.

This may be due, in part, to the fact that most compressed programs use a sequential scheduling approach in place of a parallel scheduling approach. Students take one intensive course at a time, followed by another, rather than taking several longer-term courses concurrently. Since each new course is not started until the previous one is completed, students can concentrate on mastering course material, rather than be distracted and challenged by the multitasking involved in managing several different courses simultaneously. Other argued benefits of this approach include higher levels of understanding, enhanced skill development, and greater levels of immersion and concentration (Espana, 2004; Scott & Conrad, 1992; Csikszentmihalyi, 1982). By necessity, intensive courses would need to move beyond lecture-only formats and apply different pedagogical methods, procedures, and processes. Instructors must also clearly identify expectations and requirements in advance, provide prompt feedback to students, and maintain detailed schedules and deadlines for assignments and course activities (Espana, 2004; Serdyukov et al., 2003). Group projects and collaboration are also found to be effective for intensive courses as they provide opportunities for additional discussion, reinforcement and multiple perspectives in mastering concepts (Singh & Martin, 2004).

Given the more rapid pace of an intensive scheduling format, there is typically a need to continue learning outside of the classroom, and this is where the use of electronic communication technologies can help. Employing aspects of distance learning, use of e-mail, computer conferencing, and Internet based course management systems could help to extend the learning process outside of the classroom (Wlodkowski, 2003).

BLOCK SCHEDULING

The scheduling and sequencing of courses is frequently regarded as an administrative detail having little significant relevance to learning. A review of research in this area however, has revealed that scheduling can have an impact on student success and improve learning outcomes. Traditionally the realm of high schools, block scheduling (Cawelti, 1994) is a format which allocates larger blocks of time (usually 60 minutes or more) to improve depth and intensity of learning. Use of block scheduling can bring about a greater involvement of students in the learning process, and the opportunity to use a wider variety of instructional techniques, activities, and exercises (Gaubatz, 2003; Hottenstein & Malatesta, 1993; O'Neil, 1995). Properly implemented block schedules have resulted in higher grades, better relationships among students and with instructors, and a higher and deeper level of learning overall (Gaubatz, 2003; Reid, 1995; Canady & Rettig, 1995).

MODULAR AND PROJECT-BASED LEARNING

Because adult learners desire work-related and practical emphasis in their programs, and employers of IT professionals have an expressed preference for hiring individuals with experience or degrees in a related field, bundling lessons and presenting information in the form of modules may better meet these objectives. Modules typically are set up as a "package" which contains background information, resources, relevant theory, topics, assignments and exercises, which facilitate exploration of subject matter in a more experiential, "real world" way.

To be effective, modules should be well structured and competency based, with objectives and tasks outlined and anchored in the goal of helping students apply knowledge, discover a new insight,

transfer learning to a new setting and/or acquire a new skill in a reasonable time period. Assignments and exercises should foster student understanding through experience and discovery by applying and reinforcing material taught in class or presented through in-course notes and resources (Hamilton, 2002). A modular instructional approach forms the cornerstone of the Global Business Management (GBM) program, and is outlined in the next section of this paper.

THE FDU GLOBAL BUSINESS MANAGEMENT PROGRAM: A CASE STUDY

The Global Business Management (GBM) program was designed to allow adult students to earn an undergraduate degree from the Silberman College of Business, Fairleigh Dickinson University (FDU), within four years through a "hybrid" DL approach. The program is specifically designed for adult learner students incorporating the concepts and theories previously discussed, as well as the practical emphasis associated with the expressed needs of IT employers who value practical experience in combination with attaining a four-year degree in a related field (Information Technology Association of America, 2004)

HOW DID GBM START?

The constant challenges of changing market conditions formed the impetus to assess issues relating to FDU's part time undergraduate business program, which was largely comprised of adult learners. Focus groups revealed that adults had specific educational needs which were not being met. Weeknight class schedules often conflicted with business and family obligations, the learning environment where both traditional and adult learners studied together in the same classroom did not work well, it frequently took more than four years to complete a degree, and only limited financial aid was available to part-time students.

After examining a number of approaches, the innovative design elements of the college's Executive MBA program, where retention was consistently high (above 95%), were incorporated into an accelerated undergraduate format. Specific program elements included intense courses designed for adult learners; evening and weekend scheduling; a blend of theory and practice; and the use of block and intensive scheduling which not only facilitated earlier completion, but qualified some students for financial aid.

Launched in spring 2001, the 130 credit GBM program provides students with the opportunity to earn the B.S. degree in Management, with a concentration in Global Business Administration. Although a great deal of commitment from students is required, the emphasis on andragogy and practical application of educational knowledge has facilitated highly motivated adult students in completing their undergraduate degrees.

Employing a hybrid DL instructional model geared to the strengths and interests of adult learners, the benefits of both technology and classroom interaction were combined into the course experience. Reduced time spent in the classroom was replaced by an increased emphasis on asynchronous online interaction among both students and the instructor throughout the duration of the course (Garnham & Kaleta, 2002; Young, 2002). Support for this approach was found in the concept that adult learners are self-directed, more independent, and can benefit from the flexibility of asynchronous learning (Thompson, 1988). Moreover, because of higher motivation, discipline, and time management compared with traditional college students, the hybrid instructional model would work best (Koohang & Durante, 1998).

Intensive courses are offered on Friday evenings and Saturdays, generally scheduled over 7 weeks instead of the usual 15 week semester in a block format of three different modules that utilize varying levels of face to face instruction together with hybrid distance learning. Students may reduce the credits taken in any given semester to meet family or work obligations.

Courses in the same general subject area are scheduled sequentially and configured so that GBM students take no more than 3 courses at any given time; ideally under the guidance of the same professor. This allows students to immerse themselves in a topic and for professors to reinforce key concepts from one course into the next. Within this framework, the use of Guided Independent Learning (GIL) modules as an instructional tool is encouraged.

GUIDED INDEPENDENT LEARNING: THE CONCEPT BEHIND GBM

Guided Independent Learning (GIL) uses a modular approach to course content, with an orientation towards real-world applications; instructors who serve as "mentors" rather than "lecturers;" and evaluation based more on application and performance rather than memorization. Design of GIL-based instruction modules is guided by research indicating that collaborative project-based assignments can bring about active engagement in learning which helps to improve retention of the information studied, develop adults' higher-order learning skills, and enable students to better synthesize various parts into a cohesive whole (Hafner & Ellis, 2004; Sloffer et al., 1999; Dillenbourg et al., 1996).

One way to understand the differences in technique of traditional vs. GIL-based instruction is to examine the sequence of steps that are undertaken in delivering knowledge. In a typical traditional classroom course, students are asked to read from a text before coming to class, then attend class and listen to a lecture while perhaps answering questions on what was covered.

GIL instruction requires students to independently complete a given assignment using the textbook, Internet, and other resources. Asynchronous conferencing (i.e., Blackboard) is used to review, further clarify, and develop the assignment. Students may subsequently work in teams to share knowledge and improve the submission, as needed. Finished assignments are presented in class for further discussion and analysis. Finally, students incorporate feedback received in class from the instructor or other students. This may include a preparing a revision of the assignment, completing additional work, or doing a new, additional assignment that builds upon what was learned.

The instructor is expected to be actively engaged throughout this learning process. Using online tools, the instructor first clarifies the requirements of an assignment, points to additional resources and supporting material, responds to questions, engages in discussion, offers encouragement, and poses challenge questions to help develop a deeper level of analysis and higher quality result. In the student or group presentation phase, the instructor will react to the content of the work and add feedback that supplements understanding with theoretical knowledge, lecturing where appropriate.

Two courses are examined below, to better understand how GIL (Guided Independent Learning) modules can be implemented. The first, College Writing, is an example of a course which would be helpful to adult learner students from the IT field, since the need to develop better writing, communications, and "soft skills" are paramount. The second approaches a functional business field, marketing, emphasizing practical situations and problems with an understanding of the user's perspective, while at the same time developing skills in collaboration and project management (Noll & Wilkins, 2002).

GIL: GENERAL EDUCATION--COLLEGE WRITING

ENGL 1101 College Writing Workshop is a first semester course which focuses on academic essay writing and is designed to help move students to a higher-order level of thinking required to successfully complete college-level work.

Using a GIL-based approach to improve student analytical writing abilities, students are initially required to find and email to the instructor, an article having unfamiliar subject matter, more challenging vocabulary, or an advanced writing style.

The instructor then selects one and emails it to the entire class. Students read the assigned article in advance of class, and in the next meeting, are challenged to explain/ evaluate/ question critically what was written. After the class, students individually write a reaction to the discussion, using factual examples to back their impressions/ opinions.

Class time is devoted primarily to discussion and lecture that supports/ reinforces skill building. The instructor utilizes asynchronous conferencing to check student progress, answer questions, engage critical thinking, provide encouragement, and keep students focused.

In the case of IT professionals, this course would help to develop analytical thinking, strengthen written and oral communication, and develop related abilities considered to be "critical skills" for IT professionals (Noll & Wilkins, 2002).

GIL: UPPER LEVEL BUSINESS (MARKETING)

MGMT 3360 Direct, Database and Interactive Marketing explores use of the Internet to accomplish the traditional advertising and public relations functions of creating an image, as well as building a website to achieve the sale of a product or service. The course builds upon theories of how one might effectively frame a message, target, communicate and interact with a specific audience.

One of the GIL-based modules for this course requires students to initially complete an individual assignment addressing an actual problem faced by a PR firm which is graded and subsequently used as the basis of group discussion where solutions/insights are shared. The final solutions developed by student teams are written up and displayed in the classroom.

The instructor then critiques solutions by challenging the thinking of each group and supplying new understanding through lecture, as needed. The next steps have students reviewing solutions recommended by an actual PR firm and given data on its results, followed by class discussion comparing student solutions with the actual solution. Students may defend their positions, debate relevant issues, seek clarification, and probe for additional insights regarding the solutions.

This course helps to develop the skills of students, including IT professionals, in some of the critical IT "soft skills" including collaboration and teamwork, managing projects, and being able to present ideas, both verbally and in writing. All of these are considered important to the success of professionals in the IT profession (Noll & Wilkins, 2002), together with the focused knowledge gained about effective marketing, advertising, and public relations.

FUTURE TRENDS

The development and use of Web 2.0 and constructivist/interactive technologies can be areas for continued future development. The unique features and benefits of weblogs, wikis, podcasts, and related technologies can be investigated to support adult learner education (Hsu, 2007). A greater emphasis on the proper training of instructors to more effectively teach adult learners, using

authentic and career/real-life applications, is also an area to focus further efforts and emphasis.

DISCUSSION AND CONCLUSION

The percentage of IT workers who will return to college as adult, non-traditional students is expected to increase, driven by strong global competition and the evolving role of information technology. Increasingly, employers will seek both technology and organization-driven solutions to help gain a competitive advantage in their markets. Using technology to gain productivity, redefining the value proposition and how it might be delivered, streamlining and integrating operations with an eye on overcoming complexity, and proactively addressing national security priorities are offered as some, but not all, of the identified roles that IT professionals will be expected to assume. To meet these challenges, employers will seek IT workers who possess not only practical experience, but also the higher-level cognitive skills that are typically developed in a four-year college degree (Information Technology Association of America, 2004).

Concurrently, those who seek to effectively teach the increasing number of IT professionals and other adult learners will find both challenge and opportunity, given the significant differences in learning approaches and needs between traditional undergraduate students and their adult counterparts.

Because traditional undergraduate students are young (18-21) and often lack experience and context, especially with regard to work and career orientation, it is understandable that most courses have been designed to build context, utilizing a professor/expert as the cornerstone of a classroom experience that includes lecture, note-taking, memorization and objective testing. In contrast, adult learners (including IT professionals) are likely to have significant practical and life experience, bringing to the classroom an enriched context, varying perspectives, technological savvy, and more advanced cognitive abilities. They also frequently bring a unique set of goals and personal obstacles that must be addressed, and knowledge gaps that must be closed. These differences were discussed in detail in this paper, followed by a discussion of important theories that lend insight to principles and concepts behind teaching adults, and how adults learn.

The implications which can be drawn from research in adult learning provide insight into important pedagogical considerations and issues including adult student perspectives, educational objectives, cognitive abilities, focus, and the emerging role of instructor as facilitator rather than as expert. Methods and techniques which have been identified as being effective for adult learners were also discussed and include developing assignments in real-time that require application of theory to practice and enhancement of problem-solving skills; the calculated use of distance learning to reinforce content, closing individual knowledge gaps, providing an opportunity for additional dialogue beyond the classroom; blocking and intensifying course schedules to allow adult learners to focus on only one or two content areas at a given time; and sequencing courses to reinforce key concepts and build upon new knowledge.

Although additional work needs to be done in this area, some new pedagogical approaches that have been found to provide greater benefit, satisfaction, and applicability to adult learner needs (including those of IT professionals), were offered by FDU's Global Business Management program. It is anticipated that the departure from traditional teaching methods and transition of the instructor's role from expert to coach will not only positively impact adult learners, but result in a more positive and enriched teaching experience for professors and instructors.

As the IT field continues to grow and bring about new developments at a frantic, lightning pace, the need for IT professionals who possess a well rounded background will intensify. Individuals with the capability to address issues from the technical to the managerial, all the way to that of the enterprise and industry will be in increasing demand. By providing an educational experience tailored to the specific backgrounds and needs of adult learners including those from the IT profession, it is possible to produce professionals who have the educational knowledge, broadened perspectives, and enhanced soft-skills to handle the challenges of today's complex global business environment.

REFERENCES

Anderson, T., & Garrison, D. R. (1995). Critical thinking in distance education: Developing critical communities in an audio teleconference context. *Higher Education*, *29*, 183–199. doi:10.1007/BF01383838

Applegate, L. M., Austin, R. D., & Soule, D. L. (2009). *Corporate Information Strategy and Management* (8th ed.). New York: McGraw-Hill.

Beck, P., Kung, M., Park, Y., & Yang, S. (2004). E-learning architecture: challenges and mapping of individuals in an internet-based pedagogical interface. *International Journal of Innovation and Learning*, *1*(3), 279–292. doi:10.1504/IJIL.2004.004884

Bloom, B. (1956). *The Taxonomy of educational objectives: Classification of educational goals handbook 1: The cognitive domain*. New York: McKay Press.

Brookfield, S. (1991). The development of critical reflection in adulthood. *New Education*, *13*(1), 39–48.

Canady, R., & Rettig, M. (1995). The power of innovative scheduling. *Educational Leadership*, *53*(3), 4–10.

Cawelti, G. (1994). *High School Restructuring: a national study*. Arlington, VA: Educational Research Service.

Cercone, K. (2008). Characteristics of adult learners with implications for online learning design. *AACE Journal*, *16*(2), 137–159.

Chaffee, J. (1998). *Critical thinking: The cornerstone of remedial education*. Paper presented at the Conference on Replacing Remediation in Higher Education, Stanford University, Stanford CA.

Colomo-Palacios, R., Tovar-Caro, E., Garcia-Crespo, A., & Gomez-Berbis, M. J. (2010). Identifying Technical Competences of IT Professionals. The Case of Software Engineers. *International Journal of Human Capital and Information Technology Professionals*, *1*(1), 31–43.

Csikszentmihalyi, M. (1982). *Beyond boredom and anxiety*. San Francisco, CA: Jossey and Bass.

Daniel, E. L. (2000). A review of time shortened courses across disciplines. *College Student Journal*, *34*, 298–308.

Dillenbourg, P., Baker, M., Blaye, A., & O'Malley, C. (1996). The Evolution of research on Collaborative Learning . In Spada, E., & Reiman, P. (Eds.), *Learning in humans and machine: Towards an interdisciplinary learning science* (pp. 189–221). Oxford, UK: Elsevier.

Espana, J. (2004). Teaching a research-oriented, graduate global marketing course to adult learners in a one-month format. *Journal of American Academy of Business*, *4*(1-2), 418.

Frey, B., & Alman, S. (2003). Applying adult learning theory to the online classroom. *New Horizons in Adult Education*, *17*(1), 4–12.

Garnham, C., & Kaleta, R. (2002). Introduction to hybrid courses. *Teaching with Technology Today, 8*(6).

Garrison, D. R. (1993). A cognitive constructivist view of distance education: An analysis of Teaching and learning assumptions. *Distance Education*, *14*(2), 199–211. doi:10.1080/0158791930140204

Gaubatz, N. (2003). Course scheduling formats and their impact on student learning. *National Teaching and Learning Forum*, *12*(1), 1–7.

Hafner, W., & Ellis, T. J. (2004, January 5-8). Project-Based, Asynchronous Collaborative Learning. In *Proceedings of the 37th Hawaii International Conference on System Sciences*, Waikoloa, HI.

Hamilton, K. C. (2002). *Teaching adult learners: A supplemental manual for faculty teaching in the GBM program at FDU*. Madison, NJ: FDU.

Hiltz, S. R. (1990). Evaluating the virtual classroom . In Harasim, L. (Ed.), *Online education* (pp. 134–184). New York: Praeger.

Horn, L. (1996). *Nontraditional Undergraduates*. Washington, DC: U.S. Department of Education.

Hottenstein, D., & Malatesta, C. (1993). Putting a school in gear with intensive scheduling. *The High School Magazine*, *1*(2), 28–29.

Hsu, J. (2007). Innovative Technologies for Education and Learning: Education and Knowledge-Oriented Applications of Blogs, Wikis, Podcasts, and More. *International Journal of Information and Communication Technology Education*, *3*(3), 70–89.

Information Technology Association of America. (2004, September). In *Proceedings of the Adding Value…Growing Careers: Annual Workforce Development Study,* Arlington, VA.

Jegede, O. (2002). Facilitating and sustaining interest through an on-line distance peer-tutoring system in a cooperative learning environment. *Virtual University Gazette*, 35-45.

Johnson, D., Johnson, R., & Smith, K. (1991). *Active learning: cooperation in the college classroom*. Edina, MN: Interaction Book Company.

Kim, Y., Hsu, J., & Stern, M. (2006). An Update on the IS/IT Skills Gap. *Journal of Information Systems Education, 17*(4), 395–402.

Knowles, M. (1975). *Self-directed learning: A guide for learners and teachers*. Englewood Cliffs, NJ: Prentice-Hall.

Knowles, M. (1977). *The modern practice of adult education, andragogy versus pedagogy* (8th ed.). New York: Association Press.

Knowles, M. (1980). Malcolm Knowles on 'how do you get people to be self-directed learners?'. *Training and Development Journal, 34*(5), 96–99.

Knowles, M. (1984). *Andragogy in action: Applying modern principles of adult education*. San Francisco, CA: Jossey Bass.

Knowles, M. (1990). *The adult learner: A neglected species* (4th ed.). Houston, TX: Gulf Publishing.

Knowles, M., Holton, E., & Swanson, R. (1998). *The adult learner* (5th ed.). Houston, TX: Gulf Publishing.

Koohang, A., & Durante, A. (1998). Adapting the Traditional Face-to-Face Instructional Approaches to On-line Teaching & Learning. In [Stillwater, OK: IACIS.]. *Proceedings of International Association for Computer Information Systems, 1998,* 83–92.

Kramlinger, T., & Huberty, T. (1990). Behaviorism versus Humanism. *Training and Development Journal, 44*(12), 41–45.

Lifetime Learning, 14, 49-64.

Martyn, M., & Bash, L. (2002, October 9-12). Creating new meanings in leading education. In *Proceedings of the Twenty-Second National Conference on Alternative and External Degree Programs for Adults*, Pittsburgh, PA.

McInerney, J., & Robert, T. (2004). Collaborative or cooperative learning? In Roberts, T. S. (Ed.), *Online collaborative learning: theory and practice* (pp. 203–214). Hershey, PA: IGI Global.

Mezirow, J. (1990). *Fostering critical reflection in adulthood*. San Francisco, CA: Jossey Bass.

Mezirow, J. (1997). Transformative learning. *New Directions for Adult and Continuing Education, 74,* 5–12. doi:10.1002/ace.7401

Morris, L. V., Xu, H., & Finnegan, C. L. (2005). Roles of Faculty in Teaching Asynchronous Undergraduate Courses. *Journal of Asynchronous Learning Networks, 9*(1), 65–82.

National Center for Education Statistics. (2002). *Nontraditional undergraduates (NCES Rep.)*. Washington, DC: NCES.

National Center for Research in Vocational Education. (1987). *Report on vocational education*. Berkeley, CA: NCRVE.

Noll, C. L., & Wilkins, M. (2002). Critical Skills of IS Professionals: A Model for Curriculum Development. *Journal of Information Technology Education, 1*(3), 143–154.

Nonnecke, B., & Preece, J. (2001). Why Lurkers Lurk. In *Proceedings of the AMCIS Conference*, Boston. Atlanta, GA: AIS.

O'Neil, J. (1995). Finding time to learn. *Educational Leadership, 53*(3), 11–15.

Perez Cereijo, M. (2006). Attitude as predictor of success in online training. *International Journal on E-Learning, 5*(4), 623–639.

Perry, W. G. (1970). *Forms of intellectual and ethical development in the college years: A*

Phelps, R. (2002, July 11-13). A constructivist approach to professional development in ICT Leadership. In *Proceedings of the ICEC 2002 Conference.*

Porter, M. E., & Millar, V. E. (1985, July/August). How information gives you competitive advantage. *Harvard Business Review*, 149–174.

Powers, M. J. (2005). *Effective online learning: recognizing e-learnability.* PAACE Journal of.

Reeves, T. C., Herrington, J., & Oliver, R. (2002). Authentic activities and online learning. In Goody, A., Herrington, J., & Northcote, M. (Eds.), *Quality conversations: Research and Development in Higher Education* (*Vol. 25*, pp. 562–567). Milperra, Australia: HERDSA.

Reid, L. (1995). *Perceived Effects of Block Scheduling on the Teaching of English (No. ED382950).* Washington, DC: ERIC.

scheme. New York: Holt, Rinehart, and Winston.

Schulz, B. (2003). Collaborative learning in an online environment: will it work for teacher training? In *Proceedings of the 14th Annual Society for Information Technology and Teacher Education International Conference* (pp. 503-504). Charlottesville, VA: AACE.

Scott, P. (1995). Learning experiences in intensive and semester-length classes: Student voices and. experiences. *College Student Journal, 29*(2), 207–213.

Scott, P. (1996). Attributes of High-Quality Intensive Course Learning Experiences: Student. Voices and Experiences. *College Student Journal, 30*(1), 69–77.

Scott, P., & Conrad, C. (1991). *A critique of intensive courses and an agenda for research.* Washington, DC: ERIC.

Scott, P. A. (1994). A comparative study of students' learning experiences in intensive and semester-length courses and the attributes of high-quality intensive and semester course learning experiences. In *Proceedings of the Meeting of the North American Association of Summer Sessions,* Portland, OR (pp. 370-498). Washington, DC: ERIC.

Seng, J., & Lin, S. (2004). A mobility and knowledge-centric e-learning application design method. *International Journal of Innovation and Learning, 1*(3), 293–311. doi:10.1504/IJIL.2004.004885

Singh, P., & Martin, L. R. (2004). Accelerated Degree Programs: Assessing Student Attitudes and Opinions. *Journal of Education for Business, 79*(5), 299–305. doi:10.3200/JOEB.79.5.299-305

Sloffer, S. J., Dueber, B., & Duffy, T. M. (1999). Using asynchronous conferencing to promote critical thinking: two implementations in higher education. In *Proceedings of HICSS-32,* Maui, HI. Honolulu, HI: HICSS.

Smith, K. (1995). Cooperative Learning: effective teamwork for engineering classrooms. In *Proceedings of the Frontiers in Education Conference,* Atlanta, GA (pp. 1, 2b5, 13-2b5,18). Thompson, G. (1988). Distance learners in higher education. In C. C. Gibson (Ed.), *Higher Education: Institutional Responses for Quality Outcomes* (pp. 9-24). Madison, WI: Atwood Publishing.

Subbotin, I., Serdyukova, N., & Serdyukov, P. (2003). Short-term Intensive College Instruction: What are the Benefits for Adult Learners? In C. Crawford et al. (Eds.), *Proceedings of Society for Information Technology and Teacher Education International Conference 2003* (pp. 1550-1552). Chesapeake, VA: AACE.

Trigo, A., Varajão, J., Soto-Acosta, P., Barroso, J., Molina-Castillo, F. J., & Gonzalvez-Gallego, N. (2010). IT Professionals: An Iberian Snapshot. *International Journal of Human Capital and Information Technology Professionals*, *1*(1), 61–75.

U.S. Bureau of Labor Statistics. (1999). *Occupational Outlook Handbook*. Washington, DC: U.S. Bureau of Labor Statistics.

U.S. Department of Education. (2002). *The Condition of Education 2002, NCES 2002-025*. Washington, DC: NPO.

Vygotsky, L. (1978). *Mind in Society*. Cambridge, MA: Harvard University Press.

Wahlstrom, C., Williams, B. K., & Shea, P. (2003). *The successful distance learning student*. Belmont, CA: Scratchgravel.

Wenger, E. (1998). *Communities of practice: learning, meaning, and identity*. Cambridge, UK: Cambridge University Press.

Wlodkowski, R. J. (2003). Accelerated Learning in Colleges and Universities . In *New Directions for Adult and Continuing Education* (pp. 5–15). New York: Wiley.

Young, G. (2002, March 22). Hybrid teaching seeks to end the divide between traditional and online instruction. *The Chronicle of Higher Education*, A33–A34.

Young, S. (2006). Student views of effective online teaching in higher education. *Quarterly Review of Distance Education*, *20*(2), 65–77. doi:10.1207/s15389286ajde2002_2

Zimmerman, B. J. (2001). Theories of self-regulated learning and academic achievement: an overview and analysis . In Zimmerman, B. J., & Schunk, D. H. (Eds.), *Self-regulated learning and academic achievement: theoretical perspectives* (2nd ed., pp. 1–37). Mahwah, NJ: Lawrence Erlbaum Associates.

This work was previously published in International Journal of Human Capital and Information Technology Professionals, Volume 1, Issue 3, edited by Ricardo Colomo-Palacios, pp. 15-31, copyright 2010 by IGI Publishing (an imprint of IGI Global).

Chapter 9
RSS-Based Learning Using Audio

Víctor Manuel Álvarez García
University of Oviedo, Spain

María del Puerto Paule Ruiz
University of Oviedo, Spain

Remko van Dort
Etten-Leur, The Netherlands

Juan Ramón Pérez Pérez
University of Oviedo, Spain

ABSTRACT

Specifications such as RSS feeds are opening a new channel of communication for Internet-based learning, which gives a decentralized view of web resources while maintaining the privacy of teachers and students who are consulting the information. This philosophy can be used to create personalized learning tools in which users can take control of resources they want to have access to. In this regard, RSS is XML-based, which makes it easy to complement visual access with audio interfaces, adapting the feeds to different educational contexts and learning styles. This paper discusses the use of feed syndication to create personalized feed readers accessible in visual and voice formats.

INTRODUCTION

Using web-based technologies is nowadays a part of our daily lives, offering many different ways of establishing new channels of communication. One of the technological opportunities which enable us to access information in a new form is RSS.

Originally developed by Netscape in 1999, RSS (which can stand for RDF Site Summary, Rich Site Summary, or Really Simple Syndication) is

an XML-based format that allows web developers to describe and syndicate web site content (Harmmersley, 2003). Since its creation, Really Simple Syndication (RSS) has been used on the internet as a means to retrieve information from various web sites, not linked to one another, to be read in one specific application the user can easily access. Using pull technology, the end user no longer needs to go through all the relevant web sites in order to obtain the latest updates or interesting

DOI: 10.4018/978-1-4666-0924-2.ch009

information. By subscribing to feeds available on the web, information can be selected according to personal preferences and can be delivered at the user's convenience.

The main reasons for this syndication feature to arise were the need to save time when looking for information on the web and the possibility to give users more control over the information retrieval process, personalising the information. Really Simple Syndication allows Web content to be published using a metadata format known as a "Web feed". There are two web feed formats on the market, RSS (RSS History: http://www.rssboard.org/rss-history) and Atom (Nottingham & Sayre, 2005), both using Extensible Markup Language (XML).

Although nowadays frequently used, in some cases users are unaware of the existence of RSS and are sometimes using RSS without realising it (Grossnickle, 2005). This is for instance the case for many users who use web portals, such as My Yahoo (http://my.yahoo.com/) or My MSN (http://my.msn.com/), which aggregate news and other types of information from a variety of different sources available on the web, according to the user's indicated preferences and needs. Such aggregating web sites carry out the syndication process without the user needing to know too much about the technology which lies behind it.

The area in which RSS has made its biggest breakthrough is the news sector (Asmus, Bonner, Esterhay, Lechner, & Rentfrow, 2005), as feeds are an excellent way to send out the latest news flashes by letting users subscribe to any particular news topic they wish to receive information about. Organizations are using RSS feeds to create content summaries of their web sites to attract users to come and consume their content (Glotzbach, Mohler, & Radwan, 2007). Most major news web sites such as CNN (http://www.cnn.com/), The New York Times (http://www.nytimes.com/), the BBC (http://www.bbc.co.uk/) or The Guardian (http://www.guardian.co.uk/) have a wide variety of feeds available, ranging from general topics such as ''international news'' or ''U.S. news'', to more specific topics such as ''Iraq'', ''European Union'' or ''Middle east Conflict''. This again illustrates the advantage of being able to receive personalised information, separating it from less interesting items.

In a way, newsletters sent out by email can also update a user on the latest news or information but this increases the risk of receiving unsolicited email, or spam, and when receiving RSS feeds frequently, for instance as hourly news flashes, it can obstruct email.

Feed readers usually show that new updates are available by putting the feed title in bold or using another typographical style option which visually stands out. This limits the audience which can be reached by aggregators as text does not fit well in all situations.

Thus, if we wish to enable all users to have equal access, then we have to come to the conclusion that current feed aggregators are not made to communicate to users who require to use audio while accessing material. From this necessity and with this goal in mind, the University of Oviedo has developed a software prototype called Feedo, which can communicate feeds by using both visual means and speech interaction. Although the prototype was initially created in the context of our University for educational purposes, however we can also imagine it being applied outside the educational arena, in a wide variety of contexts enabling voice access from fixed and mobile devices.

This paper explains how RSS can be used in web and audio learning. In the first section, below, we give an overview of RSS, exploring the advantages and limitations of using web feeds. The following section explores the use of RSS in education and e-learning. We then proceed to introduce Feedo, the prototype developed at the University of Oviedo for personalized web and voice-based learning using feed syndication. Finally, we present the conclusions taken from this study and point the way forward to future developments.

RSS OVERVIEW: ADVANTAGES AND LIMITATIONS

The main advantages RSS offers to users subscribing to them are the easy and effective syndication of information, the possibility to rapidly obtain relevant information, saving time browsing for information on the internet, obtaining personalised information according to the user's needs and preferences and respecting the user's privacy while receiving relevant information.

RSS guarantees the privacy of the user by not pushing but allowing content to be pulled (Hagel & Brown, 2005) and, therefore, enabling the user to have more control over the exact content of the information coming through, without having to provide an email address or any other sensitive data. It is also viewed in a separate application than email, thereby not obstructing the latter. These feed readers are, as indicated, either web-based (e.g., Bloglines: http://www.bloglines.com/) or software packages/gadgets which are installed and used separately from an internet browser (e.g., NewzCrawler: http://www.newzcrawler. com/, FeedReader: http://www.feedreader.com/). Both are available from a variety of companies, either as commercial versions or free downloads.

For the web sites sending out RSS feeds the main advantage is that it attracts people to visit the web sites in question. Feeds can be shared with other users or friends so that the number of people visiting the web site increases, attracting a new audience. Feeds can also contain advertisements, another interesting option.

Notwithstanding the clear advantages RSS offers, it should be noted that RSS also faces challenges as it is bound by certain limitations which create disadvantages in some cases. When taking a closer look at these challenges in this paper, we will mainly focus on the limitations encountered by users who need to make use of audio, instead of only visually displayed information. However, we will also touch briefly upon the general challenges RSS faces.

When summarizing these challenges we can distinguish between the problems concerning the quantity and the quality of the information, the availability of RSS, the risk of receiving too much information and data accessibility. Taking a closer look, it becomes clear that although RSS itself has a standardised format which is used on the web, the implementation depends on the publisher of each separate web site.

In our opinion, some of the limitations of RSS syndication are:

- Quantity of information included in RSS feeds: Looking at the example of RSS news feeds, in most cases the quantity of information provided in an RSS feed is limited to the title of a new article and a short summary of the information in question, normally just one or a few sentences. There are some web sites that already publish the complete content of an article via RSS, so the user does not have to visit the site for more details or to read the article in full. Although this can be a highly interesting and useful way to provide information through RSS feeds for some, this is not yet common practice and information provided through feeds remains scarce in the majority of cases. This lack of information sometimes means that it is not always clear from an RSS feed whether the feed is actually relevant to the user.

- Quality of information included in RSS: Web sites decide themselves which information they will make available through RSS feeds and which information will only be published online. In the case of news feeds, not all newspapers make Reuters news flashes available via RSS, which means that if you are subscribed to RSS feeds from one newspaper you get all headlines on a certain topic, both news flashes as well as in-depth article updates, whereas other newspapers will only provide in-depth articles or newsflashes. This is confusing for users as sites have their own policies, which often differ greatly from one another. In the case of news feeds, it remains complicated to be well informed on news items using RSS (Moeller, 2006). In general, users cannot always be completely sure they will be receiving all necessary updates and it remains vital to visit sites regularly, in order not to miss out on important information, something which RSS was actually supposed to counteract. This can be especially relevant in the case of real-time information, such as traffic reports and alerts.

- RSS availability: Not all web sites offer RSS, there still are many sites which only publish content online and which do not send out updates via RSS but might use email newsletters instead. News sites are very well represented but in other areas material is less readily available through RSS.

- Information overload: From the point of view of the person-machine interaction, RSS can increase the effectiveness in vigilance tasks (Dinges & Powell, 1985) by decreasing the cognitive load (Toffler, 1970) caused by the excess of information. Personalized information, based in the choice of relevant sources of information, gives the user the chance to read only the updates he/she wishes to receive in a certain moment. This situation favours also the usability of the sites (Nielsen, 2003; Krug, 2000), since users can make a more efficient use of them. But with updates coming in by the minute, especially when subscribed to many feeds at the same time, it can be difficult for users to deal with an apparent overload of information. This is especially the case when realising that information is at the same time coming through via email and by visiting web sites.

This is an important matter to consider, as RSS cannot be used nor implemented as a replacement of these other internet options.

- Accessibility: Feed readers create a context in which interaction with the user is carried out by using visual perception. This interaction limits the type of information, devices and users who can benefit from the feeds retrieved using RSS this way. In order to provide a broad access to Internet resources through RSS technologies, we need to complement visual interfaces with other means of communication such as live voice-based interaction.

Certainly, limitations such as RSS information overloading and accessibility are not problems derived from content syndication, but from the use we make of RSS standards. We believe that this situation can be improved by making a better use of this technology and that our research can help to offer a solution to this problem.

RSS, EDUCATION AND E-LEARNING

RSS feeds have also had a significant impact in the area of education, where syndication can offer an excellent way to improve the interaction between teachers and students (Glotzbach, Mohler, & Radwan, 2007; Anderson, 2007). Updates on new material or assignment information can be communicated to students effectively, enhancing the use of information technology in the classroom and improving the quality of communication. Teachers and students can publish their own information on the internet or search for educational material on-line and share this with their peers. Some examples where RSS has been incorporated in education (D´Souza, 2006) are:

- Bookmarking, ePortfolio's and Discussions
- Blogging
- Photo, Audio and Video Sharing

- Share Learning Objects
- Class and School Information Updates
- Productivity and Research Tools
- Website and other information Updates

Specifically, social networking adaptive technologies like blogs, wikis and the RSS process involve students in situations that require them to employ a growing assortment of cognitive skills in order to perform and solve problems in digital environments (Duffy & Bruns, 2006). But besides enabling communication, sharing and creating information in the educational activities mentioned above, RSS also makes it possible for teachers to exchange information concerning their progress and experiences, hereby improving the progress in various areas in education.

At the same time, RSS availability is improved by traditional web-based learning systems such as Moodle (http://moodle.org), Sakai (http://sakaiproject.org) or dotLRN (http://dotlrn.org), which have incorporated RSS to their already generous list of features, facilitating easier and better communication between students and teachers. The use of RSS within e-learning platforms allows to automatically generate feeds using the communication tools which are available in the system, such as the case of forums. Or they can use external RSS sources from other websites to complement the information already present for their courses.

RSS feeds are opening a new way to interoperate with learning management systems among other web-based systems. Several sources of information, including news or updates from bulletin boards, learning channels or communication tools, can now be obtained using a feed reader.

As we have explained, in certain cases it is necessary to offer feeds not only using visual means but enabling also audio access. In order to have access to educational tools and material through visual and auditive means, it is possible to create multimodal RSS feed readers. The multimodal aspect of RSS readers enables it to adapt

(Brusilovsky, 1996) to the student's needs in the e-learning environment and avoid the cognitive overload (Paule, Fernandez, Ortin, & Perez, 2008). Until now, only Adaptive Educational Hypermedia (Brusilovsky, 2001) caters to the needs of each individual student and adapts to various characteristics such as different learning styles which students have for memorizing and learning new information (Stash, Cristea, & De Bra, 2003) or the level of their knowledge (De Bra & Calvi, 1998). Learning styles are related to an understanding of learning as an active process and there are different taxonomies of the learning styles identified (Alonso, Gallego, & Honey, 2002; Dunn & Dunn, 1978; Sarasin, 1998; Felder & Silverman, 1988; Kolb, 1984). The Felder-Silverman classification mentions three dimensions: Input (visual/verbal), Organisation (inductive/deductive), and Understanding (sequential/global). However, it is the visual/verbal dimension which enables us to make a clear distinction between a visual learner who learns and remembers best what is seen - pictures, diagrams, flow charts, time lines, films and demonstrations - and a verbal learner, who learns best when using audio explanations. Therefore, if an RSS reader offers the multimodal option, creating the possibility for both visual and verbal interaction, it provides the students the possibility to select a learning style best suited to their needs.

FEEDO: A DEVELOPMENT OF A PROTOTYPE FOR PERSONALIZED WEB AND AUDIO LEARNING USING FEED SYNDICATION

Feedo is a personalized web and voice-based feed aggregator which allows teachers and students to classify their feeds into categories and read or listen to them using text or voice. Feedo's voice-interactive characteristic provides a technological solution to the limited accessibility mentioned before.

Users of educational systems which provide updates in RSS format can take advantage of this new situation which enables the user to obtain and check out the latest updates from different sites and resources in their feeds client in one glance and without having to provide any personal data.

Educational material can overcome its single-platform/single-source limitations and teachers and students can, for the first time, choose the most interesting resources for their educational goals and make an efficient use of the broad possibilities of web publishing through a personalized learning environment.

At the same time, as both RSS and Atom format for feeds syndication are XML-based, they are easy to interpret and adapt to. RSS information can be flowed into a large number of devices and provide both web and voice access to the information (Downes, 2002), enabling access to educational resources using web and voice-based applications (Figure 1). The later allows them to consult the feeds in new situations, e.g., by making a phone call or while doing common daily tasks.

Feedo, the multimodal prototype for personalized web and voice-based learning developed at the University of Oviedo, is published at Sourceforge.net (http://feedo.sourceforge.net/) and distributed under the terms of the GNU General Public License, which gives free and public access to the reader and its source code. The aforementioned characteristics provide Feedo with a great flexibility to be integrated in any on-line learning environment, enhancing current RSS modules, which cannot be accessed from audio systems.

Feedo from a User's Point of View

From the user's point of view, Feedo organizes information in categories, default categories can be managed using an administrative profile and they can include items such as 'Learning Channels', 'Personal Blogs', 'News Sites' (Figure 2), etc. Teachers and students can add and delete categories to create an educational environment of their preference. Feeds are added into categories by typing the URL of the provider, i.e. a channel for a certain subject at a University can be added into the category 'Learning channels'. 'Learning channels' can then consequently contain resources which are relevant for the user in an academic year or a semester, and can include information from subjects located at various Universities, High Schools or any other educational organization or web site.

Any information update sent out through RSS syndication can be automatically retrieved by a feed reader. Users can then use the reader to check out the title and a short summary of the information and, in case the user is interested, use the link to go to the original source and read the complete information. Feedo complements this standard behaviour of a feed reader with the possibility to listen to the information using an audio device such as an automotive multimedia device, a Voice over IP terminal or a traditional telephone (Gutiérrez, Rodríguez, Miltiadis, & Lytras 2005), enabling also audio access to the information offered through RSS syndication.

Feedo from a Technical Point View

From a technical point of view, Feedo has three main features, user personalization, feed retrieval and a multimodal adaptation.

Feedo allows users to create their own personalized learning environment based on categories and resources of their choice. Both categories and resources are database persistent and are associated to one user or session. Resources are stored using the specific RSS URL for the desired source, maintaining the privacy of the user, who does not need to give out any data to access the information. An additional database table stores feeds that have been read or listened to, keeping information about already visited feeds.

At the same time, RSS feed retrieval requires a type of software called an RSS parser, which performs the operation of checking updates from

Figure 1. Feedo process explained

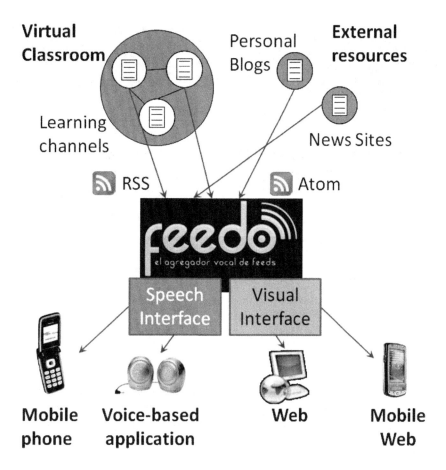

a given URL and downloads a determined number of RSS items. The current version of Feedo uses Magpie PHP RSS parser (http://magpierss. sourceforge.net/).

Multimodal adaptation, consisting in enabling web and voice access, is the most challenging task of the project. Feedo is currently considering three approximations for the solution, the use of the architectural pattern Model-View-Controller (MVC) (Reenskaug, 1979), XSLT transformations and web services (Figure 3).

The use of the pattern Model-View-Controller isolates program logic from the user interface, giving a clear separation between data manipulation and the application's appearance. This characteristic gives Feedo an obvious architectural advantage, since it needs to create different appearances depending on the access device. The current version of Feedo has been developed using Symfony Web PHP Framework (http://www. symfony-project.org/), which simplifies the use of an MVC approach in a software development.

Since feeds are provided in XML format with a well-defined structure, software can take advantage of this by applying templates using XSLT transformation. Different templates can give a different result, with appearances adapted to the access device. For example, given a resource in RSS format and using XSLT transformations, we can obtain an HTML version of the information which can be read by web browsers or a VoiceXML version which can be used by voice-based clients.

Figure 2. An example of the use of Feedo in an educational context

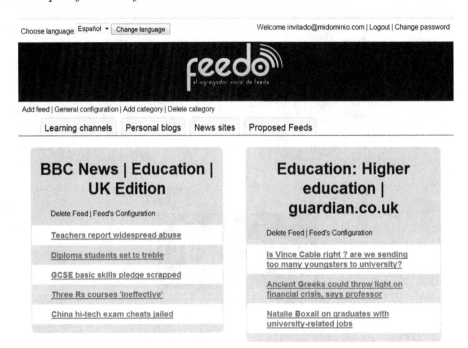

Well-designed SOA-based solutions help to improve integration with other applications (Galinec, 2010). Thus, Feedo's main functionality is also being mapped into a web services application program interface (API), which allows a seamless integration with e-learning applications such as WebCT, Moodle or Sakai. This set of web services provide a technology-independent access to Feedo's data and functionality and are an ideal solution for cases where the application client does not make use of any standard format. For example, we are using the web services API from a voice application written using the telephony platform Asterisk (http://www.asterisk.org/). Asterisk allows voice dialogs to be written using a proprietary dialog language (Asterisk AGI) or VoiceXML. Consequently, both the use of XSLT transformations or the web services API are valid approaches to access Feedo from the Asterisk voice platform.

Feedo Facing the Limitations of Present RSS Syndication

As we explained before, we think that RSS in its present form has a number of limitations. Feedo reduces some of these limitations by making a more sensible use of the technology.

From a practical point of view, Feedo provides an improvement in the quality of information being offered. The administrator has the possibility to select sources of information which are considered to be of interest to the user. These information sources are registered as "recommended Feeds" in the various "categories". The user can access these sources of information without first having to do a search to discriminate and link them in the user interface. One example of this usage are the various sections of newspapers. Very often we see that newspapers have a high quality in their printed versions but not so in their RSS

Figure 3. Multimodal access to Feedo

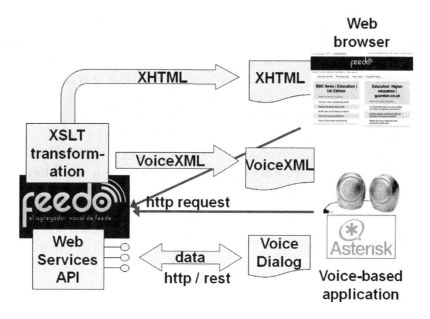

syndication. In this context, the Feedo administrator creates a filter for the information sources to go through; selecting those newspapers which he thinks are of high quality. The user can also select other sources which can be adjusted to the user's own quality criteria. An example of the use of this feature can be found in an educational context. A teacher offers his/her students those sources which are considered most adequate for the assignment, so that the student can have these ready for consultation.

The classification of information into categories in Feedo allows the user to access a larger quantity of information, without creating a cognitive overload. The categories offer the possibility to access the actual feeds the user is interested in at every moment and, if he/she considers them to be appropriate, he/she has the possibility to create new categories which collect new feeds.

In the area of accessibility Feedo offers a significant improvement when compared to present RSS readers. Although the idea of RSS being read

by using voice emerged almost immediately at the same time as RSS itself (Downes, 2002), it is not a feature integrated into current RSS readers. Feedo improves the accessibility of feeds by using speech interaction technologies. The incorporation of the use of voice means the reader can be adapted to situations in which voice needs to be used as a means of communication.

Nevertheless, using speech interaction also points directly to some of the limitations RSS has. The original source of the information is in (X) HTML, which means the structure of the information and the navigation are mainly directed at visual representation and therefore very different from one using voice. For both presentations different languages are being used, i.e., (X)HTML and VoiceXML - and although the navigation in both cases is carried out using a graph structure (Carro, 2001), the number of options and links has more limitations when using voice. This is necessary for the dialogues to remain naturalistic and not to become overcomplicated. Furthermore,

HTML also adds a number of characters which are appropriate when used for visual representation, but which need to be changed when using dialogs. The characteristic of HTML to depend on visual perception, together with the lack of structure and semantics, make it very complicated to separate the information (model) from its representation (view). We consider it necessary therefore that both the original sources as well as RSS feeds use a neutral language, which makes it possible to access the information regardless of the device or form of representation being used.

CONCLUSION AND FUTURE DEVELOPMENTS

In this paper we have analysed the use of RSS in an educational context and found that it enables new ways of communication to be established between students and teachers while at the same time allowing information to be personalised by the users themselves, selecting which educational material they wish to consult. From a technological point of view, RSS offers a useful format to interpret and adapt results. Without wanting to underestimate the advantages which RSS offers, the format also has a number of limitations among which accessibility and availability.

As to the availability, web sites are adapting more and more to the new publishing method by using pull and not push technology. This is especially the case for news sites, although it can be seen in the development of educational web sites too. Taking advantage of the proliferation of information and data published by RSS, we have developed a prototype called Feedo. Feedo can personalize access to educational material published with RSS. Feed readers traditionally are restricted to the use of a web browser to access information channels. Our prototype adds the possibility to access these channels using audio devices, which enable interaction with the user not only through visual means but also using voice

interaction. Nevertheless, we are aware that we still face certain challenges. Feedo accesses the title and the summary through web and speech interaction, but when the user wants to access the full article, it encounters that this information is published in HTML format. This can be a problem when using voice to access this type of information, which has a visual structure.

Taking into account the challenges of RSS now and looking for ways in which RSS might be implemented in the future, it is possible to imagine RSS being used to provide more in-depth information to users. This could include offering full text articles, links, video, audio and perhaps even learning objects. This will no doubt offer the recipient a broader range of interesting information, eliminating the need to check for an update, after receiving a feed.

Another developments already taking place, for instance in Microsoft Office Outlook 2007 (http://www.microsoft.com/outlook/) or Mozilla Thunderbird (http://www.mozillamessaging. com/), are combining email and RSS feeds, so the user no longer needs a separate application to read RSS feeds. Feeds are stored in a separate folder so the email facility is not obstructed.

Perhaps in the case of educational material this is even more important because users will continue to use the Internet more frequently, searching for relevant educational material, and they will need to receive more complete and accurate information in an easy-to-use application, to determine whether the article in question is relevant to them, so it can be put to use immediately.

REFERENCES

Alonso, C. M., Gallego, D. J., & Honey, P. (2002). *The learning styles*. Ediciones Mensajero.

Anderson, P. (2007). What is web 2.0? ideas, technologies and implications for education. *JISC reports*. Retrieved November 2009, from http://www.jisc.ac.uk/media/documents/techwatch/tsw0701b.pdf

Asmus, J., Bonner, C., Esterhay, D., Lechner, A., & Rentfrow, C. (2005). *Instructional design technology trend analysis*. Retrieved November 2009, from http://eduspaces.net/collinb/files/1136/2967/TrendAnalysisWeb.pdf

Brusilovsky, P. (1996). Methods and techniques of adaptive hypermedia. *User Modeling and User-Adapted Interaction, 6*(2-3), 87–129. doi:doi:10.1007/BF00143964

Brusilovsky, P. (2001). Adaptive educational hypermedia, Intelligent Computer and Communications Technology, Learning in On-Line Communities. In *Proceedings of the Tenth International PEG Conference, Digital Media Institute*, University of Technology, Tampere, Finland.

Carro, R. Mª. (2001). *Un mecanismo basado en tareas y reglas para la creación de sistemas hipermedia adaptativos: aplicación a la educación a través de Internet*. Unpublished doctoral dissertation, University Autónoma de Madrid, Spain. Retrieved November 2009, from http://www.ii.uam.es/%7Ercarro/tesis/tesis.html.

D'Souza, Q. (2006). *RSS Ideas for educators*. Retrieved November 2009, from https://www.drexel.edu/IRT/rmcweb/RSS-for-Educators.pdf

De Bra, P., & Calvi, L. (1998). AHA! an open adaptive hypermedia architecture. *New Review of Hypermedia and Multimedia, 4*, 115–139. doi:doi:10.1080/13614569808914698

Dinges, D. I., & Powell, J. W. (1985). Microcomputer analysis of performance on a portable, simple visual RT task sustained operations. *Behavior Research Methods, Instruments, & Computers, 17*, 652–655.

Downes, S. (2002). *An introduction to RSS for educational designers*. Retrieved November 2009, from http://www.downes.ca/files/RSS_Educ.htm

Duffy, P., & Bruns, A. (2006). The use of blogs, wikis and RSS in education: A conversation of possibilities. In *Proceedings of the Online Learning and Teaching Conference*, Brisbane, Australia (pp. 31-38).

Dunn, R., & Dunn, K. (1978). *Teaching students through their individual learning styles: A practical approach*. Reston, VA: Reston Publishing.

Felder, R. M., & Silverman, L. K. (1988). Learning and teaching styles in engineering education. *Journal of Engineering Education, 78*(7), 674–681.

Galinec, D. (2010). Human capital management process based on information technology models and governance. *International Journal of Human Capital and Information Technology Professionals, 1*(1), 44–60.

Glotzbach, R. J., Mohler, J. L., & Radwan, J. E. (2007). RSS as a course information delivery method. In *Proceedings of the ACM SIGGRAPH 2007 Annual Conference and Exposition*.

Grossnickle, J. (2005). RSS. *Crossing into the mainstream*. Retrieved November 2009, from http://publisher.yahoo.com/rss/RSS_whitePaper1004.pdf

Gutiérrez, J. A., Rodríguez, D., Miltiadis, D., & Lytras, M. D. (2005). Ubiquitous Computing Panorama. *Novática, 177*, 4–7.

Hagel, J., & Brown, J. S. (2005). *From push to pull: Emerging models for mobilizing resources*. Retrieved November 2009, from http://www.johnhagel.com/paper_pushpull.pdf

Hammersley, B. (2003). *Content syndication with RSS*. New York: O'Reilly & Associates.

Kolb, D. A. (1984). *Experiential learning experience as the source of learning and development.* Upper Saddle River, NJ: Prentice Hall.

Krug, S. (2000). *Don't make me think. A common sense approach to web usability.* New York: New Ryders.

Moeller, S. D. (2006). *International news and problems with the news media's RSS feeds. The International Center for Media and the Public Agenda.* Retrieved November 2009, from http://www.icmpa.umd.edu/pages/studies/rss_study_details/rss_study.html

Nielsen, J. (2003). *Usability 101: introduction to usability.* Retrieved November 2009, from http://www.alertbox.com

Nottingham, M., & Sayre, R. (2005). *The atom syndication format.* IETF.

Paule, M. P., Fernández, M. J., Ortín, F., & Pérez, J. R. (2008). Adaptation in current e-learning systems. *Elsevier Computer Standards and Interfaces, 30*(1-2), 62–70.

Reenskaug, T. (1979). *Models – Views – Controllers.* Retrieved November 2009, from http://heim.ifi.uio.no/~trygver/mvc/index.html

Sarasin, L. (1998). *Learning style perspectives: Impact in the classroom.* Madison, WI: Atwood Publishing.

Stash, N., Cristea, A., & De Bra, P. (2003) Authoring the learning styles in adaptive hypermedia. In *Proceedings of the 13th International World Wide Web Conference* (pp. 114-124).

Toffler, A. (1970). *Future shock.* New York: Bantam Books.

This work was previously published in International Journal of Human Capital and Information Technology Professionals, Volume 1, Issue 4, edited by Ricardo Colomo-Palacios, pp. 76-87, copyright 2010 by IGI Publishing (an imprint of IGI Global).

Section 3
IT Professionals in IT Projects

Chapter 10

Utilization of Project Management Software in Qatari Government Organizations:
A Field–Force Analysis

Salaheldin Ismail Salaheldin
Qatar University, Qatar

Khurram Sharif
Qatar University, Qatar

Maysarah Al Alami
Ministry of Labor & Social Affairs, Qatar

ABSTRACT

This study aims to explore the critical driving and resisting forces that promote or inhibit the implementation and use of project management (PM) software in Qatari Government Organizations in an attempt to determine whether software-based PM methodologies are being effectively implemented in the public sector organizations or not. Research hypotheses were evaluated using ANOVA and Mann- Whitney test. Findings indicated that forces that promote or inhibit software based PM implementation are significantly affected by the managerial interest and nature of existing (traditional or contemporary) PM practices. More importantly our findings identified some driving forces that promote the implementation of software-based PM methodology (SPMM) in Qatari government organizations and also identified some roadblocks that prohibit such implementations. Finally managerial implications for the successful implementation of SPMM are provided and avenues for further research are suggested.

INTRODUCTION

The 1950s marked the beginning of the modern project management era and since then, PM has been a hot topic in many sectors. The reason is that organizations invest a lot of money and efforts into projects with the expectation of realizing value, on time and within budget in order to meet their pre-defined objectives. Unfortunately too often these projects fail to deliver on these expectations. Project problems are particularly well known in areas surrounding information technology (IT)

DOI: 10.4018/978-1-4666-0924-2.ch010

investments, and governmental management of IT initiatives (Latendresse & Chen, 2003). There are numerous studies that have quantified project failure rates ranging from 50-70% which is considered to be quite high (PMI, 2004).

However recent studies indicated that there are many critical success factors (CSFs) in the improvement of project success rates. These include improved project management and delivery methodologies, training and recognizing the importance of Project Management Offices (PMO) whose entire mission is to improve project implementation and planned outcome (PMI, 2004;Hillam & Edwards, 2001). Many people would argue that the greatest contributor to this improvement is the Project Management Institute (PMI), which has published a vendor neutral body of knowledge and provides training, certification and a community of best practices for project managers. For the first time, project managers now have a common language, career path and universally recognized certification as professionals in their field. One such tool that creates an element of standardization is PM software. Software systems or functions are set of tools that are utilized to support management of project activities which may include planning, tracking, analysis and output. Some example of popular project management software are Timeline™ (by Symantic), Project™ (by Microsoft), Instaplan™ (by Instaplan), Project Scheduler™ (by Scitor), Mac Project™ (by Clavis) and Project Management™ (by Primavera Systems).

While there is no doubt that the PMI, along with the hundreds of tool and training vendors and thousands of published white papers on PM have all contributed to the improvement in project outcomes, there are a number of barriers and challenges which can impede or limit project success in government organizations. These barriers and challenges come from the complexities and unique characteristics of government projects and the nature of organization structure, culture and behaviors (Abbasi & Maharmeh, 2000; Krauth, 1999).

More importantly the review of the literature reveals that there is a gap that needs to be empirically investigated. No previous empirical study has tried to investigate the critical success factors (CSFs) related to SPMM in a developing country such as Qatar. Accordingly, the main objectives of this research are: (i) to identify the enablers promoting software-based PM implementation, (ii) to determine the inhibitors of software-based PM implementation, and (iii) to suggest recommendations and a suitable framework on how to improve the role of software-based PM in government organizations.

IMPORTANCE OF THE STUDY

The study offers an added factor to be taken into consideration, particularly when examining the effect of the CSFs for IT PM implementation. The projects that were studied and analyzed as a part of this investigation were largely related to IT. Therefore the set of CSFs evaluated were associated with successful application of PM software to effectively handle IT projects within government organizations.

More importantly, this study offers a theoretical model that can be considered as a step forward in developing an integrated model toward investigating the relationship between enablers and inhibitors and the implementation of project management software. The government sector was chosen as focus of the study because in developing countries (such as Qatar) government takes overall initiative and responsibility for launching and consequently promoting IT ventures and projects. Furthermore the study contributes by comparing the CSFs for PM implementation in the government organizations of developed and developing countries. Finally, this research adds to the body of knowledge by providing new data and empirical insights into the relationship between the CSFs of software-based PM in the Qatari government organizations.

LITERATURE REVIEW

PM software is becoming an important issue because the need for effective project management is becoming increasingly necessary in the public and private sectors of today. Hence speed, quality, and cost control are taking on increased significance in business, government, and nonprofit sectors (Wateridge, 1998). SPMM allows managers to plan and manage strategic initiatives that improve the quality of projects and services (Day et al., 2003). PM tools decrease time, control expenses, ensure quality, and enhance performance. It is one of the most important management techniques for ensuring the success of an organization (White & Fortune, 2002; Briggs et al., 2003).

All organizations, regardless of whether they small or large, at one time or another, are involved in implementing new undertakings (Huang et al., 2004). These undertakings may be diverse, such as, the development of a new product or service, the establishment of a new production line in a manufacturing enterprise, a public relations promotion campaign, or a major construction scheme. The growth and acceptance of PM is continuing to increase as resources become scarce. The application of PM concepts is an essential tool for planning, organizing, managing and control of work, which leads to better performance and increased productivity.

Companies that decided to proceed with a PM process and methodology soon found that there were more potential benefits than originally believed possible (Harold, 2000, Stevenson, 2007, and Slack *et al.*, 2007). Some of PM benefits are to: allow organizations to accomplish more work in less time and with less people, provide better control of scope changes, make the organization more efficient and effective through better organizational behavior principles, allow organizations to work more closely with our customers, provide a means for solving problems, improve quality, allow people to make good organizational decisions and increase organization's business excellence.

Although projects can be managed without a formal methodology (such as software based solutions), having one can be a big help. Hence SPMM are important for two reasons:

- First, they standardize the way in which an organization manages its projects. This allows people from anywhere in the organization to talk with one another using the same terms and the same definitions for those terms. Presenting a consistent approach to project management via standards also allows project managers to cover for one another when the need arises.
- Second, SPMM are important in that they provide new project managers with the tools to manage projects, without requiring a long learning curve (Harold, 2000; Waller, 2000).

A software methodology is a set of guidelines or principles that can be tailored and applied to a specific situation (Larry, 2002; Slack et al., 2006). In a project environment, these guidelines might be a list of things to do. A software methodology could also be a specific approach, standards, templates, forms, and even checklists used over the project life cycle. Most of such methodologies available today are usually centered on the use of tools and techniques such as PERT, Gantt Charts, Critical Path Analysis, Scheduling Techniques, Organizational Issues and Conflict Management amongst others. More importantly, PM software available today is much complex with capabilities such as: Project data summary expenditure, timing, and activity data, data management and reporting capabilities, Critical path analyses, Multi-project tracking, Impact analysis, Early-warning systems, Graphical presentations of cost, time, and activity data, Resource planning and analyses, Cost and variance analyses and Resource leveling (Larry, 2002).

A successful project can be defined in several ways. A project is commonly acknowledged as successful when it is completed on time, within budget, and in accordance with specifications and to stakeholders' satisfaction. Functionality, profitability, absence of claims and 'fitness for purpose' has also been used as measures of project success (Takim & Akintoye, 2002; Heizer & Render, 2008). De Wit (1988) remarked that a project is considered an overall success if it meets the technical performance specification and/or mission to be performed, and if there is a high level of satisfaction concerning the project's outcome among key people in the parent organization, key people in the project team and key users or clients of the project effort.

It is necessary that distinctions be made between project success and PM success. Previous studies such as: De Wit (1988), Munns & Bjeirmi (1996), and Cooke-Davies (2002) clarified that project success is measured against the overall objectives of the project while project management success is measured against cost, time, quality and performance. More importantly CSFs can be defined as 'the things that must go right in order for a project to succeed' and 'means for identifying important elements of project success' (Long & Stephen, 2004; Peter, 2006). Hence CSFs define those factors if not done right will result in a failed project. CSFs are required and necessary for successful project execution and improved team communication, focus and energy. During the planning stage, these factors should be assessed to determine if any additional preparatory tasks, management attention or control strategies must be completed prior to later activities (Quayle, 1999). A CSF generally is related to one or more objectives. CSFs are critical for reaching those objectives.

Literature suggests that there are many CSFs, a list (Figure 1) of the most important ones and their effect on project success is as follows:

RESEARCH METHODOLOGY

Research Hypotheses

In this research four hypotheses were tested as follows:

H1: There is no significant difference among different managerial levels in the Qatari government organizations concerning the critical driving factors (Enablers) promoting project management implementation.

H2: There is no significant difference among different managerial levels in the Qatari government organizations concerning the critical resisting factors (Inhibitors) inhibiting project management implementation.

H3: There is no significant difference between the Qatari government organizations which implement a PM software and those which do not implement a PM software concerning the critical driving factors (Enablers) promoting project management implementation.

H4: There is no significant difference between the Qatari government organizations which implement a PM software and those which do not implement a PM software concerning the critical resisting factors (Inhibitors) inhibiting project management implementation.

Questionnaire

To test the research hypotheses and to investigate and study the main objectives of the project, a survey was used to collect the required data. It is an attractive technique that facilitates the gathering of standardized data from many respondents with less effort and expenses than most other data gathering techniques (Fowler, 1993). Therefore, the use of a survey approach in this research is important to realize the objectives of the research. A questionnaire containing ten questions in three different main categories was designed and distributed as follows:

Figure 1. A model of the driving and resisting forces to PM software implementation

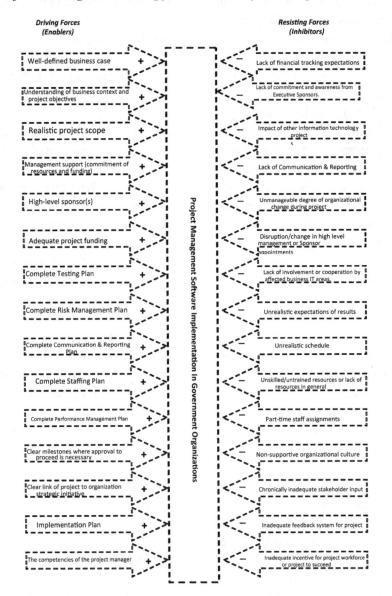

- **Questions 1-7:** Background information about the respondent (including age, education, work experience, etc.)
- **Questions 8-10:** Data about the organization's PM practices (including driving and resisting forces for implementing SPMM).

The Sample

The survey was limited to the organizations in the Qatari public sector, because of the availability of the required data. In this study, the basic criterion for the choice of the respondent was the capability of the respondent to provide the necessary information (i.e. information which helps to explore the forces that promote or inhibit PM implementation).

Consequently, three different managerial levels were targeted in this survey as follows:

- Top management (managers, executives and CEOs)
- Middle management (section heads, unit heads and project managers)
- First line (developers, technicians and specialists)

To secure data for the purpose of this project, we invited 20 well-known government organizations in Qatar to take part in the study.

Reliability and Validity of the Instrument

The instrument was examined by Cronbach's alpha which is a widely accepted index to indicate the reliability of research measures. Reliability coefficients are represented for each of the constructs (Table 1). All scales have reliability coefficients ranging from 0.88 to 0.92, which exceed the cut-off level of 0.60 (Nunnally, 1978), and all the alpha values indicate that the study's instrument is reliable. Moreover, the questionnaire was pre-tested to ensure that the wording and sequencing of the questions were appropriate and it was validated (face validity) by ten PM members from the Qatari government organizations.

DATA ANALYSIS

Profile of the Respondents

Table 2 presents the demographic profile of the respondents. The response rate was 70 per cent, i.e., 105 out of the 150 organizations claiming to have implemented or have been implementing software based PM. This is a healthy sign as it suggests that the realization of the importance of implementing the SPMM is rapidly raising among the public sector organizations in Qatar

Table 1. Internal consistency coefficients of the study variables

Constructs	Number of Items	Alpha
Critical success enablers	15	.92
Critical success inhibitors	15	.88

at all managerial levels, covering both genders, and involving different educational level and work experiences (as shown in Table 2 and Figures 2, 3, 4 and 5).

The respondents were asked to indicate the most fitting category that reflects the focus of their organizations. Our findings indicate that the majority of the respondents are working in government services organizations (39 per cent) as shown in Figure 6.

The respondents were asked to indicate the most important consideration for their organizations to acknowledge a project as successful. Table 3 shows that 'meeting stakeholders specifications and requirements' is the most important consideration in project success, and 'having met high quality standard' coming in the second place.

This finding is consistent with the PMI (2004) which indicates that the traditional project management theory stresses that project success depends on time, cost, and scope of project outputs. This can be summarized as an Iron Triangle conceptualization (PMI, 2004). These three (i.e. time, cost and scope) form the vertices with quality as a central theme (Takim & Akintoye, 2002).

It is important to note here that having our survey conducted in government organizations is the reason why the budget and time considerations came in the 3rd and 4th place respectively as government organizations, unlike the private sector, are somewhat more relaxed in terms of budget and time restrictions.

The respondents were asked to identify the most important stage in PM where the need for implementation is crucial to achieve project success. Table 4 indicates that the most important

Table 2. Demographics of respondents of the survey

	Number of respondents	Percent of respondents
Age	24	22.9
Less than 30 years	54	51.4
30-40	16	15.2
41-50	11	10.5
51-60	0	0.00
More than 60 years		
Gender	82	78.1
Male	23	21.9
Female		
Role	27	25.7
Top management	33	31.4
Middle management	45	42.9
Employee		
Working Experience	63	60.0
Less than 5 years	21	20.0
5-10	9	08.6
11-15	12	11.4
More than 15 years		
Education	5	04.8
High school degree or equivalent	15	14.2
Associate degree or some college or equivalent	53	50.5
4-year college degree or equivalent	32	30.5
Master degree or equivalent	0	0.00
Doctoral degree or equivalent		

stage of project where the need for PM is crucial is the planning or design stage with initiation stage coming in the second place.

This finding is consistent with the PMI (2004) which indicates that the traditional PM theory stresses that the most important stage of a project is the planning stage, because proper and sufficient planning is essential in all project management knowledge areas and processes (PMI 2004). The need for PM software implementation is very crucial in successful planning efforts (Larry, 2002). The need of a formal PM software is also crucial in the execution and implementation stages, but our findings shows that the respondents ranked this stage in the third place. This may also be related to the lack of PM knowledge and formal practices among the employees in the government organizations (Cook & Davis, 2003).

HYPOTHESES TESTING

Hypothesis One

There is no significant difference among different managerial levels in the Qatari government organizations concerning the Enablers promoting PM implementation.

Figure 2. Age groups

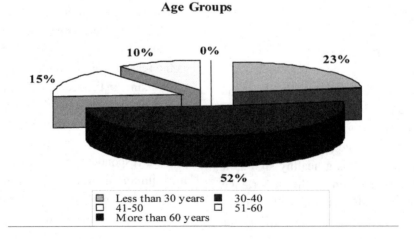

Figure 3. Working experience

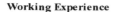

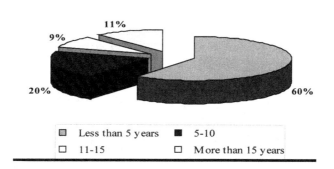

It appears from Table 5 that real differences exist between different managerial levels concerning the Enablers promoting PM implementation scored by the respondents (i.e. *H1* is relatively supported). These differences may stem from the fact that there is a lack of implementation of a formal PM methodology in these organizations, which means that each managerial level is looking into these factors from a different angle. On the other hand, it is interesting to note that these managerial levels agreed on the importance of having a well-defined business case, adequate project funding and high-level sponsors as driving forces which is fully consistent with PM literature (PMI, 2004; Peter, 2006).

Hypothesis Two

There is no significant difference among different managerial levels in the Qatari government organizations concerning the Inhibitors inhibiting PM implementation.

It appears from Table 6 that some differences exist between different managerial levels concerning the Inhibitors inhibiting PM implementation scored by respondents (i.e. *H2* is mostly supported). The findings indicate that different managerial levels mostly agreed on the same inhibiting factors, which are usually considered as the most important inhibitors in most PM literature and studies. There is a significant difference among the respondents concerning lack of commitment and awareness from executive sponsors. This may

Figure 4. Management level

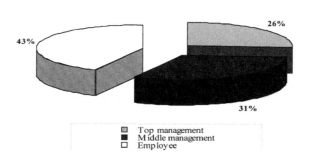

Figure 5. Education level

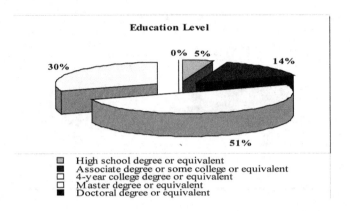

be interpreted in light of the fact that some of the top management and executive sponsors do not appreciate the real value of having a formal PM methodology.

Hypothesis Three

There is no significant difference between the Qatari government organizations which implement a PM software and those which do not implement a PM software concerning the Enablers promoting PM software implementation.

Table 7 indicates that there are some differences that exist between organizations which implement a PM software and those which do not implement a PM methodology concerning the Enablers promoting PM software implementation scored by the respondents (i.e. *H3* is mostly supported). The above findings shows that there is a consensus among these organizations that 10 out of 15 driving factors mentioned above are regarded as driving forces. These 10 factors can be considered as obvious and clear drivers no matter there is a PM implementation or not, while the

Figure 6. Government organization focus

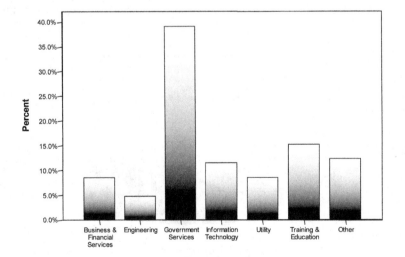

Table 3. Important considerations in project success

Consideration	Rank	Percent
Project is completed on time	4	15.2
Project is completed within specified budget	3	20
Meets stakeholders specifications & requirements	1	29.5
Meets the technical performance specification	5	11.4
Meets high quality standards	2	23.8

other 5 factors are considered to be factors where PM software and knowledge should be available to be understood and agreed on as driving factors.

Hypothesis Four

There is no significant difference between the Qatari government organizations which implement a PM software and those that do not implement a PM methodology concerning the Inhibitors inhibiting PM implementation.

Table 8 indicates that there are some differences exist between organizations which implement a PM methodology and those that do not implement a PM software concerning the Inhibitors inhibiting PM implementation scored by respondents (i.e. *H4* is mostly supported). The above findings shows that there is a consensus among these organizations that 11 out of 15 resisting factors mentioned above are regarded as inhibiting forces. These 11 factors can be considered as obvious and clear inhibitors no matter if there is a PM implementation or not while the other 4 factors are considered to be factors where PM methodology and knowledge

Table 4. Importance of PM in project stages

Project Stage	Rank	Percent
Initiation Stage	2	12.4
Planning or Design Stage	1	74.3
Execution or Implementation stage	3	9.5
Monitoring and controlling stage	4	2.9
Completion or closing stage	5	1

should be available to be understood and agreed on as resisting factors.

DISCUSSION, CONCLUSION AND MANAGERIAL IMPLICATIONS

One of the main objectives of this research was to provide some guidelines that might be of importance to promote SPMM implementation by Qatari government and public sector organizations. Within this remit, there seems to be a weak link between adequate training and knowledge base required for the successful and timely implementation of software based PM practices. It is quite likely that formal coaching and relevant mentoring is deficient or all together absent as far as proper use of PM tools, techniques and programs is concerned. Hence a strong case exists for involving suitable IT related human resource at higher, middle and lower management levels where participants are appropriately equipped with the information and the expertise required managing software solutions and formal techniques which are fundamental to successful running and conclusion of organizational projects (Wong, 2005).

More specifically, some employees utilizing sophisticated PM Software within the Qatari government IT sector may have English language handicap as most of them have Arabic educational background. This implies that these IT software users face difficulties in understanding the software applications and user instructions. This relates to the 'resisting forces' of 'lack of commitment', 'lack of involvement' and 'lack of training or provision of suitable training support'.

To overcome this deficiency, translation of software and user manual into Arabic should be considered supplemented by training and mentoring in Arabic. This exercise should be performed by bi-lingual (fluent in English and Arabic) IT professionals who understand the software context and the language context and hence are able to

Table 5. Significant levels (p-values) for the differences among different managerial levels in the Qatari government organizations concerning the Enablers.

	Enablers	ANOVA
1	Well-defined business case	.567
2	Understanding of business context and project objectives	.011
3	Realistic project scope	.395
4	Management support (commitment of resources and funding)	.000
5	High-level sponsor(s)	.582
6	Adequate project funding	.598
7	Complete Testing Plan	.023
8	Complete Risk Management Plan	.130
9	Complete Communication & Reporting Plan	.008
10	Complete Staffing Plan	.038
11	Complete Performance Management Plan	.043
12	Clear milestones where approval to proceed is necessary	.414
13	Clear link of project to organization strategic initiative	.047
14	Implementation Plan	.000
15	The competencies of the project manager	.018

-Based on a Likert scale: 1 = "not important at all"; 5 = "very important"**Significant at level .05

Table 6. Significant levels (p-values) for the differences among different managerial levels in the Qatari government organizations concerning the Inhibitors.

	Inhibitors	ANOVA
1	Lack of financial tracking expectations	.041
2	Lack of commitment and awareness from Executive Sponsors.	.000
3	Impact of other information technology projects	.333
4	Lack of communication & reporting	.285
5	Unmanageable degree of organizational change during project	.034
6	Disruption/change in high level management or Sponsor appointments	.496
7	Lack of involvement or cooperation by affected business IT areas.	.160
8	Unrealistic expectations of results	.262
9	Unrealistic schedule	.890
10	Unskilled/untrained resources or lack of resources in general	.002
11	Part-time staff assignments	.003
12	Non-supportive organizational culture	.146
13	Chronically inadequate stakeholder input	.373
14	Inadequate feedback system for project	.228
15	Inadequate incentive for project workforce or project to succeed	.395

-Based on a Likert scale: 1 = "not important at all"; 5 = "very important" **Significant at level .05

develop suitable jargon and text which conveys the intended meaning that is easily comprehended by the user with weak English. Recently (in 2008) a software house in Qatar started developing a software package which full-fills the needs of Project Management™ software (by Primavera Systems). The Arabic version of this software is intended for managing construction projects within the government sector.

Based on the results of analysis following are the main conclusion and managerial implications:

- The study demonstrates that results of forces that promote or prohibit PM implementation may vary from one organization to another; this variation may be due to the different managerial levels, existing PM software and availability of PMO.

- The findings of the current study enhance the understanding of the impact of top management support and employee involvement in the implementation of PM methodology by government organizations.

- The successful implementation of PM software in the Qatari Government sector would help to improve the quality of projects and services, and would enhance organizational performance.

- Improving workers' skills and quality consciousness through enhancing training programs is important for PM software implementation.

Table 7. Table VIII Significant levels (p-values) for the differences between PM methodology implementers and non-implementers regarding the Enablers.

	Enablers	Mann-Whitney
1	Well-defined business case	.610
2	Understanding of business context and project objectives	.503
3	Realistic project scope	.174
4	Management support (commitment of resources and funding)	.449
5	High-level sponsor(s)	.373
6	Adequate project funding	.001
7	Complete testing plan	.060
8	Complete risk management plan	.096
9	Complete communication & reporting plan	.339
10	Complete staffing plan	.322
11	Complete performance management plan	.032
12	Clear milestones where approval to proceed is necessary	.520
13	Clear link of project to organization strategic initiative	.030
14	Implementation Plan	.003
15	The competencies of the project manager	.024

-Based on a Likert scale: 1 = "not important at all"; 5 = "very important" ** Significant at level .05

Table 8. Significant levels (p-values) for the differences between PM software implementers and non-implementers regarding the Inhibitors

	Inhibitors	Mann-Whitney
1	Lack of financial tracking expectations	.019
2	Lack of commitment and awareness from Executive Sponsors.	.006
3	Impact of other information technology projects	.332
4	Lack of communication & reporting	.036
5	Unmanageable degree of organizational change during project	.481
6	Disruption/change in high level management or Sponsor appointments	.448
7	Lack of involvement or cooperation by affected business IT areas.	.633
8	Unrealistic expectations of results	.228
9	Unrealistic schedule	.423
10	Unskilled/untrained resources or lack of resources in general	.123
11	Part-time staff assignments	.016
12	Non-supportive organizational culture	.277
13	Chronically inadequate stakeholder input	.408
14	Inadequate feedback system for project	.729
15	Inadequate incentive for project workforce or project to succeed	.059

-Based on a Likert scale: 1 = "not important at all"; 5 = "very important" ** Significant at level .05

- Policy makers and top executives in government organizations should be aware that the competitive pressure affecting the public sector can be appeased through improving organization's performance and this hinges on the adoption of PM software.
- Because the implementation of PM software takes a long time, government organizations that are willing to implement it should be patient and persistent in forcing the project orientation culture.
- Government Organizations must recognize the importance of having and operating

PMO in order to better provide and support managerial, administrative, training, consulting and technical services and achieve better project success rates.

RECOMMENDATIONS FOR FUTURE RESEARCH

Several channels of future research can be pursued to better understand the critical driving and resisting forces effecting PM software implementation, as illustrated in the following list:

- Developing a deeper understanding of the driving and inhibiting forces to PM software implementation in practice remains a task that requires further attention from researchers, whatever their motivations. In so doing it also hopes to encourage researchers to go deeply into such forces by conducting case studies.
- Empirical research needs to be undertaken to evaluate the relative strength of the driving and resisting forces in the private sector.
- The current study was not specific to any particular type of government organizations. Hence, further study could be carried out with regard to specific types of government organizations
- Further studies need to be undertaken concerning the impact of organizational culture on PM software implementation. Moreover, empirical research should be conducted to evaluate the driving and resisting forces based on customers and stakeholders' points of view.

Finally, any research in this area will be determining in nature, and should place the foundation for enabling government organizations to remain competitive while satisfying the requirements of emerging environmental constraints.

REFERENCES

Abbasi, S., & Maharmeh, R. (2000). Project management practice by the public sector in a developing country. *International Journal of Project Management, 18*(2), 105–122. doi:10.1016/S0263-7863(98)00074-X

Briggs, R. O., Vreede, G. J. D., Nunamaker, J., & Sprague, R. (2003). Special issue: information system success. *Journal of Management Information Systems, 19*(4), 5–8.

Cook, A. A., & Davis, C. K. (2003). *Shifting gears to accommodate diversity: how and why an information systems project manager should customize leadership style to suit multicultural team.* Paper presented at the 2003 Southwest Decision Sciences Institute Conference (SWDSI2003) (pp. 126-31).

Cooke-Davies, T. (2002). The 'real' success factors on projects. *International Journal of Project Management, 20*(3), 185–190. doi:10.1016/S0263-7863(01)00067-9

Day, J., & Bobeva, M. (2003). Successful IS project leaders: a situational theory perspective. *Electronic Journal of Information Systems Evaluation, 6*(2), 75–86.

De Wit, A. (1988). Measurement of project success. *International Journal of Project Management, 6*(2), 321–331.

Fowler, F. J. (1993). *Survey Research Methods* (2nd ed.). Newbury Park, CA: Sage.

Harold, K. (2000). *Applied Project Management: Best Practices on Implementation.* John Wiley & Sons.

Harvey, F., & Brown, R. (1992). *The Experimental Approach to Organization Development* (4th ed.). London: Prentice-Hall.

Heizer, J., & Render, B. (2008). *Principles of Operations Management* (7th ed.). New Jersey: Prentice-Hall.

Hillam, C. E., & Edwards, H. M. (2001). A case study approach to evaluation of information technology/information systems (IT/IS) investment evaluation processes within SMEs. *The Electronic Journal of Information systems . Evaluation, 4*(2).

Huang, S., Chang, I., Li, S., & Lin, M. (2004). Assessing risk in ERP projects: identify and prioritize the factors. *Industrial Management & Data Systems, 104*(8/9), 681–690. doi:10.1108/02635570410561672

Huse, E. (1985). *Organization Development and Change* (3rd ed.). London: West Publishing.

Krauth, J. (1999). Introducing information technology in small and medium sized enterprises. *Studies in Information and Control, 8*(1).

Larry, R. (2002). *Successful Project Management* (2nd ed.). AMACOM Publishing, From PMI e-book Library.

Latendresse, P., & Chen, J. C. H. (2003). *The information age and why IT projects must not fail.* Paper presented at the 2003 Southwest Decision Sciences Institute Conference SWDSI2003 (pp. 221-5).

Long, N., & Stephen, O. (2004). A study on project success factors in large construction projects in Vietnam. *Engineering, Construction, and Architectural Management, 11*(6), 404–413. doi:10.1108/09699980410570166

Munns, K., & Bjeirmi, F. (1996). The role of project management in achieving project success. *International Journal of Project Management, 14*(2), 81–87. doi:10.1016/0263-7863(95)00057-7

Nunnally, J. (1978). *Psychometric theory.* New York: McGraw-Hill.

Peter, W. (2006). *Avoiding Project Failures: The Project Management Initiative.* http://blogs.ittoolbox.com/pm/witt/archives/avoiding-project-failures-14896.

Project Management Institute (PMI). (2004). *A Guide to the Project Management Body of Knowledge* (3rd ed.). Sylva, NC: PMI.

Quayle, M. (1999). Project management in European Aerospace plc: a case study. *Industrial Management & Data Systems, 99*(5), 221–231. doi:10.1108/02635579910282920

Slack, N., Chambers, S., & Johnston, R. (2007). *Operations Management* (5th ed.). Harlow, England: Prentice-Hall.

Slack, N., Chambers, S., Johnston, R., & Bdetts, A. (2006). *Operations and Process Management* (1st ed.). Harlow, England: Prentice-Hall.

Stevenson, W. (2007). *Operations Management* (9th ed.). Boston, USA.McGraw-Hill.

Waller, D. (2003). *Operations Management: A Supply Chain Approach* (2nd ed.). Australia: Thomson.

Wateridge, J. (1998). How can IS/IT projects be measured for success? *International Journal of Project Management, 16*(1), 59–63. doi:10.1016/S0263-7863(97)00022-7

White, D., & Fortune, J. (2002). Current practices in project management – an empirical study. *International Journal of Project Management, 20*(1), 1–11. doi:10.1016/S0263-7863(00)00029-6

Wikipedia (2007). *Force-Field Analysis,* ww.wikipedia.org.

Wong, K. Y. (2005). Critical success factors for implementing knowledge management in small and medium enterprises. *Industrial Management & Data Systems, 105*(¾),261-279.

This work was previously published in International Journal of Human Capital and Information Technology Professionals, Volume 1, Issue 1, edited by Ricardo Colomo-Palacios, pp. 1-15, copyright 2010 by IGI Publishing (an imprint of IGI Global).

Chapter 11
Team Software Process in GSD Teams:
A Study of New Work Practices and Models

Adrián Hernández-López
Universidad Carlos III de Madrid, Spain

Ricardo Colomo-Palacios
Universidad Carlos III de Madrid, Spain

Ángel García-Crespo
Universidad Carlos III de Madrid, Spain

Pedro Soto-Acosta
University of Murcia, Spain

ABSTRACT

Distributed software development is becoming the norm for the software industry today as an organizational response to globalization and outsourcing tendencies. In this new environment, centralized models for software development team building models have to be reanalyzed. Team Software Process (TSP) guides engineering teams in developing software-intensive products and is intended to improve the levels of quality and productivity of a team's software development project. In this paper, the authors assess the difficulty of using TSP in distributed software development environments. The objective of this assessment is twofold; firstly, know the general difficulty for using TSP in these environments, and secondly, know the caveats to be addressed in future software development team building models designed specifically for distributed environments.

INTRODUCTION

Software development is a collaborative and knowledge intense process where success depends on the ability to create, share and integrate information (Walz et al., 1993). This process has been

evolving since its origins in the NATO Software Engineering Conference at end of the 60's. During this evolution, new forms of software development have appeared, i.e., open-source software development (Lerner & Tirole, 2002) or outsourcing development (Sahay et al., 2003). Along with the

DOI: 10.4018/978-1-4666-0924-2.ch011

evolution of software development, the research about it has evolved and branched too. Moreover, an external but nearly related factor to software development process and its characteristics is still a top issue since, which are people (Gannon, 1979; Laughery, Jr., & Laughery, Sr., 1985); "People factors" seem to dominate "tools and techniques" as Blackburn et al. (1996) pointed in their study. Within people issue, other issues such as teams (Krishnan, 1998), people's factors (Blackburn et al., 1996), and human resources management issues such as assigning roles (Acuña & Juristo, 2004), productivity management of IT projects (Mahmood et al., 1996) or skills identification (Colomo et al., 2010; Trigo et al., 2010) as top issues in software development research.

As a key issue for software development process, quality improvement within an organization is founded on three basic pillars: processes, technologies and people. These pillars are interconnected with each other, forming an inseparable triangle on which organizations operates. In turn, software process improvement requires an effort on three levels: organization, team, people (Humphrey, 2002). For each one of these levels there are well-recognized models for its continuous improvement and quality. At organizational level, models such as CMMI (Capability Maturity Model Improvement), which based on the premise that management is convinced of the need to improve processes, facilitates the integration of traditional functions, establishes objectives and priorities for processes improvement in the guide to quality processes, and evaluates current processes; at team level, models such as TSP (Team Software Process), which guides engineers in the creation and maintenance of self-managed software teams, which plan and monitor their work, set their goals and commit to compliance with the them (Humphrey, 2000); and at individual level, models such as PSP (Personal Software Process), which shows software engineers to manage the quality of their projects, agreeing that can meet commitments to

improve their estimates and schedules and reduces defect rates in their products (Humphrey, 1995).

A software development team is defines as a team that has the implementation of a software project as its mission (Sawyer, 2004). Starting from the basic conditions presented above, Humphrey (2000) highlighted some necessary characteristics for a team to be considered an effective team: the team must be cohesive, it must have some ambitious goals, frequently receives comments on work done and should have a working framework for the tasks. In addition, globalization has led to the evolution of software development teams, and has created several types of teams with similar characteristics. Among these types are the GSD (Global Software Development) teams, geographically distributed teams, which use virtual communication channels such as email, and whose activity is focused on software development (Herbsleb & Moitra, 2001). These teams can be considered as a specification of the virtual teams (Martins et al., 2004), and are further encouraged by the relationships between customers of software development outsourcing organizations and developers (Heeks et al., 2001). GSD teams have a number of critical factors which must be considered before using a model for the management of teams in such environment. These factors are mainly the difficulty in communicating due to the geographical distances (Cramton, 2001), the cultural differences among team members (Ali Barbar et al., 2007), and the level of trust among team members (Jarvenpaa et al., 1998).

Finally, reports of TSP utilization are slim; see Callison and MacDonald (2009) for a complete bibliography. Specifically, reports of TSP utilization in distributed teams are limited to few cases; see Callison and MacDonald (2009). Distributed teams are a working style in outsourcing environments. In one of the reports of TSP utilization, Serrano and Oca (2004) assert that TSP is flexible enough to be used in outsourcing environments making some tunings but these changes were not defined. Due to the fact that these tunings are not defined across the literature, the present article aims to assess the difficulties for each activity and goal of each role defined in TSP, in order to know the tune that each role needs for outsourcing environments. The remainder of this paper is organized as follows. Firstly the issues and solutions of development teams in distributed development are presented. Secondly, TSP model is summarized. Thirdly, the difficulty of each task and goal for all roles defined in TSP is assessed using a qualitative assessment and based on the state of the art. Finally, a general overview of the assessment is discussed and conclusions are presented.

DEVELOPMENT TEAMS IN GSD, ISSUES AND SOLUTIONS

Software development is an intense human capital activity, more intense in intellectual capital (Sommerville & Rodden, 1996). Focusing on human capital, utilization of teams for the execution software development task means a set of advantages versus the execution these tasks individually (DeMarco & Lister, 1987). Within the working in teams advantages for software development tasks, a higher performance (Mizuno, 1983), a wide range of abilities and knowledge (Humphrey, 2000), and a higher capability for coordination (Faraj & Sproull, 2000) are the most noticeable ones. Despite of these advantages, there are problems that have to be addressed: Ineffective leadership; despite de fact that leadership is essential for team work (Faraj & Sambamurthy, 2006), few people are leaders by nature, so that most needs to develop leadership skills (Gorla & Jam, 2004). Among these skills, an effective team leader should motivate and inspire (Covey, 1992); Lack of commitment and cooperation; sometimes one or more team members may be unwilling to cooperate with the team (Grover et al., 1988);

Differences in contributions; contributions to the overall work of the team may vary (Curtis et al., 1988); Lack of trust (Bandow, 2004).

In addition to the issues of software development teams, the geographical distribution inherent to virtual teams carries several problems that arise from two factors inherent to the distribution; the distance between team members and the dependence of the necessary technology to allow members to communicate (Hinds & Bailey, 2003). These two factors result in various problems: distance may result in different context (Cramton, 2002), lack of familiarity with the work habits of the rest of the team members (Goodman & Leyden, 1991), cultural diversity (Mortesa & Hinds, 2001), low confidence among the members (Jarvernpaa & Leidner, 1999), technological dependence may lead to less cohesion (Strauss & McGrath, 1994), less identification with the team (Bouas & Arrow, 1996), reduced performance work (Walther & Burgoon, 1992), exclusion of certain communications (Cramton, 2001), difficult coordination (Purdy et al., 2000).

The problems associated with distance and reliance on technology can be minimized, once they have been identified, taking into account that they cannot be eliminated in its entirety (Olson & Olson, 2000). Among the ideas that can minimize these problems includes: increasing richness of communication channels (Daft & Lengeler, 1984), use of tools to share information in context (Atkins et al., 2002), increasing frequency and duration of face to face meetings (Kraut et al., 1992), share knowledge since the beginning of the creation of the team (Kraut et al., 1992), collaborative problem solving (Kirschner & van Bruggen, 2004).

Finally, it has to be highlighted that the use of distributed teams has its benefits, not all are issues and risks. Carmel (1999) listed six main potential benefits of distributed software development: mergers and acquisitions, position as global organizations, increase proximity to market, access to most talented developers, reduce development costs, and reduce time to market. Furthermore, managing software quality, which includes TSP, is further acerbated by the complexity of GSD as Muthuswamy and Crow pointed (2003).

Team Software Process (TSP)

Team Software Process (TSP) is a methodology that extends and refines the methods of CMM (Paulk et al., 1993) and PSP (Personal Software Process) (Humphrey, 1995) in order to guide engineers in creating and maintenance of software development teams, consisting of between 3 and 20 software engineers. TSP is based on the following principles: the software engineers are rigorous in their assignments and plan their work more precisely, making their own plans they commit the to reach team, engineers can balance the workload to meet schedules and / or minimize the duration of the project, they collect measurement data from each tasks in which are involved, the maximization of productivity go through the maximization of quality (Humphrey, 2000).

The use of TSP has the prerequisite of knowledge of PSP by all engineers, as this serves as a knowledge base about the practice of software engineering. As the author pointed in a later study, the lack of this knowledge is pointed as a critical factor for a successful implementation of the model (Humphrey, 2002). TSP main benefit is to show engineers how to produce quality products within planned costs and schedules on the go. Additionally, as indirect objective, TSP allows organizations to consolidate the CMM practices regarding the management and creation of software (Humphrey, 1998). With regard to the objectives sought by TSP, Humphrey (1998) notes the following ones. Firstly, TSP seeks to create self-managed teams who plan and track their work, set goals and have its processes and plans. Secondly, TSP shows to senior management a way to train and motivate their teams, and help them maintain peak performance. Thirdly, accelerates software process improvement by making the

behavior of CMM level 5 normal and expected. In last place, TSP guides organizations toward improving high maturity.

TSP uses as a basic a project management structure based on an iterative architecture of eight phases: launch, strategy, planning, requirements, high level design, implementation, integration and testing, and post-mortem. The project can start and stop at any phase or start in the first and finish in the last phase. In all of the iterations, a launch process is carried out; this process requires a work allocation of 3 or 4 days (Humphrey, 2000). During this launch process, a TSP team produces the following products (Humphrey, 1998): goals and roles for each member and for the team, a plan for the development process, a project a quality plan, a plan of support, a risk management plan and a report for project status.

TSP Analysis in GSD Environments

Once TSP model has been presented, firstly a scan of the state of the art for each activity of each role defined in TSPi has been carried in order to analysis the model in GSD environments. The focus during this scanning has been to look for problems or difficulties reports, and satisfactory reports for each activity. Some of these activities have been divided because its goal is multiple so the search of the references has been divided. The research of references has been based on three knowledge areas: outsourcing, as a framework; virtual teams, as a generic definition of working teams in outsourcing environments; GSD teams, as a specific definition of working teams for software development in outsourcing environments.

Once the state of the art has been analyzed for each activity, a qualitative measurement of criticality for each activity jointly with an explanation of the value has been done. The measurement uses the following scale: Well defined difficulties; defined difficulties for the realization of these activities have been found and widely recognized. Existence of difficulties; problems and difficulties for the correct realization of this activity have been found. These problems have not been: Difficulties not found; only satisfactory references that characterize the activity as not problematic in this environment have been found. References not found; references that manage or mention the activity in this environment have not been founded.

All TSP roles have two activities that have to be done, that is "Participate in producing the development cycle report" and "act as a development engineer". These activities are present separately in the section General Activities.

TEAM LEADER

1. Motivate the Team Members to Perform their Tasks

Motivate is one of the general tasks for a leader (Avolio & Locke, 2002). In outsourcing environments, teams are mixed, each member can be from a different organization, and therefore the ability to motivate team members becomes more important (Domberger, 1998). In addition, motivation is a risk factor in outsourcing relationships (Mehta, 2006). Taking into account these factors, this activity is assessed as *Existence of difficulties*.

2. Run the Weekly Team Meeting (Every Week)

Communication is one of the key factors for success in the ICT sector organizations (Perry et al., 1994) and in turn it is to maintain a relationship of Outsourcing in a satisfactory manner to all participants (Birks, 2007). Focus the problem of communication in meetings Outsourcing environments, the meetings are unable to be done face-to-face always because the movements are costly (Barthélemy, 2001), therefore team members have to use electronic media such as videoconferences, which are less richness methods for communication than face-to-face ones (Ebert

& De Neve, 2001). With this information, this activity is assessed as *Well defined difficulties;* the geographical categorization of outsourcing relationships has not be take into account (face-to-face meetings are less costly in nearshoring than in offshoring due to the closer geographical situation of members).

3. Report Team Status to the Instructor (Every Week)

There is a main factor that influences this activity: communication. Based on the extended conclusion that communication is a key factor for a successful outsourcing relationship (Mao et al., 2008), and with the need to use electronic communication tools in this environment (Herbsleb, 2007), this activity is assessed as *Existence of difficulties*; it can be outsourced but need some adaptations and the use of common tools for communications.

4. Help the Team in Allocating Tasks and Resolving Issues

This activity has two tasks that have been analyzed separately: allocation of tasks and resolving issues. On the one hand, the allocation of tasks in an environment of Outsourcing may resemble the one in virtual organizations in which models are used to manage and Modular Network Design (MND) that includes a step of allocating tasks (Hoogeweegen, 1999). On the other hand, the resolving issues tasks, can be explicit in the contract of Outsourcing and models for government outsourcing relationships such as eSCM (eSoucing Capability Model) provide specific practices for resolving issues based on the ideal target to build proactive and collaborative (Hyder et al., 2006; Hefley & Loesche, 2006). In contrast, it is noteworthy that the appearance of conflict environments in which team members are geographically distributed than in collocated environments, where team members are working in the same place (Jarvenpaa & Leidner, 1999).

This increase in the number of conflicts is due to two factors inherent to the geographical distribution: the distance between team members and the dependence on technology to communicate between them (Hinds & Bailey, 2003).

Both tasks of this activity are successfully carried out in open source environments, which have similar characteristics with outsourcing environments: distributed and collaborative. Regarding the allocation of tasks, there is a fundamental difference between governance and Open Source environment; in Open Source environments the allocation of tasks is typically performed by a task assignment rule from bottom to top, a rule that is opposed to the organizational processes that are implanted in a governance management environments. Finally, this activity is assessed as *Existence of difficulties*.

5. Act as Facilitator and Timekeeper for All Team Meetings

Acting as a facilitator is vital for virtual teams (Kayworth & Leidner, 2002). Nunameker et al. (2009) argued that training teams to self-facilitate is a principle for effective virtual teamwork. Paul et al. (2004) highlighted the importance of this training. Regarding to timekeeper role (Tomei, 2007) there is no literature that can shed light, so is not taken into account for the measurement of this activity. Finally, the meetings are conducted in most cases, through electronic means such as videoconferencing, which have less communicate richness face-to-face meetings.

This activity is assessed as *Existence of difficulties* because of the need to train team members as self-facilitator to make virtual meetings effective.

6. Maintain the Project Notebook

The ability to perform this activity is mainly based on the technology used for project notebook management. This tool needs to be available all time and at any place; for example web based tool

(Alshawi & Ingirige, 2003). Therefore this activity is assessed as *Difficulties not found* because only a specific tool for this environment is needed in order to successfully execute this task.

SUPPORT MANAGER

1. Lead the Team in Determining its Support Needs and in Obtaining the Needed Tools and Facilities

This activity can be summed as project infrastructure management which can be defined as a project infrastructure as the software, hardware, network, data, and content comprising the working environment of the project team. Nauman and Igbal (2005) pointed to a significantly reduction of risks commonly associated with the virtual project team approach if an integrated project infrastructure it's established. In addition, if the project infrastructure provides knowledge-base capacity, it will allow team members to collaborate on and share source code, articles, lessons learned, tips & tricks, procedures, sample deliverables, and other project artifacts. Moreover, in order to successful carry this activity out, the manager should have high communicative skills and there should be good communication channels available all the time. Finally, if the development is split around the clock, this activity may be assigned to various members so team always has a project facilitator. Considering these factor, this activity is assessed as *Existence of difficulties*.

2. Chair the Configuration Control Board and Manage the Change Control System

The usage of tools for change and configuration management emerged due to the existence of parallel developments: simultaneously various people collaborate in the same development, and due to the hard difficulties for the integration of the product without these tools. These tools may be complemented with communication tools, mostly when the team members of the development are geographically dispersed and need to communicate realized changes (Bersoff, 1992).

Generally, these tools suppose the creation of an additional layer in the organizational knowledge management (Marsh & Burke, 2001). This new layer suppose an extra work effort at the project level, on the one hand, reduce the time needed for the production and integration of new versions and therefore, as long as project growth, the cost will be reduced due to a reduction of cost needed for the generation of evolutive versions of the products (Frederick, 1981). On the other hand, these tools increase the time needed for producing changes, mostly when changes are slight and versions are frequently needed.

Leading change management to outsourcing environments, two key factors have to be considered: the automatizing of change process and the delegation of the controls for change management. Karolak (1998) views responsibility and accountability to be crucial and maintains that careful consideration can avoid many of the major problems associated with GSD. Regarding this activity, Karolak's guidance for GSD teams includes a virtual software configuration control board (SCCB). In addition, the outsourcing program manager, who is sited in service provider organization, is responsible for the change control reviews and approval. In this direction, a case study of requirement evolution in an outsourcing environment used successfully a change control system as part of requirement management (Lormans et al., 2004). Moreover, McBride (2009) argued that it can be outsourced.

Finally, because of the fact that change management is not based on tools perfectly integrated on software development process, and itself is a requirement for a satisfactory implantation (Krikkar & Crnkovic, 2007), and requires the use of additional tools for communication, this activity is assessed as *Existence of difficulties*.

3. Manage the Configuration Management System

A software configuration management (SCM) tool can assist distributed projects (Lanubile, 2009) and becomes critical due to the characteristics of the distributed development (physical distance, cultural differences, trust, communication and other factors). Moreover, it can reduce the miscommunication because it enforces a common work process and a common view of the project (Carmel & Agarwal, 2001). According to Battin et al. (2001), is more challenging for global distributed projects, and a solution could be a common SCM tool with multisite replication and a centralized bug repository. Taking into account these lessons jointly with the importance of this activity in distributed environments, it is assessed as *Existence of difficulties*.

4. Maintain the System Glossary

The maintenance of the system glossary may resemble collaborative knowledge tools such as wiki (Huettner et al., 2007). Because of this similarity, the assessment of this activity is based on the ability of such systems to manage knowledge in collaborative environments and distributed. Perhaps the best known examples of such tools are wikis, which has shown a growth of collaboration and high (Cress & Kimmerle, 2008). Because these systems can have problems if the knowledge that manage grows to large amounts of information (Eppler & Mengis, 2008), this task is assessed as *Difficulties not found*.

5. Maintain the Team's Issue- and Risk-Tracking System

This activity is based on two tracking systems, so the analysis is divided. On the one hand, in a study of tools for collaboration on distributed software teams, Lanubile (2009) presented some tools that can be used for issue tracking in distributed environments. In addition, Neef (2003) presented a successful case of issue-tracking system for global use. Moreover, issue-tracking systems can be accessed via www and used for learning about the projects history (Cubranic et al., 2005). Considering these findings, issue-tracking system for this environment has to be a collaborative and accessible for all members so this activity is measured with an 8. On the other hand, risks in distributed projects tends to be less visible (Karolak, 1998), and therefore more difficult to deal with. In this scenario, there are approaches to manage risk in distributed projects, to manage risk related to requirements, to manage risk in distributed IT projects (Prikladnicki et al., 2006).

Within these scenario, this task is assessed as *Difficulties not found*, both activities can be externalized but require an extra effort to build a system that allows these managements in the specific environment.

6. Act as the Team's Reuse Advocate

Reuse in Outsourcing is based on the ability to encourage the reuse and address intellectual property protection problems and contracts (Kim & Stohr, 1998). Outsourcing models such as eSCM-CL (eSourcing Capability Model for Client Organizations) includes a practice for the management of each of these tasks: Intellectual Property thr03 and thr04 Security & Privacy (Hefley & Loesche, 2006). Similarly the model eSCM-SP (eSourcing Capability Model for Service Providers) include: Intellectual Property thr05 and thr06 Statutory & Regulatory Compliance (Hyder et al., 2006). Based on the existence of good practices to address the problems related to reuse in this environments, jointly with the need to encourage this activity, and the independence reuse degree with respect to organizational model (Lynex & Layzell, 1998), a value of *Existence of difficulties* is obtained for the assessment of this practice.

PLANNING MANAGER

1. Lead the Team in Producing the Task Plan for the Next Development Cycle

Planning in virtual teams has more difficulties in planning activities than collocated teams. It can be explained by these additional four elements: coordination requirements, resource constraints, responsibility for progress, mapping of tasks among the members (Cascio & Shurygailo, 2003). On the one hand, the improvement in communication tools has led organizations to assign tasks to distributed groups of workers as opposed to collocated groups (Jang et al., 2000). On the other hand, the importance of a coherent distribution of tasks is a critical activity for better performance in GSD (Ebert & De Neve, 2001). Due to its criticality and because this activity can be outsourced this activity is assessed as *Existence of difficulties*.

2. Lead the Team in Producing the Schedule for the Next Development Cycle

The difficulty in achieving a schedule in environments with workers split in multiple location is higher than single site environments (Cascio & Shurygailo, 2003) due to the necessity of relying on electronic means to communicate (Jang et al., 2000) and the existence of temporal differences that reduces the available time for communications (Solomon, 1995). For these reasons, this activity is assessed as *Existence of difficulties*.

3. Lead the Team in Producing the Balanced Team Plan

One of the main motivators for the use of distributed teams is the ability to distribute the workload among different sites (Anschuetz, 1998), that is why the activity is assessed with *Difficulties not found*. This punctuation is given due to the existence of factors such as trust which hinder the measured activity (Moe & Smit, 2008).

4. Track the Team's Progress against the Plan

As Bell and Kozlowski (2002) argued the main issue for tracking and monitoring in virtual teams is the necessity of distributing the function to the team itself. In addition, the lack of face-to-face meetings restricts the ability to track progress. On the other hand, the self-directed characteristic of TSP teams reduces the criticality of this decision. Due to these factors, this activity is assessed as *Existence of difficulties* because it can be externalized, but some issues that have to be addressed.

DEVELOPMENT MANAGER

1. Lead the Team in Producing the Development Strategy

According to Casey and Richardson (2006), to be effective a successful project management virtual software team, the strategy must address the specific needs of this dynamic environment. In addition, the authors argued that "the objective may be to implement a sustained virtual software team strategy to leverage the technical experience of staff at one location with the availability of competitive cost engineers in another". In a case study of geographically distributed teams carried out by Evaristo et al. (2004) a Japan company used a development strategy that involves a "hands-on approach, with small teams being deployed into the client's facilities and keeping in touch with headquarters only for a limited amount of know-how and general directions". McCaffery et al. (2006) reported a case study of a change in software development strategy in order to continue as a significant player within the GSD industry. Considering that outsourcing represents

outsourcing represents a development strategy by itself, which is not a straightforward task, and considering the cases studies found, this activity is assessed as *Well defined difficulties*; it need to be keep in client side unless full development it outsourced.

2. Lead the Team in Producing the Preliminary Size and Time Estimates for the Products to be Produced

According to Parthasarathy (2007) the environment in which outsourcing service provides organizations do estimations is competitive and complicates the estimation process, but don't point out any limitation or difficulty for carrying this activity out. In addition, Zanoni and Audy (2004) identified size estimation as more difficult task in distributed projects due to requirement specification, test process and communication between participants being more difficult. Therefore, this activity is assessed as *Existence of difficulties*.

3. Lead the Development of the Requirements Specification (SRS)

The analysis of software requirements in global virtual teams carried out by Edwards and Sridhar (2005) indicates that this activity can be done in outsourcing environments. On the other hand, Lormas et al. (2004) reported some issues and problems in the management of software requirements evolution in outsourcing context. Moreover, Smite (2006) obtained some lessons from requirement management in GSD teams that can be useful for this environment, and indicated that this task is arduous if the process is not well defined and if the team is not prepared to work in this scenario. These lessons include for example training in soft skills, use of communication tools, and mutual knowledge. Taking into account these factors, this activity is assessed as *Existence of difficulties* because it can be outsourced but the mentioned issues need to be addressed.

4. Lead the Team in Producing the High-Level Design

The production of high-level designs can be considered as strategic function; therefore the difficulty for outsourcing it is high and can be easier to do it on mature outsourcing relationships (Fisher et al., 2008). In this direction, there are recommendations for backing in-house the high-level designs (Tiwana et al., 2008) and are pointed as a negotiation item with vendors (Lormans et al., 2004). Considering the found recommendations, this activity is assessed as *Well defined difficulties*.

5. Lead the Team in Producing the System Design Specification (SDS)

The system design specification can be created with content management software in GSD environments, but are limited when coediting a complex document (Al-Asmari & Yu, 2006). Lormans et al. (2004) carried a study of a outsource relationship which successfully included design steps from SRS to SDS, therefore this activity is assessed as *Existence of difficulties*.

6. Lead the Team in Implementing the Product

According to Zigurs (2003) virtual teams provide a unique opportunity for redefining the concept of leadership. Casey and Richardson (2006) concluded that project manager must address the specific needs of the dynamic environment. In addition, it is quite common for organizations to meet their software from outsourcing vendors (Wybo, 2007). The factors that influence this activity are the general ones: communication-distance, cultural differences, trust, etc. (House et al., 2008). With this information, this activity is assessed as *Difficulties not found*.

7. Lead the Team in Developing the Build, Integration, and System Test Plans

This activity is three-fold so the analysis has been split. Firstly, according to McMahon (2001) planning and coordinating the builds across distributed sites may be the single greatest challenge faced on virtual projects; therefore this activity is measured with a -5. Secondly, the integration plans need to minimize the dependencies across sites (Herbsleb & Grinter, 1999). In a case-study of reference models for software product integration that included distributed development (Larsson et al., 2009) pointed to four class of problems: inadequate selection and implementation of strategy, inadequate management of architecture and design, inadequate establishment or use of the integration environment, inadequate delivery of functions. For example a share integration plan in order to share points for integration and tasks may be a solution for distributed teams (Cameron, 2006). Another approach is to use an incremental integration plan (Battin et al., 2001). Kommeren and Parviainen (2007) indicate that lack of an explicit integration plan can cause inefficiency and extra complexity to integration activities.

Lastly, the system test plans may be designed for allowing dependency of task distribution (Taweel & Brereton, 2006) and following a strategy that provides predictions before the code is implemented and be capable of taking into account new information about the risk at any stage in development. Therefore, this activity is assessed as *Existence of difficulties*.

8. Lead the Team in Developing the Test Materials and Running the Tests

In a case study, Leszak and Meier (2007) presented a successful case of a large-scale global systems & software development that included software testing. In another case, Hornett (2004) reported a successful case of a virtual team that has the purpose to create and test software to ensure transferability of documents. There are no case of failures neither of problems with this activity in such environment, therefore this activity is assessed as *Difficulties not found*.

9. Lead the Team in Producing the Product's User Documentation

According to a student study carried out by Ellis (2006), interpersonal and intrapersonal interaction and communication among or between team members is needed in order to successful produce documentation. These factors can be moved to product's user documentation and be a critical factor in outsourcing environments due to the inherit problems of communication and coordination. Another key factor for producing documentation in distributed environments is the use of a shared repository (Jang et al., 2000). Taking into account these findings, this activity is assessed as *Existence of difficulties*; it can be outsourced but need a huge extra effort.

QUALITY-PROCESS MANAGER

1. Lead the Team in Producing and Tracking the Quality Plan

In a case study about pitfalls in remote team coordination, Smite et al. (2008) indicated that using a quality system was implemented and process were certified to ISO 9001:2000 standard, and jointly with weekly teleconferences to discuss urgent problems and plans, the project followed standardized guidelines for requirement specification, task management, progress reporting and monitoring, and other activities. In addition, Prikladnicki and Audy (2003) argued that the implementation of a quality model and a continuous software process improvement are very important to succeed. In other case about a distributed project, Spinellis (2006) pointed that

there are no apparent ill effects on the quality of code. This lack of difference between collocated and distributed is not reflected in the study carried out by Canfora et al. (2006). In this study, the results pointed to a link between quality and some factors of distribution settings. Such factors are coordination, communication, and development site (Raffo & Setamanit, 2005). Moreover, organizations search for competitive advantages in terms of cost, quality and flexibility in the area of software development (Prikladnicki et al., 2002), and are a motivator for investing in global software development (Prikladnicki et al., 2003). In a case study of distributed software development in offshoring and onshoring (Prikladnicki et al., 2007), the authors highlighted that the main challenges for quality management were related to difficulties in configuration management, not having a common software process among the distributed teams, and that most of the knowledge was concentrated in the supplier company, making the project documentation hard for the client organization. Considering these findings, this activity is assessed as *Existence of difficulties*.

2. Alert the Team, the Team Leader, and the Instructor to Quality Problems

Quality problems in GSD projects are not uncommon (Carmel, 1999), therefore the alert and communication of quality problems is needed in distributed environments too. Moreover, the management of quality has lead to the creation of excellence models such as eSCM (Hyder et al., 2006; Hefley & Loesche, 2006) which include quality management practices. In GSD, the channels used for communicate and alert are virtual ones instead of face-to-face, and therefore they have specific issues that need to be addressed in order be effective (Anderson et al., 2007). Considering these findings, this activity is assessed as *Existence of difficulties*.

3. Lead the Team in Defining and Documenting Its Processes and in Maintaining the Process Improvement Process

This activity may be threatened by differences in organizational cultures and management practices so the internal procedures may vary. These differences between software processes used by collaborating groups and associated process maturities may be considered as a risk category for virtual development projects (Maidantchik & da Rocha, 2002). In addition to these findings, McMahon (2001) warned about the potential danger of differences in processes and process maturities of collaborating parties in distributed development. Therefore, this activity is have risks and is assessed as *Existence of Difficulties*.

4. Establish and Maintain the Team's Development Standards

One of the main reasons of using development standards is quality assurance (Pressman, 2001). Establishing a standard for development in GSD may be done by balancing plan-driven and agile methodologies (Moe & Smite, 2008) for project management level, and for the level of development standards may be established and used but there have not been found references about this issue. This activity is assessed as *Existence of difficulties*.

5. Review and Approve all Products before Submission to the CCB

Change management in software developments represents a critical key for unique site developments. In GSD environments, it is necessary to redefine the process in order to adjust to the specific peculiarities of these environments and the synchronization between projects can support change management and make it transparent (Carmel, 1999). The centralization of revision

and acceptation tasks about products before been communicated to CCB reduces some of the lessons learned about software change management in distributed environments (Pilatti et al., 2006): working in a unique environment of configuration management and defining a coordinator for products elaboration.

Considering that this activity is not realized automatically in centralized environments and present some problems in distributed environments, this activity is assessed as *Existence of Difficulties*.

6. Act as Team's Inspection Moderator

The goal of this activity is the identification of the defects of each team member's products. During the meeting, the moderator has to focus the attention on the identification avoiding the discussions about the fix actions for each defect. So considering the meeting problems described in the GSD literature (non face-to-face, cost in travels, etc...), the specific problem for this activity is the difficulty for moderator to focus on the identification instead of the fixing of the defects. After a deep analysis of research literature there have been not found references that treat this activity in GSD environments, therefore this activity is assessed as *References not found*.

7. Act as Recorder in All the Team's Meetings

In GSD environments, meetings are mainly virtual ones and communication channels are based on technologies rather than face-to-face meetings (Anderson et al., 2007). Considering the inherent characteristics of communication technologies used for these meetings, the activity of recording the team's meetings may not represent any difficulties, and therefore this activity is assessed as *Difficulties not found*.

GENERAL ACTIVITIES

1. Participate in Producing the Development Cycle Report

The goal of development cycle report is to establish the grade of conclusion of planned work for each team participant and to identify possible improvements in future plans and similar works. Each role participate identifying which tasks have been done, which of the allocated and planned tasks have not been done for the present development cycle, and the possible improvements of these tasks. The participation on this activity is proactive because of the improvement focus of the activity for the next cycles and future projects. Based on these characteristics, the assessment of this activity is based on the proactive style jointly with the ability to generate and obtain information about the project state with participative actions.

On the one hand, proactive style in outsourcing relations is reached once the contract and the SLA down to a second dimensions and a win-win relationship is the first dimension (Lee et al., 2003). In this direction, models for government outsourcing relationships such as eSCM (eSoucing Capability Model) promote and ideal of proactive and collaborative style (Hyder et al., 2006; Hefley & Loesche, 2006). On the other hand, generating and obtaining information represent the background of GSD and there are assumed benefits such as cost reduction, cross-site modularization of development work, and the access to large skilled labor pool, closer proximity to market and customer (Conchúir et al., 2009) that makes GSD attractive for organizations if associated risks are mitigated.

Considering the presented issues, this activity is assessed as *Well defined difficulties*.

2. Act as a Development Engineer

This activity may be considered as the global activity for GSD teams; therefore the problems and issues joint with their solutions are the in-

herent ones for GSD, which have been quickly glanced across the present article, and are widely treated in research literature. Taking into account this conclusion, this activity is assessed as *Well defined difficulties*.

DISCUSSION

Once all the activities of each TSP role have been assessed and in order to sum up the obtained results, a table that summarizes each TSP role assessment are presented and discussed. Firstly, team leader's assessment results point to a general existence of difficulties which may be interpreted as an extra effort in order to carry this role in GSD environments, or an incompatibility between this role and GSD (Table 1).

Secondly, support manager's assessment results point to a less existence of difficulties and there are no well defined difficulties which may be interpreted as a possibility to d carry this role in GSD environments with a little extra effort in managing these activities (Table 2).

Thirdly, planning manager's assessment results seem parallel to support manager's which point

Table 1. Team leader assessment

Team Leader	
Activity	**Assessment Result**
Motivate the team members to perform their tasks	Existence of difficulties
Run the weekly team meeting (Every Week)	Well defined difficulties
Report team status to the instructor (Every Week)	Existence of difficulties
Help the team in allocating tasks and resolving issues	Existence of difficulties
Act as facilitator and timekeeper for all team meetings	Existence of difficulties
Maintain the project notebook	Difficulties not found

Table 2. Support manager assessment

Support Manager	
Activity	**Assessment Result**
Lead the team in determining its support needs and in obtaining the needed tools and facilities	Existence of difficulties
Chair the configuration control board and manage the change control system	Existence of difficulties
Manage the configuration management system	Existence of difficulties
Maintain the system glossary	Difficulties not found
Maintain the team's issue- and risk-tracking system	Difficulties not found
Act as the team's reuse advocate	Existence of difficulties

Table 3. Planning manager assessment

Planning Manager	
Activity	**Assessment Result**
Lead the team in producing the task plan for the next development cycle	Existence of difficulties
Lead the team in producing the schedule for the next development cycle	Existence of difficulties
Lead the team in producing the balanced team plan	Difficulties not found
Track the team's progress against the plan	Existence of difficulties

to a little extra effort in managing theses activities (Table 3).

Fourthly, development manager's assessment results have at least one result in each scale value. Assuming that having difficulties superimpose the non existence of its, the results points to an extra effort in order to carry this role in GSD environments (Table 4).

Finally, quality-process manager's results follow the results obtained for all roles which points to a general presence of difficulties so there is an extra effort needed in order to carry this role in GSD environments. There have not been found references for acting as team inspector moderator

Table 4. Planning manager assessment

Development Manager	
Activity	**Assessment Result**
Lead the team in producing the development strategy	Well defined difficulties
Lead the team in producing the preliminary size and time estimates for the products to be produced	Existence of difficulties
Lead the development of the requirements specification (SRS)	Existence of difficulties
Lead the team in producing the high-level design	Well defined difficulties
Lead the team in producing the system design specification (SDS)	Existence of difficulties
Lead the team in implementing the product	Difficulties not found
Lead the team in developing the build, integration, and system test plans	Existence of difficulties
Lead the team in developing the test materials and running the tests	Difficulties not found
Lead the team in producing the product's user documentation	Existence of difficulties

Table 5. Quality-process manager assessment

Quality-Process Manager	
Activity	**Assessment Result**
Lead the team in producing and tracking the quality plan	Existence of difficulties
Alert the team, the team leader, and the instructor to quality problems	Existence of difficulties
Lead the team in defining and documenting its processes and in maintaining the process improvement process	Existence of difficulties
Establish and maintain the team's development standards	Existence of difficulties
Review and approve all products before submission to the CCB	Existence of difficulties
Act as team's inspection moderator	References not found
Act as recorder in all the team's meetings	Difficulties not found

so it has been not assessed, but this lack of assessment doesn't influence the general result of this role (Table 5).

Figure 1. Assessment results for each role

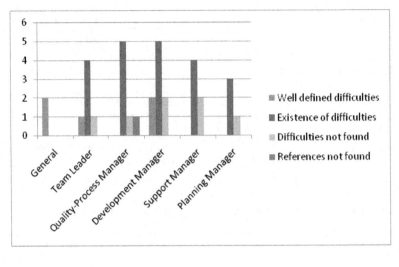

Figure 2. Assessment results

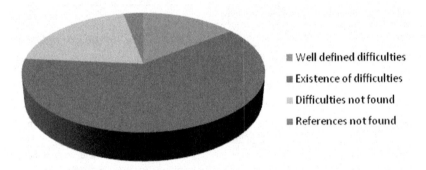

To sum up the results some figures are presented: a figure that represents the assessment for each role is presented (Figure 1), and a figure that represents the sum up of the assessment results (Figure 2).

CONCLUSION

In this the paper, the authors have found several difficulties in order to find references that treat the activities in outsourcing, GSD, or virtual team

environments. These difficulties have lead to a superficial assessment which doesn't have to be considered as the truth, but they can shed light for the utilization of TSP in these environments. On the one hand, considering the results for each role, there is not a role which have no difficulties and all roles have at least a activity that have been assessed as difficulties not found. These results point to a domination of the difficulties. On the other hand, considering the obtained results as global results, more than 75% of the activities of TSP have difficulties in order to execute them in

GSD environments. This result may indicate a difficulty in using TSP in these environments which have to be addressed in future researches with the purpose of assessing the calibration needed for each difficulty. In addition to the strong presence of difficulties for the activities, there is a little presence of difficulties not found assessments point to the same direction.

Finally, the authors propose two future works: (1) calibration of each activity in these environments, which may be done individually for each task or grouping them into categories and may lay the foundation stone for the creation of a Virtual TSP; (2) contrast the obtained results in distributed projects with the purpose of validating the results.

REFERENCES

Acuña, S. T., & Juristo, N. (2004). Assigning people to roles in software projects. *Software, Practice & Experience*, *34*(7), 675–696. doi:10.1002/spe.586

Al-Asmari, K. R., & Yu, L. (2006). Experiences in Distributed Software Development with Wiki. In R. Hamid & H. R. Arabnia (Eds.), *Proceedings of the International Conference on Software Engineering Research and Practice & Conference on Programming Languages and Compilers* (pp. 389-293). Las Vegas, NV: CSREA Press.

Ali Babar, M., Verner, J. M., & Nguyen, P. T. (2007). Establishing and maintaining trust in software outsourcing relationships: An empirical investigation. *Journal of Systems and Software*, *80*(9), 1438–1449. doi:10.1016/j.jss.2006.10.038

Alshawi, M., & Ingirige, B. (2003). Web-enabled project management: an emerging paradigm in construction. *Automation in Construction*, *12*(4), 349–364. doi:10.1016/S0926-5805(03)00003-7

Anderson, A. H., McEwan, R., Bal, J., & Carletta, J. (2007). Virtual team meetings: An analysis of communication and context. *Computers in Human Behavior*, *23*(5), 2558–2580. doi:10.1016/j.chb.2007.01.001

Anschuetz, L. (1998). Managing Geographically Distributed Teams. In *Proceedings of the IEEE Professional Communication Conference (IPCC)*, Quebec City, Canada (pp. 23-25). Washington, DC: IEEE.

Atkins, D., Boyer, D., Handel, M., Herbsleb, J., Mockus, A., & Wills, G. (2002). *Achieving speed in globally distributed project work*. Paper presented at the Human Computer Interaction Consortium, Winterpark, CO.

Avolio, B. J., & Locke, E. E. (2002). Contrasting different philosophies of leader motivation: Altruism versus egoism . *The Leadership Quarterly*, *13*(2), 169–191. doi:10.1016/S1048-9843(02)00094-2

Bandow, D. (2004). Time to create sound teamwork. *Journal for Quality and Participation*, *24*(2), 41–47.

Barthélemy, J. (2001). The hidden cost of IT outsourcing. *MIT Sloan Management*, *42*(3), 60–69.

Battin, R. D., Crocker, R., Kreidler, J., & Subramanian, K. (2001). Leveraging resources in global software development. *IEEE Software*, *18*(2), 70–77. doi:10.1109/52.914750

Bell, B. S., & Kozlowski, S. W. J. (2002). A topology of Virtual Teams: Implications for Effective Leadership. *Group & Organization Management*, *24*(14), 14–49. doi:10.1177/1059601102027001003

Bersoff, V., & Chase, R. (1982). *Software Configuration Management - An investment in Product Integrity*. Englewood Cliffs, NJ: Prentice Hall Inc.

Birks, D. F., Zainuddin, Y., Choo, A. T., Wafa, S. A., Morar, S., & Nasirin, S. (2007). Successful IT Outsourcing Engagement: Lessons from Malaysia. *The Electronic Journal of Information Systems in Developing Countries*, *30*(5), 1–12.

Blackburn, J. D., Scudder, G. D., & Van Wassenhove, L. N. (1996). Improving speed and productivity of software development: a global survey of software developers. *IEEE Transactions on Software Engineering*, *22*(12), 875–885. doi:10.1109/32.553636

Bouas, K., & Arrow, H. (1996). The development of group identity in computer and face-to-face groups with membership change. *Computer Supported Cooperative Work*, *4*(2-3), 153–178. doi:10.1007/BF00749745

Callison, R., & MacDonald, M. (2009). *A Bibliography of the Personal Software Process (PSP) and the Team Software Process (TSP)* (Tech. Rep. CMU/SEI-2009-SR-025). Pittsburgh, PA: Carnegie Mellow University, Software Engineering Institute.

Cameron, J. (2006). Governance structure, mechanisms and methods for managing collaborative eBusiness projects. *Journal on Chain and Network Science*, *6*(2), 155–174. doi:10.3920/JCNS2006.x072

Canfora, G., Cimitile, A., Di Lucca, G. A., & Visaggio, C. A. (2006). How distribution affects the success of pair programming. *International Journal of Software Engineering and Knowledge Engineering*, *16*(2), 293–313. doi:10.1142/S0218194006002756

Carmel, E. (1999). *Global Software Teams: collaborating across borders and time zones*. Upper Saddle River, NJ: Prentice Hall.

Carmel, E., & Agarwal, R. (2001). Tactical Approaches for Alleviating Distance in Global Software Development. *IEEE Software*, *18*(2), 22–29. doi:10.1109/52.914734

Cascio, W. F., & Shurygailo, S. (2003). E-Leadership and Virtual Teams. *Organizational Dynamics*, *31*(4), 362–376. doi:10.1016/S0090-2616(02)00130-4

Casey, V., & Richardson, I. (2006a). Project Management within Virtual Software Teams. In *Proceedings of the IEEE international conference on Global Software Engineering* (pp. 33-42). Washington, DC: IEEE Computer Society.

Colomo-Palacios, R., Tovar-Caro, E., Garcia-Crespo, A., & Gomez-Berbis, M. J. (2010). Identifying Technical Competences of IT Professionals. The Case of Software Engineers. *International Journal of Human Capital and Information Technology Professionals*, *1*(1), 31–43.

Conchúir, E. Ó., Ågerfalk, P. J., Olsson, H. H., & Fitzgerald, B. (2009). Global software development: where are the benefits? *Communications of the ACM*, *52*(8), 127–131.

Cramton, C. D. (2001). The mutual knowledge problem and its consequences for dispersed collaboration. *Organization Science*, *12*(3), 346–371. doi:10.1287/orsc.12.3.346.10098

Cramton, C. D. (2002). Attribution in distributed work groups. In Hinds, P. J., & Kiesler, S. (Eds.), *Distributed Work* (pp. 91–212). Cambridge, MA: MIT Press.

Cress, U., & Kimmerle, J. (2008). A systemic and cognitive view on collaborative knowledge building with wikis. *International Journal of Computer-Supported Collaborative Learning*, *3*(2), 105–122. doi:10.1007/s11412-007-9035-z

Cubranic, D., Murphy, G. C., Singer, J., & Booth, K. S. (2005). Hipikat: a project memory for software development. *IEEE Transactions on Software Engineering*, *31*(6), 446–465. doi:10.1109/TSE.2005.71

Curtis, B., Krasner, M. I., & Iscoe, N. (1988). A field study of the software design process for large systems. *Communications of the ACM, 31*(11), 1268–1287. doi:10.1145/50087.50089

DeMarco, T., & Lister, T. (1987). *Peopleware: productive projects and teams.* New York: Dorset House Publishing Co.

Domberger, S. (1999). *The contracting organization: A strategic guide to outsourcing.* New York: Oxford University Press.

Ebert, C., & DeNeve, P. (2001). Surviving global software development. *IEEE Software, 18*(2), 62–69. doi:10.1109/52.914748

Edwards, K., & Sridhar, V. (2005). Analysis of Software Requirements Engineering Exercises in a Global Virtual Team Setup. *Journal of Global Information Management, 13*(2), 21–41.

Ellis, H. J. C. (2006). An evaluation of learning in an online project-based web application design and development course. *Journal of Computing Sciences in Colleges, 21*(6), 217–227.

Eppler, M. J., & Mengis, J. (2004). The Concept of Information Overload - A Review of Literature from Organization Science, Accounting, Marketing, MIS, and Related Disciplines. *The Information Society: An International Journal, 20*(5), 1–20.

Evaristo, J. R., Scudder, R., Desouza, K. C., & Sato, O. (2004). A dimensional analysis of geographically distributed project teams: a case study. *Journal of Engineering and Technology Management, 21*(3), 175–189. doi:10.1016/j.jengtecman.2003.05.001

Faraj, S., & Sambamurthy, V. (2006). Leadership of information systems development projects. *IEEE Transactions on Engineering Management, 53*(2), 238–249. doi:10.1109/TEM.2006.872245

Faraj, S., & Sproull, L. (2000). Coordinating expertise in software development teams. *Management Science, 46*(12), 1554–1568. doi:10.1287/mnsc.46.12.1554.12072

Fisher, J., Hirschheim, R., & Jacobs, R. (2008). Understanding the outsourcing learning curve: A longitudinal analysis of a large Australian company. *Information Systems Frontiers, 10*(2), 165–178. doi:10.1007/s10796-008-9070-y

Gannon, J. D. (1979). Human factors in Software Engineering. *Computer, 12*(12), 6–7. doi:10.1109/MC.1979.1658569

Goodman, P. S., & Leyden, D. P. (1991). Familiarity and group productivity. *The Journal of Applied Psychology, 76*(44), 578–586. doi:10.1037/0021-9010.76.4.578

Gorla, N., & Lam, Y. W. (2004). Who Should Work with Whom? Building Effective Software Project Teams. *Communications of the ACM, 47*(6), 79–82. doi:10.1145/990680.990684

Grover, V., Lederer, A. L., & Sabherwal, R. (1988). Recognizing the Politics of MIS. *Information & Management, 14*(3), 145–156. doi:10.1016/0378-7206(88)90005-5

Heeks, R., Krishna, S., Nicholsen, B., & Sahay, S. (2001). Synching or sinking: Global software outsourcing relationships. *IEEE Software, 18*(2), 54–60. doi:10.1109/52.914744

Hefley, W. E., & Loesche, E. A. (2006). *eSourcing Capability Model for Client Organizations (eSCM-CL) v.1.1.* Pittsburgh, PA: Carnegie Mellon University.

Herbsleb, J. D. (2007). Global Software Engineering: The Future of Socio-technical Coordination. In *Proceedings of the International Conference on Software Engineering, 2007 Future of Software Engineering* (pp. 188-198). Washington, DC: IEEE Computer Society.

Herbsleb, J. D., & Grinter, R. E. (1999). Architectures, coordination, and distance: Conway's law and beyond. *IEEE Software, 16*(5), 63–70. doi:10.1109/52.795103

Herbsleb, J. D., & Moitra, D. (2001). Global software development. *IEEE Software, 18*(2), 16–20. doi:10.1109/52.914732

Hinds, P. J., & Bailey, D. E. (2003). Out of sight, out of synch: Understanding conflict in distributed teams. *Organization Science, 14*(6), 615–632. doi:10.1287/orsc.14.6.615.24872

Hoogeweegen, M., Teunissen, W., Vervest, P., & Wagenaar, R. (1999). Modular network design: using information and communication technology to allocate production tasks in a virtual organization. *Decision Sciences, 30*(4), 1073–1103. doi:10.1111/j.1540-5915.1999.tb00919.x

House, D., de Vreede, G. J., Wolcott, P., & Dick, K. (2008). Success Factors for the Global Implementation of ERP/HRMS Software . In Ferran, C., & Salim, R. (Eds.), *Enterprise Resource Planning for Global Economies: Managerial Issues and Challenges* (pp. 289–307). Hershey, PA: IGI Global.

Huettner, B., Brown, M. K., & James-Tanny, C. (2007). *Managing virtual teams: Getting the most from wikis, blogs, and other collaborative tools.* Plano, TX: Wordware Publishing, Inc.

Humphrey, W. S. (1995). Introducing the personal software process. *Annals of Software Engineering, 1*(1), 311–325. doi:10.1007/BF02249055

Humphrey, W. S. (1998). Three Dimensions of Process Improvement. Part III: The Team Software Process. *Crosstalk, 11*(4), 14–17.

Humphrey, W. S. (2000). *Introduction to the Team Software Process.* Reading, MA: Addison-Wesley.

Humphrey, W. S. (2002). Three Process Perspectives: Organizations, Teams, and People. *Annals of Software Engineering, 14*(1-4), 39–72. doi:10.1023/A:1020593305601

Hyder, E. B., Heston, K. M., & Paulk, M. C. (2006). *The sCM-SP v2.01: The eSourcing Capability Model for Service Providers (eSCM-SP) v2.01, Part 2: Practice Details.* Pittsburgh, PA: Carnegie Mellon University.

Jang, C. Y., Steinfield, C., & Pfaff, B. (2000). Supporting awareness among virtual teams in a web-based collaborative system: the teamSCOPE system. *ACM SIGGROUP Bulletin, 21*(3), 28–34.

Jarvenpaa, S. L., Knoll, K., & Leidner, D. E. (1998). Is Anybody Out There? The Antecedents of Trust in Global Virtual Teams. *Journal of Management Information Systems, 14*(4), 29–64.

Jarvenpaa, S. L., & Leidner, D. E. (1999). Communication and trust in global virtual teams. *Organization Science, 10*(6), 791–815. doi:10.1287/orsc.10.6.791

Karolak, D. W. (1998). *Global Software Development - Managing Virtual Teams and Environments.* Washington, DC: IEEE Computer Society Press.

Kayworth, T. R., & Leidner, D. E. (2002). Leadership Effectiveness in Global Virtual Teams. *Journal of Management Information Systems, 18*(3), 7–40.

Kim, Y., & Stohr, E. A. (1998). Software Reuse: Survey and Research Directions. *Journal of Management Information Systems, 14*(4), 113–147.

Kirschner, P. A., & van Bruggen, J. (2004). Learning and understanding in virtual teams. *Cyberpsychology & Behavior, 7*(2), 135–139. doi:10.1089/109493104323024401

Kommeren, R., & Parviainen, P. (2007). Philips experiences in global distributed software development. *Empirical Software Engineering, 12*(6), 647–660. doi:10.1007/s10664-007-9047-3

Kraut, R. E., Fish, R. S., & Chalfonte, B. (1992). Task requirements and media choice in collaborative writing. *Human-Computer Interaction, 7*(4), 375–407. doi:10.1207/s15327051hci0704_2

Krikkar, R., & Crnkovic, I. (2007). Software Configuration Management. *Science of Computer Programming, 65*(3), 215–221. doi:10.1016/j.scico.2006.10.003

Krishnan, M. S. (1998). The role of team factors in software cost and quality: an empirical analysis. *Information Technology & People, 11*(1), 20–35. doi:10.1108/09593849810204512

Lanubile, F. (2009). Collaboration in Distributed Software Development. *Lecture Notes in Computer Science, 5413*, 174–193. doi:10.1007/978-3-540-95888-8_7

Laughery, K. R. Jr, & Laughery, K. R. Sr. (1985). Human factors in software engineering: a review of the literature. *Journal of Systems and Software, 5*(1), 3–14. doi:10.1016/0164-1212(85)90003-2

Lee, J.-N., Huynh, M. Q., Kwok, R. C.-W., & Pi, S.-M. (2003). IT Outsourcing Evolution - Past, Present, and Future. *Communications of the ACM, 44*(5), 84–85. doi:10.1145/769800.769807

Lerner, J., & Tirole, J. (2002). Some simple economics of open source. *The Journal of Industrial Economics, 50*(2), 197–234. doi:10.1111/1467-6451.00174

Leszak, M., & Meier, M. (2007). Successful Global Development of a Large-scale Embedded Telecommunications Product. In *Proceedings of the Second IEEE International Conference on Global Software Engineering* (pp. 23-32). Washington, DC: IEEE Computer Society.

Lormas, M., van Dijk, H., van Deursen, A., Nocker, E., & de Zeeuw, A. (2004). Managing evolving requirements in an outsourcing context: an industrial experience report. In *Proceedings 7th International Workshop on Principles of software Evolution* (pp. 149-158). Washington, DC: IEEE Computer Society.

Lynex, A., & Layzell, P. J. (1998). Organisational considerations for software reuse. *Annals of Software Engineering, 5*(1), 105–124. doi:10.1023/A:1018928608749

Mahmood, A. M., Pettingell, K. J., & Shaskevich, A. I. (1996). Measuring productivity of software projects: A data envelopment analysis approach. *Decision Sciences, 27*(1), 57–80. doi:10.1111/j.1540-5915.1996.tb00843.x

Maidantchik, C., & da Rocha, A. R. C. (2002). Managing a worldwide software process. In *Proceedings International Workshop on Global Software Development (ICSE 2002)*, Orlando, FL.

Mao, J. Y., Lee, J. N., & Deng, C. P. (2008). Vendors' perspectives on trust and control in offshore information systems outsourcing. *Information & Management, 45*(7), 482–492. doi:10.1016/j.im.2008.07.003

Marsh, G., & Burke, M. (2001). Knowledge Management and Organizational Effectiveness: balancing the mild, the wild and the crazy. *Australasian Journal of Information Systems, 9*(1), 67–79.

Martins, L. L., Gilson, L. L., & Maynard, M. T. (2004). Virtual Teams: What Do We Know and Where Do We Go From Here? *Journal of Management, 30*(6), 805–835. doi:10.1016/j.jm.2004.05.002

McBride, N. (2009). Exploring service issues within the IT organization: Four mini-case studies. *International Journal of Information Management, 29*(3), 237–243. doi:10.1016/j.ijinfomgt.2008.11.010

McCaffery, F., Smite, D., Wilkie, F. G., & McFall, D. (2006). A proposed way for european software industries to achieve growth within the global marketplace. *Software Process Improvement and Practice, 11*(3), 277–285. doi:10.1002/spip.271

McMahon, P. E. (2001). Distributed Development: Insights, Challenges, and Solutions. *CrossTalk, 15*(11), 4–9.

Metha, A., Armenakis, A., Mehta, N., & Irani, F. (2006). Challenges and opportunities of business process outsourcing in India. *Journal of Labor Research, 27*(3), 324–338.

Mizuno, Y. (1983). Software Quality Improvement. *Computer, 16*(3), 66–72. doi:10.1109/MC.1983.1654331

Moe, N. B., & Smite, D. (2008). Understanding a lack of trust in global software development: a multiple case study. *Software Process Improvement and Practice, 13*(3), 217–231. doi:10.1002/spip.378

Mortensen, M., & Hinds, P. J. (2001). Conflict and shared identity in geographically distributed teams. *The International Journal of Conflict Management, 12*(3), 212–238. doi:10.1108/eb022856

Muthuswamy, B., & Crow, G. B. (2003). Global Software Development: Strategic Implications for U.S. Information Systems Academic Programs. *International Association for Computer Information Systems, 4*(1), 271–276.

Nauman, S., & Igbal, S. (2005). Challenges of virtual project management in developing countries. In *Proceedings of the IEEE International Engineering Management Conference,* New Foundland, Canada (pp. 579-583). Washington, DC: IEEE.

Neef, D. (2005). Managing corporate risk through better knowledge management. *The Learning Organization, 12*(2), 112–124. doi:10.1108/09696470510583502

Nichols, W., Carleton, A., Humphrey, W., & Over, J. (2009). A Distributed Multi-Company Software Project. *CrossTalk, 22*(4), 20–24.

Nunamaker, J. F., Reinig, B. A., & Briggs, R. O. (2009). Principles for effective virtual teamwork. *Communications of the ACM, 52*(4), 113–117. doi:10.1145/1498765.1498797

Olson, G. M., & Olson, J. S. (2000). Distance matters. *Human-Computer Interaction, 15*(2), 139–178. doi:10.1207/S15327051HCI1523_4

Parthasarathy, M. A. (2007). *Practical Software Estimation: Function Point Methods for Insourced and Outsourced Projects.* Boston: Addison-Wesley Professional.

Paul, S., Seetharaman, P., Samarah, I., & Mykytyn, P. P. (2004). Impact of heterogeneity and collaborative conflict management style on the performance of synchronous global virtual teams. *Information & Management, 41*(3), 303–321. doi:10.1016/S0378-7206(03)00076-4

Paulk, M. C., Curtis, B., Chrissis, M. B., & Weber, C. V. (1993). *Capability Maturity Model for Software Version 1.1* (Tech. Rep. CMU/SEI-93-TR-24). Pittsburgh, PA: Carnegie Mellon University, Software Engineering Institute.

Perry, D. E., Staudenmayer, N. A., & Votta, L. G. (1994). People, Organizations, and Process Improvement. *IEEE Software, 11*(4), 36–45. doi:10.1109/52.300082

Pilatti, L., Audy, J. L. N., & Prikladnicki, R. (2006). Software configuration management over a global software development environment: lessons learned from a case study. In *Proceedings of the 2006 international workshop on Global software development for the practitioner* (pp. 45-50). New York: ACM.

Pressman, R. S. (2001). *Software engineering: a practitioner's approach.* New York: McGraw-Hill.

Prikladnicki, R., & Audy, J. N. L. (2003). Requirements Engineering in Global Software Development: Preliminary Findings from a Case Study in a SW-CMM context. In *Proceedings of the 5ᵗʰ Simpósio Internacional de Melhoria de Processo de Software*, Pernambuco, Brazil.

Prikladnicki, R., Audy, J. N. L., Damian, D., & de Oliveria, T. C. (2007). Distributed Software Development: Practices and challenges in different business strategies of offshoring and onshoring. In *Proceedings of the Second IEEE International Conference on Global Software Engineering* (pp. 262-274).

Prikladnicki, R., Audy, J. N. L., & Evaristo, R. (2003). Global Software Development in Practice Lessons Learned. *Software Process Improvement and Practice, 8*(4), 267–281. doi:10.1002/spip.188

Prikladnicki, R., Evaristo, R., Audy, J. L. N., & Yamaguti, M. H. (2006). Risk Management in Distributed IT Projects: Integrating Strategic, Tactical, and Operational Levels. *International Journal of e-Collaboration, 2*(4), 1–18.

Prikladnicki, R., Peres, F., Audy, J. N. L., M'ora, M. C., & Perdigoto, A. (2002). Requirements specification model in a software development process inside a physically distributed environment. In *Proceedings of ICEIS*, Ciudad Real, Spain (pp. 830-834).

Raffo, D., & Setamanit, S. (2005). A Simulation Model for Global Software Development Project. In *Proceedings of the 2006 international workshop on Global software development for the practitioner* (pp. 8-14). New York: ACM.

Sahay, S., Nicholson, B., & Krishna, S. (2003). *Global IT outsourcing: software development across borders*. Cambridge, UK: Cambridge University Press. doi:10.1017/CBO9780511615351

Sawyer, S. (2004). Software Development Teams. *Communications of the ACM, 47*(12), 95–99. doi:10.1145/1035134.1035140

Serrano, M., & Montes de Oca, C. (2004). Using the Team Software Process in an Outsourcing Environment. *Crosstalk, 17*(3), 9–13.

Smite, D. (2006). Requirements Management in Distributed Projects. *Journal of Universal Knowledge Management, 1*(2), 69–76.

Smite, D., Moe, N. B., & Torkar, R. (2008). Pitfalls in Remote Team Coordination: Lessons Learned From a Case Study. *Lecture Notes in Computer Science, 5089*, 345–359. doi:10.1007/978-3-540-69566-0_28

Solomon, C. M. (1995). Global Teams: the ultimate collaboration. *The Personnel Journal, 74*(9), 49–58.

Sommerville, I., & Rodden, T. (1996). Human social and organizational influences on the software process . In Fuggetta, A., & Wolf, A. (Eds.), *Software Process (Trends in Software, 4)* (pp. 89–110). New York: John Wiley & Sons.

Spinellis, D. (2006). Global software development in the freeBSD project. In *Proceedings of the 2006 international Workshop on Global Software Development for the Practitioner* (pp. 73-79). New York: ACM.

Straus, S., & McGrath, J. E. (1994). Does the medium matter? The interaction of task type and technology on group performance and member reactions. *The Journal of Applied Psychology, 79*(1), 87–97. doi:10.1037/0021-9010.79.1.87

Taweel, A., & Brereton, P. (2006). Modelling software development across time zones. *Information and Software Technology, 48*(1), 1–11. doi:10.1016/j.infsof.2004.02.006

Tiwana, A., Bush, A. A., Tsuji, H., Yoshida, K., & Sakurai, A. (2008). Myths and paradoxes in Japanese IT offshoring. *Communications of the ACM, 51*(10), 141–145. doi:10.1145/1400181.1400212

Tomei, L. A. (2007). *Integrating information & communications technologies into the classroom.* Hershey, PA: IGI Global.

Trigo, A., Varajão, J., Soto-Acosta, P., Barroso, J., Molina-Castillo, F. J., & Gonzalvez-Gallego, N. (2010). IT Professionals: An Iberian Snapshot. *International Journal of Human Capital and Information Technology Professionals, 1*(1), 61–75.

Walther, J. B., & Burgoon, J. (1992). Relational communication in computer-mediated interaction. *Human Communication Research, 19*(1), 50–88. doi:10.1111/j.1468-2958.1992.tb00295.x

Walz, D. B., Elam, J. J., & Curtis, B. (1993). Inside a Software Design Team: Knowledge Acquisition, Sharing, and Integration. *Communications of the ACM, 36*(10), 63–77. doi:10.1145/163430.163447

Wybo, M. (2007). The IT sales cycle as a source of context in IS implementation theory. *Information & Management, 44*(4), 397–407. doi:10.1016/j.im.2007.03.001

Zanoni, R., & Audy, J. (2004). Project management model: Proposal for performance in a physically distributed software development environment. *Engineering Management Journal, 16*(2), 28–34.

Zigurs, I. (2003). Leadership in Virtual Teams: Oxymoron or Opportunity? *Organizational Dynamics, 31*(4), 339–351. doi:10.1016/S0090-2616(02)00132-8

This work was previously published in International Journal of Human Capital and Information Technology Professionals, Volume 1, Issue 1, edited by Ricardo Colomo-Palacios, pp. 32-53, copyright 2010 by IGI Publishing (an imprint of IGI Global).

Chapter 12

Identification of Patterns for the Formation of Software Development Projects Teams

Margarita André Ampuero
Instituto Superior Politécnico José Antonio Echeverría, Cuba

María G. Baldoquín de la Peña
Instituto Superior Politécnico José Antonio Echeverría, Cuba

Silvia T. Acuña Castillo
Universidad Autónoma de Madrid, Spain

ABSTRACT

The formation of software development project teams is carried out, conventionally, in an empiric manner; however, in this process, multiple factors should be considered. In literature, the works where this process is modeled are scarce, and most do not consider aspects linked to the formation of the team as a whole. In this paper, a group of patterns that contribute to the formation of software development projects teams are identified through the use of the Delphi method, psychological tests, and data mining tools. The paper identifies patterns that are validated experimentally, while psychological characteristics in the process of software team formations are exemplified.

1. INTRODUCTION

Many investigations recognize that human resources play a critical role in the success or failure of software projects (Acuña, Gómez, & Juristo, 2008a; De Carvalho, 2003; De Marco & Lister, 1999; Gorla & Wah, 2004; IEEE, 2004; Pressman, 2004; Pyster & Thayer, 2005). However, people continue to be the least formalized factor in process modeling, which tends to focus more on the technical aspect (Acuña, Juristo, & Moreno, 2006; André, Baldoquín, Acuña, & Rosete, 2008; Karn, 2006). The inadequate assignment of personnel and problems among project team members are identified as two of the main human factor related difficulties affecting software project success (Charette, 2005; Ryan, 2007). Generally, though, people are assigned to project roles, and teams are

DOI: 10.4018/978-1-4666-0924-2.ch012

formed empirically, with the resulting impact on project quality which is harder in medium-sized and large organizations. The experience of the project leader is useful in the assignment process. However, if this process occurs in an intuitive way and without an objective base, it results as poor use of the resources, not being able to satisfy the chronograms (Ngo-The & Ruhe, 2008) and it can cause dissatisfaction of personnel.

Nevertheless, although the assignment problem has been an object of study for several decades, the works where the assignment of personnel to software project teams is modeled are scarce.

In Acuña, Juristo, and Moreno (2006), De Carvalho (2003), and Ngo-The and Ruhe (2008), models are described that tackle the assignment of personal to software projects. These proposals are centered in the individual assignment of people to tasks or roles of the project and they do not consider factors associated to the formation of the team as a whole.

In this paper the main results of the process of knowledge management are shown. These are carried out to obtain patterns that contribute to formation of software development project teams, making use of Delphi, as an expert method, and of the application of psychological tests and tools for data mining. The identified patterns are validated by means of analysis of successful and unsuccessful projects teams.

This paper is structured as followed. Section 2 describes related work on models of processes for the assignment of personal to software projects and studies that consider psychological aspects in the formation of software teams. Section 3 details the main results of the process of knowledge management carried out to obtain the patterns that contribute to formation of software development project teams through the use of the Delphi method, and of the application of psychological tests and tools for data mining. Section 4 describes the validation of the identified patterns.

2. RELATED WORKS

The assignment of persons to software projects has been a topic hardly approached in software engineering literature. The models of software processes are generally centered in the technical aspects. Such that, recognized models of processes like: People-CMM (Curtis, Hefley & Miller, 2001), Personal Software Process (Humphrey, 1995), Team Software Process (Humphrey, 1998) and the Rational Unified Process (Jacobson, Booch, & Rumbaugh, 2000), although they incorporate the human factor, they do not model the assignment process of personnel to project, neither do they formalize the necessary competences for the execution of roles.

Although many authors have devoted studies to identify competences of IT professionals (e.g., Trigo et al., 2010) or software engineers (e.g., Colomo-Palacios et al., 2010), none of these studies have analyzed in deep psychological factors for the assignment of people to software development teams.

In the next subsection, works where models of processes for the assignment of personal to software projects are proposed and studies that consider psychological aspects in the formation of software teams are analyzed.

2.1. Models for the Assignment of Personal to Software Projects

In De Carvalho (2003), a management process of human resources in software development projects based in the reuse of organizational knowledge of the competences and previous assignments of personnel is proposed. According to the process, the project leaders assign people to each task of the project, taking into account the defined profile which includes competences, experiences and academic formation.

In Ngo-The and Ruhe (2008), a method of planning of releases to develop software incrementally is proposed. The method assigns functionalities to the releases, taking into consideration the technical resources, risks and budgetary restrictions, and aims to maximize the value gained (contribution of the functionality to be assigned to the release). In the assignment, productivity of human resources to execute the different types of tasks is taken into account.

The Process of Guided Software to Capacities Model (Acuña & Juristo, 2004) includes, as an original element, behavior capacities (generic competences), and it proposes two procedures: the first, to determine the capabilities of the members of the team, and the other, to assign people to roles in dependence of their capabilities and those required by the roles. The results obtained in its application demonstrate the effectiveness of considering the generic competences in the assignment process.

The evaluated proposals consider different factors in the assignment. However, the fact of not considering in the assignment process any factor that contributes to the formation of the team as a whole is common, achieving an appropriate balance, and taking into consideration the interpersonal relationships between their members, as suggested in (ISO, 2003; PMI, 2004).

2.2. Studies that Consider Psychological Aspects in the Formation of Software Teams

Although insufficient in relation to importance, the construction of software project teams has been an investigation topic from the 1960's decade. A focus it presents in a group of investigations has been the analysis of the personality in the success or failure of the software teams (De Marco & Lister, 1999; McDonald & Edwards, 2007). In Cockburn (2000), it is stated that the characteristics of people have a first order effect in software development.

In the literature several investigations are reported that approach the use of psychological tests in the formation of software teams. Only in McDonald and Edwards (2007), reference is made

to 40 works developed between 1984 and 2004. In this sense, Myers-Briggs, Belbin and 16PF are identified as three of the tests most widely used in the investigations that target the formation of software teams (McDonald & Edwards, 2007; Thomson & Holcombe, 2007). In the next paragraph a brief characterization of these tests is carried out.

The 16 Personality Factors (16PF) test is an instrument based on psychological research designed to output a very comprehensive overview of personality in the shortest possible time. It is based on measuring 16 functionally independent and psychologically significant dimensions (Catell, 1993). The 16 factors are identified with characters from A to Q4 (A-Warmth, B-Reasoning, C-Emotional Stability, E-Dominance, F-Liveliness, G-Rule Consciousness, H-Social Boldness, I-Sensitivity, L-Vigilance, M-Abstractedness, N-Privateness, O-Apprehension, Q1-Openness to Change, Q2-Self-Reliance, Q3-Perfectionism, Q4-Tension). Besides, each of the factors has negative and positive poles (extremes) based on the score. It is applied to evaluate personality traits mainly in tasks such as personnel selection. Acuña and Juristo (2004) used this test as a way to evaluate the generic competences of the people to be assigned to software project roles.

The Myers-Briggs Type Indicator (MBTI) is a self-perception test that measures four different dimensions of human preferences: Extroversion (E)/Introversion (I), Intuition (N)/Sensing (S), Thinking (T)/Feeling (F), and Judgement (J)/Perception (P). The person's psychological type is identified from the values of each dimension (of the 16 types) (Briggs, Kirby, & Myers, 1998). In software investigations the test has been used, fundamentally, to identify: the type or the pattern that prevails in the personnel of the software team (Capretz, 2003; Varvel, Adams, Pridie, & Ruiz, 2004), the most appropriate types to carry out activities (Devito, 2004) and roles (Gorla & Wah, 2004) in the development process, to evaluate the feasibility or infeasibility of the types diversity in the team (Rutherfoord, 2001), the impact of the different dimensions in the results of the project (Acuña, Gómez, & Juristo, 2008b; Yellen, Winniford, & Sanford, 1995) and in the cohesion of the team (Karn, 2006).

Belbin Team Inventory is a self-perception assessment that is useful for identifying the team roles that a person prefers or avoids. Meredith Belbin, its creator, defines team role as "our particular tendency to behave, to contribute and to be related socially", The Belbin Team Inventory identifies nine roles classified in three categories (Belbin, 2004):

- **Mental Roles:** Plant (PL), Monitor-Evaluator (ME) y Specialist (SP)
- **Action Roles:** Shaper (SH), Company Worker (CW), Completer-Finisher (CF)
- **Social Roles:** Chairman (CH), Resource Investigator (RI), Team Worker (TW).

The categories represent the dimensions of the grade of people's orientation toward the performance of tasks (action roles), toward the world of ideas (mental roles) or toward the relationships with people (social roles). The test has been used in several investigations linked to software to evaluate the impact of the different Belbin roles in the project team (Henry & Stevens, 1999; Klaus, 2001; Stevens & Henry, 2002; Thomas, 1999).

3. PROCESS OF KNOWLEDGE MANAGEMENT

In this section the results obtained from the process of knowledge management used are enunciated with the objective of obtaining patterns for the formation of software development project teams.

Very few studies exist, in the environment of software development about the impact that group factors have like: cohesion, conflict, structure of the team and coordination (Acuña, Gómez, & Juristo, 2008a). In Yang and Tang (2004), the authors

intended to determine the index of cohesion or conflict of a team in function of the reciprocally positive relationships or negatives among their members. However, in large organizations or with many new personnel it is difficult to characterize the relationships among people. The following experiment was developed with the purpose of identifying patterns that contribute to the formation of software team.

3.1 General Description of the Experiment

In the experiment carried out 336 people participated, all of whom are linked to software development, belonging to 25 organizations. Of them, 146 (44%) are professionals that work in software organizations and 190 (56%) are people that dedicated to academics (79 professors and 111 final-year engineering students of computing, belonging to two universities). Psychologists from the Center of Human Capital Formation and Development and the Universidad Autónoma de Madrid's School of Psychology participated in the experiment. The battery of tests applied were formed by six questionnaires: Myers-Briggs, Belbin, 16PF, LPC0.2, LPC0.3 (designed to identify patterns of rejection based on the factors of the 16PF test and in the dimensions of the Myers-Briggs test) and Summarize (designed to characterize the participants and it collects: general data (sex, age, career, student / professional, organization), experience in the development and management of projects, as well as preferences and rejection in function of performing functional roles).

The Belbin test was processed using two procedures: the classic (that identifies primary and secondary roles in function of the hierarchy), and a variant that takes into account both parameters: hierarchy and score. With this variant the fact of establishing the preference for a role with punctuation greater than 9 is limited, which are identified as favorite: primary, secondary and tertiary roles, according to the following rules:

- **Primary role:** hierarchy = 1, and score $\geq$ 18.
- **Secondary role:** hierarchy = 1 or 2, and $15 \leq$ score < 18.
- **Tertiary role:** hierarchy = 1, 2 or 3, and $10 \leq$ score < 15.

After processing the tests, a great volume of data was obtained, therefore, the search of patterns became a very complex task. Consequently, it was decided to apply techniques and tools for data mining. The first step was the preparation of the data which included: cleaning (with the purpose of eliminating the greatest possible number of erroneous or inconsistent data) and transformation (with the purpose of presenting the data in the most appropriate way for data mining). To achieve this, it was requested that each person completes or corrects his/her answers in the event of omissions or errors. The transformations were carried out with the help of the tool Kettle (available at http://kettle.pentaho.org/), and the main purposes were: to create new attributes and to change their type so they were easier to understand or they could be processed by the algorithms for data mining. The used tool for data mining was Weka (available at http://www.cs.waikato.ac.nz/ml/weka/).

3.2. Application of the Delphi Method

As part of the experiment, the Delphi method was applied with the purpose of identifying the contribution of the roles from Belbin to the functional invariant roles, involved in software development. Taking into consideration that success of the use of experts' methods in the process of Engineering of Knowledge depends on several factors, among them the appropriate selection of the experts to interview; the Delphi method was applied previously to identify the criteria of experts' selection. In this first stage the participants were twelve recognized professionals with at least 20 years of experience in management and development of software projects, taken from several software organizations. . The criteria for selecting experts were as follows:

- More than ten years' experience, actively and successfully participating in software development.
- Knowledge of software engineering and of technical project management.
- Have successfully directed at least three people in two or more projects of medium or high complexity.

Applying the criteria mentioned above, 34 experts were selected. These experts received a questionnaire characterizing each of the Belbin roles (features, key responsibilities in the team and accepted weakness). The experts were asked to indicate what role or functional roles in which Belbin roles impacted. Table 1 summarizes the main results of this stage.

3.3. Main Results of the Experiment

The application of both procedures in the processing of the 336 Belbin tests permitted the identification of a common behavior:

- The role Company Worker (CW) and Specialist (SP) were present in students as well as in workers (industry as well as academic); followed, generally, by Team Worker (TW), Shaper (SH) and Completer-Finisher (CF).
- In general, the least favorite roles were: Resources Investigator and Plant.
- Prevalence existed in the preference for the action roles over the mental roles and of the mental roles over the social roles.

The balance among the categories of roles was identified as a pattern to consider in the formation of software teams taking into account its presence in the processed tests and opinion emitted by experts that summarized in Table 1.

Table 1. Contribution of the Belbin roles to the functional roles

Belbin roles	Functional roles												
	Project Leader	Graphic Designer	Change Manager	Configuration Manager	Architect	Analyst	Designer	Database Designer	Programmer	Tester	Security Specialist	Quality Specialist	Documenter
Mental roles													
Plant					X	X	X		X				
Monitor-Evaluator			X		X								
Specialist		X				X	X	X	X		X		
Action roles													
Shaper	X				X							X	
Company Worker									X	X			X
Completer-Finisher		X	X	X				X	X	X		X	X
Social roles													
Chairman	X												
Team Worker			X	X								X	X
Resource Investigator						X					X		

The little difference between the prevalence of the action and the mental roles is explained by the nature of this work. In software development it is necessary that the action role prevails (SH, CW, CF) because the behavior of these roles help so that the project finishes in time and with quality. Nevertheless, software engineering is a discipline that demands creativity. The opinion of experts corroborates this position since the functional roles, associated with essential tasks such as analysis, design, and programming are associated to action roles as well as mental roles.

Another pattern identified is associated with leadership. As observed in Table 1, the experts agree that the team roles Chairman and Shaper contribute to performing the functional role, Project Leader. This relationship confirms that which is proposed in (Henry & Stevens, 1999; Klaus, 2001; Stevens & Henry, 2002). Also, an analysis of the people who participated in the experiment with at least five years of experience in project management allowed verification that 86% had among their favorite roles, Chairman or Shaper. Also, a marked preference for the role Shaper over Chairman is identified. This behavior suggests that the style of technical leadership is predominant in the software environment.

Another pattern identified is the necessity to have the presence of the creative role Plant in software projects. There was agreement in the criteria of experts on the contribution of the role Plant in the performance of the main functional roles of a project: architect, analyst, designer and programmer. These results belong together with that outlined in (Stevens & Henry, 2002).

The pattern proposed by Belbin that demands the presence of all the team roles is validated in this work because the experts associated all the team roles to at least one functional role. However, since the formation of small teams is very frequent in some software organizations, it is intended to offer the possibility of taking as a pattern: to demand the presence of at least the three categories of roles such that they accomplish the patterns identified (leadership, creativity and balance among roles categories), or to demand the presence of all the team roles.

Little preference for the roles Plant and Resources Investigator constitutes a challenge for the academic formation process of the professional given the importance that both have on team roles in software development. Previously it was discussed that the role Plant is indispensable for success of software projects. However, the necessity to establish good relationships with clients and end users and the capacity to capture ideas and to develop contacts, behavior that characterizes a Resources Investigator, is also necessary for the successful performance of a software team.

In the processing of the 336 tests of Myers-Briggs, it was detected that there was a presence of all the psychological types and that ESTJ (22%) and ISTJ (15%) prevailed. Besides, 53% of the participants had preference in the dimensions S/N and T/F for the subtype ST.

From the results obtained from processing the 288 questionnaires, LPC0.3 and of evaluating the relationship with MBTI, it was not possible to identify rules of incompatibility among the psychological types. However, when analyzing the preference and the rejection for each dimension, one could observe that, generally, people rejected the letter contrary to that of their preference. This suggests that the teams formed by people with the same type (homogeneous) could reach agreements easier; nevertheless, that would multiply their strengths as well as their weaknesses. Therefore, the potentiality of this pattern could be feasible in simple projects, with well-known technologies. However, in complex projects the diverse types led to good results. This confirms that outlined in (Rutherfoord, 2001) about the variety of strengths and weaknesses that contribute to better administrate problems that should be better managed in a project. However, it is intended to re-evaluate the

patterns that indicate the necessity of diversity of psychological types in future experiments before it is included in the team formation pattern.

Another behavior to re-evaluate in future experiments with the relationship MBTI-LPC0.3 is the prevalence for the letters E, S, T and J, and the significant percents of rejection for I, N and P.

A behavior that is proposed as a pattern and is applicable to the assignment of the Project Leader is the relationship between the functional role and the subtype E_ _J. In (Gorla & Wah, 2004) it is suggested to use the pattern ENFJ to assign a Project Leader. However, an analysis of the participants with at least five years of experience in project management, allowed verifying that 90% of them matched with the pattern E_ _J; with certain prevalence of the types ESTJ, ENTJ and ENFJ, respectively.

Of 336 persons who participated in the experiment, 302 responded the 16PF test and 305 to the LPC0.2. Nevertheless, the processing did not allow identifying any useful pattern for team formation. In 15 of the 16 factors of the 16PF, more than 50% of the participants had average scores. Except in the case of the factor N, 51% had scores in the positive pole. This result indicates that 51% of the participants are analytic with an intellectual focus that in a general way characterized the professionals of the software industry; which did not contribute significant elements to the effects of the investigation.

When evaluating the results of the questionnaire LPC0.2, it is detected that more than 50% of the participants rejected a group of behaviors: A-(55%), C-(51%), E-(67%), G-(72%), Q2+(69) and Q3-(66%). These results indicated that people are too dependent, impractical and careless. Those who did not consider the opinion of the group, did not commit themselves, and preferred to work alone as rejected. These manifestations of rejection, like in the previous case, characterized the professionals of the software industry. Nevertheless, they did not allow the identification of incompatibility patterns.

In future experiments it is proposed to investigate:

- The correspondence identified by the experts between the rest of the team roles and the functional roles.
- The relationship among types, dimensions or combinations of the MBTI, and functional roles.
- The relationship between the different factors of 16PF and the functional roles.

The above listed analyses were not possible to be carried out from the data gathered in this experiment because only the functional roles that each person preferred or rejected were registered and not those that were performed with quality. In the case of the professionals it was not possible to contact the directors since they belonged to diverse organizations. In the case of the students (although they develop real projects), the teams were very small and each student performed few of the identified roles.

Upon completion of the experiment, it was concluded that the use of the psychological tests can contribute to the formation of teams in software projects. Be that as it may, by itself it cannot identify the good engineers; neither can their results predict absolutely the quality of the execution of a job. In the formation of the team, it is necessary as stated in Acuña, Gómez, and Juristo (2008b), Turkey and Bieman (1995), and Varvel, Adams, Pridie, and Ruiz (2004) to achieve a balance among the psychological characteristics, the competences and the personnel's experience.

4. VALIDATION OF THE IDENTIFIED PATTERNS

With the purpose of validating the identified patterns for the formation of teams, a detailed analysis of the test results of the members of eight teams of projects was carried out. Six of the teams were qualified as successful, taking into account that the project concluded; the requirements specified by the user were considered and that the obtained product was used. Two of the teams were qualified as unsuccessful because the projects they developed were not concluded and the results reached were not in correspondence with the elapsed time. Table 2 summarizes the required information to carry out the analysis. The teams from 1 to 6 qualified as successful and the teams 7 and 8 were unsuccessful.

Analysis of the Successful Teams

The six projects qualified as successful adhered to each of the identified patterns:

- In all the teams, persons who carried out the role Project Leader had preference for the roles Chairman or Shaper and have E_ TJ as psychological subtype, according to the Myers-Briggs test.
- In all the teams, at least two persons existed with preference for the role Plant. Team 1, which developed the most complex project of those evaluated, contained eight people with preference for this role. The results showed that due to the nature of software development, the presence of several Plants was valuable for the teams, in spite of the inconveniences pointed out by Belbin.
- In all the teams the three categories of roles were present and there was a preference for action roles over mental roles and for mental roles over social roles. There also existed representation of all the roles as established in Belbin methodology.

In function of the results obtained, it is important to bring up a commented aspect when evaluating the results of the experiment. On one hand, there is a great diversity of psychological types in each one of the teams and on the other,

Table 2. Main results of the evaluated projects teams

Criteria	Evaluated teams								
	Successful teams							Unsuccessful teams	
	1	2	3	4	5	6		7	8
Total team members	17	10	11	7	9	9	18	9	
MBTI Results									
Project Leader (MBTI)	ESTJ	ENTJ	ESTJ	ESTJ	ESTJ	ENTJ	INFP	INTJ	
Quantity for types *(MBTI)*	7	6	8	5	6	6	10	7	
Bebin Results									
Preference for role CW-CF-SH PL-SP-ME CH-TW-RI	13-6-2 8- 4-6 2-6-3	7-4-2 2-2-5 1-2-1	9-3-2 2-2-7 1-5-1	7-4-2 2-2-3 1-2-1	13-6-1 3-2-6 1-3-1	7-7-1 3-2-6 1-4-1	8-6-3 1-11-4 4-4-7	8-5-0 0-5-1 1-5-0	
Balance among categories *Action roles* *Mental roles* *Social roles*	21 18 11	13 9 4	14 11 7	13 8 4	14 11 5	15 11 6	17 16 15	13 6 6	
Project Leader (preferred roles of leadership)	CH	SH	SH	SH	SH	CH	-	-	

the developed projects were qualified as complex. This situation contributed to reaffirm that the type diversity helped to obtain good results when faced with complex projects. This conclusion confirms what Rutherfoord (2001) said about the variety of strengths and weaknesses that contribute to better administrating problems that should be better managed in a project.

Analysis of the Unsuccessful Teams

None of the two projects qualified as unsuccessful adhered to all the identified models:

- The Project Leaders of these teams did not have as favorite roles, Chairman or Shaper but rather were roles avoided by these individuals. Also, they were introverted (even with very clear preference for introversion in function of the punctuation in this

dimension). The Project Leader of team 7 had preference for an unplanned lifestyle. This analysis allows the conclusion that in both teams, the patterns of leadership were not fulfilled.

- None of the 8 team members had preference for the role Plant. In the case of team 7 (which composed of many persons) although the pattern was satisfied, only one member had preference for this role. This situation entered in contradiction with the creativity that demanded most of the functional roles that intervened in the process of software development.

- In both teams, the three categories of roles were present. However, it is important to point out the absence of the Plant and Resources Investigator roles in team 8 because these roles were qualified as creative. Upon analysis of the balance among categories of roles, team 8 did not comply with the pattern, and although team 7 observed it, little difference existed among the preference for the mental and social roles. This fact reflected a high representation of the social roles. This situation entered into contradiction with the necessity that the software teams have of possessing one marked preference for the mental roles in function of the nature of the work.

The previous analysis allowed the conclusion that the identified patterns are useful for the formation of software development projects teams.

5. CONCLUSION

The results of the psychological tests constituted valuable information for the formation of software project teams. Myers-Briggs and Belbin tests were especially useful.

The application of the Delphi method helped to identify a group of patterns for the formation of software teams, because it permitted the views of the experts about the contribution of Belbin roles to the functional roles that intervened in software development projects to be obtained. The contribution of the Chairman or Shaper roles to the performance of the role Project Leader and the importance of the Belbin role "Plant" in the discharge of the main invariant roles of a software development project: analyst, architect, designer and programmer were pointed out by the experts. The application of the psychological tests and tools for data mining permitted the identification of patterns that contributed to the formation of teams of software projects such as the appropriate balance among the categories of team roles, the presence of the role "Plant" and the demands for the performance of the role Project Leader.

REFERENCES

Acuña, S. T., Gómez, M., & Juristo, N. (2008a). Towards understanding the relationship between team climate and software quality - a quasi-experimental study. *Empirical Software Engineering*, *13*(4), 401–434. doi:10.1007/s10664-008-9074-8

Acuña, S. T., Gómez, M., & Juristo, N. (2008b). Empirical study of how personality, team processes and task characteristics relate to satisfaction and software quality? In . *Proceedings of ESEM, 2008*, 291–293.

Acuña, S. T., & Juristo, N. (2004). Assigning people to roles in software projects. *Software, Practice & Experience*, *34*, 675–696. doi:10.1002/spe.586

Acuña, S. T., Juristo, N., & Moreno, A. M. (2006). Emphasizing Human Capabilities in Software Development. *IEEE Software*, *23*(2), 94–101. doi:10.1109/MS.2006.47

André, M., Baldoquín, M. G., Acuña, S. T., & Rosete, A. (2008). *A formalized model for the assignment of human resources to software projects*. Paper presented at the XIV Latin Ibero-American Congress on Operations Research, Cartagena de Indias, Colombia.

Belbin, R. M. (2004). *Management Teams: Why they Succeed or Fail* (2nd ed.). Oxford, UK: Butterworth Heinemann.

Briggs, I., Kirby, L. K., & Myers, K. D. (1998). *Introduction to Type. A Guide to understanding your results on the Myers-Briggs Type Indicator* (6th ed.). Anaheim, CA: Consulting Psychologists Press.

Capretz, L. F. (2003). Personality types in software engineering. *International Journal of Human-Computer Studies*, *58*(2), 207–214. doi:10.1016/S1071-5819(02)00137-4

Cattell, R. B., Cattell, A. K., & Cattell, H. E. P. (1993). *Sixteen Personality Factor Questionnaire*. Chicago: Institute for Personality and Ability Testing.

Charette, R. N. (2005). Why software fails. *IEEE Spectrum, 42*(9), 42–49. doi:10.1109/MSPEC.2005.1502528

Cockburn, A. (2000). *Characterizing People as Non-Linear, First-Order Components in Software Development*. Paper presented at the 4th International Multi-Conference on Systems, Cybernetics and Informatics, FL.

Colomo-Palacios, R., Tovar-Caro, E., Garcia-Crespo, A., & Gomez-Berbis, M. J. (2010). Identifying Technical Competences of IT Professionals. The Case of Software Engineers. *International Journal of Human Capital and Information Technology Professionals, 1*(1), 31–43.

Curtis, B., Hefley, W. E., & Miller, S. A. (2001). *Capability Maturity Model (P–CMM)* (Tech. Rep. No. CMU/SEI-2001-MM-01). Pittsburgh, PA: Software Engineering Institute.

De Carvalho, L. R. (2003). *Planejamento da alocação de recursos humanos em Ambientes de desenvolvimento de software orientados à Organização. Tese para a obtenção do grau de mestre em ciências em engenharia de sistemas e computação*. Brasil: Universidade Federal do Rio de Janeiro.

De Marco, T., & Lister, T. (1999). *Peopleware: Productives Projects and Teams* (2nd ed.). New York: Dorset House.

Devito, A., & Greathead, D. (2004). *Code review and personality: is performance linked to MBTI type?* (Tech. Rep. No. CS-TR 837). Newcastle, DE: University of Newcastle, School of Computing Science.

Gorla, N., & Wah, Y. W. (2004). Who should work with whom? Building effective software project teams. *Communications of the ACM, 47*(6), 79–82. doi:10.1145/990680.990684

Henry, S. M., & Stevens, K. T. (1999). Using Belbin's Leadership Role to Improve Team Effectiveness: An Empirical Investigation. *Journal of Systems and Software, 44*, 241–250. doi:10.1016/S0164-1212(98)10060-2

Humphrey, W. S. (1995). *A Discipline for Software Engineering*. Boston: Addison-Wesley.

Humphrey, W. S. (1998). *Managing Technical People: Innovation, Teamwork and the Software Process*. Boston: Addison-Wesley.

IEEE. (2004). *Guide to the Software Engineering Body of Knowledge-SWEBOK (2004 Version)*. Washington, DC: IEEE Computer Society.

ISO. (2003). *ISO 10006:2003. Quality management systems-Guidelines for quality management in projects*. Retrieved February 1, 2008, from http://www.iso.org

Jacobson, I., Booch, G., & Rumbaugh, J. (1999). *The Unified Software Development Process*. Boston: Addison-Wesley Professional.

Karn, J. (2006). *Empirical Software Engineering: Developer Behaviour and Preferences*. Unpublished doctoral dissertation, Department of Computer Science, University of Sheffield, South Yorkshire, UK.

Klaus, P. (2001). *Belbin's Company Worker, The Self-Perception Inventory, and Their Application to Software Engineering Teams*. Blacksburg, VA: Virginia Polytechnic Institute.

McDonald, S., & Edwards, H. M. (2007). Who Should Test Whom? Examining the use and abuse of personality tests in software engineering. *Communications of the ACM, 50*(1), 67–71.

Ngo-The, A., & Ruhe, G. (2008). A Systematic Approach for Solving the Wicked Problem of Software Release Planning. *Soft Computing, 12*(1), 95–108. doi:10.1007/s00500-007-0219-2

PMI. (2004). *A Guide to the Project Management Body of Knowledge (PMBOK® Guide)* (3rd ed.). Newtown Square, PA: Project Management Institute.

Pressman, R. S. (2004). *Software Engineering: A Practitioner's Approach.* New York: McGraw-Hill Science.

Pyster, A. B., & Thayer, R. H. (2005). Guest Editors' Introduction: Software Engineering Project Management 20 Years Later. *IEEE Software, 22*(5), 18–21. doi:10.1109/MS.2005.137

Rutherfoord, R. H. (2001). Using personality inventories to help form teams for software engineering class projects. *SIGCSE Bulletin, 33*(3), 76–76. doi:10.1145/507758.377486

Ryan, R. (2007). IT Project Management: Infamous Failures, Classics Mistakes, and Best Practices. *Mis Quarterly Executive, 6*(2), 67–78.

Stevens, K. T., & Henry, S. M. (2002). *Analyzing Software Team using Belbin's Innovative Plant Role.* Retrieved September 30, 2008, from http:///www.radford.edu/~kstevens2/

Thomas, R. (1999). *Group Dynamics and Software Engineering.* Paper presented at the Object Oriented Systems, Languages and Applications Conference, Denver, Co.

Thomson, C., & Holcombe, M. (2007). 20 Years of teaching and 7 years of research: research when you teach. In *Proceedings of 3rd South East European Formal Methods Workshop* (pp. 141-153).

Trigo, A., Varajão, J., Soto-Acosta, P., Barroso, J., Molina-Castillo, F. J., & Gonzalvez-Gallego, N. (2010). IT Professionals: An Iberian Snapshot. *International Journal of Human Capital and Information Technology Professionals, 1*(1), 61–75.

Turley, R. T., & Bieman, J. M. (1995). Competencies of exceptional and nonexceptional software engineers. *Journal of Systems and Software, 28*(1), 19–38. doi:10.1016/0164-1212(94)00078-2

Varvel, T., Adams, S. G., Pridie, S. J., & Ruiz, B. C. (2004). Team Effectiveness and Individual Myers-Briggs Personality Dimensions. *Journal of Management Engineering, 20*(4), 141–146. doi:10.1061/(ASCE)0742-597X(2004)20:4(141)

Yang, H. L., & Tang, J. H. (2004). Team Structure and Team Performance in IS Development: A Social Network Perspective. *Information & Management, 41*, 335–349. doi:10.1016/S0378-7206(03)00078-8

Yellen, R. E., Winniford, M. A., & Sanford, C. C. (1995). Extroversion and introversion in electronically supported meetings. *Information & Management, 28*, 63–74. doi:10.1016/0378-7206(94)00023-C

This work was previously published in International Journal of Human Capital and Information Technology Professionals, Volume 1, Issue 3, edited by Ricardo Colomo-Palacios, pp. 59-80, copyright 2010 by IGI Publishing (an imprint of IGI Global).

Chapter 13
Activity Driven Budgeting of Software Projects

Alexander Baumeister
Saarland University, Germany

Markus Ilg
Vorarlberg University of Applied Sciences, Austria

ABSTRACT

There are numerous forecast models of software development costs, however, various problems become apparent in context to practical application. Standardized methods, such as COCOMO II have to be calibrated at an individual operational level on the basis of the underlying database. This paper presents a new activity based approach that is based on business specific cost data that can be easily integrated into existing management accounting systems. This approach can be applied to software development projects based on the unified process in which activity driven budgeting promises several advantages compared to common tools in use. It supports enterprise specific cost forecasting and control and can be easily linked with risk analysis. In addition to the presentation of a conceptual design model, the authors present a framework for activity driven budgeting and cost management of software development projects combined with concrete implementation examples.

INTRODUCTION

With the forecast of software development costs numerous problems have to be solved and various challenges have to be met (Zaid, Selamat, Ghani, Atan, & Koh, 2008). Firstly, due to the high intensity of human resources the amount of indirect costs is relatively high, which leads to various cost assignment problems. Ongoing efforts in business-management literature to solve these cost problems have been widely discussed (e.g., Atkinson, Kaplan, Matsumara, & Young, 2007; Hicks, 2002; Horngren, Foster, Datar, Rajan, & Ittner, 2008; based on Miller & Vollman, 1985; Cooper & Kaplan, 1988). Furthermore, forecasts of the calculation's quantity structure can be problematic in various ways, depending on the software development project´s innovation level (e.g., Boehm, Abts, & Chulani, 2000; Lum et al., 2003; Pfleeger, Wu, & Lewis, 2005; Boehm, 1981; Leung & Fan, 2002).

DOI: 10.4018/978-1-4666-0924-2.ch013

A sound cost forecast is critical: it can act as an indicator for a lowest price limit calculation when discussing a development request. In case of a fixed price agreement this implies a high profit risk. Besides this, cost forecasting can function as a starting basis for internal budgeting contracts. Furthermore, the ongoing software development process constantly requires the update of costs budgeted according to the progress made. Cost forecasting helps in particular with the evaluation of adjustment provisions as well. Ultimately they may be used as a performance criterion for the project management.

Figure 1 illustrates selected further purposes of cost management in the software development lifecycle. The optimal governance of operational costs by means of cost planning and control is the principle task of software cost management (Boehm et al., 2000).

Key problem of cost forecasting in software development projects is the poor data base: Depending on the novelty of the project, the bulk of the development tasks is unknown and represents a severe hindrance to an accurate cost forecast. However, available forecast procedures are fraught with different problems (Pfleeger et al., 2005). Standard methods like COCOMO II have to be calibrated at a business specific level (Boehm et al., 2000). This preponderates if the underlying data base is not specific to the software development task (Zaid et al., 2008). Sometimes, cost forecasts can only be made when the project has made some reasonable progress. As a consequence, these approaches do not sufficiently support important decisions one has to make before the project starts; the acceptance of an order for software development may serve as an example. Furthermore, many of these approaches take a rather out-dated attitude and adapt to a traditional arrangement of software development projects in consecutive phases, for instance, requirements analysis, design, implementation, integration and system test.

The purpose of this paper is to discuss a new approach to software development cost management based on business specific cost information

Figure 1. Exemplary management purposes in the software development life cycle

project not started yet
- support of order-acceptance decisions
- assessment of external procurement alternatives
- milestone-depending cost budgeting

project is running
- supply of information about plan variances
- support of adjustment decisions
- ongoing information about remaining budgets

project terminated
- performance measurement
- information about gratification of process owners
- improvement of future development projects

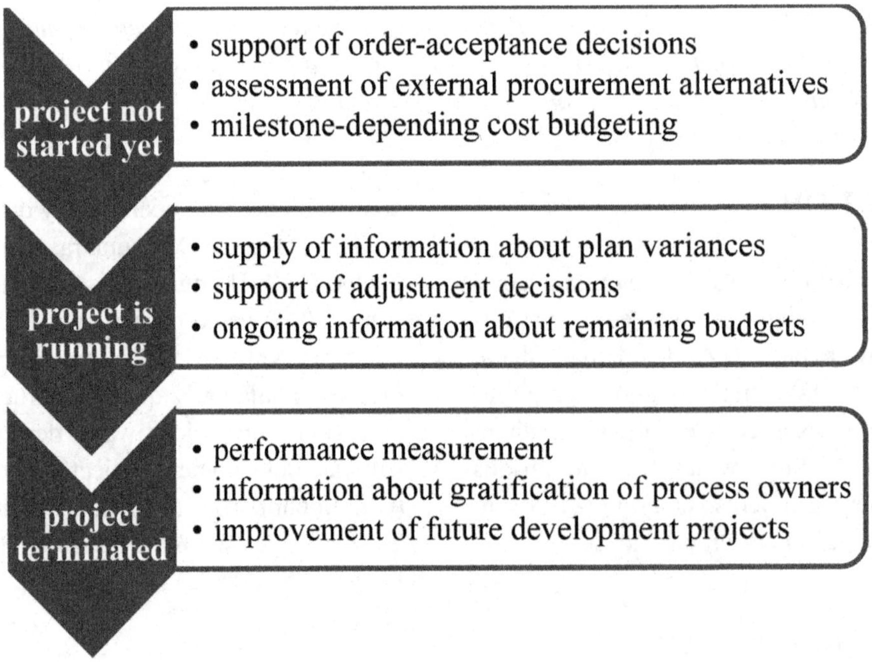

which can be easily integrated into the existing management accounting systems. This approach can be used in developmental projects according to the Unified Process. As an emerging software development process, the Unified Process, which takes a radically different approach to iterative development at heart, attempts to address the major weaknesses of other models and at the same time may serve as a means to facilitate an activity-driven approach to cost management of development projects. Boehm et al. (2000) use in their famous survey about software development cost estimation approaches four main purposes as evaluation measures: Software engineering cost models and estimation techniques should allow for

1. Budgeting,
2. Tradeoff and risk analysis,
3. Project planning and control, and
4. Software improvement investment analysis.

The approach developed in this paper contributes significantly to the first three purposes.

Existing approaches in this field can roughly be classified as algorithmic, expert-based, analogy-based or mixed (Li et al., 2007). Algorithmic techniques can be model-based as e.g. SLIM, Checkpoint or COCOMO, regression-based, learning-based as neural networks with or without regard of dynamic cost effects (e.g., Boehm et al., 2000). In the opinion of the authors, there is – although meaningful – no approach which is enterprise-specific and at the same time integrates classical managerial accounting techniques. This is a feature central to the new methodological approach presented in this paper.

In the following main aspects of the Unified Process are described. This provides a basis to analyse the principles of activity based cost management for software development. Doing so, various applications will be presented. Risk analysis of cost forecasts and cost variance analysis are accented in order to demonstrate the methods decision support suitability even more.

DEVELOPING SOFTWARE PROJECTS ACCORDING TO THE UNIFIED PROCESSS

Iterative Development as the Basic Principle of the Unified Process

Software development processes are used to make the complex task of software development manageable. An example process, which has become increasingly popular in the last few years is the Unified Process (Jacobson, Booch, & Rumbaugh, 1999; Kroll & Kruchten, 2003; Kruchten, 2003). It tries to avoid the problems commonly met in connection with other process models, like the still widely-used waterfall lifecycle, for instance, its rigidity, its lack of comprehension of the users' needs, or the danger of discovering design errors too late (Versteegen, 2005). For analysis and design in software projects, the Unified Process frequently becomes the process model of choice (Booch, Rumbaugh, & Jacobsen, 2005). The Unified Process is built up upon several of the best practices, namely use-case-driven development, tackling high-risk and high-value issues in early iterations, continuously encouraging users for evaluation and feedback etc. (Kruchten, 2003).

The key idea, however, is adaptive development in short, time boxed iterations. Within these iterations the system grows continuously, concluding any iteration with a production grade subset of the final system, which distinguishes iterative development from prototyping. Iterative development facilitates early user feedback and is also a precondition for the early mitigation of high risk issues. Iteration length is fixed within one development project. Date slippage is strongly discouraged, if the deadline cannot be met, tasks are removed from the current to a later iteration. Iterative development continuously adapts the coming iterations based on feedback. It does not try to maintain a detailed plan for the entire project, but concentrates on the next iteration. There are milestone dates and objectives at a macro level of the project, at the micro level only the near future is planned in detail. Date estimates are vague in early project stages, but they improve, as the project goes on (Larman, 2002).

Basic Dynamic Elements of the Unified Process

The Unified Process can be viewed from a static and a dynamic perspective (Figure 2). In its dynamic, schedule-oriented view, the process is partitioned into phases, namely inception, elaboration, construction and transition. The inception phase is kind of a feasibility study. It defines the approximate vision and the business case for the project and provides an approximate time and cost estimate. Its purpose is to justify the cost of further investigation or to cancel the project at this early stage. The lifecycle objective milestone (LCO) marks the end of the inception phase.

Iterative development starts with two to four iterations in the elaboration phase, where serious investigation, the implementation of the core architecture and the clarification of most of the requirements are done. High risk and high value issues are tackled, use cases are refined and time and cost estimates are recalculated on the basis of the deeper insight in the projects details. The lifecycle architecture milestone (LCA) denotes the end of the elaboration phase. The implementation of all remaining elements and preparation for deployment make up the contents of the construction phase. It is significantly longer than the other phases and ends with the initial operational capability (IOC) milestone. User and release documentation are part of the outcome of this phase. Beta tests and deployment constitute the major issues in the transition phase. The new software system is integrated with existing software applications. If the new system replaces older but critical applications, both should be run parallel at first. Workshops and in-house training ease the acceptance of the new system by its users. The product release milestone (PR) marks

the end of the transition phase (Essigkrug & Mey, 2007; Kroll & Kruchten, 2003; Larman, 2002).

Organization of the Static Dimension

The Unified Process phases elaboration, construction and transition are composed of several iterations of equal length, and each of these mini-projects constitutes a fully-fledged construction cycle. The outcome of each is a tested and integrated subsystem, which is successively refined and enlarged by subsequent iterations. Therefore, each of the Unified Process' iterations requires its own requirements analysis, design, implementation, testing and deployment activities. Together with roles, artifacts and workflows these activities make up the static view of the Unified Process (Kroll & Kruchten, 2003).

The Unified Process groups all the process elements into so called disciplines, distinguishing six core disciplines and three supporting disciplines. Typical activities within the discipline of business modelling are the analysis of the organizational structure, domain object modelling and the description of the main objectives. Within requirements use cases are written. They build a focal point of Unified Process driven projects. The design discipline covers a wide variety of design aspects, for instance databases, networks and the overall architecture. Programming and building the system is part of the implementation discipline, the proper interaction of all components is tested in the test discipline.

Installing the product at the users' machines and interconnecting with legacy systems or setting up a user help desk make up deployment. Configuration and change management, the first of the three supporting disciplines, is needed to manage the daily builds in mature project phases and to keep track of change requests. Holding on to the coarse phase plan and the construction of the iteration plan for the forthcoming iteration is subject matter of project management. The environment discipline is of prominent importance

Figure 2. Unified Process' phases and disciplines (similar to Kroll & Kruchten, 2003; Larman, 2002)

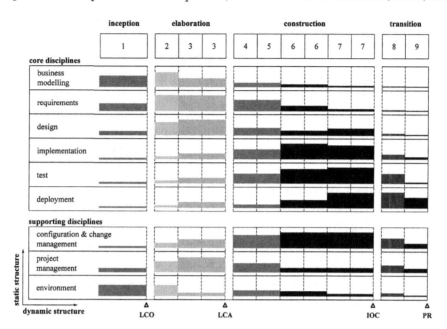

in early project phases, because it delivers the infrastructure needed to run the project (Kruchten, 2003; Versteegen, 2000).

Each of the iterations consists of all nine disciplines, however, the emphasis is on business modelling, requirements, design and environment in early project phases and shifts to construction, implementation and test as the project matures. In iteration no. 2 (Figure 2) relevance of business modelling has declined in relation to implementation and test.

ACTIVITY BASED COST MANAGEMENT OF SOFTWARE DEVELOPMENTS

Structural Affinities between the Unified Process and Activity Based Cost Systems

Taking a closer look, interesting affinities between the Unified Process and activity based cost systems can be revealed. Any iteration, for example, consists of the six core and three supporting disciplines with typical activities within each discipline. These activities correspond to the activities known in the context of activity based cost management, the disciplines make up activity groups. The identification of activities, which is usually the starting point for activity based costing, is by and large predetermined by the static structure of the Unified Process. The quantity of the activities set off by the disciplines and consequently their expenses may be differing clearly subject to iteration type and development phase. However, the main advantage when building up an activity based cost system for software developments is the consistent structure of the projects; the disciplines' types and their corresponding activities remain equal. This facilitates the creation of an activity based cost management system by default for software developments based on the Unified Process.

In its dynamic perspective, the Unified Process separates the development project into the four development phases. The iterations necessary within the development phases differ considerably in type and number for different projects. They connect software- and project-properties and the activities needed to accomplish these requirements on a quantity basis.

Iterations may therefore be interpreted as influencing components for activity costs. Iterations make up the cost drivers for activity based cost systems based on the Unified Process.

Cost functions are required to calculate total project costs, to predict the presumed costs needed to reach one of the milestones, or to determine the costs of one of the development phases. In acknowledging iterations as cost drivers, they may be used as variables in cost functions.

Theoretically, the best way to forecast the costs of a software project most precisely would be to forecast each and every individual iteration on its own. At the same time, this approach would not meet the objective of simplifying the calculation by concentrating on a small number of highly significant cost determinants. Therefore, similar iterations within each development phase should be grouped by attributes typical to software development. Nearby examples are the usage intensity of the particular disciplines, the planned number of people working on the project or the personnel structure typical for the iterations. The goal is to peel out homogenous iteration types in order to minimize the shortcomings of the cost allocation, and – at the same time – minimizing the number of iteration types to keep the budgeting approach as simple as possible. To identify the relevant attributes cluster-analytical methods can be used; they allow the adjustment of the number of clusters dependent on specific distance metrics. When taking account of attributes like personnel structure, which may lead to volatile cost behaviour for specific iterations, an alternative approach to an improved differentiation of iteration types is to implement cost driver functions depending on one or more independent variables derived from properties specific to software projects and related implementation decisions.

Iteration cost rates quote the amount of activity costs triggered by the one-time execution of the iteration or the iteration type. To calculate iteration cost rates, all activity costs concerning a specific iteration are totalled and then divided by the underlying quantity of iterations of the same type. Fundamental to this simple reckoning is the breakdown of activity costs to their causing iterations. Cost functions are incomplete if only the quantity of all iteration types priced with their iteration cost rates were employed. Additionally, other activity-independent costs have to be accounted for. In any case, direct costs concerning the cost object have to be added, for which consultancy expenses for the development project may serve as an example.

The structure of an activity based cost system for software developments according to the Unified Process is pointed out in Figure 3.

For the application of activity based costing to the pricing of software projects it is inevitable to implement it as a direct costing system. The differentiation of activity costs into costs which are dependent on activity quantities and those which are not, which is quite common to activity based costing as implemented in Europe, is based on cost splitting depending on a specific reference variable. However, just as it is the case with all other approaches based on full costing, the consideration of costs not depending on activity quantities can lead to misleading pricing decisions. In the case of Figure 3, costs independent of iterations are separated. They cannot be assigned to a specific project, but have to be considered building up a one- or multi-level contribution margin accounting.

A Framework for Activity Driven Budgeting

The preparation of budgets using activity based costing follows an output-oriented perspective. Starting with a cost centre's planned output the required quantity of activities and their respec-

Figure 3. Structure of an activity based cost system for software developments according to the Unified Process

disciplines / activities	inception iteration type 1	elaboration iteration type 2	elaboration iteration type 3	construction iteration type 4	...	construction iteration type 9	transition iteration type 10	transition iteration type 11	costs independent of iterations	Σ
business modeling										
determination of objectives	31.0 % 26,350 €	33.0 % 28,050 €	9.0 % 7,650 €	6.0 % 5,100 €	...	0.2 % 170 €	0.2 % 170 €	0.1 % 85 €	14.5 % 12,325 €	100.0 % 85,000 €
organizational analysis	16.0 % 20,000 €	25.0 % 31,250 €	13.0 % 16,250 €	8.0 % 10,000 €	...	1.5 % 1,875 €	1.0 % 1,250 €	0.5 % 625 €	21.0 % 26,250 €	100.0 % 125,000 €
documentation glossary maintenance	19.0 % 17,575 €	22.0 % 20,350 €	9.0 % 8,325 €	8.0 % 7,400 €	...	3.0 % 2,775 €	2.0 % 1,850 €	1.0 % 925 €	18.0 % 16,650 €	100.0 % 92,500 €
business rules management	7.0 % 2,485 €	23.0 % 8,165 €	24.0 % 8,520 €	13.0 % 4,615 €	...	3.0 % 1,065 €	2.0 % 710 €	1.0 % 355 €	5.0 % 1,775 €	100.0 % 35,500 €
modeling use case modeling	10.0 % 25,200 €	25.0 % 63,000 €	29.0 % 73,080 €	11.0 % 27,720 €	...	1.5 % 3,780 €	1.0 % 2,520 €	1.0 % 2,520 €	11.0 % 27,720 €	100.0 % 252,000 €
business object modeling	15.0 % 29,175 €	24.0 % 46,680 €	16.0 % 31,120 €	13.0 % 25,285 €	...	2.5 % 4,863 €	0.5 % 973 €	0.5 % 973 €	9.0 % 17,505 €	100.0 % 194,500 €
requirements					...					
environment					...					
total costs	2,554,341 €	4,473,144 €	2,622,570 €	3,507,865 €	...	1,046,016 €	2,285,565 €	365,120 €	10,222,500 €	34,986,823 €
cost driver quantities	41	52	38	85	...	18	85	40	----	----
cost driver rates	62,301 €	86,022 €	69,015 €	41,269 €	...	58,112 €	26,889 €	9,128 €	----	----

tive costs are calculated. The sound assessment of a project's budget is only ensured, if a direct costing approach to activity based costing is used. An activity driven budget is prepared according to the following six steps (Figure 6):

1. **Activity identification:** To begin with, all cost centers and the activities they are accomplishing have to be identified.

2. **Calculation of planned activity costs:** To determine relevant activity costs, it is essential to focus on planned values, i.e., planned quantities and planned costs.

3. **Determination of cost drivers:** It is possible to calculate activity quantities and activity costs for each of the activities identified. However, this approach has a tendency to become rather complex and time-consuming because of the large number of different activity types which typically can be found. Therefore it is natural to concentrate on cost drivers. They should have a more or less constant quantitative proportion to the activities they trigger. If one accomplishes to come along with rather few cost drivers to explain a great many of the activities triggered, these cost drivers can be used as reference values to simplify the budgeting process.

4. **Calculation of planned cost driver rates:** First, for all cost drivers identified in the previous step, planned activity costs for all activities employed have to be calculated. Dividing these costs with their respective cost driver quantities yields planned cost driver rates. The planned cost driver rates represent total costs per cost driver unit.

5. **Construction of the cost function:** Planning with a cost function belongs to the concept of flexible costing. It is prerequisite for budget control and the analysis of budget variances. Therefore, a cost function for the object to be budgeted has to be determined first. This cost function consists of the planned cost

driver quantities as independent variables, weighted with planned cost driver rates as calculated in the steps above. Additionally other direct costs not depending on the underlying activities may have to be considered. These activity-independent direct costs evolve of external consulting services or from the usage of external IT-resources, for instance.

6. **Forecast of independent variables, budget preparation:** To calculate the budget, the planned values of all independent variables have to be forecasted applied to the cost function.

Figure 4 shows the basic steps for an activity driven budget preparation:

Figure 4. Basic steps for activity driven budget preparation

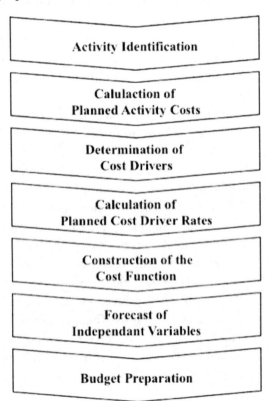

Activity Driven Cost Forecasting of Software Developments

A major issue in early stages of software developments is the lack of information concerning the quantities of the activities required. The quantity structure only gains accuracy while the project is maturing. It is exactly this problem which makes an activity based approach to cost advantageous. In using iterations as cost drivers forecasting is limited to very few key numbers. Their assessment is more likely to be reliable than the guessing of a great number of activities. Furthermore it is possible to infer quantities for the numerous activities required to complete a software development project, using the typical arrangement of iterations for average projects of similar types as a starting point. In any case, the initial analysis of the dependencies between iteration costs and activities is of particular importance.

Even though precise information about types and quantities of iterations for a new software project is not available until the end of elaboration, similarity considerations to iterations of projects already realized allow making an estimate. Estimation requires the comparability of structures of the project that has to be calculated and completed software developments serving as analogy groundwork. Furthermore, it has to be assumed that similar iterations direct to similar amounts of activities and – as a consequence – to similar activity costs. To find similar projects and iterations numerous indicators may be used, preferably indicators referring to the desired properties of the software under development or corresponding to characteristics of the development process.

Figure 5 shows the basic rationale of the similarity based estimation method. Similarity indicators are used to compare the project to be calculated with already existing projects to estimate the number of iterations necessary.

Some examples are requirements concerning the soundness of the system being developed, the number of code lines, interfaces or transaction masks, the software tools utilized or the amount of development resources procured externally. At the same time, these indicators frequently cause variables within algorithmic techniques for complexity and cost estimation like the COCOMO II (Constructive Cost Model) (Boehm et al., 2000). As these procedures do not rely on the individual project experience of the organization, calibration of these methods before to their adoption is indispensable.

Prerequisite to the sound standing of an estimate based on similarities is a database containing a sufficient amount of historic project data (cf., Li, Ruhe, Al-Emran, & Richter, 2007; Keung, Kitchenham, & Jeffery, 2008 to overview new approaches of similarity estimation). If the database does not contain any comparable projects or iterations, the similarity approach can still be employed, if adjusting computations are added to the estimation procedure. In the development of physical goods the usage of regression analysis with one or more variables is prevalent (Ehrlenspiel, Kiewert, Lindemann, & Hundal, 2007) and it may also be applied to estimates for software developments. Estimation based on similar iterations, however, is advantageous compared to other approaches, which mostly refer to the object of calculation as a whole and therefore require suf-

ficient similarity in the overall scope, whereas for software developments based on the Unified Process finding similar iterations is satisfactory. These iterations may originate from entirely different software types, an accounting application and a computer game for instance. The requirements for similarity estimation on an iteration basis are therefore less demanding, provided that information about the iterations required for the software under development is available. At the start of the project, there may be only a vague imagination of the iterations required; however, a precise idea of type and number of forthcoming iterations is a result of the elaboration phase.

Figure 3 exemplifies several activities within the discipline of business. The budget or total costs TC_h for project h (h = 1, 2,..., H) is the sum of the activity based costs C_h and all other direct costs DC_h of the project.

$$TC_h = \underbrace{\sum_{i=1}^{I} r_i \cdot x_{hi}}_{C_h} + DC_h \quad \forall \ h = 1, \ 2, \ ..., \ H,$$

(1)

r_i (i= 1, 2, 3, ...,I) denoting the iteration cost rate for iteration i and x_{hi} the quantity of cost driver i in project h. It is equal to the sum of the

Figure 5. Basic principle of similarity estimation

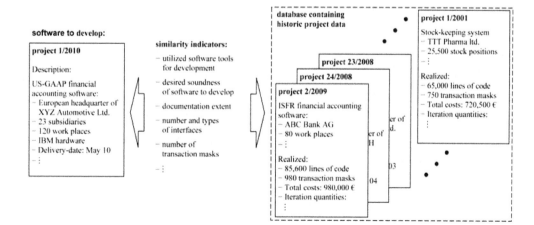

budgeted phase costs (calculated as the sum of activity based and direct costs in each development phase). The acquired cost function may be used for cost planning, ongoing budget control and the accomplishment of cost variance analysis.

Summarizing all budget costs and adding remaining fixed costs FC independent of iterations add up to an activity based enterprise cost function:

$$EC = \sum_{h=1}^{H} (C_h + DC_h) + FC \qquad (2)$$

To calculate cost estimates for price quotation or to determine a cost budget, the estimated number of iteration types for the new project is applied to cost function (1) for each of the four phases of the Unified process. Obviously, it is essential to use planned iteration cost rates as parameters to the cost function. Figure 6 illustrates an example of a phase-based, milestone-oriented budget calculation. The milestones are taken from Figure 2. The cost rates per iteration correspond with the rates of Figure 3. The planned iteration type quantity data for the software to develop are mentioned in parenthesis. They can be derived by a similarity estimation, for example directly of a best fitting single project or as an average derived from a group with partially deviating indicator values, if

Figure 6. Example for a budget calculation and a quotation pricing of the project 1/2010

phase	planned activity costs	planned direct costs	phase budget
inception	$62{,}301\ € \cdot (x_{h1} = 1)$ $= 62{,}301\ €$	*18,000 €*	*80,301 €*
elaboration	$86{,}022\ € \cdot (x_{h2} = 2)$ $+ 69{,}015\ € \cdot (x_{h3} = 2)$ $= 310{,}074\ €$	*74,100 €*	*384,174 €*
construction	$41{,}269\ € \cdot (x_{h4} = 2)$ $+ 23{,}382\ € \cdot (x_{h5} = 5)$ $+ 25{,}592\ € \cdot (x_{h6} = 0)$ $+ 35{,}596\ € \cdot (x_{h7} = 1)$ $+ 72{,}791\ € \cdot (x_{h8} = 2)$ $+ 58{,}112\ € \cdot (x_{h9} = 0)$ $= 382{,}876\ €$	*119,000 €*	*501,876 €*
transition	$+ 26{,}889\ € \cdot (x_{h10} = 2)$ $+ 9{,}128\ € \cdot (x_{h11} = 1)$ $= 62{,}906\ €$	*12,400 €*	*75,306 €*
total	*818,157 €*	*223,500 €*	*1,041,657 €*
profit charge (10 %)			*104,166 €*
risk premium (5 %)			*52,083 €*
quotation price			*1,197,906 €*

necessary statistically adjusted. The total budget can be the initial point of the quotation pricing if a profit margin can be added. In practice one or more risk-premiums may be added.

Budgeting Long-Term Projects

When budgeting long-term projects which outlive the standard planning period, financing costs have to be considered. The analogy-based determination of quantities of different iteration types still remains a helpful basis for the cost forecast, since following the Unified Process every single iteration is of the same duration. Therefore, the cumulative number of subsequent iterations can directly be used as information about the relative payment period of the related iteration costs. Figure 7 illustrates the calculation of the NPV cost budget for project 1/2010 (see figure 6 for quantities of iteration types). Having determined the relative payment period, the cost driver rates for the respective iteration are multiplied by the triggered iteration quantity. Assuming a pure successive accomplishment of all iterations, these quantities are of 0/1-type. Multiplying by the discount factors, in this example $1,05^{-\text{relative payment period}/12}$ assuming iteration periods of one month and a discount rate of 5% p.a. yields discounted cost driver rates. Analoguely, the cash flow impact of direct costs has to be analysed. Figure 6 uses the simplifying assumption that the cash flow impact of each cost driver rate is restricted to the respective phase. Only then it is the case that the accumulated cash flows of each phase are equal to the direct costs of these phases. The sum of discounted cost driver rates and discounted direct costs results in the discounted phase costs.

Important Issues Concerning Cost Control after Project-Termination

Performance control has to be restricted to cost constituents influenced by responsible managers (principle of controllability). For instance, the rise

of procurement prices cannot be accounted to the manager in charge of task and activity planning. This is why cost variances have to be separated according to deviation causes. The rationale of a differentiated deviation analysis is shown by the example of total activity based costs as in (3), with C_h denoting the cost of project h (h = 1, 2, ..., H)

$$C = \sum_{h=1}^{H} C_h = \sum_{h=1}^{H} \sum_{i=1}^{I} r_i \cdot x_{hi}. \tag{3}$$

One execution of iteration i actuates activity j q_{ij} times (j = 1, 2, ..., J). Then, denoting the cost for single execution of activity j with c_j, the iteration cost rate summarizes applying the direct calculation method to

$$r_i = \sum_{j=1}^{J} q_{ij} \cdot c_j \qquad \forall\ i = 1,\ 2,\ ...,\ I. \tag{4}$$

If the indirect method of activity based costing is used, this leads to

$$r_i = \sum_{j=1}^{J} \underbrace{\frac{q_{ij}}{\sum_{i=1}^{I} q_{ij}}}_{\alpha_{ij}} \cdot \underbrace{\overbrace{\sum_{i=1}^{I} q_{ij} \cdot c_j}^{q_j}}_{C_j} \qquad \forall\ i = 1,\ 2,\ ...,\ I,$$

$$\tag{5}$$

whereby α_{ij} is the portion of costs of activity j caused by iteration i. Obviously, the sum of all projects costs is identical to the sum of all activity costs:

$$\sum_{h=1}^{H} C_h = \sum_{j=1}^{J} C_j. \tag{6}$$

Consequently, the activities required by the iterations are subject to combined price- and quantity-variances of a higher order and it is likely, that these can be influenced by different

Figure 7. Example for a NPV budget calculation of project 1/2010

phase	relative payment period	cost driver rates	discount factors	discounted cost driver rates	direct costs	discounted direct costs	discounted phase costs
inception	1	62,301 €·1	0,99594	62,048.21 €	18,000 €	17,926.96 €	79,975.15 €
elaboration	2	86,022 €·1	0,99190	85,325.33 €	19,500 €	19,342.07 €	
	3	86,022 €·1	0,98788	84,979.12 €	12,400 €	12,249.67 €	
	4	69,015 €·1	0,98387	67,901.66 €	35,200 €	34,632.16 €	
	5	69,015 €·1	0,97988	67,626.14 €	*7,000 €*	6,859.13 €	
					74,100 €		378,915.29 €
construction	6	41,269 €·1	0,97590	40,274.42 €	9,500 €	9,271.05 €	
	7	41,269 €·1	0,97194	40,111.00 €	13,400 €	13,024.00 €	
	8	23,382 €·1	0,96800	23,069.29 €	8,100 €	7,840.77 €	
	9	23,382 €·1	0,96407	22,975.69 €	21,900 €	21,113.11 €	
	10	23,382 €·1	0,96016	22,882.46 €	5,600 €	5,376.88 €	
	11	23,382 €·1	0,95626	22,789.61 €	9,200 €	8,797.60 €	
	12	23,382 €·1	0,95238	22,697.14 €	17,500 €	16,666.67 €	
		25,592 €·0		0.00 €	0 €	0.00 €	
	13	35,596 €·1	0,94852	33,763.40 €	18,600 €	17,642.41 €	
	14	72,791 €·1	0,94467	68,763.32 €	7,300 €	6,896.08 €	
	15	72,791 €·1	0,94083	68,484.31 €	7,900 €	7,432.59 €	
		58,112 €·0		0.00 €	*0 €*	0.00 €	
					119,000 €		479,871.80 €
transition	16	26,889 €·1	0,93702	25,195.46 €	3,400 €	3,185.86 €	
	17	26,889 €·1	0,93322	25,093.22 €	5,500 €	5,132.68 €	
	18	9,128 €·1	0,92943	8,483.82 €	*3,500 €*	3,253.00 €	
					12,400 €		70,344.05 €
total		818,157 €		792,463.61 €	223,500 €	216,642.70 €	1,009,106.31 €

managers to an unequal extent, and therefore this has to be taken into account.

To break down activity costs, a differential cost analysis is needed. Having β_{jg} as the consumption rate of activity j for resource g, m_g and p_g as quantity used and price of resource g (g = 1, 2, …, G), this leads to

$$r_i = \sum_{j=1}^{J} \alpha_{ij} \cdot q_j \cdot \sum_{g=1}^{G} \beta_{jg} \cdot m_g \cdot p_g \ \forall\ i = 1,\ 2,\ ...,\ I \tag{7}$$

and a total cost of

$$C = \sum_{h=1}^{H} \sum_{i=1}^{I} \sum_{j=1}^{J} \sum_{g=1}^{G} \alpha_{ij} \cdot q_j \cdot \beta_{jg} \cdot m_g \cdot p_g \cdot x_{hi}. \tag{8}$$

The total deviation of activity costs consists in each case of one sixth-degrees, six first-degree and fifth-degrees, fifteen second- and fourth-degrees and twenty third-degrees deviations. With partial deviations $\Delta\alpha ij$ for iteration-activity-structure, Δq_j

for activity quantities, $\Delta\beta_{jg}$ for resource structure, Δm_g for resource quantity Δp_g for price and Δx_{hj} for iteration quantity this leads to

$$\Delta C = \sum_{h=1}^{H} \sum_{i=1}^{I} \sum_{j=1}^{J} \sum_{g=1}^{G} \begin{bmatrix} \Delta\alpha_{ij} \cdot \Delta q_j \cdot \Delta\beta_{jg} \cdot \Delta m_g \cdot \Delta p_g \cdot \Delta x_{hi} \\ +\Delta\alpha_{ij} \cdot \Delta q_j \cdot \Delta\beta_{jg} \cdot \Delta m_g \cdot \Delta p_g \cdot x_{hi}^{P} \\ +\vdots \\ +\alpha_{ij}^{P} \cdot q_j^{P} \cdot \beta_{jg}^{P} \cdot m_g^{P} \cdot \Delta p_g \cdot \Delta x_{hi} \\ +\Delta\alpha_{ij} \cdot q_j^{P} \cdot \beta_{jg}^{P} \cdot m_g^{P} \cdot p_g^{P} \cdot x_{hi}^{P} \\ +\alpha_{ij}^{P} \cdot \Delta q_j \cdot \beta_{jg}^{P} \cdot m_g^{P} \cdot p_g^{P} \cdot x_{hi}^{P} \\ +\alpha_{ij}^{P} \cdot q_j^{P} \cdot \Delta\beta_{jg} \cdot m_g^{P} \cdot p_g^{P} \cdot x_{hi}^{P} \\ +\alpha_{ij}^{P} \cdot q_j^{P} \cdot \beta_{jg}^{P} \cdot \Delta m_g \cdot p_g^{P} \cdot x_{hi}^{P} \\ +\alpha_{ij}^{P} \cdot q_j^{P} \cdot \beta_{jg}^{P} \cdot m_g^{P} \cdot \Delta p_g \cdot x_{hi}^{P} \\ +\alpha_{ij}^{P} \cdot q_j^{P} \cdot \beta_{jg}^{P} \cdot m_g^{P} \cdot p_g \cdot \Delta x_{hi} \end{bmatrix}. \tag{9}$$

Depending on the control purpose, corresponding deviation parts need to be eliminated to avoid misleading incentive-effects. For instance all deviations in resource prices of first and higher order, this means all terms containing Δp_g, need to be eliminated, if the person in charge is not

Figure 8. Exemplary splitting of price and quantity deviation

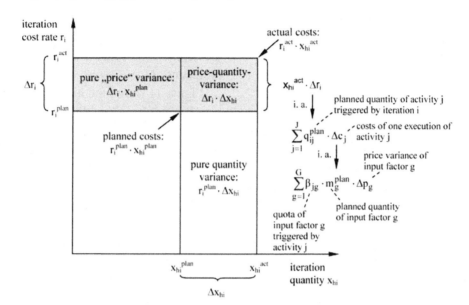

authorized for procurement. Figure exemplifies the breakdown into the plain of price deviation.

Splitting iteration costs down to the activity layer as shown above, allows for the analysis of price-, quantity or structure-dependent variances with arbitrary specificity. This facilitates research into the causing facts of reasonable cost deviations. One possible outcome of this analysis may be the awareness that some activities were needed to a significantly higher extent than expected (quantity variance), or that other activities than those originally planned have been used (structural variance). Cost management is then challenged to initiate the redesign of activities so that cost reductions in future projects become possible.

Starting Points for the Elaboration of Risk-Oriented Cost-Forecasting

A variety of risk factors have impact on development costs (Lum et al., 2003; Pfleeger et al., 2005) which often lead to a considerable cost-deviation compared to the forecasted amount (Lum et al., 2003). Therefore it seems natural to

support management decisions with a sound risk analysis, which provides information concerning cost risk and the effects of possible provisions at an early stage. In practice, this results in simple approaches like scenario analysis and sensitivity analysis, both not being based on a statistical probability approach. Sensitivity analysis investigates the impact of critical values of input variables whereas scenario analysis illustrates the effects on development costs when varying the input factors between best- and worst-case-scenarios (cf., for COCOMO II Dobán & Pataricza, 2001). Even if this provides adequate information for a first estimation of uncertainty, a thorough risk analysis based on statistical methods should explicitly be applied. A simulation approach obviously is suitable for this purpose (Lum et al., 2003).

To start with, it is convenient to consider – at a more aggregated level – the analyzed deviation categories mentioned above as risk factors themselves to provide a consistent cost planning and cost control. For instance, the deviation of iteration activity structure $\Delta\alpha_{ij}$ defines the risk that the stable correlation of the iteration as a cost driver and the resulting quantities of activities does not hold. It may then be helpful to identify the risk factors accountable for the breakup of the coherent structure.

However, this level of analysis shall not be focused here, rather the usage of risk simulation illustrated with a case study is discussed (cf., risk simulation in general Evans & Olson, 2002; Rubinstein & Melamed, 1998). Risk based modelling focuses on iteration quantities, which are derived by the similarity approach, and their respective cost rates. To simplify the matter an aggregated level of risk is considered. Starting point are the expected value estimates as shown in Figure 3 and Figure 6.

Because of its broad flexibility in application, the three-parametric Weibull-distribution is taken as a given (cf., Bronstein, Semendyayev, Musion, & Muehlig, 2002). As the location parameter γ is non-negative, modelling aberrations which may occur with the normal distribution can be avoided. Objective of the simulation is the total development cost TC of the project calculated already in an expectation value approach. Figure 9 shows the initial simulation parameters. The original expected values of Figure 3 and Figure 6 are attained by appropriate setting of scaling parameter β.

Figure 10 exemplifies the density function of the iteration cost rate no. 2 and the direct costs of project no. 1.

Figure 11 shows the histogram after 100.000 simulation runs in the Maple 11 software of waterloo Maple Inc. (sample size discussion: e.g. Ripley, 2006). The simulation leads to average development costs of the compound project structure of 1.041.200 €, which differs insignificantly from the expectation value (Figure 6) of 1.041.657 €. The risk simulation now provides a deeper insight into the cost situation. By evaluating the histogram it can be seen that cost will overrun 1.209.503 € with a probability of 10%. Analysing the distribution moments is helpful to discuss further problems, for example, the decision whether a development contract should be accepted from a risk-based point of view. The purpose would be the determination of the risk-adjusted lowest price limit taken from an expected utility comparison.

Figure 9. Initial simulation parameters for project h = 1

project's direct costs: $\alpha = 1.5$; $\beta = 81,418$ €; $\gamma = 150.000$ €		
iteration (all: $\alpha = 3$)	**cost rates**	**quantities**
– no. 1 (inception)	$\beta = 22,734$ €; $\gamma = 42,000$ €	$\beta = 0$; $\gamma = 1$
– no. 2 (elaboration)	$\beta = 22,422$ €; $\gamma = 66,000$ €	$\beta = 2.24$; $\gamma = 0$
– no. 3 (elaboration)	$\beta = 22,417$ €; $\gamma = 49,000$ €	$\beta = 2.24$; $\gamma = 0$
– no. 4 (construction)	$\beta = 22,698$ €; $\gamma = 21,000$ €	$\beta = 2.24$; $\gamma = 0$
– no. 5 (construction)	$\beta = 11,010$ €; $\gamma = 14,000$ €	$\beta = 5.6$; $\gamma = 0$
– no. 6 (construction)	$\beta = 21,940$ €; $\gamma = 6,000$ €	$\beta = 0$; $\gamma = 0$
– no. 7 (construction)	$\beta = 22,057$ €; $\gamma = 16,000$ €	$\beta = 1.12$; $\gamma = 0$
– no. 8 (construction)	$\beta = 22,119$ €; $\gamma = 53,000$ €	$\beta = 2.24$; $\gamma = 0$
– no. 9 (construction)	$\beta = 22,522$ €; $\gamma = 38,000$ €	$\beta = 0$; $\gamma = 0$
– no. 10 (transition)	$\beta = 22,049$ €; $\gamma = 7,000$ €	$\beta = 2.24$; $\gamma = 0$
– no. 11 (transition)	$\beta = 10,233$ €; $\gamma = 0$ €	$\beta = 1.12$; $\gamma = 0$

Figure 10. Density functions for exemplary input factors

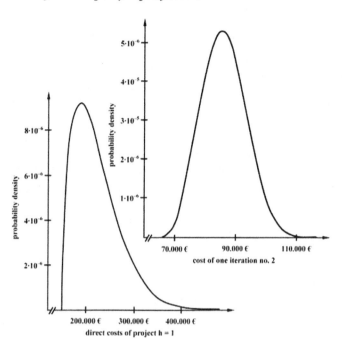

Figure 11. Simulated software development costs

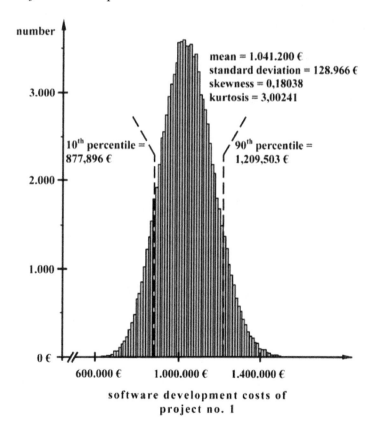

CONCLUSION

Due to its structural similarity to the Unified Process, activity based costing may be employed for cost management tasks in all phases of software development. Compared to conventional approaches the improvements are manifold. The presented approach is strictly focused on data that are specific to the developers' business, so that there is no need for business specific calibration. At the same time, this makes possible the detailed planning and control of costs. Additionally, in many companies activity based costing is already being used, which facilitates the successful adaptation of activity based cost management for software developments based on the Unified Process.

However, the quality of the similarity estimations needed to gain the quantity structure of the projects is crucial for its success. Obviously, a stable and repeated process context will be advantageous to the application of the method proposed, but in software companies with heavily changing order situations this may not be the case. The possibility to refer to similar iterations instead of projects alleviates the problem. Further, new approaches to similarity estimations may lead to an improved forecast of the quantity structure of cost estimations. Moreover, a simulation based risk analysis reveals information regarding the deviation of critical point estimations like the iteration cost rates for instance.

REFERENCES

Atkinson, A. A., Kaplan, R. S., Matsumara, E. M., & Young, S. M. (2007). *Management accounting.* Upper Saddle River, NJ: Prentice Hall.

Boehm, B. (1981). *Software engineering economics.* Upper Saddle River, NJ: Prentice Hall.

Boehm, B., et al. (Eds.). (2000). *Software cost estimation with COCOMO II.* Upper Saddle River, NJ: Prentice Hall.

Boehm, B., Abts, C., & Chulani, S. (2000). Software development cost estimation approaches - a survey. *Annals of Software Engineering, 10*(1-4), 177–205. doi:10.1023/A:1018991717352

Booch, G., Rumbaugh, J., & Jacobson, I. (2005). *The unified modelling language user guide.* Reading, MA: Addison-Wesley.

Bronstein, I. N., Semendyayev, K. A., Musion, G., & Muehlig, H. (2002). *Handbook of mathematics.* Berlin: Springer.

Cooper, R., & Kaplan, R. S. (1988). Measure costs right: Make the right decisions. *Harvard Business Review, 66*(5), 96–103.

Dobán, O., & Pataricza, A. (2001). Cost estimation driven software development process. In *Proceedings of the 27th EUROMICRO Conference* (pp. 208-213).

Ehrlenspiel, K., Kiewert, A., Lindemann, U., & Hundal, M. S. (2007). *Cost-efficient design.* Berlin: Springer.

Essigkrug, A., & Mey, T. (2007). *Rational Unified Process kompakt.* Berlin: Spektrum Akademischer Verlag. doi:10.1007/978-3-8274-2435-8

Evans, J. R., & Olson, D. L. (2002). *Introduction to simulation and risk analysis.* Upper Saddle River, NJ: Prentice Hall.

Hicks, D. T. (2002). *Activity based costing.* New York: Wiley.

Horngren, C. T., Foster, G., Datar, S. M., Rajan, M. V., & Ittner, C. (2008). *Cost accounting: A managerial emphasis.* Upper Saddle River, NJ: Prentice Hall.

Jacobson, I., Booch, G., & Rumbaugh, J. (1999). *The unified software development process*. Reading, MA: Addison-Wesley.

Keung, J. W., Kitchenham, B. A., & Jeffery, D. R. (2008). Analogy-X: Providing statistical inference to analogy-based software cost estimation. *IEEE Transactions on Software Engineering, 34*(4), 1–14. doi:10.1109/TSE.2008.34

Kroll, P., & Krutchen, P. (2003). *The rational unified process made easy*. Reading, MA: Addison-Wesley.

Kruchten, P. (2003). *The Rational Unified Process. An Introduction*. Reading, MA: Addison-Wesley.

Larman, C. (2002). *Applying UML and patterns. An introduction to object-oriented analysis and design and the unified process*. Upper Saddle River, NJ: Prentice Hall.

Leung, H., & Fan, Z. (2002). Software Cost Estimation. In S. K. Chang (Ed.), *Handbook of software engineering & knowledge engineering-Vol. 2: Emerging technologies* (pp. 307-324). River Edge, NJ: Word Scientific.

Li, J., Ruhe, G., Al-Emran, A., & Richter, M. M. (2007). A flexible method for software effort estimation by analogy. *Empirical Software Engineering, 12*(1), 65–106. doi:10.1007/s10664-006-7552-4

Lum, K., Bramble, M., Hihn, J., Hackney, J., Khorrami, M., & Monson, E. (2003). *Handbook for software cost estimation*. Pasadena, CA: Jet Propulsion Laboratory.

Miller, J. G., & Vollman, T. E. (1985). The hidden factory. *Harvard Business Review, 63*(5), 142–150.

Pfleeger, S. L., Wu, F., & Lewis, R. (2005). *Software cost estimation and sizing methods: Issues and guidelines*. Santa Monica, CA: Rand Corporation.

Ripley, B. D. (2006). *Stochastic simulation*. New York: Wiley.

Rubinstein, R. Y., & Melamed, B. (1998). *Modern simulation and modelling*. New York: Wiley.

Versteegen, G. (2000). *Projektmanagement mit dem Rational Unified Process*. Berlin: Springer.

This work was previously published in International Journal of Human Capital and Information Technology Professionals, Volume 1, Issue 4, edited by Ricardo Colomo-Palacios, pp. 14-30, copyright 2010 by IGI Publishing (an imprint of IGI Global).

Section 4
IT Professionals in Organizations

Chapter 14

Collaborative Innovation for the Management of Information Technology Resources

David O'Sullivan
National University of Ireland, Ireland

Lawrence Dooley
University College Cork, Ireland

ABSTRACT

All organisations are now facing one of the largest upheavals in business practice since the 'great depression'. Information technology organisations, who frequently lead the development of change based around ICT, are being asked to develop new products and services that add significant value for customers and to radically change their internal processes so that they are more cost effective. Innovation is process of creating positive change to any organisation and that adds value to customers – internal and external. Innovation is now widely accepted at the only sustainable engine of renewed growth for organisations. Organisations that do not embrace innovation and learn to apply its principles will simply stagnate or be obliterated by competition. ICT organisations that can learn to apply innovation effectively will become key strategic assets in driving costs down and also in adding new dimensions to product and service development. This paper presents an approach to applying innovation in any ICT based organisation, be it a service department within a larger organisation or a commercial business that generates ICT solutions for clients. The process of innovation in ICT based organisations is similar to innovation in any organisation and requires an in-depth understanding and practice of developing innovation goals, the management of innovative actions or projects, the empowerment of human capital or teams and the continuous monitoring of innovation performance. This paper presents a methodology for applying innovation and a case study of how innovation related knowledge can be managed in any ICT organisation.

DOI: 10.4018/978-1-4666-0924-2.ch014

INTRODUCTION

Today's organisations are faced with the challenge of meeting the ever increasing demands of a global customer base, whilst remaining competitive against suppliers from lower cost economies. Organisations need to constantly improve their competitive advantage and respond faster to changing markets by reducing costs, improving quality, becoming customer-driven and increasing productivity. The principal mechanism for organizational growth and sustainability is innovation. Innovation is the process of idea generation and exploitation by an organisation whose mission is to continuously add value to its customers – internal and external.

The factors that influence organisational innovation include culture, process and implementation. Factors such as fostering a risk taking environment, managing innovation continuously and portfolio management are viewed as critical for success for all types of organisations. In order to adequately address these factors and many others to be outlined later, organisations need to manage their innovation process effectively. In recent years there has been a steady growth in support for adopting a contingency approach in relation to managing organisational change, resulting in a convergence of diverse approaches to better facilitate the management of innovation. While the specific causes for the failure of innovative actions is specific to an individual organisation, there are a number of macro causes, which cuts across organisations (O'Sullivan and Dooley, 2008). These include:

1. Inadequate definition of organisational direction.
2. Ineffective mechanisms for the deployment of organisational goals to innovative actions.
3. Poor leadership of the systems innovation process
4. Poor planning in relation to generation of innovations

5. Poor implementation of proposed innovations
6. Low levels of employee participation in the innovation process
7. Ineffective results management.

Understanding these root causes of failure leads to solutions for managing innovation that can be deployed effectively in any organisation.

Understanding Innovation

Innovation is synonymous with the concept of novelty and originality (Ghislein 1963). However, this is a very narrow perspective and ignores the reality that, what may represent a trivial change for one organisation may represent a significant innovative challenge to another. Tidd et al. (2005) state that "novelty is very much in the eye of the beholder". West and Farr (1990) stress their belief that all innovation is change but emphasises that not all changes are innovation. They see the defining criteria of innovative change as "planned and desirable and must have something new to the individual". Terninko et al. (1998) cite findings from analysis of product innovation patents, that only 5% of innovations corresponded to major discoveries that resulted in solutions outside contemporary knowledge or technology. The majority of innovations analysed (95%), comprised either of conventional solutions, small inventions inside the paradigm or substantial inventions inside the technology, that bring varying levels of improvement. Adapting these findings to determine a definition of innovation, one concludes that a change that strives to improve the existing systems overall performance may be deemed an innovation.

Damanpour (1990) defines innovation as falling into three categories, namely technology, administrative and ancillary innovations. This views the potential scope for innovative change as effecting the technology application of the organisation, the interaction between the organisation's social and technical systems and the interactions that occur across the organisational boundaries.

Zaltman et al. (1973) propose that innovation may be programmed and non-programmed. Innovation can arise from a definite and directed action, or as a consequence of reacting to emerging trends (Johnston and Kaplan 1996). Zaltman et al. (1973) also categorise innovation as either instrumental or ultimate. Ultimate innovations are considered ends in themselves, where as instrumental innovations are undertaken to facilitate the subsequent introduction of an ultimate innovation. An innovative change does not have to contribute directly to organisational wellbeing, but instead can be a supporting development towards the achievement of another major innovation. The final dimension defined by Zaltman et al. (1973) is that innovation may be routine and radical in its nature. A routine innovation may be viewed as the introduction of something similar to previous organisational practice, although its specifics are new to the organisation. A radical innovation, is also new in its specifics to the organisation, but differs fundamentally to existing organisational systems and results in larger and more disruptive change (Johnston and Kaplan 1996). Innovation, like other types of change, may traverse a number of different spectrums. Urabe et al. (1988) define innovation as a concept that incorporates the entire development process from generation of a potential idea to its successful implementation.

A number of theorists emphasise their belief that the value of innovation lies in its contribution to profits. Urabe et al. (1988) describe innovation as "an economic concept rather than a technological one... [that] does not constitute innovation if it creates no growth or pure profit". While incorporating this information into our understanding of innovation, an assumption is made that profit seeking adopts a long-term perspective in relation to organisational growth. Another issue that this definition of innovation raises is that not all innovation is economically valuable from its initial conception. In reality, it may often be difficult to justify certain innovations on strictly financial grounds as many benefits associated with a proposed innovation may be indirect and cut cross functional boundaries. The adoption of a high level systems view of the organisation that evaluates the innovation relative to its contribution to achieving organisational goals is one way of overcoming this difficulty.

Roberts (1988) views innovation consisting of two interrelated elements: the generation of the idea and; the subsequent conversion of that idea into a useful application. Kanter (1983) also defines innovation, viewing it as "the process of bringing any new problem solving idea into use …it is the generation, application and implementation of ideas, processes, products and services". Drucker (1995) views the process of innovation as the various paths that innovative ideas follow from conception to approval and implementation. The seeds of innovation are ideas and problem solutions and the successful transition into innovations depends on the effectiveness of innovation process management (Urabe et al. 1988). When discussing ideas relative to innovation, Duggan (1999) argues the importance of the ability to move an original idea through to beneficial implementation, to an organisation's competitiveness. Ekvall (1991) when discussing the development of a creative organisational culture, emphasises the concept of idea-management, where a focus is placed on "finding and taking care of ideas in the organisations operations ".

Ideas can originate either as a reaction to a certain situation, that compels the organisation into action or as a proactive action to exploit a new development (Sadler 1995). Van de Ven et al. (1989) indicate that innovation can originate from "a recombination of old ideas, a schema that challenges the present order, or a formula or unique approach that is perceived as new by the individuals involved". An innovative idea therefore can originate from a broad spectrum of sources. Potential innovative sources include customer complaints, corrective action systems, suggestion boxes, supplier developments and benchmarking studies. Drucker (1985) asserts his belief that the source of innovative opportunity arise from (1) unexpected occurrences, (2) incongruities, (3) process needs, (4) market changes as well as changes in (5) demographics, (6) perception and (7) new knowledge. King (1990) notes a diffusion bias towards innovation being imported from outside the organisation, rather than internally generated. A possible reason for this may be that it is easier to adapt the creativity of someone else, than develop and maintain a creative organisational environment. Cumming (1999) identifies a vast myriad of facilitating factors that contribute to the conception, development and successful application of potential innovations.

Drawing these various perspectives of innovation together, certain parameters can be determined. Innovation may be viewed as a change that adds value to an organisation that traverses the radical and incremental rates of change. Innovation may be viewed as driven from a planned and unplanned perspective and between process and product focused. Systems innovation can focus on development of existing and 'new' processes, as well as process development to support development of a new product (Utterback 1994). Irrespective of the type of innovation, its overall objective is to contribute to an organisation's economic wellbeing, either directly or indirectly in a manner novel to the individual organisation.

Innovation is a process of generating and converting ideas into outputs which increase customer value (Roberts, 1988). Innovative ideas can range from replacement of existing computing equipment to the deployment of computers to new business processes. The innovation process will naturally involve unsuccessful ideas. These are seen as a natural by-product of the innovation process. In order for some ideas to succeed many more will need to fail. Organizations can learn from these failures and bring new knowledge (and sometimes technology) to use in future innovative actions that may benefit the organization. The company who can successfully sift out the good from the bad ideas will be more adaptable than

those that cannot. When managing the innovation process, destroying poor ideas early on allows scarce resources to be released and re-focused on new ideas. The goal of every organization is the successful development of 'good' ideas that are valued by their customers. The emerging perspective by specialists in the field of innovation is to define innovation in the broadest context possible. One reason for this is that by defining it too tightly, it may have a detrimental effect on creativity by excluding certain avenues of investigation.

Operations and Innovation

Simplifying an organization down to its most basic level, it can be said to consist of two core activities - operations and innovation. Operations relate to all of the activities that provide an existing service or product to a customer and that includes customer service, software backups and routine systems maintenance. Operations is focused on the 'here and now requirements' facing the organization. Innovation, on the other hand, consists of all activities that change operations and are focused on how requirements of customers will be met in the future. Activities such as machine replacement, automation of operations, software development, systems analysis and so on are processes of innovation and typically carried out through projects or initiatives. In many organizations tension exists between operating the system that provides existing products for the customer and changing the system in order to add more value to the customer. Innovation disrupts the established operations process and consequently incurs resistance. Organizations naturally avoid disruption and instinctively try to maintain the status quo and resist innovative change. Innovative organizations on the other hand, embrace the challenge of maintaining a balance between serving the needs of the customer and meeting emerging future needs.

A useful way to visualize the relationship between the operations and innovation activities is presented in Figure 1. This figure illustrates an 'activity diagram' with two activities labelled with active verbs: 'Operate' and 'Innovate'. The first activity 'Operate' converts orders from customers into goods and services that meet customer orders. Other inputs include raw materials and resources (bottom face) such as product specifications and processes. All three inputs are required to produce the output. The second activity 'Innovate' is about making beneficial changes to products, processes and services. It has an entirely different set of inputs and outputs. The major input is new demands from customers and other major stakeholders. These new demands can stimulate the generation of ideas and new ideas can be converted into new product specifications and new processes for the 'operate' activity. The relationship between 'Innovate' and 'Operate' is symbiotic. One serves the customers, the other changes the way the customer is served. This figure is of course simplified and incomplete but it serves to illustrate graphically the two core activities in any organization. While the majority of innovation output is focused on improving operations activity, certain innovation output is actually focused on the innovation activity itself. Thus, the organization not only strives to change

operations in terms of new products, processes and services but it also changes the means by which the innovation process itself is achieved.

Radical vs. Incremental Innovation

Innovation can be classified as either radical or incremental. Radical innovation is about making major changes in systems such as installing a new ERP process. When examining innovation, it is often the impact rather than the size of the project that we are interested in. The term radical often refers to the level of contribution it makes to the efficiency or revenue of the organization (MacLaughlin, 1999). We can visualize radical innovation as a 'step change' in some measure of growth such as revenue or efficiency. Most organizations engage in some form of radical innovation over their lifetime. While it is radical innovations that often make the headlines, most organizations elect to spread their risk by also undertaking smaller or incremental innovations. Incremental innovation is less ambitious in both its scope and potential returns for the organization but consequently has less associated risks. Apart from requiring fewer resources, incremental inno-

Figure 1. Operations and Innovation

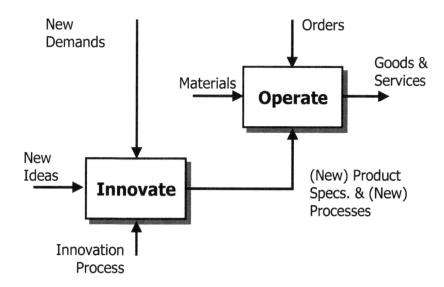

vations consist of smaller endeavours making them easier to manage than their larger counterparts. If an organisation successfully implements enough incremental innovations then it can sometimes lead to the similar levels of growth as those driven by radical innovation. Figure 2 gives an example of one organisations innovation portfolio across the incremental-radical spectrum. This graphical representation shows that the organisation has structured its innovation portfolio so that the majority of its actions are supporting or building on its existing offering, with only a small number of actions focus on radical innovation.

There are advantages and disadvantages to both incremental and radical innovation. Radical innovation has the advantage of creating a step change in growth. The disadvantage is the high level of risk and high cost of failure. The advantages of incremental innovation are lower risk and the possibility of achieving a smaller degree of growth. However, the disadvantage is the comparative slowness to reach growth targets before competitors, leading to a loss of competitive advantage. As a result of this, management decisions involve a mix of innovative actions and influenced by diverse factors such as attitude

within the organization towards risk-taking, the availability of funds and the pressures from the external environment.

INNOVATION PROCESS

"The innovation process itself is often not very well understood within organisations. Ideas are not generated in any conscious or systematic way. The ideas which are thrown up *ad hoc*, are rarely well managed through the phases of implementation" (Henry and Walker 1991). Successful organisations require a process for "ensuring the usefulness of the innovations that are implemented, without stifling all change" (Farr and Ford 1990). Tidd et al. (2005) state that the real success of innovation "lies in being able to repeat the trick, to manage the process consistently so that success, whilst never guaranteed, is more likely". The ability to manage the innovation process is an essential competence of any organization, but they must first understand the workings of the process to be successful. The path followed by innovative concepts from their initial generation as ideas through to its eventual consumption by

Figure 2. Radical and incremental innovation (adapted from (Henderson, 2007) and (Wheelwright and Clark, 1992)

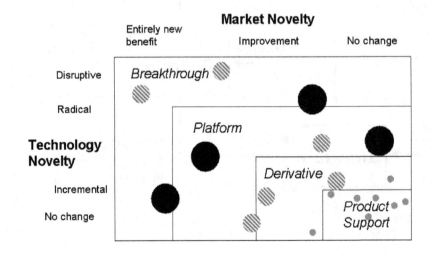

the intended market can vary greatly (Tidd et al., 2005). The process of innovation can be described in terms of the interaction between four key sub processes. Figure 3 illustrates these processes as: Idea Generation, Opportunity Recognition, Development and Realization. There are two related sub processes associated with Opportunity Recognition and these are: Organizations Goals and Available Resources.

The first stage in our perspective of the innovation process relates to the creative activity of generating an opportunistic idea. This stage involves the continuous scanning of the internal and external environment of the organization for threats and opportunities which might be developed into an innovation by the organization. The presence of an organizational culture that encourages creativity and empowerment can significantly support this phase of the process. Various stimuli can lead to the creation of an idea and range from reading magazines and observing problems to visiting other organizations and having informal discussions with colleagues and customers.

The second stage of the process is opportunity recognition where the relative opportunity of developing the idea into a new product, process or service is assessed and evaluated relative to others. This phase of the process relates to deciding which innovative ideas are pursued by the organization and which are deemed outside its interest. The undertaking of innovative actions is both expensive and resource intensive on any organization and even large organizations need to decide between which ideas to pursue. How this decision is made is complex and involves trade-offs including correlation with the strategic goals and resources available to the organization, the organizations current capability, the mix of innovations already being developed, the actions of competitors and the emerging signals from the external environment. Similarly, this evaluation of prospective innovations is not a once off, but occurs periodically along the innovation process to ensure that the organization is investing in 'positive' innovations. Cooper (1988) refers to these decision points as 'stage-gates' where unsuitable projects are 'killed-off' to allow extra resources to be directed towards more suitable innovations. The difficulty at this second phase of the process is that the organization does not possess a crystal ball to see into the future and thus cannot know for certain which ideas will be winners or losers. They can only make the most enlightened decision they can, based on available knowledge and continue to periodically screen their portfolio of developing innovations for appropriateness. As a consequence of this phase, ideas are often im-

Figure 3. Innovation process

proved, merged with other ideas or in many cases shelved or abandoned. An important test for an idea is that it matches the goals of the organization and available resources – people, skills and financial funds that the organization has available.

If an opportunity is suitably attractive for the organization then it progresses to the next stage of the process to be further developed. This phase relates to the development of the idea or solution into a potential innovation that is ready for launch to its internal or external market. The development of an innovation can be highly resource intensive for any organization, both in terms of financial and human resources required. The selection of the innovations by organizations is constrained by the available budget and the existing portfolio of innovative actions underway. Certain innovations may require competencies and skills that are in scare supply or even absent from the organization and thus this can also hinder the implementation of certain innovations. Organizations must carefully project manage the innovative actions to ensure success. Part of managing the implementation of these actions is the constant scanning of the external environment for emerging trends that may alter the trajectory of the innovation. The implementation phase of the innovation is usually undertaken as a team approach (due to the diverse competencies required) and involves making the initial idea tangible in a form that best meets customer demands. At the end of the development phase of the process, the initial idea has been developed into a product, process or service which the organization views as capable of meeting user requirements and benefiting the organisation going forward.

The realisation phase of the innovation process relates to the launch to 'operations' and is where the customer makes the final evaluation of the innovation. Understanding customer needs and requirements is essential to ensure the eventual offering to the market meets these needs. A strong alignment between the two needs increases the likelihood that the innovation's initial adoption

will be a success. While Figure 3 illustrates the realization phase following the development phase, it is a truer reflection of reality to view these phases as overlapping. Information regarding customer needs is an essential input to the development phase and information concerning the innovations attributes is necessary to begin educating and preparing 'operations'. The objective of the realization phase of the process is to develop an innovation for the end user that meets their requirements and is readily adopted. The realization phase will encompass activities such as commissioning, validation and training to facilitate successful adoption.

Many researchers propose a new phase to the innovation process – learning. Learning requires the organization to analyze the previous phases of the innovation process and to identify areas where the innovation process itself can be improved. In this way, even innovative actions which are abandoned or end in failure can recoup benefit since the organization can learn from its mistakes and avoid repeating them in the future. Similarly, the new knowledge acquired from undertaking the innovations can also be used as input to the idea generation phase that may lead to future innovations. Over time the organizations effectiveness at managing its innovation process improves, which will increase the success of its future innovative actions.

Services Innovation

Much writing in the field of innovation has focused on the development of products. However, in first world economy, service based organisations are overtaking traditional manufacturing in contribution to economic growth. Service industries in areas such as finance, IT services, education, transportation, health, and government make up the vast majority of organizations in any economy. These organizations also need to innovate continuously so they can offer increased levels of service to their customers and the overall performance of the economy. Service can be defined as a sequence of overlapping value creating activities. Others choose to define service in terms of performance, where client and provider co-produce value. The unique characteristics of services, such as intangibility, customer contact, inhomogenity and perishable production also offer significant scope for innovation. A key attribute of a service is a very high level of interaction with the end customer or user during the creation and delivery of the service. The customer is often unable to separate the service from the individual delivering the service (e.g. inhomogenity) and so will make value assumptions based on impressions of the service, the people delivering the service and any product delivered as part of the service. Another characteristic of some service organizations is that their output may often be perishable or consumable; therefore the product or service is consumed or used as soon as possible upon delivery, for example help desk activities. As a consequence of this, the timing of the delivery and customer perception of value are crucial to success. Organisations that are service based must incorporate these factors into their innovation effort. For the remainder of this paper, we will focus on how innovation within an Information Technology service based organisation is structured and effectively managed.

Innovation Funnel

The innovation funnel provides a solution for effectively managing innovation through controlling the interaction of goals, actions, teams and results used in the innovation process (Dooley and O'Sullivan, 2003). The funnel illustrates how goals, actions, teams and results interact with each other to deliver innovation in any organization – see Figure 4. The funnel metaphor is not new and can be traced back to the seminal work of Hayes, Wheelwright and Clark (1984) in relation to the research and development funnel. The innovation funnel can be visualized as

containing four arrows flowing around a funnel. Each arrow represents the flow of goals, actions, teams and results. Actions enter the wide mouth of the funnel and represent among other things, ideas and solutions to problems. These actions flow towards to the neck of the funnel where they are screened relative to their opportunity for the organization. The neck of the funnel is constrained by two arrows – goals and teams. These constraints loosen or tighten depending on the availability of teams and the goals defined by the organization. Tightly defined goals can be visualized as closing the neck of the funnel resulting in fewer actions flowing through. The availability of more teams on the other hand can be visualized as opening the neck of the funnel and allowing more actions to be developed. As actions are implemented, they impact on the organization's fortunes. The final arrow reflects this impact. Results flow from the narrow end of the funnel and represent information concerning the relationships between goals, actions and teams. This arrow flows back towards goals representing the impact of results on the process of defining and redefining goals.

An important aspect of the innovation funnel is the relationships generated between goals, actions, teams and results. Ideas, for example, that cannot easily be related with goals will find it difficult to proceed into the funnel. This has two affects; firstly the individuals or teams generating the ideas will study the goals more closely in order to generate an idea that matches better. Secondly, good ideas that are not easily associated with goals will begin to impact on the definition of the goals ultimately leading to a redefinition of goals in order to allow the good ideas through. This is a natural learning process within an innovation community. When goals change there is a knock on effect in the generation of ideas that meet these goals, because the innovation community in now tuned to having new ideas meet the new organizational goals. The process offers the innovation community the ability to alter the innovation process in response to chang-

Figure 4. Innovation funnel

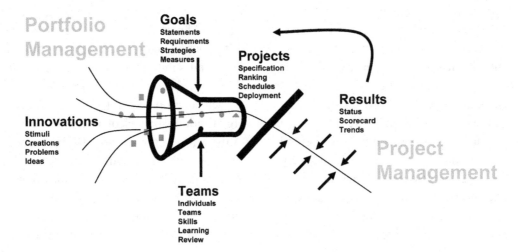

ing demands of stakeholders and the environment. The main body of the funnel can be said to represent 'portfolio management' where the innovation process is about creating the optimum balance between ideas, goals and resources. The latter end of the funnel represents 'project management' where ideas that successfully proceed through the funnel are implemented as projects and progress through various stage gates.

Architecture for Innovation

The innovation management process as initially defined in this article and later illustrated through the innovation funnel needs to be operationalised and deployed in the organisation. We now turn our attention to how such as innovation management toolset can be developed using technology such as collaborative workspaces for asynchronous distributed collaboration. Innovation goals for example can be defined using knowledge elements such as Statements (e.g. mission statement) and Indicators. Innovation actions will be defined through elements such as problems, ideas and projects. Innovation teams can be defined and codified through individuals, teams and training plans but also through performance appraisals.

Innovation results can be defined through exceptions and reports. All of these knowledge elements can combine and interact with each other through relational databases and information technology to create a sophisticated knowledge management system for managing innovation in any organization. Over time, as the organization can build upon core knowledge elements and add new dimensions to innovation such as organisation and information models and customer complaints and warranties. The power of the system will increase as elements are added and most importantly interact with each other to illuminate a holistic innovation management process (see Figure 5). Figure 5 illustrates a large number of knowledge elements using to store and share innovation related data within one ICT organisation. All elements are represented by plurals or groups of concepts (i.e. words that end with the letter 's'). We will now expand this architecture into an intranet based collaborative workspace.

Innovation in IT Organisations

The IT sector traverses the product-service spectrum, and is populated by organisations that deliver generic and bespoke software, technology

Figure 5. Architecture for innovation

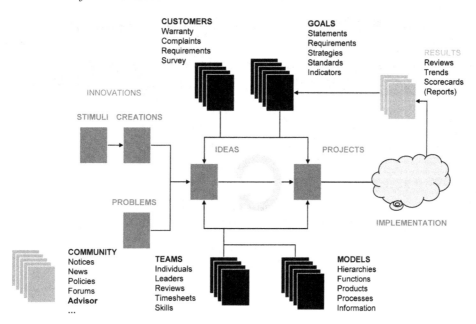

infrastructure, technical support and consultancy. These organisations are important for co-designing products and services for external customers and designing new systems for operational use by internal customers. Adopting the information architecture of the innovation funnel presented earlier, an IT organisation is able to structure and manage its innovation process using a number of knowledge elements accessible through one innovation portal. Figure 6 presents the innovation portal for one ICT organisation. This portal provides the organisation with an 'innovation dashboard' of up to date innovation related information. The portal structure also allows the organisation to integrate the goals, actions, teams and results together to manage their innovation process, while building resources and community to support their innovation effort.

The portal illustrated in Figure 6 has been deployed using a number of technologies including Microsoft Sharepoint, Lotus Domino, Web Site Languages and Semantic Web Languages. The system architecture is comprised of a number of tables or lists each of which represents one innovation element (e.g. indicators or ideas). Tables or Lists can be linked hierarchically and each element or record can have a relationship or association with any another. In this way all records regardless of their table can form a complex network of concepts and associations. In this way end users can infer various meanings from the knowledge base. In most organisations the relationships between records or concepts is kept simple. Figure 7 illustrates a number of screen shots from the system.

BUILDING COMMUNITIES

Building an innovation management system for a single IT department within a large organisation represents only one part of all of the innovation taking place across the organisation and across an extended organisation that includes suppliers, distributors and even customers. We now focus our attention towards innovation management across a

Figure 6. Innovation dashboard for an IT department

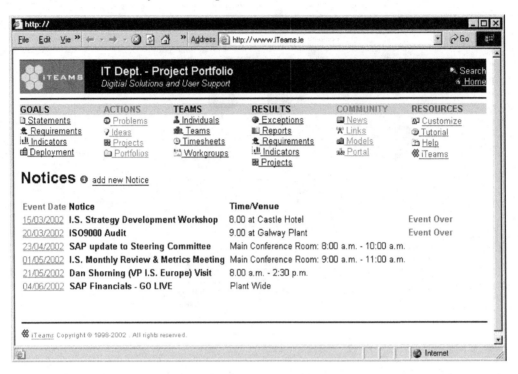

much broader community of innovation – we call this extended innovation that incorporates many different innovation funnels. An examination of literature in this regard highlights two central notions about the nature of innovation: (1) innovations are understood as 'interactive learning processes' and; (2) these learning processes are 'socially embedded' (Moodysson, 2007). Communities of organisations are becoming more common as a legitimate means of innovation, entered into for strategic motives including risk sharing, to access new markets and technologies, to speed product development and commercialisation, and to pool complementary knowledge and skills. Many organizations in knowledge intensive sectors choose to leverage inter-organisational networks as an important source of creativity and innovation (Powell et al, 1996). Such leverage offers collaborating organizations strategic flexibility (Sanchez, 1997) by enhancing their ability to redefine and expand their knowledge resource base. However, learning through net-

works depends upon the extent to which the various organizations possess "absorptive capacity" (Cohen and Levinthal, 1990) to recognize the value of the new knowledge and the dynamic capabilities (Teece et al, 1997) required to exploit them. Powell (1998) observes "When uncertainty is high, organisations interact more, not less, with external parties in order to access both knowledge and resources. Hence, the locus of innovation is found in networks of learning, rather than in individual firms." These inter-organisational knowledge networks collaborate for the purpose of generating 'new' knowledge for future exploitation. Knowledge networks function because key individuals have gained status as 'knowledge brokers' (Hargadon, 2003), possessing the ability to cross knowledge and organisational boundaries. These 'boundary spanners' (Donaldson and O'Toole, 2007) provide weak ties that nurture the flow of knowledge both within the network and between the network and the larger external environment (Granovetter, 1976). The value of

Figure 7. Other sample screen shots

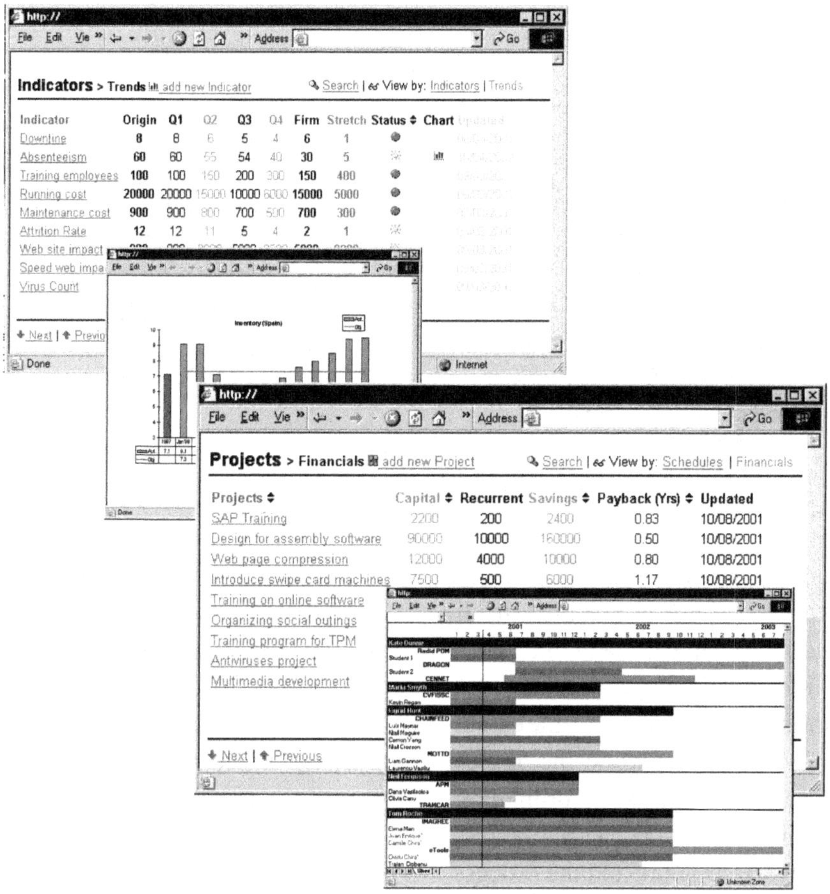

Indicators > Trends | add new Indicator   Search | View by: Indicators | Trends

Indicator	Origin	Q1	Q2	Q3	Q4	Firm	Stretch	Status	Chart	Updated
Downtime	8	8	6	5	4	6	1			
Absenteeism	60	60	55	54	40	30	5			
Training employees	100	100	150	200	300	150	400			
Running cost	20000	20000	15000	10000	6000	15000	5000			
Maintenance cost	900	900	800	700	500	700	300			
Attrition Rate	12	12	11	5	4	2	1			
Web site impact										
Speed web impa										
Virus Count										

Next | Previous

Inventory (Spain)

Projects > Financials | add new Project   Search | View by: Schedules | Financials

Projects	Capital	Recurrent	Savings	Payback (Yrs)	Updated
SAP Training	2200	200	2400	0.83	10/08/2001
Design for assembly software	90000	10000	160000	0.50	10/08/2001
Web page compression	12000	4000	10000	0.80	10/08/2001
Introduce swipe card machines	7500	500	6000	1.17	10/08/2001
Training on online software					
Organizing social outings					
Training program for TPM					
Antiviruses project					
Multimedia development					

Next | Previous

these individuals lies not only in their ability to traverse network boundaries but also in their ability to make sense of the dynamic complexity within which the network exists (Senge, 1994) and combine knowledge to generate new linkages and ideas (Best, 2001). Their value is that they initiate learning activities between organizations, establish new linkages for enriching knowledge and connect the innovation activity with wider scientific and institutional networks (Powell et al, 1996; Murray, 2002).

Organisations that participate in a network are committed to each other through mutual reliance and relationships. The extent of organisational 'embeddness' (Granovetter, 1985) within a network will influence the routines and behaviour practiced within the network and their ability to generate new knowledge. The network form is denoted by nodes of complementary strengths and inter-dependencies, medium to high commitment exhibited between partners and a culture of adaptability and mutual benefit (Powell, 1990). When analysing functioning networks, the four basic elements of reciprocity, interdependence, loose coupling and power-trust relations are evident (Grabher, 1993). The extent of each of these elements within a network will be dependent upon factors such as context, necessity and partner legacy issues. Partner legacy issues can include past social and professional relations, organisational reputational standing, industrial power \ size or even the degree of exclusivity of specific knowledge. Each of these elements influences the structure of the network, as well as its routines of

Figure 8. Clusters of innovation lead IT organisations

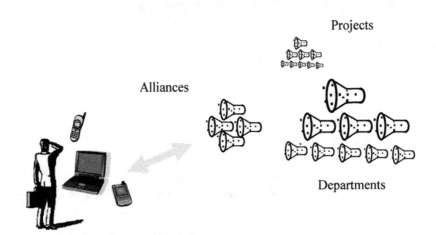

practice. Networks will evolve over time, based on the way each of these elements manifests itself within the network. While each network manifestation will be unique, Grandori and Soda (1995) attempt to categorise networks based on the extent of formalisation within the network, the degree of centralisation and the mix of co-ordinating mechanisms within the network. These factors will affect the network structure and the process of relational contracting between the organisational nodes.

CONCLUSION

IT organisations must continuously innovate in terms of product, process, market and business model to remain sustainable. They innovate to enhance competitive advantage over other organisations and improve profitability. The desire to develop radical innovations that occupy 'new' market space often requires an organisation to move significant distance from its existing competencies and capabilities. As this distance increases so does the risk of failure in undertaking the prospective innovation. This has led to a shift in innovation perspective from concentration on developing internal organisational competencies to support innovation, to the 'new' perspective of inter-organisational collaborative networks. Future organisational innovation activity will be exemplified by continuous innovation, achieved by inter-organisational networks exploring opportunities through horizontal and self-managed systems. The trend towards inter-organisational collaboration is driven by increased global competition and shortening product lifecycles, increased complexity and cost of the innovations being undertaken and a more discerning market. The model of collaborative innovation allows an organisation certain advantages such as access to deficient internal skills and capabilities, distribution of the associated risks and costs across the network partners and ultimately the enhancing of their ability to deliver the innovation to the market.

REFERENCES

Best, M. H. (2001). *The New Competitive Advantage: The Renewal of American Industry*. UK: Oxford University Press.

Cohen, W. M., & Levinthal, D. A. (1990, March). Absorptive Capacity: A New Perspective on Learning and Innovation. *Administrative Science Quarterly, 35*(1), 128–152. doi:10.2307/2393553

Cooper, B. (1988). *Winning at new products.* London: Kogan Page.

Cumming, B. (1999). Understanding Innovation form the cradle to the grave. In M. Zairi (Ed.), *Best Practice: Process innovation management.* Oxford: Butterworth-Heinemann.

Damanpour, F. (1990). Innovation effectiveness, adoption and organisational performance. In M.A. West & J.L. Farr (Eds.), *Innovation and Creativity at Work.* Chichester: Wiley.

Donaldson, B., & O'Toole, T. (2007). *Strategic Market Relationships: From Strategy to Implementation.* Chichester: John Wiley & Sons.

Dooley, L., & O'Sullivan, D. (2003). Developing a software infrastructure to support systemic innovation through effective management. *The International Journal of Technological Innovation and Entrepreneurship (Technovation), 23*(8), 689–704.

Drucker, P. F. (1985). *Innovation and Entrepreneurship: Practice and principles.* London: Heinemann.

Duggan, R. (1999). Idea Generation: Creative problem solving and innovation. In M. Zairi (Ed.), *Best Practice: Process innovation management.* Oxford: Butterworth-Heinemann.

Ekvall, G. (1991). The Organisational Culture of Idea-Management: A creative climate for the management of ideas. In J. Henry & D. Walker (Eds.), *Managing Innovation.* London: Sage Publishing.

Farr, J. L., & Ford, C. M. (1990). Individual Innovation. In M.A. West & J.L. Farr (Eds.), *Innovation and Creativity at Work.* Chichester: Wiley.

Ghislein, B. (1963). Ultimate criteria for two levels of creativity. In C. Taylor & F. Barron (Eds.), *Scientific Creativity: Its recognition and development.* New York: Wiley.

Grabher, G. (1993). *The embedded firm: on the socioeconomics of industrial networks.* New York: Routledge Publishing.

Grandori, A., & Soda, G. (1995). Inter-firm networks: antecedents, mechanisms and forms. *Organization Studies, 16*(2), 183–214. doi:10.1177/017084069501600201

Grannovetter, M. S. (1985). Economic action and social structure: problem of embeddedness. *American Journal of Sociology, 91*, 481–510. doi:10.1086/228311

Hayes, R. H., Wheelwright, S. C., & Clarke, K. B. (1988). *Dynamic Manufacturing: Creating the learning organisation.* New York: The Free Press.

Henderson, R. (2007). *Developing and Managing a Successful Technology and Product Strategy (MIT Lecture Notes).*

Henry, J., & Walker, D. (1991). *Managing Innovation.* London: Sage Publishing.

Johnston, R.E., & Kaplan, S. (1996, June). Harnessing the Power of Strategic Innovation. *Journal of Creativity and Innovation Management, 5*.

Kanter, R. M. (1983). *The Change Masters.* New York: Simon & Schuster.

King, N. (1990). Innovation at work: the research literature. In M.A. West & J.L. Farr (Eds.), *Innovation and Creativity at Work.* Chichester: Wiley.

MacLaughlin, I. (1999). *Creative Technological Change: The Shaping of Technology and Organizations.* London: Routledge

Moodysson, J. (2007). *Sites and Modes of Knowledge Creation: on the Spatial Organization of Biotechnology Innovation* (Ph.D. Thesis), Lund, Dept of Social and Economic Geography, Lund University, Sweden.

Murray, F. (2002). Innovation as co-evolution of scientific and technological networks: exploring tissue engineering. *Research Policy, 31*(8/9), 1389–1404. doi:10.1016/S0048-7333(02)00070-7

O'Sullivan, D., & Dooley, L. (2008). *Applying Innovation*. California: Sage Publications.

Powell, W. (1990). Neither market nor hierarchy: network forms of organization. In B.M. Staw & L.L. Cummings (Eds.), *Research in Organizational Behavior* (pp. 295-336). JAI Press.

Powell, W., Koput, K. W., & Smith-Doerr, L. (1996). Interorganizational collaboration and the locus of innovation: Networks of learning in biotechnology. *Administrative Science Quarterly, 41*, 116–145. doi:10.2307/2393988

Powell, W. W. (1998). Learning from Collaboration: Knowledge and Networks in the Biotechnology and Pharmaceutical Industries. *California Management Review, 40*(3), 228–240.

Roberts, E. M. (1988). Managing invention and innovation. *Research-Technology Management, 31*(1), 11–29.

Sadler, P. (1995). *Managing Change*. Sunday Times Business Skills, London: Kogan Page.

Sanchez, R. (2001). *Knowledge Management and Organizational Competence*. UK: Oxford University Press.

Senge, P. M. (1994). The Leader's New Work: Building Learning Organizations. In C. Mabey & P. Iles (Eds.), *Managing Learning*. UK: Thompson Learning.

Teece, D. J., Pisano, G., & Shuen, A. (1997). Dynamic capabilities and strategic management. *Strategic Management Journal, 7*(18), 509–533. doi:10.1002/(SICI)1097-0266(199708)18:7<509::AID-SMJ882>3.0.CO;2-Z

Terninko, J., Zusman, A., & Zlotin, B. (1998). *Systematic Innovation: An introduction to TRIZ (Theory of Inventive Problem Solving)*, Boca Raton, Fl: CRC Press.

Tidd, J., Bessant, J., & Pavitt, K. (2005). *Managing Innovation – Integrating Technological, Market and Organizational Change* (3rd ed.). Chichester: John Wiley & Sons.

Utterback, J. M. (1994). *Mastering the dynamics of innovation*. Boston: Harvard Business School Press.

Van de Ven, A. H., Angle, H. L., & Poole, M. S. (1989). *Research on the management of innovation: The Minnesota studies*. New York: Harper & Row.

West, M. A., & Farr, J. (1990). *Innovation and Creativity at work*. Chichester: Wiley.

Wheelwright, S. C., & Clark, K. B. (1992). *Revolutionizing Product Development: Quantum leaps in speed, efficiency and quality*. New York: The Free Press.

Zaltman, G., Duncan, R., & Holbeck, J. (1973). *Innovation and Organizations*. New York: Wiley.

This work was previously published in International Journal of Human Capital and Information Technology Professionals, Volume 1, Issue 1, edited by Ricardo Colomo-Palacios, pp. 16-30, copyright 2010 by IGI Publishing (an imprint of IGI Global).

Chapter 15

The Organizational Management as Instrument to Overcome the Resistance to the Innovative Process:
An Application in the Canary Company

Zamira Acosta
La Laguna University, Spain

Jaime Febles
La Laguna University, Spain

ABSTRACT

Changes in economic activity on a global scale affect organizations due to modifications on their decision criteria, but also for the permanent character of the change. This situation implies an increase of the competition and also the appearance of new markets and opportunities. On the other hand the innovation not only offers major possibilities to guarantee the organization's survival but also it allows to increase their competitive capacity; even turning into a generating element of the change and vice versa. But it will be the organization that inserts appropriately the above mentioned innovation, or that uses it better, the one that will be more competitive. The management of the organizational change, in this sense, turns into an influential factor in the creation of future and in the promotion of the available possibilities. This paper analyzes organizational management more adapted to the innovative processes of the Canary companies, as well as the underlying differences in the types of compared enterprises.

INTRODUCTION

The companies, to be able to compete on an increasingly competitive and globalized market, need to be provided with new strategies that allow them to confront successfully the environ-

ment challenges. The change can be defined like any modification from one state to other, which is observed in the environment and possesses a relatively lasting character (Collerette & Delisle, 1988). The organizational perspective takes sense in this work considering the narrow relation ex-

DOI: 10.4018/978-1-4666-0924-2.ch015

isting between the organizational structures and strategies with the internal and external context that surrounds them.

Even more, since it happens in this study, if we are talking about small and medium enterprises, to which it turns out to be more difficult to face this situation for their scarce resources availability, as well as the resistance to its introduction on the part of the managers. Another reason that makes difficult the change introduction, both in the small and in the big company, is the need that the changes are supported by the values and attitudes of their personnel; which is part of the managerial culture. Therefore, the commitment of the worker is important at the time of initiating the changes and he must become a participant in these. Like that, he will feel more protagonists of the processes and not harmed by them.

The main problem to be conquered is the resistance to the changes that, in natural form, appears before any innovation process, which turns out to have higher impact social than technological, having to be overcome the prejudice of the personnel, since this implies a change in their work routine. Therefore, it turns out to be interesting to study and to analyze the reactions and answers of the personnel involved in the implementation of an innovation. Emphasizing both the positive aspects and the negatives of the introduction of innovations, not only from the point of view of the process but also of the persons involved in the same one, since it might be the generational difference, an important aspect to facilitate its implantation, because the recent generations have a high facility to use the new technologies, since they have been educated in this ambience.

Most of the companies feel comfortable realizing business as they have always realized them. Therefore to cross the threshold towards the change of the internal processes or new ways of carrying on business, product of the innovations, placed the organizations in a discomfort area, that not always they are ready to confront, well for fear that the things will not be equal, or worse the things might go badly. Refusing in some cases to confront the fast changes generated in the new technologies, because a technological phobia of some organizations, what leads them to lose important sources of competitive advantages and even to disappear of the market.

With regard to our study, we will try not only to explore the predisposition in the Canary companies for the implantation of innovative processes, but also we will analyze, from the organizational perspective, so much the aspects relative to the organizational structure that are favouring to the changes as well as those that create resistance conditions. Likewise, we will try to investigate the aspects relating to the predominant individual attitudes, so much in the companies that prefer the innovation as in those which show not to prefer the same one. It is through this way as we will try to discover differences on behaviour between the companies that prefer the innovation with regard to those which do not show to have it, having like final objective, the search of satisfactory conditions that favor the implantation of the innovative process.

The paper is structured in six sections. After this introduction, in the second and third sections the theoretical background is reviewed. The fourth part explains the objectives and methodology of our research, followed by a brief description of the sample. In the fifth section, we provide the results of the empirical analysis. Finally, the six parts summarize the principal conclusions and suggest future research.

EVOLUTION OF THE STRATEGIC ENVIRONMENT AND MANAGERIAL ATTITUDES OPPOSITE TO THE CHANGE

At the present time it is possible to speak about a constant that is the change, the permanent change, the globalization and the increasing competitiveness, characterized by political, economic, social, cultural and technological transformations, force the enterprises to change. These changes affect the society in all the levels, and the organizations are not precisely the exception of the rule, because inside them the change affects to all the aspects, it breaks the work routines, it modifies the habits and alters the traditional decision criteria.

The changes in the economic activity on a global scale, explained partly, for the constant technological innovation, together with the processes of economic integration of the markets, the globalization of the production or the descent of the barriers to the commerce (Gómez-Mejías & Balkin, 2003), they take to the globalization of the markets. This situation supposes the appearance of new opportunities and markets for the enterprises, but at the same time, it causes an enormous increase of the competition.

The technological research and the innovation allow us to increase in the competitive capacity, in the contributions of the human capital and the financial profitability, both in the large firms and in the small and medium. Even when a small-scale enterprise carries out an effort in this sense the effect on his managerial activity is proportionally bigger than the obtained by a large firm. This leads us to thinking that innovation is one of the strategic processes of the company.

Referring to that particularly O'Brien and Marakas (2005) indicates, the companies are expanding global markets for their products and services, using global manufacture establishments to made or to assemble products, gathering money on global capital markets, forming alliances with global associates and fighting against global competitors for clients from all the world. The manage and the achievement of these strategic changes would be impossible without Internet, intranets and other global information networks and telecommunications that constitute the central nervous system of today's global companies. In this line, the technological innovation has been a generating element of changes and vice versa.

But is the organization that uses it better and manages to insert it successfully in its culture and in its development strategies, the one that will be more competitive and its process more efficient. As Hammer and Champy (1993) support, the real power of the technology is not in that it could make to work better the old processes, but, in that it allows the organizations to break the rules and to create new ways of working, that is to say, to redesign.

On the other hand, there are few enterprises able of creating an innovation as such, in product, service or process, something completely new on the market developed in its department of R&D. Often when one alludes to the technological innovation incorporated by a company we are referring to the form and grade in which it applies an innovation

Figure 1. Evolution of the market conditions

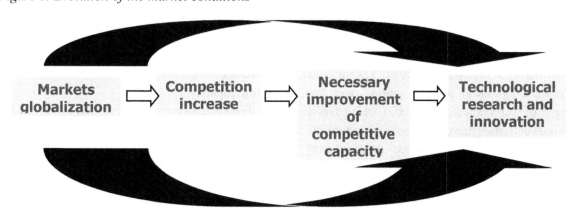

generated and experienced on another ambience (Lope, 1996). It is therefore the introduction of innovations proceeding mainly from the exterior of the enterprise, what allows considering it innovative. Even more in an environment as Canary Island where predominates small firms, without infrastructure or financial capacity to support the high cost that need a research and development department.

To stand up to the continuous evolution of the market conditions, the enterprises can have three different attitudes: to continue with their traditional activity without bearing in mind the environment changes, adapting themselves little by little with light successive modifications to the new conditions, or, to advance with the change through the innovation.

The first attitude in a global, dynamic and competitive environment is untenable. The second one would lead us to introduce in the enterprise what traditionally we call improvement or incremental innovations, referred to modifications that they are implemented in the processes, products or services, in order to raise its services or to attract a specific market, but these innovations don't cause a rupture with the used processes or the products offered previously by the firm.

The third option supposes the incorporation into the enterprise of radical innovations in products or processes, what implies a completely rupture with the previous situation. New technological applications or deep changes are realized in the processes, or in the products and services offered by the firms. Here the risk of failure rises, but if it is realized successfully, the reached competitive advantage is larger.

In this sense the Spanish industry has suffered important structural transformations over the course of last years (Cotec, 2007), being faced towards activities more innovative and more intensive technologically, to favour its adaptation to the new competitive frame of economic activity globalization. The Spanish companies are every day more sensitive to the importance that

has the introduction of innovations, so much through modifications or improvements in their productive processes as in the final products, and they realize a hefty effort to start steps directed to improve the technological development and, therefore, they aptitude to be competitive.

Nevertheless, the innovation is the result of a complex and interactive process in which takes part technologies, human resources, professional training, organizational capacities, designs, and other intangible factors of the managerial activity. It is therefore, the art of transforming the knowledge into wealth and quality of life (Nuñez & Gómez, 2005). In this line Kuczmarski (1995) expresses that although it is not possible to touch, to smell, to listen, to view or to try, the innovation is possible to feel, to think and to perceive. The innovation can be well described as an attitude that penetrates and spreads, which, it allows to the companies to go beyond the present and to create a future vision. In this way the innovation would be a mental attitude inherent the human being, which has an important consequence in the organizational answer to the same one that we will analyze in the following section.

THE RESISTANCE TO THE INNOVATIVE PROCESS

The innovation implies change, as is gathered in some definitions like those of Knight (1967), Drucker (1986), or Nelson and Winter (1982) that define it as a change that needs considerable grade of imagination and that constitutes a relatively deep rupture with the established ways of doing the things; with it fundamentally it creates a new capacity.

The changes not necessary lead to significant improvement. The only fact of introducing a managerial innovation is not a guarantee of an increased productivity. So that the implantation of an innovation produces some results, it is necessary to fulfil several requisites like to know deeply

Figure 2. Answers opposite the change

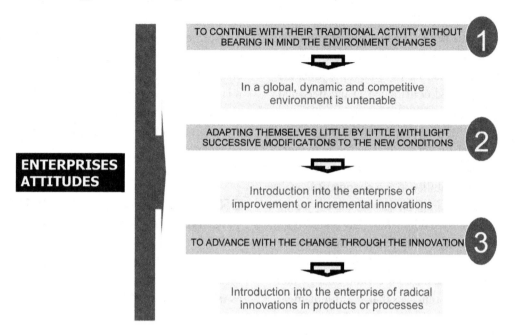

the processes of the company, to plan in detail the needs, to carry out the introduction gradually and, as Edwards, Ward, and Bytheway (1991) supports, to determine the form in which the applications have to be development, how they are going to be acquired, used, controlled and managed the necessary technological and human resources to satisfy the company needs. It would be necessary to add to all this, the need to identify the available skills inside the organization, looking for the best methodologies to start up the innovation, consulting the experts, propitiating a discussion ambience about the best practices.

The innovation projects in the organizations generally provoke transformations of certain importance, that is to say, they are not simply small modifications, but rather they imply higher modifications that affect the structure, the processes and the most important thing, the human capital that integrates them. For all this it is necessary to consider equally the technical dimension and the human one, like the only alternative to guarantee a successfully implantation.

One of the difficulties of the change introduction is that some persons can perceive the effects of the change as beneficial, while others look at them like harmful or, even like unnecessary, therefore they resist to it on having been affected in different ways. The answer will depend on their personal perceptions and on their adaptive capacity. These persons who resist to the changes usually have certain emotional wear, product of the tensions, the worry and anxiety that affect the individual personality during a period of change. Some times, the obstacles to the change are environmental factors that make difficult the acceptance and application of the change. This attitude is named resistance to change, characterized by the barrier rising by the fear to the unknown, for suspicion towards the indicators of the change, or for feelings of threatened safety (Nuñez & Gómez, 2005).

The resistance alludes to any thought or action directed against a change (Harrington, Conner, & Horney, 2000). Robbins (1989) indicates that the sources of resistance to a change are of individual and organizational character.

The individual resistance sources to the change reside in basic human features like the perceptions, personalities and needs. To that we can add the surprise and fear before the unknown, the modifications in power relations or removal of jobs, the low self-esteem and confidence in the personal capacities (Robbins, 1989). Sometimes, what is rejected is not the introduction of the innovation but the moment or the form that the managers want to implant it, the worker cannot understand his role or responsibility in the change process.

Also we can meet persons who usually resist to all the changes and others that only resist some of them, depending on the features of the above mentioned changes. Added to that, the attitude of the workers opposite to a certain change can be different in the time, so that we might meet persons who at first resist but later they are flexible, or vice versa (Collerette & Delisle, 1988).

While the rejection or resistance in the organizations come from the companies conserving nature opposite to the change, which is caused by their structural inertia, the threat to the established resource distribution, or to the established power relations (Robbins, 1989).

An important problem is that the organizations are not prepared for the unexpected things. The stable structures produce and preserve their own stability, being opposed to their own change (Escorsa & Valls, 1997). The innovation implies that the managers introduce, or allow, a little disorder and flexibility, they must allow to create and to change, which will make to appear contingencies in the functioning of their companies.

It is proceeding also to indicate that the resistance to change is not necessary negative, rather it is absolutely normal. Therefore the idea would be to make use of the process of feedback generated by the same one (García, 2005), since it informs us about the importance that the system attaches to the objectives of the change, also it informs us about the system grade of permeability and opening with regard to the change and, also it can reveal to the managers mistakes in the development of

their projects of change or in the approach used to implant them.

Before these resistance, and since it is not possible to brake the change that appears like a constant around the companies (Mullins, 1993), it is necessary to give up formal structures and to choose more flexible structures, as the used ones by the informal organizations, that promotes indefinite relations and favor the personnel spontaneity.

ORGANIZATIONAL PARAMETERS IN THE INNOVATIVE ENTERPRISE

Many authors have studied the innovative organizations. Already from the 70s studies appear as those of Twiss (1974) that suggest the need to use matricidal organizations in any innovative process, the models of Atkinson (1984), Toffler (1985) or Handy (1990), which distinguishes the trefoil organization, the federal organization or the triple i organization, all of them looking for the flexibility. In the same line there are many studies, between them we will emphasize Mintzberg and Quinn (1988) who consider that the innovation demands a very flexible configuration, he names it adhocracy, characterized by the decentralization, orientation to the needs of the clients, functioning through projects, matricidal, few level structures, work teams, fluid and informal communications, knowledge before authority. Nevertheless in Mintzberg's theory does not stand out the importance of a committed manager team that leads the company to the change, able of transmitting this feeling to the whole company.

Other authors, like Morcillo (1997), propose to look for the flexibility of the company to innovate through different forms of external relations as, between others, the enterprise alliance or the organization in network. Nevertheless this is not the objective of our paper; we try to study the organizational design in the internal level which allows us to introduce the innovations in the company with the minimal resistance.

Figure 3. Resistance to change and organizational design

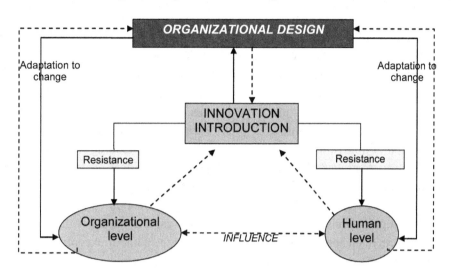

Being studying small and medium companies, we start already from a point necessary for a better introduction of innovations; they are provided with small units. Because of this they can answer more quickly, they are more flexible and closer which helps them to encourage the initiative.

As soon as the company is organized in flexible form it is necessary to proceed to a reduction of the number of levels. The structures with few levels facilitate the initiative, they improves the communication and the responsibilities, elements that all the authors agree in considering like necessary for the success in the incorporation of changes.

The work in team turns out to be essential, for the introduction of innovations; it can be settled with temporary character to put into practice the project innovation, or with permanent character for the work continued in the company (García, 2005). It is necessary to promote the collective effort and, in the moments of new hiring, there will be selected those persons who show capacities related with the work in team. At individual level, the jobs must be understood in terms of value added to the process in which they are taking part. The inflexibility in the jobs description has to be eliminated, favouring the rotation and, additionally, it is necessary to consider the personal contribution to the work in team.

A substantial change to be developed is the investment in human capital; in particular in the least qualified levels of the organization, it is necessary to form the personnel or to hire workpeople who dominate the knowledge necessary for the introduction of innovation. It will be necessary to dedicate a lot of time to the training, without losing efficacy in the daily work, which will have to allow the professional auto development as well as the continuous learning and the development of skills (Kotter & Schlesinger, 1979). Never the use of the whole available talent will be limited. This training must reach also the intermediate managers, because they are entrusted to guide and to supervise the process of implementation of the innovation.

The management style will be based on the leadership. The leaders will have to be converted into the promoters of the innovative change, and they must lead the basic processes, impelling them and motivating the workpeople to prevent from developing attitudes of resistance (García, 2005). This support will begin in the high levels of the company (Kotter, 1996), which will have to be involved, from the first moment, in the process of introduction of innovations; determining with precision the scope and objectives of the innovation and allocating the necessary resources. They must have the enough knowledge to start, to develop and to evaluate the innovative process. And it will continue with the intermediate managers who will take part in the design of the plans and will be compromised with the results. As a reinforcement of all these behaviours the companies will establish evaluation and reward systems for those employees who impel, support and contribute to the process of introduction of innovations.

In all levels it is necessary to assume the risks (Kotter, 1996) inherent in the innovation, it is not possible to innovate without assuming risks, in particular in the levels of high responsibility, and this implies the development of an aptitude to accept a consistent level of mistakes and resistances, which they will have to be solved in an efficient way. It is necessary to eliminate the traditional system of punishment to the mistakes, learning of the same ones, for this motive the personnel should acquire confidence and safety in that the introduction of innovations will not have negative effects for them.

Following the realized review of the literature, to avoid in greater measurement the resistance of the workpeople to the implantation of innovations, the company will have to carry out a cultural change based on the development of a favourable attitude to the introduction of innovation, through a higher communication, initiative, creativity, participation and collaboration.

A critical element of the change is the communication (Kotter & Schlesinger, 1979), for this reason, from the beginning, it will be established a high level of dialogue and honesty in the relations, both between the managers and with the personnel. It is necessary to encourage the informative transparency. In this way the enterprises will try to promote a favourable attitude before the changes, especially before those of innovative character, which can generate more suspicion for its novelty. The un-favourable attitudes must be diminished or controlled (Kotter & chlesinger, 1979), through negotiations or agreements, so

that they do not turn into conducts that prevent the initiative (García, 2005).

In support to the previous idea there is essential the promotion of the creativity of the personnel through the development of new tools and job methodologies (Escorsa & Valls, 1997). It is necessary to carry out the recognition of the efforts and achievements, to request suggestions, work in team, to encourage initiatives, challenges, development of ideas, as well as any other procedure that helps to involve the personnel in the process of innovation.

At the same time the widespread and active participation, without exceptions, of all the personnel of the company (Kotter & Schlesinger, 1979), must be used like the best mechanism of motivation and identification of the employees with the process of introduction of the innovation, which will avoid the rejection of the same ones to the realized changes.

Finally a basic element will be the joint responsibility in the objectives, with the necessary delegation, which is essential at the time of generating a climate of confidence (Kotter, 1996). It is necessary to encourage the collaboration and cooperation in all levels, delegating and granting real power to low level personnel to adopt and to put into practice some decisions, whenever they know better the processes than the proper managers.

RESEARCH OBJECTIVES AND METHODOLOGY

The first objective of the present research is focused on the analysis of the organizational aspects that could influence the resistance to the innovative change, confronting the above mentioned aspects between the innovative companies and not innovative ones, to obtain a first approach to the organizational efficiency of the Canary innovative companies. For it the following hypotheses will be analyzed:

Theorem 1: The Canary companies that show major preference to the innovation also do it for the introduction of flexibility in their structures.

Theorem 2: The Canary companies that show major preference to the innovation tend to consider in major measurement the communication.

Theorem 3: The training is highly valued by the Canary companies that support the innovation.

Theorem 4: The Canary companies that show major preference to the innovation also do it for the decentralization and the participation.

Theorem 5: The Canary companies that value the innovation express to realize major efforts to encourage the initiative and the creativity.

We will analyze secondly the predisposition to the innovation by the Canary enterprises, attending on the form of the same ones, distinguishing if it is realized in the products and services or in the processes of the company.

At the same time we will evaluate the resistance to change by the Canary enterprises in the context of the importance that the companies grant to the variables of the environment.

Because the economy of Canary Island is characterized by the predominance of the small and medium companies, and their survival and competitiveness, which will depend on the adaptation to the changes in the environment, is fundamental for the development and creation of employment. In last place we will explore the grade of sensibility to the changes that the Canary managers perceive in the direction of their companies, which can favor the implantation of the innovative process.

This analysis, that will have exploratory character, will be carried out through the processing of the information generated by the Informative Head Office about the Canary Enterprises, which corresponds to the Research Contract 981201 of FYDE-CajaCanarias and the University of La Laguna. The information was obtained during the first four-month period of 2004, through a questionnaire that was completed by personalized interviews.

The population universe, study object, is formed by the set of manufacturing companies, construction, commercial and service companies that operate in the Canary Islands.

The companies varied in size from 1 to 1300 workers. The ages of the firms ranged from 1 year for the youngest up to 123 years the most ancient.

The used questionnaire gathers questions up from the most significant variables related to the constructs contemplated in the introduction of this work, as we observe in Figure 4. There are innovation and technology variables that allow us to verify positions about innovation in process, products and services. It is valued some elements of organizational design in the company, its culture, as well as some important variables for the enterprise management, of which we will analyze the resistance to the changes and the adaptation to the changes.

The questionnaire has been tested in advance through previous works, as well as managed inside a wider project of investigation, above mentioned, which observes the established requirements.

All the questions are quantified using a five point Likert scale that changes from (1), which is interpreted as a low influence level, up to (5), which represents a very high level. Additional questions ask for specific responses including number of employees, age of the firm or number of levels in the hierarchy.

The interview is realized to individuals with managing functions.

The sample is composed by 449 enterprises that develop their activities in Canary Islands and after our treatment finally used 401.

Figure 4. Analyzed variables

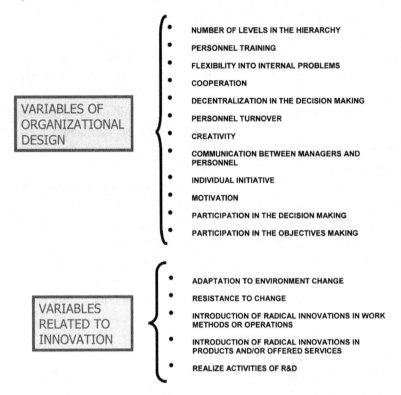

DATA AND RESULTS ANALYSIS

The analysis of the organizational design parameters that help the companies to overcome the resistances to change on having introduced innovation, we have realized it in comparative form. That is to say, we oppose the companies that affirm to realize innovations with the companies that declare not to innovate and, also with regard to the companies of the whole of the sample. For a clearer presentation of the results there have been prepared the Figures 4 and 5 that show the analysis of some of the variables that allow us to evaluate the hypothesis.

The data, showed in the Figure 5, allows us to confirm with enough clarity the preferences for creativity, training, flexibility into the internal problems, adaptation to the change of the environment, individual initiative and decentralization of the decision making in the innovative compa-

nies. This result allows us to accept the hypotheses 1, 3 and 5. Nevertheless we can not verify the hypothesis 2 since the communication level, between managers and personnel, is the same in the whole of companies of the sample, both innovative and not innovative enterprises. The latter result can be as regards the limited size of the companies that might favour the communication.

In the Figure 6 we describe another group of variables related to the five hypotheses to be evaluated. We emphasize from this figure the great difference of higher appreciation of the participation, so in the decision making as in the objectives making, which takes place in the innovative companies with regard to the rest of enterprises. We also observe higher decentralization of the decision making in the innovative companies, as we argue previously about Figure 5. All of this allows us to accept the hypothesis 4, although we

Figure 5. Comparative of design variables between the innovative companies and not innovative ones (I)

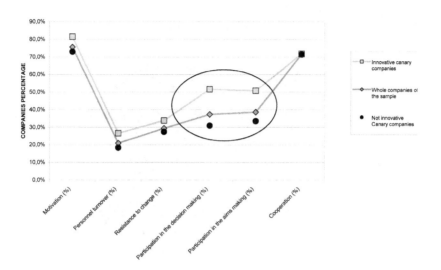

must admit that, in general, the decentralization level is low valued, for the whole sample, without overcoming 25% of the companies.

At the same time we observe higher appreciation of the motivation and personnel turnover in the innovative companies, nevertheless they are accompanied of a higher level of resistance to the change.

We want to stand out the high level of cooperation expressed in the Canary firms, appears equally in all companies of the sample, which coincides and might be related with the high levels of communication, also expressed by the managers.

The analysis of the data from the used questionnaire, showed in figure 7, allows us to confirm the predominance of the small and medium company in the Canary Islands, with 93.27% of the whole of companies of the samples. Emphasizing the high number of micro companies, with less than 10 employees (Comisión de las Comunidades Europeas, 2003), it supposes 45.64% of the analyzed Canary companies. If also we consider the small and medium enterprises, of less than 250 employees (Comisión de las Comunidades Europeas, 2003), the percentage of companies of limited size in the Canary economy is 93%, is for this reason that our study is focus principally

on the problems of resistance to the introduction of the innovation in the small and medium firms. These data do not disagree too much of the rest of Spain where any more than 99% of the Spanish companies belongs to the group of the small and medium company (DIRCE, 2006).

The small and medium company is not provided with resources to carry out big investments in R&D, which we verify on having observed the low consideration of the item realize R&D in the Canary enterprises, where only 17.71%, express to realize some R&D inside the company. This is not an impediment for the small and medium firms to carry out an introduction of innovations in their products or processes since, as Lope (1996) supports, these companies can introduce and develop small innovations in continued form making use of an innovation generated and experienced on another ambience. The innovation can come from other companies, technological institutes, research centres, university departments, or from the public institutions, the important thing is to obtain access to it and to manage its implementation.

Spain presents a considerable delay in innovative matter as regards the average values of the principal European indicators and, although the data of growth of last years are positive (López,

Figure 6. Comparative of design variables between the innovative companies and not innovative ones (II)

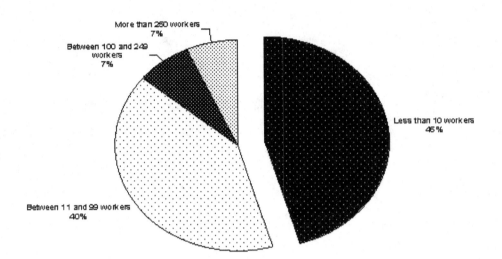

Montes, & Vázquez, 2007), an important effort is still necessary in the resources assigned to the innovation. According to the National Institute of Statistics (INE, 2006) in the period of our study there were in Spain 47,529 innovative companies, that is to say, 27% of the whole of companies of 10 or more employees. It is not possible to compare this data with those of our analysis because this data are not considering the micro companies, very important part of the Canary managerial sector; because of this reason we take it only in sense of guidance. The data of our study, which are given next in Figure 8, considers this group of enterprises, they show us that in Canary Islands 18.95% of the firms have preference to realize innovations in methods of work and operations, while 24.19% show to realize innovations in products and services.

The Canary companies that express a high resistance to the changes, like the introduction of innovations, represent a 29.43% of the analyzed enterprises in our database, and in 48.88% they state an average resistance, that is showed next in Figure 9. Therefore from the perspective of the Canary managers, at the time of introducing changes in their companies, some resistance is going to arise in 78.31% of the situations.

In last place we can observe also that the Canary managers have a high appreciation of the importance of the adaptation to the change of the environment, confirming this affirmation 58.10% of the companies analyzed in the sample, as we can see in Figure 4. This affirmation, expressed by the interviewed managers, creates the beginning conditions that might favor the introduction of innovations in the company.

CONCLUSION

As regards the studied variables, we want to emphasize from the two typologies of companies that we distinguish, (those who show to have high propensity towards the innovation with regard to that ones which haven't it), that the underlying differences have to do principally with the leading role of the persons. This reveals the improvement opportunities in the organizational management that open for these Canary companies, being able to develop an integration frame that canalizes the behavior of the persons towards priority objectives.

We state at the same time coherence in the answers expressed by the set of polled managers as it is observed in the variable participation, which

Figure 7. Number of employees in canary enterprises

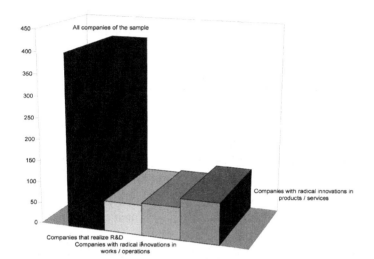

is converted into the concept most differentiated between the Canary innovative and not innovative companies. Everything previously commented also allows us to discern that both typologies have a wide sense of the identity with their group of belonging. This is also perceptible in the interactions with the rest of organizational variables. At the same time there are appreciated important differences between the companies compared in

this work. That is to say the innovative Canary companies show a major development of the variables of creativity, individual initiative and participation, from this it might be interpreted that they contemplate successful methods to favor open thoughts, facilitating in this way, the reduction of the resistance and the introduction of innovations.

In spite of the advantages that are attributed to the activities of the information technology

Figure 8. Combined analysis of R&D and types of innovation

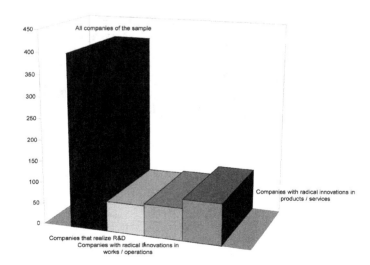

companies, the knowledge of the innovative process is still scarce in the same ones. Through this study we can also analyze and explain what information sources are essential to improve the results, as well as what organizational resources are necessary to combine with the information technologies by the persons in charge of the same ones to be able to promote the innovations.

About the importance of the training of the human capital of the company, our work confirms in the case of the innovative Canary companies, the existence of a higher preference to develop the capacities of the personnel. Making possible thus to can reduce the individual resistance, as for that it might increase the safety of the employee and his skills to confront the changes.

It is necessary to realize therefore, an effort to train workers, starting by base personnel on which is sustained the innovative effort, they are going to prepare the product or service offered to the clients and to influence in the quality of the product offered by the firm. But, although it is important that formation exists in the base, it must exist in the enterprises intermediate and high control levels. The managers must direct the

introduction as well as the starting of the innovation and, hardly they will be able to give commands, instructions, detect bugs or supervise activities that they do not control themselves. Bearing in mind that at present it has a tendency that the managers lead more than order and, to be able to lead needs specific train.

The personnel, before the introduction of innovations, not always resist to the innovative change for itself, sometimes it depends on the ambience or on the general politics of the company, and most of the generated resistance can be avoidable. The Canary enterprise is provided with an advantage to overcome the resistance to change, this is the flexibility that their small size gives to them.

This major flexibility of the innovative Canary companies, is also reinforced and facilitated, as we appreciate, by a major preference for the personnel turnover, and in this way, they deepen in coherence as regards the not innovative companies of the sample, which present these features in less measurement.

The Canary managers declare to incorporate innovations between their competitive strategies, in a similar percentage to the realized in the rest of

Figure 9. Resistances to change perception of canary managers

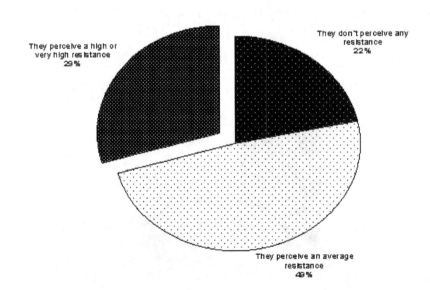

the country. A major introduction of innovations is observed in products and services opposite to the innovations in processes.

The higher predisposition to the adaptation to the change of the innovative companies, with regard to not innovative ones, in the analysis of the Canary companies, allows us to reinforce the idea of that the innovative change is not only a possible generating strategy of advantages to compete in the environment, but also a sign of coherence and of a determined will.

But at the same time, we verify that this innovation, resultant from a major adaptation to the change, also faces the company to a new challenge, the natural need to manage the resistance to the modifications that they are trying to start up, that will be individual or organizational resistances.

In next studies, not only we will try to overcome the limitations imposed by the exploratory character of this work, we will apply other measurements tools, and we will consider to increase the number of variables and the relations to study.

REFERENCES

Atkinson, J. (1984, August). Manpower Strategier for Flexible Organizations. *Personal Management, 28-31.*

Collerette, P., & Delisle, G. (1988). *La planificación del cambio.* México: Editorial Trillas.

Comisión de las Comunidades Europeas. (2003). *Recomendación de la Comisión, de 6 de mayo de 2003.* Sobre la definición de microempresas y pequeñas y medianas empresas: Bruselas.

Cotec (2007). *Informe Tecnología e innovación en España.* Madrid, Spain: Fundación Cotec para la innovación tecnológica.

DIRCE. (2006). *Directorio Central de Empresas.*

Drucker, P. (1986). *Innovation and entrepreneurship.* London: William Heinemann Ltd.

Edwards, C., Ward, J., & Bytheway, A. (1991). *The Essence of Information Systems.* London: Prentice-Hall International.

Escorsa, P., & Valls, J. (1997). *Tecnología e innovación en la empresa. Dirección y gestión.* Barcelona, Spain: Ediciones de la Universitat Politécnica de Catalunya.

García, G. (2005). Herramienta para el diagnóstico de la resistencia al cambio durante el desarrollo de proyectos mayores. *Estudios gerenciales, 96*(3), 57-106.

Gómez-Mejías, L., & Balkin, D. (2003). *Administración.* Madrid, Spain: McGraw-Hill.

Hammer, M., & Champy, J. (1993). *Reengineering the Corporation: A Manifesto for Business Revolution.* New York: Harper Collins Publishers.

Handy, C. (1990). *The age of unreason.* Boston: Harvard Business School.

Harrington, J., Conner, D., & Horney, N. (2000). *Project Change Management: Applying Change Management to Improvement Projects.* New York: McGraw-Hill.

INE. (2006). *Encuesta sobre Innovación Tecnológica en las Empresas.* Instituto Nacional de Estadística.

Knight, K. E. (1967). A descriptive model of the intrafirm innovation process. *The Journal of Business, 40*(4), 478–496. doi:10.1086/295013

Kotter, J. P. (1996). *Leading change.* Boston: Harvard Business School Press.

Kotter, J. P., & Schlesinger, L. A. (1979). Choosing strategies for change. *Harvard Business Review, 57,* 106–114.

Kuczmarski, T. (1995). *Innovation: Leadership Strategies for the Competitive Edge.* New York: McGraw-Hill/Contemporary Books.

Lope, A. (1996). *Innovación tecnológica y cualificación*. Madrid, Spain: Consejo Económico y Social, Departamento de Publicaciones.

López, N., Montes, J. M., & Vázquez, C. J. (2007). *Cómo gestionar la innovación en las PYMES. La Coruña*. Galicia, Spain: Netbiblo.

Mintzberg, H., & Quinn, J. (1988). *The Strategy Process: Concepts, Contexts and Cases*. Englewood Cliffs, NJ: Prentice Hall.

Morcillo, P. (1997). *Dirección estratégica de la tecnología e innovación: un enfoque de competencias*. Madrid, Spain: Editorial Civitas.

Mullins, L. J. (1993). *Management and Organizational Behaviour*. London: Pitman Publication.

Nelson, R., & Winter, S. (1982). *An Evolutionary Theory of Economic Change*. Cambridge, MA: Harvard University Press.

Nuñez, M., & Gómez, O. (2005). El factor humano: resistencia a la innovación tecnológica. *Revista Orbis, 1*(1), 23–34.

O'brien. J., & Marakas, G. M. (2005). *Management Information System* (7th ed.). New York: McGraw-Hill.

Robbins, S. P. (1989). *Organizational Behavior: Concepts, Contro-versies, and Applications*. Englewood Cliffs, NJ: Prentice Hall.

Toffler, A. (1985). *The adaptative corporation*. New York: McGraw-Hill.

Twiss, B. C. (1974). *Managing Technological innovation*. London: Longman.

This work was previously published in International Journal of Human Capital and Information Technology Professionals, Volume 1, Issue 2, edited by Ricardo Colomo-Palacios, pp. 49-64, copyright 2010 by IGI Publishing (an imprint of IGI Global).

Chapter 16
GOTOPS:
Code of Technoethics Governance

Helena Campos
Universidade do Minho, Portugal

Luís Amaral
Universidade do Minho, Portugal

ABSTRACT

Information Systems Technology (IST) has an increasingly central role in today's globalised information society. In this regard, it is imperative to recognise the impossibility of a technological life without ethics. As typical components for an ethics program, the authors use Codes of Ethics/Conduct/Practices (CE/CC/CP) as some professions (physicians, lawyers, etc.) have adopted them. The codes are instrumental in developing sound relations with various stakeholders to reduce the number of legal proceedings and contingencies, negotiate conflicts of interest, and ensure the fulfillment of the law. In view of this, the codes should be dynamic and not static documents, used for the advancement in easy reading, understanding, and structure. This will be instrumental for their followers to more easily consult and understand them, and find guidelines for their key ethical problems and concerns. This paper proposes the voluntary GOTOPS code of the techno ethics governance, that is, ethical problems raised by IST.

INTRODUCTION

Human potentials are the most important resources nowadays (Galenic, 2010) and with the support of IST any person could connect and interact with another one, in any place in the world, and improve your work. However, the globalisation raised ethical concerns that only a deep and joint interdisciplinary reflection can lessen by searching for and suggesting paths that promote awareness and consequently socially responsible ethical practices (Campos & Amaral, 2007a, 2007b).

In this globalised information society, one still has to add the real scenario, of all the other dimensions – social, environmental and economic (*triple bottom line*) – supported by the IST. Therefore, besides the image and reputation of all professionals of other business areas and IST users - that need IST for the development of his profession – one has to point out the image, repu-

DOI: 10.4018/978-1-4666-0924-2.ch016

tation, and responsibility of the IST Professionals (ISTP) to guarantee technological sustainability (Johnson, 2005).

The management of any business area requires a set of activities that cover planning, implementation and control through formal and informal means. At the same time, every business management should include common typical techniques and instruments of ethics management (statements of values, CE/CC/CP, ethics committees, Social Responsibility (SR) programmes, among others) whose main role is the management of the ethical behaviour of the collaborators, the management of relations with the stakeholders and the evaluation of the ethical performance of an organization. Amongst the instruments mentioned, to be pointed out are the CE/CC/CP as they are statements that explicitly outline the desired and expected conduct and practice of the professionals from the ethical point of view within an organisation or profession (Campos, 2007a). This practice is already quite common in many European countries and the USA (Campos & Amaral, 2006c).

The confirmation of the importance of ethics in the field of the IST – here called "Technoethics"; the awareness of the many concerns and ethical dilemmas that emerged with globalisation; the recognition of the need for technoethical management and the urgency for ethical leadership on the part of the respective relevant authority are unquestionable findings that led us to the themes of the CE/CC/CP as the first instrument necessary for technoethical management. In line with this confirmation – the need of ethics for the technological civilisation - the objective of the present work is the presentation of a voluntary code of Technoethical Governance for Sustainable Portuguese Organisations (GOTOPS) that was created and that fully includes ethical problems raised by development and utilization of the IST. So, this study pursues the importance of the CE/CC/CP for IST. As it presents the first code for ISTP in Portugal, which until now was nonexistent; its approach is innovative.

RESEARCH APPROACH

The elaboration and implementation of a code is not an ad-hoc process (Campos & Amaral, 2007a, 2007b) but a development process (process of tasks) that undergoes the articulation of possible mechanisms for the construction and sustainability of the code and for the renovation of the energies that led to its development. In this context, once the integrated process of the tasks was constructed, the approach followed consisted of proceeding with the implementation of this process to construct and support the GOTOPS code in an interactive and user-friendly way, resulting in a uniform, dynamic and interactive code, and the first in Portugal of technoethics governance for a sustainable organisation, business and IST. Thus, the GOTOPS code referred to aims at promoting the responsibility and sustainability of Portuguese organisations through the involvement of its top governance bodies (Abramo, 2000; Berleur et al., 2004; Birkett & Barbera, 1999; Brown, 2003; Campos, 2005; Driscroll & Hoffman, 2000; Initiative, 1998; Navran, 2003; Richard et al., 2002; Webley, 2001).

Work Carried Out

The construction of the GOTOPS code was an integrated process of tasks (already developed and validated) supported by: (1) the comparative analysis of the CE/CC/CP already constructed and validated in the IST area [Campos & Amaral, 2006c]; (2) the DIORCODES model (**DI**rectives of **OR**ientation for **CODES**) for the development process of a code (Campos & Amaral, 2007a); (3) the set of ten guidelines for writing a code and by the PROECO prototype (Prototype for Structure of a Code) that provides the structure (form and content) of a code (Campos & Amaral, 2007b) and (4) by the SSIGOTOPS system (Sustainability and Interactive Support of the GOTOPS code) of automatic support (Campos & Amaral, 2009a) – included in the points that follow.

Comparative Analysis of Codes of Ethics in the IST Area

When analysing the literature in the ambit of the CE/CC/CP developed in the IST areas, it was concluded that in all the prefaces the main objective is to get the professions inherent to IST to be considered the most influential in the future of our society (Campos & Amaral, 2006c). From the comparative analysis of 20 organisations of international reference that were studied in the IST area, it has to be pointed out that a CE is a more condensed version that describes a set of general standards and aspirations or ideals (fundamental ethical principles of an organisation or profession) at the highest level of abstraction. A CC states how the fundamental ethical principles must be complied with, and therefore requires a higher degree of detail. A CP governs as the person they apply to and executes his work technically (Campos & Amaral, 2006c).

DIORCODES Model for the Development Process of an Efficient Code

The DIORCODES model proposed for the development process of a code includes the possibility of the code being constructed (15 steps) or not (11 steps) by the organisation (Campos & Amaral, 2007a). The exclusion of four steps is due to the fact that there is no leadership participation in the construction of the code as the code is a voluntary one.

Directives for Writing a Code / PROECO Prototype

To define how to write and to structure (form and content) a code, if it is CE, CC and/or CP, becomes an obligatory task before its construction. The quality of the writing and structure of a code is fundamental for the professionals to find the guidelines for their problems and key ethical concerns (Campos & Amaral, 2007b). Thus, we want a structure as uniform and automatised as possible for the code, with its application aimed at both areas business/IST. The essential items of a code considered in the PROECO prototype are in Table 1. One has to point out that the instantiation of the GOTOPS code was followed the structure of the prototype PROECO proposed (Campos & Amaral, 2007b).

SSIGOTOPS System

The tool is a system of the web-based type and uses the Internet as communication infrastructure. Above all it is a proof-of-concept in relation to the proposed GOTOPS code. For that purpose, a system was developed based on the WEB architecture on a Database.

The SSIGOTOPS (Campos & Amaral, 2009a) has a system of authentication (*login and password*) established in the database. It is thus ensured that the content of the application will only be visualized by 'authorised' users. The SSIGOTOPS objective is to dynamise and automatises the GOTOPS code, thus differentiating it from all the already existing codes that are on paper.

GOTOPS VOLUNTARY CODE

The GOTOPS code aims to be an 'interactive ethical guide or book' with the necessary ethical components (ingredients) to enable any organisation to construct its own code adjusted to its own culture and mission. The GOTOPS code aims at being the starter, to motivate organisations to have a CE/CC/CP, thus allowing them to choose the most important and significant ethical components – main ethical principles, conducts and practices – previously defined by GOTOPS, so as to establish the objectives of ethical character that the organization intends to achieve and pursue, internally and externally, considering the different interested parties (Campos & Amaral, 2009b). The

Table 1. PROECO Prototype for the form and content of a code

Draft of a prototype for the form and content of a code
1. Explanatory and creative title
2. Presentation of commitment from highest authority
3. Presentation of writing and approval committee
4. Introduction
• *Mission*
• *Spirit*
• *Purpose/Aim of the code*
• *Context*
• *How it must be use*
5. Key Ethics, Conduct and Specific Practices Statements
6. Implementation and operationalisation of the code
7. Monitorisation and sustainability of the code
8. Disclosure of evolution of the ethical performance of the organisation

great objective of GOTOPS is to be applicable to any organisation that intends to have a CE/CC/CP without having to develop it, just needing to adapt it to its own reality and dimension in a quick and interactive manner. The organization also has the flexibility to choose the categorization and character or degree of specificity of the code it wishes to have.

Ethics Statements, Professional Conduct and Professional Practices

The key ethics, conduct and good practices statements are the core of the codes (Campos & Amaral, 2006c). They consist of the definition of principles and/or procedures that the organization or profession believes in and wishes to fulfil (Campos & Amaral, 2006c; Crane & Matten, 2004).

With the GOTOPS code, which is based on basic ethical principles (CE) accompanied by a detailed set of rules (guidelines) of conduct (CC) for the ISTP's behaviour and good practice (CP) for performance of the IST profession (Campos & Amaral, 2009b), the target for the ISTP, as professionals in planning, development, management and implementation of the IST (knowledgeable

and influential in the construction, maintenance, storage, access and manipulation of IST), is to carry out a role that is distinct from professionals of other areas and from the end users with regards to quality, efficiency and responsibility in the production of IST. As, in what concerns IST, all the other professionals are only responsible for the correct use of the IST. Thus, the ISTP have the responsibility to facilitate the technological performance of other professions and to be proactive technoethical role models.

Ethics Statements – Code of Ethics (CE)

What distinguishes an ISTP before society or the public is knowledge about IST, its theories and methods, what can be done or not with the IST and how to do it. In the meantime, knowledge brings responsibilities and a principle that is generally accepted in all societies is that the greater the power and authority a person has in any organization the greater the responsibility that person has. Therefore, there is a set of interconnected responsibilities that in an ethical and careful manner may allow for a lighter and more rewarding atmosphere for any professional, taking into account all the relationships that each one has with him/herself, with the family and with all that is an active part and is related to his/her professional performance – country, public, colleagues and peers, profession, professional judgements, product, with his/her relevant authority and in the management and leadership of his/her subordinates (Section 5 in Table 2).

The presence of these fundamental Ethical Statements (ten fields of responsibility) found general international acceptance. This is due to the fact that the ISTP has responsibilities and duties towards each one of them:

- The professionals establish a 'kind of national and social contract', with country and with public, according to which they are allowed to exercise a certain profession, sometimes with certain privileges and in exchange they undertake to exercise their profession in a manner that is beneficial to the country and to society which, at the very least, means not to cause damage and, at the most, respect the health, environment, safety and well-being not only of the present generations but also of the future ones. That is the origin of the need for professionals to acquire and maintain the highest ethical standard, aiming at the best for the country and for the society to which they belong;

- There is also a 'work ethics' of the professionals before their relevant authority (employers, clients, managers or leaders) namely with regards to protection of the employer's interests in situations where the employer frequently does not have the ability to technically supervise the professional's work and where the relationship is established based on trust. And the same happens with the client, who generally do not have the knowledge to judge whether the solution proposed is correct or not, or

is the best one. Good relations between the parties are important for both as a substantial part of the work must be done in groups, with the coordination and collaboration of several people;

- With regards to their product, the professionals have the responsibility to ensure it meets the highest standards (quality, modifications, updates, safety, tests etc.);

- In their professional judgments they have to be as honourable as possible, namely with regards to conflicts of interest, comments and opinions that must be expressed within their level of competence;

- The leaders and managers with supervisory positions must be examples of responsible ethical conduct and leadership, in order to encourage their subordinates to carry out their responsibilities with motivation and professional dedication;

- In general, the profession deals with aspects of the ethical behaviour that must be avoided so as not to discredit the profession itself. It usually has priority in relation to rules with regards to colleagues because, if a colleague repeatedly does not carry out his/her duties, he/she may be denounced so that the profession is not harmed;

- Respect, support and caution not to take discriminatory actions must always be present in the relationship between the professionals and their colleagues and peers. In particular with regards to collaboration between colleagues of the same profession that usually share the same interests. Although this may be subject to different interpretations.

- The professional has his/her origin in a family. Integrity and ethics must be constructed from inside to outside and, as the family is the first system of orientation, education and learning – the moral guide and fundamental stone of ethical teaching - [Sousa, 1996; White, 1996] its presence has become fundamental. It is essential that ethical behaviour should start within the family for a child to more easily become an 'ethical professional'. There must be balance between family life and professional life. And for that balance to be achieved several actors have their share of responsibility: (1) the organisation – must take into account the effort and dedication it demands from its professional, always taking care to safeguard the central core of his/her family; (2) the professional – must bear in mind that when he/she arrives home, his/her family do not want the successful professional but an attentive person with the desirc to invest in his/her family environment. The parents, the teachers and the chiefs, in this hierarchy, are responsible for the good training of these young professionals. In this context, professional ethics is a result of personal ethics (Sousa, 1996; White, 1996);

- Every professional has responsibilities to him/herself. It seems reasonable to say that if you do not respect yourself, you will hardly be able to respect others, if you are not feeling good with yourself, you will hardly feel good about others; that if you are not persevering, i.e., if you do not have the capacity to voluntarily sustain an activity that implies a long task – to be ethical - you will hardly be so – "Ethics is intrinsic to the individual" (Neves, 2008).

The ten fundamental ethical principles presented identify the ethically responsible relationships in which the individuals, groups and organisations participate and the main responsibilities within those relationships. Therefore, the CE is made up of these ten "Ethical Statements" (Section 5, Table 2.) related to behaviours and decisions of the ISTP, including users, educators, managers and supervisors, as well as the instructors and students of the profession (Couger, 1989).

Professional Conduct – Code of Conduct (CC)

After the main fields of responsibility of the ISTP were identified and defined, it was necessary to identify the important rules and/or professional conducts to be followed in order to fulfil those fields of responsibility, aiming at greater detail and depth in the support and guidance given to making better ethical decisions. The set of all the Professional Conducts make up the CC, whose support basis was the study of the IFIP (Berleur & d'Udekem-Gevers, 1996b). The professional conducts are divided into five great categories (Section 5 in Table 2) each one arranged sequentially (3 levels - category, subcategory and sub subcategory) in hierarchical manner and detailing the specificities of the ethical relations between the ISTP and specific interested parties.

Professional Practices – Code of Practices (CP)

The process of identifying and defining good professional practices for the planning, development, management, implementation and utilisation of the ISTP implied the orderly classification and structuring of the ISTP's competences and skills, through the reuse of the SFIA[1] framework (Skills Framework for the Information Age). This set of Professional Practices gave origin to the CP. This code allows the ISTP immediate access only to the good critical practices to be followed for ethical, competent and professional performance of his/her functions (Section 5 in Table 2). Given the changing nature of the IST industry and the great alteration in the roles, this code is more dynamic requires more frequent review in relation to the CE and CC.

GOTOPS Code Presentation

Figures 1-9 show the structure of the GOTOPS code.

Figure 1. Structure of GOTOPS code

GOTOPS Code
1. Title
Technoethical Governance of Sustainable Portuguese Organisations (GOTOPS) *"Work Ethically for Technological Sustainability and Governance"*
2. Presentation of the commitment from the relevant authority
It is hereby declared that this organisation undertakes to comply with the GOTOPS code
3. Presentation of the writing and approval committee
Written by: Approved by:

Figure 2. Structure of GOTOPS code (Cont.)

GOTOPS Code	
2. Introduction	
Mission	The mission of the GOTOPS code is to be an instrument to help the top governance members of the organisations to include the principles of sustainable development at IST level in their activities and decisions.
Purpose	It aims at the possibility and need to extend the range of work of the top governance bodies and of the main ethical principles established by the organisation at technological level. In this sense, the basic motivations are the following:

• The growing social consensus about the need for a sustainable technoethical development:

The top governance bodies of the organizations must meet society's growing demand that the organisations not only pursue maximum profitability of their actions but that they so in coherence with the principles of sustainable development– in space and time – from the economic, environmental social point of view and, especially in this code, in planning, development, management, implementation and utilisation of the IST.

• From shareholders' satisfaction to stakeholders' satisfaction

Top directive bodies (leaders and managers) must take into account that the organisations and, therefore, their top governance bodies, cannot just consider the requirements and needs of their investors and clients, but also those of all the people and organisations that have some type of interest or influence in their activities at consubstantial level – shareholders and investors, collaborators, strategic partners; contextual – creators of opinion and knowledge, local communities, countries and societies, public administration and contractual – suppliers, financial institutions and clients.

• Ethical aspects of sustainable technoethical development:

The organization and its top governance bodies in particular, must interiorise that sustainable technoethical development foresees and demands, in the first place, ethical commitment on the part of the top management, which is then followed by all the stakeholders. |
| Spirit | The content aims at being the promoter, inspirer and guide of the principles sustainable development in the IST area of organisation governance |
| Context | Type of the code: corporative and professional

Sphere of application : local and national

Source: scientific research work

End-users of the code: the GOTOPS code is for all ISTP, whatever their degree, and IST students and users

Character or degree of the specificity: generic, specific and specialised

Origin : voluntary code

Promulgation : |

Figure 3. Structure of GOTOPS code (Cont.)

GOTOPS Code

4. Introduction (cont.)

How it must be used	**CE versus CC versus CP** The code is divided into three sections – The **Code of Ethics** (CE), the **Code of Conduct** (CC) and the **Code of Practice** (CP). Although the first, (CE) and the second (CC) are specifically for ISTP, it aims at the possibility of being applicable to these professionals regardless of their role or specific area of specialisation. They were conceived with a set of fundamental ethical principles (CE - abstract) explained through directives and guidelines of professional conduct (CC - detailed) that indicate the acceptable behaviour for each ISTP that works in the industry to clearly comply with the fundamental ethical principles defined by the CE. Moreover, the ultimate objective is for it to be applied to other professionals, since all professionals use IST. Thus the indissociation of the dichotomy "business/IST" is impossible in a global information society. The third (CP) is a set of guidelines on acceptable good practices in the IST profession.
Terminology	The Code makes a reference to 'you', the IST Professional (ISTP), to show that it is necessary that the ISTP assume a personal commitment. Relevant Authority – This term is used to identify the person (employers, clients, managers and leaders) that has authority over the individual activity you develop. Top management / Leadership – individual or group of individuals responsible for the formal management/leadership of the organization at the highest level. Client – Any person, organisation or department, before which a member has undertaken the responsibility to supply IST services, whatever the type. Client also means other departments within the organisation of the member in question. Organisation – Any legal private or public entity (company, enterprise, institution, university, firm, governmental department, etc.), corporate body or not, profitable or non-profitable, that has its own functional and administrative structure, in which the member (collaborator, supplier, consultant, student or a volunteer) assumes an individual position in the sphere of his/her professional practice. User – Any person, department, organisation or other entity served by IST. System – The set of electronic equipment and software that together supply a specific service – it also includes any application that involves the use of computers. The term *system* may be interpreted as non-computational operative procedures like office systems, manual, communication and electro-mechanic processes. Information Systems and Technology(IST) – Set of different practices or intervention activities of IS and IT. Stakeholder – People, groups, or organisations that affect or are affected by the activities of an organization. Besides the shareholders, the stakeholders are internal and external (collaborators, clients, suppliers and subcontractors, local community, regulatory authorities, employers' associations and trade unions). Code – the term "Code" is used following the practice of other works carried out for improving governance in the organisations, and not with the dictionary meaning of the word.

EMPIRIC VALIDATION

The GOTOPS code was validated through a real case study taken from the literature, aiming at the access, handling and its utilisation in an interactive and automatic manner, i.e., by SSIGOTOPS system (Campos & Amaral, 2009a). Another validation was through the direct contributions of the MBA and MSC students.

Figure 4. Structure of GOTOPS code (Cont.)

GOTOPS Code

2. Ethics Statements, Professional Conducts and Practices

Ethics Statements – **Code of Ethics (CE)**

This code should be considered the ethical basis of professional commitment. It is a summary of the ethical values the professionals are expected to follow. It points out the aspirations in a high level of abstraction which are expressed as principles that should influence the ISTP to consider who is affected by their work.

RESPONSIBILITY TO
COUNTRY
PUBLIC
RELEVANT AUTHORITY
PRODUCT
PROFESSIONAL JUGEDMENTS
LEADERSHIP AND MANAGEMENT
PROFESSION
PEERS AND COLLEAGUES
FAMILY
SELF

CE

The CE contains ten fundamental ethical principals related to the behaviours and decisions of the ISTP. The principles identify the ethically responsible relationships within which the individuals, groups and organisations participate and the main obligations those relationshipsimply.

Professional Conducts – **Code of Conduct (CC)**

The CC is extremely important as it explains how the commitments assumed in the CE are expressed in rules, clarifying and formally stating the ethical requirements that are important in order to achieve those commitments. The code determines your personal and professional conduct whilst a collaborator of the organization and details the categories to follow in order to comply with each of the fields of responsibility stated in the CE. It is a guideline of the professional conduct necessary to be able to follow each fundamental principle included in the CE.

The five big categories listed below are divided into subcategories which, in turn, can be subdivided into subsubcategories. It is worth pointing out that they may not necessarily be followed by all the fields of responsibility of the CE, since it is the field of responsibility in question that determines which categories, subcategories and subsubcategories are to be followed. For example, if it is the 'Profession' field of responsibility within the first category – **Respectful general attitude** – subdivided into 5 subcategories, it is enough to follow 'Respect for the prestige and promotion of the profession'.

The dynamic and demanding context of the ISTP profession requires a code that is adaptable and relevant to new situations as they occur. The code offers support to the ISTP that need to act positively in a certain case, documenting the ethical situation of the profession.

Professional Conducts

1.   Respectful general attitude

- Respect for the interests or rights of the people involved
- Respect for the prestige and promotion of the profession
- Respect for the well-being, public health, environment and quality of life
- Respect for the quality of life of the people involved
- Respect for the well-being of the Global Information Society

---

CONTRIBUTIONS

The main contribution obtained with the development of the research work carried out was the creation of a technoethics governance code for the ISTP and help the Portuguese organisations to adhere to technological sustainability without having to spare dedicated collaborators exclusively to its elaboration. In addition, the sustainability and automatic and interactive support of the code, allows that in a simple and friendly way the ISTP, of any one organisation, could easily and frequently

Figure 5. Structure of GOTOPS code (Cont.)

GOTOPS Code

5. Ethics Statements, Professional Conducts and Practices (cont.)

Professional Conducts (cont.)

3. Production and information flow
- Information flow to the parties or people involved
- Information towards the public
- Comprehensive/Detailed information
- Production of tests, evaluations, results or specifications
- Information flow from the parties or people involved

4. Attitude regarding the regulations
- Respect for the code (compliance with the code)
- Respect for the existing laws relating to professional work
- Respect for IST and the professionals standards
- Development of standards
- Knowledge and development of the law
- Development of the code itself
- Sanctions for violation or breach of the code

Professional Practices – **Code of Practices (CP)**

We advise following the guidelines in the CP that are relevant in relation to the exercise of your functions and specific practical responsibilities. To facilitate consultation, the CP is divided into SIX ORGANISATIONAL COMPETENCES (ORGC):

1. **Strategy and Planning**
2. **Development**
3. **Business Change**
4. **Service Provision**
5. **Procurement and Support Management**
6. **Ancillary Skills**

The 6 ORGC subdivide into 17 Operational Competences (OPC) that, in their turn, are divided into 78 Professional Skills (PS). Through the SP one can visualise which are the most important and representative PS to exercise the respective necessary operational skill to execute the organisational competence in question.

The set of all the good practices to be followed in each PS constitute the common practical guidelines included in the CP and which include:

a) Relevant common practices for all IST professionals;

b) Key-practices for specific IST competences;

c) Practices to be applied in the field of specific flows of business or education.

consult it, whenever in doubt or in need of clarification with regards to the technoethical conduct and practice to be followed in the exercise of his IST profession.

The fundamental contribution of this study consists in a innovative GOTOPS code, the first code for consultation, updating, and automatic handling in Portugal. As all the existing codes are

Figure 6. Structure of GOTOPS code (Cont.)

GOTOPS Code
5.   Ethics Statements, Professional Conducts and Practices (Cont.)

Professional Conducts – **CC** (Cont.)

Professional Conducts

2.   *Personal/Institutional   Qualities: Conscientiousness   and   Honesty;   Positive   Attitude, Competence and Efficiency; Integrity, Objectivity and Independence*

- **Consciousness and Honesty**
  - Acceptance of responsibility
  - Acceptance of integrity
  - Professionalism
  - Credit to work done by others
  - Trust, Loyalty and Goodwill (Image, Reputation, Promotion, 'Good Name')
  - Concern to meet overall objectives
  - Courage of one's convictions
  - Avoid injury to others

- **Positive Attitude**
  - Appeal to respect requirements, contracts or agreements
  - Appeal to conscientious work
  - Voluntary work
  - Be correct and not take discriminatory actions
  - Promotion of progress in the profession

- **Competence and efficiency**
  - Professional development and training
  - Limitation of work within the field of competence
  - General Competence

- **Integrity, Objectivity and Independence**
  - Objectivity and Independence
  - Integrity
  - Conflicts of interest

3.   *Promotion of privacy of information and data integrity*

- Confidentiality
- Privacy (Web, Data Base, Encryption, E-mail, Anonymity, Spamming)
- Respect for the rights of property
  - Ownership of property
  - Intellectual Property (copyright, patents, trademarks)
- No to computer crime, no to information piracy or misuse
- No to access and unauthorised use
- Data Integrity

Figure 7. Structure of GOTOPS code (Cont.)

GOTOPS Code		
5. Ethics Statements, Professional Conducts and Practices (cont.)		
<u>Professional Practices</u> – CP (Cont.)		
It is advisable to follow all the common practices even though you only have to select the practices pertaining to certain competences and flows in the tool. Here lies the flexi-manipulation, handling and updating of the tool.		
Organisational Competences (ORGC)	**Operational Competences (OPC)**	**Professional Skills (PS)**
Strategy and planning	Information Strategy	Information Management
	Advice and Guidance	Consultancy
		Technical Expertise
	Business/Information Systems Strategy and Planning	Research
		Innovation
		Improvement of Business Processes
		Strategic application of information systems
		Business risk management
		Information Security
		Information assurance
	Technical Strategy and Planning	Systems architecture
		Monitoring of Emerging Technology
		Continuity management
		Software development process
		Network planning
		Methods and tools
Development	Systems Development	Systems development management
		Data analysis
		Systems design
		Network design
		Database design
		Programming/software development
		Safety Engineering
		Web site specialisation
		Systems testing
	Human Factors	Systems ergonomics
		Content creation
		Non-functional needs analysis
		Usability evaluation
		Human factors integration

in paper, that explains the strictness and low rate of consultation and knowledge of those codes.

FUTURE WORK

For the future, we propose right now the translation of the code to the universal language (English) and the progressive and continuous improvement of the GOTOPS code and the SSIGOTOPS system.

Figure 8. Structure of GOTOPS code (Cont.)

GOTOPS Code		
5. Ethics Statements, Professional Conducts and Practices (cont.)		
Professional Practices – CP (cont.)		
Organisational Competences (ORGC)	**Operational Competences (OPC)**	**Professional Skills (PS)**
Development (Cont.)	Installation and Integration	Systems integration
		Porting/software integration
		Systems installation/decommissioning
Business Change	Business Change Management	Business analysis
		Programme management
		Project management
		Business process testing
		Planning and management of change implementation
		Organisation design and implementation
		Benefits management
	Relationship Management	Stakeholder relationship management
Service Provision	Infrastructure	Configuration management
		Change management
		Capacity management
		System software
		Security administration
		Radio frequency engineering
		Availability management
		Financial management for IST
	Operation	Data protection
		Application support
		Management and operations
		Network control and operation
		Database administration
		Service level management
	User Support	Network support
		Problem management
		Helpdesk and incident management

In the near future, we should aim to include a discipline of professional technoethics in the undergraduate courses curricula, to make aware students of need and importance of technoethics in their future professional life (Couger, 1989). Through the use of the GOTOPS code, the approach of technoethics in a pedagogical perspective takes the students to interiorize fundamental technoethics concepts which will serve them as basic principles and practices when confronted with problems in their professional careers – today's students will be tomorrow's professional.

Figure 9. Structure of GOTOPS code (Cont.)

GOTOPS Code		
5. Ethics Statements, Professional Conducts and Practices (cont.)		
<u>Professional Practices – CP (cont.)</u>		
Organisational Competences (ORGC)	**Operational Competences (OPC)**	**Professional Skills (PS)**
Procurement and Support Management	Supply Management	Procurement
		Supplier relationship management
	Quality	Quality management
		Quality assurance
		Quality standards
		Compliance audit
		Safety assessment
	Resource Management	Project office
		Asset management
		Information systems coordination
		Client services management
		Professional development
		Resourcing
Ancillary skills	Education and Training	Education and training management
		Creation and maintenance of training materials
		Education and training delivery
	Sales and Marketing	Account management
		Marketing
		Sales
		Sales support
6. Implementation and operationalisation of the code		
7. Monitorisation and sustainability of the code		
8. Disclosure of evolution of the ethical performance of the organisation		

CONCLUSION

The fact that, the GOTOPS code supports ethical decisions through sustainability and automatic support permits emphasising the analysis of real situations that involve a variety of topics (e.g. ´Intellectual property´, ´Privacy´, ´Confidentiality´, ´Quality of the Professional work´, ´Justice and discrimination´, ´Risks caused by software´, ´Conflicts of interest´, ´Non-authorised access´) that demand ethical positions and that are ever more present in the lives of the organisations and professionals.

As the first voluntary code of technoethical governance in Portugal, this code is not simply to judge the nature of questionable acts; it also has an important educational function. As it thoroughly and completely expresses the rules and behaviours about technoethical issues, it is a means for educating students, users, ISTP and trainee professionals about the technoethical obligations of all.

The GOTOPS code supported by the SSIGO-TOPS system aims to be dynamic in the sense of constant updates and because it is automatically supported, those updates may be obtained much more quickly and efficiently. These updates come from the utilization of the code itself, whether in organisational, academic and/or scientific (research) environment.

REFERENCES

Abramo, C. W. (2000). *Formulação e implantação de código de ética em empresas - reflexões e sugestões*. São Paulo, Brazil: Instituto Ethos de Empresas e Responsabilidade Social.

Berleur, J., & d'Udekem-Gevers, M. (1996b). *IFIP Framework for ethics: codes of ethics/conduct for computer societies - The experience of IFIP*. London: Chapman & Hall.

Berleur, J., Duquenoy, P., Holvast, J., Jones, M., Kimppa, K., & Sizer, R. (2004). *Criteria and prodecures for developing codes of ethics or of conduct*. International Federation for Information Processing.

Birkett, W., & Barbera, M. (1999). *Codifying power and control - ethical codes, codes in action contents (Tech. Rep.)*. Sydney, Australia: University of New South Wales, The Australian Centre for Management Accounting Development.

Brown, J. (2003). *Ten writing tips for creating an effective code of conduct*. Washington, DC: Ethics Resource Center.

Campos, H. (2005). Ética e tecnologia - uma parceria que pode dar certo. *Revista Pessoal, 38.*

Campos, H. (2006a, May/June). Gestão ética nos negócios: não há responsabilidade social sem ética nos negócios. *Recursos humanos magazine, 44.*

Campos, H. (2006b, November). Dossier «Ética Empresarial» Reportagem: Do que é que se fala... *Revista Pessoal, 51.*

Campos, H., & Amaral, L. (2006c, September). Codes of ethics in IST: comparative analisys. In *Proceedings of the International Conference Softwars 2006*, Universidade do Minho, Guimarães, Portugal.

Campos, H., & Amaral, L. (2007a, January). Proposta de um modelo para o processo de desenvolvimento de um código de ética/conduta/práticas. In *Proceedings of the International Conference CAPSI 2006 - 7ª Conferência da Associação Portuguesa de Sistemas de Informação*, Universidade de Aveiro, Aveiro, Portugal.

Campos, H., & Amaral, L. (2007b, November). *Structure and writing of a code of ethics/conduct/practices*. Paper presented at the International Conference ICT, Transparency and Social Responsibility, Lisboa, Portugal.

Campos, H., & Amaral, L. (2009a, February). *Sytem of interactive sustainability and support for GOTOPS code -SSIGOTOPS*. Paper presented at the IADIS International Conference e-Society 2009, Barcelona, Spain.

Campos, H., & Amaral, L. (2009b, October). *Code of tecnoethics governance for the sustainable portuguese organisations - GOTOPS code*. Paper presented at the CENTERIS'2009 - Conference on ENTERprise Information Systems – aligning technology, organizations and people, Ofir, Portugal.

Couger, J. D. (1989). Preparing IS Students To Deal with Ethical Issues. *Management Information Systems Quarterly, 13*(2), 211–218. doi:10.2307/248930

Crane, A., & Matten, D. (2004). *Business Ethics: a european perspective - Managing Citizenship and Sustainability in Age of Globalization*. New York: Oxford University Press.

Driscroll, D.-M., & Hoffman, W. M. (2000). *Ethics Matters: How to Implement Values-driven management*. Washington, DC: Ethics Resource Center.

Galenic, D. (2010). Human Capital Management Process Based on Information Technology Models and Governance. *International Journal of Human Capital and Information Technology Professionals*, *1*(1), 44–60.

Initiative, J. (1998). *Voluntary Codes: A Guide for Their Development and Use*.

Johnson, D. G. (2005, September 16). Corporate excellence, ethics and the role of I.T. In *Proceedings of the 2nd International Forum, Business Ethics and Corporate Social Responsibility in a Global Economy*, Milano, Italy.

Navran, F. (2002, September. (2003, July). Seven Steps For Changing the Ethical Culture of an Organization. *Ethics Today Online*, *1*, 15.

Neves, J. C. (2008). *A ética é intrínseca ao indivíduo*. Retrieved February 22, 2008, from http://www.ver.pt/conteudos/ver_mais_Etica.aspx?docID=287

Ricard, J. E., Rodriguez, M. Á., Blasco, D. J. L., Elorriaga, D. J. F., & Castilla, D. M. L. (2002). *Código de gobierno para la empresa sostenible - Guía para su implantación*. Barcelona: IESE Business School - Universidad de Navarra.

Sousa, J. V. (1996). *Cartas ao editor*. Retrieved November 8, 2006, from http://www.airpower.maxwell.af.mil/apjinternational/apj-p/2tri97/carta.html

Webley, S. (2001). *Eight Steps for a Company Wishing To Develop Its Own Corporate Ethics Programme*. London: Institute of Business Ethics.

White, M. G. E. (1996). *Personal Ethics versus Professional Ethics*. Airpower Journal.

ENDNOTE

[1]   http://www.sfia.org.uk

This work was previously published in International Journal of Human Capital and Information Technology Professionals, Volume 1, Issue 3, edited by Ricardo Colomo-Palacios, pp. 54-68, copyright 2010 by IGI Publishing (an imprint of IGI Global).

Chapter 17
An eAgriculture–Based Decision Support Framework for Information Dissemination

Leisa J. Armstrong
Edith Cowan University, Australia

Dean A. Diepeveen
Department of Agriculture and Food Western Australia, Australia

Khumphicha Tantisantisom
Edith Cowan University, Australia

ABSTRACT

The ability of farmers to acquire knowledge to make decisions is limited by the information quality and applicability. Inconsistencies in information delivery and standards for the integration of information also limit decision making processes. This research uses a similar approach to the Knowledge Discovery in Databases (KDD) methodology to develop an ICT based framework which can be used to facilitate the acquisition of knowledge for farmers' decision making processes. This is one of the leading areas of research and development for information technology in an agricultural industry, which is yet to utilize such technologies fully. The Farmer Knowledge and Decision Support Framework (FKDSF) takes information provided to farmers and utilizes processes that deliver this critical information for knowledge acquisition. The framework comprises data capture, analysis, and data processing, which precede the delivery of the integrated information for the farmer. With information collected, captured, and validated from disparate sources, according to defined sets of rules, data mining tools are then used to process and integrate the data into a format that contributes to the knowledge base used by the farmer and the agricultural industry.

DOI: 10.4018/978-1-4666-0924-2.ch017

INTRODUCTION

The livelihoods of the world's population are still largely dependent on the production of food and other agricultural products (World Bank, 2006; Diao et al., 2007). The vast majority of the population, for example in Sub-Saharan Africa, relies directly on agriculture (Diao et al., 2007). The increase in the global population, that has resulted in a doubling of the world's population in the 40 years to 1999 and forecasted to increase to 9 billion in the next 30 years (U.S. Census Bureau, 2009), has necessitated improved food production systems. This has been further facilitated by the pressures of climate change, world trade and problems with the global economy which have made it even more important for the agricultural industry to improve the efficiency of food production. Information remains the most effective tool for the farmer to acquire knowledge, make decisions and communicate knowledge (Kalusopa, 2005). Any improvements in the dissemination of appropriate agricultural information facilitate and enhance farmer knowledge and engender greater capacity to respond to other factors influencing food production.

Considerable efforts have been made by government and university research sectors to find ways to improve rural livelihoods. Studies have investigated the role of information and communication technologies to support agriculture production systems. The term eAgriculture has been coined to describe the enhancement of agriculture and rural development through improved information exchange, communication and learning processes (eAgriculture.org, 2009). eAgriculture has also been defined as "An emerging field, which combines agricultural informatics, agricultural development and entrepreneurship" (Amin et al., 2007). The Food and Agriculture Organization (2000) emphasized the importance of information dissemination to farmers by stating that "information and knowledge play a key role in ensuring food security and sustainable development". Other

studies by Richardson (1997) have suggested the Internet and communication technologies be used to contribute substantially to rural and remote communities, including improving healthcare, education and agricultural productivity.

AGRICULTURAL INFORMATION DISSEMINATION

The dissemination, "to spread or give out something, especially news, information, ideas, etc., to a lot of people" (Cambridge University Press, 2009), or delivery, "the carrying and turning over of letters, goods, etc., to a designated recipient or recipients" (Dictionary.com, LLC, 2009), of agricultural information is integral to facilitating the adoption of new farm technologies. The farmer needs to be aware of the best practices and advances in farm management and breeding. Information on general agronomy practices such as seeding, fertilizer, pest management, harvesting and marketing provides the knowledge base for farmers to make informed decisions. This is supported by Umber (2006) who reported that, for information to be used effectively by growers, it needs to be delivered in a format that can be easily integrated into grower decision making. However, this may only be effective if farmers have the skills to interpret this data and to make decisions relevant to their individual situations (Armstrong et al., 2007).

The timing of disseminating the information is important. Information provided before cropping could include various crop management strategies such as scheduling of seeding activities (Krishna Reddy & Ankaiah, 2005; Tiwari, 2008), improved seedlings (Irivwieri, 2007), input price and availability (Rao, 2004; Tiwari, 2008) and soil fertility (Ekoja, 2004). Other types of useful information may play crucial roles in improving the amount and the quality of products during the growing season. Weather information (Rao, 2004; Tiwari, 2008), fertilizer supply (Ekoja, 2004), fertilizer use in terms of amount and timing (Krishna Reddy & Ankaiah, 2005), pest surveillance and management (Ekoja, 2004; Ratnam, Krishna Reddy, & Reddy, 2005; Rao, 2004; Tiwari, 2008), type and dosage of pesticides (Krishna Reddy & Ankaiah, 2005), weed control (Ekoja, 2004), and disease management (Ratnam, Krishna Reddy, & Reddy, 2005; Tiwari, 2008) have all been reported as types of agricultural information disseminated to farmers. Post season information may include marketing advice (International Institute for Communication and Development, 2006), where financial planning and market prices are likely to be required (International Institute for Communication and Development, 2006; Irivwieri, 2007; Tiwari, 2008).

AGRICULTURAL INFORMATION RESOURCES

The information provided to farmers may be derived from a number of providers. Government meteorological organizations may provide information on current and long term weather with other meteorological forecasts (Jensen & Thysen, 2003). National and regional research institutes and government agencies may provide expert advice services (Jensen & Thysen, 2003), dedicated information and extension services in Agriculture departments (International Institute for Communication and Development, 2006). For example, in Australia, federal research organizations, such as the Commonwealth Scientific and Industrial Research Organisation (CSIRO), state government Departments of Agriculture or Primary Industries, university centres of excellence and private consultants constitute the main providers of relevant agricultural information. The Internet also facilitates the provision of agricultural information. For example, research by Malhan and Rao (2007) has reported on two web portals: the AGMARKNET, which provides daily market price reports, and the Indian Farmers

Fertilizer Cooperative Limited (IFFCO) which delivers required information straight to its kiosks in rural areas.

USE OF INTERNET AND COMMUNICATION TECHNOLOGIES (ICT) IN AGRICULTURE

The dissemination of agricultural information to farmers has been reported through the use of various ICT media. Telephony and mobile phone usage by farmers has been advantageous due to its capability of delivering voice and data with continuing reductions in cost (Bertolini, 2004 cited in Munyua, Adera, & Jensen, 2008; Mangstl, 2008). Mobile phone usage by farmers has been used for a variety of purposes such as acquiring the latest weather information via SMS (Jenson, 2003), spraying schedules, money transfer (Hafkin & Odame, 2002, cited in Munyua, Adera & Jensen, 2008), providing relevant information and taking images (Parikh, 2009).

The Internet may also provide an effective means of communication for farmers. Several research projects have reported the establishment of Internet portals to deliver agricultural information including the iKisan.com project (Tiwari, 2008), the TARAhaat project (Tiwari, 2008) and the e-Choupal project (Rao, 2007), the i-Village and the Gydanroot projects in local languages (Tiwari, 2008) and the Zee Interactive Learning System for its communication satellites (Sood, 2001). Studies have reported a cost effective delivery of agricultural information through community television and radio services (Hassan et al., 2008); Kweku, 2006, cited in Munyua, Adera, & Jensen, 2008; Parikh, 2009). CD and DVD usage for delivery of agricultural learning modules have proved to be viable dissemination media (Anandaraja et al., 2009; Pye et al., 2003, cited in Munyua, Adera, & Jensen, 2008; Parikh, 2009; Sheriff, 2009). The use of these self learning modules has been found to reduce dependency on technical staff for acquiring new agricultural knowledge. Other technologies such as radio-frequency identification (RFID) have been used to capture and transmit agriculture information to farmers (Munyua, Adera, & Jensen, 2008). Other research studies have reported the use of geographic information systems (GIS) to gather relevant information about farming villages (Tiwari, 2007).

Research by Ratnam et al. (2005) has demonstrated the use of a web-based expert system (e-Sagu) which assists farmers to improve productivity by providing customized information in a timely and personalized manner. This was achieved through the use of text and digital photographs to collect information about crop situations to formulate advice for farmers. The e-Sagu system consists of five components: farmers, coordinators, agricultural experts, agricultural information systems and communication systems (Ratnam, Krishna Reddy, & Reddy, 2006). Farmers register with the system and provide information to local coordinators who are responsible for several farmers. Various data are collated and specific advice is provided for each farm. The benefits that were reported from this system included reductions in time, money and energy through more effective use of agricultural experts (Ratnam, Krishna Reddy, & Reddy, 2006). However, opportunities exist for greater support for the agricultural experts to provide advice and suggestions for individual farming situations (Krishna Reddy, Ramaraju, & Reddy, 2007). Farmers also played a significant role in improving this recommendations system. Problems did occur when some farmers did not follow expert advice, which resulted in suboptimal outcomes in crop productivity (Ratnam, Reddy, & Reddy, 2006).

DECISION MAKING BY FARMERS

Research on decision making has suggested that the process of making decisions has been reported to be a series of sequential steps, comprising:

identify the problem, generate alternative solutions, evaluate and choose, implement (McKenna & Martin-Smith, 2005). Recent decision making theory suggests a more chaotic and complex cycle (McKenna & Martin-Smith, 2005). In an agricultural context, only a few attempts have been made to develop decision making systems which allow the delivery of customizable information for farmers cropping practices (Graham et al., 2002). The type of information used for decision making is varied and includes climate, marketing, price information, production and cultivation techniques, plant nutrients and water usage, education and health, current stock information, diseases and insect information (Amin et al., 2007). Other recent studies have reported the decision making process in terms of the adoption of new technologies and initiatives such as water management (Schwarz & McRae-Williams, 2009).

This paper will develop a framework based on information dissemination to support decision making of farmers. A common scenario of a farmer seeking information on selecting crop varieties in order to increase grain quality and production will be used to demonstrate the validity of the proposed framework. The development of this framework follows earlier attempts to identify agricultural information dissemination frameworks. For example, research reported by Krishna Reddy and Ankaiah (2005) described the AgriIDS framework. This framework is outlined in Figure 1. The framework shows the process for the delivery of location specific expert agricultural knowledge to farming communities in India. The participants in this framework include farmers (end users), coordinators (a group of farmers who have data-entry skills) and agriculture experts.

It is clear that further work is needed to establish the role that information and communication technologies may have in farmers' decision making processes. These frameworks need to take into account the varied delivery technologies, such as the Internet and mobile technologies, which may contribute to farmers acquiring ap-

Figure 1. An agriculture information dissemination system. Source: Adapted from Krishna Reddy & Ankaiah (2005)

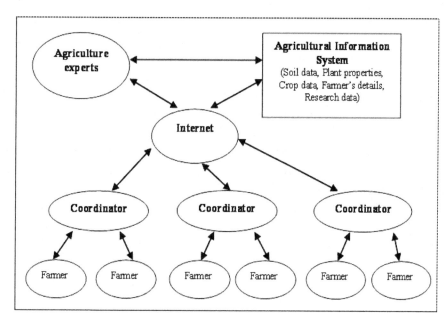

propriate knowledge. Similarly, further work is needed to distinguish between users with differing competencies in using the Internet and other technologies.

The Australian Agricultural Industry

The Australian agricultural industry is primarily large scale, export orientated enterprises that are profit driven and not subsidized by government. Farmers have had to overcome unfavourable environmental conditions, which in turn have produced highly specialised agricultural systems, skills and technologies (Arumapperuma, 2005). Cropping systems are often large scale with cereal/legume/pasture rotations. Southern Australia has a Mediterranean climate in which farmers are heavily reliant on infrequent rain events for growing winter crops (Pearson et al., 1995). The climate is also characterized by drought and poor nutrient soils. Farmers use high technology farm machinery and must employ very strategic management practices to maximize profit. Farmers

also need to produce crops with high yields and of consistent quality for specialized export markets. As a consequence, farmers are reliant on accurate location and farming-specific information to assist decision making for all aspects of their cropping, e.g. choosing varieties, herbicide spraying and fertilizer application.

The delivery of agricultural information in the Western Australian agriculture sector is disparate in nature. Both government and private consultants are responsible for this process. Information is provided from various sources including paper-based publications, websites, agricultural advisors and other farmers. Farmers value the customized information they receive on farm practices and crop performance provided for their local situation. Such customized information contributes to the farmer knowledge base. Farmers may acquire this knowledge through gathering information from neighbouring farmers, farmer demonstrations and research-based field experiments. However, acquiring this information and then distributing it locally is often a challenge. Field days and agricultural advisors are still the preferred methods of delivery. More recently, the Internet is playing a vital role in improving the availability of these resources. Mobile services may also provide opportunities to transform the way information is delivered to farmers. Improvements in Internet connectivity have promoted the establishment of some dedicated websites which provide crop variety information. State government departments, such as the Department of Agriculture and Food (DAFWA), provide websites which offer downloadable reports and the ability to compare varieties (Department of Food and Agriculture, Western Australia, 2007).

Dedicated decision-aid systems allow farmers to ask "what-if" questions about recommended crop varieties. Such "what-if" information has been delivered for several years by DAFWA via a downloadable Microsoft Excel workbook that can run on the growers' computers (Department of Food and Agriculture, Western Australia, 2007). The problem with this method of delivery is that the program needs to be downloaded regularly to get the latest variety comparison information. There is now a need to improve the delivery of such farmer-oriented decision tools via the Internet and mobile technologies. Other factors may influence the ability of farmers to use information and knowledge for decision making. For example, anecdotal evidence would suggest that farmers vary in their approaches to seeking information and adopting new technologies.

FARMER KNOWLEDGE AND DECISION SUPPORT FRAMEWORK

This research draws on knowledge gained from the practices used by agricultural scientists, extension officers, agricultural consultants and DAFWA experts in the production, delivery and use of cropping based information. The authors have many years of professional practice in the area of crop variety testing and plant breeding research. The

Farmer Knowledge Decision Support Framework (FKDSF) was created using the Unified Modelling Language (Object Management Group, 2008) as it is considered to be an industry standard system and modelling framework which has been used frequently in the analysis and design of ICT-based software systems.

The FKDSF was developed using two commonly used modelling diagrams, the case scenario diagram and the sequence diagram. These modelling diagrams were then integrated with the information flow process model formulated as inputs, process and outputs. This was further refined for a specific scenario based on "A farmer wanting to improve his crop grain quality". The model framework provides alternative decision-making processes incorporating the ability to cycle through each user case decision. The final stage in the development of the framework was to use sequence diagrams to map the information flow and decision making process for individual scenarios.

The FKDSF is a framework which takes inputs, processes and collates these inputs and outputs as a decipherable data set as a flow of information. The framework comprises a series of steps which include data capture, analysis and data processing and precedes the delivery of integrated information to the farmer. Information is collected from disparate sources, collated and validated according to defined set of rules. It is then processed and further integrated, by using data mining tools and other technologies, into a format more readily used by the farmer.

The Farmer Knowledge Decision Support Framework (FKDSF) has been proposed in order to explain the general flow of crop related information from the perspective of the farmer. The framework can be used to identify the data types, granularity and where they will use information in the process. It is designed to identify, at an abstract industry level, where researchers and information generators can best support the

Table 1. Types of Information Participants

Type	Description
User	Farmers, farm groups, general public, consultants, industry groups
Facilitator	Consultants, agricultural scientists, extension officers, seed company representatives
Generator	Private research organizations, government agencies, farmer groups, seed companies

Table 2. Input, Process and outputs in the system

Stage	Description	Example
Inputs	Get general information	Publications, library, Internet sites, other farmers, field trial days
Process	Search, collate, analyse, filter and customize information	Internet searches, expert systems, decision aids, statistical analysis, data mining
Outputs	Report customized information	Crop variety guides, farm bulletins, Internet sites, farm manuals, ready reckoners, search engines, web applications

delivery of cropping information to improving farmer decision making.

Three types of participants are central to the information provision process: the information generators, the facilitators and the users. Information generators make available the information to the information facilitators who receive, filter and process the information into a customizable format for the information users. An elaboration of the types of participants and information in the system is outlined below in Table 1 and Table 2.

The information flow process used to develop the generic FKDSF is shown in Figure 2. The use

Figure 2. Farmer knowledge and information flow process

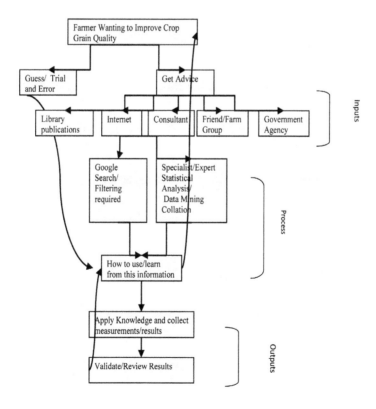

Figure 3. Farmer decision process use case diagram

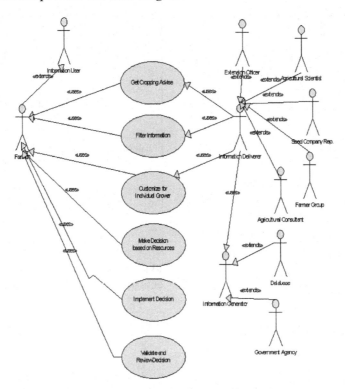

case diagram displayed in Figure 3 was used to illustrate the system from a farmer's perspective, outlining the actors and the user cases that describe the processes in the system. These processes are: Get advice, Filter information, Customize information, Make decision, Implement decision, and Validate and review decision.

The FKDSF may also be used to show how information flow and decision- making vary for different farmers and situations. The use of UML sequence diagrams allows a close examination of the information process and the interaction between the participants in the system. An example is demonstrated in Fig. 4 which highlights differences in the approach of two types of farmers, traditional farmers and innovative farmers.

Traditional farmers are characterized as those who prefer to use printed materials such as the *Crop Variety Sowing* guides (Department of Food

and Agriculture, Western Australia, 2007), have limited skills in the use of the Internet, and/or are limited by access to the Internet. These farmers also prefer to have face-to-face contact with other growers and agricultural consultants. Innovative farmers are characterized as being willing to collate their own information using multiple sources and formats. They are skilled in searching the Internet and will seek advice using expert systems and other decision aids.

DISCUSSION

A comparison between the farmer approaches found that the traditional farmer approach took fewer information seeking steps and relied on help from recipe-based publications and consultants to make decisions. This information is likely to be

Figure 4. (a.) Traditional farmers' crop variety decision processes. (b.) Innovative farmers' crop variety decision processes.

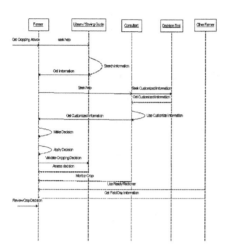

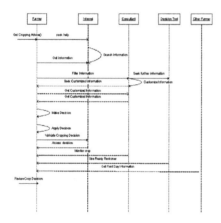

generalized and not necessarily customized. The innovative farmers make greater individual efforts and skills to perform their own initial searches for collation of information. Any interaction with the consultants is targeted at gathering unknown information and adds to the complexity of the process. Moreover this refinement leads to greater customization of information. Examination of the sequence diagrams shows it is possible to establish where information flow and decision-making processes might break down and/or result in inaccurate information being provided to the farmer.

The agriculture industry is faced with a number of challenges and must explore all avenues to overcome the bottlenecks which exist in technology transfer to the farmer. The delivery of customized information and acquisition of knowledge by farmers for decision making has been shown to be vastly improved by the use of data mining technologies (Armstrong et al., 2007). Additionally, by making these eAgriculture technologies available in real time via the Internet, the process of decision making might be further enhanced.

The ultimate goals of developing this framework were firstly to see how new technologies, such as the use of the Internet and data mining techniques, can fit into the process and secondly to identify, and provide solutions for, information delivery problems and bottlenecks. This framework extends on other attempts to describe the dissemination of agricultural information by Krishna Reddy and Ankaiah (2005).

This research paper has explored how the development of a ICT based framework might be used to understand how these processes can be improved. Farmers must be able to make informed decisions in order to improve their farming practices if their businesses are to remain profitable. In order to understand how this process may be improved, there is a need to elaborate the information flow and decision making processes.

The proposed FKDSF provides a mechanism for agricultural scientists and extension specialists to map all aspects of the information flow process accurately and to decide where there is a need to concentrate efforts to assist in farmer decision making. At a higher industry level, it could be used to improve the likelihood of farmers receiving the most appropriate information to make valid decisions.

The benefit of using such a framework is that it may be applied to specific scenarios and decision making. In addition, it may be used as a supportive tool and to establish where new technologies, such as the use of the Internet and data mining, might fit into the process. In the example scenarios provided in this paper, the framework was effectively tailored for Western Australian growing conditions and farmer practices. The framework might easily be applied to other agricultural decision making processes such as animal husbandry or pasture management. Other research studies have shown that the delivery of customizable information for decision making using ICT technologies is possible (Krishna Reddy & Ankaiah, 2005; Ratnam et al., 2005). It is envisioned that this framework might be used as a basis for further refinements in eAgriculture systems such as the development of an online farm management system to provide structured support for researchers and extension specialists to assist farmers in their decision making.

REFERENCES

Amin, M. R., Saleheen, S., Kibria, R., & Karmakar, C. K. (2007). *An effective approach for implementing E-Agriculture in Bangladesh*. Retrieved September 24, 2009, from http://wwwi4donline. net/ATF/2007/fullpapers/MDRUHUL_AT-F07ABS130.pdf

Anandaraja, N., Sujhi, G., Gayathri, G., Ramasubramanian, M., & Rathakrishnan, T. (2009). *Technology enabled farm women*. Retrieved July 3, 2009, from http://www.i4donline.net/ sept07/1434.pdf

Armstrong, L. J., Diepeveen, D., & Vagh, Y. (2007). *Data mining can empower growers' crop decision making*. Paper presented at the T2: Technology and Transformation. 3rd Transforming Information and Learning Conference, Perth, Australia.

Arumapperuma, S. (2006). Agricultural innovation system in Australia. *Journal of Business Systems . Governance and Ethics, 1*(4), 15–25.

Bertolini, R. (2004). *Strategic thinking: making information and communication technologies work for food security in Africa*. Cited in H. Munyua, E. Adera, & M. Jensen (2008), Retrieved September 6, 2007, from http://www.ifpri.org/ pubs/ib/ib27.pdf

Cambridge University Press. (2009). *Cambridge Advanced Learner's Dictionary Online Dictionary*. Retrieved November 20, 2009, from http://dictionary.cambridge.org/define.asp? key=22599&dict=CALD

Department of Agriculture and Food. Western Australia (DAFWA). (2007). *e-Variety Profiler for Western Australia*. Retrieved December 2, 2009, from http://www.agric.wa.gov.au/content/ fcp/evarietyprofiler_2006.htm

Diao, X., Hazell, P., Resnick, D., & Thurlow, J. (2007). *The role of agriculture in development: Implications for Sub-Saharan Africa*. Washington, DC: IFPRI.

Dictionary.com. LLC. (2009). *Delivery*. Retrieved November 9, 2009, from http://dictionary.reference.com/browse/delivery eagriculture.org. (2009). *What is eAgriculture?* Retrieved April 5, 2009, from http://eagriculture.org/

Ekoja, I. I. (2004). Sensitising users for increased information use: the case of Nigerian farmers. *African Journal of Library . Archives and Information Science, 14*(2), 193–204.

Food and Agriculture Organization of the United Nations (FAO). (2000). *The role of information and communication technologies in rural development and food security*. Retrieved September 24, 2009, from http://www.fao.org/sd/CDdirect/ CDre0055.htm

Graham, P. J., Linnegar, M., & Kealy, M. (2002). *Better Information delivery to Rice Growers - A pilot rice bulletin. Rural Industries Research and Development Report*. Retrieved September 27, 2009, from http://www.rirdc.gov.au/reports/ RIC/02-100.pdf

Hafkin, N. J., & Odame, H. H. (2002). *Gender, ICTs and agriculture. A situation analysis for the 5th Consultative Expert Meeting of CTA's ICT Observatory meeting on gender and agriculture in the information society.* Retrieved from http://www.cta.int/observatory2002/background_paper.pdf

Hassan, M. S., Hassan, M. A., Samah, B. A., Ismail, N., & Shaffril, H. A. M. (2008). Use of information and communication technology (ICT) among agri-based entrepreneurs in Malaysia. In *Proceedings of the World Conference on Agricultural Information and IT,* Atsugi, Japan (pp. 753-762).

International Institute for Communication and Development. IICD. (2006). *ICTs for agricultural livelihoods: Impact and lessons learned from IICD supported activities.* The Hague: The Netherlands: IICD.

Irivwieri, J. W. (2007). Information needs of illiterate female farmers in Ethiopia East local government area of Delta State. *Library Hi Tech News, 9*(10), 38–42. doi:10.1108/07419050710874278

Jensen, A. L., & Thysen, I. (2003). Agricultural information and decision support by SMS. In *Proceedings of the EFITA 2003 Conference,* Debrecen, Hungary (pp. 286-292).

Kalusopa, T. (2005). The challenges of utilizing information communication technologies (ICTs) for the small-scale farmers in Zambia. *Library Hi Tech, 23*(3), 414–424. doi:10.1108/07378830510621810

Krishna Reddy, P., & Ankaiah, R. (2005). A framework of information technology-based agriculture information dissemination system to improve crop productivity. *Current Science, 88,* 1905–1913.

Krishna Reddy, P. K., Ramaraju, G. V., & Reddy, G. S. (2007). eSagu: a data warehouse enabled personalized agricultural advisory system. In *Proceedings of the SIGMOD 07,* Beijing, China (pp. 910-914).

Kweku, A. K. (2006). *Demystifying ICT diffusion and use among rural women in Kenya.* Unpublished paper presented to ProLISSA 2006.

Malhan, I. V., & Rao, S. (2007). Impact of globalization and emerging information communication technologies on agricultural knowledge transfer to small farmers in India. In *Proceedings of the World Library and Information Congress: the 73rd IFLA General Conference and Council,* Durban, South Africa (pp. 1 -20).

Mangstl, A. (2008). Emerging issues, priorities and commitments in e-Agriculture. *Agriculture Information Worldwide, 1*(1), 5–6.

McKenna, R. J., & Martin-Smith, B. M. (2005). Decision making as a simplification process: new conceptual perspectives. *Management Decision, 43,* 821–836. doi:10.1108/00251740510603583

Munyua, H., Adera, E., & Jensen, M. (2008). Emerging ICTs and their potential in revitalizing small scale agriculture in Africa. In *Proceedings of the World Conference on Agricultural Information and IT,* Atsugi, Japan (pp. 707-718).

Object Management Group. (2008). *Unified Modelling Language Specification ™ (UML®) 2.1.2.* Retrieved May 28, 2008, from http://www.omg.org/technology/documents/modeling_spec_catalog.htm#UML

Parikh, T. S. (2009). Engineering rural development. *Communications of the ACM, 52*(1), 54–63. doi:10.1145/1435417.1435433

Pearson, J., Norman, D. W., & Dixon, J. (1995). *Sustainable dryland cropping in relation to soil productivity - FAO Soils Bulletin 72.* Retrieved November 20, 2009, from http://www.fao.org/docrep/v9926e/v9926e00.htm#Contents

Pye, D., Stephenson, J., Harris, S., Lee, B., & Leask, M. (2003). *Using ICTs to increase the effectiveness of community-based, non-formal education for rural people in sub-Saharan Africa: The CERP Project Final report*. Retrieved December 18, 2009, from http://www.nfer.ac.uk/research-areas/pimsdata/summaries/using-ict-to-increase-the-effectiveness-of-community-based-non-formaleducation-for-rural-people-in-sub-saharan-africa-the-cerp-project.cfm

Rao, N. H. (2007). A framework for implementing information and communication technologies in agricultural development in India. *Technological Forecasting and Social Change, 74*(4), 491–518. doi:10.1016/j.techfore.2006.02.002

Rao, S. S. (2004). Role of ICTs in India's rural community information systems. *Info, 6*(4), 261–269. doi:10.1108/14636690410555663

Ratnam, B. V., Krishna Reddy, P., & Reddy, G. S. (2005). eSagu: An IT based personalized extension system prototype: Analysis of 51 farmers' case studies. *International Journal of Education and Development using Information and Communication Technology, 2*, 79-94.

Richardson, D. (1997). *The internet and rural and agricultural development – an integrated approach*. Retrieved September 24, 2009, from http://www.fao.org/docrep/w6840e/w6840e00.htm

Schwarz, I., & McRae-Williams, P. (2009). *Farmer behaviour and enterprise change as a result of the Wimmera Mallee Pipeline – One year on*. A report prepared for the Victorian Department of Primary Industries, Horsham, Australia.

Sheriff, F. R. (2009). *Village Information Centers in Tamil Nadu, TANIVAS, Chennai, India: e-Empowering resource poor farmers*. Retrieved July 3, 2009, from http://www.i4donline.net/articles/current-article.asp?Title=Village-information-centres-in-Tamil-Nadu,TANUVAS,Chennai,India&articleid=2241&typ=Features

Sood, A. D. (2001). How to wire rural India: the problems and possibilities of digital development. *Economic and Political Weekly, 36*(43), 4134–4141.

Tiwari, S. P. (2008). Information and communication technology initiatives for knowledge sharing in agriculture. *Indian Journal of Agricultural Sciences, 78*(9), 737–747.

Umber, A. (2006). *Farming Practices in Australian Grain Growing – the means for Productive and Environmental Sustainability*. Australia: Grain Council.

United States. Department of Agriculture (USDA). (2009). *USDA Rice Baseline, 2004-13*. Retrieved August 20, 2009, from http://www.ers.usda.gov/Briefing/rice/2004baseline.htm

United States. Census Bureau, Population Division. (2009). *World population: 1950 – 2050*. Retrieved November 8, 2009, from http://www.census.gov/ipc/www/idb/worldpopgraph.php

World Bank. (2006). *Africa development indicators*. Washington, DC: World Bank. Retrieved April 10, 2009, from http://siteresources.worldbank.org/INTSTATINAFR/Resources/adi2007_final.pdf

This work was previously published in International Journal of Human Capital and Information Technology Professionals, Volume 1, Issue 4, edited by Ricardo Colomo-Palacios, pp. 1-13, copyright 2010 by IGI Publishing (an imprint of IGI Global).

Chapter 18
Social Networks and Young People:
A Case Study

Neuza Ferreira
International Association for Scientific Knowledge (IASK), Portugal

ABSTRACT

This paper aims at stating the main advantages and implications of Web 2.0 by analysing popular social networks in Portugal and addressing some examples of their utility. The authors present results of an empirical study applied to young people, aged between 12 and 20 years old, in a specific Portuguese region. In the first part of the study, main characteristics and differences between Web 1.0 and Web 2.0 are presented. In addition, results of empirical research and concluding remarks are presented and discussed. Achieved results seem to be particularly relevant for academics and industry professionals who might be interested in the application of new technologies for communication and socialization purposes.

INTRODUCTION

Social networking is based on people's socialization in a virtual environment, where a person can chat with friends, show photo albums, see movies, listen to music and be a member of clubs and associations. Basically, it is what is done in daily life: socialising, talking, joining groups of interest and sharing with friends and family. According to Miguel (2009), we have witnessed, therefore, the passage from the Internet based on consultation of websites for a few minutes, the use of the e-mail for advice and, later, the use of the mIRC – a full featured Internet Relay Chat –, which is based on knowing people and talking with friends, to the era of the Internet based on sharing in the production and personalization of contents. Initially, the cell phone was just a function of the portable telephone, and the photographs that few models could take were of mediocre quality, and accessing the Internet from them was too expensive. Today, with a very cheap phone we can take pictures with a high resolution, access the Internet easily and upload from it. It is in this stage that the microblogging (like Twitter), Youtube (mainly for video sharing) or Wikipedia (online encyclopaedia) arise.

DOI: 10.4018/978-1-4666-0924-2.ch018

Following Miguel (2009), the networks provide a public image that we want to pass and we can make a personal media network (so there is no need to recur to traditional media to express ideas, opinions, photos, etc.).

Based on a study carried out by Damásio et al (2009, p. 29), the Internet is not only a simple reality because it is based on a complex activity consisting of the *"e-mail, games, online newspapers, chat rooms, blogs and social communities such as Youtube or HI5, not to speak of the microblogging like Twitter"*. The transition from traditional media to new media seems to be closely related to the activity that is done, not only with technology, being a constitutive aspect of the differences in Internet use. The same study (Damásio et al., 2009) shows, however, that people up to 18 years old continue to predominantly use the TV media, followed by the Internet, particularly upon the activities that consist of forms of customization and personal expression.

This study's main objective consists of studying the possibilities of Web 2.0 and the activities undertaken by young people in online social networks in Alverca do Ribatejo, Portugal. In order to operationalize this, a questionnaire was administered to 100 young people aged between 12 and 20 years old. Then it will deal with the transition from Web 1.0 to Web 2.0, and then there will be a key approach to social networks,

followed by the presentation of the case study and final conclusions.

CHANGING OF THE "WEB 1.0" TO "WEB 2.0"

The so-called "Web 2.0" is very distinct from the "Web 1.0" and, according to Coutinho et al (2007, p. 199), *"people began to produce its own documents and publish them automatically on the network without the need for a further knowledge of programming and sophisticated computing environments"*. The shift from the paradigm "Web 1.0" to "Web 2.0" was very fast, and it is therefore important to present some differences between them (Figure 1).

According to Table 1, it is possible to draw some conclusions: previously, individuals had a role as mere spectators, while now, besides the access to information, people can also produce it, create and edit Web pages, use the servers for free, and have numerous tools. Thus, blogs, Wikipedia and *Hi5* are examples of some of these tools available on the Web. These tools can also be categorized as presented in Table 1. According to a study carried out by Cardoso (2007) at the national level, young people between 13 and 18 years old have at least one computer at home (over 50%), have Internet connection at home (87.3%)

Figure 1. Comparison between "Web 1.0" and "Web 2.0"

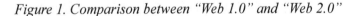

Web 1.0	Web 2.0
- User is a consumer of the information;	- User is a consumer and producer of the information;
- Difficulties encountered in programming and acquisitioning of specific software to create web pages;	- Facilities for creating and editing online pages;
- To have a space on the network, most of the servers are paid;	- The user has multiple servers to serve out his pages for free;
- Smaller number of tools and possibilities.	- Number of tools and unlimited possibilities.

Source: Coutinho *et al* (2007)

or use it at school (47.9%), friends' or relatives' home (20.3%) and even in *cybercafes* (8.3%).

In addition to these results, in terms of sociability, the majority of young people (82.3%) used chat rooms to communicate with people who they know from other places, including the school. It is in these virtual places that many admit to show themselves as they really are (62%), whereas a part admits pretending sometimes to be other people (mostly young girls). Moreover, half of young people participate in chats or newsgroups, 38.4% date or combine meetings with friends over the Internet, browsing blogs is done mostly by young people between 13 and 15 and about 20% of the people download music network, read sports news or broadcast their pictures or their family's. For activities, young people between 13 and 18 carry out, in order of importance, the following tasks: search for information related studies (84%), send files (~35%), play online games (~35%), send photos (~30%) and enter in chat rooms or virtual communities (~30%). A study conducted by Nielsen (2008) presents the ranking of the best-used social networks in the U.S., as shown in Table 2.

In Table 2, it can be observed that in the U.S. *MySpace* is the most used social network, having grown 1% in 2008. Despite a lower number of users than *MySpace*, surprisingly *Facebook*, as *LinkedIn* or *Tagged.com*, had a growth above 100% (116%, 193% and 330%, respectively).

In the paradigm of the social Web, "Web 2.0" has become the new "buzzword" and *Google*, *MySpace*, *Flickr*, *Wikipedia* or *Hi5* became its icons. In its structure, social web is based on platforms that enable the connection between people, the ability to produce and share content, to create frameworks that can increase participation and to extract and process knowledge back to share it. Some of the trends of this paradigm point to the need for awareness on the part of companies regarding benefits that "Web 2.0" can offer them, in a perspective of integrated marketing communication. This means that companies

Table 1. Categorization of "Web 2.0" Tools

Categories	"Web 2.0" Tools	"Web 2.0" Features
Applications that exist only on the Internet, which effectiveness increases with the number of registered users.	Google Docs, Wikipedia, Youtube, Skype, eBay, Hi5, MySpace, Orkut, etc.	• Enables the creation of social networking; • Tools for collaborative writing; • Online communication tools; • Easy access to videos; • Elimination of dependence on physical media for data storage; • Easy and fast storage of text and files.
Applications that can work offline and have advantages if they are online.	Picasa Photos, Google Map, Mapquest, iTunes, etc.	

must rethink the way they communicate with their public in seeking to achieve their confidence in order to make people be willing to share content with their friends about the brands that they like more or which have repeatedly made through

Table 2. Top 10 Sites of Social Networks in the U.S.

Site	Sept-07 UA (000)	Sept-08 UA (000)	YOY Growth
Myspace.com	58,581	59,352	1%
Facebook	18,090	39,003	116%
Classmates Online	13,313	17,075	28%
LinkedIn	4,075	11,924	193%
Windows Live Spaces	10,275	9,117	-11%
Reunion.com	4,845	7,601	57%
Club Penguin	3,769	4,224	12%
AOL Hometown	7,685	3,909	-49%
Tagged.com	898	3,857	330%
AOL Community	4,017	3,079	-23%

these new channels of communication. One example of promotion in these terms was the *Dove* "Campaign for Real Beauty" that culminated in online conversations, as well as its transmission on *Youtube* and in the blogosphere.

On the other hand, some risks associated to this paradigm were pointed out. According to a *Diário de Notícias*' report (*in* Jesus, 2009), there are some studies that have confirmed that continuous exposure on social networks tends to diminish our ability to concentrate and we become more selfish. The neurologist coordinator of one of these studies indicates that, in cultural and psychological terms, future generations will have less ability to initiate relationships with other people and their identity is more fragile. However, doubts remain about the future implications of networks, since it is a recent phenomenon that has generated much speculation.

In terms of security, an article by Almeida (2009) shows some of the worrying aspects of social networks based on the ease with which people expose their intimacy, and this fact becomes even more alarming when young people are involved. This suggests the need to start thinking about information and data regulation (Trigo et al., 2010). In Portugal there is a website dedicated to this concern that *"seeks to help users of social networks to think about their safety (...) warning (...) to some of the cares of a virtual social network"* (Almeida, 2009).

On the other hand, there is still a concern about the activities of children without parental supervision, which has led to the creation of a number of initiatives in schools to teach children ways to defend themselves against the dangers of the Internet, developed by *Microsoft Portugal* and the Association of Entrepreneurs for Social Inclusion (Ferreira et al., 2009).

Paradoxically, this "fashion" of social networking websites seems promising because, according to Gustavo Cardoso (*in* Jesus, 2009), they have always existed because *"in our life we are building our network, which includes family, friends, school and work, although this notion is not structured in our head"*. In fact, according to *Marktest* (*in* Brito, 2009), Portugal is the third European country that uses social networks, peaking in March 2009 a total of 4 million hours devoted to them. Moreover, as early as December, *"72.9% of Internet users has more than 15 years and accessed the computer from home"*, having visited at least one social networking website (Brito, 2009).

The differences between the online and offline social spaces were pointed out by Danah Boyd (*in* Rettberg, 2008), based on four keys features (Table 3).

According to Table 3, the main characteristics of online social spaces are the persistence, the ability to search, the replication and the existence of invisible audience. Therefore, the offline social spaces do not allow further access to information

Table 3. Comparison of Online and Offline Social Spaces

Features	Online Social Spaces	Offline Social Spaces
Persistency	• The information that arises is seen / heard / read and can be accessed later.	• The social conversations are ephemeral.
Demand	• Each person can find anyone.	• Ease of finding someone is lower.
Replication	• The pictures or conversations can be replicated / modified.	• The conversations can be played but never linked to the original.
Invisible Audiences	• It is not known exactly who can see our profiles.	• When you talk to someone you can see who is talking.

due to their short-life feature. On the other hand, it has a capacity of less demand than the online space. In terms of replication, reproduction is never connected directly to the original and it is possible to know who is talking while in the online space this is not always the case.

SOCIAL NETWORKS: EXAMPLES OF ADOPTION

Facebook

In 2004, what seemed to be a joke created by Zuckerberg (CEO, executive director), resulted in an exponential growth, and *Facebook* has currently about a thousand employees. Originally, *Facebook* was created with the aim of *"giving people the opportunity to replicate in the Internet what they do every day in real life"* (Miguel, 2009). This social network has more than 100 million users (124 million, more precisely), watching a daily increase of 250 thousand new members (Miguel, 2009). Additionally, it is geared to a target population over 25 years, being used by politicians or celebrities for self-promotion. According to Rettberg (2008), *Facebook* has very innovative services, in which users can register at a regional level. Users can view the profiles of other members, but they can only see the name and the profile picture of a user who is not a member of their network, depending on the profile of privacy adopted by them. So, there is the possibility of an agreement of "friendship" between members that do not belong to the same network, allowing more detailed view of the profiles.

MySpace

This network was created in 2003, with 114 million users and it is used mainly by bands and fans. It has been a way of adapting to the demands of the music industry, serving to self-promotion and mass marketing (Miguel, 2009).

Hi5

This network is certainly the one that has more impact on more than 25 countries worldwide. Being created in 2003 and turning to a younger audience, it has more than 70 million users. Its use is based, in general, on the creation of communities, promotion of celebrities and marketing activities (Miguel, 2009). In Portugal, it presents itself as the leading social networks, with 87% of the time devoted to these networks, followed by *Facebook, Twitter, MySpace, Orkut* and *LinkedIn* (Brito, 2009).

Orkut

Orkut is a social network that has a localized use, focusing mainly in countries like India, the U.S. and Brazil. Being established in 2004, it has currently 120 million users and serves as a *"community building, maintaining and expanding the network of contacts and promotion of celebrities, music and products"* (Miguel, 2009). *Orkut* is based on the idea of raising the maximum number of friends. As its membership has fallen, mostly in the U.S. and Brazil, there were some problems with the language, because the Americans could not understand the messages in Portuguese. This network has become very popular in Iran, but it was eventually banned by the Iranian government because the meetings and the combination of profiles clashed with the Muslim culture (Rettberg, 2008).

Twitter

Built in 2006, this is the latest network that includes 2 million users. In terms of orientation, it is directed to an audience that spends a lot of time on the Internet, in the case of a system for *microblogging*. For this reason, it is used to *"maintain and expand the network of contacts and create virtual communities"* (Miguel, 2009).

Examples of Adoption

Social networks such as *Facebook*, *MySpace* or *Twitter* eventually draw the attention of companies to their potential users. *IKEA*, for example, used these networks to recruit employees (and received 800 *curricula* in one day), making it easy to *"pass the names and contacts at hand"* (Catarina Tendeiro – *IKEA in* Miguel, 2009) and avoiding the expenditure of amounts on ads.

More recently, we have watched the famous campaign of Barack Obama in the U.S., which used the *Facebook* (besides other networks) to raise support and funding in a viral way (i.e., asking a person to recruit 10 people to their cause and, in turn, each of these new people would have to recruit 10 more, and so on). *Twitter* has also been used by Obama, followed by the Foreign Minister of the United Kingdom, David Millibard, who has been using it to *"increase the proximity between politicians and citizens"* (Miguel, 2009).

In contrast, another example is the improperly disclosed information in cyberspace, such as in *MySpace* or *Hi5*, which can cause damage to people's lives (e.g., exclusion of a process of job application by the existence of improper information in these spaces).

The high adherence of youth to social networks has created an opportunity for a number of actors who surrendered to their advantages, such as politicians and journalists, among others. One example is *Juventude Socialista*, which created a social support network to José Sócrates (Portuguese Prime Minister) similar to *Facebook* or *Hi5*, which main opportunities are to create personal areas of their users, to invite friends, to upload files, as well as a discussion forum (*in* Lusa, 2009).

Additionally, the *Guarda Nacional Republicana* (GNR) has adhered to four platforms: *Sapo Vídeos*, *Youtube*, *Flickr* and *Twitter* in order *to "put there the new activities of the Guard, show the new equipment and operations"* (Robalo, 2009). One of the objectives is based on the placement of images and videos of the most relevant

activities and to attract more people into the GNR. Also, one of the brands that have surrendered to social networks was *Super Bock*, which joined *Facebook* and *MySpace*, in which it is updating the brand activities, hobbies, product launches and also campaigns, responding to questions and comments from users (Barroso, 2009).

Finalising the examples, another entity that has followed the new technologies also surrendered to *MySpace*: the Portuguese Catholic Church (Carvalho, 2009). In this space it provides evidence for priests, religious and laity individuals, prayers for download in *ipod* and a space for communication with other people.

SOCIAL NETWORKS AND YOUNG PEOPLE: A CASE STUDY

Inquiry by Questionnaire

For further analysis of the activities carried out in social networks, a questionnaire was designed (see *Appendix 1*) which consisted of three main sections: (1) Internet use, (2) *blogs* and (3) social networks. The questionnaire was based on another one, applied with some regularity worldwide, but in which Portugal has not been included yet (*Universal MacCann*, 2008). In the questionnaire closed-ended questions were used, with the use of *Likert* scales. For limitations of various kinds (e.g., time), Cronbach's alphas were not calculated. However, after production, the questionnaire was tested in 10 randomly chosen people, and their contribution was important to define the final structure of the questionnaire.

Sample

After being tested, the questionnaire was administered to 100 young people aged between 12 and 20 years, who had in common the fact of being students. In addition, all of them lived in the same location (Alverca do Ribatejo, Portugal).

Results

As mentioned, the questionnaire consisted of three main parts, in which questions were asked about the various activities undertaken by young people. In the first part of the questionnaire, the questions focused on issues related to ownership of computers with Internet access and the tasks tested in this environment.

To start, in terms of data reporting, as can be seen in Figure 2., most of the respondents were female (55%).

In the age group, most belonged to the group of 16-18 years (50%), followed by the group of 12-15 years (26%), and finally the group of over 18 years (24%) as can be observed in Figure 3..

The educational level of respondents fell on high school education, followed by primary education and, finally, higher education (see Figure 4.).

For the first part of the questionnaire – The Use of the Internet – as shown in Figure 5., all respondents answered affirmatively when asked about the ownership of a computer.

In Figure 6., when asked whether they used to access the Internet from home, the majority of the respondents answered positively (98%), while only 2% answered negatively.

Similarly to what occurred in the first question, all respondents answered that they usually access the Internet (Figure 7.).

In terms of type of Internet access, in Figure 8. we can see that most people access it via ADSL (40%), followed by 35% who have cable internet and 25%, who have the mobile Internet.

In Figure 9., in terms of frequency of Internet access, 68% respondents said they access it every day, 8% stated that they access four days a week, the same figure (8%) accessing less than three days a week, while 6% said they access three days a week, and Internet access five and six days a week were mentioned by 5% of the respondents, respectively.

With respect to hours spent online, in Figure 10. it can be observed that most young people reported spending daily from one to two hours on the Internet (32), followed by 28 who reported spending more than four hours, while a significant number stated spending two to three hours on the Internet, although some noted that they are three to four hours (9) and less than one hour (5).

With regard to the tasks that young people have tried on the Internet, considering multiple answers (Figure 11.), it is worth noticing that the most experienced task was the viewing of video clips online (91), followed by visiting websites

Figure 2. Gender of respondents

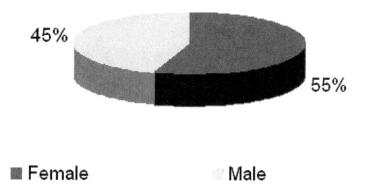

Figure 3. Age group of respondents

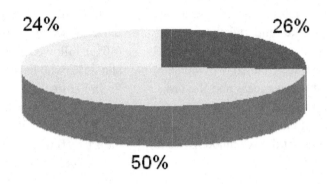

24% 26%

50%

■ 12-15 Years ▪ 16-18 Years More than 18 Years

for sharing photos (79), managing a profile in an existing social network (71) and uploading photos to a website for sharing photos (58). The remaining tasks have focused on reading blogs (58), in making comments on blogs (49), in reading personal blogs (47), in carrying out weekly podcasts (37), in upload videos to sharing video websites (32), the initiation of a blog (31), in making com-

ments on websites about news (24) and, finally, the subscription of RSS Feed (9).

In Figure 12. the values on a scale from 1 to 5 (1 = rarely and 5 = daily), in what regards activities on the Internet, are presented. Thus, it seems clear that the viewing of video clips online is often performed (3), as well as visiting websites, photo sharing (2.89) and the management of an

Figure 4. Education

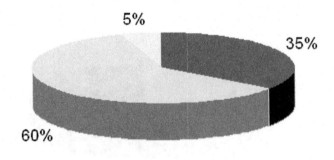

5% 35%

60%

■ Primary Education ▪ High School Education Higher Education

Figure 5. Computer ownership

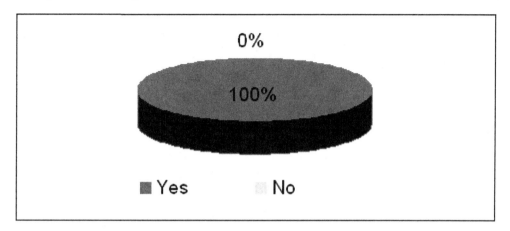

existing social network profile (2.82). From another perspective, the activity that most repeats is still the viewing of video clips online (3), whereas all other activities had the same value (1). Paradoxically, the activity with the lowest subscription was RSS feed and it is rarely performed (1.21).

The responses obtained in the second part of the questionnaire – *Blogs* – are outlined below. When asked about the *blog* ownership, most respondents answered negatively (77%) while only 23% have a *blog*, as shown in Figure 13.

As confirmed in Figure 14., considering multiple answers, from the 23 respondents who have a blog, 14 indicated that the topics that are often placed are "others", followed by music (13), sports (8) and games (7), while the topics on management (1) or celebrities (1) are the least discussed. Within the topic "other", some said it was related to school subjects and daily life.

On the next question, young people indicated that the content they tend to place on their blog are the pictures (19), music (15) and videos (13) and relegated to the last place are applications that reproduce content from other websites (3)

Figure 6. Internet access from home

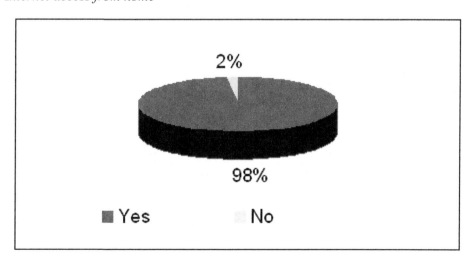

Figure 7. – Internet access use

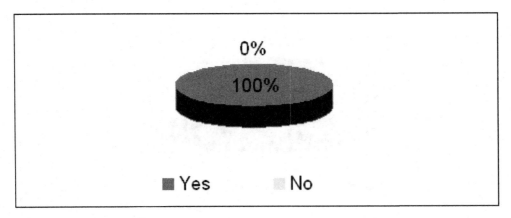

and stories from other blogs (3), as shown in Figure 15..

In Figure 16., it can be observed that 57% of respondents (including those with blogs and those who do not have one), stated they do not usually read blogs, while 43% said they read blogs.

Therefore, the 43 people who said they read blogs indicated that the topics that are more often read are those related to music (39), their relatives or friends (38) and games (28), as shown in Figure 17..

In Figure 18. we can observe the degree of correlation with the indicated five statements, and the one which contracted a more positive correlation was the one that indicated that blogging was an important way to socialize with friends, which, in a scale from 1 to 5, obtained 3.2.

In the third part of the questionnaire, dedicated to social networks, the majority of respondents said that they have a profile on an existing social network (72%), while only 28% responded negatively, as shown in Figure 19..

Concerning the possession of a social network profile, as confirmed in Figure 20., the major choice fell on Hi5 (68), followed by MySpace (11) and Facebook (8), and the least incidence was LinkedIn (1).

With regard to activities in the social network, most respondents send messages to friends (69), place pictures online (67) and recently listened

Figure 8. Type of internet access

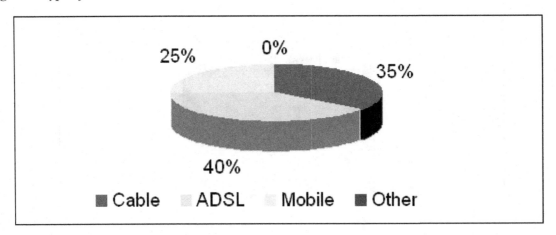

Figure 9. Frequency of internet access

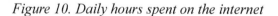

to favorite music (45), contrasting with the branding promotion (2), as shown in Figure 21..

Regarding the frequency of social networks' use (see Figure 22.), on a scale from 1 to 5, most respondents chose a frequent use of Hi5 (4), and in terms of replay value that the responses occurred more, it was 5 (daily).

In Figure 23. it was analysed the frequency of use of tasks for each social network, so that, on

a scale from 1 to 5 (1= rarely and 5 = daily), *Hi5* was again the most targeted, with a total of 2 078 responses, and it is used quite frequently to post comments (3) and to see photos (3). For the remaining networks, the second best one was *MySpace* (which, despite its use being rare, mainly focuses on viewing photos), followed by *Facebook* and *Blogger* (with a rare use, focusing on reading the posts respectively).

Figure 10. Daily hours spent on the internet

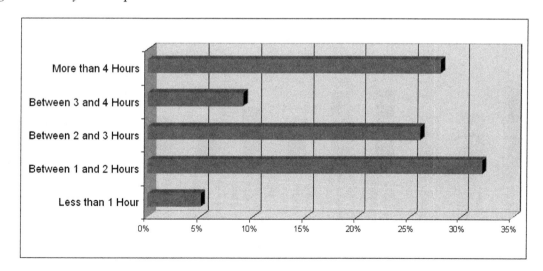

Figure 11. Internet tasks experimented

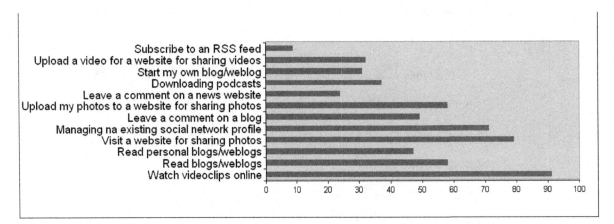

CONCLUSION

This study sought to address the possibilities of "Web 2.0", focusing on the analysis of the most used social networks, with the introduction of examples, and in the preparation of a questionnaire with a group of young people living in the same location.

For an analysis of "Web 2.0", the literature shows that "Web 2.0" has the same advantages in socializing through the Internet comparing to real life and it may go beyond, because the Internet is not a single reality, and consists of a series of activities that make it complex. Furthermore, social networks appear as a way to convey a public image and to form a kind of personal media. Therefore, the main differences between the "Web 1.0" and "Web 2.0" are based on the way they process information (shift from consumer to producer), user-friendliness with Web pages in free access to the network and tools available. The advantages of "Web 2.0" have increased the

Figure 12. Frequency performance of online activities

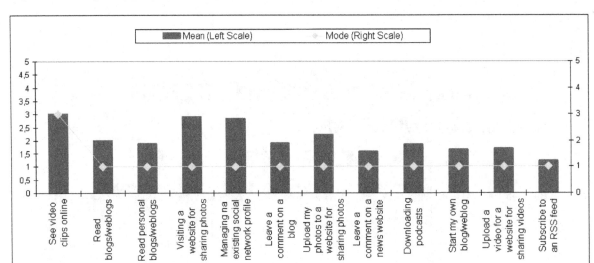

Figure 13. Owning blog

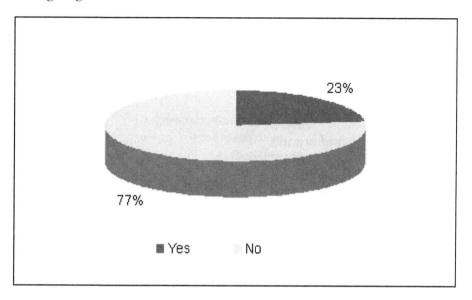

interest of companies as a way to obtain benefits from this environment in terms of communication with their audiences. The importance of social networks has gained weight and it was found out that young people between 13 and 18 years communicate over the Internet with people they already know from other places (including school), which indicates that in most cases they show themselves as they really are. Some of the risks associated to this paradigm heavily rely on its regulatory issues. The increased level of safety, concerns about the exposure of the individual's

Figure 14. Topics more placed in blogs

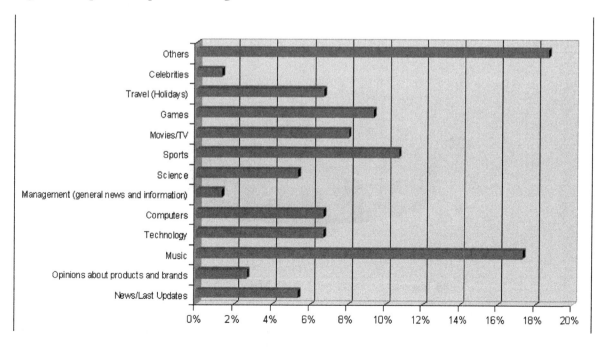

Figure 15. Content more placed in blogs

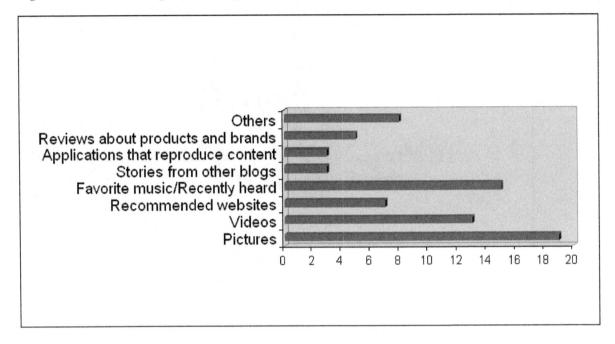

privacy and, more relevantly, the youngest's privacy. Moreover, there is much concern about the future implications of their use, particularly on issues related to the loss of ability to concentrate and increased selfishness.

From the obtained data, it was possible to realize that this study is consistent with another one made by Cardoso (2007) in terms of computer ownership and Internet connection by young people, as well as the interest in music and the

Figure 16. Reading blogs

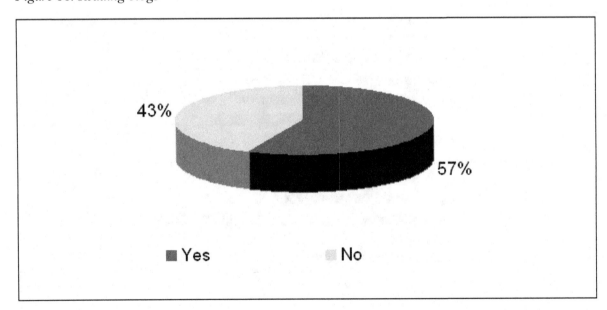

Figure 17. Topics more frequently read

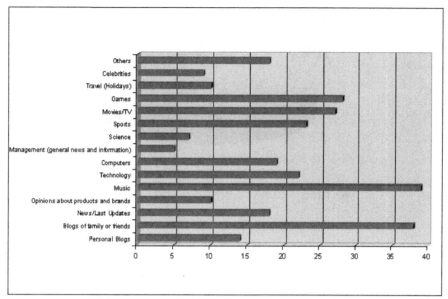

transmission of pictures online. Moreover, the same happens with activities, sending photos, games and online access to virtual communities. In the remaining results of this study, we observed that the involvement of young people with the

Internet is almost daily, with one to two hours of time devoted to it everyday. Another interesting aspect is the fact that most people have already experienced a series of online tasks, such as viewing video clips and visiting websites for sharing

Figure 18. Opinion about indicated statements

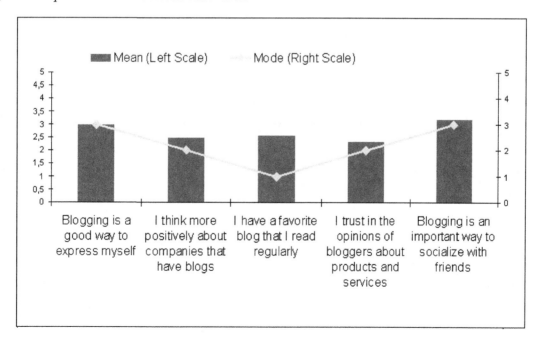

Figure 19. Possession of a social network profile

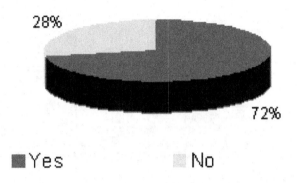

photos, meeting the main activities carried out in social networks (view photos). Among the important aspects, it is the relation of possession of blogs to read them because, although most people do not have a blog, they also state that they often read them. Comparatively, those who have blogs like that but have not read them, the topic which had the largest figure was music. With regard to social networks, most people have a profile, being *Hi5* the most indicated network, reaching out to its leadership role at a national level (Rettberg, 2008). Therefore, the *LinkedIn* network was indicated only by a person, oddly placed in the age group above 18 years with a

Figure 20. Possession of a profile by social network

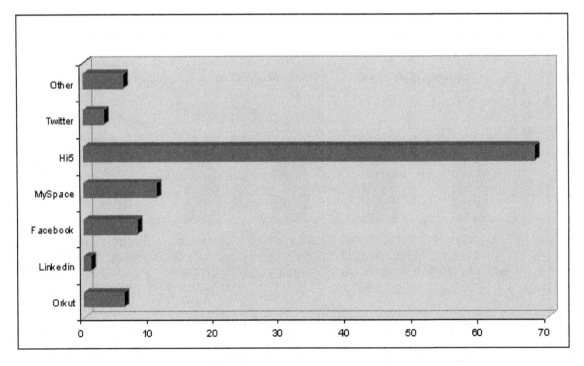

Figure 21. Activities performed in social networking

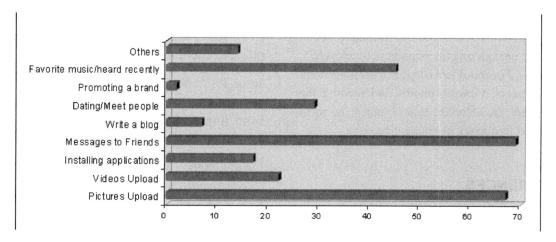

Figure 22. Frequency of use of social networks

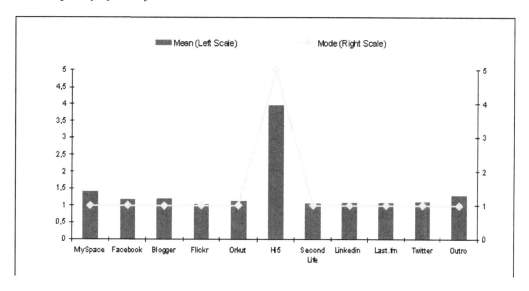

Figure 23. Frequency of tasks by social network

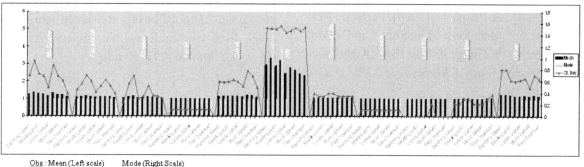

Obs.: Mean (Left scale)   Mode (Right Scale)

higher education degree, existing some connection between the features of *LinkedIn* and its audience. Finally, in terms of activities performed by social network, considering the popular networks (*Hi5*, *MySpace*, *Facebook* and *Blogger*), the placement of comments, viewing photos and reading the posts were the activities that obtained the most increased frequency of application.

REFERENCES

Almeida, P. (2009). *Redes Virtuais são Espaço Sem Lei*. Retrieved from http://dn.sapo.pt/inicio/opiniao/interior.aspx?content_id=1219447

Barroso, M. (2009). *Empresas Descobrem Mundo Virtual*. Retrieved from http://dn.sapo.pt/bolsa/interior.aspx?content_id=1217875

Brito, P. (2009). *Portugal é o Terceiro País da Europa nas Redes Sociais*. Retrieved February 22, 2009, from http://dn.sapo.pt/inicio/tv/interior.aspx?content_id=1151669

Cardoso, G. (Coord.) (2007). *E-Generation: Os Usos de Media pelas Crianças e Jovens em Portugal*. CIES-ISCTE.

Carvalho, R. (2009). *Igreja Usa MySpace para Recrutar Religiosos*. Retrieved April 27, 2009, from http://dn.sapo.pt/inicio/portugal/interior.aspx?content_id=1213325

Coutinho, C., & Junior, J. (2007). Blog e Wiki: Os Futuros Professores e as Ferramentas da Web 2.0. In . *Proceedings of SIIE, 2007*, 199–204.

Damásio, M., & Poupa, C. (2009). Perfis de Actividades de Utilizadores da Internet: Um Estudo Comparativo Profiling On-Line Users Activities: A Comparative Study. *Observatorio (OBS). Journal, 8*, 28–39.

Ferreira, A., & Lourenço, T. (2009). *Crianças Navegam na Internet sem o Controlo dos Pais*. Retrieved February 11, 2009, from http://dn.sapo.pt/inicio/interior.aspx?content_id=1172586

Jesus, P. (2009). *Estão as Redes Sociais a Mudar o Nosso Cérebro?* Retrieved February 26, 2009, from http://dn.sapo.pt/inicio/portugal/interior.aspx?content_id=1154229

Lusa. (2009). *"Site" de Apoio a Sócrates cria "Rede Social" Semelhante ao Facebook ou Hi5*. Retrieved April 12, 2009, from http://dn.sapo.pt/Inicio/interior.aspx?content_id=1199713

Miguel, J. (2009). Viver na Rede. *Visão, 838*, 76–82.

Nielsen. (2008). *Nielsen Online Provides Fastest Growing Social Networks for September 2008*. Retrieved May 20, 2009, from http://blog.nielsen.com/nielsenwire/wp-content/uploads/2008/10/press_release24.pdf

Rettberg, J. (2008). *Blogging: Digital Media and Society Series* (pp. 68–83). New York: Polity Press.

Robalo, H. (2009). *GNR Adere às Novas Tecnologias da Internet*. Retrieved February 16, 2009, from http://dn.sapo.pt/Inicio/interior.aspx?content_id=1172861

Trigo, A., Varajão, J., Soto-Acosta, P., Barroso, J., Molina-Castillo, F., & Gonzales-Gallego, N. (2010). IT professionals: An Iberian snapshot. *International Journal of Human Capital and Information Technology Professionals, 1*(1), 61–75.

Universal MacCann. (2008). *Power to the People Social Media Tracker*. Retrieved April 20, 2009, from www.universalmccann.com/Assets/wave_3_20080403093750.pdf

This work was previously published in International Journal of Human Capital and Information Technology Professionals, Volume 1, Issue 4, edited by Ricardo Colomo-Palacios, pp. 31-54, copyright 2010 by IGI Publishing (an imprint of IGI Global).

APPENDIX

QUESTIONNAIRE

The use of the Internet for social and entertainment ends by young people of Alverca do Ribatejo (Portugal)
    Contact: neuzaclaudia@hotmail.com
    Obs.: This questionnaire has academic purposes and the confidentiality of answers will be naturally guaranteed. The document ends with the sentence "End of the Questionnaire".
    Form Instructions:
    Correct:⊠ Incorrect:■ ☑

I: The Use of the Internet

1. Do you have a computer?
    (Tick your answer, according to the filling instructions).
    - Yes
    - No
2. Do you have access to the Internet from home?
    (Tick your answer, according to the filling instructions).
    - Yes
    - No
3. Do you often access the Internet?
    (Tick your answer, according to the filling instructions).
    - Yes
    - No
    (If you answered *No*, please follow to question 20)
4. What kind of Access do you have?
    (Tick your answer, according to the filling instructions).
    - Cable
    - ADSL
    - Mobile
    - Do Not Know/No Answer
5. How often do you access the Internet?
    (Tick your answer, according to the filling instructions).
    - Less than 3 days a week
    - 3 days a week
    - 4 days a week
    - 5 days a week
    - 6 days a week
    - Everyday

6. How many hours, per day, do you spend on the Internet?
   (Tick your answer, according to the filling instructions).
   - Less than 1 hour
   - Between 1 and 2 hours
   - Between 2 and 3 hours
   - Between 3 and 4 hours
   - More than 4 hours

7. Considering the use of the Internet, which one (s) of the following tasks have you already experienced?
   (Tick your preferred answer (s), according to the filling instructions).
   - Watching *videoclips online*
   - Read blogs/*weblogs*
   - Read personal blogs/*weblogs*
   - Visiting a website for sharing photos
   - Manage an existing social network profile
   - Leave a comment on a blog
   - Upload my photos to a website for sharing photos
   - Leave a comment on a news website
   - Make podcast downloads
   - Start my own blog/*weblog*
   - Uploading a video for a website for sharing videos
   - Subscribe to an RSS feed

8. How often do you perform the following tasks?
   (Tick your answer for each item, considering a scale from 1 to 5 (1= Rarely and 5 = Daily).
   ① ② ③ ④ ⑤ Watching *videoclips online*
   ① ② ③ ④ ⑤ Read blogs/*weblogs*
   ① ② ③ ④ ⑤ Read personal blogs/*weblogs*
   ① ② ③ ④ ⑤ Visiting a website for sharing photos
   ① ② ③ ④ ⑤ Manage an existing social network profile
   ① ② ③ ④ ⑤ Leave a comment on a blog
   ① ② ③ ④ ⑤ Upload my photos to a website for sharing photos
   ① ② ③ ④ ⑤ Leave a comment on a news website
   ① ② ③ ④ ⑤ Make podcast downloads
   ① ② ③ ④ ⑤ Start my own blog/*weblog*
   ① ② ③ ④ ⑤ Uploading a video for a website for sharing videos
   ① ② ③ ④ ⑤ Subscribe to an RSS feed

II: Blogs

9. Do you have a blog?
   (Tick your answer, according to the filling instructions).
   - Yes
   - No

   (If you answered *No*, please follow to question 12)

10. When you write in your blog, what are the topics that you usually write?
    (Tick your preferred answer (s), according to the filling instructions).
    - News/Last Updates
    - Opinions about products and brands
    - Music
    - Technology
    - Computers
    - Management (general news and information)
    - Science
    - Sports
    - Movies/TV
    - Games
    - Travel (Holidays)
    - Celebrities
    - Others

11. When you write in your blog, what do you usually put?
    (Tick your preferred answer (s), according to the filling instructions).
    - Pictures
    - Videos
    - Recommended *Websites*
    - Favorite music/Recently heard
    - Stories from other blogs
    - Applications that reproduce content from other websites (*e.g.* pictures of a site for sharing photos)
    - Reviews about products and brands
    - Others

12. Do you often read blogs?
    (Tick your answer, according to the filling instructions).
    - Yes
    - No

    (If you answered *No*, please follow to question 15)

13. When you read blogs, which of the following topics you read most often?
    (Tick your preferred answer (s), according to the filling instructions).
    - Personal blogs
    - Blogs from relatives or friends
    - News/Last Updates
    - Opinions about products and brands
    - Music
    - Technology
    - Computers
    - Management (general news and information)
    - Science
    - Sports

- Movies/TV
- Games
- Travel (Holidays)
- Celebrities
- Others

14. What is your opinion about the following expressions?

(Tick your answer for each item, considering a scale from 1 to 5 (1= totally disagree and 5 = totally agree).

① ② ③ ④ ⑤ *Blogging* is a good way to express myself

① ② ③ ④ ⑤ I think more positively about companies that have blogs

① ② ③ ④ ⑤ I have a favorite blog that I read regularly

① ② ③ ④ ⑤ I trust in the opinions of bloggers about products and services

① ② ③ ④ ⑤ *Blogging* is an important way to socialize with friends

III: Social Networks

15. Do you have any social network profile?

(Tick your answer, according to the filling instructions).

- Yes
- No

(If you answered *No*, please follow to question 20)

16. In which?

(Tick your preferred answer (s), according to the filling instructions).

- *Orkut*
- *Linkedin*
- *Facebook*
- *MySpace*
- *Hi5*
- *Twitter*
- Outro

17. What kind of things do you do with your social network profile?

(Tick your preferred answer (s), according to the filling instructions).

- Pictures *Upload*
- Vídeos *Upload*
- Installing applications
- Messages to friends
- Write a blog
- Dating/Meet people
- Promoting a brand
- Favorite music/heard recently
- Others

18. Which one (s) of the following social networking sites do you use?
     (Tick your answer for each item, considering a scale from 1 to 5 (1= rarely and 5 = daily).
     ① ② ③ ④ ⑤ *MySpace*
     ① ② ③ ④ ⑤ *Facebook*
     ① ② ③ ④ ⑤ *Blogger*
     ① ② ③ ④ ⑤ *Flickr*
     ① ② ③ ④ ⑤ *Orkut*
     ① ② ③ ④ ⑤ *Hi5*
     ① ② ③ ④ ⑤ *Second Life*
     ① ② ③ ④ ⑤ *Linkedin*
     ① ② ③ ④ ⑤ *Last.fm*
     ① ② ③ ④ ⑤ *Twitter*
19. How often do you do the following tasks by social network?
     (Tick your answer for each item, considering a scale from 1 to 5 (1= rarely and 5 = daily).
     See Table A.

IV: Characterization of the Respondent

20. What is your gender?
     (Tick your answer, according to the filling instructions).
     - Female
     - Male
21. How old are you?
     (Tick your answer, according to the filling instructions).
     - 12 - 15 Years
     - 16 - 18 Years
     - + than 18 Years
22. What are your educational qualifications?
     (Tick your answer, according to the filling instructions).
     - Primary School
     - High School Education
     - Higher Education

End of Questionnaire

Thank you very much for your collaboration! ☺

Table A. Please mark your responses for question 19

	MySpace	*Facebook*	*Blogger*	*Flickr*	*Orkut*	*Hi5*	*Second Life*	*Linkedin*	*Last.fm*	**Twitter**	**Other**
Watching viedos	① ② ③ ④ ⑤	① ② ③ ④ ⑤	① ② ③ ④ ⑤	① ② ③ ④ ⑤	① ② ③ ④ ⑤	① ② ③ ④ ⑤	① ② ③ ④ ⑤	① ② ③ ④ ⑤	① ② ③ ④ ⑤	① ② ③ ④ ⑤	① ② ③ ④ ⑤
Watching photos	① ② ③ ④ ⑤	① ② ③ ④ ⑤	① ② ③ ④ ⑤	① ② ③ ④ ⑤	① ② ③ ④ ⑤	① ② ③ ④ ⑤	① ② ③ ④ ⑤	① ② ③ ④ ⑤	① ② ③ ④ ⑤	① ② ③ ④ ⑤	① ② ③ ④ ⑤
Reading posts	① ② ③ ④ ⑤	① ② ③ ④ ⑤	① ② ③ ④ ⑤	① ② ③ ④ ⑤	① ② ③ ④ ⑤	① ② ③ ④ ⑤	① ② ③ ④ ⑤	① ② ③ ④ ⑤	① ② ③ ④ ⑤	① ② ③ ④ ⑤	① ② ③ ④ ⑤
Make a comment	① ② ③ ④ ⑤	① ② ③ ④ ⑤	① ② ③ ④ ⑤	① ② ③ ④ ⑤	① ② ③ ④ ⑤	① ② ③ ④ ⑤	① ② ③ ④ ⑤	① ② ③ ④ ⑤	① ② ③ ④ ⑤	① ② ③ ④ ⑤	① ② ③ ④ ⑤
Videos *Upload*	① ② ③ ④ ⑤	① ② ③ ④ ⑤	① ② ③ ④ ⑤	① ② ③ ④ ⑤	① ② ③ ④ ⑤	① ② ③ ④ ⑤	① ② ③ ④ ⑤	① ② ③ ④ ⑤	① ② ③ ④ ⑤	① ② ③ ④ ⑤	① ② ③ ④ ⑤
Photos *Upload*	① ② ③ ④ ⑤	① ② ③ ④ ⑤	① ② ③ ④ ⑤	① ② ③ ④ ⑤	① ② ③ ④ ⑤	① ② ③ ④ ⑤	① ② ③ ④ ⑤	① ② ③ ④ ⑤	① ② ③ ④ ⑤	① ② ③ ④ ⑤	① ② ③ ④ ⑤
Music *Upload*	① ② ③ ④ ⑤	① ② ③ ④ ⑤	① ② ③ ④ ⑤	① ② ③ ④ ⑤	① ② ③ ④ ⑤	① ② ③ ④ ⑤	① ② ③ ④ ⑤	① ② ③ ④ ⑤	① ② ③ ④ ⑤	① ② ③ ④ ⑤	① ② ③ ④ ⑤
Access to links	① ② ③ ④ ⑤	① ② ③ ④ ⑤	① ② ③ ④ ⑤	① ② ③ ④ ⑤	① ② ③ ④ ⑤	① ② ③ ④ ⑤	① ② ③ ④ ⑤	① ② ③ ④ ⑤	① ② ③ ④ ⑤	① ② ③ ④ ⑤	① ② ③ ④ ⑤
Files *download*	① ② ③ ④ ⑤	① ② ③ ④ ⑤	① ② ③ ④ ⑤	① ② ③ ④ ⑤	① ② ③ ④ ⑤	① ② ③ ④ ⑤	① ② ③ ④ ⑤	① ② ③ ④ ⑤	① ② ③ ④ ⑤	① ② ③ ④ ⑤	① ② ③ ④ ⑤

Chapter 19
Technological Dissemination in the Portuguese Payments System:
An Empirical Analysis to the Region of Santarém

Sara Pinto
Polytechnic Institute of Santarém, Portugal

Fernando Ferreira
Polytechnic Institute of Santarém and CASEE - University of Algarve, Portugal,
& University of Memphis, USA

ABSTRACT

Nowadays, few would contest that the contribution of ICT – Information and Communication Technologies – for the progress of the payments system in Portugal has been significant. The continuous irruption of new payment forms, as well as the emergence of more attractive and profitable offers, triggers countless changes. In fact, there has been an organizational restructuring of the banks, aiming at achieving higher efficiency levels, resulting from the use of ICT. In broad terms, the payments system in Portugal has been revealing high levels of modernity. However, is that adhesion to ICT similar in all the regions that are part of the Portuguese territory? The main goal of this study focuses on an empirical analysis which allows to investigate the degree of convergence, regarding the technological dissemination for banking purposes, between the region of Santarém and the national trends.

INTRODUCTION

Presently, Portugal has one of the most revolutionary and developed European payments systems (*cf.* Ferreira, 2005; BP, 2007b; Expresso, 2009). The ICT – Information and Communication Technologies – have not been strange to that characterization (for a general overview of the impact of ICTs on markets' structure, see Hannan & McDowell, 1990; Coombs, Saviotti & Walsh, 1997; Laranja, Simões & Fontes, 1997; Trigo, Varajão, Soto-Acosta, Barroso, Molina-Castillo & Gonzales-Gallego, 2010). In fact, several studies

DOI: 10.4018/978-1-4666-0924-2.ch019

have been put forward, aiming at spreading this reality and presenting the Portuguese example as a case study (see, for instance, Guimarães, 1999; Ferreira, 2002 and 2003; Monteiro Barata, 1996a and 1996b).

The main motive for this paper consists of investigating whether the region of Santarém has the same trends as the rest of the country, concerning the adoption of the new technologies for banking purposes. Therefore, the methodological framework is made aiming at investigating the degree of convergence between the region of Santarém and the national trend.

The methodology used focused on techniques of direct enquiry (*i.e.* questionnaire surveys) directed to the resident and/or active population in Santarém, in order to assess the diffusion and technological assimilation patterns in the region's banking sector.

The paper is organized into four main points: (1) methodological framework, (2) presentation and analysis of the results, (3) recommendations and (4) final conclusions.

METHODOLOGICAL FRAMEWORK

ICTs have changed the Portuguese payments system, with the operations being easier and less costly (Ferreira & Cravo, 2004). Different institutions, such as SIBS – *Sociedade Interbancária de Serviços* – and the BP – Bank of Portugal –, have been revealing evolutions at the national level, betting on new channels of services distribution and in the introduction of new payment forms, which has changed significantly the consumers' preferences. Presently, these preferences are even more evident, being the ATM – *Automatic Teller Machine* – and the payment cards the main choices of the bank clients (BP, 2007a). In national terms, both the ATM and the Homebanking service are in an expansion stage, with an ever growing number of adherent clients (regarding the national trends of adhesion to these services, see SIBS, 2008a).

The banks' investment on ICT has triggered changes concerning the number of employees per bank branch, causing for their decrease, however increasing the demand levels in terms of workers' competences, knowledge and qualifications (APB, 2009).

Basically, this research aims at comparing what occurs in the region of Santarém to the rest of the country. For data collection, a questionnaire was elaborated (see *Appendix*), following the guidelines proposed by Hill & Hill (2005), and settled in four blocks: (1) a first block composed of questions related to the characterization of the present tendencies; (2) a second block composed of questions which may allow to investigate on the expected benefits; (3) a third block with questions that may allow to analyse the innovation of the payment system and, finally, (4) a fourth block composed of questions aiming at characterizing the inquired sample.

Likert Scales

A questionnaire survey may play a fundamental role in an empirical research, in order that the previously defined hypotheses may be verified (Hill & Hill, 2005). Within the scope of this research, questions of dichotomous answer and/or of closed answer have been used, as they allow an easier and faster statistical treatment (Bell, 2008). In particular, Lickert scales from 1 to 5 (1 = less favourable option and 5 = more favourable option) have been used, aiming at scoring the answers according to the degree of concordance or discordance (Lickert, 1932).

Questionnaire Testing

Still in what concerns the questionnaire framing, it is important to mention that the questionnaire was tested in a small sample of 10 individuals in order to guarantee whether the document was fit to be implemented. The surveyed individuals were asked to answer with comments and to make remarks about the questions. This testing process allowed the detection of some flaws, namely in the structure which had initially been determined, in the existence of ambiguous words, in poorly structured questions and in possibly repetitive questions.

The surveys were directly administered by one of the researchers, so that, in the presence of any doubts, clarification would be immediate and null answers would be avoided.

Sample Type

Concerning the sample, a great number of factors have been considered, namely the cost underlying the execution of the questionnaires and the available time, among others. Hence, the questionnaire was administered to a convenience or accidental sample, were the selection of the sample meets the convenience of the research (Baranãno, 2004). However, that fact cannot jeopardize the results reached, as, as referred by some authors (*e.g.* Monteiro Barata, 1996a; Ferreira, 2003), if we consider that, in an opinion survey, the number of respondents tends to decrease, then the difference between a random sample and an accidental sample is not as big as it would initially be expected.

Limitations of the Application

Bearing in mind the initially defined objectives, some factors limited this research. One of the reasons that contributed most to those limitations concerns the restricted availability in monetary terms, hence the use of a convenience sample. Another reason has to do with the fact that such a research always needs more time than the initially foreseen, besides requiring great attention and availability. Related to the limitations are also the availability of the respondents and the truthfulness of the opinions.

PRESENTATION AND ANALYSIS OF RESULTS

The analysis and interpretation of results obtained through direct enquiry techniques (*i.e.* questionnaire surveys) will be presented according to the main themes encompassed in the questionnaire.

2 Sample Characterization

The questionnaire surveys, directed to the Santarém's resident and/or active population, through a convenience or accidental sample, focused on both genders and involved a total of 100 ques-

Figure 1. Gender

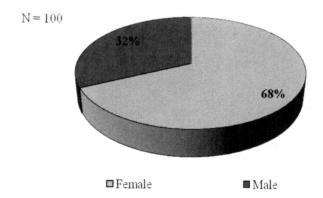

N = 100

□ Female   ■ Male

Figure 2. Age Groups

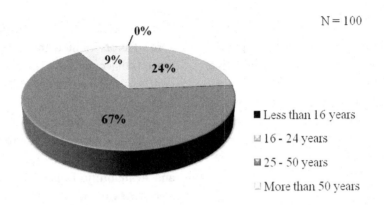

tionnaires. 68% of the respondents were female (Figure 1).

Based on Figure 2, we can see that 67% of the respondents are between 25 and 50 years old, followed by 16 and 24 years old (24%); 9% are over 50 years old and people under 16 years old were not inquired.

In turn, Figure 3 characterizes the sample according to the marital status of the respondents. Here, the supremacy of the marital status married is to be highlighted, with 44%, followed by single (39%), divorced (13%) and widow (with only 4%).

Regarding education, most respondents holds secondary education (55%), followed by higher education (23%) and basic education (18%) (Figure 4).

Figure 5 illustrates the professional status of the respondents, where the majority is an employee (59%). Students and business people are equalled, with about 16%.

It has been verified that the average respondent is female, is between 25 and 50 years old, is married, holds a secondary education and is an employee.

Present Trends

After implementing the questionnaires to the Santarém's inhabitants, it was verified that 18%

Figure 3. Marital Satus

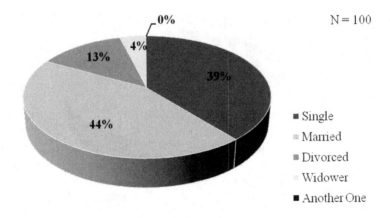

Figure 4. Education

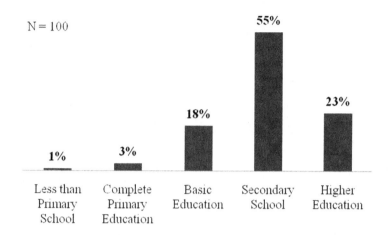

Figure 5. Professional Status

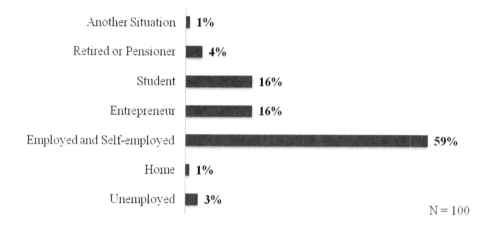

does not know the meaning of the expression Payments System. However, most of them is aware of and understands what the expression represents (Figure 6).

According to Figure 7, and based on a 1 to 5 Lickert scale (1 = never used and 5 = very used), it can be observed that Santarém's inhabitants do not use the telephone so much, preferring ATMs to perform their banking transactions. Bank branches, Internet and APT – *Automatic Payment Terminals* – are similar in terms of use by Santarém's inhabitants. In national terms, ATMs are

the electronic channel that registers more operations (*cf.* SIBS, 2008a).

Concerning payment means, payment cards and cash are the most valued ones in the region of Santarém, both with maximum classification attributed (mode of 5), whereas the check is the least used one, with a mode of 2 (Figure 8). In Portugal, payment cards are also the first option, but the check is not the least used payment form (*cf.* BP, 2007a).

Most Santarém's inhabitants have two payment cards (37%) and all of them possess at least a payment card (Figure 9), which is in accordance

Figure 6. Awareness of the Expression Payments System

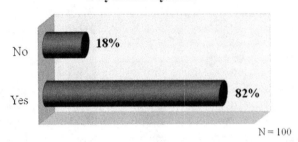

Figure 7. Degree of Use by Channels

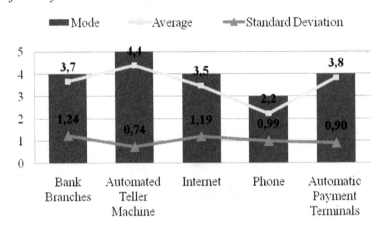

Figure 8. Most Used Instruments

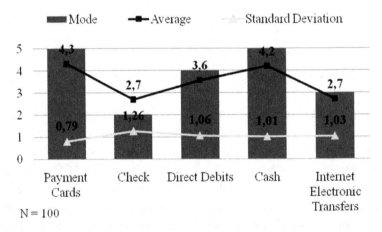

to what occurs in Portugal (*cf.* SIBS, 2008b; INE, 2009).

Figure 10 represents the most performed operations in the ATM service, which allows people to perform countless operations. Withdrawals and purchases are the most used operations by Santarém's inhabitants (16% and 15%, respectively); low value payments, such as parking (7%) and

Figure 9. Number of Payment Cards

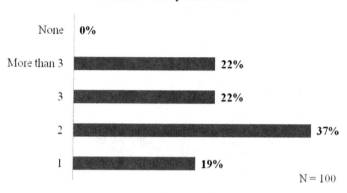

Figure 10. Most Performed ATM Operations

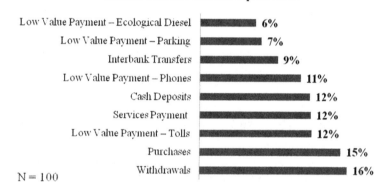

diesel (6%) are the ATM least requested operations.

At the national level, the situation is quite the opposite, as purchases hold the first position, followed by withdrawals and low value payments, such as tolls and telephones (*cf.* Ferreira, 2003). Specifying the operation ATM Services Payment, which encompasses a multitude of services, cell phones loading prevails (28%), followed by purchases payment (26%) and the purchase of theatre and/or shows tickets (13%). Low value payments (*e.g.* ecological diesel and parking) are the most devalued ATM operations (6% and 7%, respectively) (Figure 11).

ICTs have modified the banks action and services offered. These institutions have increas-

ingly fewer employees per bank branch. On average, there are 10 employees per bank branch (*cf.* APB, 2009). However, in the region of Santarém, 45% of the respondents states to meet between 5 and 6 employees and about 40% states to meet between 1 to 4 employees. None of the respondents has admitted to see more than 10 employees per bank branch (Figure 12).

Expected Benefits

The several instruments of electronic payment offer clients the possibility of performing a number of operations, to which benefits are associated (Figure 13).

Figure 11. Most Performed Operations at the Services Payment

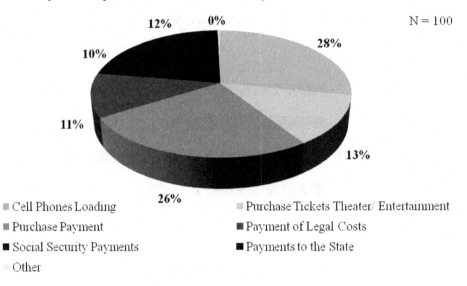

Figure 12. Number of Employees per Bank Branch

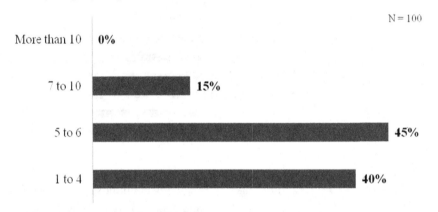

Figure 13. Benefits Associated to Electronic Instruments

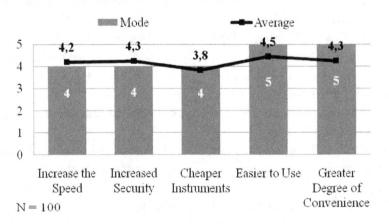

Figure 14. Check

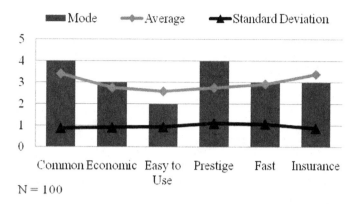

Based on a Lickert scale (1 = total disagreement and 5 = total agreement), respondents consider that electronic instruments are user-friendly and quite convenient, both having been attributed maximum score. In practice, respondents see them as fast, secure and cheap (Figure 13), which meets the national trends (*cf.* BP, 2007a). The second question of this group focused on the identification of the advantages attributed to each payment instrument, based on a Lickert scale similar to the previous one.

Check

In national terms, the check is seen as an expensive instrument and being less and less used nowadays.

The same occurs in region of Santarém (Figure 14), where it is considered neither a user-friendly nor an economic instrument.

It is also possible to see that respondents do not attribute prestige to those who use this form of payment. For them, the check is common, fast and secure, obtaining a satisfactory score in these parameters (mean of 2.54, in a 1 to 5 scale).

Effects

Observing Figure 15, it is clear that Effects are loosing weight in the choices of Santarém's inhabitants, similarly to what happens in national terms (*cf.* BP, 2007a).

Figure 15. Effects

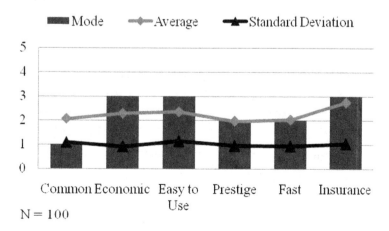

Figure 16. Interbank Electronic Transfers

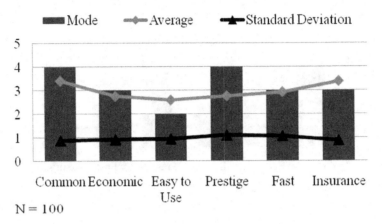

N = 100

Respondents do not regard this instrument as a regular preference, consider it neither common nor fast, do not attribute prestige to those who use this form of payment, but consider it economic, user-friendly and secure, with a mean of 2.24.

IET

The analysis of Figure 16 enables us to see that prestige and easy access to IET – *Interbank Electronic Transfers* – are the main valued attributes by the Santarém's active or resident population, both of them with a mode of 4 points. Notwithstanding this result, they do not consider this service as user-friendly (mode of 2 points). Moreover,

they see it as an average service regarding costs, speed and safety.

Direct Debits

Through the analysis of the results from the questionnaires concerning the advantages associated to Direct Debits, it becomes clear that respondents highly value this payment instrument and score it well in general terms. In a 1 to 5 scale, the 4 prevails. However, they give it average scores in economic and prestige terms (Figure 17).

Figure 17. Direct Debits

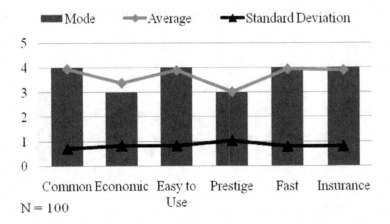

N = 100

Figure 18. ATM

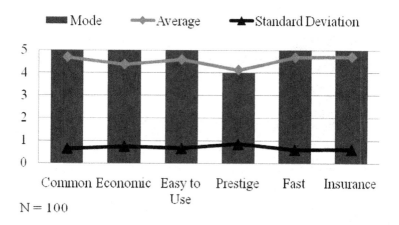

ATM

Figure 18 illustrates the advantages associated to ATM, which, in general terms, is seen as the most complete payment instrument. It has been scored the highest rating in all parameters, except for the association of this service to prestige and to status. It is regarded as a secure, fast, user-friendly, rather cheap and very common instrument.

Figure 19 clearly shows that respondents have associated benefits to each payment instrument, gathering the Check and the Effects the least as-sociated benefits. Furthermore, respondents' preferences go to ATM, which is considered to be the most complete of all the payment instruments, followed by Direct Debits.

In global terms, this group has allowed to conclude that people see electronic payment instruments as advantageous and rather efficient, as they allow performing operations quickly and safely.

Figure 19. Benefits Associated to the Payment Instruments (Mode)

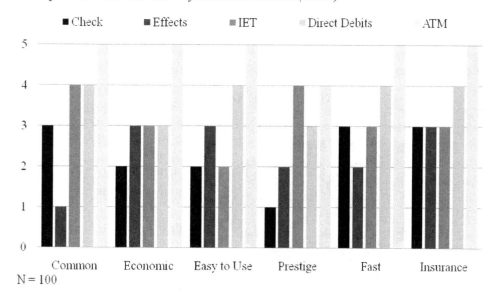

Figure 20. Adhesion to MB PHONE Service

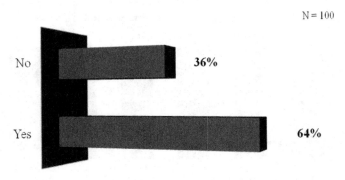

N = 100

No   36%

Yes   64%

Innovation and Evolutional Perspectives

Technological progress has triggered countless changes, which caused for the appearance of new innovative and modern payment services. Therefore, we are observing a progressive replacement of the checks and effects by the electronic payment instruments, such as direct debits and IETs. In the region of Santarém, respondents prefer those instruments which are user-friendly, cheap, fast, convenient and safer.

The appearance of new e-channels, such as MB PHONE, MB NET, MB CODE and MB SPOT, aims at facilitating citizens' lives, providing countless services.

MB PHONE Service

According to data from 2008 (SIBS, 2008b), MB PHONE is expanding at the national level. However, according to Figure 20, we can see that 36% of respondents admit neither to know this service nor what it consists of. The remaining 64% know and use MB PHONE.

Enquiries (*e.g.* balances) are the most valued and requested operations (86%), followed by services payment (9%) and other operations, with only 5% (Figure 21).

Santarém's trends meet what happens at the national level, where the MB PHONE has increasingly more followers, who choose to perform operations through the telephone (SIBS, 2008b).

Figure 21. Operations Performed by MB PHONE

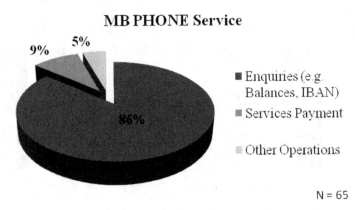

MB PHONE Service

9%   5%

86%

■ Enquiries (e.g. Balances, IBAN)

■ Services Payment

■ Other Operations

N = 65

Figure 22. Degree of Relevance of Electronic Channels

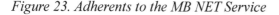

Electronic Channels Relevance

Figure 22 illustrates the degree of relevance that respondents attributed to each channel, when performing their banking operations. Based on a 1 to 5 Lickert scale (1 = not relevant at all and 5 = very relevant), it has been verified that respondents value ATMs (in terms of mode, the 5 prevailed, mean of 4.4. and standard deviation of only 0.66). According to the respondents' assessment, APT – *Automatic Payment Terminals* – followed, with a mean of 3.8 and showing, likewise, a small standard deviation of 0.81. E-channels, such as: MB CODE, MB NET, MB PHONE and MB SPOT, are very close, with a mode of 3. However, in terms of mean, there are distinctions, and the

MB SPOT is the one that shows up, with a mean of 3.4 (Figure 22).

Summing up, according to the respondents, the most relevant electronic channel is the ATM, which presents more usefulness and underlies people's everyday lives. APTs are the second most important channel for the respondents, whereas other e-channels are still in an expansion stage.

MB NET Service

For the Santarém's population, purchasing through the Internet is not very useful, since only 37% of the respondents refer to have used this service (Figure 23).

In national terms, there is a huge increase of this service, having been registered, in 2008, about

Figure 23. Adherents to the MB NET Service

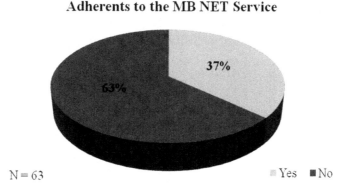

Figure 24. Use of MB SPOT

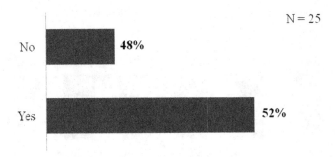

900 thousand operations performed, with approximately 450 thousand cards, both debit and credit ones (SIBS, 2008b). In the region of Santarém, this service does not have many followers, as respondents admit to prefer personally purchasing goods or services.

MB SPOT Service

The MB SPOT service is the newest SIBS's bet. It consists of the offer of a wide range of operations, while a person is purchasing a given good or service. Figure 24 accounts for the MB SPOT degree of use.

In the region of Santarém there are already followers of this kind of service, but they claim that there are few devices in the shops. According to Figure 24, 52% of respondents refer to know and use this service. However, 48% admit not to use this very recent electronic channel.

Homebanking

Based on the data from Figure 25, it is possible to see that 58% of the respondents stated that they use this service, whereas the remaining 42% do not.

In Figure 26 it is possible to observe the opinions of the respondents who use this service. They consider it very fast in performing operations, quite secure, user-friendly and very efficient. All parameters revealed high scores.

Some respondents also consider it quite convenient, as it allows people not to move, that is, it is enough to access the Internet and bank access codes to perform any kind of banking operation. Exception is, naturally, made to cash withdrawal.

RECOMENDATIONS

Bearing in mind the limitations previously referred to in this paper, further investigation on this topic

Figure 25. Use of the Homebanking Service

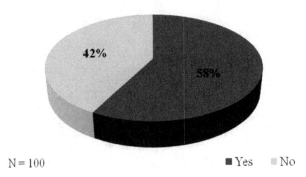

Figure 26. Characterization of the Homebanking Service

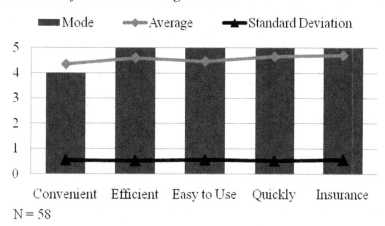

N = 58

will have to consider the several practical constraints that may occur. Moreover, the use of a more grounded sampling process is recommended, so that conclusions may be drawn and extrapolated to the Universe under study. There is always, naturally, the need to consider the existence of scarce resources (*e.g.* time, money, access to information and motivation (Baranãno, 2004)). Finally, it is recommended that data collection is made by the investigator himself, in order to draw as much information as possible from the respondents. It is important to bear in mind the existing difficulty concerning respondents' adhesion.

CONCLUSION

One of the most evident conclusions lays on the fact that, both at the national level and in Santarém, ATM is the most valued channel by people, who regard it as fast, secure, user-friendly, common to all people and cheap. Throughout this paper, it is possible to verify that ICT were (and are) an important lever towards the modernization of the payment systems. The Portuguese payment system is characterized as innovative and deeply developed, and each Portuguese citizen has, on average, at least two credit and/or debit cards. The same occurs in the region of Santarém (37%). As to bank restructuring in terms of employees

per bank branch, it has been found out that, in Santarém, the figure is placed between 5 and 6 employees (45%), in contrast to what happens at the national level, where there are, on average, 10 employees per bank branch.

In conclusion, there is a gradual replacement of the scriptural payment instruments by the electronic ones, the use of the check is becoming obsolete, respondents consider it difficult to use and not at all cheap.

Therefore, it can be said that the degree of convergence between the region of Santarém and the national trends, regarding technological spreading in the payment system, is considered as high. However, it is important to bear in mind that this study is merely exploratory and, thus, more complex, wide and thorough analyses should follow, so that results may be extrapolated.

REFERENCES

APB – Associação Portuguesa de Bancos. (2009). *Actividade bancária 2008*. Retrieved March 10, 2009, from http://www.apb.pt/Publicacoes/ S%C3%ADntese+de+2008/

Baranãno, A. (2004). *Métodos e técnicas de investigação em gestão* (1st ed.). Lisbon: Edições Sílabo.

Bell, J. (2008). *Como realizar um projecto de investigação* (4th ed.). Lisbon: Editora Gradiva.

BP – Bank of Portugal. (2007a). *Relatório dos sistemas de pagamentos e de liquidação interbancária.* Available online at http://www.bportugal.pt/bank/payments/rel_sp2007_p.pdf [10 March 2009].

BP – Bank of Portugal. (2007a). *Relatório dos sistemas de pagamentos e de liquidação interbancária.* Retrieved March 10, 2009, from http://www.bportugal.pt/bank/payments/rel_sp2007_p.pdf

Coombs, R., Saviotti, P., & Walsh, V. (1987). *Economics and technological change.* New Jersey: Rownam & Littlefield.

Expresso. (2009). *As melhores agências estão em Portugal.* Retrieved March 20, 2009, from http://aeiou.expresso.pt/economia/noticiario?p=arquivo

Ferreira, F. (2002). *Inovação tecnológica no sistema financeiro português: Evolução e perspectivas.* Master Dissertation in Economics and Business Sciences, Faculty of Economics, University of Algarve.

Ferreira, F. (2003). *Inovação tecnológica no sistema financeiro português: Evolução e perspectivas.* Coimbra: Pé-de-Página Edition.

Ferreira, F. (2005). Impacto tecnológico na estrutura do sector financeiro em Portugal: Ensaio empírico e pistas para uma reflexão. *Portuguese Journal of Management Studies, X*(1), 71–87.

Ferreira, F., & Cravo, P. (2004). Technological progress: An important variable in the Portuguese banking system structure reform? *Proceedings of the IADIS International Conference www/Internet 2004* (II), October, Madrid, Spain, 1139–1142.

Guimarães, M. (1999). *As transferências electrónicas de fundos e os cartões de débito.* Coimbra: Livraria Almedina.

Hannan, T., & McDowell, J. (1990). The impact of technology adoption on market structure. *The Review of Economics and Statistics, 72*(1), 164–168. doi:10.2307/2109755

Hill, M., & Hill, A. (2005). *Investigação por questionário* (2nd ed.). Lisbon: Edições Sílabo.

INE – Instituto Nacional de Estatística. (2009). *População residente em Santarém.* Retrieved April 2, 2009, from http://www.ine.pt

Laranja, M., Simões, V., & Fontes, M. (1997). *Inovação tecnológica. Experiências das empresas portuguesas.* Lisbon: Texto Editora.

Likert, R. (1932). A technique for the measurement of attitudes. *Archives de Psychologie, 22*(140), 1–55.

Monteiro Barata, J. (1996a). *Inovação nos serviços: sistemas e tecnologias de informação e competitividade no sector bancário em Portugal.* Doctoral Thesis in Economics, ISEG/UTL.

Monteiro Barata, J. (1996b). Mutação tecnológica na banca em Portugal. Uma perspectiva para o final do século. *Revista da Banca, 39*, 5–34.

SIBS. (2008b). *Estatísticas.* Retrieved March 10, 2009, from http://www.sibs.pt/pt/estatisticas/

Trigo, A., Varajão, J., Soto-Acosta, P., Barroso, J., Molina-Castillo, F., & Gonzales-Gallego, N. (2010). IT professionals: An Iberian snapshot. *International Journal of Human Capital and Information Technology Professionals, I*(1), 61–75.

APPENDIX

Survey

Technological Dissemination in the Santarém's Banking System
    Contact: SaraDGPinto@gmail.com
    Obs.: This survey has academic objectives and the confidentiality of the answers will be naturally ensured. The document ends with the expression "End of the Survey".

Filling Instructions:

Correct: ■ Incorrect: ☒ ☑

I: Present Trends

1. Do you know what a Payment System is?
    (Tick your answer, according to the filling instructions)
    - Yes
    - No
    (If you answered *NO*, please request an explanation)
2. Regarding the following distribution channels, how often do you use each one of them to perform banking transactions?
    (Tick your answer for each item, considering a scale from 1 to 5 (1= never used and 5= very used))
    ① ② ③ ④ ⑤ Bank Branches
    ① ② ③ ④ ⑤ Automated Teller Machine
    ① ② ③ ④ ⑤ Internet
    ① ② ③ ④ ⑤ Phone
    ① ② ③ ④ ⑤ Automatic Payment Terminals
3. Regarding the following payment means, how often do you use each one of them to perform banking transactions?
    (Tick your answer for each item, considering a scale from 1 to 5 (1= never used and 5= very used))
    ① ② ③ ④ ⑤ Payment Cards
    ① ② ③ ④ ⑤ Check
    ① ② ③ ④ ⑤ Direct Debits
    ①② ③ ④ ⑤ Cash
    ①② ③ ④ ⑤ Internet Electronic Transfers
4. How many debit and/or credit cards do you have/use?
    (Tick your preferred answer, according to the filling instructions)
    - 1
    - 2
    - 3
    - + 3
    - None
    (If you answered *NONE*, please proceed to question 7)

5. Which is your most performed ATM operation?
    (Tick your preferred answer, according to the filling instructions)
    - Purchases
    - Cash Deposits
    - Withdrawals
    - Low Value Payment – Parking
    - Low Value Payment – Ecological Diesel
    - Low Value Payment – Tolls
    - Low Value Payment – Phones
    - Services Payment
    - Interbank Transfers

6. Which is your most performed operation at the services payment?
    (Tick your preferred answer, according to the filling instructions)
    - Cell Phones Loading
    - Purchase Tickets Theater/ Entertainment
    - Purchase Payment
    - Payment of Legal Costs
    - Social Security Payments
    - Payments to the State
    - Other

7. On average, how many employees do you see at the bank branch where your main bank account is?
    (Tick your preferred answer, according to the filling instructions)
    - 1 to 4
    - 5 to 6
    - 7 to 10
    - + 10

II: Expected Benefits

8. What are the main benefits brought by electronic payment instruments?
    (Tick your answer for each item, considering a scale from 1 to 5 (1= total disagreement and 5= total agreement))
    ① ② ③ ④ ⑤ Increase the Speed
    ① ② ③ ④ ⑤ Increased Security
    ① ② ③ ④ ⑤ Cheaper Instruments
    ① ② ③ ④ ⑤ Easier to Use
    ① ② ③ ④ ⑤ Greater Degree of Convenience

9. Which are the main advantages associated to each payment instrument?
    (Tick your answer for each item, considering a scale from 1 to 5 (1= total disagreement and 5= total agreement))

	Check	Effects	IET	Direct Debits	ATM
Common	① ② ③ ④ ⑤	① ② ③ ④ ⑤	① ② ③ ④ ⑤	① ② ③ ④ ⑤	① ② ③ ④ ⑤
Economic	① ② ③ ④ ⑤	① ② ③ ④ ⑤	① ② ③ ④ ⑤	① ② ③ ④ ⑤	① ② ③ ④ ⑤
Easy to Use	① ② ③ ④ ⑤	① ② ③ ④ ⑤	① ② ③ ④ ⑤	① ② ③ ④ ⑤	① ② ③ ④ ⑤
Prestige	① ② ③ ④ ⑤	① ② ③ ④ ⑤	① ② ③ ④ ⑤	① ② ③ ④ ⑤	① ② ③ ④ ⑤
Fast	① ② ③ ④ ⑤	① ② ③ ④ ⑤	① ② ③ ④ ⑤	① ② ③ ④ ⑤	① ② ③ ④ ⑤
Insurance	① ② ③ ④ ⑤	① ② ③ ④ ⑤	① ② ③ ④ ⑤	① ② ③ ④ ⑤	① ② ③ ④ ⑤

III: Innovation

10. Do you know what MB PHONE means?
     (Tick your preferred answer, according to the filling instructions)
     - Yes
     - No
     (If you answered *NO*, please proceed to question 15)
11. For what purposes do you use the MB PHONE service?
     (Tick your preferred answer, according to the filling instructions)
     - Enquiries (*e.g.* Balances, IBAN)
     - Services Payment
     - Other Operations
12. What degree of relevance do you give to each one of the following electronic channels?
     (Tick your answer for each item, considering a scale from 1 to 5 (1= not relevant at all and 5= very relevant))
     ① ② ③ ④ ⑤ ATMs
     ① ② ③ ④ ⑤ MB CODE
     ① ② ③ ④ ⑤ MB NET
     ① ② ③ ④ ⑤ MB PHONE
     ① ② ③ ④ ⑤ MB SPOT
     ①② ③ ④ ⑤ Automatic Payment Terminals
13. Did you get the MB NET service by activating your credit or debit card?
     (Tick your preferred answer, according to the filling instructions)
     - Yes
     - No
     (If you answered *NO*, proceed to question 15)
14. Do you know the term MB SPOT?
     (Tick your preferred answer, according to the filling instructions)
     - Yes
     - No
15. Do you use *Homebanking* services?
     (Tick your preferred answer, according to the filling instructions)
     - Yes
     - No

(If you answered *NO*, proceed to question 17)

16. How do you characterize your *Homebanking* service?

(Tick your answer for each item, considering a scale from 1 to 5 (1= really bad and 5= very good))

① ② ③ ④ ⑤ Convenient

① ② ③ ④ ⑤ Efficient

① ② ③ ④ ⑤ Easy to Use

① ② ③ ④ ⑤ Quickly

① ② ③ ④ ⑤ Insurance

IV: Sample's Characterization

17. What is your gender?

(Tick your answer, according to the filling instructions)

- Female
- Male

18. How old are you?

(Tick your answer, according to the filling instructions)

- Less than 16 years
- 16 - 24 years
- 25 - 50 years
- More than 50 years

19. Which is your marital status?

(Tick your answer, according to the filling instructions)

- Single
- Married
- Divorced
- Widower
- Another One

20. What are your educational qualifications?

(Tick your answer, according to the filling instructions)

- Less than Primary School
- Complete Primary Education
- Basic Education
- Secondary School
- Higher Education

21. What is your professional status?

(Tick your answer, according to the filling instructions)

- Unemployed
- Home
- Employed and Self-employed
- Entrepreneur
- Student
- Retired or Pensioner
- Another Situation

End of the Survey

Thank you for your collaboration!

Compilation of References

Abbasi, S., & Maharmeh, R. (2000). Project management practice by the public sector in a developing country. *International Journal of Project Management, 18*(2), 105–122. doi:10.1016/S0263-7863(98)00074-X

Abramo, C. W. (2000). *Formulação e implantação de código de ética em empresas - reflexões e sugestões.* São Paulo, Brazil: Instituto Ethos de Empresas e Responsabilidade Social.

Abran, A., Bourque, P., Dupuis, R., & Moore, J. W. (2004). *SWEBOK. Guide to the Software Engineering Body of Knowledge.* Los Alamitos, CA: IEEE Computer Society.

Acuña, S. T., Gómez, M., & Juristo, N. (2008a). Towards understanding the relationship between team climate and software quality - a quasi-experimental study. *Empirical Software Engineering, 13*(4), 401–434. doi:10.1007/s10664-008-9074-8

Acuña, S. T., Gómez, M., & Juristo, N. (2008b). Empirical study of how personality, team processes and task characteristics relate to satisfaction and software quality? In. *Proceedings of ESEM, 2008,* 291–293.

Acuña, S. T., & Juristo, N. (2004). Assigning people to roles in software projects. *Software, Practice & Experience, 34*(7), 675–696. doi:10.1002/spe.586

Acuña, S. T., Juristo, N., & Moreno, A. M. (2006). Emphasizing Human Capabilities in Software Development. *IEEE Software, 23*(2), 94–101. doi:10.1109/MS.2006.47

Adler, P. S., & Kwon, S. W. (2002). Social capital: Prospects for a new concept. *Academy of Management Review, 27*(1), 17–40. doi:10.2307/4134367

Ahuja, M. K. (2002). Women in the information technology profession: A literature review, synthesis and research agenda. *European Journal of Information Systems, 11*(1), 20–34. doi:10.1057/palgrave/ejis/3000417

Aigner, D. J., & Cain, G. G. (1977). Statistical theories of discrimination in labor markets. *Industrial & Labor Relations Review, 30*(2), 175–187. doi:10.2307/2522871

Al-Asmari, K. R., & Yu, L. (2006). Experiences in Distributed Software Development with Wiki. In R. Hamid & H. R. Arabnia (Eds.), *Proceedings of the International Conference on Software Engineering Research and Practice & Conference on Programming Languages and Compilers* (pp. 389-293). Las Vegas, NV: CSREA Press.

Albrecht, J., Björklund, A., & Vroman, S. (2003). Is there a glass ceiling in Sweden? *Journal of Labor Economics, 21*(1), 145–177. doi:10.1086/344126

Ali Babar, M., Verner, J. M., & Nguyen, P. T. (2007). Establishing and maintaining trust in software outsourcing relationships: An empirical investigation. *Journal of Systems and Software, 80*(9), 1438–1449. doi:10.1016/j.jss.2006.10.038

Almeida, P. (2009). *Redes Virtuais são Espaço Sem Lei.* Retrieved from http://dn.sapo.pt/inicio/opiniao/interior.aspx?content_id=1219447

Alonso, C. M., Gallego, D. J., & Honey, P. (2002). *The learning styles.* Ediciones Mensajero.

Alshawi, M., & Ingirige, B. (2003). Web-enabled project management: an emerging paradigm in construction. *Automation in Construction, 12*(4), 349–364. doi:10.1016/S0926-5805(03)00003-7

Amanda Roan, G. W. (2007). Women, information technology and 'waves of optimism': Australian evidence on 'mixed-skill' jobs. *New Technology, Work and Employment*, 22(1), 21–33. doi:10.1111/j.1468-005X.2007.00181.x

Amason, A. C., & Sapienza, H. (1997). The effects of top management team size and interaction norms on cognitive and affective conflict. *Journal of Management*, 23(4), 495–507. doi:10.1016/S0149-2063(97)90045-3

Amin, M. R., Saleheen, S., Kibria, R., & Karmakar, C. K. (2007). *An effective approach for implementing E-Agriculture in Bangladesh*. Retrieved September 24, 2009, from http://wwwi4donline.net/ATF/2007/fullpapers/MDRUHUL_ATF07ABS130.pdf

Anandaraja, N., Sujhi, G., Gayathri, G., Ramasubramanian, M., & Rathakrishnan, T. (2009). *Technology enabled farm women*. Retrieved July 3, 2009, from http://www.i4donline.net/sept07/1434.pdf

Ancona, D. G., & Caldwell, D. F. (1992). Demography and design: Predictors of new product team performance. *Organization Science*, 3(3), 321–341. doi:10.1287/orsc.3.3.321

Anderson, P. (2007). What is web 2.0? ideas, technologies and implications for education. *JISC reports*. Retrieved November 2009, from http://www.jisc.ac.uk/media/documents/techwatch/tsw0701b.pdf

Anderson, A. H., McEwan, R., Bal, J., & Carletta, J. (2007). Virtual team meetings: An analysis of communication and context. *Computers in Human Behavior*, 23(5), 2558–2580. doi:10.1016/j.chb.2007.01.001

Anderson, T., & Garrison, D. R. (1995). Critical thinking in distance education: Developing critical communities in an audio teleconference context. *Higher Education*, 29, 183–199. doi:10.1007/BF01383838

André, M., Baldoquín, M. G., Acuña, S. T., & Rosete, A. (2008). *A formalized model for the assignment of human resources to software projects*. Paper presented at the XIV Latin Ibero-American Congress on Operations Research, Cartagena de Indias, Colombia.

Ang, S., & Slaughter, S. (2000). The missing context of information technology personnel: a review and future directions for research. In R. Zmud (Ed.), *Framing the domains of IT management: Projecting the future through the past* (pp. 305-327). Cincinnati, Ohio: Pinnaflex Education Resources.

Anschuetz, L. (1998). Managing Geographically Distributed Teams. In *Proceedings of the IEEE Professional Communication Conference (IPCC)*, Quebec City, Canada (pp. 23-25). Washington, DC: IEEE.

APB – Associação Portuguesa de Bancos. (2009). *Actividade bancária 2008*. Retrieved March 10, 2009, from http://www.apb.pt/Publicacoes/S%C3%ADntese+de+2008/

Applegate, L. M., Austin, R. D., & Soule, D. L. (2009). *Corporate Information Strategy and Management* (8th ed.). New York: McGraw-Hill.

Armstrong, L. J., Diepeveen, D., & Vagh, Y. (2007). *Data mining can empower growers' crop decision making*. Paper presented at the T2: Technology and Transformation. 3rd Transforming Information and Learning Conference, Perth, Australia.

Arulampalam, W., Booth, A. L., & Bryan, M. L. (2006). Is there a glass ceiling over Europe? Exploring the gender pay gap across the wages distribution. *Industrial & Labor Relations Review*, 60(2), 163–186.

Arumapperuma, S. (2006). Agricultural innovation system in Australia. *Journal of Business Systems. Governance and Ethics*, 1(4), 15–25.

Asmus, J., Bonner, C., Esterhay, D., Lechner, A., & Rentfrow, C. (2005). *Instructional design technology trend analysis*. Retrieved November 2009, from http://eduspaces.net/collinb/files/1136/2967/TrendAnalysisWeb.pdf

Atkins, D., Boyer, D., Handel, M., Herbsleb, J., Mockus, A., & Wills, G. (2002). *Achieving speed in globally distributed project work*. Paper presented at the Human Computer Interaction Consortium, Winterpark, CO.

Atkinson, J. (1984, August). Manpower Strategier for Flexible Organizations. *Personal Management*, 28-31.

Atkinson, A. A., Kaplan, R. S., Matsumara, E. M., & Young, S. M. (2007). *Management accounting*. Upper Saddle River, NJ: Prentice Hall.

Avolio, B. J., & Locke, E. E. (2002). Contrasting different philosophies of leader motivation: Altruism versus egoism. *The Leadership Quarterly, 13*(2), 169–191. doi:10.1016/S1048-9843(02)00094-2

Babcock, C. (1996). Taking the long view on IS expertise. *Computerworld, 30*(51).

Baker, S. J. D. R. (2007). Modeling and Understanding Students' Off-Task Behavior in Intelligent Tutoring Systems. *Proceedings of ACM SIGCHI conference on Human Factors in Computing Systems*, 1059-1068.

Bandow, D. (2004). Time to create sound teamwork. *Journal for Quality and Participation, 24*(2), 41–47.

Baranãno, A. (2004). *Métodos e técnicas de investigação em gestão* (1st ed.). Lisbon: Edições Sílabo.

Barber, A. E., & Daly, C. L. (1996). Compensation and Diversity: New Pay for a New Workforce? In Kossek, E. E., & Lobel, S. A. (Eds.), *Managing Diversity: Human Resource Strategies for Transforming the Workplace.* Cambridge, UK: Blackwell.

Barney, J. B. (1991). Firm resources and sustained competitive advantage. *Journal of Management, 17*, 99–120. doi:10.1177/014920639101700108

Barroso, M. (2009). *Empresas Descobrem Mundo Virtual*. Retrieved from http://dn.sapo.pt/bolsa/interior.aspx?content_id=1217875

Barthélemy, J. (2001). The hidden cost of IT outsourcing. *MIT Sloan Management, 42*(3), 60–69.

Bassellier, G., Reich, B. H., & Benbasat, I. (2001). IT Competence of Business Managers: A Definition and Research Model. *Journal of Management Information Systems, 17*(4), 159–182.

Battin, R. D., Crocker, R., Kreidler, J., & Subramanian, K. (2001). Leveraging resources in global software development. *IEEE Software, 18*(2), 70–77. doi:10.1109/52.914750

Baxter, J., & Wright, E. O. (2000). The glass ceiling hypothesis: A comparative study of the United States, Sweden, and Australia. *Gender &. Society, 14*(2), 275–294.

Becker, B. E., & Gerhart, B. (1996). The impact of human resource management on organizational performance: Progress and prospects. *Academy of Management Journal, 39*(4), 779–801. doi:10.2307/256712

Becker, G. S. (1957). *The Economics of Discrimination.* Chicago: University of Chicago Press.

Beck, P., Kung, M., Park, Y., & Yang, S. (2004). E-learning architecture: challenges and mapping of individuals in an internet-based pedagogical interface. *International Journal of Innovation and Learning, 1*(3), 279–292. doi:10.1504/IJIL.2004.004884

Behling, R., Behling, C., & Sousa, K. (1996). Software Re-engineering: Concepts and Methodology. *Industrial Management & Data Systems, 96*(6), 3–10. doi:10.1108/02635579610126836

Belbin, R. M. (2004). *Management Teams: Why they Succeed or Fail* (2nd ed.). Oxford, UK: Butterworth Heinemann.

Bell, B. S., & Kozlowski, S. W. J. (2002). A topology of Virtual Teams: Implications for Effective Leadership. *Group & Organization Management, 24*(14), 14–49. doi:10.1177/1059601102027001003

Bell, J. (2008). *Como realizar um projecto de investigação* (4th ed.). Lisbon: Editora Gradiva.

Berger, F., & Ghei, A. (1995). Employment tests: A facet of hospitality hiring. *Cornell hotel and restaurant administration quarterly, 36*(6).

Berleur, J., & d'Udekem-Gevers, M. (1996b). *IFIP Framework for ethics: codes of ethics/conduct for computer societies - The experience of IFIP.* London: Chapman & Hall.

Berleur, J., Duquenoy, P., Holvast, J., Jones, M., Kimppa, K., & Sizer, R. (2004). *Criteria and prodecures for developing codes of ethics or of conduct.* International Federation for Information Processing.

Bersoff, V., & Chase, R. (1982). *Software Configuration Management - An investment in Product Integrity.* Englewood Cliffs, NJ: Prentice Hall Inc.

Bertolini, R. (2004). *Strategic thinking: making information and communication technologies work for food security in Africa.* Cited in H. Munyua, E. Adera, & M. Jensen (2008), Retrieved September 6, 2007, from http://www.ifpri.org/pubs/ib/ib27.pdf

Best, M. H. (2001). *The New Competitive Advantage: The Renewal of American Industry.* UK: Oxford University Press.

Bilodeau, N., & Singh, L. (2007). The *marriage of process and data governance: key to BPM and SOA initiatives' success.* BPMInstitute.org.

Birkett, W., & Barbera, M. (1999). *Codifying power and control - ethical codes, codes in action contents (Tech. Rep.).* Sydney, Australia: University of New South Wales, The Australian Centre for Management Accounting Development.

Birks, D. F., Zainuddin, Y., Choo, A. T., Wafa, S. A., Morar, S., & Nasirin, S. (2007). Successful IT Outsourcing Engagement: Lessons from Malaysia. *The Electronic Journal of Information Systems in Developing Countries, 30*(5), 1–12.

Blackburn, J. D., Scudder, G. D., & Van Wassenhove, L. N. (1996). Improving speed and productivity of software development: a global survey of software developers. *IEEE Transactions on Software Engineering, 22*(12), 875–885. doi:10.1109/32.553636

Blake, R. R., & Mouton, J. S. (1982). *Productivity: the human side.* New York: Amacom.

Blau, F. D., & Ferber, M. (1986). *The Economics of Women, Men, and Work.* New Jersey: Prentice-Hall.

Blau, F. D., & Kahn, L. M. (1996). Wage structure and gender earnings differentials: An international comparison. *Economica, 63*(250), 29–62. doi:10.2307/2554808

Blau, F. D., & Kahn, L. M. (1999). Analyzing the gender pay gap. *The Quarterly Review of Economics and Finance, 39*(5), 625–646. doi:10.1016/S1062-9769(99)00021-6

Blau, P. M. (1964). *Exchange and power in social life.* New York: John Wiley.

Bloom, B. (1956). *The Taxonomy of educational objectives: Classification of educational goals handbook 1: The cognitive domain.* New York: McKay Press.

Boehm, B. (1981). *Software Engineering Economics.* Englewood Cliffs: Prentice-Hall.

Boehm, B., Horowitz, E., Madachy, R., Reifer, D., Clark, B. K., Steece, B., et al. (2000). *Software Cost Estimation with COCOMO II.* Upper Saddle River: Prentice Hall.

Boehm, B. (1981). *Software engineering economics.* Upper Saddle River, NJ: Prentice Hall.

Boehm, B., et al. (Eds.). (2000). *Software cost estimation with COCOMO II.* Upper Saddle River, NJ: Prentice Hall.

Boehm, B., Abts, C., & Chulani, S. (2000). Software development cost estimation approaches - a survey. *Annals of Software Engineering, 10*(1-4), 177–205. doi:10.1023/A:1018991717352

Bolton, R., & Bolton, D. G. (1984). *Social Style / Management Style.* New York: A.M.A.

Bontis, N., & Choo, C. W. (2001). *Strategic management of intellectual capital and organizational knowledge.* New York: Oxford University Press.

Booch, G., Rumbaugh, J., & Jacobson, I. (2005). *The unified modelling language user guide.* Reading, MA: Addison-Wesley.

Boraas, S., & Rodgers, W. M. (2003). How does gender play a role in the earnings gap? *Monthly Labor Review, 126*(3), 9–15.

Borman, W. C., & Hallman, G. L. (1991). Observation Accuracy for assessors of work sample performance. *The Journal of Applied Psychology, 76*(4).

Bouas, K., & Arrow, H. (1996). The development of group identity in computer and face-to-face groups with membership change. *Computer Supported Cooperative Work, 4*(2-3), 153–178. doi:10.1007/BF00749745

Bourdieu, P. (1986). The forms of capital. In Richardson, J. G. (Ed.), *Handbook of Theory and Research in Sociology of Education* (pp. 241–258). New York: Greenwook.

Bourque, P., Buglione, L., Abran, A., & April, A. (2004). Bloom's Taxonomy Levels for Three Software Engineer Profiles. In *Proceedings of the Eleventh Annual International Workshop on Software Technology and Engineering Practice* (STEP'04).

Boxall, P. (1998). Achieving competitive advantage through human resource strategy: towards a theory of industry dynamics. *Human Resource Management Review, 8*(3), 265–288. doi:10.1016/S1053-4822(98)90005-5

BP – Bank of Portugal. (2007a). *Relatório dos sistemas de pagamentos e de liquidação interbancária.* Available online at http://www.bportugal.pt/bank/payments/rel_sp2007_p.pdf [10 March 2009].

BP – Bank of Portugal. (2007a). *Relatório dos sistemas de pagamentos e de liquidação interbancária.* Retrieved March 10, 2009, from http://www.bportugal.pt/bank/payments/rel_sp2007_p.pdf

Brewster, C. (1999). Strategic Human Resource Management: the value of different paradigms. *Management International Review, 39*(3), 45–64.

Briggs, I., Kirby, L. K., & Myers, K. D. (1998). *Introduction to Type. A Guide to understanding your results on the Myers-Briggs Type Indicator* (6th ed.). Anaheim, CA: Consulting Psychologists Press.

Briggs, R. O., Vreede, G. J. D., Nunamaker, J., & Sprague, R. (2003). Special issue: information system success. *Journal of Management Information Systems, 19*(4), 5–8.

Brito, P. (2009). *Portugal é o Terceiro País da Europa nas Redes Sociais.* Retrieved February 22, 2009, from http://dn.sapo.pt/inicio/tv/interior.aspx?content_id=1151669

Bronstein, I. N., Semendyayev, K. A., Musion, G., & Muehlig, H. (2002). *Handbook of mathematics.* Berlin: Springer.

Brookfield, S. (1991). The development of critical reflection in adulthood. *New Education, 13*(1), 39–48.

Brown, J. (2003). *Ten writing tips for creating an effective code of conduct.* Washington, DC: Ethics Resource Center.

Brusilovsky, P. (2001). Adaptive educational hypermedia, Intelligent Computer and Communications Technology, Learning in On-Line Communities. In *Proceedings of the Tenth International PEG Conference, Digital Media Institute*, University of Technology, Tampere, Finland.

Brusilovsky, P. (1996). Methods and techniques of adaptive hypermedia. *User Modeling and User-Adapted Interaction, 6*(2-3), 87–129. doi:doi:10.1007/BF00143964

Buchinsky, M. (1994). Changes in the U.S. wage structure 1963-1987: Application of quantile regression. *Econometrica: Journal of the Econometric Society, 62*(2), 405–458. doi:10.2307/2951618

Buchinsky, M. (1998). The dynamics of changes in the female wage distribution in the USA: A quantile regression approach. *Journal of Applied Econometrics, 13*(1), 1–30. doi:10.1002/(SICI)1099-1255(199801/02)13:1<1::AID-JAE474>3.0.CO;2-A

Burke, R. (1999). *Project Management: Planning & Control Techniques.* New York: John Wiley and Sons Ltd.

Burt, R. S. (1992). The social structure of competition. In Nohria & Eccles (Eds.), *Networks and organizations structure, form, and action* (pp. 57-82). Boston, MA: Harvard Business School Press.

Calabrese, G., & Erbetta, F. (2005). Outsourcing and firm performance: evidence from Italian automotive suppliers. *International Journal of Automotive Technology and Management, 5*(4), 461–479. doi:10.1504/IJATM.2005.008585

Callahan, D., & Pedigo, B. (2002). Educating Experienced IT Professionals by Addressing Industry's Needs. *IEEE Software, 19*(5), 57–62. doi:10.1109/MS.2002.1032855

Callison, R., & MacDonald, M. (2009). *A Bibliography of the Personal Software Process (PSP) and the Team Software Process (TSP)* (Tech. Rep. CMU/SEI-2009-SR-025). Pittsburgh, PA: Carnegie Mellow University, Software Engineering Institute.

Cambridge University Press. (2009). *Cambridge Advanced Learner's Dictionary Online Dictionary.* Retrieved November 20, 2009, from http://dictionary.cambridge.org/define.asp? key=22599&dict=CALD

Cameron, J. (2006). Governance structure, mechanisms and methods for managing collaborative eBusiness projects. *Journal on Chain and Network Science, 6*(2), 155–174. doi:10.3920/JCNS2006.x072

Campos, H. (2005). Ética e tecnologia - uma parceria que pode dar certo. *Revista Pessoal, 38.*

Campos, H. (2006a, May/June). Gestão ética nos negócios: não há responsabilidade social sem ética nos negócios. *Recursos humanos magazine, 44.*

Campos, H. (2006b, November). Dossier «Ética Empresarial» Reportagem: Do que é que se fala... *Revista Pessoal, 51.*

Campos, H., & Amaral, L. (2006c, September). Codes of ethics in IST: comparative analisys. In *Proceedings of the International Conference Softwars 2006*, Universidade do Minho, Guimarães, Portugal.

Campos, H., & Amaral, L. (2007a, January). Proposta de um modelo para o processo de desenvolvimento de um código de ética/conduta/práticas. In *Proceedings of the International Conference CAPSI 2006 - 7ª Conferência da Associação Portuguesa de Sistemas de Informação*, Universidade de Aveiro, Aveiro, Portugal.

Campos, H., & Amaral, L. (2007b, November). *Structure and writing of a code of ethics/conduct/practices.* Paper presented at the International Conference ICT, Transparency and Social Responsibility, Lisboa, Portugal.

Campos, H., & Amaral, L. (2009a, February). *Sytem of interactive sustainability and support for GOTOPS code -SSIGOTOPS.* Paper presented at the IADIS International Conference e-Society 2009, Barcelona, Spain.

Campos, H., & Amaral, L. (2009b, October). *Code of tecnoethics governance for the sustainable portuguese organisations - GOTOPS code.* Paper presented at the CENTERIS'2009 - Conference on ENTERprise Information Systems – aligning technology, organizations and people, Ofir, Portugal.

Canady, R., & Rettig, M. (1995). The power of innovative scheduling. *Educational Leadership, 53*(3), 4–10.

Canfora, G., Cimitile, A., Di Lucca, G. A., & Visaggio, C. A. (2006). How distribution affects the success of pair programming. *International Journal of Software Engineering and Knowledge Engineering, 16*(2), 293–313. doi:10.1142/S0218194006002756

Capretz, L. F. (2003). Personality types in software engineering. *International Journal of Human-Computer Studies, 58*(2), 207–214. doi:10.1016/S1071-5819(02)00137-4

Carbonell, J. G., Larkin, J. H., & Reif, F. (1983). *Towards a General Scientific Reasoning Engine* (Tech. Rep. pp. 445-457). Computer Science Department.

Cardoso, G. (Coord.) (2007). *E-Generation: Os Usos de Media pelas Crianças e Jovens em Portugal.* CIES-ISCTE.

Cardoso, A. R. (1996). Women at work and economic development: Who's pushing what? *The Review of Radical Political Economics, 28*(3), 1–34. doi:10.1177/048661349602800301

Carmel, E. (1999). *Global Software Teams: collaborating across borders and time zones.* Upper Saddle River, NJ: Prentice Hall.

Carmel, E., & Agarwal, R. (2001). Tactical Approaches for Alleviating Distance in Global Software Development. *IEEE Software, 18*(2), 22–29. doi:10.1109/52.914734

Carro, R. Mª. (2001). *Un mecanismo basado en tareas y reglas para la creación de sistemas hipermedia adaptativos: aplicación a la educación a través de Internet.* Unpublished doctoral dissertation, University Autónoma de Madrid, Spain. Retrieved November 2009, from http://www.ii.uam.es/%7Ercarro/tesis/tesis.html.

Carvalho, R. (2009). *Igreja Usa MySpace para Recrutar Religiosos.* Retrieved April 27, 2009, from http://dn.sapo.pt/inicio/portugal/interior.aspx?content_id=1213325

Casado-Lumbreras, C., Colomo-Palacios, R., Gomez-Berbis, M. J., & Garcia-Crespo, A. (2009). Mentoring Programmes: A Study of the Spanish Software Industry. *International Journal of Learning and Intellectual Capital, 6*(3), 293–302. doi:10.1504/IJLIC.2009.025046

Cascio, W. F., & Shurygailo, S. (2003). E-Leadership and Virtual Teams. *Organizational Dynamics, 31*(4), 362–376. doi:10.1016/S0090-2616(02)00130-4

Casey, V., & Richardson, I. (2006a). Project Management within Virtual Software Teams. In *Proceedings of the IEEE international conference on Global Software Engineering* (pp. 33-42). Washington, DC: IEEE Computer Society.

Cash, E., Yoong, P., & Huff, S. (2004). The impact of E-commerce on the role of IS professionals. *The Data Base for Advances in Information Systems, 3*(3), 50–63.

Cattell, R. B., Cattell, A. K., & Cattell, H. E. P. (1993). *Sixteen Personality Factor Questionnaire.* Chicago: Institute for Personality and Ability Testing.

Cawelti, G. (1994). *High School Restructuring: a national study*. Arlington, VA: Educational Research Service.

Cercone, K. (2008). Characteristics of adult learners with implications for online learning design. *AACE Journal*, *16*(2), 137–159.

Chaffee, J. (1998). *Critical thinking: The cornerstone of remedial education*. Paper presented at the Conference on Replacing Remediation in Higher Education, Stanford University, Stanford CA.

Champy, J. (1997). It's not who you hire, it's who you keep. *Computerworld*, *31*(39).

Chao, G. T., Walz, P. M., & Gardner, P. D. (1992). Formal and Informal Mentorships: A Comparison on Mentoring Functions and Contrast with Nonmentored Counterparts. *Personnel Psychology*, *45*, 619–636.

Charette, R. N. (2005). Why software fails. *IEEE Spectrum*, *42*(9), 42–49. doi:10.1109/MSPEC.2005.1502528

Chatman, J. A., & Flynn, F. J. (2001). The influence of demographic heterogeneity on the emergence and consequences of cooperative norms in work teams. *Academy of Management Journal*, *44*(5), 956–974. doi:10.2307/3069440

Chesebrough, P. H., & Davis, G. B. (1983). Planning a career path in information systems. *Journal of Systems Management*, *34*(1), 6–13.

Chitiris, L. (2001). *Human Resources Management*. Athens, Greece: Publications Interbooks.

CIOMAG. (2007). The STATE of the CIO '07. *CIO Magazine*.

Círculo de progreso (2005). *Informe Infoempleo 2005: Oferta y Demanda del empleo cualificado en España*. Madrid, Spain: Círculo de Progreso.

Cockburn, A. (2000). *Characterizing People as Non-Linear, First-Order Components in Software Development*. Paper presented at the 4th International Multi-Conference on Systems, Cybernetics and Informatics, FL.

Cohen, D., & Prusak, L. (2001). How to invest in social capital. *Harvard Business Review*, *79*(5), 86–93.

Cohen, W. M., & Levinthal, D. A. (1990, March). Absorptive Capacity: A New Perspective on Learning and Innovation. *Administrative Science Quarterly*, *35*(1), 128–152. doi:10.2307/2393553

Cole, G. A. (1999). *Management theory and practice* (5th ed.). Edinburgh, UK: Letts.

Coleman, J. S. (1988). Social capital in the creation of human capital. *American Journal of Sociology*, *94*, 95–120. doi:10.1086/228943

Collerette, P., & Delisle, G. (1988). *La planificación del cambio*. México: Editorial Trillas.

Colomo-Palacios, R., Gomez-Berbis, M. J., Garcia-Crespo, A., & Puebla-Sánchez, I. (2008). Social Global Repository: Using Semantics and Social Web in Software Projects. *International Journal of Knowledge and Learning*, *4*(5), 452–464. doi:10.1504/IJKL.2008.022063

Colomo-Palacios, R., Tovar-Caro, E., Garcia-Crespo, A., & Gomez-Berbis, M. J. (2010). Identifying Technical Competences of IT Professionals. The Case of Software Engineers. *International Journal of Human Capital and Information Technology Professionals*, *1*(1), 31–43.

Colwill, J., & Townsend, J. (1999). Women, leadership and information technology: The impact of women leaders in organizations and their role in integrating information technology with corporate strategy. *Journal of Management Development*, *18*(3), 207–216. doi:10.1108/02621719910261049

Comisión de las Comunidades Europeas. (2003). *Recomendación de la Comisión, de 6 de mayo de 2003*. Sobre la definición de microempresas y pequeñas y medianas empresas: Bruselas.

Conchúir, E. Ó., Ågerfalk, P. J., Olsson, H. H., & Fitzgerald, B. (2009). Global software development: where are the benefits? *Communications of the ACM*, *52*(8), 127–131.

Constantine, L. (2001). *Peopleware Papers: The Notes on the Human Side of Software*. Englewood Cliffs, NJ: Prentice-Hall.

Cook, A. A., & Davis, C. K. (2003). *Shifting gears to accommodate diversity: how and why an information systems project manager should customize leadership style to suit multicultural team.* Paper presented at the 2003 Southwest Decision Sciences Institute Conference (SWDSI2003) (pp. 126-31).

Cooke-Davies, T. (2002). The 'real' success factors on projects. *International Journal of Project Management, 20*(3), 185–190. doi:10.1016/S0263-7863(01)00067-9

Coombs, R., Saviotti, P., & Walsh, V. (1987). *Economics and technological change.* New Jersey: Rownam & Littlefield.

Cooper, B. (1988). *Winning at new products.* London: Kogan Page.

Cooper, R., & Kaplan, R. S. (1988). Measure costs right: Make the right decisions. *Harvard Business Review, 66*(5), 96–103.

Cotec (2007). *Informe Tecnología e innovación en España.* Madrid, Spain: Fundación Cotec para la innovación tecnológica.

Cotter, D. A., Hermsen, J. M., Ovadia, S., & Vanneman, R. (2001). The glass ceiling effect. *Social Forces, 80*(2), 655–682. doi:10.1353/sof.2001.0091

Couger, J. D. (1989). Preparing IS Students To Deal with Ethical Issues. *Management Information Systems Quarterly, 13*(2), 211–218. doi:10.2307/248930

Coutinho, C., & Junior, J. (2007). Blog e Wiki: Os Futuros Professores e as Ferramentas da Web 2.0. In *Proceedings of SIIE, 2007*, 199–204.

Cramton, C. D. (2001). The mutual knowledge problem and its consequences for dispersed collaboration. *Organization Science, 12*(3), 346–371. doi:10.1287/orsc.12.3.346.10098

Cramton, C. D. (2002). Attribution in distributed work groups. In Hinds, P. J., & Kiesler, S. (Eds.), *Distributed Work* (pp. 91–212). Cambridge, MA: MIT Press.

Crane, A., & Matten, D. (2004). *Business Ethics: a european perspective - Managing Citizenship and Sustainability in Age of Globalization.* New York: Oxford University Press.

Cress, U., & Kimmerle, J. (2008). A systemic and cognitive view on collaborative knowledge building with wikis. *International Journal of Computer-Supported Collaborative Learning, 3*(2), 105–122. doi:10.1007/s11412-007-9035-z

Csikszentmihalyi, M. (1982). *Beyond boredom and anxiety.* San Francisco, CA: Jossey and Bass.

Cubranic, D., Murphy, G. C., Singer, J., & Booth, K. S. (2005). Hipikat: a project memory for software development. *IEEE Transactions on Software Engineering, 31*(6), 446–465. doi:10.1109/TSE.2005.71

Cukier, W., Shortt, D., & Devine, I. (2002). Gender and information technology: Implications of definitions. *SIGCSE Bulletin, 34*(4), 142–148. doi:10.1145/820127.820188

Cumming, B. (1999). Understanding Innovation form the cradle to the grave. In M. Zairi (Ed.), *Best Practice: Process innovation management.* Oxford: Butterworth-Heinemann.

Curtis, B. (2002), Human Factors in Software Development. In J.J. Marciniak (Ed.), *Encyclopedia of Software Engineering* (pp. 598-610). Willey & Sons.

Curtis, B., Hefley, W.E., & Miller, S.A. (2001). *People Capability Maturity Model (P-CMM®) Version 2.0.* CMU/SEI-2001-MM-01.

Curtis, B., Krasner, M. I., & Iscoe, N. (1988). A field study of the software design process for large systems. *Communications of the ACM, 31*(11), 1268–1287. doi:10.1145/50087.50089

D'Souza, Q. (2006). *RSS Ideas for educators.* Retrieved November 2009, from https://www.drexel.edu/IRT/rmcweb/RSS-for-Educators.pdf

Damanpour, F. (1990). Innovation effectiveness, adoption and organisational performance. In M.A. West & J.L. Farr (Eds.), *Innovation and Creativity at Work.* Chichester: Wiley.

Damásio, M., & Poupa, C. (2009). Perfis de Actividades de Utilizadores da Internet: Um Estudo Comparativo Profiling On-Line Users Activities: A Comparative Study. *Observatorio (OBS). Journal, 8*, 28–39.

Daniel, E. L. (2000). A review of time shortened courses across disciplines. *College Student Journal, 34*, 298–308.

Davies, M. F., & Kanaki, E. (2006). Interpersonal characteristics associated with different team roles in work groups. *Journal of Managerial Psychology, 21*(7), 638–650. doi:10.1108/02683940610690187

Davila, T., Epstein, M. J., & Shelton, R. (2006). *Making Innovation Work: How to Manage It, Measure It, and Profit from It"*. Wharton School Publishing.

Day, J., & Bobeva, M. (2003). Successful IS project leaders: a situational theory perspective. *Electronic Journal of Information Systems Evaluation, 6*(2), 75–86.

De Bra, P., & Calvi, L. (1998). AHA! an open adaptive hypermedia architecture. *New Review of Hypermedia and Multimedia, 4*, 115–139. doi:doi:10.1080/13614569808914698

De Carvalho, L. R. (2003). *Planejamento da alocação de recursos humanos em Ambientes de desenvolvimento de software orientados à Organização. Tese para a obtenção do grau de mestre em ciências em engenharia de sistemas e computação*. Brasil: Universidade Federal do Rio de Janeiro.

De la Rica, S., Dolado, J. J., & Llorens, V. (2005). *Ceilings and floors: Gender wage gaps by education in Spain* (Discussion Paper No. 1483). Bonn, Germany: Institute for the Study of Labor.

De Marco, T., & Lister, T. (1985). Programmer Performance and the effects of the workplace. In *Proceedings of the 8th International Conference on Software Engineering* (pp. 268-272).

De Marco, T., & Lister, T. (1999). *Peopleware: Productive Projects and Teams* (2nd ed.). New York: Dorset House.

De Wit, A. (1988). Measurement of project success. *International Journal of Project Management, 6*(2), 321–331.

Delery, J. E., & Doty, D. H. (1996). Modes of theorizing in Strategic Human Resource Management: Test of Universalistic, Contingency, and Configurational performance predictions. *Academy of Management Journal, 39*(4), 802–835. doi:10.2307/256713

DeMarco, T., & Lister, T. (1987). *Peopleware: productive projects and teams*. New York: Dorset House Publishing Co.

Department of Agriculture and Food. Western Australia (DAFWA). (2007). *e-Variety Profiler for Western Australia*. Retrieved December 2, 2009, from http://www.agric.wa.gov.au/content/fcp/evarietyprofiler_2006.htm

Devito, A., & Greathead, D. (2004). *Code review and personality: is performance linked to MBTI type?* (Tech. Rep. No. CS-TR 837). Newcastle, DE: University of Newcastle, School of Computing Science.

Dewayne, E. P., Adam, A. P., & Lawrence, A. V. (2000). Empirical Studies of Software Engineering. In *Proceedings of International Conference on Software Engineering* (pp. 345-355).

Dewey, J. (1916). *Democracy and Education*. New York: The Macmillan.

Dex, S., & Sloane, P. J. (1988). Detecting and removing discrimination under equal opportunities policies. *Journal of Economic Surveys, 2*(1), 1–27. doi:10.1111/j.1467-6419.1988.tb00034.x

Diao, X., Hazell, P., Resnick, D., & Thurlow, J. (2007). *The role of agriculture in development: Implications for Sub-Saharan Africa*. Washington, DC: IFPRI.

Dictionary.com. LLC. (2009). *Delivery*. Retrieved November 9, 2009, from http://dictionary.reference.com/browse/delivery eagriculture.org. (2009). *What is eAgriculture?* Retrieved April 5, 2009, from http://eagriculture.org/

Dillenbourg, P., Baker, M., Blaye, A., & O'Malley, C. (1996). The Evolution of research on Collaborative Learning. In Spada, E., & Reiman, P. (Eds.), *Learning in humans and machine: Towards an interdisciplinary learning science* (pp. 189–221). Oxford, UK: Elsevier.

Dimou, N. (2003). *Personnel Management* (2nd ed.). Athens, Greece: Ellin.

Dinges, D. I., & Powell, J. W. (1985). Microcomputer analysis of performance on a portable, simple visual RT task sustained operations. *Behavior Research Methods, Instruments, & Computers, 17*, 652–655.

DIRCE. (2006). *Directorio Central de Empresas*.

Dobán, O., & Pataricza, A. (2001). Cost estimation driven software development process. In *Proceedings of the 27th EUROMICRO Conference* (pp. 208-213).

Domberger, S. (1999). *The contracting organization: A strategic guide to outsourcing.* New York: Oxford University Press.

Donaldson, B., & O'Toole, T. (2007). *Strategic Market Relationships: From Strategy to Implementation.* Chichester: John Wiley & Sons.

Dooley, L., & O'Sullivan, D. (2003). Developing a software infrastructure to support systemic innovation through effective management. *The International Journal of Technological Innovation and Entrepreneurship (Technovation), 23*(8), 689–704.

Downes, S. (2002). *An introduction to RSS for educational designers.* Retrieved November 2009, from http://www.downes.ca/files/RSS_Educ.htm

Dresner, H., Linden, A., Buytendijk, F., Friedman, T., Strange, K., Knox, M., & Camm, M. (2002). *The business intelligence competency center: an essential business strategy.* Gartner, Inc.

Driscoll, D.-M., & Hoffman, W. M. (2000). *Ethics Matters: How to Implement Values-driven management.* Washington, DC: Ethics Resource Center.

Drucker, P. F. (1985). *Innovation and Entrepreneurship: Practice and principles.* London: Heinemann.

Drucker, P. (1986). *Innovation and entrepreneurship.* London: William Heinemann Ltd.

Drucker, P. F. (1992). The new society of organizations. *Harvard Business Review, 70*(5), 95–104.

Duffy, P., & Bruns, A. (2006). The use of blogs, wikis and RSS in education: A conversation of possibilities. In *Proceedings of the Online Learning and Teaching Conference*, Brisbane, Australia (pp. 31-38).

Duggan, R. (1999). Idea Generation: Creative problem solving and innovation. In M. Zairi (Ed.), *Best Practice: Process innovation management.* Oxford: Butterworth-Heinemann.

Dunn, R., & Dunn, K. (1978). *Teaching students through their individual learning styles: A practical approach.* Reston, VA: Reston Publishing.

Dvorak, D. E. (1988). *References, resumes and other lies.* Industry Week.

Eagly, A. H., & Steffan, V. J. (1984). Gender Stereotypes Stem from the Distribution of Women and men into Social Roles. *Journal of Personality and Social Psychology, 46,* 735–754. doi:10.1037/0022-3514.46.4.735

Ebert, C., & DeNeve, P. (2001). Surviving global software development. *IEEE Software, 18*(2), 62–69. doi:10.1109/52.914748

Edwards, C., Ward, J., & Bytheway, A. (1991). *The Essence of Information Systems.* London: Prentice-Hall International.

Edwards, K., & Sridhar, V. (2005). Analysis of Software Requirements Engineering Exercises in a Global Virtual Team Setup. *Journal of Global Information Management, 13*(2), 21–41.

Ehrlenspiel, K., Kiewert, A., Lindemann, U., & Hundal, M. S. (2007). *Cost-efficient design.* Berlin: Springer.

Ekoja, I. I. (2004). Sensitising users for increased information use: the case of Nigerian farmers. *African Journal of Library. Archives and Information Science, 14*(2), 193–204.

Ekvall, G. (1991). The Organisational Culture of Idea-Management: A creative climate for the management of ideas. In J. Henry & D. Walker (Eds.), *Managing Innovation.* London: Sage Publishing.

Ellis, H. J. C. (2006). An evaluation of learning in an online project-based web application design and development course. *Journal of Computing Sciences in Colleges, 21*(6), 217–227.

Enns, H. G., Huff, S. L., & Golden, B. R. (2001). How CIOs obtain peer commitment to strategic IS proposals: barriers and facilitators. *The Journal of Strategic Information Systems, 10*(1), 3–14. doi:10.1016/S0963-8687(01)00041-5

Eppler, M. J., & Mengis, J. (2004). The Concept of Information Overload - A Review of Literature from Organization Science, Accounting, Marketing, MIS, and Related Disciplines. *The Information Society: An International Journal, 20*(5), 1–20.

Escorsa, P., & Valls, J. (1997). *Tecnología e innovación en la empresa. Dirección y gestión.* Barcelona, Spain: Ediciones de la Universitat Politécnica de Catalunya.

Espana, J. (2004). Teaching a research-oriented, graduate global marketing course to adult learners in a one-month format. *Journal of American Academy of Business*, 4(1-2), 418.

Essigkrug, A., & Mey, T. (2007). *Rational Unified Process kompakt*. Berlin: Spektrum Akademischer Verlag. doi:10.1007/978-3-8274-2435-8

Evans, J. R., & Olson, D. L. (2002). *Introduction to simulation and risk analysis*. Upper Saddle River, NJ: Prentice Hall.

Evaristo, J. R., Scudder, R., Desouza, K. C., & Sato, O. (2004). A dimensional analysis of geographically distributed project teams: a case study. *Journal of Engineering and Technology Management*, 21(3), 175–189. doi:10.1016/j.jengtecman.2003.05.001

Expresso. (2009). *As melhores agências estão em Portugal*. Retrieved March 20, 2009, from http://aeiou.expresso.pt/economia/noticiario?p=arquivo

Fairhurst, G. T., & Snavely, B. K. (1983). Majority and token minority group relationships: Power acquisition and communication. *Academy of Management Review*, 8(2), 292–300. doi:10.2307/257757

Falkenberg, L. (1990). Improving the Accuracy of Stereotypes within the Workplace. *Journal of Management*, 16(1), 107–118. doi:10.1177/014920639001600108

Faraj, S., & Sambamurthy, V. (2006). Leadership of information systems development projects. *IEEE Transactions on Engineering Management*, 53(2), 238–249. doi:10.1109/TEM.2006.872245

Faraj, S., & Sproull, L. (2000). Coordinating expertise in software development teams. *Management Science*, 46(12), 1554–1568. doi:10.1287/mnsc.46.12.1554.12072

Farr, J. L., & Ford, C. M. (1990). Individual Innovation. In M.A. West & J.L. Farr (Eds.), *Innovation and Creativity at Work*. Chichester: Wiley.

Felder, R. M., & Silverman, L. K. (1988). Learning and teaching styles in engineering education. *Journal of Engineering Education*, 78(7), 674–681.

Ferreira, A., & Lourenço, T. (2009). *Crianças Navegam na Internet sem o Controlo dos Pais*. Retrieved February 11, 2009, from http://dn.sapo.pt/inicio/interior.aspx?content_id=1172586

Ferreira, F. (2002). *Inovação tecnológica no sistema financeiro português: Evolução e perspectivas*. Master Dissertation in Economics and Business Sciences, Faculty of Economics, University of Algarve.

Ferreira, F., & Cravo, P. (2004). Technological progress: An important variable in the Portuguese banking system structure reform? *Proceedings of the IADIS International Conference www/Internet 2004* (II), October, Madrid, Spain, 1139–1142.

Ferreira, F. (2003). *Inovação tecnológica no sistema financeiro português: Evolução e perspectivas*. Coimbra: Pé-de-Página Edition.

Ferreira, F. (2005). Impacto tecnológico na estrutura do sector financeiro em Portugal: Ensaio empírico e pistas para uma reflexão. *Portuguese Journal of Management Studies*, X(1), 71–87.

Fisher, J., Hirschheim, R., & Jacobs, R. (2008). Understanding the outsourcing learning curve: A longitudinal analysis of a large Australian company. *Information Systems Frontiers*, 10(2), 165–178. doi:10.1007/s10796-008-9070-y

Fletcher, C. (1992). Ethics and the job interview. *Personnel management*.

Food and Agriculture Organization of the United Nations (FAO). (2000). *The role of information and communication technologies in rural development and food security*. Retrieved September 24, 2009, from http://www.fao.org/sd/CDdirect/CDre0055.htm

Ford, G., & Gibbs, N. E. (1996). *A Mature Profession of Software Engineering*. Technical CMU/SEI-96-TR-004, Pittsburgh, PA: Software Engineering Institute, Carnegie Mellon University.

Fowler, F. J. (1993). *Survey Research Methods* (2nd ed.). Newbury Park, CA: Sage.

Frey, B., & Alman, S. (2003). Applying adult learning theory to the online classroom. *New Horizons in Adult Education*, 17(1), 4–12.

Friedman, T. (2005). *Data integration forms the technology foundation of EIM*. Gartner, Inc.

Fujimoto, T. (2005). *Imagination of Information Design*. Tokyo, Japan: Pleiades Publisher.

Fukuyama, F. (1995). *Trust: The social virtues and the creation of prosperity*. New York: The Free press.

Fyock, C. D. (1991). *Expanding the talent search: 19 ways to recruit top talent*. H.R Magazine.

Gaertner, S. L., Mann, J. A., Dovidio, J. F., Murrell, A. J., & Pomare, M. (1990). How does cooperation reduce intergroup bias? *Journal of Personality and Social Psychology*, *59*(4), 692–704. doi:10.1037/0022-3514.59.4.692

Galinec, D. (2010). Human capital management process based on information technology models and governance. *International Journal of Human Capital and Information Technology Professionals*, *1*(1), 44–60.

Galinec, D., & Vidović, S. (2007). Methodology framework for process integration and service management. [Faculty of Organization and Informatics Varaždin - University of Zagreb.]. *Journal of Information and Organizational Sciences*, *31*(1), 37–49.

Gannon, J. D. (1979). Human factors in Software Engineering. *Computer*, *12*(12), 6–7. doi:10.1109/MC.1979.1658569

García, G. (2005). Herramienta para el diagnóstico de la resistencia al cambio durante el desarrollo de proyectos mayores. *Estudios gerenciales, 96*(3), 57-106.

Garcia-Crespo, A., Colomo-Palacios, R., Gomez-Berbis, M. J., & Mencke, M. (2009a). BMR: Benchmarking Metrics Recommender for Personnel issues in Software Development Projects. *International Journal of Computational Intelligence Systems*, *2*(3), 257–267. doi:10.2991/ijcis.2009.2.3.7

Garcia-Crespo, A., Colomo-Palacios, R., Gomez-Berbis, M. J., & Paniagua-Martin, F. (2008b). A Case of System Dynamics Education in Software Engineering Courses. *IEEE Multidisciplinary Engineering Education Magazine*, *3*(2), 52–59.

Garcia-Crespo, A., Colomo-Palacios, R., Gomez-Berbis, M. J., & Tovar-Caro, E. (2008a). The IT Crowd: Are We Stereotypes? *IT Professional*, *10*(6), 46–49. doi:10.1109/MITP.2008.134

Garcia-Crespo, A., Colomo-Palacios, R., Gomez-Berbis, M. J., & Tovar-Caro, E. (2009b). IT Professionals' Competences: High School Students' Views. *Journal of Information Technology Education*, *8*, 45–57.

García, J., Hernández, P. J., & López-Nicolás, A. (2001). How wide is the gap? An investigation of gender wage differences using quantile regression. *Empirical Economics*, *26*(1), 149–167. doi:10.1007/s001810000050

Gardeazabal, J., & Ugidos, A. (2005). Gender wage discrimination at quantiles. *Journal of Population Economics*, *18*(1), 165–179. doi:10.1007/s00148-003-0172-z

Garnham, C., & Kaleta, R. (2002). Introduction to hybrid courses. *Teaching with Technology Today, 8*(6).

Garrison, D. R. (1993). A cognitive constructivist view of distance education: An analysis of Teaching and learning assumptions. *Distance Education*, *14*(2), 199–211. doi:10.1080/0158791930140204

Gaubatz, N. (2003). Course scheduling formats and their impact on student learning. *National Teaching and Learning Forum*, *12*(1), 1–7.

Genovese, Y., & Hayward, S. (2008). *What Does It Mean to Implement a BPP?* Gartner, Inc.

Ghislein, B. (1963). Ultimate criteria for two levels of creativity. In C. Taylor & F. Barron (Eds.), *Scientific Creativity: Its recognition and development*. New York: Wiley.

Glotzbach, R. J., Mohler, J. L., & Radwan, J. E. (2007). RSS as a course information delivery method. In *Proceedings of the ACM SIGGRAPH 2007 Annual Conference and Exposition*.

Goles, T., Hawk, S., & Kaiser, K. M. (2008). Information technology workforce skills: The software and IT services provider perspective. *Information Systems Frontiers*, *10*, 179–194. doi:10.1007/s10796-008-9072-9

Gómez-Mejías, L., & Balkin, D. (2003). *Administración*. Madrid, Spain: McGraw-Hill.

Goodman, P. S., & Leyden, D. P. (1991). Familiarity and group productivity. *The Journal of Applied Psychology, 76*(44), 578–586. doi:10.1037/0021-9010.76.4.578

Gorla, N., & Wah, Y. W. (2004). Who should work with whom? Building effective software project teams. *Communications of the ACM, 47*(6), 79–82. doi:10.1145/990680.990684

Grabher, G. (1993). *The embedded firm: on the socio-economics of industrial networks.* New York: Routledge Publishing.

Graham, P. J., Linnegar, M., & Kealy, M. (2002). *Better Information delivery to Rice Growers - A pilot rice bulletin. Rural Industries Research and Development Report.* Retrieved September 27, 2009, from http://www.rirdc.gov.au/reports/RIC/02-100.pdf

Grandori, A., & Soda, G. (1995). Inter-firm networks: antecedents, mechanisms and forms. *Organization Studies, 16*(2), 183–214. doi:10.1177/017084069501600201

Grannovetter, M. S. (1985). Economic action and social structure: problem of embeddedness. *American Journal of Sociology, 91*, 481–510. doi:10.1086/228311

Grossnickle, J. (2005). RSS. *Crossing into the mainstream.* Retrieved November 2009, from http://publisher.yahoo.com/rss/RSS_whitePaper1004.pdf

Grover, V., Lederer, A. L., & Sabherwal, R. (1988). Recognizing the Politics of MIS. *Information & Management, 14*(3), 145–156. doi:10.1016/0378-7206(88)90005-5

Gruenfeld, D. H., Matorana, P. V., & Fan, E. T. (2000). What do groups learn from their worldiest members? Direct and indirect influence in dynamic teams. *Organizational Behavior and Human Decision Processes, 82*, 45–59. doi:10.1006/obhd.2000.2886

Guimarães, M. (1999). *As transferências electrónicas de fundos e os cartões de débito.* Coimbra: Livraria Almedina.

Gutiérrez, J. A., Rodríguez, D., Miltiadis, D., & Lytras, M. D. (2005). Ubiquitous Computing Panorama. *Novática, 177*, 4–7.

Hafkin, N. J., & Odame, H. H. (2002). *Gender, ICTs and agriculture. A situation analysis for the 5th Consultative Expert Meeting of CTA's ICT Observatory meeting on gender and agriculture in the information society.* Retrieved from http://www.cta.int/observatory2002/background_paper.pdf

Hafner, W., & Ellis, T. J. (2004, January 5-8). Project-Based, Asynchronous Collaborative Learning. In *Proceedings of the 37th Hawaii International Conference on System Sciences*, Waikoloa, HI.

Hagel, J., & Brown, J. S. (2005). *From push to pull: Emerging models for mobilizing resources.* Retrieved November 2009, from http://www.johnhagel.com/paper_pushpull.pdf

Hamilton, K. C. (2002). *Teaching adult learners: A supplemental manual for faculty teaching in the GBM program at FDU.* Madison, NJ: FDU.

Hammer, M., & Champy, J. (2003). *Reengineering the Corporation: A Manifesto for Business Revolution.* Collins Business Essentials.

Hammersley, B. (2003). *Content syndication with RSS.* New York: O'Reilly & Associates.

Handy, C. (1990). *The age of unreason.* Boston: Harvard Business School.

Hannan, T., & McDowell, J. (1990). The impact of technology adoption on market structure. *The Review of Economics and Statistics, 72*(1), 164–168. doi:10.2307/2109755

Harold, K. (2000). *Applied Project Management: Best Practices on Implementation.* John Wiley & Sons.

Harrington, J., Conner, D., & Horney, N. (2000). *Project Change Management: Applying Change Management to Improvement Projects.* New York: McGraw-Hill.

Harrison, D. A., Price, K. H., & Bell, M. P. (1998). Beyond relational demography: Time and the effects of surface and deep-level diversity on work group cohesion. *Academy of Management Journal, 41*(1), 96–107. doi:10.2307/256901

Hartmann, N. (1933). *Das Problem des geistigen Seins: Untersuchgn zur Grundlegung d. Geschichtsphilosophie u. d. Geisteswissenschaften.* Berlin: de Gruyter.

Hartog, J., Pereira, P. T., & Vieira, J. A. C. (2001). Changing returns to education in Portugal during the 1980s and early 1990s: OLS and quantile regression estimators. *Applied Economics, 33*(8), 1021–1037.

Harvey, F., & Brown, R. (1992). *The Experimental Approach to Organization Development* (4th ed.). London: Prentice-Hall.

Hassan, M. S., Hassan, M. A., Samah, B. A., Ismail, N., & Shaffril, H. A. M. (2008). Use of information and communication technology (ICT) among agri-based entrepreneurs in Malaysia. In *Proceedings of the World Conference on Agricultural Information and IT,* Atsugi, Japan (pp. 753-762).

Hayes, R. H., Wheelwright, S. C., & Clarke, K. B. (1988). *Dynamic Manufacturing: Creating the learning organisation.* New York: The Free Press.

Heeks, R., Krishna, S., Nicholsen, B., & Sahay, S. (2001). Synching or sinking: Global software outsourcing relationships. *IEEE Software, 18*(2), 54–60. doi:10.1109/52.914744

Hefley, W. E., & Loesche, E. A. (2006). *eSourcing Capability Model for Client Organizations (eSCM-CL) v.1.1.* Pittsburgh, PA: Carnegie Mellon University.

Heizer, J., & Render, B. (2008). *Principles of Operations Management* (7th ed.). New Jersey: Prentice-Hall.

Henderson, R. (2007). *Developing and Managing a Successful Technology and Product Strategy (MIT Lecture Notes).*

Henry, J., & Walker, D. (1991). *Managing Innovation.* London: Sage Publishing.

Henry, S. M., & Stevens, K. T. (1999). Using Belbin's Leadership Role to Improve Team Effectiveness: An Empirical Investigation. *Journal of Systems and Software, 44,* 241–250. doi:10.1016/S0164-1212(98)10060-2

Herbsleb, J. D. (2007). Global Software Engineering: The Future of Socio-technical Coordination. In *Proceedings of the International Conference on Software Engineering, 2007 Future of Software Engineering* (pp. 188-198). Washington, DC: IEEE Computer Society.

Herbsleb, J. D., & Grinter, R. E. (1999). Architectures, coordination, and distance: Conway's law and beyond. *IEEE Software, 16*(5), 63–70. doi:10.1109/52.795103

Herbsleb, J. D., & Moitra, D. (2001). Global software development. *IEEE Software, 18*(2), 16–20. doi:10.1109/52.914732

Herschel, G. (2004). *AGF gains visibility through customer segmentation.* Gartner, Inc.

Hicks, D. T. (2002). *Activity based costing.* New York: Wiley.

Hillam, C. E., & Edwards, H. M. (2001). A case study approach to evaluation of information technology/information systems (IT/IS) investment evaluation processes within SMEs. *The Electronic Journal of Information systems. Evaluation, 4*(2).

Hill, M., & Hill, A. (2005). *Investigação por questionário* (2nd ed.). Lisbon: Edições Sílabo.

Hiltz, S. R. (1990). Evaluating the virtual classroom. In Harasim, L. (Ed.), *Online education* (pp. 134–184). New York: Praeger.

Hindle, T. (2001). *How to recruit and select.* Athens, Greece: Ellinika Grammata.

Hinds, P. J., & Bailey, D. E. (2003). Out of sight, out of synch: Understanding conflict in distributed teams. *Organization Science, 14*(6), 615–632. doi:10.1287/orsc.14.6.615.24872

Holincheck, J. (2008). *The Impact of SOA on HCM Applications.* Gartner, Inc.

Hoogeweegen, M., Teunissen, W., Vervest, P., & Wagenaar, R. (1999). Modular network design: using information and communication technology to allocate production tasks in a virtual organization. *Decision Sciences, 30*(4), 1073–1103. doi:10.1111/j.1540-5915.1999.tb00919.x

Horngren, C. T., Foster, G., Datar, S. M., Rajan, M. V., & Ittner, C. (2008). *Cost accounting: A managerial emphasis.* Upper Saddle River, NJ: Prentice Hall.

Horn, L. (1996). *Nontraditional Undergraduates.* Washington, DC: U.S. Department of Education.

Hottenstein, D., & Malatesta, C. (1993). Putting a school in gear with intensive scheduling. *The High School Magazine, 1*(2), 28–29.

Hough, L. M. (1990). Criterion - related validities of personality constructs and the effect of response distortion on those validities. *The Journal of Applied Psychology,* 74.

House, D., de Vreede, G. J., Wolcott, P., & Dick, K. (2008). Success Factors for the Global Implementation of ERP/HRMS Software. In Ferran, C., & Salim, R. (Eds.), *Enterprise Resource Planning for Global Economies: Managerial Issues and Challenges* (pp. 289–307). Hershey, PA: IGI Global.

Hsu, J. (2007). Innovative Technologies for Education and Learning: Education and Knowledge-Oriented Applications of Blogs, Wikis, Podcasts, and More. *International Journal of Information and Communication Technology Education, 3*(3), 70–89.

Huang, S., Chang, I., Li, S., & Lin, M. (2004). Assessing risk in ERP projects: identify and prioritize the factors. *Industrial Management & Data Systems, 104*(8/9), 681–690. doi:10.1108/02635570410561672

Huettner, B., Brown, M. K., & James-Tanny, C. (2007). *Managing virtual teams: Getting the most from wikis, blogs, and other collaborative tools.* Plano, TX: Wordware Publishing, Inc.

Humphrey, W. S. (1998). *Managing Technical People: Innovation, Teamwork and the Software Process.* Reading, MA: Addison-Wesley.

Humphrey, J., & Schmitz, H. (1998). Trust and interfirm relations in developing and transition economies. *The Journal of Development Studies, 34*(4), S32–S61. doi:10.1080/00220389808422528

Humphrey, W. S. (1995). *A Discipline for Software Engineering.* Boston: Addison-Wesley.

Humphrey, W. S. (1995). Introducing the personal software process. *Annals of Software Engineering, 1*(1), 311–325. doi:10.1007/BF02249055

Humphrey, W. S. (1998). *Managing Technical People: Innovation, Teamwork and the Software Process.* Boston: Addison-Wesley.

Humphrey, W. S. (1998). Three Dimensions of Process Improvement. Part III: The Team Software Process. *Crosstalk, 11*(4), 14–17.

Humphrey, W. S. (2000). *Introduction to the Team Software Process.* Reading, MA: Addison-Wesley.

Humphrey, W. S. (2002). Three Process Perspectives: Organizations, Teams, and People. *Annals of Software Engineering, 14*(1-4), 39–72. doi:10.1023/A:1020593305601

Hunt, J. W. (1984). The shifting focus of the personnel function. *Personnel Management, 16*(2), 14–18.

Huse, E. (1985). *Organization Development and Change* (3rd ed.). London: West Publishing.

Hyder, E. B., Heston, K. M., & Paulk, M. C. (2006). *The sCM-SP v2.01: The eSourcing Capability Model for Service Providers (eSCM-SP) v2.01, Part 2: Practice Details.* Pittsburgh, PA: Carnegie Mellon University.

Iacocca, L., & Novak, W. (1984). *Iacocca: An Autobiography.* New York: Bantam.

Ibarra, H., & Andrews, S. B. (1993). Power, social influence and sensemaking: Effects of network centrality and proximity on employee perceptions. *Administrative Science Quarterly, 38*(2), 277–303. doi:10.2307/2393414

IEEE. (2004). *Guide to the Software Engineering Body of Knowledge-SWEBOK (2004 Version).* Washington, DC: IEEE Computer Society.

INE – Instituto Nacional de Estatística. (2009). *População residente em Santarém.* Retrieved April 2, 2009, from http://www.ine.pt

INE. (2006). *Encuesta sobre Innovación Tecnológica en las Empresas.* Instituto Nacional de Estadística.

INE. (2007). *Lista das 1000 maiores empresas portuguesas. Ficheiro de Unidades Estatísticas - FUE - Base Belém:* Instituto Nacional de Estatística.

Information Technology Association of America. (2004, September). In *Proceedings of the Adding Value...Growing Careers: Annual Workforce Development Study,* Arlington, VA.

Initiative, J. (1998). *Voluntary Codes: A Guide for Their Development and Use.*

International Institute for Communication and Development. IICD. (2006). *ICTs for agricultural livelihoods: Impact and lessons learned from IICD supported activities.* The Hague: The Netherlands: IICD.

Irivwieri, J. W. (2007). Information needs of illiterate female farmers in Ethiopia East local government area of Delta State. *Library Hi Tech News, 9*(10), 38–42. doi:10.1108/07419050710874278

ISO. (2003). *ISO 10006:2003. Quality management systems-Guidelines for quality management in projects.* Retrieved February 1, 2008, from http://www.iso.org

Jackson, S. E., & Álvarez, E. B. (1992). Working through diversity as a strategic imperative. In Jackson, S. E. (Ed.), *Diversity in the workplace: Human resource initiatives* (pp. 13–29). New York: Guilford Press.

Jacobson, B. (1999). Diversity management process of transformational change. In *Proceedings of the Total E-Quality Management Conference*, Nuremberg, Germany.

Jacobson, I., Booch, G., & Rumbaugh, J. (1999). *The Unified Software Development Process.* Boston: Addison-Wesley Professional.

Jacobson, I., Booch, G., & Rumbaugh, J. (1999). *The unified software development process.* Reading, MA: Addison-Wesley.

Jang, C. Y., Steinfield, C., & Pfaff, B. (2000). Supporting awareness among virtual teams in a web-based collaborative system: the teamSCOPE system. *ACM SIGGROUP Bulletin, 21*(3), 28–34.

Jarvenpaa, S. L., Knoll, K., & Leidner, D. E. (1998). Is Anybody Out There? The Antecedents of Trust in Global Virtual Teams. *Journal of Management Information Systems, 14*(4), 29–64.

Jarvenpaa, S. L., & Leidner, D. E. (1999). Communication and trust in global virtual teams. *Organization Science, 10*(6), 791–815. doi:10.1287/orsc.10.6.791

Jegede, O. (2002). Facilitating and sustaining interest through an on-line distance peer-tutoring system in a cooperative learning environment. *Virtual University Gazette*, 35-45.

Jehn, K. A. (1997). A qualitative analysis of conflict type and dimensions in organizational groups. *Administrative Science Quarterly, 42*(3), 234–257. doi:10.2307/2393737

Jensen, A. L., & Thysen, I. (2003). Agricultural information and decision support by SMS. In *Proceedings of the EFITA 2003 Conference*, Debrecen, Hungary (pp. 286-292).

Jesus, P. (2009). *Estão as Redes Sociais a Mudar o Nosso Cérebro?* Retrieved February 26, 2009, from http://dn.sapo.pt/inicio/portugal/interior.aspx?content_id=1154229

Johnson, D. G. (2005, September 16). Corporate excellence, ethics and the role of I.T. In *Proceedings of the 2nd International Forum, Business Ethics and Corporate Social Responsibility in a Global Economy*, Milano, Italy.

Johnson, D., Johnson, R., & Smith, K. (1991). *Active learning: cooperation in the college classroom.* Edina, MN: Interaction Book Company.

Johnston, R.E., & Kaplan, S. (1996, June). Harnessing the Power of Strategic Innovation. *Journal of Creativity and Innovation Management, 5.*

Jones, D., Pringle, J., & Shepherd, D. (2000). Managing diversity´ meets Aotearoa/New Zealand. *Personnel Review, 29*(3), 364–380. doi:10.1108/00483480010324715

Kalusopa, T. (2005). The challenges of utilizing information communication technologies (ICTs) for the small-scale farmers in Zambia. *Library Hi Tech, 23*(3), 414–424. doi:10.1108/07378830510621810

Kandola, R., & Fullerton, J. (1994). Diversity: More than just an empty slogan. *Personnel Management, 26*(4), 46.

Kantas, A. (1995). *Organisational and industrial psychology.* Athens, Greece: Greek Letters.

Kanter, R. M. (1983). *The Change Masters.* New York: Simon & Schuster.

Karn, J. (2006). *Empirical Software Engineering: Developer Behaviour and Preferences.* Unpublished doctoral dissertation, Department of Computer Science, University of Sheffield, South Yorkshire, UK.

Karolak, D. W. (1998). *Global Software Development - Managing Virtual Teams and Environments*. Washington, DC: IEEE Computer Society Press.

Kayworth, T. R., & Leidner, D. E. (2002). Leadership Effectiveness in Global Virtual Teams. *Journal of Management Information Systems*, *18*(3), 7–40.

Kee, H. J. (2006). Glass ceiling or sticky floor? Exploring the Australian gender pay gap. *The Economic Record*, *82*(259), 408–427. doi:10.1111/j.1475-4932.2006.00356.x

Keller, R. T. (2001). Cross-functional project groups in research and new product development: Diversity, communications, job stress, and outcomes. *Academy of Management Journal*, *44*(3), 547–555. doi:10.2307/3069369

Kempf, T., & Soejarto, A. (2003). *Answerthink delivers metric-based process improvements*. Gartner, Inc.

Keung, J. W., Kitchenham, B. A., & Jeffery, D. R. (2008). Analogy-X: Providing statistical inference to analogy-based software cost estimation. *IEEE Transactions on Software Engineering*, *34*(4), 1–14. doi:10.1109/TSE.2008.34

Kiker, B. F., & Santos, M. C. (1991). Human capital and earnings in Portugal. *Economics of Education Review*, *10*(3), 187–203. doi:10.1016/0272-7757(91)90043-O

Kimball, R. (2002). *The data warehouse toolkit: the complete guide to dimensional modeling*. Wiley.

Kim, Y., Hsu, J., & Stern, M. (2006). An Update on the IS/IT Skills Gap. *Journal of Information Systems Education*, *17*(4), 395–402.

Kim, Y., & Stohr, E. A. (1998). Software Reuse: Survey and Research Directions. *Journal of Management Information Systems*, *14*(4), 113–147.

King, N. (1990). Innovation at work: the research literature. In M.A. West & J.L. Farr (Eds.), *Innovation and Creativity at Work*. Chichester: Wiley.

Kirschner, P. A., & van Bruggen, J. (2004). Learning and understanding in virtual teams. *Cyberpsychology & Behavior*, *7*(2), 135–139. doi:10.1089/109493104323024401

Kitchenham, B., Budgen, D., Brereton, P., & Woodall, P. (2005). An investigation of software engineering curricula. *Journal of Systems and Software*, *74*(3), 325–335. doi:10.1016/j.jss.2004.03.016

Klaus, P. (2001). *Belbin's Company Worker, The Self-Perception Inventory, and Their Application to Software Engineering Teams*. Blacksburg, VA: Virginia Polytechnic Institute.

Knight, D., Pearce, C. L., Smith, K. G., Olian, J. D., Sims, H. P., Smith, K. A., & Floods, P. (1999). Top management team diversity, group process and strategic consensus. *Strategic Management Journal*, *20*(5), 445–465. doi:10.1002/(SICI)1097-0266(199905)20:5<445::AID-SMJ27>3.0.CO;2-V

Knight, K. E. (1967). A descriptive model of the intrafirm innovation process. *The Journal of Business*, *40*(4), 478–496. doi:10.1086/295013

Knowles, M. (1975). *Self-directed learning: A guide for learners and teachers*. Englewood Cliffs, NJ: Prentice-Hall.

Knowles, M. (1977). *The modern practice of adult education, andragogy versus pedagogy* (8th ed.). New York: Association Press.

Knowles, M. (1980). Malcolm Knowles on 'how do you get people to be self-directed learners?'. *Training and Development Journal*, *34*(5), 96–99.

Knowles, M. (1984). *Andragogy in action: Applying modern principles of adult education*. San Francisco, CA: Jossey Bass.

Knowles, M. (1990). *The adult learner: A neglected species* (4th ed.). Houston, TX: Gulf Publishing.

Knowles, M., Holton, E., & Swanson, R. (1998). *The adult learner* (5th ed.). Houston, TX: Gulf Publishing.

Koenker, R., & Bassett, G. (1978). Regression quantiles. *Econometrica: Journal of the Econometric Society*, *46*(1), 33–50. doi:10.2307/1913643

Kolb, D. A. (1984). *Experiential learning experience as the source of learning and development*. Upper Saddle River, NJ: Prentice Hall.

Kommeren, R., & Parviainen, P. (2007). Philips experiences in global distributed software development. *Empirical Software Engineering, 12*(6), 647–660. doi:10.1007/s10664-007-9047-3

Koohang, A., & Durante, A. (1998). Adapting the Traditional Face-to-Face Instructional Approaches to Online Teaching & Learning. In [Stillwater, OK: IACIS.]. *Proceedings of International Association for Computer Information Systems, 1998,* 83–92.

Kotter, J. P. (1996). *Leading change.* Boston: Harvard Business School Press.

Kotter, J. P., & Schlesinger, L. A. (1979). Choosing strategies for change. *Harvard Business Review, 57,* 106–114.

Kovacs, P. J., Caputo, D., Turchek, J., & Davis, G. A. (2006). A survey to define the skill sets of selected information technology professionals. *Issues in Information Systems Journal, 7*(1), 242–246.

Kramlinger, T., & Huberty, T. (1990). Behaviorism versus Humanism. *Training and Development Journal, 44*(12), 41–45.

Krauth, J. (1999). Introducing information technology in small and medium sized enterprises. *Studies in Information and Control, 8*(1).

Kraut, R. E., Fish, R. S., & Chalfonte, B. (1992). Task requirements and media choice in collaborative writing. *Human-Computer Interaction, 7*(4), 375–407. doi:10.1207/s15327051hci0704_2

Krikkar, R., & Crnkovic, I. (2007). Software Configuration Management. *Science of Computer Programming, 65*(3), 215–221. doi:10.1016/j.scico.2006.10.003

Krishna Reddy, P. K., Ramaraju, G. V., & Reddy, G. S. (2007). eSagu: a data warehouse enabled personalized agricultural advisory system. In *Proceedings of the SIGMOD 07,* Beijing, China (pp. 910-914).

Krishna Reddy, P., & Ankaiah, R. (2005). A framework of information technology-based agriculture information dissemination system to improve crop productivity. *Current Science, 88,* 1905–1913.

Krishnan, M. S. (1998). The role of team factors in software cost and quality: an empirical analysis. *Information Technology & People, 11*(1), 20–35. doi:10.1108/09593849810204512

Kruchten, P. (2003). *The Rational Unified Process. An Introduction.* Reading, MA: Addison-Wesley.

Krug, S. (2000). *Don't make me think. A common sense approach to web usability.* New York: New Ryders.

Kuczmarski, T. (1995). *Innovation: Leadership Strategies for the Competitive Edge.* New York: McGraw-Hill/Contemporary Books.

Kweku, A. K. (2006). *Demystifying ICT diffusion and use among rural women in Kenya.* Unpublished paper presented to ProLISSA 2006.

Lanes, W. J. (2001). What is Engineering Management? *IEEE Transactions on Engineering Management, 48*(1), 107–110. doi:10.1109/17.913170

Lankau, M. J., & Scandura, T. A. (2002). An investigation of personal learning in mentoring relationships: content, antecedents, and consequences. *Academy of Management Journal, 45*(4), 779–790. doi:10.2307/3069311

Lanubile, F. (2009). Collaboration in Distributed Software Development. *Lecture Notes in Computer Science, 5413,* 174–193. doi:10.1007/978-3-540-95888-8_7

Laranja, M., Simões, V., & Fontes, M. (1997). *Inovação tecnológica. Experiências das empresas portuguesas.* Lisbon: Texto Editora.

Larman, C. (2002). *Applying UML and patterns. An introduction to object-oriented analysis and design and the unified process.* Upper Saddle River, NJ: Prentice Hall.

Larry, R. (2002). *Successful Project Management (2nd ed.).* AMACOM Publishing, From PMI e-book Library.

Latendresse, P., & Chen, J. C. H. (2003). *The information age and why IT projects must not fail.* Paper presented at the 2003 Southwest Decision Sciences Institute Conference SWDSI2003 (pp. 221-5).

Lau, D. C., & Murnighan, J. K. (1998). Demographic diversity and faultlines: The compositional dynamics of organizational groups. *Academy of Management Review, 23*(2), 325–340. doi:10.2307/259377

Laughery, K. R. Jr, & Laughery, K. R. Sr. (1985). Human factors in software engineering: a review of the literature. *Journal of Systems and Software*, 5(1), 3–14. doi:10.1016/0164-1212(85)90003-2

Lazerson, M. (1995). A new phoenix: Modern putting-out in the modern knitwear industry. *Administrative Science Quarterly*, 40(1), 34–59. doi:10.2307/2393699

Leana, C. R., & Van Buren, H. J. III. (1999). Organizational Social Capital and Employment Practices. *Academy of Management Review*, 24(3), 538–555. doi:10.2307/259141

Ledwith, S., & Colgan, F. (1996). *Women in organizations. Challenging gender politics. Management, work and organizations*. New York: Macmillan Business.

Lee, P. (2001). Technopreneurial Inclinations and Career Management Strategy among Information Technology Professionals. In *Proceedings of the 34th Hawaii International Conference on System Sciences*.

Lee, D., Trauth, E., & Farwell, D. (1995). Critical Skills and Knowledge Requirements of IT Professionals: A Joint Academic/Industry Investigation. *MIS Quarterly*, 19(3), 313–340. doi:10.2307/249598

Lee, J.-N., Huynh, M. Q., Kwok, R. C.-W., & Pi, S.-M. (2003). IT Outsourcing Evolution - Past, Present, and Future. *Communications of the ACM*, 44(5), 84–85. doi:10.1145/769800.769807

Lee, P. C. B. (2006). Information Technology Professionals' Skill Requirements in Hong Kong. *Contemporary Management Research*, 2(2), 141–152.

Leigh, A. (2001). *20 ways to manage better*. London: Chartered Institute of Personnel and Development.

Lerner, J., & Tirole, J. (2002). Some simple economics of open source. *The Journal of Industrial Economics*, 50(2), 197–234. doi:10.1111/1467-6451.00174

Lesser, E., & Cothrel, J. (2001, spring/summer). Fast friends: Virtuality and social capital. *Knowledge Directions*, 66-79.

Leszak, M., & Meier, M. (2007). Successful Global Development of a Large-scale Embedded Telecommunications Product. In *Proceedings of the Second IEEE International Conference on Global Software Engineering* (pp. 23-32). Washington, DC: IEEE Computer Society.

Lethbridge, T. C. (2000). What Knowledge Is Important to a Software Professional? *Computer*, 33(5), 44–50. doi:10.1109/2.841783

Leung, H., & Fan, Z. (2002). Software Cost Estimation. In S. K. Chang (Ed.), *Handbook of software engineering & knowledge engineering- Vol. 2: Emerging technologies* (pp. 307-324). River Edge, NJ: Word Scientific.

Li, E. Y., McLeod, R., & Rogers, J. C. (2001). Marketing information systems in Fortune 500 companies: a longitudinal analysis of 1980, 1990, and 2000. *Information & Management*, 38(5), 307–322. doi:10.1016/S0378-7206(00)00073-2

Li, J., Ruhe, G., Al-Emran, A., & Richter, M. M. (2007). A flexible method for software effort estimation by analogy. *Empirical Software Engineering*, 12(1), 65–106. doi:10.1007/s10664-006-7552-4

Likert, R. (1932). A technique for the measurement of attitudes. *Archives de Psychologie*, 22(140), 1–55.

Likert, R. (1961). New patterns of Management. *Industrial & Labor Relations Review*, 17(2), 336–338.

Likert, R. (1967). *The Human Organisation*. New York: McGraw-Hill.

Lin, C., & Pervan, G. (2003). The practice of IS/IT benefits management in large Australian organizations. *Information & Management*, 41(1), 13–24. doi:10.1016/S0378-7206(03)00002-8

Lin, N. (2001). *Social capital: A theory of social structure and action*. New York: Cambridge University Press.

Litecky, C. R., Arnett, K. P., & Prabhakar, B. (2004). The paradox of soft skills versus technical skills in IS hiring. *Journal of Computer Information Systems*, 45(1), 69–76.

Liu, C., & Arnett, K. P. (2000). Exploring the factors associated with Web site success in the context of electronic commerce. *Information & Management*, 38(1). doi:10.1016/S0378-7206(00)00049-5

LMI Government Consulting. (2009). *Organizations and human capital*. Retrieved January 10th, 2009 from http://www.lmi.org/organizations/organizations.aspx. LMI Headquarters, McLean.

Long, N., & Stephen, O. (2004). A study on project success factors in large construction projects in Vietnam. *Engineering, Construction, and Architectural Management, 11*(6), 404–413. doi:10.1108/09699980410570166

Lope, A. (1996). *Innovación tecnológica y cualificación*. Madrid, Spain: Consejo Económico y Social, Departamento de Publicaciones.

López, N., Montes, J. M., & Vázquez, C. J. (2007). *Cómo gestionar la innovación en las PYMES. La Coruña*. Galicia, Spain: Netbiblo.

Lormas, M., van Dijk, H., van Deursen, A., Nocker, E., & de Zeeuw, A. (2004). Managing evolving requirements in an outsourcing context: an industrial experience report. In *Proceedings 7th International Workshop on Principles of software Evolution* (pp. 149-158). Washington, DC: IEEE Computer Society.

Lum, K., Bramble, M., Hihn, J., Hackney, J., Khorrami, M., & Monson, E. (2003). *Handbook for software cost estimation*. Pasadena, CA: Jet Propulsion Laboratory.

Lusa. (2009). *"Site" de Apoio a Sócrates cria "Rede Social" Semelhante ao Facebook ou Hi5*. Retrieved April 12, 2009, from http://dn.sapo.pt/Inicio/interior.aspx?content_id=1199713

Lynex, A., & Layzell, P. J. (1998). Organisational considerations for software reuse. *Annals of Software Engineering, 5*(1), 105–124. doi:10.1023/A:1018928608749

Machado, J. A. F., & Mata, J. (2000). *Counterfactual decomposition of changes in wage distributions using quantile regression*. Paper presented at the Econometric World Society Conference, Seattle.

Machado, J. A. F., & Mata, J. (2001). Earning functions in Portugal 1982-1994: Evidence from quantile regressions. *Empirical Economics, 26*(1), 115–134. doi:10.1007/s001810000049

MacLaughlin, I. (1999). *Creative Technological Change: The Shaping of Technology and Organizations*. London: Routledge

Mahmood, A. M., Pettingell, K. J., & Shaskevich, A. I. (1996). Measuring productivity of software projects: A data envelopment analysis approach. *Decision Sciences, 27*(1), 57–80. doi:10.1111/j.1540-5915.1996.tb00843.x

Maidantchik, C., & da Rocha, A. R. C. (2002). Managing a worldwide software process. In *Proceedings International Workshop on Global Software Development (ICSE 2002)*, Orlando, FL.

Malhan, I. V., & Rao, S. (2007). Impact of globalization and emerging information communication technologies on agricultural knowledge transfer to small farmers in India. In *Proceedings of the World Library and Information Congress: the 73rd IFLA General Conference and Council*, Durban, South Africa (pp. 1 -20).

Mangstl, A. (2008). Emerging issues, priorities and commitments in e-Agriculture. *Agriculture Information Worldwide, 1*(1), 5–6.

Mao, J. Y., Lee, J. N., & Deng, C. P. (2008). Vendors' perspectives on trust and control in offshore information systems outsourcing. *Information & Management, 45*(7), 482–492. doi:10.1016/j.im.2008.07.003

Marsh, G., & Burke, M. (2001). Knowledge Management and Organizational Effectiveness: balancing the mild, the wild and the crazy. *Australasian Journal of Information Systems, 9*(1), 67–79.

Martin, C. D. (1998). Is computer science a profession? *ACM SIGCSE Bulletin, 30*(2), 7–8. doi:10.1145/292422.296068

Martins, L. L., Gilson, L. L., & Maynard, M. T. (2004). Virtual Teams: What Do We Know and Where Do We Go From Here? *Journal of Management, 30*(6), 805–835. doi:10.1016/j.jm.2004.05.002

Martins, P. S., & Pereira, P. T. (2004). Does education reduce wage inequality? Quantile regression evidence from 16 countries. *Labour Economics, 11*(3), 355–371. doi:10.1016/j.labeco.2003.05.003

Martyn, M., & Bash, L. (2002, October 9-12). Creating new meanings in leading education. In *Proceedings of the Twenty-Second National Conference on Alternative and External Degree Programs for Adults*, Pittsburgh, PA.

Mathis, R. L., & Jackson, J. H. (1994). *Human resource management*. St. Paul, MN: West Publishing.

Matsuura, S. (2007). Software Engineering Education Based on Practical Software Development Experiments. *Transactions of Information Processing Society of Japan, 48*(8), 2578–259.

Maylor, H. (2003). *Project Management* (3rd ed.). London: Pearson Education Limited.

McBride, N. (2009). Exploring service issues within the IT organization: Four mini-case studies. *International Journal of Information Management, 29*(3), 237–243. doi:10.1016/j.ijinfomgt.2008.11.010

McCaffery, F., Smite, D., Wilkie, F. G., & McFall, D. (2006). A proposed way for european software industries to achieve growth within the global marketplace. *Software Process Improvement and Practice, 11*(3), 277–285. doi:10.1002/spip.271

McConnell, S. (2003). *Professional Software Development*. Boston, MA: Addison-Wesley.

McDaniel, M. A. (1989). Biographical constructs for predicting employee suitability. *The Journal of Applied Psychology, 74*(6). doi:10.1037/0021-9010.74.6.964

McDaniel, M. A., Whetzel, D. L., Schmidt, F. L., & Maurer, S. D. (1994). The validity of employment interviews: A comprehensive review and meta-analysis. *The Journal of Applied Psychology, 79*(4), 599–616. doi:10.1037/0021-9010.79.4.599

McDonald, M., Begin, J., & Fortino, S. (2009). *Meeting the Challenge: The 2009 CIO agenda*. Gartner Executive Programs, Gartner, Inc.

McDonald, S., & Edwards, H. M. (2007). Who Should Test Whom? Examining the use and abuse of personality tests in software engineering. *Communications of the ACM, 50*(1), 67–71.

McInerney, J., & Robert, T. (2004). Collaborative or cooperative learning? In Roberts, T. S. (Ed.), *Online collaborative learning: theory and practice* (pp. 203–214). Hershey, PA: IGI Global.

McKenna, R. J., & Martin-Smith, B. M. (2005). Decision making as a simplification process: new conceptual perspectives. *Management Decision, 43*, 821–836. doi:10.1108/00251740510603583

McLeod, R. (1995). Systems theory and information resources management: Integrating key concepts. *Information Resources Management Journal, 18*(2), 5–14.

McMahon, P. E. (2001). Distributed Development: Insights, Challenges, and Solutions. *CrossTalk, 15*(11), 4–9.

McMurtrey, M. E., Downey, J. P., Zeltmann, S. M., & Friedman, W. H. (2008). Critical Skill Sets of Entry-Level IT Professionals: An Empirical Examination of Perceptions from Field Personnel. *Journal of Information Technology Education, 7*, 101–120.

Messick, D. M., & Mackie, D. M. (1989). Intergroup relations. *Annual Review of Psychology, 40*, 45–81. doi:10.1146/annurev.ps.40.020189.000401

Metha, A., Armenakis, A., Mehta, N., & Irani, F. (2006). Challenges and opportunities of business process outsourcing in India. *Journal of Labor Research, 27*(3), 324–338.

Mezirow, J. (1990). *Fostering critical reflection in adulthood*. San Francisco, CA: Jossey Bass.

Mezirow, J. (1997). Transformative learning. *New Directions for Adult and Continuing Education, 74*, 5–12. doi:10.1002/ace.7401

Miguel, J. (2009). Viver na Rede. *Visão, 838*, 76–82.

Miller, J. G., & Vollman, T. E. (1985). The hidden factory. *Harvard Business Review, 63*(5), 142–150.

Mincer, J., & Polachek, S. (1974). Family investments in human capital: Earnings of women. *The Journal of Political Economy, 82*(2), 76–108. doi:10.1086/260293

Ministerio de Administraciones Públicas, M. A. P. Secretaría de Estado para la Administración Pública. Consejo Superior de Informática (2001). MÉTRICA: versión 3 Madrid, Spain: Ministerio de Administraciones Públicas.

Mintzberg, H., & Quinn, J. (1988). *The Strategy Process: Concepts, Contexts and Cases*. Englewood Cliffs, NJ: Prentice Hall.

Misic, M. M., & Graf, D. K. (2004). Systems analyst activities and skills in the new millennium. *Journal of Systems and Software, 71*(1-2), 31–36. doi:10.1016/S0164-1212(02)00124-3

Miyake, N., & Masukawa, H. (2000). Relation-making to sensemaking: Supporting college students' constructive understanding with an enriched collaborative note-sharing system. *Fourth international conference of the learning sciences*, 41-47.

Mizuno, Y. (1983). Software Quality Improvement. *Computer*, *16*(3), 66–72. doi:10.1109/MC.1983.1654331

Moeller, S. D. (2006). *International news and problems with the news media's RSS feeds. The International Center for Media and the Public Agenda*. Retrieved November 2009, from http://www.icmpa.umd.edu/pages/studies/rss_study_details/rss_study.html

Moe, N. B., & Smite, D. (2008). Understanding a lack of trust in global software development: a multiple case study. *Software Process Improvement and Practice*, *13*(3), 217–231. doi:10.1002/spip.378

Mohrman, S. A., Finegold, D., & Mohrman, A. M. (2003). An empirical model of the organization knowledge system in new product development firms. *Journal of Engineering and Technology Management*, *20*(1-2), 7–38. doi:10.1016/S0923-4748(03)00003-1

Monteiro Barata, J. (1996a). *Inovação nos serviços: sistemas e tecnologias de informação e competitividade no sector bancário em Portugal*. Doctoral Thesis in Economics, ISEG/UTL.

Monteiro Barata, J. (1996b). Mutação tecnológica na banca em Portugal. Uma perspectiva para o final do século. *Revista da Banca*, *39*, 5–34.

Moodysson, J. (2007). *Sites and Modes of Knowledge Creation: on the Spatial Organization of Biotechnology Innovation* (Ph.D. Thesis), Lund, Dept of Social and Economic Geography, Lund University, Sweden.

Morcillo, P. (1997). *Dirección estratégica de la tecnología e innovación: un enfoque de competencias*. Madrid, Spain: Editorial Civitas.

Morris, L. V., Xu, H., & Finnegan, C. L. (2005). Roles of Faculty in Teaching Asynchronous Undergraduate Courses. *Journal of Asynchronous Learning Networks*, *9*(1), 65–82.

Mortensen, M., & Hinds, P. J. (2001). Conflict and shared identity in geographically distributed teams. *The International Journal of Conflict Management*, *12*(3), 212–238. doi:10.1108/eb022856

Mueller, R. E. (1998). Public-private sector wage differentials in Canada: Evidence from quantile regressions. *Economics Letters*, *60*(2), 229–235. doi:10.1016/S0165-1765(98)00110-4

Mullins, L. J. (1993). *Management and Organizational Behaviour*. London: Pitman Publication.

Munchns, G. (1992). *Check references for safer selection*. H.R. Magazine.

Munns, K., & Bjeirmi, F. (1996). The role of project management in achieving project success. *International Journal of Project Management*, *14*(2), 81–87. doi:10.1016/0263-7863(95)00057-7

Munyua, H., Adera, E., & Jensen, M. (2008). Emerging ICTs and their potential in revitalizing small scale agriculture in Africa. In *Proceedings of the World Conference on Agricultural Information and IT*, Atsugi, Japan (pp. 707-718).

Murray, F. (2002). Innovation as co-evolution of scientific and technological networks: exploring tissue engineering. *Research Policy*, *31*(8/9), 1389–1404. doi:10.1016/S0048-7333(02)00070-7

Muthuswamy, B., & Crow, G. B. (2003). Global Software Development: Strategic Implications for U.S. Information Systems Academic Programs. *International Association for Computer Information Systems*, *4*(1), 271–276.

Nahapiet, J., & Ghoshal, S. (1998). Social Capital, Intellectual capital, and the organizational advantage. *Academy of Management Review*, *23*(2), 242–266. doi:10.2307/259373

National Center for Education Statistics. (2002). *Nontraditional undergraduates (NCES Rep.)*. Washington, DC: NCES.

National Center for Research in Vocational Education. (1987). *Report on vocational education*. Berkeley, CA: NCRVE.

Nauman, S., & Igbal, S. (2005). Challenges of virtual project management in developing countries. In *Proceedings of the IEEE International Engineering Management Conference*, New Foundland, Canada (pp. 579-583). Washington, DC: IEEE.

Navran, F. (2002, September. (2003, July). Seven Steps For Changing the Ethical Culture of an Organization. *Ethics Today Online*, *1*, 15.

Neef, D. (2005). Managing corporate risk through better knowledge management. *The Learning Organization*, *12*(2), 112–124. doi:10.1108/09696470510583502

Nelson, R., & Winter, S. (1982). *An Evolutionary Theory of Economic Change*. Cambridge, MA: Harvard University Press.

Neves, J. C. (2008). *A ética é intrínseca ao indivíduo*. Retrieved February 22, 2008, from http://www.ver.pt/conteudos/ver_mais_Etica.aspx?docID=287

Ngo-The, A., & Ruhe, G. (2008). A Systematic Approach for Solving the Wicked Problem of Software Release Planning. *Soft Computing*, *12*(1), 95–108. doi:10.1007/s00500-007-0219-2

Nichols, W., Carleton, A., Humphrey, W., & Over, J. (2009). A Distributed Multi-Company Software Project. *CrossTalk*, *22*(4), 20–24.

Nickerson, R. S., Perkins, D. N., & Smith, E. E. (1985). *The Teaching of Thinking*. Hillsdale, NJ: Lawrence Erlbaum.

Nielsen, J. (2003). *Usability 101: introduction to usability*. Retrieved November 2009, from http://www.alertbox.com

Nielsen. (2008). *Nielsen Online Provides Fastest Growing Social Networks for September 2008*. Retrieved May 20, 2009, from http://blog.nielsen.com/nielsenwire/wp-content/uploads/2008/10/press_release24.pdf

Noll, C. L., & Wilkins, M. (2002). Critical Skills of IS Professionals: A Model for Curriculum Development. *Journal of Information Technology Education*, *1*(3), 143–154.

Nonnecke, B., & Preece, J. (2001). Why Lurkers Lurk. In *Proceedings of the AMCIS Conference*, Boston. Atlanta, GA: AIS.

Nottingham, M., & Sayre, R. (2005). *The atom syndication format*. IETF.

Nunamaker, J. F., Reinig, B. A., & Briggs, R. O. (2009). Principles for effective virtual teamwork. *Communications of the ACM*, *52*(4), 113–117. doi:10.1145/1498765.1498797

Nuñez, M., & Gómez, O. (2005). El factor humano: resistencia a la innovación tecnológica. *Revista Orbis*, *1*(1), 23–34.

Nunnally, J. (1978). *Psychometric theory*. New York: McGraw-Hill.

O'brien. J., & Marakas, G. M. (2005). *Management Information System* (7th ed.). New York: McGraw-Hill.

O'Neil, J. (1995). Finding time to learn. *Educational Leadership*, *53*(3), 11–15.

Oaxaca, R. (1973). Male-female wage differentials in urban labor markets. *International Economic Review*, *14*(3), 693–709. doi:10.2307/2525981

Object Management Group. (2008). *Unified Modelling Language Specification™(UML®)2.1.2*. Retrieved May 28, 2008, from http://www.omg.org/technology/documents/modeling_spec_catalog.htm#UML

Olson, G. M., & Olson, J. S. (2000). Distance matters. *Human-Computer Interaction*, *15*(2), 139–178. doi:10.1207/S15327051HCI1523_4

O'Sullivan, D., & Dooley, L. (2008). *Applying Innovation*. California: Sage Publications.

Otter, T., & Holincheck, J. (2009). Key Issues in Human Capital Management Software, Gartner, Inc.

Parikh, T. S. (2009). Engineering rural development. *Communications of the ACM*, *52*(1), 54–63. doi:10.1145/1435417.1435433

Parthasarathy, M. A. (2007). *Practical Software Estimation: Function Point Methods for Insourced and Outsourced Projects*. Boston: Addison-Wesley Professional.

Paule, M. P., Fernández, M. J., Ortín, F., & Pérez, J. R. (2008). Adaptation in current e-learning systems. *Elsevier Computer Standards and Interfaces*, *30*(1-2), 62–70.

Paulk, M. C., Curtis, B., Chrissis, M. B., & Weber, C. V. (1993). *Capability Maturity Model for Software Version 1.1* (Tech. Rep. CMU/SEI-93-TR-24). Pittsburgh, PA: Carnegie Mellon University, Software Engineering Institute.

Paul, S., Seetharaman, P., Samarah, I., & Mykytyn, P. P. (2004). Impact of heterogeneity and collaborative conflict management style on the performance of synchronous global virtual teams. *Information & Management, 41*(3), 303–321. doi:10.1016/S0378-7206(03)00076-4

Pearson, J., Norman, D. W., & Dixon, J. (1995). *Sustainable dryland cropping in relation to soil productivity - FAO Soils Bulletin 72*. Retrieved November 20, 2009, from http://www.fao.org/docrep/v9926e/v9926e00.htm#Contents

Perez Cereijo, M. (2006). Attitude as predictor of success in online training. *International Journal on E-Learning, 5*(4), 623–639.

Perry, D. E., Staudenmayer, N. A., & Votta, L. G. (1994). People, Organizations, and Process Improvement. *IEEE Software, 11*(4), 36–45. doi:10.1109/52.300082

Peter, W. (2006). *Avoiding Project Failures: The Project Management Initiative.* http://blogs.ittoolbox.com/pm/witt/archives/avoiding-project-failures-14896.

Pfleeger, S. L., Wu, F., & Lewis, R. (2005). *Software cost estimation and sizing methods: Issues and guidelines*. Santa Monica, CA: Rand Corporation.

Phelps, R. (2002, July 11-13). A constructivist approach to professional development in ICT Leadership. In *Proceedings of the ICEC 2002 Conference.*

Pilatti, L., Audy, J. L. N., & Prikladnicki, R. (2006). Software configuration management over a global software development environment: lessons learned from a case study. In *Proceedings of the 2006 international workshop on Global software development for the practitioner* (pp. 45-50). New York: ACM.

PMI. (2004). *A Guide to the Project Management Body of Knowledge (PMBOK® Guide)* (3rd ed.). Newtown Square, PA: Project Management Institute.

Polyzos, S. (2004). *Management and Planning of Projects*. Athens, Greece: Kritiki.

Porter, M. E., & Millar, V. E. (1985, July/August). How information gives you competitive advantage. *Harvard Business Review*, 149–174.

Portugal, Ministério do Trabalho e da Solidariedade Social (2006). *Quadros de Pessoal*. In magnetic media.

Powell, W. (1990). Neither market nor hierarchy: network forms of organization. In B.M. Staw & L.L. Cummings (Eds.), *Research in Organizational Behavior* (pp. 295-336). JAI Press.

Powell, W. W. (1998). Learning from Collaboration: Knowledge and Networks in the Biotechnology and Pharmaceutical Industries. *California Management Review, 40*(3), 228–240.

Powell, W., Koput, K. W., & Smith-Doerr, L. (1996). Interorganizational collaboration and the locus of innovation: Networks of learning in biotechnology. *Administrative Science Quarterly, 41*, 116–145. doi:10.2307/2393988

Powers, M. J. (2005). *Effective online learning: recognizing e-learnability*. PAACE Journal of.

Pressman, R. S. (2001). *Software engineering: a practitioner's approach*. New York: McGraw-Hill.

Preston, J. A. (1999). Occupational gender segregation: Trends and explanations. *The Quarterly Review of Economics and Finance, 39*(5), 611–624. doi:10.1016/S1062-9769(99)00029-0

Prikladnicki, R., & Audy, J. N. L. (2003). Requirements Engineering in Global Software Development: Preliminary Findings from a Case Study in a SW-CMM context. In *Proceedings of the 5th Simpósio Internacional de Melhoria de Processo de Software*, Pernambuco, Brazil.

Prikladnicki, R., Audy, J. N. L., Damian, D., & de Oliveria, T. C. (2007). Distributed Software Development: Practices and challenges in different business strategies of offshoring and onshoring. In *Proceedings of the Second IEEE International Conference on Global Software Engineering* (pp. 262-274).

Prikladnicki, R., Peres, F., Audy, J. N. L., M'ora, M. C., & Perdigoto, A. (2002). Requirements specification model in a software development process inside a physically distributed environment. In *Proceedings of ICEIS*, Ciudad Real, Spain (pp. 830-834).

Prikladnicki, R., Audy, J. N. L., & Evaristo, R. (2003). Global Software Development in Practice Lessons Learned. *Software Process Improvement and Practice, 8*(4), 267–281. doi:10.1002/spip.188

Prikladnicki, R., Evaristo, R., Audy, J. L. N., & Yamaguti, M. H. (2006). Risk Management in Distributed IT Projects: Integrating Strategic, Tactical, and Operational Levels. *International Journal of e-Collaboration, 2*(4), 1–18.

Project Management Institute (PMI). (2004). *A Guide to the Project Management Body of Knowledge* (3rd ed.). Sylva, NC: PMI.

Putnam, R. D. (1995). Bowling slone: America's declining social capital. *Journal of Democracy, 6*(1), 65–78. doi:10.1353/jod.1995.0002

Pye, D., Stephenson, J., Harris, S., Lee, B., & Leask, M. (2003). *Using ICTs to increase the effectiveness of community-based, non-formal education for rural people in sub-Saharan Africa: The CERP Project Final report.* Retrieved December 18, 2009, from http://www.nfer.ac.uk/research-areas/pimsdata/summaries/using-ict-to-increase-the-effectiveness-of-community-based-non-formaleducation-for-rural-people-in-sub-saharan-africa-the-cerp-project.cfm

Pyster, A. B., & Thayer, R. H. (2005). Guest Editors' Introduction: Software Engineering Project Management 20 Years Later. *IEEE Software, 22*(5), 18–21. doi:10.1109/MS.2005.137

Quayle, M. (1999). Project management in European Aerospace plc: a case study. *Industrial Management & Data Systems, 99*(5), 221–231. doi:10.1108/02635579910282920

Raffo, D., & Setamanit, S. (2005). A Simulation Model for Global Software Development Project. In *Proceedings of the 2006 international workshop on Global software development for the practitioner* (pp. 8-14). New York: ACM.

Rao, N. H. (2007). A framework for implementing information and communication technologies in agricultural development in India. *Technological Forecasting and Social Change, 74*(4), 491–518. doi:10.1016/j.techfore.2006.02.002

Rao, S. S. (2004). Role of ICTs in India's rural community information systems. *Info, 6*(4), 261–269. doi:10.1108/14636690410555663

Ratnam, B. V., Krishna Reddy, P., & Reddy, G. S. (2005). eSagu: An IT based personalized extension system prototype: Analysis of 51 farmers' case studies. *International Journal of Education and Development using Information and Communication Technology, 2*, 79-94.

Reagans, R., & Zuckerman, E. (2001). Networks, diversity, and productivity: the social capital of corporate R&D teams. *Organization Science, 12*(4), 502–517. doi:10.1287/orsc.12.4.502.10637

Reenskaug, T. (1979). *Models – Views – Controllers.* Retrieved November 2009, from http://heim.ifi.uio.no/~trygver/mvc/index.html

Reeves, T. C., Herrington, J., & Oliver, R. (2002). Authentic activities and online learning. In Goody, A., Herrington, J., & Northcote, M. (Eds.), *Quality conversations: Research and Development in Higher Education* (Vol. 25, pp. 562–567). Milperra, Australia: HERDSA.

Reid, L. (1995). *Perceived Effects of Block Scheduling on the Teaching of English (No. ED382950).* Washington, DC: ERIC.

Rettberg, J. (2008). *Blogging: Digital Media and Society Series* (pp. 68–83). New York: Polity Press.

Ricard, J. E., Rodriguez, M. Á., Blasco, D. J. L., Elorriaga, D. J. F., & Castilla, D. M. L. (2002). *Código de gobierno para la empresa sostenible - Guía para su implantación.* Barcelona: IESE Business School - Universidad de Navarra.

Richard, O. C., & Johnson, N. B. (2001). Understanding the Impact of Human Resource Diversity Practices on Firm Performance. *Journal of Managerial Issues, 2*, 177–195.

Richard, O. C., & Shelor, R. M. (2002). Linking top management team age heterogeneity to firm performance: juxtaposing two mid-range theories. *International Journal of Human Resource Management, 13*(6), 958–974. doi:10.1080/09585190210134309

Richardson, D. (1997). *The internet and rural and agricultural development – an integrated approach.* Retrieved September 24, 2009, from http://www.fao.org/docrep/w6840e/w6840e00.htm

Riordan, C. M., & Shore, L. M. (1997). Demographic diversity and employee attitudes: An empirical examination of relational demography within work units. *The Journal of Applied Psychology, 82*(3), 342–358. doi:10.1037/0021-9010.82.3.342

Ripley, B. D. (2006). *Stochastic simulation.* New York: Wiley.

Robalo, H. (2009). *GNR Adere às Novas Tecnologias da Internet.* Retrieved February 16, 2009, from http://dn.sapo.pt/Inicio/interior.aspx?content_id=1172861

Robbins, S. P. (1989). *Organizational Behavior: Concepts, Contro-versies, and Applications.* Englewood Cliffs, NJ: Prentice Hall.

Roberts, E. M. (1988). Managing invention and innovation. *Research-Technology Management, 31*(1), 11–29.

Robertson, I., et al. (1990). The validity of situational interviews for administrative jobs. *Journal of organizational psychology, 11.*

Robertson, I., & Makin, P. (1986). Management and selection. A survey and critique. *Journal of Occupational Psychology, 59*(1), 45–58.

Roth, P. L., & Camprion, J. E. (1992). An analysis of the predictive power of the panel interview and pre-employment tests. *Journal of Occupational and Organizational Psychology, 65.*

Rubinstein, R. Y., & Melamed, B. (1998). *Modern simulation and modelling.* New York: Wiley.

Rummler, G., & Brache, A. (1990). *Improving Performance: How to Manage the White Space on the Organization Chart.* Jossey Bass Business and Management Series.

Rutherfoord, R. H. (2001). Using personality inventories to help form teams for software engineering class projects. *SIGCSE Bulletin, 33*(3), 76–76. doi:10.1145/507758.377486

Ryan, R. (2007). IT Project Management: Infamous Failures, Classics Mistakes, and Best Practices. *Mis Quarterly Executive, 6*(2), 67–78.

Saavedra, R. P., Earley, C. P., Dyne, L. V., & Lee, C. (1993). Complex interdependence in task-performing groups. *The Journal of Applied Psychology, 78*(1), 61–72. doi:10.1037/0021-9010.78.1.61

Sackman, H., Erikson, W. J., & Grant, E. E. (1968). Exploratory Studies comparing online and offline programming performance. *Communications of the ACM, 11*(1), 3–11. doi:10.1145/362851.362858

Sadler, P. (1995). *Managing Change.* Sunday Times Business Skills, London: Kogan Page.

Sahay, S., Nicholson, B., & Krishna, S. (2003). *Global IT outsourcing: software development across borders.* Cambridge, UK: Cambridge University Press. doi:10.1017/CBO9780511615351

Saiedian, H., Bagert, D., & Mead, R. N. (2002). Software Engineering Programs: Dispelling the Myths and Misconceptions. *IEEE Software, 19*(5), 35–41. doi:10.1109/MS.2002.1032852

Sakellariou, C. (2004). Gender-earnings differentials using quantile regressions. *Journal of Labor Research, 25*(3), 457–468. doi:10.1007/s12122-004-1024-7

Sanchez, R. (2001). *Knowledge Management and Organizational Competence.* UK: Oxford University Press.

Sarasin, L. (1998). *Learning style perspectives: Impact in the classroom.* Madison, WI: Atwood Publishing.

Sawyer, S. (2004). Software Development Teams. *Communications of the ACM, 47*(12), 95–99. doi:10.1145/1035134.1035140

scheme. New York: Holt, Rinehart, and Winston.

Schmid, A. A. (2003). Discussion: Social capital as an important level in economic development policy and private strategy. *American Journal of Agricultural Economics, 85*(3), 716–719. doi:10.1111/1467-8276.00473

Schulz, B. (2003). Collaborative learning in an online environment: will it work for teacher training? In *Proceedings of the 14th Annual Society for Information Technology and Teacher Education International Conference* (pp. 503-504). Charlottesville, VA: AACE.

Schwarz, I., & McRae-Williams, P. (2009). *Farmer behaviour and enterprise change as a result of the Wimmera Mallee Pipeline – One year on.* A report prepared for the Victorian Department of Primary Industries, Horsham, Australia.

Scott, P. A. (1994). A comparative study of students' learning experiences in intensive and semester-length courses and the attributes of high-quality intensive and semester course learning experiences. In *Proceedings of the Meeting of the North American Association of Summer Sessions,* Portland, OR (pp. 370-498). Washington, DC: ERIC.

Scott, P. (1995). Learning experiences in intensive and semester-length classes: Student voices and. experiences. *College Student Journal, 29*(2), 207–213.

Scott, P. (1996). Attributes of High-Quality Intensive Course Learning Experiences: Student. Voices and Experiences. *College Student Journal, 30*(1), 69–77.

Scott, P., & Conrad, C. (1991). *A critique of intensive courses and an agenda for research.* Washington, DC: ERIC.

SEDISI. (2004). *Estudio sobre Salarios y Política Laboral en el Sector Informático.* Madrid, Spain: SEDISI.

Seibert, S. E., Kraimer, M. L., & Liden, R. C. (2001). A social capital theory of career success. *Academy of Management Review, 44*(2), 219–237. doi:10.2307/3069452

Seitanidis, P. (1987). *Personnel Evaluation* (2nd ed.). Athens, Greece: Galaios.

Senge, P. M. (1994). The Leader's New Work: Building Learning Organizations. In C. Mabey & P. Iles (Eds.), *Managing Learning.* UK: Thompson Learning.

Seng, J., & Lin, S. (2004). A mobility and knowledge-centric e-learning application design method. *International Journal of Innovation and Learning, 1*(3), 293–311. doi:10.1504/IJIL.2004.004885

Serrano, M., & Montes de Oca, C. (2004). Using the Team Software Process in an Outsourcing Environment. *Crosstalk, 17*(3), 9–13.

Shaw, M. (2002). Software Engineering Education: A Roadmap. In *Proceedings of International Conference on Software Engineering* (pp. 371-380).

Sheriff, F. R. (2009). *Village Information Centers in Tamil Nadu, TANIVAS, Chennai, India: e-Empowering resource poor farmers.* Retrieved July 3, 2009, from http://www.i4donline.net/articles/current-article.asp?Title=Village-information-centres-in-Tamil-Nadu,TANUVAS,Chennai,India&articleid=2241&typ=Features

Sherman, A., Bohlander, G., & Snell, S. (1998). *Managing human resources.* Cincinnati, OH: South-Western College.

SIBS. (2008b). *Estatísticas.* Retrieved March 10, 2009, from http://www.sibs.pt/pt/estatisticas/

Singh, P., & Martin, L. R. (2004). Accelerated Degree Programs: Assessing Student Attitudes and Opinions. *Journal of Education for Business, 79*(5), 299–305. doi:10.3200/JOEB.79.5.299-305

Slack, N., Chambers, S., & Johnston, R. (2007). *Operations Management* (5th ed.). Harlow, England: Prentice-Hall.

Sloffer, S. J., Dueber, B., & Duffy, T. M. (1999). Using asynchronous conferencing to promote critical thinking: two implementations in higher education. In *Proceedings of HICSS-32*, Maui, HI. Honolulu, HI: HICSS.

Smite, D. (2006). Requirements Management in Distributed Projects. *Journal of Universal Knowledge Management, 1*(2), 69–76.

Smite, D., Moe, N. B., & Torkar, R. (2008). Pitfalls in Remote Team Coordination: Lessons Learned From a Case Study. *Lecture Notes in Computer Science, 5089*, 345–359. doi:10.1007/978-3-540-69566-0_28

Smith, K. (1995). Cooperative Learning: effective teamwork for engineering classrooms. In *Proceedings of the Frontiers in Education Conference*, Atlanta, GA (pp. 1, 2b5, 13-2b5,18). Thompson, G. (1988). Distance learners in higher education. In C. C. Gibson (Ed.), *Higher Education: Institutional Responses for Quality Outcomes* (pp. 9-24). Madison, WI: Atwood Publishing.

Smith, K. G., Smith, K. A., Olian, J. D., Sims, H. P., & Scully, J. A. (1994). Top management team demography and process: The role of social integration and communication. *Administrative Science Quarterly, 39*(3), 412–438. doi:10.2307/2393297

Snell, S. A. (1999). Social capital and strategic HRM: It's who you know. *HR. Human Resource Planning*, *22*(1), 62–65.

Snell, S. A., Lepak, D. P., & Youndt, M. A. (1999). Managing the architecture of intellectual capital: Implication for strategic human resources management. *Research in Personnel and Human Resources Management, 4*, 175–193.

Sohal, A. S., & Ng, L. (1998). The role and impact of information technology in Australian business. *Journal of Information Technology, 13*(3), 201–217. doi:10.1080/026839698344846

Solomon, C. M. (1995). Global Teams: the ultimate collaboration. *The Personnel Journal, 74*(9), 49–58.

Sommerville, I., & Rodden, T. (1995). Human, *social and organizational influences on the software process*. Technical Report CSEG/2/1995, Cooperative Systems Engineering Group, Computing Department, Lancaster University (pp. 1–21).

Sommerville, I., & Rodden, T. (1996). Human social and organizational influences on the software process. In Fuggetta, A., & Wolf, A. (Eds.), *Software Process (Trends in Software, 4)* (pp. 89–110). New York: John Wiley & Sons.

Sood, A. D. (2001). How to wire rural India: the problems and possibilities of digital development. *Economic and Political Weekly, 36*(43), 4134–4141.

Sousa, J. V. (1996). *Cartas ao editor*. Retrieved November 8, 2006, from http://www.airpower.maxwell.af.mil/apjinternational/apj-p/2tri97/carta.html

Spinellis, D. (2006). Global software development in the freeBSD project. In *Proceedings of the 2006 international Workshop on Global Software Development for the Practitioner* (pp. 73-79). New York: ACM.

Stanton, E. S. (1982). *Reality-Centered People Management Key to Improved Productivity*. New York: Amacom.

Stash, N., Cristea, A., & De Bra, P. (2003) Authoring the learning styles in adaptive hypermedia. In *Proceedings of the 13th International World Wide Web Conference* (pp. 114-124).

Stenzel, T. F. (2001). Why is there a gender wage gap and how can we fix it? *Employee Rights Quarterly, 2*(2), 1–7.

Stevens, K. T., & Henry, S. M. (2002). *Analyzing Software Team using Belbin's Innovative Plant Role*. Retrieved September 30, 2008, from http:///www.radford.edu/~kstevens2/

Stevenson, W. (2007). *Operations Management* (9th ed.). Boston, USA. McGraw-Hill.

Storr, A. (2006). *Fraud*. Philadelphia: Naxos/Audiofy.

Straus, S., & McGrath, J. E. (1994). Does the medium matter? The interaction of task type and technology on group performance and member reactions. *The Journal of Applied Psychology, 79*(1), 87–97. doi:10.1037/0021-9010.79.1.87

Sturm, R. (1996). When quality of service, not crisis management, is the real standard. *Communications Week, 625*.

Subbotin, I., Serdyukova, N., & Serdyukov, P. (2003). Short-term Intensive College Instruction: What are the Benefits for Adult Learners? In C. Crawford et al. (Eds.), *Proceedings of Society for Information Technology and Teacher Education International Conference 2003* (pp. 1550-1552). Chesapeake, VA: AACE.

Sukhoo, A., Barnard, A., Eloff, M. M., Van der Poll, J. A., & Motah, M. (2005). Accommodating soft skills in software project management. *Issues in Informing Science and Information Technology, 2*, 691–704.

Tadman, M. (1989). The past predicts the future. *Security management, 33*(7).

Taweel, A., & Brereton, P. (2006). Modelling software development across time zones. *Information and Software Technology, 48*(1), 1–11. doi:10.1016/j.infsof.2004.02.006

Teece, D. J., Pisano, G., & Shuen, A. (1997). Dynamic capabilities and strategic management. *Strategic Management Journal, 7*(18), 509–533. doi:10.1002/(SICI)1097-0266(199708)18:7<509::AID-SMJ882>3.0.CO;2-Z

Terninko, J., Zusman, A., & Zlotin, B. (1998). *Systematic Innovation: An introduction to TRIZ (Theory of Inventive Problem Solving)*, Boca Raton, Fl: CRC Press.

Terrell, K. (1992). Female-male earnings differentials and occupational structure. *International Labour Review, 131*(4), 387–404.

Thomas, R. (1999). *Group Dynamics and Software Engineering*. Paper presented at the Object Oriented Systems, Languages and Applications Conference, Denver, Co.

Thomson, C., & Holcombe, M. (2007). 20 Years of teaching and 7 years of research: research when you teach. In *Proceedings of 3rd South East European Formal Methods Workshop* (pp. 141-153).

Tidd, J., Bessant, J., & Pavitt, K. (2005). *Managing Innovation – Integrating Technological, Market and Organizational Change* (3rd ed.). Chichester: John Wiley & Sons.

Tiwana, A., Bush, A. A., Tsuji, H., Yoshida, K., & Sakurai, A. (2008). Myths and paradoxes in Japanese IT offshoring. *Communications of the ACM, 51*(10), 141–145. doi:10.1145/1400181.1400212

Tiwari, S. P. (2008). Information and communication technology initiatives for knowledge sharing in agriculture. *Indian Journal of Agricultural Sciences, 78*(9), 737–747.

Toffler, A. (1970). *Future shock*. New York: Bantam Books.

Toffler, A. (1985). *The adaptative corporation*. New York: McGraw-Hill.

Tomayko, J., & Hazzan, O. (2004). *Human aspects of Software Engineerng*. Hingham, MA: Charles River Media.

Tomei, L. A. (2007). *Integrating information & communications technologies into the classroom*. Hershey, PA: IGI Global.

Trauth, E. M. (2002). Odd girl out: An individual differences perspective on women in the IT profession. *Information Technology & People, 15*(2), 98–118. doi:10.1108/09593840210430552

Trigo, A., Varajão, J., Soto-Acosta, P., Barroso, J., Molina-Castillo, F. J., & Gonzalvez-Gallego, N. (2010). IT Professionals: An Iberian Snapshot. *International Journal of Human Capital and Information Technology Professionals, 1*(1), 61–75.

Trigo, A., Varajão, J., Soto-Acosta, P., Barroso, J., Molina-Castillo, F., & Gonzales-Gallego, N. (2010). IT professionals: An Iberian snapshot. *International Journal of Human Capital and Information Technology Professionals, 1*(1), 61–75.

Tsui, A. S., Egan, T., & O'Reilly, C. A. III. (1992). Being different: Relational demography and organizational attachment. *Administrative Science Quarterly, 37*(4), 549–579. doi:10.2307/2393472

Turley, R. T., & Bieman, J. M. (1995). Competencies of Exceptional an Non-Exceptional Software Engineers. *Journal of Systems and Software, 28*(1), 19–38. doi:10.1016/0164-1212(94)00078-2

Turley, R. T., & Bieman, J. M. (1995). Competencies of exceptional and nonexceptional software engineers. *Journal of Systems and Software, 28*(1), 19–38. doi:10.1016/0164-1212(94)00078-2

Twiss, B. C. (1974). *Managing Technological innovation*. London: Longman.

U.S. Bureau of Labor Statistics. (1999). *Occupational Outlook Handbook*. Washington, DC: U.S. Bureau of Labor Statistics.

U.S. Department of Education. (2002). *The Condition of Education 2002, NCES 2002-025*. Washington, DC: NPO.

U.S. Department of Labor. (2009). Occupational Outlook Handbook, 2008-09 Edition Retrieved April 12, 2009, from http://www.bls.gov/oco/oco2003.htm

Umber, A. (2006). *Farming Practices in Australian Grain Growing – the means for Productive and Environmental Sustainability*. Australia: Grain Council.

United States. Census Bureau, Population Division. (2009). *World population: 1950 – 2050*. Retrieved November 8, 2009, from http://www.census.gov/ipc/www/idb/worldpopgraph.php

United States. Department of Agriculture (USDA). (2009). *USDA Rice Baseline, 2004-13*. Retrieved August 20, 2009, from http://www.ers.usda.gov/Briefing/rice/2004baseline.htm

Universal MacCann. (2008). *Power to the People Social Media Tracker*. Retrieved April 20, 2009, from www.universalmccann.com/Assets/wave_3_20080403093750.pdf

Utterback, J. M. (1994). *Mastering the dynamics of innovation*. Boston: Harvard Business School Press.

Van de Ven, A. H., Angle, H. L., & Poole, M. S. (1989). *Research on the management of innovation: The Minnesota studies*. New York: Harper & Row.

Van der Vegt, G., & Janssen, O. (2003). Joint impact of interdependency and group diversity on innovation. *Journal of Management, 29*(5), 729–751. doi:10.1016/S0149-2063_03_00033-3

van Solingen, R., Berghout, E., Kusters, R., & Trienekens, J. (2000). From process improvement to people improvement: enabling learning in software development. *Information and Software Technology, 42*(14), 965–971. doi:10.1016/S0950-5849(00)00148-8

Varajão, J., Ferreira, N., Fraga, M. d. G., & Amaral, L. (2008, Dezembro de 2008). Outsourcing de Sistemas de Informação nas empresas nacionais. *Revista CXO*.

Varajão, J., Trigo, A., Figueiredo, N., & Barroso, J. (2007, Maio). 2007). TI nas empresas nacionais. *Revista CXO, 2*, 19–23.

Varajao, J., Trigo, A., Figueiredo, N., Barroso, J., & Bulas-Cruz, J. (2009). Information systems services outsourcing reality in large Portuguese organisations. *Int. J. Bus. Inf. Syst., 4*(1), 125–142. doi:10.1504/IJBIS.2009.021606

Varvel, T., Adams, S. G., Pridie, S. J., & Ruiz, B. C. (2004). Team Effectiveness and Individual Myers-Briggs Personality Dimensions. *Journal of Management Engineering, 20*(4), 141–146. doi:10.1061/(ASCE)0742-597X(2004)20:4(141)

Vaxevanidoy, M., & Reklitis, P. (2008). *Human Resources Management Theory and Act*. Athens, Greece: Propobos.

Venkatesh, V., & Morris, M. G. (2000). Why don't men ever stop to ask for directions? Gender, social influence, and their role in technology acceptance and usage behavior. *Management Information Systems Quarterly, 24*(1), 115–139. doi:10.2307/3250981

Versteegen, G. (2000). *Projektmanagement mit dem Rational Unified Process*. Berlin: Springer.

Vieira, J. A. C., Cardoso, A. C., & Portela, M. (2005). Gender segregation and the wage gap in Portugal: An analysis at the establishment level. *The Journal of Economic Inequality, 3*(2), 145–168. doi:10.1007/s10888-005-4495-8

Vieira, J. A. C., & Pereira, P. T. (1993). Wage differential and allocation: An application to the Azores islands. *Economia, 17*(2), 127–159.

Vygotsky, L. (1978). *Mind in Society*. Cambridge, MA: Harvard University Press.

Wahlstrom, C., Williams, B. K., & Shea, P. (2003). *The successful distance learning student*. Belmont, CA: Scratchgravel.

Walker, G., Kogut, B., & Shan, W. (1997). Social capital, structural holes and the formation of an industry network. *Organization Science, 8*(2), 109–125. doi:10.1287/orsc.8.2.109

Waller, D. (2003). *Operations Management: A Supply Chain Approach* (2nd ed.). Australia: Thomson.

Walther, J. B., & Burgoon, J. (1992). Relational communication in computer- mediated interaction. *Human Communication Research, 19*(1), 50–88. doi:10.1111/j.1468-2958.1992.tb00295.x

Walz, D. B., Elam, J. J., & Curtis, B. (1993). Inside a Software Design Team: Knowledge Acquisition, Sharing, and Integration. *Communications of the ACM, 36*(10), 63–77. doi:10.1145/163430.163447

Wardle, C., & Burton, L. (2002). Programmatic efforts encouraging women to enter the information technology workforce. *SIGCSE Bulletin, 34*(2), 27–31. doi:10.1145/543812.543824

Wasserman, S., & Galaskiewicz, J. (1984). Some generalizations of p1: External constraints, interactions, and non-binary relations. *Social Networks, 6*, 177–192. doi:10.1016/0378-8733(84)90016-9

Watad, M. M., & DiSanzo, F. J. (1998). Transforming IT/IS infrastructure and IS personnel issues. [MCB UP Ltd.]. *Business Process Management Journal, 4*(4), 322–332. doi:10.1108/14637159810238228

Wateridge, J. (1998). How can IS/IT projects be measured for success? *International Journal of Project Management, 16*(1), 59–63. doi:10.1016/S0263-7863(97)00022-7

Webley, S. (2001). *Eight Steps for a Company Wishing To Develop Its Own Corporate Ethics Programme*. London: Institute of Business Ethics.

Wenger, E. (1998). *Communities of practice: learning, meaning, and identity*. Cambridge, UK: Cambridge University Press.

Werther, W. B. Davis, Jr., & Davis, K. (1996). *Human resources and personnel management* (5th ed.). New York: McGraw-Hill.

West, M. A., & Farr, J. (1990). *Innovation and Creativity at work*. Chichester: Wiley.

Wheelwright, S. C., & Clark, K. B. (1992). *Revolutionizing Product Development: Quantum leaps in speed, efficiency and quality*. New York: The Free Press.

White, D., & Fortune, J. (2002). Current practices in project management – an empirical study. *International Journal of Project Management, 20*(1), 1–11. doi:10.1016/S0263-7863(00)00029-6

White, M. G. E. (1996). *Personal Ethics versus Professional Ethics*. Airpower Journal.

Wiersema, M. F., & Bird, A. (1993). Organizational demography in Japanese firms: Group heterogeneity, individual dissimilarity, and top management team turnover. *Academy of Management Journal, 36*(5), 996–1025. doi:10.2307/256643

Wikipedia (2007). *Force-Field Analysis,* ww.wikipedia.org.

Wlodkowski, R. J. (2003). Accelerated Learning in Colleges and Universities. In *New Directions for Adult and Continuing Education* (pp. 5–15). New York: Wiley.

Wong, K. Y. (2005). Critical success factors for implementing knowledge management in small and medium enterprises. *Industrial Management & Data Systems, 105*(¾), 261-279.

Wood, R. M. (2003). *Uncovering BPI*. Retrieved February 15th, 2009 from http://www.gantthead.com/article.cfm?ID=184452. Gantthead.

World Bank. (2006). *Africa development indicators*. Washington, DC: World Bank. Retrieved April 10, 2009, from http://siteresources.worldbank.org/INTSTATINAFR/Resources/adi2007_final.pdf

Wright, P. M., & McMahan, G. C. (1992). Theoretical perspectives for strategic human resource management. *Journal of Management, 18*(2), 295–320. doi:10.1177/014920639201800205

Wright, P. M., & Snell, S. A. (1998). Toward a Unifying Framework for Exploring Fit and Flexibility in Strategic Human Resource Management. *Academy of Management Review, 23*(4), 756–772. doi:10.2307/259061

Wu, J. H., Chen, Y. C., & Chang, C. (2007). Critical IS professional activities and skills/knowledge: A perspective of IS managers. *Computers in Human Behavior, 23*(6), 2945–2965. doi:10.1016/j.chb.2006.08.008

Wybo, M. (2007). The IT sales cycle as a source of context in IS implementation theory. *Information & Management, 44*(4), 397–407. doi:10.1016/j.im.2007.03.001

Yang, H. L., & Tang, J. H. (2004). Team Structure and Team Performance in IS Development: A Social Network Perspective. *Information & Management, 41*, 335–349. doi:10.1016/S0378-7206(03)00078-8

Yellen, R. E., Winniford, M. A., & Sanford, C. C. (1995). Extroversion and introversion in electronically supported meetings. *Information & Management, 28*, 63–74. doi:10.1016/0378-7206(94)00023-C

Youndt, M., & Snell, S. A. (2004). Human resource configuration, intellectual capital and organizational performance. *Journal of Managerial Issues, 16*(3), 337–360.

Young, G. (2002, March 22). Hybrid teaching seeks to end the divide between traditional and online instruction. *The Chronicle of Higher Education*, A33–A34.

Young, S. (2006). Student views of effective online teaching in higher education. *Quarterly Review of Distance Education, 20*(2), 65–77. doi:10.1207/s15389286ajde2002_2

Zaltman, G., Duncan, R., & Holbeck, J. (1973). *Innovation and Organizations*. New York: Wiley.

Zanoni, R., & Audy, J. (2004). Project management model: Proposal for performance in a physically distributed software development environment. *Engineering Management Journal, 16*(2), 28–34.

Zapounidis, K., Kalfakakou, G., & Athanasiou, V. (2008). Theories and Models of Motivation and Leadership, Case Study Application. In *Proceedings of the PM-04 - 4ᵗʰ SCPM & 1ˢᵗ IPMA/MedNet Conference on Project Management Advances, Training & Certification in the Mediterranean.*

Zenger, T. R., & Lawrence, B. S. (1989). Organizational demography: The differential effect of age and tenure distribution on technical communication. *Academy of Management Journal, 32*(2), 353–376. doi:10.2307/256366

Zevgraridis, S. (1985). *Organisation and Management.* Thessaloniki, Greece: Kiriakidis Bros.

Zigurs, I. (2003). Leadership in Virtual Teams: Oxymoron or Opportunity? *Organizational Dynamics, 31*(4), 339–351. doi:10.1016/S0090-2616(02)00132-8

Zimmerman, B. J. (2001). Theories of self-regulated learning and academic achievement: an overview and analysis. In Zimmerman, B. J., & Schunk, D. H. (Eds.), *Self-regulated learning and academic achievement: theoretical perspectives* (2nd ed., pp. 1–37). Mahwah, NJ: Lawrence Erlbaum Associates.

About the Contributors

Ricardo Colomo-Palacios is an Associate Professor at the Computer Science Department of the Universidad Carlos III de Madrid. His research interests include applied research in Information Systems, software project management, people in software projects and social and Semantic Web. He received his PhD in Computer Science from the Universidad Politécnica of Madrid (2005). He also holds a MBA from the Instituto de Empresa (2002). He has been working as Software Engineer, Project Manager and Software Engineering Consultant in several companies including Spanish IT leader INDRA. He is also an Editorial Board Member and Associate Editor for several international journals and conferences and Editor in Chief of International Journal of Human Capital and Information Technology Professionals.

* * *

Jaime Febles Acosta is doctor in Economy and Business Management and master on Business Management from La Laguna University, Spain. He is professor of Business Organization and Enterprise Economy in the Faculty of Business and Economic Sciences of La Laguna University and tutor professor of the National University of Distance Education (UNED). He is also Director of the University Institute of the Enterprise of La Laguna University (IUDE). He has taken part in research projects related with the application of the Rasch Model to the Business Administration and with the strategic bases for the management of small and medium companies. He is co-author of scientific publications about the management style of the Canary businessman, as well as the study of the external and internal factors which determine the orientation of the strategic culture of the companies.

Luís Amaral, Born in 1960, holds a Ph.D. on Information Systems obtained at University of Minho in 1994. He is Associate Professor at Department of Information Systems in the School of Engineering of University of Minho where he teaches courses on information systems management and information systems planning to undergraduate and postgraduate degrees. He is also involved in research projects in the area of methodologies for organizational intervention activities such as; Information Systems Management, Information Systems Planning and Information Systems Development. He has supervised several master and doctoral dissertations, and is author of several scientific publications presented at international conferences and published in scientific and technical journals. Since 2005 is the President of the board of directors of CCG - Centro de Computação Gráfica. Pro-Rector at University of Minho since July 2006.

Helena Campos is an Independent Consultant and Researcher at Porto, Portugal. She graduated in Applied Mathematics and Computation, from Portucalense University and received a MBA (1992) and an MSc (1993) degree in Management and Marketing – School of Business CaixaVigo – Vigo, Spain; a MSC (1996) and a PhD (2009) degree in Information Systems Technology from University of Minho – Guimarães, Portugal. She teaches courses on Technoethics to postgraduate degree. She develops consultant work and research at the Technoethics area. She is member of the APG (Portuguese Association Managers), and is a member of IADIS (International Association for Development of the Information Systems). Her research includes technoethics governance for sustainable portuguese organizations. She has published several papers in refereed conference proceedings in these areas.

Fernando Ferreira is an Adjunct Professor at the Polytechnic Institute of Santarém, Portugal, and an Adjunct Research Professor at the University of Memphis, TN, USA. He holds a PhD in Quantitative Methods Applied to Economics and Management from the University of Algarve, Portugal. He has authored peer-reviewed papers and made many conference presentations. He is an Editorial Board Member of the *International Journal of Innovation and Learning (IJIL), International Journal of Intercultural Information Management (IJIIM)* and *International Journal of Information and Operations Management Education (IJIOME)*. His main research interests are Banking and Multiple Criteria Decision Analysis.

Takayuki Fujimoto (Ph.D, M.S, B.Edu) received the Doctor degree of Informatics (Ph.D.) from Graduate School of Science and Engineering in Yamagata University in 2007. He also received Master degree of Science in Japan Advanced Institute of Science and Technology in 2003 and Bachelor degree of Education in Waseda University in 2001. Currently, He is a lecturer of Dep. of Computational Science and Engineering, Toyo University. His main area of study include Information Design, Artificial Intelligence, and Electronic Education, e-Learning Support Systems, University Information Support Systems based on Information Reuse and Integrations, and E-Activity. He is a member of IEEE, and several others. He is a conference organizing IEEE IWEA 2007.

Darko Galinec was born in Zagreb, 1967. He obtained a PhD (2009) and MSc ("Program and Information Engineering", 2000) in information science from Faculty of Organization and Informatics at University of Zagreb. He obtained a BSc from Faculty of Economics ("Economic cybernetics") at the same university (1991). His research interests include of fuzzy logic, enterprise application integration (EAI) and command and control information systems (C2IS) interoperability. His work has appeared or is forthcoming in such scientific books and journals as *Encyclopedia of Multimedia Technology and Networking 2ⁿᵈ Edition* (Information Science Reference, USA), *International Journal of Information Systems in Service Sector* (IGI Publishing, USA), *Journal of Information and Organizational Sciences* (University of Zagreb, Croatia), *Journal of Behavioral and Applied Management* (The Institute of Behavioral and Applied Management, USA) and in refereed conference proceedings as well. He completed specialized training programs at Oxford Saïd Business School: "CIO Academy" (2008) and NATO CIS School: "Communications and Information Systems Orientation for Cooperation Partners Course" (2001). As senior lecturer, he teaches EAI at Polytechnic of Zagreb. Also, he serves as Editorial Review Board Member for International Journal of Human Capital and Information Technology Professionals (IGI Publishing, USA) and Editorial Board member for *International Journal of Society Systems Science* (Inderscience Publishers, UK).

Victor Manuel Alvarez Garcia has a M.Sc. in Computer Science (2004) and is, since 2006, an Associate Professor at the Department of Computer Science, University of Oviedo, where he is also doing his Thesis research in voice interactive learning. He has worked as an external consultant for several Telecommunications companies in Finland and the United Kingdom, involved in Mobile, VoIP and IVR development. Victor is also the author of several publications in e-learning. His current research interests are: eLearning and Audio Learning, Voice Browsers, Voice over IP and Interactive Voice Applications, Web, Mobile and Open-source software development.

Angel García-Crespo is the Head of the SofLab Group at the Computer Science Department in the Universidad Carlos III de Madrid and the Head of the Institute for promotion of Innovation Pedro Juan de Lastanosa. He holds a PhD in Industrial Engineering from the Universidad Politécnica de Madrid (Award from the Instituto J.A. Artigas to the best thesis) and received an Executive MBA from the Instituto de Empresa. Professor García-Crespo has led and actively contributed to large European Projects of the FP V and VI, and also in many business cooperations. He is the author of more than a hundred publications in conferences, journals and books, both Spanish and international.

Karin Hamilton is the Administrative Director for Graduate and Global Programs at the Silberman College of Business at Fairleigh Dickinson University. She has extensive experience in both business and academic administration in the areas of strategic and tactical planning, project management and training and development. She has written numerous guides and manuals that have been used by business professionals, educational administrators, faculty and students. Her research interests are primarily in learning, pedagogy and use of technology to improve learning outcomes. Karin was one of the two originators of the GBM program: an innovative pedagogical framework for teaching adult learners using a partial distance-learning format. She received her M.B.A. at Fairleigh Dickinson University and her B.A. at Valparaiso University.

Adrián Hernández López is a PhD student at the Computer Science Department of the Universidad Carlos III de Madrid in Spain. His research interests include applied research in People in IT, Human Aspects in IT and Software Process Improvement. He finished his Bachelor's degree in Computer Science on 2007 and his Master's degree in IT Science specialized on Software Engineering on 2009 at the Universidad Carlos III de Madrid. He has been working as software engineer in several companies including Telefónica and INDRA.

Jeffrey Hsu is an Associate Professor of Information Systems at the Silberman College of Business, Fairleigh Dickinson University. He is the author of numerous papers, chapters, and books, and has previous business experience in the software, telecommunications, and financial industries. His research interests include human-computer interaction, e-commerce, IS education, and mobile/ubiquitous computing. He is Managing Editor of the International Journal of Data Analysis and Information Systems (IJDAIS), Associate Editor of the International Journal of Information and Communication Technology Education (IJICTE), and is on the editorial board of several other journals. Dr. Hsu received his Ph.D. in Information Systems from Rutgers University, a M.S. in Computer Science from the New Jersey Institute of Technology, and an M.B.A. from the Rutgers Graduate School of Management.

Macarena López-Fernández, PhD, is an associate professor in the Organization Department of the University of Cádiz, where she teaches Human Resource Management. She was visiting fellow at Limerick and Manchester Universities where she worked toward completing her PhD in Social Capital and Diversity. Her work has been presented at top international and Spanish conferences.

Glykeria Kalfakakou Diploma of Civil Engineering (Aristotle University of Thessaloniki, 1976), PhD in Civil Engineering (Aristotle University of Thessaloniki, 1987); Professor of the Civil Engineering Department, Faculty of Engineering, Aristotle University of Thessaloniki; Vice-President of the Civil Engineering Department of Aristotle University of Thessaloniki; Research interest: investments' evaluation, graphics theory, decision tress, linear programming; Member of the PM Greece association.

Fernando Martín-Alcazar, PhD, is the Dean of the Faculty of Economic of the University of Cádiz, where he is currently leading two funded research projects, both focusing on the effects of HR strategies on a group's social capital. He has published his work in the field of HRM in peer-reviewed international journals such as the International Journal of Human Resource Management, British Journal of Management and Journal of Knowledge Management.

Tokuro Matuso (Ph.D, M.S, B.Edu) is an associate professor at Graduate School of Science and Engineering in Yamagata University since 2006. He received the Doctor degree of Engineering from Dept. of Computer Science at Nagoya Institute of Technology in 2006. He is a member of AAAI and IEEE. He is a conference chair / program chair of IEEE/ACIS ICIS 2010, ACIS SNPD 2009, IEEE/ACIS IWEA 2007-2009, IEEE/WIC/ACM ECBS 2008-2009, ACAN 2005-2009, IEEE PRIWEC 2006. He is a principal investigator of Grant for Doctorate Receiver (NEC Foundation, 2007-2008), Research grants for young researchers (Japan Ministry of Education, 2006-2008, 2009-2012), Research Grant (Japan Science Research Foundation, 2003-004) and more than other 25 research grants in years past.

Raquel Mendes has been a Professor of Economics at the School of Management of the Polytechnic Institute of Cavado and Ave, since 1997; Ph.D. student in Economic Sciences; Master's Degree in Economic and Social Studies, 2002; Graduate in Public Administration,1997.

Juan Ramón Pérez Pérez is a Lecturer in Department of Computer Science at the University of Oviedo. He received his M.Sc. degree in Computer Science in 1996 and his Ph.D. from the University of Oviedo in 2006. From 1995 to 1999 he worked for an information technologies company in the research and development departments, building specific development environments and database connectors. He obtained a position as an Associate Lecturer at the University of Oviedo in 2000. He has participated actively in several national projects related with e-learning systems, and he is at the moment involved in a national research project based on adaptive systems. His PhD. topic is about collaborative development environment on the web. His research interests are focused on collaborative systems on the Internet, social software, adaptive systems and e-learning systems at functional and architectural levels. He is author of several publications in JCR journals about these topics.

Sara Pinto is a junior researcher and works in a private bank. She holds a BA (2009) from the School of Management and Technology of the Polytechnic Institute of Santarém, Portugal. Presently, she is enrolled in a Master's degree program at the University of Évora, Portugal. Her major research interests are focused on the relationship between ICT impact and banking system. Some of her works have been published nationally and internationally.

Maria del Puerto Paule Ruiz is Lecturer for the Department of Computer Science at the University of Oviedo. She received her M.Sc. degree in Computer Science in 1997 and her Ph.D from the University of Oviedo in 2003. She has participated actively in several regional and national projects related with adaptive educational and context-aware e-learning systems, and is at the moment involved in a national research project based on adaptive systems. Currently she is working on national and European proposals on Mobile Learning, Speech interactive e-learning and Adaptive e-learning systems. She is the author of several publications in major journals. Her current research interests are: Adaptive e-learning, Audio e-learning, Mobile learning, Web and Mobile development and Open-source software development.

Pedro M. Romero-Fernández, PhD, is an associate professor in the Organization Department of the University of Cádiz. His teaching experience (more than 15 years) spans the broad range of strategy, human resources, and management. Together with Professor Martín-Alcázar, he has published in top national and international journals as the British Journal of Management and the Journal of Business Research.

Zamira Acosta Rubio is master on Business Management from the La Laguna University, Spain. She is professor of Business Organization with the Department of Economy and Business Management, La Laguna University, since 1990, professor of Skills of Management and Organization in the University School of Computer Engineering and tutor professor of the National University of Distance Education (UNED). She is also member of the University Institute of the Enterprise of La Laguna University (IUDE). The fields of interests of her research include technology and innovation, enterprises organization and R&D. She has shared scientific publications related with the innovation in the small and medium firms and with the characteristics of the enterprises in the Canary Islands.

Pedro Soto-Acosta is a Professor of Management at the University of Murcia (Spain). He holds a PhD in Management Information Systems (MISs) and a Master's degree in Technology Management from the University of Murcia. He received his BA in Accounting and Finance from the Manchester Metropolitan University (UK) and his BA in Business Administration from the University of Murcia. He attended Postgraduate Courses at Harvard University (USA). His work has been published in journals such as the European Journal of Information Systems, the International Journal of Information Management, the Information Systems Management, and the Journal of Enterprise Information Management, among others.

Remko van Dort, The Netherlands, finished his business and marketing studies at the ISAIP school in Angers, France (2001). He has developed his language skills in English, French and Spanish and has worked in worked in the area of technical support and customer service in The Netherlands as well as abroad. He has also worked in the area of distance learning and worked together with the University of Oviedo on a number of papers concerning the use of audio in distance learning and has worked in the same field of expertise during an internship at the DeMontfort University in Leicester, United Kingdom. His current research interests are: e-learning platforms, Voice Interactive Learning and Open-Source software development.

John Wang is a professor in the Department of Management and Information Systems at Montclair State University, USA. Having received a scholarship award, he came to the USA and completed his Ph.D. from Temple University. He has published over 100 refereed papers and six books that are related to information systems, data mining, and operations research. He has also developed several computer software programs based on his research findings.

Konstantinos C. Zapounidis Diploma of Civil Engineering (Aristotle University of Thessaloniki, 1999), MSc in Construction (Project) Management (Heriot-Watt University, Edinburgh, 2000); Project Manager IPMA certified (Level D); Project Manager of European projects and proposals in Pieriki Anaptixiaki S.A.; Phd cand. and visitor Lecturer of MSc courses in Aristotle University of Thessaloniki; Member of conferences' scientific committees and papers' reviewer; Invited Speaker to European Commissions' conferences and workshops; Project and risk management research interest; Member of the PM Greece association.

Index